AF607979

MILTON AND QUESTIONS OF HISTORY

Essays by Canadians Past and Present

EDITED BY FEISAL G. MOHAMED
AND MARY NYQUIST

Milton and Questions of History

Essays by Canadians Past and Present

UNIVERSITY OF TORONTO PRESS
Toronto Buffalo London

Toronto Buffalo London
www.utppublishing.com

ISBN 978-1-4426-4392-5 (cloth)

Library and Archives Canada Cataloguing in Publication

Milton and questions of history : essays by Canadians past and present / edited by Feisal G. Mohamed and Mary Nyquist.

Includes bibliographical references and index.
ISBN 978-1-4426-4392-5

1. Milton, John, 1608–1674 – Criticism and interpretation. 2. Milton, John, 1608–1674 – Political and social views. 3. Historical criticism (Literature)– Canada. I. Mohamed, Feisal G. (Feisal Gharib), 1974– II. Nyquist, Mary Ellen, 1947–

PR3588.M47 2012 821'.4 C2012-900314-X

This book has been published with the help of a grant from the Canadian Federation for the Humanities and Social Sciences, through the Aid to Scholarly Publications Program, using funds provided by the Social Sciences and Humanities Research Council of Canada.

University of Toronto Press acknowledges the financial assistance to its publishing program of the Canada Council for the Arts and the Ontario Arts Council.

Canada Council for the Arts Conseil des Arts du Canada

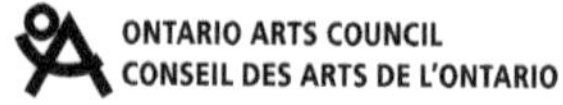

University of Toronto Press acknowledges the financial support of the Government of Canada through the Canada Book Fund for its publishing activities.

in memory of
Hugh R. MacCallum,
Balachandra Rajan,
and
Jay Macpherson

Contents

Acknowledgments

Thanks must go first to the authors of this volume's 'present' essays, which were thoughtfully and engagingly written in response to a slightly quixotic invitation. Deserving special mention is Paul Stevens, who supported the volume with a partial subvention through the Canada Research Chair Programme.

We are also very grateful to Erin Reynolds, a graduate research assistant at the University of Toronto who worked assiduously on the manuscript, and to Suzanne Rancourt, Barb Porter, and Miriam Skey at the University of Toronto Press for their indispensable support in bringing this volume to fruition. Enormous thanks go to Andrew Hall, a graduate research assistant at the University of Illinois, who indexed this substantial volume with great efficiency.

For granting permissions we are grateful to the following presses: Cornell University Press, Everyman Library UK, Random House UK, Oxford University Press, University of North Carolina Press, and the University of Toronto Press. Citations are provided on the first page of each reprinted chapter.

One of the great privileges of preparing this collection has been dialogue with that generation of scholars to whom it pays tribute: Eleanor Cook, Hugh MacCallum, Jay Macpherson, Balachandra Rajan, and Ernest Sirluck. We dedicate the volume to the late Macpherson, a gifted scholar and poet, and to the late MacCallum and Rajan, two remarkable Miltonists and generous teachers. All three passed away while the volume was still in progress. The pleasure they expressed when first learning of this project will, we hope, in some way be passed on to readers.

A Note on Texts

Unless otherwise indicated, all references to Milton's poetry in non-reprinted chapters are to *Paradise Lost*, ed. Barbara K. Lewalski (Oxford, 2007), and *Complete Shorter Poems*, ed. Stella P. Revard (Oxford, 2009). References to Milton's prose are to the *Complete Prose Works*, 8 vols, in 10, ed. Don M. Wolfe et al. (New Haven, 1953–82), and are indicated in parentheses by the abbreviation *YP*.

Introduction

FEISAL G. MOHAMED AND MARY NYQUIST

I

With the resurgence of interest in formalism leading, in some quarters, to skirmishes between New Formalism and New Historicism, this may be a good moment to revisit conflicts between New Criticism and historical scholarship that began in the late thirties and often centred on Milton. The Canadian scholars whose publications we have archived in this volume participated in these debates, sometimes explicitly, sometimes not. New Criticism set itself against what, in his 1948 address to the MLA, Douglas Bush drily calls 'the old scholarship.' If symmetry were in order, the Old Scholarship might be re-christened 'Old Historicism,' nomenclature unceremoniously implicit, anyway, in the emergence of 'New Historicism.' One of the difficulties with 'Old Historicism,' however, is that the programmatic historical contextualization of literary texts was not at the time really that old, having arisen with the professionalization of literary studies. Another is that its practitioners were as committed to the interpretation of distinctively *literary* texts – with poetry exemplifying the essence of literariness – as were the New Critics, which is why the rubric A.S.P. Woodhouse introduces into the debate, 'Historical Criticism,' is probably the most appropriate. In an exchange with Cleanth Brooks published in the 1951 volume of *PMLA*, Woodhouse argues that Historical Criticism does not lead away from the text merely to correct errors but, on the basis of hypotheses and the sedulous gathering of evidence, opens up 'new and fruitful ways of looking at the poem under consideration.'[1] Amid numerous areas of principled disagreement, proponents of both New Criticism and Historical Criticism share not only a common goal but also a set of assumptions about the uniqueness of creative literature, literary forms, and language. These assumptions have since been questioned, whether in the course of a more interdisciplinary historicization of both literary and extra-literary texts, or in tandem with the epistemological doubt that theorists of the 1970s and 1980s cast on the possibility of acquiring knowledge that is non-relational or extra-textual.

With the exception of Northrop Frye's essay on *Lycidas*, all of the roughly mid-twentieth century pieces collected here engage extra-literary texts, by Milton, his contemporaries, or writers who have been influenced by Milton. A.S.P. Woodhouse, Ernest Sirluck, and Arthur Barker significantly shaped the academic study of Milton's political works that is now considered indispensable to an understanding of seventeenth-century political philosophy as well as of Milton's poetry. So forcefully yet painstakingly articulated in his prose works are Milton's politico-theological commitments that his oeuvre seriously challenges the disciplinary boundaries of literary study, certainly more than any other major English literary figure. This challenge has often been contained, however, by the disjunction institutionalized in the academy between political philosophy and literary studies, or by the demarcation of hierarchical relations between poetry and prose within Milton studies. The convoluted history of a national, and, then, transnational, desire to exalt Milton the poet at the expense of Milton the controversialist and theologian is finally beginning to be told, Nicholas von Maltzahn having undertaken the process of rigorously analysing its divergent narrative threads. Similarly influential, though, has been the contrary tendency to disparage Milton's poetry on the basis of the repugnancy of his religious and political views. This, famously, is the stance taken by T.S. Eliot and adopted by the early twentieth-century critics who imbibe his hostility to Milton, many of whom are associated with New Criticism.

Directly addressed in the essay by Douglas Bush that opens the present collection, such hostility elicits defensive attitudes that have often been a feature of Milton studies. In this published version of his 1944 Messenger Lectures, Bush claims that Milton 'is one of the great portions of that heritage for which the war has been fought.' Not surprisingly, Milton's dedication to 'liberty,' which qualifies him for this honour, becomes a central preoccupation of post-war scholarship, produced when 'liberty' is promoted by Cold War ideology as a glorious universal to be safeguarded by the capitalist West. In responding to this era's demands, the mid-century Canadian scholars represented here generally presuppose that liberty's significance alters, even for Milton over the course of his career as a writer, and that whatever meanings liberty had for Milton and his contemporaries in revolutionary England are not the same as for, say, Milton's Romantic successors. Even when defence enters into their historical contextualization of Milton's texts, they often avoid glossing over unpleasant truths. Woodhouse, for example, observes in his introduction to the Putney debates, first published in 1938 and excerpted here, that the Puritan doctrine of 'the equality of believers implies their superiority to unregenerate men. And this superiority, so long as dogma is unimpaired, or in the secular field uncircumvented, will continue to oppose an effective barrier against a wider equalitarianism.'

Along with other aspects of his political vision that may make him uncongenial to modern readers, Milton's limited commitment to equality, whether marital, civil, or national, has often been contested. In an ironic historical twist, by the later decades of the twentieth century, Milton's defenders were frequently employing New Critical interpretative strategies. Recently, apologists for a gentler, less doctrinaire Milton have advocated the use of (very loosely) formalist strategies to liberate the aesthetic pleasures of Milton's poetry from heavy-handed, didactic historicism. In the context of this contemporary, self-styled 'New Milton Criticism,' it is instructive to return to the exchange between Cleanth Brooks and Douglas Bush in the late 1940s and early 1950s over Marvell's *Horatian Ode.* Bush opposes Brooks's frequent recourse to ambiguity, irony and indeterminacy – the mainstay of New Criticism – by arguing that 'the result, if not the aim, of Mr. Brooks's inquiry is, in large measure, to turn a seventeenth-century liberal into a modern one.' Brooks, Bush charges, writes under the sway of an assumption that 'a sensitive, penetrating, and well-balanced mind like Marvell could not really have admired a crude, single-minded, and ruthless man of action like Cromwell.' 'This is a prejudice,' Bush continues, 'natural enough in a good modern liberal, who is bound to see Cromwell, even the Cromwell of 1650, as a sort of Puritan Stalin.' The stakes are equally high when it comes to Marvell's stanza on Cromwell's conquest of the Irish. Brooks takes the lines to be ironic, while Bush, in a scathing rebuttal, reads them as straightforward praise for the success of Cromwell's Irish campaign, insisting that 'we really must accept the unpalatable fact that [Marvell] wrote as an Englishman of 1650,' a point he elaborates with reference to Milton's *Observations on the Articles of Peace.*[2]

This is not to imply that Bush or any of the other mid-century critics archived here were grappling in a sustained way with the difficult issues raised by England's expansionist ideology and colonialist practices – with the important exception of Balachandra Rajan, who devoted the latter part of his career to their exploration, having earlier dedicated two decades of humanitarian public service to a newly independent India. Critical distance from the United States' self-forged identity as the sole, unrivalled progenitor of political liberty likely contributed to Canadian scholarly interest in seventeenth-century precursors to Enlightenment liberalism. But Canada's colonial status appears not to have inspired a desire to critique English imperialism. In this era, students were generally encouraged to immerse themselves in *The Faerie Queene* and *Paradise Lost* or *The Mutabilitie Cantos* and *Lycidas* while remaining blissfully ignorant that Spenser also wrote *A View of the Present State of Ireland* and Milton the *Observations.* Nor, unsurprisingly – despite Frye's sometimes humourous, trenchant comments on Milton's masculinism – was gender a category receiving thoughtful, historicized analysis. In *Puritanism and Liberty*, his edition of the Putney debates, for example, Woodhouse includes an excerpt from *Petition of Women, Affecters and Approvers of the Petition of Sept. 11, 1648*, to which he gratuitously appends the comment, 'It is improbable that this petition was actually composed by the women. Its principles are none the less interesting' (367–9). Scholarship emerging since Woodhouse wrote these words suggests that Katherine Chidley played a large role in composing the petition, and has produced awareness of an outburst of public activism and literary productivity on the part of women engaged in radical politics, thereby transforming our sense of what is probable in the civil war and restoration periods.[3]

With these caveats, not only controversial political issues but formal literary properties and major, structural poetic patterns receive historical contextualization at the hands of the mid-century Canadian scholars represented here. At times, that project's defence of Milton from Eliotean disparagement works very subtly. Only implicitly responding to Eliot's declaration that Milton's poetry suffers from 'the hypertrophy of the auditory imagination at the expense of the visual and tactile' (cited by Bush in the essay reprinted here), Frye concedes that '[t]he precision of Milton's poetry is aural rather than visual, musical rather than pictorial,' but associates the predominance of sound over image with the iconoclasm of radical Protestantism as well as with Milton's contemporaries Rembrandt and Claude Lorrain, in whose paintings 'we find the same mysterious shadows and diffused brilliance that we find in Milton's hell and heaven.' (In *Milton, Mannerism, and Baroque*, Roy Daniells later develops a complex, historicist analysis of relations between the period's poetry and movements in the visual arts.)[4] Similarly inspired is Frye's observation in the essay on *Lycidas* included here that 'Milton was even by seventeenth-century standards an unusually professional and impersonal poet.' At this point Frye is distinguishing 'literary' from 'personal' sincerity, but his remark dismisses the portrait Eliot and Leavis draw of Milton the harsh, self-aggrandizing egotist while at the same time deftly assigning Milton mastery of the impersonality that Eliot believes to be the acme of artistry.

Given Frye's conviction that literary texts inhabit their own, autonomous field of significance, the New Critical tenet that appears in his *Lycidas* essay is scarcely unexpected: 'We notice that a law of diminishing returns sets in as soon as we move away from the poem itself.' It is more surprising to come across Bush divorcing aesthetic effects from knowledge of the poet's life. In *A Milton Evening*, a slim MLA volume in which various luminaries provide a favourite passage from the writings of Bush and C.S. Lewis, W.K. Wimsatt cites Bush tentatively asserting the relative autonomy of literary texts: 'If the drama [*Samson Agonistes*] did not in itself move us greatly, our biographical knowledge would not bring it to life ... [I]f we had time to look at all of Milton's poems I think we should find that their effect does not depend upon biographical information.'[5] The critics commemorated here would likely not have disagreed with this, though with differing provisos about the reach of 'biographical.' A desire to preserve poetry's privileged status in the Christian humanist tradition expresses itself in even the most historicist of their analyses of the prose. Yet it co-exists with a commitment to understanding how Milton's poetry and prose may be interrelated. Woodhouse's influential articles on Milton's poetry, for example, attempt to marry historicist concerns with literary analysis, especially analysis of thematic and structural patterning.[6] Barker, too, relies on close reading in his articles on patterning in Milton's poetry, while Hugh MacCallum builds upon Barker's arguments for the poetic patterning and unity of the Nativity Ode.[7] All three put into practice a principle Woodhouse formulates about interrelations between Milton's literary and extra-literary productions: 'Whatever may be said of some other poets, Milton's aesthetic patterns rely on a foundation, or rather perhaps a framework, of conceptual thought, and they cannot be elucidated without reference to it.'[8]

Balachandra Rajan is not entirely in agreement with this, holding that literary criticism and historical scholarship are fundamentally different methodologically. 'For scholarship,' Rajan states in the first chapter of *'Paradise Lost' and the Seventeenth Century Reader*, 'tends to simplify and separate. It isolates elements in order to see them more clearly. But in literary criticism the terms which are given by scholarship are fused in the transmuting unity of a pattern, and the totality which is thus recreated is often not predictable from its component parts.' Rajan argues that Milton's *De doctrina Christiana* is not really all that important to *Paradise Lost*, which goes out of its way to present heterodox views 'discreetly and doubtfully.'[9] In his chapter '*Paradise Lost*,' excerpted here, Rajan proposes that the explanation a literary critic offers for a given textual phenomenon should be sought in the text's own internal organization, and that a given literary interpretation is to be evaluated by 'the standard of poetic achievement it implies.'[10] Rajan does not, however, imagine that the politico-theological presuppositions of *Paradise Lost* are timeless or immediately apprehensible by twentieth and twenty-first century readers. Instead, he explicates them with reference to a set of beliefs that Milton could assume his seventeenth-century readers would share – views Rajan illustrates by citations from or references to a formidably wide range of early modern texts – and a set of formal patterns and correspondences developed in *Paradise Lost* itself. Aware that Rajan has flagged important, theoretical issues, Woodhouse correctly describes Rajan's major contribution to the study of *Paradise Lost* as having limited its historicism to an interest in 'the intellectual commonplaces of the age' – what might later be characterized as its discursive context – at the expense of Milton's distinctive theological and political views. In its privileging of historical commonplaces and aesthetic analysis, Woodhouse states, Rajan's work 'approaches as near as Historical Criticism well may to the concerns and methods of the New Criticism.'[11]

II

'You do have to ask,' Rajan mused when first learning of this volume, 'whether Canadian Miltonists amount to anything more than Miltonists teaching in Canada.'[12] Rajan's own long career in Canada, and the fact that his tercentenary tribute to *Paradise Lost* is the only previous all-Canadian collection, make him particularly well placed to wonder.[13] But his career also suggests that Miltonists teaching in Canada could sometimes have uncanny connections, personal if not intellectual. Struggling to finish his Cambridge doctorate during the Second World War, Rajan called upon a fellow student of Milton serving in the Canadian Army to furnish him with books from North America relevant to the dissertation, later to become *'Paradise Lost' and the Seventeenth-Century Reader*. That soldier was Ernest Sirluck, whose career illustrates a pattern that may give

Milton studies in Canada its main principle of coherence: procession and return from that *fontanus plenitudo* A.S.P. Woodhouse.

More than the other mid-century critics assembled here, Ernest Sirluck is content to concentrate on what Woodhouse calls 'extra-aesthetic' concerns. Not coincidentally, David Wootton mentions Sirluck's introduction to the second volume of the Yale edition of Milton's *Complete Prose Works* (1959), together with Laslett's introduction to Locke's *Two Treatises* (1960) and Pocock's *Ancient Constitution* (1957), as studies whose exemplary historical contextualization of political theory predates by a decade those of Quentin Skinner and other members of the Cambridge School.[14] Over the course of preparing that edition, one of Sirluck's encounters in the British Museum's North Library suggests that to the outside observer something of a distinct voice in Milton studies had emerged from Canada. 'Olivier Lutaud of the Sorbonne,' Sirluck reports, 'was there working on Milton. When he found that I was engaged on the Yale Milton he said he did not much admire the published volume [volume 1, edited by Don M. Wolfe]; he much preferred the work of the Toronto Miltonists. He grew more hopeful on learning that I had done my thesis under Woodhouse and Barker.'[15] What cheered Lutaud, himself a student of England's revolutionary period, is presumably the historicism of the Toronto Miltonists Woodhouse and Barker, who had already published *Puritanism and Liberty* (1938) and *Milton and the Puritan Dilemma* (1942).[16]

In 1937, his third year of undergraduate studies at the University of Manitoba, Sirluck registered in the lectures of a 'whimsically mustachioed' newcomer on campus, Roy Daniells, who recently graduated from the University of Toronto where Woodhouse had joined the faculty in 1928 after himself teaching at Manitoba.[17] That was a fortuitous overlap: Daniells would soon return to his undergraduate alma mater, the University of British Columbia, where he would become department chair and establish its creative writing program. The pull east to Toronto, and to Woodhouse, would soon draw Sirluck, who completed his graduate studies – with time out for decorated service in the War – under the guidance of Woodhouse, known to be a great tutor, and his young protégé, Arthur Barker. Both Sirluck and Barker would move for a time to Illinois – to the Universities of Chicago and Illinois, respectively – before returning to Canada. Sirluck entered administration at the University of Toronto, later returning to Manitoba as president, and Barker took up a position at the University of Western Ontario. In their American sojourns, each would leave a significant imprint on Milton studies south of the border, Sirluck supervising the doctoral dissertation of Barbara Lewalski, and Barker supervising Diane McColley's dissertation on Milton's Eve.[18] It was Woodhouse who passed along to Sirluck a project for which he could not find the time: editing of the second volume of the Yale edition of Milton's prose.[19] The meticulous care of Sirluck's introduction to the prose of 1643–8 would mark a new direction for the study of mid-seventeenth century political treatises as well as for the edition as a whole, and would change permanently the scholarly understanding of *Areopagitica.*

Precision in the handling of seventeenth-century sources gained significant reinforcement from a fellow undergraduate Torontonian and contemporary of Woodhouse's, Douglas Bush. Their friendship would later produce the second volume of the variorum edition of Milton's poems, a task originally assigned to Woodhouse and completed after his sudden passing by Bush.[20] Here was yet another way, in terms not of production but reception, that history proved invaluable to the study of literature. Bush sensibly proposes that the 'scholar needs to be critical and the critic scholarly,' explaining his resistance both to an over-emphasis on the texture of an individual work and to the 'factual and external' research of his rigidly philological training at Harvard in the 1920s.[21] We reprint the opening chapter of Bush's *'Paradise Lost' in Our Time,* with its critique of the 'modern reaction to Milton' of Eliot and F.R. Leavis. As in his 1948 MLA address, Bush objects to an overly ingenious search for ambiguity and paradox, associated for him with an elitist aestheticism: 'When complexity and ambiguity have become a fetish, there seems to be no check upon interpretative irresponsibility except the limits of the critic's fancy.'[22] (That comment could have been plucked from current debate over the 'New Milton Criticism.') The scholarly practices so eloquently defended by Bush and Woodhouse are, of course, engaged in by many scholars of the mid- and later twentieth century who are not connected with Bush, Toronto, or Woodhouse in their graduate training – Balachandra Rajan, Alan Rudrum, and P.G. Stanwood come to mind[23] – and would persist in many corners after Woodhouse's passing in October 1964 brought an end to his benevolent guidance of English at Toronto.

Bush did his undergraduate degree in Classics at Victoria College, while Woodhouse enrolled in Modern History at University College, and yet by Bush's account the two did not meet until 1921, when both were graduate students at Harvard.[24] Though Bush could praise the poetic achievements of Eliot and other moderns, he was in his element when lamenting the decline of Christian humanist knowledge and values.[25] His survey of seventeenth-century literature preceding the Restoration shows that he could summon as clear and authoritative a portrait of the period's history as Woodhouse ever did.[26] Yet he was more interested in the contours of a broad literary history running from the classics to the Romantics, the historical meta-narrative of which unapologetically pits the high-minded virtues of Christian humanism against various forms of philistinism and iniquity. His work is punctuated by haughty blasts at a fallen age, whether speaking of Milton's *Of Education* – 'the curriculum Milton proposed, which shocks the degenerate modern, becomes much less shocking when judged by contemporary standards of work' – or defending God the Father – 'even if Milton's God were presented with the compelling imaginative force of Satan (which no poet could achieve), he would still be antipathetic to an age that has changed "sinful" to "antisocial."'[27] Much as such statements can shade toward cranky grumbling, Bush's satiric edge leads him openly to denounce Pound's flirtations with fascism and to remain sceptical of his Harvard professor Irving Babbitt, whose 'New Humanism' sought to generate an aristocracy of learning and laid the foundation for later conservative movements in the humanities.[28]

Bush's moralizing moments and critical insights are discussed below in an essay by John Leonard, an eminently discerning evaluator of Bush's work as critic, scholar, and editor. Leonard describes how Bush's Christian humanist intellectual historiography leads him to use right reason, or *recta ratio,* as a means of bringing Milton closer to more conservative thinkers, such as Richard Hooker and Jeremy Taylor. As Leonard shows, right reason is equally discernible among such radicals as John Lilburne, Richard Overton, and John Cook. More open to complexity and contradiction, he finds, is Bush's handling of literary allusion, which is especially praiseworthy in his readings of *Paradise Lost* and his editing of the Nativity Ode, where Bush with Woodhouse carefully unpacks the contradictions surrounding Pan without seeking to resolve them.

Woodhouse adheres more fully than Bush to what might now be considered historicism, though with a strong affinity for Whig paradigms. For Woodhouse the Puritan emphasis on individual belief is fundamental to the development of liberal, democratic principles. By separating the orders of nature and grace, Puritanism left the natural world to the governance of human reason while the spiritual order, open to the operation of divine grace, remains an order of individual conscience and spiritual practice. In this volume are excerpted those portions of the introduction to

Puritanism and Liberty where Woodhouse articulates his helpful terms and taxonomies: the orders of nature and grace; the principle of segregation; Parties of the Right, Independents of the Centre, Independents of the Left. This clear-sighted introduction, we hope, will not become neglected by students of the period; after an astonishing run, Woodhouse's invaluable book has fallen out of the favour of print, its most recent release being a 1992 Everyman edition. The history of the principle of liberty that is his concern, as Hugh MacCallum describes it in his reflections on the study of Milton at Toronto, would become something of a 'ground-note' for those students and colleagues whom Woodhouse influenced.

Woodhouse continues to awaken affection. When asked to comment on his rumoured disparagement of female scholars, Jay Macpherson and Eleanor Cook, former students and colleagues of his at the University of Toronto, adamantly rejected the notion that it had any substance, both having had years of respectful, intellectually and professionally supportive interactions with him. The rumour could have arisen, they reflected, from resentment felt in many Canadian universities about the extent of Woodhouse's power. Though he did not hire women at University College, this, they explained, was because he accepted the Oxbridge or Seven Sisters model of separate women's colleges, not from any personal objection to female colleagues or scholars, whom he always spoke of with respect. Cook, whom Woodhouse once offered to recommend for a position in the United States, brings back undergraduate memories in which appear 'a large, slightly stooped man with a deceptively bland face and demeanour. Behind this calm, possessed style was a mind like a steel trap (as we say) and a charming, slightly ironic sense of humour. He would have made a good secret agent in that his face and manner gave little away, rather like George Smiley's.' Yet Macpherson remembers one occasion on which this equanimity did give way. Having remained behind after an undergraduate exam, Macpherson seized the opportunity to ask Woodhouse if it were true that he and Rosamond Tuve were going to get married. When Woodhouse appeared startled, Macpherson mentioned that Tuve had been overheard calling him 'darling.' Bowing his head and blushing deeply, Woodhouse murmured, 'She calls even [a colleague, Harold] Wilson "darling."'[29]

III

Annabel Patterson opens an essay on institutional and intertextual connections between Spenser and Milton in *Critical Inquiry* (1990) by recalling her first teaching assignment at the University of Toronto in 1963, which included a course on Spenser and Milton she describes as 'a famous cornerstone course carrying the stamp of the formidable Renaissance scholar A.S.P. Woodhouse, known affectionately if disrespectfully to his students as Professor Nature-and-Grace.'[30] In the discussion of authorial and institutional processes of canon-formation that follows, Patterson uses historicist methods rigorously to critique the assumptions underlying Woodhouse's pairing of Spenser and Milton, supported, she argues, by Sirluck's annotations on Milton's comment in *Areopagitica* that Spenser is 'a better teacher than *Scotus* or *Aquinas*.' 'Sirluck,' Patterson argues, 'spoke for the profession,'

> taking the comment in *Areopagitica* as grounds for establishing Milton as Spenser's pupil in classical ethics, Christian Neoplatonism, and Reformation nationalism. But the value of this connection resides in a particular view of the function of literature, one that is itself a product of classical ethics, Christian Neoplatonism, and Reformation nationalism. As a better teacher than Scotus or Aquinas, Spenser appears in the position that poetry occupied with respect to philosophy for Sir Philip Sidney, and which, in turn, Spenser-and-Milton as a couple have come to occupy in the academic canon – that is to say, an effective conveyance of certain traditional values, including the value of tradition itself.[31]

As Patterson reconstructs and interprets the historical record, however, the filiations Milton chooses to establish with Spenser are not poetic and ethico-philosophical but relate to radical religious reform and nationalism. The bonds between the two writers are 'predominantly political, polemical, and full of hostilities – not between Spenser and himself, but between them both and their mutual opponents' – including, of course, the Irish.[32] In Patterson's critique, Woodhouse and Sirluck are wistful proponents of a Christian humanism that their historicist methods not only expound but extol.

Cook recounts that Woodhouse began the Spenser-Milton course with a section on the Church Fathers in order to differentiate an ascetic tradition hostile to the senses and to art from a more inclusive, aesthetic-positive tradition. The aim, Cook explains, was to challenge current stereotypes about Puritanism, a purpose shared by Woodhouse's *Puritanism and Liberty*. This reframing seemed especially urgent since, at the time, the mid-seventeenth century English revolution was known primarily as 'the Puritan revolution.' As Elizabeth Sauer and Nicholas von Maltzahn demonstrate in this volume, the Puritan revolution was often important to historical meta-narratives, ranging from the familiar, Whig narratives of liberty's progressive unfolding or of a modern, civic religion that emerges in late seventeenth-century England to a narrative of the energies of the Scottish Enlightenment finding their way to Canadian education through Thomas McCulloch, the first president of Dalhousie University. Those energies, von Maltzahn shows, could be recruited to highly problematical ends in the anti-communism and Eurocentric brand of multiculturalism influentially advanced by Watson Kirkconnell. Sauer points out that enlisting Milton in this history can also paper over key developments and contradictions in the poet's thought. Drawing on her important co-edited collection, *Milton and Toleration*, and on Sharon Achinstein's recent article on the 'Cold War Milton,' Sauer situates the initial appearance of *Puritanism and Liberty* in 1938 among early twentieth-century efforts to draw England's civil-war period into a Whig history – pointing to the work of S.R. Gardiner, W.K. Jordan, and William Haller – and in mounting tensions in Europe between forces of liberty and absolutism. The tendency of *Puritanism and Liberty* to present itself as an anthology of primary documents, Sauer shows, often does not take into account Woodhouse's active hand in arranging it according to the values avowed in the introduction. Though he encourages scholarly contextualization and analysis of Milton's prose, Woodhouse's stress on Milton's liberationist Puritanism – best illustrated, in his view, by *Areopagitica* – obscures some of the internal tensions of Milton's thought. In its careful selection of excerpts and texts, *Puritanism and Liberty* can at times suggest that Milton is in essential harmony with the Levellers while simultaneously anticipating John Stuart Mill.

Although Barker, like Woodhouse, views the prose works as worthy of study in themselves and as fundamental to comprehension of the poetry, he is less invested than Woodhouse in Whig historiography, and more concerned with Milton's increasing sympathies over the 1650s with the left wing of Reformed thought. Barker finds Milton's views on liberty opposed to those of the nineteenth-century liberals who had enlisted him in their cause, and in this respect anticipates such intellectual historians as Quentin Skinner and Paul A. Rahe.[33] Though Michael Fixler would for a time cast doubt on Barker's comparison of Milton and the younger Sir Henry Vane, current scholarship significantly reinforces connections between Milton and Vane, and with Restoration nonconformists.[34] Indeed, so much current work seems to engage the issues central to Barker's seminal book that we have decided not to reprint an excerpt from it, choosing instead a complete piece and one relatively neglected: his article from the 1942 volume of the *University of Toronto Quarterly* arising by his own admission from Woodhouse's famous graduate seminar on the origins of Romanticism. In this perceptive essay on the reception of *Paradise Lost*, Barker charts eighteenth-century handling of Milton's troubling adherence to and departure from classical decorum as it prepares the way for the dynamic Satanism of Blake and Shelley. Barker argues that Milton's poetic sublimity, admired by Joseph Addison, becomes enthusiastically celebrated as a means of either downplaying or defending the irregularities of his epic, with the result that the opening two books and the War in Heaven receive lavish attention and praise. Aristotelian probability, Barker shows, slips imperceptibly into a stress on Satan's humanity, and then into a sympathetic portrait of his noble suffering. In this piece, Barker seems to anticipate the historicist approach to literary categories to which critics of Milton are just now turning their attention more fully.[35]

In his handling of Milton's political theory, and by extension of the liberal tradition claiming it as foundational, Sirluck is more reluctant than either Woodhouse or Barker to situate Milton's prose in an historical meta-narrative. The prose works, and especially the polemical prose works, cannot in Sirluck's view be divorced from the specific moments in England's civil-war period in which they intervened; they have tactical and immediate aims, and should not be expected to unfold intellectual histories not yet written. Sirluck's doctoral dissertation, lamentably unpublished, argues that Milton advances a political theory grounded in natural law in his 1649 tracts, *The Tenure of Kings and Magistrates* and *Eikonoklastes*, only to abandon the idea in the *Defenses* – under pressure from such groups as the Levellers on the left and the Presbyterians on the right – in favour of a government of the enlightened. When he seeks disestablishment of the church and limits on the authority of the state, Milton returns to naturalistic theory in *A Treatise of Civil Power* (1659), shortly thereafter to return to arguments for government by the enlightened in *The Readie and Easie Way* (1660) when he wished to prevent the restoration of Stuart monarchy at any cost. 'Although with certain differences in theory,' Sirluck concludes, Milton 'supports whatever group dominates the Revolution until the second dissolution of the Rump; he does this although it means his political theory suffers from ambiguity, fundamental inner contradiction, and frequent reversal.'[36]

Milton is more revolutionary than political philosopher in Sirluck's view, which is not that far from Frye's in the introduction to his edition of *'Paradise Lost' and Selected Poetry and Prose* (1951). 'After Cromwell's death,' Frye writes, Milton 'proposed that the power of holding the new republic together should be entrusted to a permanent senate, a sort of reconstituted Long Parliament. He thus never arrived at what we should now consider a liberal or democratic position, partly because, being in a revolutionary situation, he was trying to see what would fit that situation, not what would be on paper the best form of government.'[37] In the essay written for this volume, Patterson returns to this proposal, made in *The Readie and Easie Way to Establish a Free Commonwealth*, a tract that has traditionally occupied an embarrassed place in Milton's oeuvre, in part, she argues, because of presuppositions about the religious cast of Milton's political thought, in part because Milton's revisions have not been given adequate attention. Patterson finds in Milton's carefully formulated and revised recommendations a perceptive anticipation of political conflicts that would trouble England in the reign of Charles II. In warning against a restored monarchy, Milton predicts that the sins of the father will be writ large in the son, and that the constitutional issue of personal rule would return with a Stuart king. Milton was, Patterson shows, quite correct.

Yet Milton's persistent opposition to tyranny does not, Sirluck argues, give *Areopagitica* the preternatural power of articulating the quintessential, liberal-democratic value of opposition to censorship so much as it makes an occasional appeal to the Erastian element in Parliament best poised to curtail the rising influence of the Presbyterian party. Sirluck's positioning of *Areopagitica* has proven to be a foundation of later work on Milton's most famous prose tract, forming significant background to the readings of Abbe Blum, Nigel Smith, Christopher Kendrick, and Thomas Fulton.[38] As with Barker, the strong influence and wide availability of the introduction to the second volume of the Yale edition of Milton's prose makes a reprint seem unnecessary. We include here the article '*Areopagitica* and a Forgotten Licensing Controversy,' which identifies one of the first discernible influences of Milton's tract upon licensing debates, a moment that is still often forgotten in discussions of the tract's reception.

Milton's poetic and polemical responses to the theological controversies of his time are of central, consuming interest for Hugh MacCallum, who illuminates Milton's political commitments by reframing their theological underpinnings and expression. The essay we reprint here, 'Milton and Figurative Interpretation of the Bible,' situates and examines Protestant exegetical principles with MacCallum's characteristic erudition and clarity. It begins with a distinction reminiscent of Woodhouse between 'knowledge' and 'grace' before exploring the tension between literal and figurative readings of scripture in Milton's writings. Surveying Reformed critiques of figurative interpretation, it finds Milton assuming and, even, extending them in both *De doctrina Christiana* and the poetry. In his recent obituary of MacCallum, Paul Stevens describes the transformative effect of his first reading of the essay:

> When I first read this essay as an undergraduate at the University of London in the early 1970s, it seemed like a voice from another world. Its unusual learning, measured tone, and the elegant unfolding of its thesis made the polemics of Eliot and Leavis, with which we were saturated, and even the interventions of the much admired Empson and Ricks, suddenly seem partisan, subjective, and indeed amateurish in their ignorance of anything to do with Milton other than their endless scrutiny of the poems.[39]

MacCallum's historicist approach to Reformed theology culminates in *Milton and the Sons of God*, which explores Milton's heterodox views of the divine Son and Father and their implications for humanity's filial relationship to the Godhead.[40] Before his passing in 2008, MacCallum offered us his reflections in 'The Study of Milton at Toronto in Mid-Century,' which provides insight on the major figures active in that moment – though regrettably, as is typical of MacCallum's retiring personality, his account is silent on his own interventions.

Tensions between New and Historical Criticism are interestingly crystallized by Rosamond Tuve in her response to Empson's reading of Herbert's 'Sacrifice' when she says: 'For much that is "outside" a poem to us was well inside it to our forefathers, and still is to some readers.'[41] To many twenty-first century ears, Tuve's unselfconscious 'our' reinforces the import of her formulation, as it brings up issues of socio-cultural positionality and the means of acquiring (or being unable to acquire) relevant 'cultural capital,' issues that rarely get addressed, either in these debates or at present, though they are perhaps especially pertinent to Milton studies. At the same time, in succinct, non-theoretical language, Tuve disturbs any fixed boundary between what is 'inside' and 'outside' a text. From this vantage point, relations between 'inside' and 'outside' appear somewhat mystified in Frye's critical practice, since when writing about specific literary texts he often effortlessly finds cultural, intellectual, and political histories 'inside' them. His theoretical pronouncements, on the other hand, insist that literature comprises its own, autonomous history: that literature *is* context (to adapt the title of the essay reprinted here), being, as it were, its own inside. As MacCallum presents it in the reflections written for this volume, Frye would come to similar conclusions about Milton as did Woodhouse and Barker, though Frye views Milton's poetry as a site exposing or resolving tensions that are literary rather than conceptual or political. Frye's debt to Woodhouse is especially evident in *The Return of Eden*, with its distinction between the orders of nature and grace.[42] These become in the present essay an Aristotelian taxonomy of four orders: the order of grace, the order of human nature, the order of physical nature, and the disorder of the unnatural. In Milton's elegy, the figure of Lycidas is associated with all four orders together with archetypes such as Orpheus, Adonis, and Saint Peter. For Frye, archetypes and generic conventions are constitutive elements of literary expression, a mode of expression that stands quite apart from personal sincerity. The moment Wordsworth gives poetic expression to his grief over the death of Lucy she inescapably becomes, for Frye, 'a Proserpine figure.'

Despite the hints of Woodhouse's influence, and despite the ostensible expansiveness of Frye's famous witticism in that essay – 'there is such a variety of even legitimate critics. There are critics who can find things in the Public Records Office, and critics who, like myself, could not find the Public Records Office' – Peter C. Herman argues below for the fundamental anti-historicism of Frye's aim scientifically to evaluate the mythic order.[43] Drawing on the arguments of his recent book, *Destabilizing Milton* (2005), Herman finds Frye's essay on *Lycidas*, and especially its dismissal of Samuel Johnson's charge of the poem's lack of sincerity, to be performing the disciplinary work of asserting the poem's unity. Frye's suspicion of historicism, Herman avers, might explain the relatively scant attention paid to the influential critic's work on Milton, for all that Milton seems to have been a consistent presence in his work.[44] In turning attention to Frye's omnibus articles on Canadian literature, however, Herman finds Frye admitting precisely those qualities deemed 'external' to Anglo-American literature, and speculates on the historical and biographical causes of this apparent inconsistency.

Frye's decision to consider *Paradise Lost* under the category of 'high mimesis' is the starting point of Feisal G. Mohamed's contribution to this volume. Noting the high regard in which Frye held Woodhouse, Mohamed wonders whether Frye might not have shared Woodhouse's vision of transmitting the wisdom of the ancients and have had an

Arnoldian streak of his own, despite his conviction that moralizing was not the business of the literary critic (Arnoldian tones can definitely be heard in Bush's essay). While Milton's epic has often been considered a precursor of the low-mimetic novel, Mohamed's interest lies in its satiric energies and its affinities with mock epic, both of which, he argues, perform a critique of the authority traditionally held by epic and tragedy as classical genres. In showing how Milton can fruitfully be paired with Jonson and Fielding, and that mock epic has a history and contemporary presence relevant to Milton's epic, Mohamed suggests the limitations of a critical tradition that showcases the classical lineage of *Paradise Lost.*

IV

In addition to reflections and essays engaging a critical past, we include here several essays pointing in new directions. Querying the portrait of Milton the artist uncomplicated in his energetic Protestantism, Elizabeth Hodgson explores allusions to the cloister in *Areopagitica* and *Il Penseroso.* In her essay, Hodgson raises questions about Milton's early career of the kind that have come to the fore in the recent biography of Gordon Campbell (not widely known to have Canadian roots) and Thomas N. Corns, with its sceptical eye to the tradition of Milton as 'puritan son of puritan father, educated by puritans, writing on puritan themes against puritan enemies until the failure of a puritan revolution requires him to redirect those energies into the definitive puritan poem.'[45] One of the unities of Milton studies in Canada, Hodgson indirectly reminds us, is confessional, itself an expression of various Protestant commitments.

Engaging issues of critical historiography, Phillip J. Donnelly examines *Areopagitica* in order to characterize and evaluate Milton's fundamental disagreement with Machiavelli's conception of history. Where Machiavelli presents history as a struggle against the disruptive energies of *fortuna* as they are opposed by *virtù,* history is for Milton a participation in the 'story of Scripture' (*YP* 2: 387), especially as that story is revealed in the Creation, Fall, and Eschaton. These differing meta-narratives explain the emphasis on coercion and deception in Machiavelli's politics against the desire in *Areopagitica* to eliminate a tool of state coercion so that virtue has a better chance of flourishing. In the course of his careful, comparative analysis of Milton and Machiavelli, Donnelly evaluates the immediate rhetorical aims of *Areopagitica* in light of Sirluck's scholarship and of recent questions raised about Sirluck's views by Markus Klinge.

In the spirit of Nabil Matar's work on Islamic influence in seventeenth-century England, and of recent interest in the 1649 translation of the Qur'an, Muhammad Sid-Ahmad explores the possible influence of Abubakr Ibn Tufayl on Milton's portrait of Adam in *Paradise Lost.* Persuasively demonstrating the importance of the study of Arabic in early modern Cambridge and Oxford, and the currency of Ibn Tufayl's *Hayy bin Yaqzan,* particularly in the Hartlib circle during the time at which Milton was writing his epic, Sid-Ahmad suggests that this influential Arabic text, which is known to have been important to Daniel Defoe's *Robinson Crusoe,* may subtly inform Milton's representation of Adam's creation and first moments of consciousness as recalled by Adam in book 8 of *Paradise Lost.*

The final word among these articles goes to Balachandra Rajan, who explores the question of eco-justice in the Ludlow masque. Rajan briefly compares Milton's revision of the masque, a dramatic subgenre specific to its historical moment, with his challenge to the epic's imperial claims in *Paradise Lost,* which, he beautifully says, 'implements the epic undertaking with unapproachable grandeur and as it does so sinks a spear into its heart.' Milton's challenge to the masque involves a reformation of its aesthetic of conspicuous consumption, which has in the intervening centuries become a major feature of advanced capitalism and, now, a global preoccupation. Through the Lady's lengthy riposte, Rajan points out, Milton introduces concerns relating to social and ecological justice to which he does not return. In *Paradise Lost,* Milton may suggest that nature is self-endangering rather than self-balancing, yet he also assigns humankind 'Dominion absolute' over 'Beast, Fish, Fowl,' a gesture Rajan refers to as 'assertive eco-imperialism.' In this, his last essay, Rajan intervenes strongly in an emerging eco-criticism, and does so in the powerful timbre long characteristic of his critical voice.

How little Milton could have imagined when in *Areopagitica* he used 'Canada' as a synecdoche for the Western tip of creation that it would be the home of some of his fittest readers – all the more fit for lacking unanimity as staunch as any January could freeze together. It is hoped that this collection, conceived as a tribute to and critique of Milton's mid-twentieth century Canadian scholars, will helpfully situate and illuminate the critical enterprises in which they engaged and which often haunt, unperceived, those of the present. Woodhouse concludes his theoretical discussion by claiming that Historical Criticism and New Criticism 'need each other,' a harmonious note on which to close. Yet such harmony brings out the *basso continuo* that sounds quietly in the background of much mid-century Canadian scholarship on Milton. Its sonorous tone is captured by Rajan when he reflects in *'Paradise Lost' and the Seventeenth-Century Reader* on how the certainties that *Paradise Lost* represents were threatened even as it was being written:

> The power of a great writer to order a tradition, to endow it with some kind of retrospective logic, is among the chief forces which keep traditions alive. And the tradition which *Paradise Lost* attempts to keep in being, the massive, unchallengeable synthesis of knowledge it asserts, is one far richer and far more reassuring than the fragile, limited substitutes which have replaced it.[46]

To the extent that historical criticism involves not only reinterpreting but also revivifying the past, it may make earlier historical eras home to nostalgic idealization. As he became committed to studying early modern imperialism, Rajan significantly qualified his view of the reassuring substantiality of the tradition *Paradise Lost* preserves. The longer and broader the historical vista, the more clearly it appears that Milton's poetry and prose synthesize traditions as various and potentially incommensurate as those in the popular, literary, scholarly, and political traditions they have inspired.

While this volume was being prepared for publication, a 'Public Observance in Solidarity with the People of Haiti' was held at the Great Hall in Hart House at the University of Toronto (Hart House was not open to women until the early 1970s). At an emotional point in a moving ceremony, one of the speakers looked up to read the words inscribed on the frieze extending along the walls of the Great Hall. The words served as a reminder that Haiti has forcibly been denied the fruits of the independence it formally gained in 1804. But they applied to the struggle for renewal that was emerging from the rubble, the Haiti whose people, it was hoped, will be more strongly united than ever as they rebuild their nation: 'Methinks I see in my mind a noble and puissant nation rousing herself like a strong man after sleep, and shaking her invincible locks.' Neither *Areopagitica* nor Milton's name was mentioned, and would anyway have been lost in the sounds of original Haitian music and pan drums. Unattributed, decontextualized, the words read aloud were more sampling than citation. Against the historical background of Milton's involvement in early modern Euro-colonialism, they could plausibly be given an ironic, post-modern spin. Yet the history of Milton's reception includes decolonization movements (beginning, of course, with the New England colonies), and is, in any case, ongoing, open-ended, in the making.

NOTES

1 A.S.P. Woodhouse, 'The Historical Criticism of Milton,' *PMLA* 66 (1951): 1033–44.
2 Douglas Bush, 'Marvell's "Horatian Ode,"' (1952), 351, 342, 349–50, rpt. *Seventeenth-Century English Poetry: Modern Essays in Criticism,* ed. William R. Keast (Oxford, 1962). Cleanth Brooks's 'Marvell's "Horatian Ode"' (1946) and 'A Note on the Limits of "History" and the Limits of "Criticism"' (1953) also appear in this collection, 321–40, 352–8.
3 See Ian J. Gentles, 'Chidley, Katherine (fl. 1616–1653),' *Oxford Dictionary of National Biography* (Oxford, 2004; online ed., Jan 2008). On women and radical politics in the period, see for example, Patricia Higgins, 'The Reactions of Women, with Special Reference to Women Petitioners,' in *Politics, Religion and the English Civil War,* ed. Brian Manning (London, 1973), 179–222; Sharon Achinstein, 'Women on Top in the Pamphlet Literature of the English Revolution,' *Women's Studies* 24.1 (1994): 131–63; Catharine Gray, *Women Writers and Public Debate in Seventeenth-Century England* (New York, 2007); and Marcus Nevitt, *Women and the Pamphlet Culture of Revolutionary England, 1640–1660* (Aldershot, 2006).
4 Roy Daniells, *Milton, Mannerism, and Baroque* (Toronto, 1964).
5 *A Milton Evening in Honor of Douglas Bush and C.S. Lewis* (New York, 1954), 6; the volume provides a biographical summary on p.7. Wimsatt quotes Douglas Bush, 'The Critical Significance of Biographical Evidence, John Milton,' *English Institute Essays* (1946), 10, 17, 18. See also in *A Milton Evening,* William Haller's fitting application of Bush's words on Milton ('His Christian humanism ... becomes as he grows old a noble anachronism in an increasingly modern and mundane world' [3]), and D.C. Allen's poetic tribute (1):

> Let profane scorners, Leavites and the rest
> Who round about our epic altar push,
> Owles Cuckoes, Asses, Apes, and Doggs that press
> Beware the thunder in this burning Bush.

6 See A.S.P. Woodhouse, 'The Argument of Milton's *Comus,*' *UTQ* 11 (1941–2): 46–71; '*Comus* Once More,' *UTQ* 19 (1949–50): 218–23; 'Milton's Pastoral Monodies,' in *Studies in Honour of Gilbert Norwood,* ed. Mary Estelle White (Toronto, 1952), 261-78; 'The Pattern of *Paradise Lost,*' *UTQ* 22 (1952–3), 109–27; 'Theme and Pattern in *Paradise Regained,*' *UTQ* 25 (1955–6): 167–82; '*Samson Agonistes* and Milton's Experience,' *Transactions of the Royal Society of Canada,* 3rd ser., 43 (1949): Section 2, 157–75; 'Tragic Effect in *Samson*

Agonistes,' UTQ 28 (1958–9): 205–22; see also Woodhouse's lesser known *Milton the Poet*, Sedgwick Memorial Lecture (Vancouver, 1955).

7 Hugh MacCallum, 'The Narrator of Milton's "On the Morning of Christ's Nativity,"' in *Familiar Colloquy: Essays Presented to Arthur Edward Barker* (Ottawa, 1979), 179–95; Arthur E. Barker, 'The Pattern of Milton's *Nativity Ode*,' *UTQ* 10 (1941): 167–81; 'Structural Pattern in *Paradise Lost*,' *Philological Quarterly* 28 (1949): 17–30; 'Structural and Doctrinal Pattern in Milton's Later Poems,' in *Essays in English Literature from the Renaissance to the Victorian Age*, ed. Millar MacLure and F.W. Watt (Toronto, 1964), 169–94.

8 Woodhouse, 'Historical Criticism,' 1041.

9 Balachandra Rajan, *'Paradise Lost' and the Seventeenth Century Reader* (London, 1947), 35, 36–7.

10 Rajan, *'Paradise Lost' and the Seventeenth Century Reader*, 51.

11 Woodhouse, 'Historical Criticism,' 1037.

12 Balachandra Rajan, Letter to Feisal Mohamed, 23 April 2007.

13 Balachandra Rajan, ed., *'Paradise Lost': A Tercentenary Tribute* (Toronto, 1969).

14 Interview with Mary Nyquist, February 2009. *Divine Right and Democracy: An Anthology of Political Writing in Stuart England*, ed. David Wootton (London, 1986), 12.

15 Ernest Sirluck, *First Generation: An Autobiography* (Toronto, 1996), 196.

16 See Olivier Lutaud, *Les Niveleurs, Cromwell et la république* (Paris, 1963); and *Des révolutions d'Angleterre à la Révolution française; le tyrannicide et Killing no murder (Cromwell, Athalie, Bonaparte)*, Archives internationales d'histoire des idées 56 (The Hague, 1973).

17 Sirluck, *First Generation* , 47; F.E.L. Preistley, 'A.S.P. Woodhouse 1895–1964,' *Proceedings and Transactions of the Royal Society of Canada*, 4th ser., 33 (1965): 183–8.

18 Barker's influence in Canada is attested in the Festschriften *Milton Reconsidered: Essays in Honor of Arthur E. Barker*, ed. John Karl Franson, Elizabethan and Renaissance Studies [Salzburg] 49 (1976); and *Familiar Colloquy: Essays Presented to Arthur Edward Barker*, ed. Patricia Bruckmann (Ottawa, 1978). The latter of these provides a brief account of Barker's career (5) and a bibliographical list of his major publications, as well as his supervisions (227–30).

19 See Sirluck, *First Generation*, 178–9.

20 In the original *Variorum Commentary on the Poems of John Milton*, under the general editorship of Merritt Y. Hughes, Douglas Bush handled the Latin and Greek poems in volume 1 (New York, 1970), and completed the volume on the minor English poems, the task of A.S.P. Woodhouse left unfinished by his death, vol. 2 [in three parts] (New York, 1972).

21 Douglas Bush, 'A.S.P. Woodhouse: Scholar, Critic, Humanist,' *Essays in English Literature from the Renaissance to the Victorian Age*, ed. Millar MacLure and F.W. Watt (Toronto, 1964), 321.

22 Bush, 'The New Criticism: Some Old-Fashioned Queries,' *PMLA* 64 (1949): 19.

23 Many of Rajan's most influential writings on Milton are collected in *Milton and the Climates of Reading: Essays by Balachandra Rajan*, ed. Elizabeth Sauer (Toronto, 2006). Recent Festschriften attest to the influence of Rudrum and Stanwood: *Of Paradise and Light: Essays on Henry Vaughan and John Milton in Honor of Alan Rudrum*, ed. Donald R. Dickson and Holly Faith Nelson (Newark, DE, 2004); and *Wrestling with God: Literature and Theology in the English Renaissance*, ed. Mary Ellen Henley and W. Speed Hill, special issue of *Early Modern Literary Studies* 7 (2001), 9 June 2009 http://extra.shu.ac.uk/emls/si-07/si-07toc.htm.

24 Bush, 'A.S.P. Woodhouse,' 320–1.

25 See Bush, 'The New Criticism,' 13; *The Renaissance and English Humanism*, The Alexander Lectures (1939; Toronto, 1965), 13. See also Bush's defence of pastoral against Samuel Johnson in *John Milton: A Sketch of His Life and Writings* (New York, 1964), 62–3. Bush's own classicism is evident everywhere in his work, but see especially *Prefaces to Renaissance Literature* (Cambridge, MA, 1965); *Mythology and the Renaissance Tradition in English Poetry*, rev. ed. (New York, 1963); and *Mythology and the Romantic Tradition in English Poetry* (Cambridge, MA, 1937).

26 See, for example, the introductory chapter 'The Background of the Age' in *English Literature in the Earlier Seventeenth Century*.

27 Bush, *English Literature in the Earlier Seventeenth Century*, 16; *John Milton: A Sketch*, 154; see also *Prefaces to Renaissance Literature*, 44–5. See also the dark view of modernity in *English Poetry: The Main Currents from Chaucer to the Present*, 2nd ed. (London, 1965): 'Many of the spectres that have haunted this generation are, directly or indirectly, the offspring of science, not merely new weapons of mass-destruction but more insidious, everyday enemies of order and security – the decay of religious faith and of moral values, the predominance of a purely naturalistic view of life and man, the mechanization of both external existence and the individual personality, the change from communal stability to the urban atomizing of society, and so on' (192).

28 See Bush, 'A.S.P. Woodhouse,' 321: 'Arthur recognized Babbitt's aesthetic and critical shortcomings and the degree of prejudice in his crusading zeal, but, like some other good minds, he, without being a blind disciple, valued such passionate concern with moral ideas that mattered.' Babbitt

distinguishes humanism from humanitarianism: 'The humanitarian lays stress almost solely upon breadth of knowledge and sympathy ... The humanist is more selective in his caresses ... The humanist, then, as opposed to the humanitarian, is interested in the perfecting of the individual rather than in schemes for the elevation of mankind as a whole'; Irving Babbitt, *Literature and the American College: Essays in the Defense of the Humanities* (Boston, 1908), 7–8.

29 Interview with Mary Nyquist, February 2009.

30 Annabel Patterson, 'Couples, Canons, and the Uncouth: Spenser-and-Milton in Educational Theory,' *Critical Inquiry* 16 (1990): 773.

31 Patterson, 'Couples, Canons,' 777.

32 Patterson, 'Couples, Canons,' 781.

33 See Arthur E. Barker, *Milton and the Puritan Dilemma* (1942; Toronto, 1976), xi and xiv; Quentin Skinner, *Liberty Before Liberalism* (1998; Cambridge, 2006); and Paul A. Rahe, *Against Throne and Altar: Machiavelli and Political Theory under the English Republic* (Cambridge, 2008).

34 Michael Fixler, *Milton and the Kingdoms of God* (London, 1964).

35 Nicholas von Maltzahn, 'The War in Heaven and the Miltonic Sublime,' *A Nation Tranformed*, ed. Alan Houston and Steve Pincus (Cambridge, 2001), 154–79; and Victoria Kahn, 'Aesthetics as Critique: Tragedy and *Trauerspiel* in *Samson Agonistes*,' *Reading Renaissance Ethics*, ed. Marshall Grossman (New York, 2007), 104–27.

36 Ernest Sirluck, 'Milton and the Law of Nature,' diss. University of Toronto, 1948, 218; 23 June 2009, available in *ProQuest Digital Dissertations.*

37 Frye, introduction to *'Paradise Lost' and Selected Poetry and Prose, Northrop Frye on Milton and Blake*, ed. Angela Esterhammer, Collected Works of Northrop Frye 16 (Toronto, 2005), 9.

38 See Abbe Blum, 'The Author's Authority: *Areopagitica* and the Labour of Licensing,' in *Re-Membering Milton*, ed. Mary Nyquist and Margaret W. Ferguson (New York, 1988), 74–96; Nigel Smith, '*Areopagitica*: Voicing Contexts, 1643–45,' in *Politics, Poetics, and Hermeneutics in Milton's Prose*, ed. David Loewenstein and James Grantham Turner (Cambridge, 1990), 103–22; Christopher Kendrick, *Milton: A Study in Ideology and Form* (New York, 1986), 19–51; and Thomas Fulton, '*Areopagitica* and the Roots of Liberal Epistemology,' *English Literary Renaissance* 34 (2004): 44.

39 Paul Stevens, 'Hugh MacCallum, 1928–2008: In Memoriam,' *Milton Quarterly* 42 (2008): 249.

40 H.R. MacCallum, *Milton and the Sons of God: The Divine Image in Milton's Epic Poetry* (Toronto, 1986).

41 Rosamond Tuve, 'On Herbert's "Sacrifice,"' *Kenyon Review* 12 (1950): 54.

42 Frye, *The Return of Eden: Five Essays on Milton's Epics*, in *Northrop Frye on Milton and Blake*, ed. Angela Esterhammer, vol. 16 of *The Collected Works of Northrop Frye* (Toronto, 2005), 60.

43 For an alternate view of Frye's relationship to historical criticism, see A.C. Hamilton, *Northrop Frye: Anatomy of His Criticism* (Toronto, 1990), 45–80.

44 Frye not only published the essay on *Lycidas* and *The Return of Eden*, but also edited *'Paradise Lost' and Selected Poetry and Prose* (New York, 1951). See also his 'New Directions from Old,' *Myth and Myth-Making*, ed. Richard Ohmann (New York, 1962), 66–82; 'The Problem of Spiritual Authority in the Nineteenth Century,' *Literary Views: Critical and Historical Essays*, ed. Carroll Camden (Chicago, 1964), 145–58; 'The Revelation to Eve,' *Paradise Lost: A Tercentenary Tribute*, 18–47 (reprinted in *The Stubborn Structure: Essays on Criticism and Society* [Ithaca, NY, 1970], ch.9); and *Spiritus Mundi: Essays on Literature, Myth, and Society* (Bloomington, IN, 1976), ch. 7. For further details on these items, see Robert D. Denham, *Northrop Frye: An Annotated Bibliography of Primary and Secondary Sources* (Toronto, 1987); and Angela Esterhammer, introduction to *Northrop Frye on Milton and Blake*, xvii–xxxiv.

45 Gordon Campbell and Thomas N. Corns, *John Milton: Life, Work, and Thought* (Oxford, 2008), 1.

46 Balachandra Rajan, *'Paradise Lost' and the Seventeenth Century Reader*, 58–9.

MILTON AND QUESTIONS OF HISTORY

Essays by Canadians Past and Present

REPRINTS

1 The Modern Reaction to Milton*

DOUGLAS BUSH

Among the generality of people the number who prefer *Paradise Lost* to the current best seller is probably smaller than the number who prefer Bach to a 'name band,' and no one would expect either group to be very large. But among the musical, even those who have an imperfect sympathy with Bach would not dream of sniffing at the *B Minor Mass*, while many of the literary sniff freely at *Paradise Lost* though such persons, who shy away from Milton's biblical story and learned seriousness, will embrace with enthusiasm the often ponderous erudition and philosophizing of Thomas Mann's novel of Joseph. However, we are not much concerned with the legendary terrors which, in many minds, envelop a poet identified with religious themes and sublimity of imagination and tone. We are concerned with the critical reaction against Milton and *Paradise Lost* in particular which has been a very audible phenomenon of the past twenty-five years or more. That reaction, to be sure, has made small headway among those who really know Milton, and it has involved only a few critics, but it has for the most part been carried on with the kind of arrogant self-confidence which these same critics regard as one of Milton's central defects, and in literary criticism, as in other forms of propaganda, confident assertion goes a long way. So far as the reaction has embodied genuinely critical ideas, it has of course been salutary. We do not want to admire Milton or any other writer by tradition and blind faith, and if antagonism of any sort compels us to re-examine his credentials and our own feelings and opinions, it is all to the good.

---

* Originally appearing in *'Paradise Lost' in Our Time* (New York, 1948), comprising Bush's 1944 Messenger Lectures at Cornell University.

This modern reaction is the subject of our first hour, and I must apologize to the audience, especially to those members of it who are here for the last time, for what seems the unavoidable necessity of approaching Milton by a controversial road. In the three lectures that follow, we shall be looking directly at Milton and much less at his critics, but it is impossible to discourse on *Paradise Lost* without taking account of the recent wave of hostility, a wave which appears to have carried a shoal of young intellectuals along with it. If there be any people who think that the rise or fall of Milton's fame is not of much moment in a war-torn world, we may remember that poetry has outlived many wars and that Milton is one of the great portions of that heritage for which the war has been fought, that, as Wordsworth wrote when Europe lay under the heel of Napoleon,

> We must be free or die, who speak the tongue
> That Shakespeare spake; the faith and morals hold
> Which Milton held.

Millions of people nowadays are anxious lest, having won the war, we fail to achieve lasting peace; but it would also be calamitous if, possessing such a poet and prophet as Milton, we should show ourselves unworthy of the possession. For indifference or hostility to him is not a mere matter of liking or disliking a particular poet; it belongs to the much larger question whether the tastes and standards of our generation reflect spiritual health or disease. It is rather doubtful if we do hold the faith and morals which Milton held.

Nineteenth-century liberalism often inclined critics of that age to recoil from Milton's religious beliefs, or supposed beliefs, while they celebrated his passion for liberty and his transcendent art and music. The modern critics have carried on one nineteenth-century impulse by summarily dismissing or denouncing Milton's religious ideas, and they have gone much further in attacking his poetic art as well. Their dethronement of Milton was necessary to the enthronement of Donne. The enormous modern vogue of Donne was in part solidly based on the great virtues of a kind of writing which had been inadequately appreciated. That kind of writing, to which the name 'metaphysical' has long been attached, may be briefly defined as poetry which simultaneously embraces diverse planes of experience and is characterized by realistic immediacy, particularity, and complexity, by a fusion of thought and feeling, by the interplay of irony and wit, and by diction, syntax, and rhythms which belong to the genius of common speech. But the vogue of Donne, however solidly based, was attended with a good deal of extravagance, and with some degree of snob appeal; many young people hastened to worship a difficult poet who had not been 'clapper-clawed with the palms of the vulgar.' That for Mr. T.S. Eliot the exaltation of one kind of writing should require the denigration of another is quite understandable, since a highly original poet can seldom enjoy poetry which is not akin to his own and which he cannot 'use,' but such narrowness of sensibility is rather less natural in Mr. Eliot's unpoetic satellites.

Donne was not the only representative of 'metaphysical' poetry set up against the classicist Milton. There were Donne's successors and also, and especially, Dante, Shakespeare, and George Chapman. But the critics were not altogether consistent in their consideration of poetic art and poetic substance. They were sufficiently aware of the substance and meaning of poetry to be allergic to Milton's ideas as well as his style, but they did not apparently observe that their admired models of sensibility and expression, Dante, Shakespeare, and Chapman, were in their religious and ethical creed more or less close to Milton and very remote from most of themselves.

Further, the reaction against Milton coincided at some points with a reaction against the romantic poets of the early nineteenth century. To defeatist intellectuals of the 'Armistice' period, 1918–1939, any form of idealism was anathema, whether romantic or Miltonic. The sceptical, cynical, and sensual irresponsibility of Jack Donne was, or seemed to be, very modern, and was much more congenial than either romantic faith in humanitarian progress or Milton's more strenuous and exacting faith in God, order, and individual righteousness.

While the personal opinions of a literary scholar, as he is frequently reminded by literary gentlemen, are of no account whatever, I should like, just to keep the record straight, to say that I have great admiration for Mr. Eliot's poetry and have more than once so testified in print; and that I have as much admiration for Donne as is good for anyone, and a perhaps excessive admiration for Chapman, Herbert, Vaughan, and Marvell. If I raise my voice against the sometimes fantastic adulation of Donne and the sometimes fantastic depreciation of Milton, it is not because I dislike metaphysical poetry. I have merely pointed out some of the less valid reasons which have gone along with valid ones in establishing the cult of Donne; and I do not think that a right view of Milton's greatness necessitates uncritical disparagement of the metaphysicals, or vice versa. I do think that the house of poetry, nondramatic poetry, has many mansions, and that Milton still occupies the royal suite. And I think it is important for us in these times that we should relive the experience of Milton, that a multitude of readers to whom he can give much should not be alienated by a small but dogmatic chorus of opinion. There is indeed ground for belief that the righting of our poetical perspective was under way before the war began, and that the war will be found to have completed the process. Viewed against the scope and stress of a world conflict, Milton's stature, and Donne's, somehow assume their true proportions.

Whether or not that belief commands assent, we are considering the modern reaction against Milton. With that movement one would certainly not associate Mr. Oliver Elton and Sir Herbert Grierson, yet these eminent scholar-critics may be mentioned as men of nineteenth-century vintage who, with all their aesthetic admiration, have apparently been unable to see in *Paradise Lost* a great religious poem. And the late Archbishop of Canterbury doubtless spoke for some laymen when he declared that Milton's longer poems bored him stiff. But the active campaign against Milton has been conducted by younger guerrilla warriors. We might begin by naming Mr. Ezra Pound, though we shall pass him by, since his notion of Milton is not of much more value than his notion of, say, his own learning or of Fascism. Nor shall we linger with Mr. Herbert Read, whose studies of Wordsworth and Shelley indicate some capacity for aberration, and whose opinion of Milton is comprehended in that of critics to be mentioned later. Mr. Wilson Knight is a fire worshiper whom *Paradise Lost* leaves cold, or at least with a mixture of chills and fever. In 1939 Mr. Knight produced a long critique, mainly of the epic, entitled 'The Frozen Labyrinth.' In 1942, having felt the impact of the war, Mr. Knight mounted the architect of the frozen labyrinth in a chariot of wrath as the great apostle of national liberty and destiny. One may respect the feeling behind the change while thinking that Milton might have preferred relatively intelligible criticism to a whirlwind apotheosis.

For a clear statement of a common attitude we may go to Mr. Middleton Murry. Mr. Murry acknowledges some sort of greatness in Milton, but sees in him a repellent type of secularized Protestantism:

> ... his apparent peculiarity is that he is overweeningly confident in the natural man, or at least in the natural reason of man ...
>
> On the moral and spiritual side I find it easy enough to place him: he is, simply, a bad man of a very particular kind, who is a bad man because he is so sublimely certain of being a good one ... But these defences of Milton teach us nothing; they tell us nothing new. They are irrelevant to our dissatisfaction with Milton: which is that a poet so evidently great, in some valid sense of the word, should have so little intimate meaning for

> us. We cannot make him real. He does not, either in his great effects or his little ones, touch our depths. He demonstrates, but he never reveals. He describes beauty beautifully; but truth never becomes beauty at his touch.[1]

This judgment is typical of both the religious romantic and the secular romantic. Mr. F.R. Leavis expresses a similar dislike of Milton:

> He has 'character,' moral grandeur, moral force; but he is, for the purposes of his undertaking, disastrously single-minded and simple-minded. He reveals everywhere a dominating sense of righteousness and a complete incapacity to question or explore its significance and conditions. This defect of intelligence is a defect of imagination. He offers as ultimate for our worship mere brute assertive will, though he condemns it unwittingly by his argument and by glimpses of his own finer human standard. His volume of moral passion owes its strength too much to innocence – a guileless unawareness of the subtleties of egotism – to be an apt agent for projecting an 'ordered whole of experience.'[2]

But Mr. Leavis is more interested in the technique and tone of poetry than in its moral values, and his main concern is the stiff, heavy English of *Paradise Lost.*

A further roll call of rebel angels would indicate that they say pretty much the same things, and we shall give our attention to two or three representatives. Much the most important, both in priority and in authority, is Mr. Eliot. Mr. Leavis' essay, cited a moment ago, begins with these smug words:

> Milton's dislodgment, in the past decade, after his two centuries of predominance, was effected with remarkably little fuss. The irresistible argument was, of course, Mr. Eliot's creative achievement; it gave his few critical asides – potent, it is true, by context – their finality, and made it unnecessary to elaborate a case.

Apparently Mr. Eliot's critical asides, though potent, were not quite final, since the complete demolition of Milton required twenty-five pages from Mr. Leavis. However, the central fact was that the poetic world was not big enough to contain both Milton and Mr. Eliot, and Milton had to go. Whatever the motives of Mr. Eliot's camp followers and others, his own sniping at Milton has been a kind of oblique – and quite needless – justification of his own poetry.

Perhaps the most potent of all Mr. Eliot's ideas was that, in the unified sensibility of the metaphysical poets, thought and feeling and the most diverse kinds of experience were fused, whereas Milton, who lacked that capacious and flexible sensibility, made a baneful divorce between thought and feeling and imposed that dissociation upon his successors up to our own day. Such a doctrine, involving not only the metaphysicals and Milton but the whole range of English poets, would seem to require a considerable analysis of a vast and various body of writing before it could be launched even as a hypothesis. But Mr. Eliot covered the ground in a few pages or paragraphs, and among all moderns who profess critical intelligence this has been a standard dogma ever since. One might exclaim, as Dr. Johnson did about Goldsmith's debts, 'Was ever poet so trusted before?' Of Mr. Eliot's place in poetry there can be no question, and his criticism is already classical in one sense; it has become a part of English literary history because it has been the main agent in effecting a revolution in taste. But the other or 'classicist' meaning of 'classical' seems rather less evident. Although Mr. Eliot has chosen that label for himself and wears the mantle of authority, his critical essays, with all their ordered lucidity and insight and impersonal traditionalism, are not seldom more valuable in illuminating their author than in illuminating their subjects. They may be utterances of that 'Inner Voice' for which Mr. Eliot once chided Mr. Murry and others, and to the inner voice one may, in Mr. Eliot's own phrase, remain an inner deaf-mute.

In 1936 Mr. Eliot went about the business of iconoclasm more directly in a short essay called 'A Note on the Verse of John Milton.'[3] The modest title is a reminder that a commando raid by Mr. Eliot is equivalent to full-scale invasion. While Milton is not, apparently, a good poet, he is admitted, reluctantly, to be a very great one, but, like Mr. Murry, Mr. Eliot is puzzled to decide in what Milton's greatness consists:

> As a man, he is antipathetic. Either from the moralist's point of view, or from the theologian's point of view, or from the psychologist's point of view, or from that of the political philosopher, or judging by the ordinary standards of likeableness in human beings, Milton is unsatisfactory.

If we are not disposed to accept a simple 'Off with his head!' we may ask to what kind of moralist, theologian, psychologist, political philosopher, and human being Milton is unsatisfactory. All that emerges from the supposedly universal verdict is that Mr. Eliot does not like the mind and personality of Milton; and his way of saying so illustrates his agreement with the remark he once quoted from Rémy de Gourmont, that it is a man's great effort, if he is sincere, to erect his personal impressions into laws.

As theologian and political thinker Milton may be antipathetic to Mr. Eliot, as he was on similar grounds to Dr. Johnson; it does not follow that he is antipathetic to a large number of other intelligent people. As for 'the psychologist,' all of us rest under his disapproval, and the nature of Milton's special obliquity one may be unable to guess. What indictment can be lodged by 'the moralist' is not clear, unless it is that, like some of the Church fathers, Milton could be violent in controversy and that, like some other upright men, he accepted the execution of King Charles.[4] If these things are what disturbed Mr. Eliot's 'moralist,' we may observe that, in writing a eulogy of Lancelot Andrewes and his sermons, Mr. Eliot did not think it necessary to mention what has troubled other admirers, the saintly bishop's approval of the infamous Countess of Essex' infamous plea for divorce and his acceptance of, or share in, the sending of a heretic to the stake.

Finally, although Mr. Eliot may not like what he knows of Milton as a human being (and although one may doubt if Isaiah or Aeschylus or Dante was very likeable), there is plentiful evidence in Milton's writings and in the early biographies that he liked and was liked by a varied circle of friends, that he had, as Miss Darbishire says, the genius for friendship. And his funeral was attended not only by 'all his learned and great friends' but by 'a friendly concourse of the vulgar.'[5]

So much for Milton the bad man. Since it is axiomatic in modern criticism that our concern is with an author's works and not his personal character, this would seem an irrelevant topic if it were not that the anti-Miltonists use their prejudice against the man as a ready and easy way to establish a prejudice against his poetry. They seldom use that approach to Donne, in spite of the abundant material at hand – and quite apart from Donne's early libertinism, which is indeed an asset, being so much more human and attractive than Milton's strict virtue. I have no desire to prove Milton a saint, which he was not. But those of us who do not feel qualified to cast stones at him might pause for a minute to recall another judgment, familiar though it is, delivered by a man nearer to Milton in literary stature, as well as in time, than any modern:

Milton! thou shouldst be living at this hour:
England hath need of thee: she is a fen
Of stagnant waters: altar, sword, and pen,
Fireside, the heroic wealth of hall and bower,

Have forfeited their ancient English dower
Oh! raise us up, return to us again;
And give us manners, virtue, freedom, power.
Thy soul was like a Star, and dwelt apart;
Thou hadst a voice whose sound was like the sea:
Pure as the naked heavens, majestic, free,
So didst thou travel on life's common way,
In cheerful godliness; and yet thy heart
The lowliest duties on herself did lay.

We may ask ourselves which view of Milton comes nearer the mark.

Having disposed of Milton the man and the thinker, Mr. Eliot speaks of his bad influence. As regards the pseudo-Miltonism of many eighteenth-century poets, he admits that a good deal of the responsibility may devolve upon those poets themselves, but he affirms that 'Milton's poetry could only be an influence for the worse, upon any poet whatever ... that Milton's bad influence may be traced much farther than the eighteenth century, and much farther than upon bad poets,' and that it is 'an influence against which we still have to struggle.'[6] Mr. Eliot seems to have forgotten his own dictum, uttered apropos of Seneca, that 'the influence of any man is a different thing from himself';[7] and we should hesitate to blame Mr. Eliot for the not always successful efforts of his imitators.

But all our guns are spiked by the next pronouncement. Of what the critic has to say against Milton he considers that 'the only jury of judgement is that of the ablest poetical practitioners' of his own time![8] One defect in the logic of this declaration has been pointed out by Mr. C.S. Lewis that we cannot, on such terms, even know who are the ablest poetical practitioners of our time, or whether Mr. Eliot is a poet, nor can Mr. Eliot himself know without begging the question. Another large fallacy is less abstract. Throughout the eighteenth and nineteenth and early twentieth centuries a successive series of Eliots might have appealed to the judgment of the ablest poetical practitioners of their times, and they would have got a series of unanimous or almost unanimous verdicts that Milton was the greatest and best of English nondramatic poets. It appears, however, that almost the whole array of English poets for over two hundred years were merely wrong, while the judgment of the ablest poets of our time is infallible and final. Who make up this great tribunal Mr. Eliot does not indicate. The only modern poet mentioned in the essay is Mr. Pound, whose infallibility we may be forgiven for doubting.

If other able poets of our time have testified against Milton, I do not remember their names; but I do remember that such modernist poets as Allen Tate, John Crowe Ransom, and Yvor Winters have manifested their admiration. Again, under the show of authority, we are listening to Mr. Eliot's inner voice.

The main thesis of Mr. Eliot's essay is that throughout his poetry Milton lacks a visual imagination and that he sacrifices to sound the naturalness of speech and the vitality of words; whereas Shakespeare conveys the feeling of being in a particular place at a particular time, and offers perpetual novelty in his combinations of words, Milton's language is vague, artificial, and conventional. One hardly needs to point out how uncritical is the anti-Miltonist habit here illustrated, the open or tacit setting up of Shakespeare's realistic dramatic speech as a standard by which to try the wholly different nondramatic poetry of Milton – though one might expect the author of *The Waste Land* and *Ash-Wednesday*, *Murder in the Cathedral*, and *The Family Reunion*, to be aware of such a fundamental difference.

Mr. Eliot first quotes the lines from *Macbeth* on 'The temple-haunting martlet' and 'Light thickens,' and then, by way of contrast with Shakespeare's naturalness and particularity, gives us three bits of conventional artifice from Milton's early work. One is a line from a lyric in the little masque, *Arcades* –

> O'er the smooth enamell'd green –

in which 'enamell'd' is marked for censure. Since Marvell has all the virtues Milton lacks, and has none of the Miltonic vices, we may wonder if Mr. Eliot also condemns Marvell's picture of Bermuda:

> He gave us this eternal Spring,
> Which here enamels every thing.

Milton is not trying to make us see and feel grass; he wishes, like Marvell, to suggest something finer than mere nature provides.

Mr. Eliot's second example of conventional artifice is from the opening of *Comus*:

> paths of this drear Wood,
> The nodding horror of whose shady brows
> Threats the forlorn and wand'ring Passenger.

Milton is personifying his symbolic wood by way of heightening its sinister darkness. Mr. Eliot presumably does not like 'nodding horror,' presumably because he sees the phrase as a bit of eighteenth-century poetic diction. But at the time Milton was writing it was a novelty. As Mr. Geoffrey Tillotson has shown the use of English derivatives in their classical meaning was beginning in the early seventeenth century, and such words – like some of Mr. Eliot's classicisms of diction – had an effect comparable to the metaphysical wit and surprise. Granted that these lines of Milton's have no special distinction, they show already a touch of that suggestive vagueness which can be as essential for its purpose as particularity.

That Mr. Eliot's demand for particularity is purely arbitrary dogma is made very clear by his third example. The imagery in 'L'Allegro' and 'Il Penseroso,' he says, is all general, and he quotes:

While the Plowman near at hand,
Whistles o'er the Furrow'd Land,
And the Milkmaid singeth blithe,
And the Mower whets his scythe,
And every Shepherd tells his tale
Under the Hawthorn in the dale.

Mr. Eliot must surely be the only critic who ever complained of these buoyant lines. 'It is not,' he says, 'a particular ploughman, milkmaid, and shepherd that Milton sees (as Wordsworth might see them); the sensuous effect of these verses is entirely on the ear, and is joined to the concepts of ploughman, milkmaid, and shepherd.'[9] One would have thought it obvious that realistic particularity would be quite out of place in a 'landscape with figures,' in ideal pictures designed to express and evoke contrasted moods. One wonders if the ploughman should have been individualized with the swollen ankles of Simon Lee, or if the name of poetry should be denied to such generalized pastoral images as: 'The Lord is my shepherd; I shall not want. He maketh me to lie down in green pastures: he leadeth me beside the still waters.'

The lack of new life in Milton's language, Mr. Eliot continues, appears even in his most mature work, and he quotes *Samson Agonistes*:

The Sun to me is dark
And silent as the Moon,
When she deserts the night,
Hid in her vacant interlunar cave.

The description of the moon's darkness as silence, an arresting figure used by Virgil and Dante, gains fresh power, as Mr. Tillyard points out, on the lips of the blind Samson. But what Mr. Eliot dislikes is 'vacant' and 'cave,' and his dislike – to follow Mr. Tillyard further – arises from ignorance of the ancient astronomical idea Milton employs, that of the moon's retiring into a cave between her bright appearances, an idea which is here related, with concentrated, subtle, and ironic indirectness, to Samson's present but temporary impotence.[10]

A tortuous style, says Mr. Eliot, is not necessarily a dead one, when its peculiarity is aimed at precision; only when complication is dictated by a demand of verbal music, instead of by any demand of sense. He then compares a speech of Satan's with a passage in Henry James, whose intricate utterance is aimed at precision and not merely at sound. The complication of a Miltonic sentence, on the other hand, is 'a complication deliberately introduced into what was a previously simplified and abstract thought. The dark angel here is not *thinking* or conversing, but making a speech carefully prepared for him; and the arrangement is for the sake of musical value, not for significance. A straightforward utterance, as of a Homeric or Dantesque character, would make the speaker very much more real to us; but reality is no part of the intention.'[11] This is the Miltonic speech, a speech delivered by Satan to his followers after God has proclaimed Christ as His Son and the Messiah:

Thrones, Dominations, Princedoms, Virtues, Powers,
If these magnific Titles yet remain
Not merely titular, since by Decree
Another now hath to himself Ingross't
All Power, and us eclipst under the name
Of King anointed, for whom all this haste
Of midnight march, and hurried meeting here,
This only to consult how we may best
With what may be devis'd of honours new
Receive him coming to receive from us
Knee-tribute yet unpaid, prostration vile,
Too much to one, but double how endur'd,
To one and to his image now proclaim'd?

One may be unable to see what is complicated or tortuous in these lines. The sense is plain and the whole speech reveals Satan's thwarted ambition and passionate resentment. Further, the critic has failed to grasp Milton's intention. We are told that Satan is not thinking or conversing, as he should be. Of course he is not. He is the leader of a rebellion making a speech of exhortation to his followers, flattering and arousing them by recalling what splendid titles and powers they have enjoyed and are now being deprived of. In such a situation rhetorical magniloquence is essential to the effect he desires. We might, by the way, put beside Milton part of 'a straightforward utterance' from Dante:

> The next triad, that in like manner bourgeons in this sempiternal spring which the nightly Aries despoils not, perpetually sing Hosannah with three melodies, which sound in the three orders of joy wherewith it is threefold. In this hierarchy are the three divinities, first Dominations, and then Virtues; the third order is of Powers. Then, in the two penultimate dances, the Principalities and Archangels circle; the last is wholly of Angelic sports. These orders all gaze upward, and downward so prevail, that toward God all are drawn, and all draw.[12]

Is this speaker so obviously 'thinking or conversing,' even in the lucidity of a prose translation? Is she so 'very much more real to us' than the angry Satan?

Mr. Eliot quotes two more specimens of Milton's rhetoric. One is the geographical passage in the eleventh book of *Paradise Lost* where Michael, beginning his revelation of human history to Adam, takes him up a high hill like that

> Whereon for different cause the Tempter set
> Our second Adam in the Wilderness,
> To show him all Earth's Kingdoms and thir Glory.

We could not have a plainer declaration of Milton's purpose. Then comes the compendious and suggestive survey of the great empires and rich cities of the world, the realms of khan and mogul, czar and sultan, all symbols of the power and pomp and vanity of earthly kings and all familiar in history and books of travel. And this is what Mr. Eliot (with the support of that sensitive Miltonic critic, Richard Bentley) pronounces not serious poetry, but rather a solemn game.[13]

The other passage is from 'Lycidas':

> Whether beyond the stormy Hebrides,
> Where thou perhaps under the whelming tide

Visit'st the bottom of the monstrous world;
Or whether thou to our moist vows denied,
Sleep'st by the fable of Bellerus old,
Where the great vision of the guarded Mount
Looks toward Namancos and Bayona's hold.

'Than which,' says Mr. Eliot, 'for the single effect of grandeur of sound, there is nothing finer in poetry.'[14] The critic's thesis makes this left-handed praise. He does not observe that the geographical allusions are presented with great visual power, the full power of the best Miltonic mixture of the precise and the vague. Nor does he perceive that the purpose and effect of these allusions, which are only and greatly heightened by the sound, are to give us an overwhelming sense of the littleness and helplessness of man in a world of natural forces which God does not seem to control. Finally, we might ask if these lines are an example of Milton's pervasive deadness of language, or of his pervasive failure to fuse thought and feeling?

Mr. Eliot's general conclusions must be quoted in full:

> A disadvantage of the rhetorical style appears to be, that a dislocation takes place, through the hypertrophy of the auditory imagination at the expense of the visual and tactile, so that the inner meaning is separated from the surface, and tends to become something occult, or at least without effect upon the reader until fully understood. To extract everything possible from *Paradise Lost,* it would seem necessary to read it in two different ways, first solely for the sound, and second for the sense. The full beauty of his long periods can hardly be enjoyed while we are wrestling with the meaning as well; and for the pleasure of the ear the meaning is hardly necessary, except in so far as certain key-words indicate the emotional tone of the passage. Now Shakespeare, or Dante, will bear innumerable readings, but at each reading all the elements of appreciation can be present. There is no interruption between the surface that these poets present to you and the core. While, therefore, I cannot pretend to have penetrated to any 'secret' of these poets, I feel that such appreciation of their work as I am capable of points in the right direction; whereas I cannot feel that my appreciation of Milton leads anywhere outside of the mazes of sound. That, I feel, would be the matter for a separate study, like that of Blake's prophetic books; it might be well worth the trouble, but would have little to do with my interest in the poetry. So far as I perceive anything, it is a glimpse of a theology that I find in large part repellent, expressed through a mythology which

> would have been better left in the Book of Genesis, upon which Milton has not improved. There seems to me to be a division, in Milton, between the philosopher or theologian and the poet ...[15]

This curious mixture of ultrasophistication and naïveté leaves us with the exponent of an odious theology who has only one gift, that of creating mazes of sound. It is a verdict we might have expected Mr. Eliot to render upon Swinburne. It is puzzling to guess how he could call Milton a very great poet indeed.

To go through an essay item by item, in the fashion of a seventeenth-century controversialist, is not a correct or mature or exciting procedure, but it has this advantage: it enables us to say that every time Mr. Eliot quotes and directly comments upon the text of Milton he clearly betrays a lack of perception and understanding. And these misread bits of Milton are the representative basis of his large generalizations. When all his evidence is unreliable, not even a jury of poets could give authority to his judgment. Would Mr. Eliot accept the judgments of a critic who read his own poetry, or that of his favorites, in the same spirit?

It should be said here that in his wise address to the Classical Association in 1942 Mr. Eliot coupled Shakespeare and Milton as our two greatest poets, and in a paragraph on Milton uttered what may have amounted to a palinode.[16] But even such a palinode, if it was one, cannot alter the fact that Mr. Eliot has done more than any other individual to turn a generation away from Milton – a fact doubly regrettable because Mr. Eliot and Milton, as poets in the classical-Christian tradition, are indissolubly allied against naturalistic disorder.

The unsupported, unexamined generalizations that we have reviewed are the kind of thing which passes current among anti-Miltonists, who follow the well-known principle that what they tell us three times must be true. Let us take one further example, which might be called semiofficial, since it comes from the introduction to the *Oxford Book of Christian Verse* (1940). In surveying his chief writers the editor, Lord David Cecil, says:

> Donne takes first place among English Christian poets. For he alone is equally interesting as Christian and as poet ... And religion was to him so stimulating a subject that there was hardly an aspect of it that did not fire him to poetry.

We shall not pause to question these very questionable remarks but will proceed to what is of more direct interest. Milton, Lord David declares,

> was not essentially a religious poet. He was a philosopher rather than a devotee. His imagination was lucid and concrete, unlit by heavenly gleams; theology to him was a superior branch of political science, the rule of reason and the moral law as exhibited in the working of the cosmos. Nor was his moral sensibility a Christian one. The Stoic virtues, fortitude, temperance, above all, moral independence, were what he valued. He did not live by faith, scorned hope, and was indisposed to charity; while pride, so far from being the vice which Christianity considers it, was to Milton the mark of a superior nature. As an exponent of the Christian spirit he cannot compare with Donne or Herbert. But if he is not our greatest religious poet, he is the greatest of English poets who have made religion their subject ... As an exposition of Christian belief *Paradise Lost* and *Paradise Regained* are failures. In *Paradise Lost* All-holy God and innocent Adam are made equally irritable and egotistic; Christ in *Paradise Regained* is an austere, unsympathetic classical philosopher. But for mastery of design, for distinction of style, for sustained grandeur of conception, Milton surpasses every other poet whose works are quoted in this collection.[17]

Here we have the good old story, considerably heightened on the adverse side. Not to speak of other matters of opinion or prejudice, on which one could say something, one would like some evidence for the assertion concerning Milton's want of faith, hope, and even charity (the anti-Miltonists' own peculiar virtue!) and his high esteem for unchristian pride. The nature of the poet's religious thought and feeling had been made pretty clear, before Lord David wrote, by a number of Miltonists, but one surmises that his pronouncements were based on boyhood recollections of Milton and Sir Walter Raleigh's book. The anti-Miltonists in general, like Congreve's Petulant, do not need learning, they rely altogether on their parts. It is worth noting that the author of a leading article on Lord David's book, in the semiofficial organ of English criticism, the London *Times Literary Supplement*, quoted some of his chief dicta on Milton and acquiesced in them as a matter of course, with only a slight peripheral qualification. So long as such ex-cathedra verdicts can be delivered from such quarters, so long are mere scholars justified in opposing them.

Since this hostility to Milton has developed almost wholly in his own country,[18] and since such Englishmen as Messrs. Tillyard, Charles Williams, C.S. Lewis, and R.W. Chambers – not to mention the work of American scholars – have written sensitive and cogent expositions and defenses of Milton, it may be said, or thought, that there can be no occasion for another and inevitably less sensitive and cogent defense. There is no adequate reply to that. But by way of extenuation one may say, first, that one has one's own view of Milton and feels moved to express it; secondly, that most 'general readers' here as well as in England seem to rest in the nineteenth-century notion of verbal and musical beauties divorced from obsolete substance; and, thirdly, that a good many bright American undergraduates have been infected by the modernist reaction and of late years have poured forth with monotonous glibness the dogmas of the 'metaphysical' and anti-Miltonist creed though it should be added that some other bright, or perhaps brighter, undergraduates have remained proof against the fear of holding an unfashionable opinion.

Much as I should like to speak of Milton's other works, early and late, we are focusing our attention upon *Paradise Lost* because it has borne the brunt of the attack. And we shall look first at some of the central principles of Milton's religious and ethical thought. If any excuse be needed for such a natural enterprise, we may find one in the opening words of Mr. Eliot's essay on 'Religion and Literature':

> Literary criticism should be completed by criticism from a definite ethical and theological standpoint. In so far as in any age there is common agreement on ethical and theological matters, so far can literary criticism be substantive. In ages like our own, in which there is no such common agreement, it is the more necessary for Christian readers to scrutinize their reading, especially of works of imagination, with explicit ethical and theological standards. The 'greatness' of literature cannot be determined solely by literary standards; though we must remember that whether it is literature or not can be determined only by literary standards.[19]

As we have seen, Mr. Eliot allows that Milton belongs, in a pernicious way, to literature, but he contradicts the sound theory just quoted by saying that the exploration of Milton's repellent ideas would have little to do with his own interest in the poetry. In the face of such inconsistency we can only appeal from Philip prejudiced to Philip unprejudiced.

If we needed any negative excuse for considering Milton's thought, in addition to that provided by the anti-Miltonists' unanimous ignorance, we might find it in Mr. Logan Pearsall Smith's *Milton and His Modern Critics* (1940–1941). On the positive side of his argument Mr. Smith did not go much beyond an ardent but rather slight eulogy of Milton's art and music. Milton was assuredly always an artist, and in general, most of us may think, a great artist, but he did not prayerfully and repeatedly dedicate his life and faculties to the manipulation of vowels and consonants. If a reputedly great poet has no other claim upon us than his style and sound, however wonderful these may be, we might better admit that he is dead and read poets who still have something to say. But before we assent too readily to the conventional view that *Paradise Lost* is a monument to dead ideas, and the poet's art the decoration on a tomb, we may ask, first, what those ideas were, and, secondly, if they are in essence so remote from us and our world, if they are not, rather, very close to what many modern thinkers have been declaring are necessary to our own necessary regeneration. Nowadays old and young are full of zeal for a better world, and that of course is fine. But, to judge from the millions of words poured into print and into the air, much of that zeal is directed toward making other people better, or making more and better gadgets. In all his major poems Milton is occupied with the far more real and fundamental problem, of making one's self better. And he makes us better not merely through his imaginative and 'poetical' beauties but through the total effect of his religious and ethical theme, through his profound concern with 'man, the heart of man, and human life.'

NOTES

1 [John] Middleton Murry, *Studies in Keats New and Old*, 2nd ed. (1930; London: Oxford University Press, 1939), 110, 121–2.

2 F.R. Leavis, *Revaluation: Tradition & Development in English Poetry* (London: Chatto and Windus, 1936), 58. The essay first appeared in *Scrutiny* in 1933.

3 T.S. Eliot, ['A Note on the Verse of John Milton,'] *Essays and Studies by Members of the English Association* 21 [, ed. Herbert Read] (Oxford: Clarendon Press, 1936) [, 32–40].

4 It may be added that Milton's character and career have been scanned with peculiar zeal by a Swedish and a French scholar, and that the main charges they have been able to manufacture are: first, that Milton could not have visited Galileo as he said he had because the scientist was kept under surveillance – a kind of circumstantial argument which, applied to a case three centuries old, seems rather nebulous; and, secondly, that Milton, with the President of the Council, contrived to have a prayer from Sidney's *Arcadia* inserted in some issues of *Eikon Basilike* in order that Milton could 'smear' that dangerous book by exposing the passage. Without going into this matter, one can say that the witness invoked was a notorious rogue and that the modern arguments, apart from any question of Milton's character,

do not even make sense in themselves. A recent and vigorous discussion of the case is R.W. Chambers, 'Poets and their Critics: Langland and Milton,' *Proceedings of the British Academy* 27 (1941) [: 109–54].

5 A little later Mr. Eliot speaks of 'the peculiar education' Milton received as one of his liabilities. It was the same kind of education as that of the other seventeenth-century poets whom Mr. Eliot admires, the kind of classical-Christian education which Mr. Eliot has written two admirable essays to uphold as a prime need of our time. There was nothing in the least peculiar about Milton's education, unless that it was broader, and pursued with more intensity, than some other men's.

6 [Eliot, 'A Note,' 33.] (References to Eliot's pagination not provided in Bush's essay.)

7 T.S. Eliot, *Selected Essays, 1917–1932* (London: Faber and Faber, 1932), 132–3; (New York: Harcourt Brace, 1932), 113. In later remarks on Milton (see page 18 below), Mr. Eliot takes his earlier and sounder position.

8 [Eliot, 'A Note,' 33.]

9 [Ibid., 34.]

10 E.M.W. Tillyard, *The Miltonic Setting Past and Present* ([Cambridge:]Cambridge University Press; New York: Macmillan, 1938), 101–2.

11 [Eliot, 'A Note,' 36.]

12 Dante Alighieri, *The Divine Comedy*, trans. C.E. Norton (Boston: Houghton Mifflin, 1902), *Paradise*, xxviii.

13 Cf. Tillyard, *The Miltonic Setting*, 93.

14 [Eliot, 'A Note,' 39.]

15 [Ibid., 38.]

16 T.S. Eliot, *The Classics and the Man of Letters* (London: Oxford University Press, 1942).

17 Lord David Cecil, ed., *Oxford Book of Christian Verse* (Oxford: Clarendon Press, 1940), xvii, xxi–xxii.

18 One might add such a piece of crude fictional slander as Robert Graves's *Wife to Mr. Milton* (London: Cassell, 1943; New York: Creative Age Press, 1944).

19 T.S. Eliot, 'Religion and Literature,' *Essays Ancient and Modern* (London: Faber and Faber, 1936), 93; (New York: Harcourt Brace, 1936), 92.

2 From the Introduction to *Puritanism and Liberty**

A.S.P. WOODHOUSE

[11] The Debates have a special value, even beyond the pamphlet literature of the day, in giving us a spontaneous and unconscious revelation of the Puritan mind as it wrestles with its problems, practical and theoretic, in an effort not merely to justify a policy and battle down opposition, but to arrive at truth and agreement. There are the sharpest cleavages of opinion between the Independents and their allies to the Left, and they sometimes develop an acrimony in debate that suggests outlooks absolutely alien from each other. But even where they differ most markedly, they talk a common language very foreign to our ears; and all their differences are at last reducible to one: the point at which a revolutionary ideal must compromise with the demands of actual life, including those of order, tradition, sentiment, and vested interest. If the leaders on both sides came to the debate with a policy to advance, and with their minds largely closed, the other participants (who also reveal the Puritan temper and ideology) came both to convince and to be convinced; their presence and intervention are the necessary links between the opponents.[…]

[14] The chief interest of the Debates, and of the Supplementary Documents, is the light they throw on the Puritan mind. But if they are not to be misinterpreted they must be studied in connection with the situation in which the Puritans find themselves.

---

* The 1938 J.M. Dent edition has been used as a source text for this selection, though pagination is the same in all printings of *Puritanism and Liberty: Being the Army Debates (1647–49) from the Clarke Manuscripts*. Page numbers of the original are provided in square brackets, which are also used to indicate our emendations. Woodhouse's square brackets have been converted to angled ones.

II

Among the victors in the First Civil War (with their history of conflicting principles and interests temporarily controlled by the necessity of defeating the enemy) only one point was held in common: the restored King must be so bound that he could never exercise the arbitrary rule, civil and ecclesiastical, for whose overthrow the war had been fought. Beyond this general principle, disagreements at once emerged: first, as to the means of achieving the desired end, and what constituted satisfactory guarantees of its endurance; secondly, and more fundamentally, as to the disposition of the effectual sovereignty, taken from the King. Had that sovereignty been civil alone the problem would have presented enormous difficulties, but it was also ecclesiastical. In the Puritan revolution the religious problem may not have been – was not, in fact – more important than the civil, but in itself it was certainly the more difficult solution, and it so combined with the civil problem as to render it, too, well-nigh insoluble.

Among the victors four main groups may be roughly distinguished. Each has a particular set of principles to advance, and a particular set of interests to guard, in the proposed religious settlement; and each is not only influenced in its whole policy by the interests, but, in varying degrees, takes the colour of its political thinking from the principles. Three of the groups fall under the general designation of *Puritan*; the fourth stands apart, for its guiding principle is secular, not religious, and its interest in the ecclesiastical settlement, while lively, is negative. This [15] fourth group, known in the Long Parliament as the Erastians, is ineffectual in so far as it lacks the party organization which the two main Puritan groups possess, but influential through its power to combine with either of them and because it fully expresses the secular and anticlerical spirit of the nation, the spirit which will accept passively any settlement in the church so long as that settlement is powerless to tyrannize or to endanger the peace.

The first of the three religious groups, the Presbyterian, had led the attack on absolutism and dominated the earlier phases of the struggle with Charles. Though it had lost the military ascendancy it once possessed, it could still generally command a majority in Parliament, and it hoped (with or without Scottish aid) to effect a settlement of the kingdom in its own interests. It stood for adherence to the Covenant, the establishment of Presbyterianism on the general lines laid down by the Westminster Assembly, and the suppression of every other doctrine and order. It was opposed to toleration, and was in general less interested in liberty than reform. Its alliance with the Scots was its potential military strength and its actual political weakness, for in moments when national feeling ran high its majority in Parliament became a minority. But English Presbyterianism is not to be confounded with Scottish. Few indeed wished to see the Scottish church duplicated in England. Not only did the Presbyterian Party in Parliament rely on the Erastians to make its majority effective; its own adherents (as Baillie and his fellow Commissioners had lamented) were tainted with Erastianism. They would have a national Presbyterian church, and would suppress its rivals, but the church should be controlled by the state. In civil matters the Party was the most conservative of the revolutionaries(agreeing well enough with the Erastians herein); it was the Party of the Right in the Puritan coalition, finding its chief support among the aristocrats who had adhered to the Parliamentary cause, and the wealthy merchants of London, and fearing and hating the Parties of the Left for their civil, quite as much as their religious principles. The Presbyterians wished to limit the objectives of the revolution: to assert the effectual sovereignty not of the people but of Parliament, and to preserve at all costs the sanctity of property, whether real, personal, or political (the historic rights of the Crown and the material possessions of the Church alone excepted). The monarchy, shorn of its power, they would cherish in the interests of a lasting settlement – an assurance that the revolution had not been so very revolutionary after [16] all, and a guarantee that it should go no further. (Had not God given the Israelites kings, and whenever they could do so with impunity, had not that model people knocked them about?) The King was indeed essential to their scheme, and the time was to come when they would sacrifice almost anything but the church settlement to gain him. He refused their terms and ruined himself and them. The Party of the Right is unrepresented in the Army Debates except in so far as the Independent officers agree with its civil policy or regard its opinion as something to be opposed only with caution.

To the spirit of this civil policy, the Independents, or the Party of the Centre, as we may call them,[1] did not at first demur. But they were alarmed at its conjunction with an ecclesiastical ideal at variance with their own. The Independents were the heirs of the Presbyterians' former military ascendancy, and between winning victories and opposing the hated Scots, they were sometimes able to gain a majority in Parliament. A common distrust of Presbyterian clericalism also enabled them to rely up to a point on the support of the Erastians.[2] But even more than the Presbyterians', their majority, when achieved, was highly precarious. Being astute politicians they knew that Parliament (or at all events this Parliament) would never settle the religion of the nation on their plan. Accordingly they were (or pretended to be) satisfied with a state-controlled Presbyterian establishment, so long as a toleration, of the general kind demanded by the Dissenting Brethren in the Assembly, were assured; and even for this they seemed content to wait, evidently sharing to some extent Cromwell's comfortable assurance that heaven was on their side and would presently afford them an opportunity of taking what they wanted. Thus, partly through force of circumstances, but partly through a logical development of their own basic doctrines, the Independents became the party of toleration. This fact gave them an immense advantage outside Parliament; for it enabled [17] them to draw support from the Parties of the Left, almost unrepresented in the House of Commons, but strong in the Army, on which in the last analysis the Independents relied. As time went on an increasing rift between Independents and Presbyterians became apparent in the matter of the civil settlement. Like the Presbyterians (and Erastians), the leaders retained their respect for property, real, personal, and political. This is the burden of Ireton's impassioned argument at Putney: 'All the main thing that I speak for, is because I would have an eye to property' (57).[3] But they grew progressively less attached to the notion of the effectual sovereignty of Parliament, progressively more sensible of its tyranny; and, while loath to break with the existing Parliament, they sought a settlement which should put a definite limit to its life, and provide securely against the power of the restored King but also against the self-perpetuating tyranny of Parliaments in future. They discovered that if new presbyter was but old priest writ large, new Parliament also bore a striking resemblance to old King. To the monarchy itself they were certainly prepared to be not less generous than the Presbyterians, provided the King could be brought to their policy of discountenancing ecclesiastical tyranny, of ending the present Parliament, and of accepting the principle of biennial Parliaments – from whose power (as also from the King's) certain fundamental matters should be reserved, and whose institution should be preceded by certain electoral reforms. These are some of the provisions of the Independents' scheme of settlement, the *Heads of the Proposals* (422–6). But their attachment to monarchy was, like their attachment to Parliament, less deeply grounded than the Presbyterians'; it was more a matter of policy than of principle. The Independents could divest themselves of it when the moment came – when heaven (to adopt their own language) held forth the opportunity of other things; the Presbyterians could not. Independency is inherently the more radical creed. This does not mean that it is necessarily more democratic. In drawing support from the Parties of the Left, Independency allied itself with the one genuinely democratic party thrown up by the Puritan revolution, the Levellers, and temporarily even adopted some of their principles. But its immediate purpose served, the alliance dissolved, leaving the Levellers sadder and (as regards the Independents at least) wiser men. To gauge the cleavage between the Independents and their allies one has only to read the Putney Debates.

The Parties of the Left, the sectaries, religious and political, [18] were a heterogeneous company among whom the winds of doctrine assumed the proportions of a tempest. They were descended from the Separatists and Anabaptists, as the Independents were from the more sedate Congregationalists, and were, so to speak, the Independents' poor relations.[4] Among themselves they agreed in little save the belief in a total separation of church and state and the demand for liberty of conscience, both which tenets are logical developments of parts of the Independents' own creed, and the latter of them a main ground of the alliance between the sects and the Independent Party. Two significant types of opinion emerge among the sectaries. The one is recognizable as predominantly democratic in tendency, and ultimately secular in aim, though it maintains its emphasis on liberty of conscience and at times adopts the language of religious enthusiasm. This is the opinion of the Levellers (already mentioned), the political doctrinaires led by Lilburne, Overton, Wildman, and others. It appealed more or less definitely to many of the rank-and-file in the New Model, to the Agitators (old and new), and even to some of the higher officers such as Colonel Rainborough. The second type of opinion is at bottom neither democratic in tendency nor secular in aim. It emphasizes not the rights of the people, but the privileges of the Saints, and it looks forward to the millennium (which always seems to be just around the corner) when the Saints shall inherit the earth and rule it with, or on behalf of, Christ (232–47, 390–6). This is the type of opinion held by the Fifth Monarchy Men, the religious doctrinaires (if the title may be awarded to one group when there are so many highly qualified claimants). Much less effectively organized in 1647–9 than the Levellers, this party had an advantage in the experience of victorious warfare through which the Army had passed, and in the Army's susceptibility to religious enthusiasm. One cannot gauge the precise extent of its influence in the lower ranks. Probably that influence was very considerable, for up to a point it could [19] coalesce with democratic opinion. Among the higher officers Colonel Harrison and Lieutenant-Colonel Goffe are definite adherents, and others, including Cromwell himself, are not untouched by its spell.

Such, in brief, are the main groups into which the Puritans fall. As political forces these parties operate in three corporate but not homogeneous bodies, the Parliament, the City, and the Army;[5] and membership in each of these bodies partially, though only partially, cuts across party alignments and loyalties. (1) The Presbyterians' majority in Parliament (even after they were relieved of the odium of a Scottish army on English soil) was always insecure. Yet in a less overt way, the Presbyterian Party dominated Parliament up to the very moment of Pride's purge; for they, with the Erastians, were in a special sense the Parliamentary party, insistent on the sovereignty of Parliament, determined that the regal powers and functions should be transferred to it, and that there should be no dissolution of the existing Parliament till all was settled and the kingdom safe – if ever. In these views the Parliament as a whole acquiesced, and even the Independent Party in Parliament (as distinct from the Independents of the Army and their allies) were influenced by the 'interest' of Parliament and of themselves as members of that august body: they could be induced to submit to Pride's purge, but nothing could persuade the resulting Independent House of Commons to dissolve. Equally instructive to contemplate is the long struggle in Cromwell between the Leader of the Army and the member of the House of Commons. (2) In the oligarchy which ruled the City the power of the Presbyterians was far more secure than in the House of Commons,[6] and it was therefore a special object of the Army's distrust. It generally acted in collusion with the Presbyterian leaders in Parliament. But the City, like the Parliament, was jealous of its independence and had its own special interests, material and political, to guard, and on occasion these interests [20] conflicted with the needs of the Parliamentary party and the Presbyterian cause. (3) The Army was a corporate body in a sense somewhat different from Parliament and City, but no less real. Its *ethos* was as pronounced as theirs. All that it lacked was appropriate organs of expression, and these, with a remarkable initiative, it proceeded to create. The Army became, indeed, at once a sort of fourth estate in the realm, and a body not less representative than the (not very representative) Parliament at Westminster. It contained men of every shade of

Puritan opinion, and no doubt a substantial number quite indifferent to the special ideals of the various Puritan parties and intent only on the soldiers' material needs and grievances. But the political activities of the Army were dominated by two groups working in uneasy cooperation, the Independents, including many of the higher officers, and the Parties of the Left, finding their chief strength in the lower officers and the common troopers. These, and especially the leading Independents (Cromwell and Ireton, with a group of loyal colonels) shaped for the Army a policy which was in general harmony, but certainly not identical, with the policy of the Independent Party in Parliament. The Army had its own sense of corporate being and its own special needs and interests, in which officers and men of no close party affiliations could share. At the head of the Army, a symbol of its existence as a separate entity, stood Fairfax, of whom Gardiner remarks: 'most likely no one in England – probably not Fairfax himself – knew whether he was a Presbyterian or an Independent.'

A Parliament insecurely, but until Pride's purge fairly constantly, dominated by the Presbyterians; an Army increasingly dominated by the Independents; the City where the Presbyterian interest prevailed; at a distance the Scots, and at home a vast but relatively unorganized mass of Royalist and Anglican discontent, and a smaller but more articulate body of popular and radical discontent; and finally, the endless and futile machinations of Charles – this (with a brief interruption, of the Second Civil War) is the general scene presented by the two years between February 1647 and January 1649.[…]

[39] The Puritan turned to the theological aspects of a question as naturally as the modern man turns to the economic; and his first instinct was to seek guidance within the covers of his Bible – or was it rather to seek there justification for a policy already determined on other, on political and economic, grounds?[…] Granted the theological mode of argument is in some sort a 'rationalization,' granted even the disingenuousness with which it is often pursued; that does not dispose of the matter. The terms in which the Puritan insists that the argument shall be carried on, are real to him, and of first-rate historical importance because they are the terms in which he views his world. Ignore the terms, or misunderstand them, and the Puritan mind has eluded you. The Puritan viewed the world as a twofold system, a scheme of *nature* and a scheme of *grace*. The two were interrelated: because God was the creator and supreme ruler of them both, and because they had a common subject-matter in man, and a common object, the good. Man as *man*

belonged to the natural order; the elect belonged also to the order of grace. The author of *The Ancient Bounds* writes (247–8):

> Christ Jesus, whose is the kingdom, the power, and the glory, both in nature and in grace, hath given several maps and schemes of his [40] dominions ... both of his great kingdom, the world, his dominions at large which he hath committed to men to be administered in truth and righteousness, in a various form as they please ... and also his special and peculiar kingdom, the kingdom of grace. Which kingdoms though they differ essentially or formally, yet they agree in one common subject-matter (man and societies of men) though under a diverse consideration. And not only man in society, but every man individually, is an epitome, either of one only or of both these dominions: of one only, so every natural man (who in a natural consideration is called *microcosmus,* an epitome of the world), in whose conscience God hath his throne, ruling him by the light of nature to a civil outward good and end; of both, so every believer who, besides this natural conscience and rule, hath an enlightened conscience carrying a more bright and lively stamp of the kingly place and power of the Lord Jesus, swaying him by the light of faith or scripture, and such a man may be called *microchristus,* the epitome of Christ mystical.

There was a goodness appropriate to the natural order; and there was a goodness appropriate to the order of grace, which, while it included the natural goodness, also (because spiritual) transcended it. The views taken of the precise relation of these separate, yet interrelated orders, colour the Puritans' thought, and condition the terms – and perhaps more than the terms – of their particular and practical demands, as, for instance, that of Roger Williams for the absolute separation of church and state (the social organs of grace and nature) with complete liberty of conscience, or again the demand of others for the subjection of the natural man, and his institutions, to the church – or the Saints (241–7). God was the lawgiver of the two orders. Israel was a model (so ran the simpler view), and in the Bible might be read the precepts by which all men ought to be governed: 'Though the laws be few and brief, yet they are perfect and sufficient, and so large as the wisdom of God judged needful for regulating judgment in all ages and nations. For no action or case doth, or possibly can, fall out in this or other nations ... but the like did, or possibly might, fall out in Israel.'[7] If one was to escape the conclusion which the Old Testament enforced in a particular issue (as, for example, in the question of the magistrate's power in religion), it could be only by an appeal to the New Testament, with an elaborate argument tending to prove that Israel was 'typical,' that its law (or some part of its law) was abrogated by the appearance of Christ, who was the 'antitype,' and that Israel [41] furnished, therefore, no literal model for life under the Gospel. Beside precept and model, there was prophecy. Daniel and Revelation afforded a key to events, past and present, and a vision of the future. From these books the Millenarians derived a view of history and a motive of revolution. And the pattern exhibited coloured the thought of many who could not be described as active adherents, so that one may speak of Millenarian doctrine as in a sense typical.

The cultural and disciplinary value to the Puritan mind, of all this biblical study, formal theological reasoning, and eager and disputatious searching into the purposes of God, is rarely, I think, appreciated to the full. It was on such studies that the logical faculty of Roger Williams was formed. Narrow and one-sided as the Puritan mind is apt to be, it is never flaccid. In their attitude toward reason the Puritans differed widely among themselves, ranging from the extremes of voluntarism and obscurantism to almost pure rationalism; but whatever the avowed attitude, their tacit reliance in the exposition of dogma and text was on logical thought: no one was ever more insistent on hearing a reason for the faith that was in you. That is why Puritanism carried its own special mental discipline. The Debates furnish abundant illustration of the dominance of dogmatic religion and scriptural reference; it appears in connection with every subject discussed, and (though in varying degrees) in all the participants. Unbelievably remote as the argument often seems, its general level attests the bracing effect of the Puritan discipline on ordinary minds. Nor must the limits which it set to inquiry be exaggerated. Dogma, brought into hourly relation with life, led men beyond dogma. Especially is this true of the group who separated most sharply the two orders of nature and grace. But this is to anticipate.

According to the Puritan notion, God spoke in the first instance through his word – the dominance of dogmatic religion means Puritan scripturism; but there were two other modes of learning his will. There was the mode of immediate religious experience. If dogmatic religion is heavily represented in the Debates, so is experiential. There are moments when one could hardly parallel the atmosphere at Putney outside the walls of Little Bethel. Yet to the Puritans it seems perfectly natural. They listen to each others' experiences and are duly edified and impressed. Even the hard-headed Ireton is strangely moved (21–2). The exposition of dogma and text make their claim upon reason, but in these experiences imagination and emotion have their play: the [42] Puritan imagination is fired, and the passions necessary to great, and sometimes desperate enterprises, are kindled. And there is a community of feeling not less important than intellectual agreement; this, too, religious experience, enjoyed in common, fosters. But the thing has its dangers. Cromwell finds that he is without anything to report 'as in the name of the Lord' (102), and is a little fearful lest 'carnal imaginations' may pass themselves off as promptings from heaven (104). He prefers, because it seems more objective, the testimony of events. That is God's third mode of revealing his will. The Puritan lives in a world of particular providences. God has 'owned' the Army by the success he has vouchsafed.[8] Let the Army pursue its course, but let it not outrun its commission or seize an opportunity before God has given one; and guidance will not fail. We have seen the Army on its momentous march to London, 'there to follow Providence as God shall clear our way.' The way was cleared to Pride's purge and the judicial murder of the King.

The sense of special insight into, and co-operation with, the purposes of God, is a distinguishing mark of the Puritan, and it sets him at a distance from other men. It is both a strength and a weakness. At its worst it issues in self-righteousness. (All the publicans and sinners were on one side, said Chillingworth, all the scribes and Pharisees on the other.) But it nerved the arm and brought an access of courage, which on any other premise, would have been reckless. Like everything else in the Puritan's outlook, the separation from his fellows rested on a dogmatic basis: the doctrine of predestination taught him that it was from the beginning. The Saint alone belonged to the order of grace, with its special equipment, its privileges, and its duties. The possible inferences from this fact were various, but so long as the dogma remained unimpaired, or uncircumvented, the attitude towards the natural man was constant. 'Men as men,' said Ireton, 'are corrupt and will be so' (174).

If this account of the dominant place held by religion in the Puritan mind is even approximately correct, no wonder the religious issue bulked so large in the Civil War and the subsequent settlement. 'The interest of England is religion,' said Hugh Peter (138). 'Kings, and Armies, and Parliaments,' said another speaker, 'might have been quiet at this day if they would have let Israel alone' (147). And the religious issue is not [43] isolated. It complicates, and is complicated by, the civil.[9] Nor does the connection depend merely on the fact observed above, that each section of the Puritan Party has both religious and civil interests to guard, and religious and civil aims to secure. There is perpetual interaction between the two struggles. Passion generated in the one is available for the prosecution of the other. And here the primacy of the religious struggle appears: in it Puritan idealism burns with its steadiest flame, and religion exercises its influence not only directly by intrusion into the civil sphere, but indirectly by analogy. Milton speaks of 'the best part of our liberty, which is our religion'; and the Puritan's whole conception of liberty is (as we shall see) deeply coloured by his religious thought, while the second and partially incompatible object of his concern, positive reformation, is equally so coloured.

The zeal for positive reform[10] is one of the most constant and indisputable notes of Puritanism. 'Reform the universities ... Reform the cities ... the countries ... the Sabbath ... the ordinances, the worship of God ... *Every plant which my heavenly Father hath not planted shall be rooted up.*'[11] Alike in Presbyterians, Congregationalists, and the sects, the ideal of the 'holy community,'pure in doctrine and exemplary in life, is dominant; but with very different effects upon political thought and action. By the strictest and most logical of the Separatists the ideal is recognized as applicable to, and attainable by, the elect alone; and it operates within the limits of a voluntary religious community made up of visible Saints, with no attempt to influence the state save by exhortation and example. Wherever, on the other hand, the ideal is combined with that of a national church, an attempt will be made to bring the nation into outward conformity with the standard of the godly. The non-elect and the unbelievers are (as Troeltsch puts it) disciplined for the glory of God and the peace and welfare of the church. Thus the effect of what is at bottom the same motive would appear to be totally different in the Puritans of the Right and of the Left, with those of the Centre [44] occupying the interval between them. But this does not exhaust the possibilities. A further distinction has to be drawn among the Puritans of the Left, where the idea of a national church, at least in its Presbyterian form, has no place. It is among some of the sectaries, whose church organization is Separatist and who (for their own purposes) join in the plea for liberty of conscience, that the ideal of the 'holy community' assumes its most menacing aspect, the doctrine of the rule of the Saints. And the rule of the Saints means the enforcement of the standards of the 'holy community' upon the nation at large, as the Millenarians frankly avow. If the idea of toleration is one ground of alliance between the Parties of the Centre and Left, this opposing idea is certainly another. Puritanism was not only committed in all sections to the ideal of the 'holy community,' but, in most of them, strongly drawn to the establishment of its reign outside the body of the elect, where, since persuasion could be of no avail, reform must be by coercion.

Its zeal for reformation results in part from the fact that the Puritan temper is in general active rather than contemplative. Though its official creed repudiates works as a *means* of salvation, it emphasizes them as a *sign*; and the Puritan has an overwhelming sense of one's responsibility to use every effort for advancing the kingdom of God. 'It is action,' says Baxter, 'that God is most served and honoured by.'[12] And the predilection comes out repeatedly in different forms. There is a vein – even here it is not the dominant vein – of pure contemplation in Anglican literature. The Puritans on the other hand, despite their addiction to experiential religion, seem very often deficient in the higher and more disinterested kinds of mysticism. Milton is the least mystical of all great religious poets. And in his hands spiritual concepts like 'Christian liberty' are capable of being wrested from the contemplative to the active sphere. This is not to deny an element of mysticism in some of the Puritans. Cromwell can remind the Council of the Army, eager to dictate the settlement of the kingdom, that the best government 'is but a moral thing ... it is but dross and dung in comparison of Christ' (97). They appear to disagree with him – and when the time comes Cromwell too will act. In Roger Williams a more unfaltering sense of the mystical quality of religious experience tends to set it apart, thus assigning religion to the contemplative spirit, but to the active reserving all the rest of life. Where no such separation occurs the strong Puritan impulse to action results in the constant [45] intrusion of religion into the secular sphere in an effort to enforce the standards of the holy community upon the world, and in a marked tendency to press on, in the name of that ideal, from the quest for religious liberty to the quest for political power.

Within limits the spirit of Puritanism is not only active, but experimental. Naturally the experimental spirit will be operative only in those sections of the party which conceive that the necessary point of compromise between the ideal and the demands of actual life has not yet been reached. For the rest, and notably for the Presbyterians, the period of its operation is already past. For the Independents, and much more markedly for the sects, the point is not yet reached.[13] The Bible embodies a revelation complete and unalterable; but there is still room for progressive comprehension, progressive interpretation;[14] and it is here that free discussion can (as Milton maintains in the *Areopagitica*) minister to the discovery of the truth and to agreement in the truth. 'I am verily persuaded,' said John Robinson to the departing Pilgrims, 'the Lord hath more truth yet to break forth out of his holy word ... I beseech you remember it is an article of your church covenant that you be ready to receive whatever truth shall be made known to you from the written word of God ... It is not possible that the Christian world should come so lately out of such thick Antichristian darkness and that perfection of knowledge should break forth at once.'[15] The Apologetical Narrators, the most moderate of Congregationalists, resolve 'not to make our present judgment and practice a binding law unto ourselves for the future' and could wish that this principle 'were (next to that most supreme, namely to be in all things guided by the perfect will of God) enacted as the most sacred law of all other ... in [46] Christian states and churches throughout the world.'[16] The Christian, Henry Robinson urged, ought continually to grow not only from grace to grace, but from knowledge to knowledge.[17] 'The true temper and proper employment of a Christian is always to be working like the sea, and purging ignorance out of his understanding and exchanging notions and apprehensions imperfect for more perfect, and forgetting things behind to press forward' (259). 'To be still searching what we know not, by what we know,' said Milton, 'still closing up truth to truth as we find it ... this is the golden rule in theology as well as in arithmetic.'[18] The exponents of toleration, says another writer, 'count not themselves perfect but stand ready to receive further light, yea though from the meanest of the brethren.'[19] This experimental spirit, this eager quest of truth (whether adequately or inadequately conceived), with the attendant confidence in truth's power to guard itself and to prevail if given an open field, is the deepest and most abiding element in the Puritan campaign for liberty of conscience. There it joins hands with other traditions of free inquiry coming down from the Renaissance, as appears in quotations from Charron (260–1), and in John Goodwin's argument:

> If so great and considerable a part of the world as America is ... was yet unknown to all the world besides for so many generations together, well may it be conceived ... that ... many truths, yea and those of main concernment and importance, may be yet unborn and not come forth out of their mother's womb – I mean the secrets of the scripture to see the light of the sun ... <No> man is completely furnished for the ministry of the Gospel ... who is not as well able to make some new discovery, and to bring forth something of himself [47] in the things of God in one kind or other, as to preach the common and received truths ... That is neither new nor unjustifiable by the practice of wise men, to examine, yea and to impugn

> received opinions. He that will please to peruse the first book of Doctor Hakewell's learned *Apology of the Power and Providence of God &c.* shall meet with great variety of instances ... in divinity, philosophy, in ecclesiastical history, in civil or national history, in natural history of opinions which had a long time been received, and yet were at last suspected, yea and many of them evicted and rejected upon due examination ... There are many errors (erroneously so called) in the Christian world which are made of the greatest and choicest truths; yea and which doubtless will be redeemed from their captivity and restored to their thrones and kingdoms by diligence, gifts and faithfulness of the approaching generation.[20]

Transferred to the political field, the experimental spirit manifests itself chiefly in the Levellers. But it is shared in some degree by the official body of the Independents and underlies the idea of the Debates.

An attitude tentative, yet confident and expectant, was further fostered by the rapid march of events. The break in the ordered procession of the traditional in church and state seemed to the more visionary to place the ideal within their reach. 'God,' wrote the Leveller leaders, 'hath so blessed that which has been done as thereby ... to afford an opportunity which these six hundred years has been desired, but could never be attained, making this a truly happy and wholly free nation.'[21] 'God's people, as well as worldlings,' said Henry Robinson, 'have their times to fish in troubled waters.'[22] The circumstances of the period fostered in those whose minds already contained the germs, both utopianism and the iconoclasm which, for the active temper, is inseparable from it.

Already in the *Grand Remonstrance* there is a suggestion of the utopian spirit in the programme of reforms which its framers outline;[23] Charles, indeed, specifically complains of 'that new Utopia of religion and government into which they endeavour to transform this kingdom.'[24] Here again Puritanism met other currents of thought: the still-living tradition of Renaissance utopianism (always more academic than the Puritan), embodied in the work of a More and a Campanella; the teaching of Bacon, [48] now commencing to find eager disciples and to shape its own august memorial, the Royal Society (a dream of the New Atlantis come true); the cult of Comenius, assiduously fostered by Samuel Hartlib, who had plans for the reform of everything from beehives to the state, not to mention a scheme, the special department of his friend John Dury, for the reunion of Protestant Christendom. Whatever the intentions of the Long Parliament, there were plenty of persons ready to point the way to Utopia: in education (to mention only the most important examples), Hartlib, Dury, Milton, Petty, John Webster, and William Dell; in the organization of society and the state, Hartlib, Harrington, Milton, Vane, Baxter, Hugh Peter, Henry Robinson, the Levellers in general, and Richard Overton in particular (see 335–8), the Millenarians with their vision of rule by the Saints, and Gerrard Winstanley with his communist *Law of Freedom in a Platform.* All these writers, with the exception of Harrington and Petty, definitely belong to the Puritan parties (and even they have connections with the Puritans). Up to a point the outcropping of utopianism may further illustrate the beginnings of a trend away from dogmatic and towards humanitarian religion, or, in the case of the Levellers, Harrington, and Petty, a definite process of secularization; but Baxter, Vane, Dell, and the Millenarians certainly manifest no drift from dogma, on whose acceptance, indeed, their utopias depend. And all exhibit qualities recognized elsewhere in the products of the Puritan mind – above all the Puritan impulse to action; for these are not utopias in the sense of Sir Thomas More, but somewhat visionary schemes of reform to be actually attempted, utopias in the sense of Charles I's indignant protest. They may, like the *Areopagitica,* even repudiate 'Atlantic and utopian politics.' Typical is John Cook's *Unum Necessarium,* which pleads for the control of the drink trade and the relief of the poor (including free medical service): 'I am not of their opinion that drive at a parity, to have all men alike. *'Tis but a utopian fiction.* The scripture holds forth no such thing: *the poor ye shall have always with you.* But there ought to be no beggar in England, for they live rather like beasts than men.'[25] Fostered by the unsettled state of English institutions, and supplemented by various intellectual influences, this utopianism takes its rise in the Puritan mind and temper, and constitutes an important element in the Army Debates.

Hand in hand with utopianism goes iconoclasm. The common effort to destroy religious institutions of a thousand years had [49] confirmed this trait in the Puritan mind, even when the purpose was to replace them with a sterner rule and 'not to loose the golden reins of discipline and government in the church.'[26] 'And for the extirpation of prelacy,' wrote John Saltmarsh, 'though it be a government riveted into our laws and usages ... yet let us not like the Jews lose our Gospel with holding our Laws too fast. I know this kingdom hath ever been a retentive nation of customs and old constitutions ... And hence it is that reformation ... hath been with such little power and duration ...'[27] Though fostered by the revolution in the church the triumph of iconoclasm was but partial in the end; for some of the deepest instincts of the national temper (as Saltmarsh hints) were ranged against it, and these kept cropping up – in the Puritans themselves. Only in the Parties of the Left is iconoclasm willingly adopted and unhesitatingly pursued. Beyond a certain point, the Independents are drawn into it not by choice, but by the force of circumstances. In November 1647, Ireton defends 'the fundamental constitution' from Leveller attacks. By November 1648, he has had to retreat from this position: 'the fundamental constitution' gives too little ground for beheading monarchs and establishing republics in their place.[28] The subject leads into a [50] consideration of the appeal to natural rights, which must be reserved for our consideration of liberty; but we may glance at the Puritan attitude to custom, precedent, and history, taking Milton as our example.[29] No sooner has he attacked the problem of religious liberty and reform than he decides that change cannot be too 'swift and sudden provided still it be from worse to better.' Custom, he discovers, is 'a natural tyrant' in religion and in the state, a tyrant which has an ally in man's fallen nature – 'a double tyranny of custom from without and blind affections within.' Custom, it is assumed as self-evident, always enters into alliance with error, never with truth: '... Error supports custom, custom countenances error, and these two between them would persecute and chase away all truth and solid wisdom out of human life were it not that God,. rather than man, once in many ages calls together the prudent and religious counsels of men, deputed to repress the encroachments and to work off the inveterate blots and obscurities wrought upon our minds by the subtle insinuating of custom and error.' In this passage is implied the Puritan view of history (the view which informs Adam's vision in *Paradise Lost*): deterioration is its note, but deterioration relieved by sudden interventions of God in behalf of truth and righteousness, as seen in the prophets of old, pre-eminently in the earthly ministry of Christ, and recently, after twelve hundred years of increasing darkness, in the Reformation, whose work England was called on to complete, 'even unto the reformation of reformation.' The view can best be characterized as the direct antithesis of Burke's: history is not 'the known march of the ordinary providence of God'; it is a protracted wandering from the way, relieved by sudden interventions of God's *extraordinary* providence. The common elements of theism and idealism in the two thinkers make the comparison legitimate and significant. For Milton theism does not validate the actual, does not dispose him to seek for evidences of the ideal in the actual, or in history which is the record of the actual. Though other influences contribute to form his mind, there is strong indication that in this he speaks for Puritanism: and he is at one with the Independent John Cook, who repudiates 'the puddles of history,'[30] and with the Levellers, [51] who dismiss the past as vicious and irrelevant: '... Whatever our forefathers were, or whatever they did or suffered, or were enforced to yield unto, we are men of the present age and ought to be absolutely free from all kinds of exorbitancies, molestations, and arbitrary power.'[31] It is in connection with the plea for liberty that Puritan iconoclasm most frequently appears; but the attitude was learned in connection with church reform. 'Let them chant while they will of prerogatives,' said Milton, 'we shall tell them of scripture; of custom, we of scripture; of acts and statutes, still of scripture.' [...]

[53] More or less closely connected with the feeling for liberty are Puritan individualism and Puritan equalitarianism, each with its appropriate dogmatic basis, whose fuller discussion may also be postponed. Here one must recognize, however, countertendencies and counter-associations in the Puritan mind. Puritan individualism speaks most significantly of all in the voice of conscience. The Puritan asserts the right and duty of thinking for himself. Those in authority (the Agents observe to Fairfax) may demand an unquestioning obedience, but a man is finally answerable to his own conscience (436n) – that is (in Ireton's phrase) to 'conscience obliging above or against human and outward constitutions' (459). The consciences of common men were a new phenomenon in politics, and one that has never since disappeared. Ideally, to assert one's right of private judgment should be to concede the same right to every one else. But it is not always thus that the celebrated Nonconformist conscience has reasoned – and we understand the Puritan conscience the better if we give it its later name. Some of its associations are with liberty, but not all. For it can argue that all it pleads for is the autonomy of the illuminated conscience and that this it denies to no man. Again, in regard to Puritan equalitarianism it is sufficient to observe that the equality of believers implies their superiority to unregenerate men. And this superiority, so long as dogma is unimpaired, or in the secular field uncircumvented, will continue to oppose an effective barrier against a wider equalitarianism.

The two processes, the impairing of dogma and its circumvention, must be clearly distinguished. Both are present in Puritanism of the Left, and each has its place in the history of liberty and equality.

Of the forces counteracting, and ultimately impairing, the dogmatic attitude we have noticed one, the principle of the progressive interpretation of truth. With its operation (as also with the ineptitude of amateur theologians) may be associated the rapid multiplication of sects and heresies which Thomas Edwards deplores.[32] Standing in varying relations to the Puritan movement, [54] the new opinions consist either in some exaggeration of the dominant Calvinistic creed (a repudiation of some compromise which it had sanctioned) or in a reaction, theological or ethical, against some part of that creed and its inferences. For our present purpose the latter type alone is directly important, though the very multiplication of opinions, whatever their character, would do something to weaken the authority of dogma as such. Most significant of all is the reaction against the Calvinistic dogma of predestination as that dogma is set forth by Prynne (232–3) and others. The reaction, which extends far beyond the ranks of the Puritans, represents a shift towards a rational theology and a humanistic, even a humanitarian, religion. As the Cambridge Platonists were to demonstrate, Arminianism was pre-eminently the doctrine of Christian rationalism[33] and Christian humanism, re-reading the stern pronouncements of the Reformation in the mellow light of the Renaissance. The Calvinists were quick to point out its affinities with the Pelagian heresy, whose effect was to eliminate divine grace and substitute a gospel of self-help. This is a gospel comfortable to human nature (All men, said Culverwel, are naturally born Pelagians), and one whose role in the making of the modern mind is self-evident.[34] It is not surprising then to find some of the sectaries going far beyond the Arminian position proper, hinting the sufficiency and the natural goodness of human nature and calling in question the doctrine of original sin. But apart from these dubious inferences, and by its central attack on the extreme form of the Calvinistic doctrine of predestination, of absolute election and reprobation, Arminianism weakens the theological basis of Puritan *in* equalitarianism, of the conception of an aristocracy of the elect, and thus undermines the most formidable of the barriers separating Puritanism from democracy.

Other forces are at work among the sectaries to a similar end. Two may be distinguished, though not so as to exclude their mutual influence. For, as Chesterton observes, heterodoxies, often of the most opposite kinds, will flock together. In seventeenth-century England (as in the Europe of the Reformation) [55] currents which in spirit belong to no religious tradition but rather to libertinism, seek a temporary alliance with radical Protestant thought. In Overton there is a militant naturalism and a thinly veiled hostility to dogmatic religion. He champions the mortalist heresy in the name of scripture and reason and advances a materialistic view of man and the world.[35] He claims to have attempted a proof of the main truths of revelation from nature and reason;[36] it is difficult to judge of his motives, but the method seems to link him with the beginnings of Deism. He is perfectly familiar with Puritan doctrine and can use it on occasion. He talks of the order of nature in terms reserved by the more orthodox for the order of grace, by the simple expedient of omitting all reference to the Fall ([Introduction] 69). He seizes upon the radical plea for liberty of conscience put forward on religious grounds by Roger Williams and others, and gives it his own emphasis.[37] Wildman can also speak the language of the Saints:[38] on the most extreme Separatist ground, he argues against the magistrate's power in matters of religion, developing the doctrine of the two orders in a direction which might lead to either scepticism or fideism, and incidentally in one diametrically opposed to Overton's boasted effort to deduce the truths of revelation from nature (168–9). By Walwyn a subtler method is used. His aim is to inculcate a sentiment. He adapts (sometimes almost out of recognition) such parts of Puritan doctrine as he can use, while undermining, rather than openly assailing, the rest. The doctrine of Christian liberty, detached from its dogmatic basis, becomes an invitation to free oneself from the oppression of religious ordinances; Eden is approximated to the life of the golden age, and of Montaigne's happy savages; the Fall is thus interpreted as a forsaking of nature for human 'inventions,' and the rule of the Gospel as an injunction to return to a natural simplicity; the genuine (and at this time somewhat neglected) humanitarian element in Christianity is emphasized at the expense of every other, and, more dubiously, it is presented as a militant and revolutionary creed. It is not without significance that Walwyn here affects to be expounding the [56] doctrines of the Familists.[39] Such teaching carries us over from the sceptics to the mystics, who tend to undermine dogma in the act of reinterpreting it. This is the second force to which we referred above. The influential teaching of Winstanley may serve as an example, whose blend of the practical with the mystic points on to Quakerism. His method of interpreting the Bible is frankly allegorical. The unfallen state is one in which the indwelling God (variously described as Reason and as Universal Love) rules the life of man. The Fall means the intrusion of self-love, which is followed by the curse. This, however, can be but temporary; for Reason or Universal Love must triumph, and mankind be restored to its primal perfection (375–89).[40] By this and other such reinterpretations of the Christian scheme (in which some of the essential dogmas of Calvinism are omitted and the whole takes on a universalist colouring) Winstanley builds the theological foundations of his social teaching.

A fourth influence is less theoretic. Apart from the varying notes of naturalism and scepticism detected in some of their leaders, there was among the Levellers a marked transfer of interest from religion to the world. But even in the leaders the drift from Puritan belief and sentiment is by no means constant. There appears to have been no such drift in John Lilburne, the most influential of them all. His earliest sufferings had been in the cause of liberty of conscience, and eight years later he published an account of his religious experience at this time.[41] Increasingly preoccupied with secular concerns, and thrown into association with Overton and Walwyn, he seems, nevertheless, to have [57] remained a religious enthusiast to the end. And wherever he deals with religion he appears as a rigorous Separatist who could readily subscribe to all the teachings of Williams's *Bloody Tenent.*[42] More significant still is the fact that all the Levellers, when arguing in favour of religious liberty, do so on the grounds set forth in that great book, which is as orthodox as it is radical.

For the undermining of dogma is not a necessary prelude to a contribution by Puritanism to liberty or even equality. While there are enemies to be encountered, an uncritical religious enthusiasm, not too careful of logical consequences, may do yeoman service. But before the contribution can be one of ideas, and unequivocal in its logical bearings, limits must be set to the drawing of inferences from religious dogma in the secular sphere. The way actually taken by true Puritans depends on no serious undermining of dogma itself, but on quite another process which leaves the reign of dogma in religion unimpaired. With this we come to the final characteristic of Puritan thought. If it is ignored, one cannot gauge correctly the relation of Puritanism to political liberty and secular progress. That characteristic is a tendency, already hinted, to distinguish sharply between religion and the rest of life, to segregate the spiritual from the secular, and to do this, in the first instance, for the sake of religion, though with momentous consequences for the life of the world. As in the case of the Puritan concern for liberty itself, the characteristic is of the utmost importance; and, once more, it is problematical because it manifests itself only in some of the Puritans, and those not the majority, and because it would seem to run counter to one of the characteristics already fully established: the tendency of the Puritan mind to carry the implications of dogma into secular life. Like the Puritan concern for liberty, it obviously requires to have its status examined and vindicated.

The groups in which the new characteristic appears are roughly identical with those already cited as exhibiting most clearly the Puritan concern for liberty and as setting limits to the Puritan zeal for positive reform. In the Party of the Right, the Presbyterians, the new characteristic is absent;[43] but so is it also in the [58] Millenarians, and in the other groups (of the Centre and Left)who share in any appreciable degree their vision of the future. On the other hand, in those groups of the Left who are most deeply devoted to liberty of conscience and from whom proceeded the main Puritan argument and effort in behalf of political liberty, the new characteristic is very strongly marked. In the Independents, the Centre Party, it clearly emerges, but less decisively than in these. From the facts thus baldly set forth, one might predict a close relation between the new characteristic – the tendency to segregate the spiritual and the secular – and the effective emergence of the Puritan concern for liberty. The segregation of the spiritual and the secular is indeed the means by which the concern for liberty frees itself in the secular sphere from other and countervailing impulses, and disposes of all those particular inferences from dogma which are inimical to liberty. If the concern for liberty is an authentic characteristic of the Puritan mind, so also is this, the necessary mode of its transfer to the secular field. But the proof need not rest here. As in the case of the concern for liberty, the separation of the spiritual and the secular (or what we may for brevity call the *principle of segregation*) is traceable to the foundations of Puritan thought. In discussing the Puritan conception of man and the world, we observed as a constant feature the recognition of a twofold system, an order of nature and an order of grace, and we remarked on the extent to which the different views taken of the precise relation subsisting between the two orders coloured Puritan thought. It is upon an extreme interpretation of this dogma of the two orders that the principle of segregation depends. The two orders are separate and opposed. God indeed is the creator and ruler of them both, but he rules them by different dispensations, and the goods which pertain to them are totally different (for, though spiritual goodness no doubt assumes all the natural virtues, it also transcends them). What God has thus divided, the Christian may not seek to join. He must not (for example), through mistaken zeal, try to bring the natural man under a rule meant only for the elect. In all his thinking, indeed, he must be mindful of the distinction of the two orders. This principle, thoroughly applied, imposes severe limits upon the intrusion of dogma into secular life. In other words, it completely secularizes one division of existence. But the principle is derived not from any conscious reaction against dogma as such, but from a confident and extreme appeal to one of the basic dogmas of the Puritan creed. The correctness of this interpretation is, I think, confirmed by the fact that for many who apply the principle [59] of segregation the reign of dogma in the spiritual sphere remains (for a long time at least) unassailed.

The practical manifestations of this principle, and its less immediate results, are far-reaching indeed. The most obvious manifestation, the perfect example in action, is the insistence by Puritans of the Left on the absolute separation of church and state, the social organs of grace and nature respectively. That this insistence becomes the groundwork of a plea for complete liberty of conscience illustrates the close connection between the principle of segregation and the Puritan concern for liberty. But the alliance does not stop short with religious liberty; the reasoning which issues in a purely spiritual view of the church issues just as certainly in a purely secular view of the state. This in itself invites a reconsideration of the state's origin, function, and sanctions. It does not follow that the reconsideration will be democratic in tendency; but it may be so, and the invitation is the first service of the Puritan principle of segregation to the cause of liberty and equality. There is a second service. We have seen that Puritanism nourishes both a concern for liberty and a sentiment of equality (and this it does without reference to the principle of segregation). But both terms require to be qualified: it is *Christian* liberty, and it is the equality of *believers*. The natural man can claim no share in these privileges, which belong to a higher order, the order of grace. The sense of a fundamental *inequality* underlies both the concern for liberty and – the paradox is only seeming – the sentiment of equality itself. In other words: when the order of nature and the order of grace are considered together, the superiority of the latter will always assert itself. The principle of segregation enters to insist that they must be considered apart. That is its second service. But there is a third. Puritanism fosters the impulse to reform in the interests of righteousness, and this impulse (we have seen) runs or may run, counter to a concern for liberty. Viewing Puritanism as a whole, we detected a potential and unresolved conflict between these two motives. The incentive to reform belongs to the order of grace, but it may be translated into action in the order of nature. To such a passage from one order to the other the principle of segregation once more opposes a barrier. At least it insists that the attempt to reform the world shall be in the terms appropriate to the world, the terms not of religion but of natural ethics. Indeed where the principle is carried to its logical conclusion, as it is in Roger Williams, it resolves the conflict between the two motives of liberty and reform. This is the third and final service.

[60] But is not the principle of segregation a two-edged sword? Will it not, logically applied, cut off from the secular sphere the liberalizing as well as the reactionary influences of Puritanism, at least in so far as these are grounded in dogma? Theoretically it should. Indeed, in so far as the principle is anticipated by Luther it has precisely that result: Christian liberty, he reiterates, has no bearing on politics. Furthermore, Separatism in essence means separation from the world and its cares. But the predominantly active character of the Puritan temper – not to mention the instincts of human nature, even when sanctified – may be depended on to forestall that result. And the segregation of the spiritual and the secular cannot in practice mean that all influence of the one upon the other will cease. The lessons learned in the conventicle will not be forgotten in the forum. But we may look for a new mode of influence: not the direct influence of intrusion, but the indirect influence of *analogy*. There is a spiritual equality in the order of grace: is there not an analogous equality in the order of nature? This is but one of a dozen points at which analogically Puritanism could reinforce the cause of liberty and equality.

In briefest outline, and too abstractedly perhaps (but illustration will follow), we have suggested the importance of the principle of segregation in its bearing on liberty. The principle opened to the Puritan other developments in the secular field: it enabled him to adopt Baconian ideas in education as readily as democratic ideas in politics, and in the next century it contributed to make some of the Dissenting academies outposts of the Enlightenment and of radical thought. With the true Puritan, religion remains the first concern: the principle – one might almost call it the device – of segregation prevents (or rather, as the subsequent history of Dissent seems to show, postpones) the repercussion upon his dogmatic creed, of radical and naturalistic ideas adopted in a secular sphere.

NOTES

1 That is, in relation to the other Puritan groups and with care not to be confused by Cromwell's term 'the middle party' (419), which he applies to the Erastians with other loosely attached elements in the House of Commons.

2 In principle, Independency, with its ideal of an exclusive and divinely appointed church, was of course opposed to Erastianism; and there were Independent attacks on the Erastianism of the Presbyterian Prynne (see

Certain Brief Observations on Master Prynne's Twelve Questions, 1644; and *Calumny Arraigned and Cast*, 1645). On the other hand, the separation of church and state, in proportion as the Independents were willing to make it absolute, would have the effect of rendering impossible the religious tyranny that the Erastians dreaded.

3 [Woodhouse's parenthetical references are to *Puritanism and Liberty* – Eds.]

4 It would be a mistake to exaggerate the sharpness of the line separating parties, or to overlook the fact that a logical development of certain Independent principles would easily carry one over the line. Progressive movement towards the Left is illustrated by Milton and Roger Williams: it is another source of the sects. Thomas Edwards affected to think a pure Independent a *rara avis*, a mistake in the other direction. Space does not permit me to speak of the relation of parties before the meeting of the Long Parliament, when the principles to be expressed after 1640 were taking shape. Much light on this subject may be expected from forthcoming works by Professor M.M. Knappen and Professor William Haller. See also the admirable account in Perry Miller, *Orthodoxy in Massachusetts* ([Chicago,] 1934), 1–10.

5 In an early Declaration <E. 390 (26)> the Army significantly speaks of the City and itself as 'bodies': why should the Army's petitions 'be apprehended as a putting of conditions upon Parliament more than all other petitions have been, from counties, from corporations, and especially from the City of London, being a body more numerous, more closely compacted, more near to the Parliament, and more plentifully furnished with money and all things else to back and carry on their desires than the Army is … ?' (5).

6 Among the citizens Presbyterian sympathies also prevailed, tinged, like the oligarchy's, with Erastianism. But in the City and surrounding municipalities, there was a vigorous minority whose allegiance was divided between the Independents and the Parties of the Left.

7 William Aspinwal, *Description of the Fifth Monarchy* ([London,] 1653), 10 [11]. Presbyterians appealed with like confidence to the Old Testament.

8 Not all the Puritans are satisfied with such reasoning. 'But success alone is not a rule for wise men to go by …' (*The Ancient Bounds* [London, 1645], 55).

9 A different account of the priority of the religious struggle is given in *An Answer to Mr. William Prynne's Twelve Questions* ([London,] 1644): the needed civil reforms might have been effected without an appeal to arms had not Episcopalian fears and Presbyterian ambitions complicated and forced the issue.

10 It is necessary to distinguish between positive and negative reforms. The latter term may designate the reforms whose object is merely the removal

of abuses and of restrictions upon the individual; the former may designate new interference with the individual for his or the community's benefit or in the interests of righteousness or efficiency.

11 Thomas Case, *Two Sermons to the Commons* ([London,] 1641), 21–2 [Second Sermon, 22].

12 Richard Baxter, *Christian Directory*[, 4 vols] ([London,] (1678), 1:336.

13 The effort of Independency to replace Presbyterianism as the latter was replacing Episcopacy could be best rationalized in terms of progressive comprehension: '<D>oth Master Prynne think we have no more light discovered in these days about church-government than the godly had in former days? Or must all the Saints be regulated by former patterns? Then should Episcopacy be more followed than Presbytery' (*Certain Brief Observations,* 1644, p. 7).

14 *The Independent Catechism* (1647) associates progressive comprehension of truth with an approaching millennium. The companion *Presbyterian Catechism,* issued by the same publisher, but a fair presentation of Presbyterian beliefs, is significantly silent on both progressive knowledge and the millennium. According to [Roger] Williams, however, even the Presbyterians 'profess to want more light' (*Queries of Highest Consideration,* [London,] 1644).

15 [Daniel] Neal's *History of the Puritans*[, 5 vols] ([London,] 1822) 2:110–11; cf. Edward Winslow, *Hypocrisy Unmasked* ([London,] 1646), 97.

16 [Thomas Goodwin *et al.,*] *Apologetical Narration* ([London,] 1644), 10. The tentative and experimental spirit of Independency is one of the reproaches levelled against it by the Presbyterian ministers, irritated by the Dissenting Brethren's demand for toleration coupled with a wary and largely politic refusal to set forth a counter-scheme of settlement: '[T]hey profess reservations and new lights for which they will no doubt expect the like toleration and so *in infinitum*' (*Letter of the Ministers of London, to the Assembly, against Toleration,* 1646, 2–3). A clever satire makes the ministers complain: 'The Independents will ever be looking for further light, and go on still in reformation, and would carry the people along with them "to grow in grace and in the knowledge of Jesus Christ" ... by which means things will never be settled perfectly whilst the Church is militant. Therefore Independency is a mischief to the Church' (*Certain Additional Reasons to Those in A Letter by the Ministers of London to the Assembly,* 1646, 6).

17 Henry Robinson, *Liberty of Conscience* ([London,] 1644), 50.

18 [John] Milton, *Areopagitica, Prose Works,* [5 vols, ed. J.A. St. John (London, 1848–90),] 2:90.

19 *A Paraenetic for Christian Liberty* ([London,] 1644), 34.

20 John Goodwin, *Imputatio Fidei* ([London,] 1642), preface.
21 *A Manifestation from Lieutenant Col. John Lilburn, Mr. William Walwyn, Mr. Thomas Prince, and Mr. Richard Overton* (14 April 1649), 3.
22 Henry Robinson, *Liberty of Conscience* (1644), preface.
23 Husband's *Exact Collection* ([London,] 1643), 15–16, 19–20.
24 Husband's *Exact Collection*, 315.
25 John Cook, *Unum Necessarium* ([London,] 1648), 36.
26 *Grand Remonstrance.*
27 John Saltmarsh, *A Solemn Discourse upon the Covenant* ([London,] 1644), 6.
28 Ireton is forced to execute a partial retreat on the related subject of the binding character of engagements. At Putney he declares them to be inescapable. A year later in the *Remonstrance of the Army* (460) he does not reverse the decision, but he provides a very pretty example of Puritan casuistry by indicating how, without doing so, he can set the Covenant aside. The Covenant indeed constituted a recurrent stumbling-block to the Independents and the Parties of the Left. Hugh Peter chose simply to ignore it: he had it administered to him 'as he thought, twenty times, and saw nothing in it that men should make such a stir about it' (Thomas Edwards, *Gangraena*, [3 parts, London, 1645–6,] part 3, 123). The spokesmen of the Left at Putney take up the position that no engagement is binding if, and when, it conflicts with the claims of justice and right, or with the safety of the people (which is the supreme law). They are merely giving reasoned expression to a rather obscure tendency in the Puritan mind to regard no bargain as binding once it has ceased to be advantageous – especially to the children of grace. This form of iconoclasm is fairly widespread (cf. Milton's treatment of the marriage contract in *The Doctrine and Discipline of Divorce*). The same idea could be expressed in the language of religious enthusiasm. Buff-Coat remarks ecstatically: 'Whatsoever obligation I should be bound unto, if afterwards God should reveal himself, I would break it, if it were an hundred a day' (34). Though the principle had been invoked by the Independents in their struggle for religious liberty, and by the Parliament in its struggle with Charles, Ireton voices the alarm of the Centre Party: 'When I hear men speak of laying aside all engagements, to consider only that wild or vast notion of what in every man's conception is just or unjust, I am afraid and do tremble at the boundless and endless consequences of it' (27).
29 *Of Reformation, Reason of Church Government, Tenure of Kings and Magistrates, Doctrine and Discipline of Divorce: Prose Works*, 2:410, 503, 2; 3:171–2; 2:485.
30 G.P. Gooch, *English Democratic Ideas in the Seventeenth Century*[, 2nd ed.] ([Cambridge,] 1927), 159.

31 [Richard Overton,] *Remonstrance of Many Thousand Citizens* (7 July 1646), 5.

32 Thomas Edwards, *Gangraena,* 3 parts (1645–6).

33 This is illuminatingly explained in Joseph Glanvil's 'Free Philosophy and Anti-fanatical Religion' (*Essays* [*on Several Important Subjects in Philosophy and Religion*], [London,]1676). In Puritan pamphlets the term 'Arminian' is loosely used to designate the whole Laudian position, but usually with some reference to the attitude on predestination which was felt to be basic (see Godfrey Davies, 'Puritan *vs.* Arminian,' *Huntington Library Bulletin,* April 1934, [pp. 157–179]).

34 See the suggestive analysis in T.E. Hulme's *Speculations* ([London,] 1924), 46–71.

35 Cf. R<ichard> O<verton>, *Man's Mortality* (1643; enlarged 1655).

36 *Picture of the Council of State* (1649), 28 (quoted by [William] Haller, [ed.], *Tracts* [*on Liberty in the Puritan Revolution,* 1638–1647, 3 vols (New York: 1934)], 1:96). Overton and Walwyn both sign the *Manifestation* (14 April 1649), in which the Leveller leaders protest their belief in God and the Bible.

37 Martin Mar-Priest [Richard Overton], *The Arraignment of Mr. Persecution* ('Europe,' 1645), 14–17, 22–6.

38 *Putney Projects* (1647), 1: 'God's present great design ... is the shaking of the powers of the earth and marring the pride of all flesh. Isaiah 2. 11: *The lofty looks of man shall be humbled and the haughtiness of men shall be bowed down, and the Lord shall be exalted in that day* ... To-day is this scripture fulfilled ...'

39 I have tentatively adopted Professor Haller's ascription of *The Power of Love* (1643) to Walwyn (*Tracts* 1:121–7; 2:271–303).

40 Cf. *The Mystery of God Concerning the Whole Creation: Mankind* ([London,] 1648); *A New-Year's Gift for the Parliament and Army* ([London,] 1650); L.H. Berens, *The Digger Movement* ([London,] 1906), 44. The name for God, 'the Universal Love,' points to a connection with Familist teaching, the alternative name 'Reason,' points as clearly to rationalist thought (see further, below, [Introduction], 94). The whole conception is coloured by opposition to Calvinism and by incipient naturalism. In his attack on the clergy in *The Law of Freedom in a Platform* ([London,] 1652), 58, he declares: '... To know the works of God within the creation is to know God himself, for God dwells in every visible work or body. And indeed if you would know spiritual things, it is to know how the spirit or power of wisdom and life ... dwells within and governs both the several bodies ... in the heavens above, and ... the earth below ... for to reach God beyond the creation ... is a knowledge beyond the ... capacity of man to attain ...'

41 John Lilburne, *Innocency and Truth Justified* ([London,] 1646). The account is dated 11th November 1638. We hear of his disagreement with Walwyn's views on religion (*England's Lamentable Slavery,* [London,] 1645, 1).

42 Cf. Lilburne's *Nine Arguments* ([London,] 1644), kindly lent to me by Professor Haller. Lilburne finally became a Quaker, and there is a hint of his repudiation of all church organization in his *Legal Fundamental Liberties* ([London,] 1649), 39, in a contemptuous reference to 'their <Cromwell and Ireton's> champions in all their pretended churches of God, either Independent or Anabaptistical.'

43 Save in so far as it is adumbrated in that limited doctrine of the two kingdoms common to Puritan and Jesuit theory (see J.N. Figgis, *Divine Right of Kings*).

3 Literature as Context: Milton's *Lycidas**

NORTHROP FRYE

I should like to begin with a brief discussion of a familiar poem, Milton's *Lycidas*, in the hope that some of the inferences drawn from the analysis will be relevant to the theme of this conference. *Lycidas*, then, is an elegy in the pastoral convention, written to commemorate a young man named Edward King who was drowned at sea. The origins of the pastoral are partly Classical, the tradition that runs through Theocritus and Virgil, and partly Biblical, the imagery of the twenty-third Psalm, of Christ as the Good Shepherd, of the metaphors of 'pastor' and 'flock' in the Church. The chief connecting link between the traditions in Milton's day was the Fourth or Messianic Eclogue of Virgil. Hence it is common enough to have pastoral images echoing both traditions at once, and not surprising to find that *Lycidas* is a Christian poem as well as a humanistic one.

In the Classical pastoral elegy the subject of the elegy is not treated as an individual, but as a representative of a dying spirit of nature. The pastoral elegy seems to have some relation to the ritual of the Adonis lament, and the dead poet Bion, in Moschus' poem, is celebrated with much the same kind of imagery as Bion himself uses in his lament for Adonis. The phrase 'dying god,' for such a figure in later pastoral, is not an anachronism: Virgil says of Daphnis, for example, in the Fifth Eclogue: 'deus, deusille, Menalca.' Besides, Milton and his learned contemporaries, Selden, for example, or Henry Reynolds, knew at least as much about the symbolism of the 'dying god' as any modern student could get out of *The Golden Bough*, which depends mainly on the same Classical sources

* Originally appearing in *Comparative Literature: Proceedings of the Second Congress of the International Comparative Literature Association*, ed. Werner P. Friedrich, *UNC Studies in Comparative Literature* 23 (Chapel Hill, NC, 1959): 44–55.

that were available to them. The notion that twentieth-century poets differ from their predecessors in their understanding or use of myth will not bear much scrutiny. So King is given the pastoral name of Lycidas, which is equivalent to Adonis, and is associated with the cyclical rhythms of nature. Of these three are of particular importance: the daily cycle of the sun across the sky, the yearly cycle of the seasons, and the cycle of water flowing from wells and fountains through rivers to the sea. Sunset, winter and the sea are emblems of Lycidas' death; sunrise and spring of his resurrection. The poem begins in the morning, 'Under the opening eyelids of the morn,' and ends with the sun, like Lycidas himself, dropping into the western ocean, yet due to rise again as Lycidas is to do. The imagery of the opening lines, 'Shatter your leaves before the mellowing year,' suggests the frosts of autumn killing the flowers, and in the great roll-call of flowers towards the end, most of them early blooming flowers like the 'rathe primrose,' the spring returns. Again, the opening invocation is to the 'Sisters of the sacred well,' and the water imagery carries through a great variety of Greek, Italian and English rivers to the sea in which the dead body of Lycidas lies.

Lycidas, then, is the 'archetype' of Edward King. By an archetype I mean a literary symbol, or cluster of symbols, which are used recurrently throughout literature, and thereby become conventional. A poetic use of a flower, by itself, is not necessarily an archetype. But in a poem about the death of a young man it is conventional to associate him with a red or purple flower, usually a spring flower like the hyacinth. The historical origin of the convention may be lost in ritual, but it is a constantly latent one, not only in literature but in life, as the symbolism of the scarlet poppies in the First World War shows. Hence in *Lycidas* the 'sanguine flower inscrib'd with woe' is an archetype, a symbol that recurs regularly in many poems of its kind. Similarly Lycidas himself is not only the literary form of Edward King, but a conventional or recurring form, of the same family as Shelley's Adonais, the Daphnis of Theocritus and Virgil, and Milton's own Damon. King was also a clergyman and, for Milton's purposes, a poet, so, having selected the conventional archetype of King as drowned young man, Milton has them to select the conventional archetypes of King as poet, and of King as priest. These are, respectively, Orpheus and Peter.

Both Orpheus and Peter have attributes that link them in imagery with Lycidas. Orpheus was also an 'enchanting son,' or spirit of nature; he died young, in much the same role as Adonis, and was flung into the water. Peter would have drowned too without the help of Christ; hence Peter is not named directly, but only as 'The Pilot of the Galilean

Lake,' just as Christ is not named directly, but only as 'Him that walked the waves.' When Orpheus was torn to pieces by the Maenads, his head went floating 'Down the swift Hebrus to the Lesbian shore.' The theme of salvation out of water is connected with the image of the dolphin, a conventional type of Christ, and dolphins are called upon to 'waft the hapless youth' just before the peroration begins.

The body of the poem is arranged in the form ABACA, a main theme repeated twice with two intervening episodes, as in the musical rondo. The main theme is the drowning of Lycidas in the prime of his life; the two episodes, presided over by the figures of Orpheus and Peter, deal with the theme of premature death as it relates to poetry and to the priesthood respectively. In both the same type of image appears: the mechanical instrument of execution that brings about a sudden death, represented by the 'abhorred shears' in the meditation on fame, and the 'grim two-handed engine' in the meditation on the corruption of the Church. The most difficult part of the construction is the managing of the transitions from these episodes back to the main theme. The poet does this by alluding to his great forerunners in the pastoral convention, Theocritus of Sicily, Virgil of Mantua, and the legendary Arcadians who preceded both:

> O fountain Arethuse, and thou honour'd flood,
> Smooth-sliding Mincius, crown'd with vocal reeds . . .

and later:

> Return, Alpheus, the dread voice is past
> That shrunk thy streams: return, Sicilian Muse.

The allusion has the effect of reminding the reader that this is, after all, a pastoral. But Milton also alludes to the myth of Arethusa and Alpheus, the Arcadian water-spirits who plunged underground and reappeared in Sicily, and this myth not only outlines the history of the pastoral convention, but unites the water imagery with the theme of disappearance and revival.

In pastoral elegy the poet who laments the death is often so closely associated with the dead man as to make him a kind of double or shadow of himself. Similarly Milton represents himself as intimately involved with the death of Lycidas. The theme of premature death is skilfully associated in the opening lines with the conventional apology for a 'harsh and crude' poem; the poet hopes for a similar elegy when he dies, and at the end he accepts the responsibilities of survival and turns 'Tomorrow to fresh woods, and pastures new,' bringing the elegy to a full rich *tierce de Picardie* or major chord. By appearing himself at the beginning and end of the poem, Milton presents the poem as, in a sense, contained within the mind of the poet.

Apart from the historical convention of the pastoral, however, there is also the conventional framework of ideas or assumptions which forms the background of the poem. I call it a framework of ideas, and it may also be that, but in poetry it is rather a framework of images. It consists of four levels of existence. First is the order revealed by Christianity, the order of grace and salvation and of eternal life. Second is the order of human nature, the order represented by the Garden of Eden in the Bible and the Golden Age in Classical myth, and which man in his fallen state can, up to a point, regain through education, obedience to law, and the habit of virtue. Third is the order of physical nature, the world of animals and plants which is morally neutral but theologically 'fallen.' Fourth is the disorder of the unnatural, the sin and death and corruption that entered the world with the fall.

Lycidas has his connections with all of these orders. In the first place, all the images of death and resurrection are included in and identified with the body of Christ. Christ is the sun of righteousness, the tree of life, the water of life, the dying god who rose again, the saviour from the sea. On this level Lycidas enters the Christian heaven, and is greeted by the 'Saints above' 'In solemn troops, and sweet societies,' where the language echoes the Book of Revelation. But simultaneously Lycidas achieves another apotheosis as the Genius of the shore, corresponding to the Attendant Spirit in *Comus*, whose habitation is said to be a world above our own, identified, not with the Christian heaven, but with Spenser's Gardens of Adonis. The third level of physical nature is the world of ordinary experience, where death is simply a loss, and those who mourn the death have to turn to pick up their tasks again. On this level Lycidas is merely absent, 'to our moist vows denied,' represented only by the empty bier with its flowers. It is on this level too that the poem is contained within the mind of the surviving poet, as on the Christian level it is contained within the body of Christ. Finally, the world of death and corruption holds the drowned corpse of Lycidas, which will soon come to the surface and 'welter to the parching wind.' This last is an unpleasant and distressing image, and Milton touches it very lightly, picking it up again in an appropriate context:

> But swoln with wind and the rank mist they draw,
> Rot inwardly ...

In the writing of *Lycidas* there are four creative principles of particular importance. To say that there are four does not mean, of course, that they are separable. One is convention, the reshaping of the poetic material which is appropriate to this subject. Another is genre, the choosing of the appropriate form. A third is archetype, the use of appropriate, and therefore recurrently employed, images and symbols. The fourth, for which there is no name, is the fact that the forms of literature are autonomous: that is, they do not exist outside literature. Milton is not writing an obituary: he does not start with Edward King and his life and times, but with the conventions and archetypes that poetry requires for such a theme.

Of the critical principles illustrated by this analysis, one will be no surprise to the present audience. *Lycidas* owes quite as much to Hebrew, Greek, Latin and Italian traditions as it does to English. Even the diction, of which I have no space to speak, shows strong Italian influence. Milton was of course a learned poet, but there is no poet whose literary influences are entirely confined to his own language. Thus every problem in literary criticism is a problem in Comparative Literature, or simply of literature itself.

The next principle is that the provisional hypothesis which we must adopt for the study of every poem is that that poem is a unity. If, after careful and repeated testing, we are forced to conclude that it is not a unity, then we must abandon the hypothesis and look for the reasons why it is not. A good deal of bad criticism of *Lycidas* has resulted from not making enough initial effort to understand the unity of the poem. To talk of 'digressions' in *Lycidas* is a typical consequence of a mistaken critical method, of backing into the poem the wrong way round. If, instead of starting with the poem, we start with a handful of peripheral facts about the poem, Milton's casual knowledge of King, his ambitions as a poet, his bitterness against the episcopacy, then of course the poem will break down into pieces corresponding precisely to those fragments of knowledge. *Lycidas* illustrates, on a small scale, what has happened on a much bigger scale in, for example, the criticism of Homer. Critics knowing something about the fragmentary nature of heroic lays and ballads approached the *Iliad* and the *Odyssey* with this knowledge in mind, and the poems obediently split up into the pieces that they wished to isolate. Other critics came along and treated the poems as imaginative unities, and today everyone knows that the second group were more convincing.

The same thing happens when our approach to 'sources' becomes fragmentary or piecemeal. *Lycidas* is a dense mass of echoes from previous literature, chiefly pastoral literature. Reading through Virgil's Eclogues with *Lycidas* in mind, we can see that Milton had not simply read or studied these poems: he possessed them; they were part of the material he was shaping. The passage about the hungry sheep reminds us of at least three other passages: one in Dante's *Paradiso*, one in the Book of Ezekiel, and one near the beginning of Hesiod's *Theogony*. There are also echoes of Mantuan and Spenser, of the Gospel of John, and it is quite possible that there are even more striking parallels with poems that Milton had not read. In such cases there is not *a* source at all, no one place that the passage 'comes from,' or, as we say with such stupefying presumption, that the poet 'had in mind.' There are only archetypes, or recurring themes of literary expression, which *Lycidas* has recreated, and therefore re-echoed, yet once more.

The next principle is that the important problems of literary criticism lie within the study of literature. We notice that a law of diminishing returns sets in as soon as we move away from the poem itself. If we ask, who is Lycidas? the answer is that he is a member of the same family as Theocritus' Daphnis, Bion's Adonis, the Old Testament's Abel, and so on. The answer goes on building up a wider comprehension of literature and a deeper knowledge of its structural principles and recurring themes. But if we ask, who was Edward King? What was his relation to Milton? How good a poet was he? we find ourselves moving dimly in the intense inane. The same is true of minor points. If we ask, why is the image of the two-handed engine in *Lycidas*? we can give an answer, along the lines suggested above, that illustrates how carefully the poem has been constructed. If we ask, what is the two-handed engine? there are forty-odd answers, none of them completely satisfactory; yet the fact that they are not wholly satisfactory hardly seems to be important.

Another form of the same kind of fallacy is the confusion between personal sincerity and literary sincerity. If we start with the facts that *Lycidas* is highly conventional and that Milton knew King only slightly, we may see in *Lycidas* an 'artificial' poem without 'real feeling' in it. This red herring, though more common among third-rate romantics, was dragged across the study of *Lycidas* by Samuel Johnson. Johnson knew better, but he happened to feel perverse about this particular poem, and so deliberately raised false issues. It would not have occurred to him, for example, to question the conventional use of Horace in the satires of Pope, or of Juvenal in his own. Personal sincerity has no place in literature, because personal sincerity as such is inarticulate. One may burst into tears at the news of a friend's death, but one can never spontaneously burst into song, however doleful a lay. *Lycidas* is a passionately sincere poem, because Milton was deeply interested in the structure and symbolism of funeral elegies, and had been practising since adolescence on every fresh corpse in sight, from the university beadle to the fair infant dying of a cough.

If we ask what inspires a poet, there are always two answers. An occasion, an experience, an event, may inspire the impulse to write. But the impulse to write can only come from previous contact with literature, and the formal inspiration, the poetic structure that crystallizes around the new event, can only be derived from other poems. Hence while every new poem is a new and unique creation, it is also a re-shaping of familiar conventions of literature, otherwise it would not be recognizable as literature at all. Literature often gives us the illusion of turning from books to life, from second-hand to direct experience, and thereby discovering new literary principles in the world outside. But this is never quite what happens. No matter how tightly Wordsworth may close the barren leaves of art and let nature be his teacher, his literary forms will be as conventional as ever, although they may echo an unaccustomed set of conventions, such as the ballad or the broadside. The pretence of personal sincerity is itself a literary convention, and Wordsworth makes many of the flat simple statements which represent, in literature, the inarticulateness of personal sincerity:

> No motion has she now, no force:
> She neither hears nor sees.

But as soon as a death becomes a poetic image, that image is assimilated to other poetic images of death in nature, and hence Lucy inevitably becomes a Proserpine figure, just as King becomes an Adonis:

> Rolled round in earth's diurnal course
> With rocks, and stones, and trees.

In Whitman we have an even more extreme example than Wordsworth of a cult of personal statement and an avoidance of learned conventions. It is therefore instructive to see what happens in *When Lilacs Last in Dooryard Bloomed.* The dead man is not called by a pastoral name, but neither is he called by his historical name. He is in a coffin which is carried the length and breadth of the land; he is identified with a 'powerful western fallen star'; he is the beloved comrade of the poet, who throws the purple flower of the lilac on his coffin; a singing bird laments the death, just as the woods and caves do in *Lycidas*. Convention, genre, archetype, and the autonomy of forms are all illustrated as clearly in Whitman as they are in Milton.

Lycidas is an occasional poem, called forth by a specific event. It seems, therefore, to be a poem with a strong external reference. Critics who cannot approach a poem except as a personal statement of the poet's thus feel that if it says little about King, it must say a good deal about Milton. So, they reason, *Lycidas* is really autobiographical, concerned with Milton's own preoccupations, including his fear of death. There can be no objection to this unless Milton's conventional involving of himself with the poem is misinterpreted as a personal intrusion into it.

For Milton was even by seventeenth-century standards an unusually professional and impersonal poet. Of all Milton's poems, the one obvious failure is the poem called *The Passion*, and if we look at the imagery of that poem we can see why. It is the only poem of Milton's in which he is preoccupied with himself in the process of writing it. 'My muse,' 'my song,' 'my Harp,' 'my roving verse,' 'my Phoebus,' and so on for eight stanzas until Milton abandons the poem in disgust. It is not a coincidence that Milton's one self-conscious poem should be the one that never gets off the ground. There is nothing like this in *Lycidas*: the 'I' of that poem is a professional poet in his conventional shepherd disguise, and to think of him as a personal 'I' is to bring *Lycidas* down to the level of *The Passion*, to make it a poem that has to be studied primarily as a biographical document rather than for its own sake. Such an approach to *Lycidas* is apt to look most plausible to those who dislike Milton, and want to see him cut down to size.

One more critical principle, and the one that I have written this paper to enunciate, seems to me to follow inevitably from the previous ones. Every poem must be examined as a unity, but no poem is an isolatable unity. Every poem is inherently connected with other poems of its kind, whether explicitly as *Lycidas* is with Theocritus and Virgil, or implicitly, as Whitman is with the same tradition, or by anticipation, as *Lycidas* is with later pastoral elegies. And, of course, the kinds or genres of literature are not separable either, like the orders of pre-Darwinian biology. Everyone who has seriously studied literature knows that he is not simply moving from poem to poem, or from one aesthetic experience to another: he is also entering into a coherent and progressive discipline. For literature is not simply an aggregate of books and poems and plays: it is an order of words. And our total literary experience, at any given time, is not a discrete series of memories or impressions of what we have read, but an imaginatively coherent body of experience.

It is literature as an order of words, therefore, which forms the primary context of any given work of literary art. All other contexts: the place of *Lycidas* in Milton's development; its place in the history of English poetry; its place in seventeenth-century thought or history, are secondary and derivative contexts. Within the total literary order certain structural and generic principles, certain configurations of narrative and imagery, certain conventions and devices and *topoi*, occur over and over again. In every new work of literature some of these principles are reshaped.

Lycidas, we found, is informed by such a recurring structural principle. The short, simple, and accurate name for this principle is myth. The Adonis myth is what makes *Lycidas* both distinctive and traditional. Of course if we think of the Adonis myth as some kind of Platonic idea existing by itself, we shall not get far with it as a critical conception. But it is only incompetence that tries to reduce or assimilate a poem to a myth. The Adonis myth in *Lycidas* is the structure of *Lycidas*. It is in *Lycidas* in much the same way that the sonata form is in the first movement of a Mozart symphony. It is the connecting link between what makes *Lycidas* the poem it is and what unites it to other forms of poetic experience. If we attend only to the uniqueness of *Lycidas*, and analyze the ambiguities and subtleties of its diction, our method, however useful in itself, soon reaches a point of no return to the poem. If we attend only to the conventional element, our method will turn it into a scissors-and-paste collection of allusive tags. One method reduces the poem to a jangle of echoes of itself, the other to a jangle of echoes from other poets. If we have a unifying principle that holds these two tendencies together from the start, neither will get out of hand.

Myths, it is true, turn up in other disciplines, in anthropology, in psychology, in comparative religion. But the primary business of the critic is with myth as the shaping principle of a work of literature. Thus for him myth becomes much the same thing as Aristotle's *mythos*, narrative or plot, the moving formal cause which is what Aristotle called the 'soul' of the work and assimilates all details in the realizing of its unity.

In its simplest English meaning a myth is a story about a god, and Lycidas is, poetically speaking, a god or spirit of nature, who eventually becomes a saint in heaven, which is as near as one can get to godhead in ordinary Christianity. The reason for treating Lycidas mythically, in this sense, is conventional, but the convention is not arbitrary or accidental. It arises from the metaphorical nature of poetic speech. We are not told simply that Lycidas has left the woods and caves, but that the woods and caves and all their echoes mourn his loss. This is the language of that curious identification of subject and object, of personality and thing, which the poet has in common with the lunatic and the lover. It is the language of metaphor, recognized by Aristotle as the distinctive language of poetry. And, as we can see in such phrases as sun-god and tree-god, the language of metaphor is interdependent with the language of myth.

I have said that all problems of criticism are problems of Comparative Literature. But where there is comparison there must be some standard by which we can distinguish what is actually comparable from what is merely analogous. The scientists discovered long ago that to make valid comparisons you have to know what your real categories are. If you are studying natural history, for instance, no matter how fascinated you may be by anything that has eight legs, you cannot just lump together an octopus and a spider and a string quartet. In science the difference between a scientific and a pseudo-scientific procedure can usually be spotted fairly soon. I wonder if literary criticism has any standards of this kind. It seems to me that a critic practically has to maintain that the Earl of Oxford wrote the plays of Shakespeare before he can be clearly recognized as making pseudo-critical statements. I have read some critics on Milton who appeared to be confusing Milton with their phallic fathers, if that is the right phrase. I should call them pseudo-critics; others call them neo-classicists. How is one to know? There is such a variety of even legitimate critics. There are critics who can find things in the Public Records Office, and there are critics who, like myself, could not find the Public Records Office. Not all critical statements or procedures can be equally valid.

The first step, I think, is to recognize the dependence of value-judgments on scholarship. Scholarship, or the knowledge of literature, constantly expands and increases; value judgments are produced by a skill based on the knowledge we already have. Thus scholarship has both priority to value judgments and the power of veto over them. When Thomas Rymer called *Othello* a bloody farce, he was not making a bad value-judgment; he was making a correct value-judgment based on impossibly narrow scholarship. Most of the famous howlers of criticism are of this kind.[1] The second step is to recognize the dependence of scholarship on a co-ordinated view of literature. A good deal of critical taxonomy lies ahead of us. We need to know much more than we do about the structural principles of literature, about myth and metaphor, conventions and genres, before we can distinguish with any authority a real from an imaginary line of influence, an illuminating from a misleading analogy, a poet's original source from his last resource. The basis of this central critical activity that gives direction to scholarship is the simple fact that every poem is a member of the class of things called poems. Some poems, including *Lycidas,* proclaim that they are conventional, in other words that their primary context is in literature. Other poems leave this inference to the critic, with an appealing if often misplaced confidence.

NOTES

1 [These two sentences, beginning 'When Thomas Rymer' and ending 'of this kind,' do not appear in later versions of the essay: the reprint in *Milton's 'Lycidas': The Tradition and the Poem,* ed. C.A. Patrides (New York, 1961), 200–11; and in Frye's *Fables of Identity* (New York, 1963), 119–29 – Eds.]

4 Milton and Figurative Interpretation of the Bible*

HUGH MACCALLUM

'The letter killeth,' said St. Paul, 'but the spirit giveth life.' In the history of the study of the Bible, two influential interpretations of this statement have frequently vied with each other. One interpretation conceives of the life-giving spirit in terms of knowledge, the other in terms of grace. The first view results in Christian symbolism; it identifies the work of the spirit with the comprehension of metaphorical or figurative expressions, maintaining that spiritual understanding arises from a gradual realization of the true meaning of signs. This theory leads finally to allegorical interpretation of the Bible. The alternative view of the Pauline injunction results in a theory of Christian liberty. This explanation associates the letter with the outward and compulsory law and the spirit with grace. It contrasts bare and servile conformity with the spiritual freedom which enables the Christian to comprehend the intention behind the letter, maintaining that spiritual understanding arises when the commands of the Bible are interpreted in such a way as to establish the reign of love. The first view, then, interprets St. Paul's assertion in a manner that leads to contemplation, the second in a manner that leads to action. The history of the conflict between the rival interpretations provides a profound commentary on the roles of mind and will in Christian experience.

Some writers, like St. Augustine, embrace both interpretations of the Pauline injunction. In his *De doctrina Christiana*, Augustine develops the first of the two explanations:

> 'The letter killeth but the spirit giveth life.' For when what is said figuratively is taken as if it were said literally, it is understood in a carnal manner.

* Originally appearing in the *University of Toronto Quarterly* 31 (1962): 397–415.

> And nothing is more fittingly called the death of the soul than when that in it which raises it above the brutes, the intelligence namely, is put in subjection to the flesh by a blind adherence to the letter. For he who follows the letter takes figurative words as if they were proper, and does not carry out what is indicated by a proper word into secondary signification ... Now it is surely a miserable slavery of the soul to take signs for things, and to be unable to lift the eye of the mind above what is corporeal and created, that it may drink in eternal light.[1]

Here the spirit is associated with figurative meaning, the flesh with the letter; the passage as a whole is an attack on the sense-bound imagination and a plea for insight into Christian symbolism. On the other hand, Augustine is one of the great exponents of the alternative theory concerning St. Paul's meaning. In *De spiritu et littera* he develops this second explanation: 'I wish to show ... that the apostle's words: "the letter killeth but the spirit giveth life," do not refer primarily to the figurative modes of speech – though that sense may also fit them – but rather to the law's express forbidding of evil.'[2] He proceeds to elaborate the theory that the law, that is, the letter, makes sin manifest but provides no escape from death, and that only with the aid of the spirit can man slip the fetters of sin and freely fulfil the law through charity.

The Reformers considered that only this latter interpretation of the passage is valid. It is the second view that Luther has in mind when he expresses his fear that through the authority of Erasmus 'some will be led to defend the literal, that is the killing, sense of the Scripture of which Lyra and almost all the commentators after Augustine are full.'[3] Augustine is excepted from the condemnation because he grasped the crucial distinction between Law and Gospel, not because he recommended a figurative reading of Scripture. Thus Luther advises a friend to read Augustine's books against the Pelagians, 'especially the one on the Spirit and the Letter.'[4] It is Calvin, however, who best sums up the Protestant view of this matter in his commentary on the crucial passage in 2 Corinthians 3.6:

> The exposition contrived by Origen has got into general circulation – that by the *letter* we ought to understand the grammatical and genuine meaning of Scripture, or the *literal* sense (as they call it), and that by the *spirit* is meant the allegorical meaning, which is commonly reckoned to be the *spiritual* meaning. Accordingly, during several centuries, nothing was more commonly said, or more generally received, than this – that Paul here furnishes us with a key for expounding Scripture by allegories, while nothing is

> farther from his intention. For by the term *letter* he means outward preaching, of such a kind as does not reach the heart; and, on the other hand, by *spirit* he means living doctrine, of such a nature as *worketh effectually* ... on the minds of men, through the grace of the Spirit.[5]

The theory of Christian symbolism, which on so many occasions had been associated, either explicitly or implicitly, with the spirit which saves the believer from the dead letter, is here openly rejected by Calvin. The terms 'letter' and 'spirit' do not refer to the 'exposition' of the Word, but to its 'influence and fruit.' Thus figurative interpretation is sharply isolated from spiritual apprehension.

There is no doubt about Milton's attitude to this controversial issue. His view of spiritual understanding is in essential agreement with the view of Luther and Calvin. This can be seen in any of the celebrations of the living spirit which are scattered throughout his writings. Thus, for example, he explains that a failure to understand the difference between letter and spirit corrupted the Church and made the Reformation necessary: '... men came to scan the scriptures by the letter, and in the covenant of our redemption, magnified the external signs more than the quickening power of the Spirit ...' (3.1:3).[6] Characteristically, this is a plea for faith, not figurative interpretation. Milton has in mind, not Origen's distinction between a carnal letter and a spiritual mystery hidden in allegories, but rather Calvin's distinction between outward, formal knowledge and inward, living apprehension. Such a living apprehension of Scripture, which for Milton arises both from faith and from charity, makes the regenerate man 'victorious under the guidance of the living Spirit, not under the dead letter' (4:75). Milton envisages escape from bondage to the letter in the manner of Luther and Calvin or of the Augustine of *De spiritu et littera*: '... we being freed from the works of the law, no longer follow the letter, but the spirit; doing the works of faith, not of the law' (16:151).

In thus aligning himself with reformed thought, Milton abandoned much of the ancient tradition of multiple-level, figurative interpretation; those elements which he retained, he modified drastically. The purpose of the present study is to examine certain aspects of this process of rejection and adaptation. More precisely, its purpose is to investigate the role which Milton assigned to biblical imagery. Two areas of imagery are particularly relevant: the first includes those images used to describe the nature and actions of God; the second those images which are drawn from biblical history and read typologically. Such a study is, I believe, a necessary preliminary to a full understanding of Milton's use of imagery in his poetry.

We may begin by observing the distrust of metaphor as an instrument of religious knowledge which pervades Milton's later prose works. Anyone who associates the poetic temperament with a love of imagery, metaphor, and 'double-talk' is bound to feel some surprise on remembering that these works were written by a major poet. The desire to limit the authority of metaphor and the distrust of figurative modes of expression appear frequently, often explicitly, and they are particularly evident in Milton's theological work, *De doctrina Christiana.* In this review of Christian belief, undertaken with the aim of removing all hesitation and doubt concerning the chief principles of religious doctrine, Milton eschews metaphors and seeks directness and logical accuracy. 'In drawing up a law,' he writes, 'as in composing a definition, it is necessary that the most exact words should be used, and that they should be interpreted not in their metaphorical, but in their proper signification' (15:127–9). This is the bias of his method. When he finds it necessary to use metaphorical language, he does so with caution, as in the following comment on predestination: 'If an argument of any weight in the discussion of so controverted a subject can be derived from allegorical and metaphorical expressions, mention is frequently made of those who are written among the living, and of the book of life, but never of the book of death' (14:93). Even the language of the sacraments must be read as metaphoric hyperbole; a clear understanding is gained only when figurative expressions are stripped away to reveal the causes underlying the institution of the sacraments and the nature of the contract on which they depend (16:193–9). On the whole, then, it is safe to say that *De doctrina Christiana* reveals a quest for exact and literal definitions and a distrust of deductions based on metaphorical statements.

However, one soon grows aware that a number of Milton's key theological terms – 'election,' 'adoption,' 'engrafting into Christ,' 'the law written on the heart,' and so on – contain a seemingly figurative element. Yet when employing such terms, Milton frequently writes as if they were to be read literally, and not in any figurative sense. Since all these terms are scriptural, this tendency is to be explained partly by his belief that the theologians should adhere closely to the very words of the Bible. But it also reflects a definite theory concerning the way in which Scripture accommodates itself to the human imagination.

Milton's doctrine of accommodation has often been noted by critics, but its implications remain in need of further examination.[7] The first step in his argument is the assertion of the importance of revelation to man's knowledge of God: no one, he argues, can have right thoughts of God with nature or reason alone as his guide, 'independent of the word, or message, of God' (14:31). Even when aided by Scripture, however, man's knowledge of God necessarily remains imperfect, for the finite mind cannot hope to know the real nature of the deity. God has made as full a revelation of himself as man can receive, and the safest approach is to form in the mind

> such a conception of God, as shall correspond with his own delineation and representation of himself in the sacred writings. For granting that both in the literal and figurative descriptions of God, he is exhibited not as he really is, but in such manner as may be within the scope of our comprehensions, yet we ought to entertain such a conception of him, as he, in condescending to accommodate himself to our capacities, has shown that he desires we should conceive (14:31–33).

The descriptions of God found in Scripture are not pictures of God in himself but of God as he wishes to appear. They have no metaphysical validity outside the sphere of human perception. Yet they are all that is available to man, and he must learn to rest content with them. To speculate further is to indulge in 'vague cogitations and subtleties.'

Some ambiguity is present in Milton's discussion. Scripture, of course, frequently depicts God as if he were a man. Is it possible that he really exists in such a form? Milton will not say. God either is or is not such as he represents himself to be: if the representation is accurate, then the argument rests; if not, it is still true that this is the way he wishes to be apprehended. 'For such knowledge of the Deity as was necessary for the salvation of man, he has himself of his goodness been pleased to reveal abundantly.' The whole problem remains in human terms, and Milton is unwilling to leave any scope for metaphysical or mystical speculation. God is in the position of the Kantian 'thing-in-itself'; his real nature, as opposed to his perceived nature, is a presupposition which can never be verified. We see God through the glass of Scripture, and whether that glass is transparent and colourless, or whether it is merely translucent, or possibly even warped and tinted, we cannot say. Nor need it concern us. The anthropomorphic picture of God is a hypothesis, but a hypothesis presented by God himself.

In employing this hypothesis we must be careful and yet bold. When we read that 'it repented Jehovah that he had made man,' we should believe that he really did repent; yet we should also remember that in this case 'repentance' does not imply inadvertency. Similar qualifications must be supplied when we think of God's 'grief,' his 'rest,' and his 'fear.' In short, 'what is imperfection and weakness when viewed in reference to ourselves' must be considered 'as most complete and excellent when imputed to God.' At first glance these qualifications suggest the mystic's formula for describing God: 'This is He, neither is this He.' What kind of repentance, one might object, does not involve inadvertency, and how can the omnipotent suffer fear? Surely Milton is setting up a system by which all affirmations made of God are ultimately negated? The emphasis, however, consistently falls on affirmation. All the necessary moral and theological doctrines can be worked out in terms of the anthropomorphic picture of himself which God has provided:

> For however we may attempt to soften down such expressions by a latitude of interpretation, when applied to the Deity, it comes in the end to precisely the same. If God be said 'to have made man in his own image, after his likeness' ... and that too not only as to his soul, but also as to his outward form ... why should we be afraid of attributing to him what he attributes to himself ...[8]

Milton's suspicion of metaphor and the symbolic use of images finds here its theological ground.

Doctrines of accommodation appear frequently in Reformation theology (both Luther and Calvin thought of themselves as upholding anthropomorphism). Nevertheless Milton's doctrine is unusually daring and thoroughgoing. This becomes apparent as soon as it is compared with other contemporary versions. Most of these are what might be called theories of *social* accommodation. They take the position that the Bible was written for a popular audience consisting largely of simple, uneducated people. Moses, averred John Colet, spoke 'not according to his own powers of comprehension, but according to the comprehension of the multitude'; thus Moses taught the rude multitude in the manner of a 'popular poet.'[9] Well over a century later, Spinoza, describing how the Bible teaches basic moral doctrines to the ignorant by means of figures and anthropomorphic images, took the startling step of suggesting that Moses and the other writers of the Bible possessed essentially the same powers of comprehension as the multitude which they taught; they were men of strong imaginations who lacked clear and distinct ideas.[10] Not many of Milton's contemporaries would have assented to this unorthodox view, but most found it useful to resort to the theory that the writers of the Bible often addressed themselves to the capacities of the vulgar sort.

Whether the vulgar are defined in terms of their lack of clear and distinct ideas, or of their failure to penetrate Neoplatonic metaphysics, or of their scientific ignorance, the final effect of these theories of social accommodation is to induce the student to read between the lines, to penetrate behind the veils of imagery to the hidden meaning. Milton's doctrine, on the other hand, centres attention unwaveringly on the Bible itself. His theory has nothing to do with social classes or the historical development of cultures; it could be called *epistemological*, in the sense that it defines the limits of man's comprehension. The whole drift of his argument is calculated to encourage the reader to rest in the words and images of Scripture, not to penetrate behind them. Thus while the tendency of theories of social accommodation is to explain away the anthropomorphic descriptions of God, Milton's doctrine requires the acceptance of them at face value, without any distinction between the 'tenor' and the 'vehicle.' He will not permit the assumption that the initiate may find a more esoteric doctrine behind the simplicity of scriptural expressions: 'There is no need then that theologians should have recourse here to what they call anthropopathy – a figure invented by the grammarians to excuse the absurdities of the poets on the subject of heathen divinities' (14:33).[11]

In one other respect, Milton's doctrine is unusual. For most theologians, the gap between human understanding and the divine nature is bridged through Christ. Since in orthodox thought the Son is believed to be perfect God and perfect Man, he provides unqualified and direct knowledge of God. This is an ultimate form of accommodation; yet it is more than that, for as the Athanasian Creed puts the matter, Christ is both God and Man 'not by the conversion of the Godhead into flesh; but by taking of the Manhood into God.' For Milton, however, the Incarnation had a more restricted significance. The Son is not co-eternal with the Father, he believed, nor does the Son equal the Father in power and knowledge. Being the first of God's creatures the Son cannot bring us into direct contact with the divine essence itself, which is incommunicable. True, the Son is the perfect image of the Father; but since Christ is the image by which we see and hear God, he cannot be one with God (14:401). Milton's doctrine of accommodation, then, lacks the traditional sanction which orthodox trinitarians found in the Incarnation.[12]

The second area of our study is that of typology. The subject offers an opportunity to examine Milton's attitude to biblical metaphors and images against the background provided by an ancient and pervasive tradition. Recent scholarship has clarified the role of typology in patristic and mediaeval exegesis and has explored the complex relations of typology and allegory.[13] It is not always recognized, however, that the Reformers, despite their antipathy to subtle exegetical speculations, were deeply influenced by the typological tradition.

It is true, of course, that attacks on allegorical and multiple-level interpretation were frequent in the writings of Luther, Calvin, and their successors. The kind of interpretation which they rejected is best epitomized by the hermeneutics of Origen. Origen maintained that every passage in Scripture has a spiritual meaning, and he frequently exalted this meaning at the expense of the literal sense. Reacting to such systematic allegorizing, the Reformers stressed the 'literal' or 'plain' or 'historical' sense of Scripture. By these terms they meant, as a rule, the *single* meaning intended by the author of the passage under consideration. William Ames, Milton's contemporary, was merely echoing the conventional view when he wrote that 'there is only one sence to one place of Scripture; because otherwise the sence of the Scripture should be not onely not cleare and certaine but none at all: for that which doth not signifie one thing, signifieth certainly nothing.'[14] This antagonism to multiplicity of meaning is clearly reflected in *De doctrina Christiana*, where Milton writes that 'no passage of Scripture is to be interpreted in more than one sense' (16:263). As a rule, the Reformation writers rounded out their argument by maintaining that allegory is a rhetorical device, a legitimate accommodation of biblical texts to new circumstances by the preacher; they insisted, however, that as a rhetorical device allegory belongs to homiletics, not exegesis. Milton is in complete agreement with the Protestant theologians on this issue. Although not averse to employing allegories, even allegories in the Alexandrian manner, he indicates when he does so that he considers himself to be inventing, not interpreting.[15]

The Reformers' suspicion of allegorical exegesis did not, however, involve the complete rejection of typological criticism. Believing the union of typology and philosophical allegory to be an error introduced by the Alexandrians and perpetuated by the Schoolmen, they attempted to renew the pure typology of the New Testament and particularly of the Pauline epistles. The scope which Protestant exegetes allowed themselves for such criticism varied considerably, but all were willing to admit that many scriptural passages must be understood typically. This admission appears at first sight inconsistent with the theory of 'one sense to one place.' The problem, however, was resolved by a new argument which we may call the doctrine of the compound sense. John Weemes' presentation of this wide-spread argument is thoroughly conventional and was quite possibly known to Milton. Weemes accepts as his starting point the principle that 'there is but one literall sense in the Scriptures.' This sense, he argues, may be either simple or compound. The compound sense, however, 'is not taken here to make two senses out of one Scripture (for that were contradictory) but onely it showes the diverse wayes how the severall parts of a Scripture have beene fulfilled either literally or figuratively.' Thus, for example, the injunction 'neither shall ye break a bone thereof' (Exod 12.46) was fulfilled literally in the Paschal Lamb and figuratively in the crucifixion of Christ. The two meanings of such passage make up a single sense, and this sense is the literal meaning of the passage; that is, it is the meaning intended by the author.[16]

Milton accepted the doctrine of the compound sense. In *De doctrina Christiana,* having asserted the theory of 'one sense to one place,' he adds that 'this sense is sometimes a compound of the historical and the typical.' He then illustrates the compound sense by a traditional example of typology: 'out of Egypt have I called my son ... may be explained in a double sense, as referring partly to the people of Israel, and partly to Christ in his infancy' (16:263). The highly conventional nature of Milton's discussion at this point is indicated by the fact that, as Professor Maurice Kelly has shown, the passage in question is taken directly from Wollebius' *Compendium theologiae Christianae.*[17] The view contained in the passage, however, was operative in Milton's treatment of the Bible. Many passages in his prose, and several in his poetry, show its influence. A particularly clear and full illustration can be found in his treatment of Melchisedec as a type in *The Likeliest Means to Remove Hirelings.* The interchange between Melchisedec and Abram, he maintains, can be explained on two distinct levels of meaning. In blessing Abram and his army and refreshing them with bread and wine, Melchisedec was incited by two forces: first, by the secret providence of God, which intended him for a type of Christ and his priesthood; secondly, by his gratitude to Abram, who had freed the borders of Salem from the enemy. Abram's gift of a tenth of the spoils was likewise the product of a double motive: first, he was inspired by secret providence to act in such a way as to foreshadow the excelling of the priesthood of Levi by the priesthood of Christ; secondly, he was guided by his feeling of thankfulness and reverence to Melchisedec. Thus the story contains both historical and typological levels of significance. As representation, it depicts human beings in a moral context; as typology, it provides a prefiguration of Christ. The characters, however, are unaware of the secret meaning which they dramatize.

Milton's handling of this episode reveals how sharply he distinguished between types and examples. Such a distinction was a commonplace in Protestant-Puritan exegesis, as can be seen in such representative compendiums of typology as Samuel Mather's *The Figures or Types of the Old Testament* and Thomas Taylor's *Christ Revealed: or the Old Testament Explained.*[18] By accepting this view, these writers placed themselves within a tradition which had been forcefully asserted centuries before in the writings of St. Augustine. In *Contra Faustinum,* a work which is among other things a textbook of typology, Augustine remarks that 'when actions are related or recorded as types, the merit or demerit of the agents is a matter of no importance, as long as there is a true typical relation between the action and the thing typified.'[19] Not all Protestant critics were willing to put the matter quite so starkly. Mather, for example, would add the qualification that 'no wicked man individually considered ever was or could be a type of Christ.'[20] But concerning the main issue – that a type is a prefiguration of something to come in which the motives of the human agents who elaborate the type are not of importance – there was general agreement.

Distinct from examples, types are also differentiated from simple prophecy. They are veiled and indirect forecasts rather than open and literal predictions. Metaphor is of the essence of typology. 'There was and is *a double use of types* and parables,' wrote Mather, 'and of that whole way of Argument by Similitude and Comparison: They do both *darken* and *illustrate*: if explained and understood, they do exceedingly enlighten and illustrate: but if not explained, they are like a Puddle, they cast a dark mist and cloud upon the thing.'[21] In the simplest typology, the metaphorical element arises because both type and antitype are embedded in history, the relation being one of correspondence between events, persons, or objects. Such 'similar situation' typology did not in itself appeal strongly to the Reformers, however. The Protestant-Puritan view of the antitype was usually affected by the belief that the inwardness and spirituality of the Gospel stand in sharp contrast to the externality of the Law. As Mather observed, '*God never had but one way only to save men by*; but it had divers fashions and forms, divers outward discoveries and manifestations; in those times in a more legal manner, but afterwards more like itself, in a more Evangelical manner.'[22] This view led the Protestant writers to stress the spiritual nature of the antitype and to contrast this with the external and outward nature of the type. This tendency is very evident in Milton's writing. Thus he observes that all the 'sumptuous things' under the Law were made 'to signifie the inward beauty and splendors of the Christian Church' (3:191). Thus, too, Michael's narrative of the history of the world in the last two books of *Paradise Lost* shows a movement 'From Shadowie types to truth, from Flesh to Spirit'(12.303). Milton reveals little interest in that traditional form of typology in which an external event in the Old Testament prefigures an equally external event in the New; the Protestant bias of his thought consistently caused him to emphasize the inward and spiritual nature of the antitype.

Further problems arise, however, when attention is turned to the variety of significates possible to types. Mather's remarks can again be taken as fairly representative: 'Types,' he observes, 'relate not only to the Person of Christ, but to his Benefits, and to all Gospel Truths and Mysteries, even to all New-Testament Dispensations.'[23] As this implies, a threefold pattern can be discerned in typical events: the type can refer to the life of Christ, to the life of the Church and the individual Christian within it, or the mysteries of eternity. In traditional terminology, these three forms are called allegory (this technical sense must be distinguished sharply from the general meaning), tropology, and anagogy. Mather and Taylor did not use this nomenclature, but many Protestant exegetes with less antipathy to scholasticism drew upon it without hesitation.[24] Whether the technical terms were employed or not, however, most Reformers accepted a large body of multiple-level typological interpretation, purged it of what they considered extraneous philosophical elements, and reconciled it to their conception of the plain meaning of Scripture by the doctrine of the compound sense.

Milton's comments on types are more conservative and reserved than those of most Reformation writers. Not only does he avoid the finer theoretical distinctions among types, but he is unusually restrained in his usage. Examples of the various forms can be culled from his writings: Joshua as a type of Jesus is allegory; the manna as type of the Lord's supper is tropology; the translation of Elijah as a type of perfect glorification is anagogy (16: ch.3, 197, 337). It is clear, however, that Milton was not concerned to stratify his types in this fashion. One can say only that his typological strategy varies from one writing to another. In the anti-episcopal tracts, for example, anagogic interpretation is prominent. Believing that the advent of the millennium was imminent, he used types to prefigure that apocalyptic event. In the world history contained in the last books of *Paradise Lost*, on the other hand, the typology focusses on the man of faith as the prefiguration of Christ. Modelled on the Epistle to the Hebrews (11–13) and Stephen's speech before the Sanhedrin in Acts (7.1–53), this typology is, in the technical sense, allegorical. Whatever may be the typological drift of a given piece of Milton's writing, however, one always finds his characteristic emphasis on the spiritual and evangelical nature of the antitype.

Having accepted a modified version of traditional typological theory, the Reformers were faced with the problem of defining the limits of such exegesis. Typology has a tendency to slip into systematic allegory, as can be seen in St. Paul's allegory of Ishmael and Isaac (Gal 4.21–31), and the Reformation critics wished to keep that tendency firmly in check. All agreed on the general principle which ought to control the exegete: identification of types should depend on the text of Scripture, not on the whim of the individual. But what constitutes scriptural justification of a typological interpretation? Those types which Christ and the apostles explicitly identify were, of course, universally accepted. But many commentators agreed with Samuel Mather that 'express Scripture' is only one of several methods by which Scripture makes types known. Types, Mather argues, may be indicated by etymology, by analogy between events, and by similarities of phrasing in different parts of the Bible.[25] Rules such as these leave the door open for a wide variety of typological interpretations, and the results obtained by their application will clearly depend to a large extent on the learning, common sense, and theological commitments of the interpreter employing them.

Milton is unusually strict in his practice of typology. Most of the types found in *De doctrina Christiana* can be identified by 'express Scripture.' This is not always true of the patterns of correspondence developed in some of the more polemical works, but Milton would no doubt have admitted that in these works he was employing typology partly as a rhetorical and homiletic device. In general agreement with the Reformed tradition concerning the limits of typological interpretation, he was more severe than many of his contemporaries in his strictures on its abuse. His comments lack the expansiveness present in the speculations of Weemes or Mather or Taylor. Even in the early tracts, where his practice is more flamboyant than in his later works, he attacks the belief that each event in the Old Testament must be answered by an event in the New: '… if this method may be admitted of interpreting those prophetical passages concerning Christian times in a punctuall correspondence, it may, with equal probability, be urged upon us, that we are bound to observe some monthly solemnity answerable to the new moons, as well as the Lord's day which we keep in lieu of the sabbath' (3.1:206). Years later, when considering in *De doctrina Christiana* the typological parallels among the sacraments of the Old Testament and those of the New, he writes that 'there is ... no necessary analogy between circumcision and baptism; and it is our duty not to build our belief on vague parallels, but to attend exclusively to the institution of the sacrament itself, and regard its authority as paramount' (16:181). Vague parallels must not be used to enforce a strict correspondence between Old and New Testament times. Because one event prefigures another in certain respects, it does not follow that there must be a series of perfect analogies between them, and outward, external similarities are particularly misleading. Many of the traditional correspondences, Milton felt, are in reality but fugitive and insignificant parallels. Types must be established with discretion, and those who analyse them should have a clear apprehension of the spiritual and evangelical nature of the antitype.

Imagery and metaphor play a subordinate role in Milton's conception of biblical interpretation and in the theology which he elaborates from his study of the Bible. The tendency to restrict the function of metaphorical modes of understanding is apparent everywhere: it can be seen in his manner of reading sacramental language as hyperbole, in his attempt to base doctrine on the plainest passages of the Bible and to use words in their proper significations when seeking definitions, and in his theory that the anthropomorphic picture of God provided by Scripture defines the limits of human comprehension. The same restraint can be seen in his attitude to the tradition of typology. He upholds the Protestant rejection of multiple meanings, rejects allegory as an instrument of exegesis, permits a compound sense but prefers types clearly established by the New Testament, denies all authority to types in matters of doctrine and discipline, and stresses the spirituality of the antitype.

Milton's comments on Scripture can at best provide only an uncertain guide to his views concerning poetry. What is said about the Word of God will not necessarily be applicable to the words of man, and when applicable, may be so only indirectly and by analogy. Nonetheless, our present study emphasizes certain views which are relevant to an understanding of Milton's poetry and particularly to a study of his poetic imagery. Much recent criticism has been preoccupied with the conception of figurative communication implied by the use of imagery in his poetry. Since he made few critical pronouncements which deal directly with this aspect of poetry, his remarks concerning biblical imagery are of special value. Two tendencies in recent criticism of his poetry may, I believe, be reassessed in the light of the views of imagery and metaphor which we have noticed.

The first is the tendency to read Milton's poetry in the light of traditional allegorical and typological theory. An example of this kind of criticism in a simple form is provided by Professor F.M. Krouse's *Milton's Samson and the Christian Tradition.* Professor Krouse maintains that since typological criticism of the Samson story was a commonplace of Protestant as well as Catholic exegesis, Milton would have altered the story significantly if he had wished to counteract the contemporary reader's tendency to see Christ in Samson. Since no corrective alterations were made, Krouse concludes that allegorical duality was part – perhaps even the centre – of the meaning the poet intended his tragedy to possess.[26] A much subtler attempt to associate Milton with the allegorical tradition has recently been made by Professor Rosemond Tuve in her learned and persuasive study of five early poems. Her approach differs from Krouse's in that she is not concerned primarily with biblical typology, but with extensions of allegorical techniques to the treatment of ethical and non-scriptural subjects. Milton, she holds, wrote in a deeply figurative manner, for an audience thoroughly accustomed to reading allegorically. His figurative habits melt indistinguishably into those of 'the modified, medieval background against which we see him.' If we wish, Professor Tuve argues, we can find 'the familiar medieval four-fold meanings' in Milton's poetry, although we shall be wise, she adds, if we ape the writers of the Middle Ages in their unrigorous and sporadic application of these meanings.[27]

Such views stand in need of some qualification. Metaphoric and symbolic modes of understanding were, we know, an important element in Milton's milieu; he wrote, as Professors Tuve and Krouse have reminded us, for an audience adept at reading allegorically. Yet he also belonged to a religious movement which assumed a critical and highly selective attitude toward traditional symbolism, and he was somewhat more severe than the average Reformed theologian in his strictures on metaphorical modes of thought. For this reason I find Professor Krouse's contention concerning *Samson Agonistes* unconvincing. It is improbable that Milton would invest the biblical subject-matter employed in his poetry with more typological significance than his exegetical principles permitted to it. The simple fact that Milton's contemporaries were familiar with the idea of allegorical duality does not justify us in assuming that such duality is essential to the meaning of the poetic drama, particularly since the assumption ignores Milton's expressed views concerning typology.[28]

On the other hand, it is quite possible that, when dealing with subject-matter that is not explicitly scriptural, Milton might have felt free to follow the example of many Renaissance poets by drawing upon mediaeval fourfold meanings. If, as Miss Tuve maintains, he did so, then we may conclude that he separated rather sharply the technique proper to the poet from those employed by the writers of the Bible. I suggest, however, that in Milton's poetry these 'meanings' do not usually exist apart from the literal sense. Unlike the Alexandrian and scholastic theories, the Protestant doctrine of types unites the literal and the typical senses, and this rejection of independent secondary significations left its mark on Milton's poetry.

The second tendency found in recent criticism of Milton's imagery has arisen from the assumption that he envisaged the function of the Christian poet in terms of the framework provided by Renaissance Neoplatonism. Milton, it has been argued,[29] saw a basic similarity between the accommodation of truth provided by the Bible and that provided by the poet. Believing that the world of fact is merely an image of divine reality, he developed a doctrine of scriptural accommodation which held that the Bible adapted eternal and hidden verities to the imagination of man through the symbolic use of images. Believing in the high office of the Christian poet, he concluded that his poetry was also a revelation through sensible images of the truth of God. According to this view, then, Milton considered that the inspired poet employs a symbolic method which is essentially the same as that used by the prophets, the apostles, and the 'penmen' of the Bible.

This assessment has some validity and usefully relates Milton to a very powerful current of Renaissance thought. Yet it also subtly distorts his position. His doctrine of scriptural accommodation lacks the characteristic emphasis of Renaissance Neoplatonism. It does not encourage the student to purify his spiritual sight in order to penetrate ever more deeply into the mysteries reflected in the dark glass of Scripture, nor does it urge him to pass through the sensible veil of imagery to the divine ray of revelation. On the contrary, Milton's doctrine insists that the Christian should rest content with that conception of deity which God made manifest, for 'it is best to be ignorant of what God wills should remain unknown' (15:271). Instead of attempting to dissolve the figures, the student should accept them as if they were literal, and proceed to deduce moral and doctrinal positions from them. In a manner opposed to all but the most purely ethical Neoplatonism, Milton's theory prevents the extrapolation of metaphysical or mystical theories from the concrete imagery of the Bible. This view of scriptural accommodation, however, clearly does not provide a model for the Neoplatonic conception of the poet's act of accommodation. Although Milton appears to have held that in some sense he was continuing the work of the biblical poets, I see no evidence that he considered a Neoplatonic conception of symbolism to be a mark of his office.

Milton's comment on the single sense of Scripture also indicates a point of view antagonistic to most forms of Renaissance Neoplatonism. Erasmus expressed a common tenet of such philosophy when he argued in his *Enchiridion* that even the Gospel has flesh and spirit and that in order to proceed from the former to the latter we must learn to read allegorically. Milton, as we have seen, rejects the association of the letter with the body and the complementary association of figurative awareness with the spirit. The spiritual understanding of the letter requires the apprehension of the letter through faith and charity rather than the substitution of an allegorical meaning for the literal one. Thus Milton's Protestant belief in the spirit as inseparable from the letter reminds one, not of the metaphysics of Christian Neoplatonism, but of his own 'biblical' philosophy of monism in which matter and spirit are ultimately indistinguishable.

Milton gained much from the ancient figurative traditions which had been inherited and modified by writers of the Renaissance. Recent scholarship has provided a new insight into this debt. In our examination of his use of traditional symbolism, however, we should not neglect the manner in which its significance is conditioned and qualified by his Reformation tenets. Milton reveals throughout his life, and most intensely in his late works, a belief that the order and coherence sought by the symbol-making imagination are dangerous and liable to enslave man and force the spirit. Reacting against those forms of religious speculation which delight in veiled mysteries, mysteries partially hidden by the very symbols through which they are bodied forth, Milton held that Scripture is plain and perspicuous in all things necessary to salvation and that its revelation is adapted to the mind as physical light to the eye (3:33).

NOTES

1 [Augustine of Hippo] *The Works of… Augustine*, ed. M. Dods (Edinburgh, 1892), 9:86.

2 [Augustine,] *Later Works*, trans. and ed. John Burnaby (London, 1955), 199.

3 [Martin Luther,] *Luther's Correspondence and Other Contemporary Letters,* [2 vols,] trans. and ed. Preserved Smith (Philadelphia, 1913), 1:44.
4 Ibid., 43 [42].
5 [John Calvin,] *Commentary on ... Corinthians,* [2 vols,] trans. John Pringle, Calvin Translation Society (Edinburgh, 1848–9), 1:175[passage quoted is on 2:172].
6 Citations in the text from Milton's prose are from *The Works of John Milton,* ed. Frank Allen Patterson (New York: Columbia University Press, 1931–38), 18 vols.
7 See George N. Conklin, *Biblical Criticism and Heresy in Milton* (New York, 1949), ch. 2, and A.J.A. Waldock, *'Paradise Lost' and Its Critics* (Cambridge, 1947), 19–20.
8 As R.M. Frye has observed – *God, Man and Satan* (Princeton, 1960), 14 – Milton in this passage makes essentially the same point as that made by Raphael in his famous aside to Adam:

what surmounts the reach
Of human sense, I shall delineate so,
By lik'ning spiritual to corporal forms,
As may express them best, though what if Earth
Be but the shadow of Heav'n, and things therein
Each to other like, more than on Earth is thought? (*PL* 5.571–6)

Both passages are most relevant to presentation of deity in the poem. M.M. Ross – *Poetry and Dogma* (Rutgers University Press, 1954) – suggests that Raphael's titillating question 'gives to metaphor a nervous life by making it *reach* even when it cannot, must not, touch.' Although this may be the aesthetic effect of placing Raphael's observation at the opening of his narrative, I suggest that Milton's intention was the opposite of that attributed to him by Ross. Raphael is saying that Adam (and the reader) need not seek a highly figurative interpretation of his story, since the likening of spiritual to corporeal forms is a perfectly adequate way of revealing his moral and theological lessons. Milton's conception of scriptural accommodation contrasts sharply both with the philosophical view which approaches God through analogies and with the mystical view which maintains that an apprehension of divine mysteries is achieved through a transcendence of the ordinary categories of the understanding. As well as opposing scholastic philosophy, he was antagonistic to the kind of speculation epitomized in the following observation by Plotinus: 'He that would speak exactly must not name it [the One] by this name or that; we can but circle, as it were, about its circumference, seeking to interpret in speech our experience of it, now shooting near the mark, and again disappointed of our aim by reason of the antinomies we find in it' (*Enn.* 6.9.3, trans. E.R. Dodds, *Select Passages Illustrating Neoplatonism* [London, 1923], 57). Milton's doctrine appears designed to suppress just such probing of mysteries, so popular among the Renaissance followers of Plotinus. On the Italian Platonist as mystagogue, see Edgar Wind, *Pagan Mysteries in the Renaissance* (New Haven, 1958), Introduction and ch. 1.

9 Letters to Radulphus on the first chapter of Genesis, as quoted by F. Seebohm, *The Oxford Reformers*[, 3rd ed.] (London, 1887), 51–7.

10 Benedictus Spinoza, *Tractatus Theologico-Politicus*, in *the Chief Works of Benedict de Spinoza*, [2 vols,] trans. and ed. R.H.M. Elwes (London, 1887), 1:28.

11 Many analogues to Milton's doctrine of accommodation can be found in Reformation writing. Thus Luther in his commentary on Genesis asserts that anthropomorphic terms provide the only means of talking about God: 'It is absolutely necessary that when God reveals himself to us, He should do so under some veil of representation' (*Commentary on … Genesis*, trans. Henry Cole [Edinburgh, 1858], 37). Yet in his commentary Luther shows a strong tendency to pass by means of allegory from the concrete imagery of Genesis, the veils, to abstract theological generalization.

12 See, for example, Augustine's *De civitate Dei*, 1.2, 'Of the knowledge of God, which none can attain but through the mediator between God and man, Christ Jesus.' In the same vein, Dante's final vision in the *Paradiso* is of the second person of the Trinity.

13 On patristic and mediaeval attitudes to allegorical interpretation, see particularly the following works: Jean Danièlou, *Origène* (Paris, 1948), and *Sacramentum futuri* (Paris, 1950); R.M. Grant, *The Letter and the Spirit* (London, 1957); R.P.C. Hanson, *Allegory and Event* (London, 1959); Henri de Lubac, *Exégèse Mediévale: Les Quatre Sens de l'Écriture* (Paris, 1959[–1964]), 2 vols; Beryl Smalley, *The Study of the Bible in the Middle Ages*, rev. ed. (New York, 1952). Most writers agree on distinguishing fairly sharply between allegory and typology. On this distinction see Erich Auerbach, 'Figura,' trans. Ralph Manheim in *Scenes from the Drama of European Literature* (New York, 1956); Charles Donahue, 'Patristic Exegesis,' in *Critical Approaches to Medieval Literature*, ed. Dorothy Beth[u]rum (New York, 1960), and K.J. Woolcombe, 'The Biblical Origins and Patristic Development of Typology,' in G.W. Lampe and K.S. Woolcombe, *Essays on Typology* (London, 1957). Little has yet been done to apply the discoveries made by these scholars to Renaissance and Reformation literature.

14 William Ames, *The Marrow of Sacred Divinity* (London, 1643), 151.

15 See, for example, his allegory 'something different from that in Philo Judaeus concerning Amalek, though happily more significant,' in *The*

Doctrine and Discipline of Divorce (3:435). The theory that allegory is an application of Scripture, and hence a matter of homiletics, was ubiquitous. See Luther, *Commentary on ... Genesis*, 24, and *Table Talk*, ed. and trans. William Hazlett (London, 1857), 326; William Tyndale, *Doctrinal Treatises*, ed. Henry Walter, Parker Society (Cambridge, 1848), 422–6. Heinrich Heppe provides further evidence of the widespread acceptance of this view in *Reformed Dogmatics*, rev. and ed. Ernst Bizer, trans. G.T. Thomson (London, 1950), 38.

16 John Weemes, *The Christian Synagogue*, in *Works*[, 4 vols.] (London, 1637), 1:320. See also his 'Exercitation XX' in *Works*, 3:177. Another clear summary of the distinction between the *sensus literalis simplex* and the *sensus literalis compositus* can be found in a passage cited by Heppe (*Reformed Dogmatics*, 37) from Amandus Polanus' *Syntagma Theologiae Christianae*. Frequently the distinction was illustrated by the unity of the literal and mystical significance of the Sacraments. Like Weemes, Whitaker employs this analogy, *A Disputation of Holy Scripture*, trans. W. Fitzgerald, Parker Society (Cambridge, 1849), 407.

17 Maurice Kelly, 'Milton's Debt to Wollebius' *Compendium Theologiae Christianae*,' *PMLA* 50 (1935): [156–65,] 158.

18 *Christ Revealed* appeared in 1635, but *Figures* was not published until 1683, twelve years after the author's death. The books are similar in aim and design, although Mather's, which was originally a series of sermons, is more ambitious. They reflect widespread Protestant-Puritan beliefs, and both draw on the theory of typology sketched by Calvin in his commentaries. On Calvin's typology, see R.S. Wallace, *Calvin's Doctrine of Word and Sacrament* (Edinburgh, 1953).

19 Augustine of Hippo, *Works*, ed. Dods, 5:474.

20 Mather, *Figures*, 63.

21 Mather, *Figures*, 11.

22 Mather, *Figures*, 8.

23 Mather, *Figures*, 56.

24 See, for example, William Whitaker, *Disputation of Holy Scripture*, 403–9, and Weemes, *The Christian Synagogue*. At the opposite pole from Tyndale, whose derision of the 'chopological' senses runs throughout his discussions of allegory in *A Prologue into ... Leviticus* and *The Obedience of a Christian Man*, Weemes shows considerable familiarity with mediaeval four-fold interpretation.

25 Mather, *Figures*, 53–5.

26 F. Michael Krouse, *Milton's Samson and the Christian Tradition* (Princeton, NJ, 1949), 122–4.

27 Rosemond Tuve, *Images and Themes in Five Poems by Milton* (Cambridge, Mass., 1957), 5, 12.

28 The inclusion of Samson among the men of faith in the Epistle to the Hebrews (11.32) lends some scriptural justification to the belief that he is a type of Christ. Krouse, however, has in mind the 'similar situation' typology which he discovers in the treatment of the Samson story by several Protestant commentators. Agreeing with Krouse that there is no internal evidence which would lead us to read *Samson Agonistes* as a continuous allegory, I cannot accept his verdict that adequate external evidence exists for such a reading. Alexandrian allegorists had explained away the sins of the Old Testament saints by appealing to the spiritual sense, and this strategy was popular in the Renaissance, as even Erasmus' *Enchiridion* testifies. Thomas Haynes, whose *The General View of the Holy Scriptures* (London, 1640) provides Krouse's chief example of Protestant typological interpretation of Samson, is prepared to elevate 'spiritual' above moral considerations; thus, for example, he argues that Dalila's betrayal of Samson typifies Judas' betrayal of Christ. Many Reformers, however, preferred to treat such issues morally and in terms of their theological conception of faith: 'Such things happened them for our ensample, not that we should counterfeit their evil; but if ... we yet fall ... that we despair not' (Tyndale, 'Prologue to ... Genesis,' in *Doctrinal Treatises*, ed. Henry Walter, Parker Society [Cambridge, 1848], 400). This is far closer to the heart of *Samson Agonistes* than the views of such an allegorist as Haynes.

29 See particularly J.H. Hanford's admirable essay, 'That Shepherd, Who First Taught the Chosen Seed,' *UTQ* 8 (1938–9): 403–19. See also Tuve, *Images and Themes*, 159; and Basil Willey, *The Seventeenth Century Background* (London, 1957), 70.

5 *Paradise Lost**

BALACHANDRA RAJAN

In my previous chapter I tried to suggest some of dangers of using Milton's systematic prose in order to elucidate his poetry. I implied that for the understanding of *Paradise Lost* we could rely on nothing except the poem itself and that therefore our immediate, though not our only business as critics, was to find out what Milton's words meant to Milton's audience. Now there are two things which you can say of a poet's audience at the outset. It has first a structure of literary expectation based on its experience of previous poetry of the kind presented. You can challenge this if you like and violate it if you dare to; but you are writing with your left hand if you choose to completely ignore it. It has secondly a structure of topical expectation, that is, it only sanctions a literary form because it serves as a vehicle for its preoccupations and for the poetic definition of the problems which obsess it.

I do not pretend of course that these sentences say one tenth of what can be said of an audience. I have written them only to suggest that there is a tradition, a literary past which a successful poem must modify and at the same time a fund of present idiom and experience which that tradition must interpret and control. It is only very rarely that a poem achieves this union. I believe that *Paradise Lost* is such a poem and in the next few pages I shall try to press this assertion home. But to keep any such demonstration within manageable limits I must refer it continually to the requirements I have outlined. I shall begin therefore with a sketch

* This selection comprises the first, third, and fourth parts of chapter 3, *'Paradise Lost,'* in *'Paradise Lost' and the Seventeenth-Century Reader* (London, 1947). Editors' emendations are indicated in square brackets; Rajan's square brackets have been converted to angled ones.

of the specific literary tradition which *Paradise Lost* inherits. Tracing the chief modifications which Milton makes to this tradition I shall attempt to show that these are poetically justifiable. Finally I shall allude to the central problem of England in the Puritan Revolution, the problem of liberty without licence, and suggest there is in *Paradise Lost* a considered poetic treatment of this problem. Much as I admire Milton I will not say that he solves it. But his vocabulary is different from ours, his assumptions are fundamentally different, and at the very least the conclusions which result should help to elucidate our own.

There is now no doubt (thanks to American research which is all too often ignored) that *Paradise Lost* in its major outlines, and to a surprising extent in its detail and imagery, follows what is known as the hexaemeral genre.[1] This began as a commentary on the six days of the Creation, of which Philo's in the first century A.D. is a conspicuous early example. Something like eighty hexamerons were subsequently written by the Fathers culminating in the work of Ambrose and Basil.[2] After this the genre declined in popularity. There were of course developments from it such as the 'Caedmonian Genesis' and much of the material provided by the Fathers was retained and elaborated in theological encyclopaedias, books of sentences and 'Mirror Literature.' But on the whole little was done to serve as precedents for Milton's epic. The mediaeval craft cycles may seem a different story. As Mr. Dustoor persuasively points out, they say a good deal that is said in *Paradise Lost*.[3] But this is not at all surprising since they begin at the beginning and end at the Day of Judgment. On closer examination the similarities are less striking than the differences. The chronology bears little resemblance to that of *Paradise Lost*. The angels are usually created on the first day and fall on the day of their creation. The conspicuous exception is the Towneley cycle where the date of angelic creation is not clear and the fall takes place on the fifth day.[4] Usually also it is a tenth, not a third, of the heavenly host which rebels.[5] Estimates of the time taken by the fall vary from three days to forty and this gives God plenty of time to prepare Hell for their reception, Hell being part of the world and generally at its centre. Accounts of the battle in Heaven are limited to a few lines which say no more than is said in Revelation. The literature does provide the elements of a character for Satan; but its most important function is to popularize a set of concepts to which all temporal events can be referred. After this a tradition can be assumed and much of Elizabethan literature seems to assume it.

With the Renaissance the classical hexamerons were once more made available. According to Thibaut de Maisières, the revival of interest in this genre began with the publication of Ambrose's hexameron in 1527 and Basil's in 1532, both with prefaces by Erasmus. In 1560 Avitus, Dracontius, Cyprian, Hilary and Marius Victor were brought together in a single volume.[6] Side by side with this revival came a flood of commentaries on Genesis. The best known of these, that of Pererius, was issued in 1590, and had run into at least seven editions by 1622. Its thirteen hundred pages were formidable enough,[7] but even this was surpassed by Mersenne's enormous and unfinished folio volume. These commentaries were pillaged by Raleigh and Browne. It is an open question whether Milton drew on them to any great extent,[8] but even if he did not, what matters is that they helped to disseminate that curious and extensive learning which is so obvious a feature of his epic. More important for our purposes, however, is the mass of epic and dramatic poetry (of which the best known example is Du Bartas's *La Sepmaine*) which grew up around this body of information. Much of this writing is intolerably tedious, and because we are unable to read it, we are only too apt to infer that it did not exist, or could have existed only as a movement of minor importance. Nothing could be further from the truth. The movement was European in its dimensions, it was founded on information which was part of the popular heritage, and it was therefore direct and powerful in its appeal, in its manipulation of the common core of sentiment which it could take for granted in each member of its audience.

So when Milton came to write his epic he did not write it on a *tabula rasa.* Behind the thunder of his great argument were massed the reverberations of a literary past. Those echoes and cadences may not have been defined but Milton caught them in a defining harmony. Before *Paradise Lost* you could exhaust yourself on the reading of innumerable hexamerons and wonder why men of genius had squandered their talents upon them. After *Paradise Lost* you saw that tradition set in order and could understand for the first time its symmetry and purpose. 'Tous les *Hexamérons,*' writes Thibaut de Maisières, 'semblent s'unir dans une sorte de lignée généalogique pour faire éclore, après des générations d'efforts, cette oeuvre complète, qui les résume tous, qui les voue à l'oubli et qui étient leur race ayant atteint la perfection.'[9] It is well said, but one must add in qualification that a work of art need not extinguish the tradition it fulfils. On the contrary it may compel us to review it. The present changes our perception of the past just as the past controls our perception of the present.

Such observations may seem too obvious to be worth recording. But it is this potency in a work of art, this ability to revise and order a tradition, this power in a great poet to be in the fullest sense critical of all that he inherits, which writers on Milton's hexaemeral affiliations ignore. There is a sense in which Professor McColley's work on the sources of *Paradise Lost* and Professor Taylor's study of Milton's use of Du Bartas are almost too successful. The very weight of the evidence which they muster, the irresistible catalogues of precedents, the authorities massed behind what seem to us casual minutiae, batter and overwhelm the reservations of the reader. Yet though such compilations are undeniably impressive it is difficult to imagine the inventive powers of Milton as surrendered wholly to conventions, however august. He is, as Professors McColley and Taylor would be the first to admit, an innovator as well as a traditionalist. But most important of all he is a poet, and to a poet the voices of tradition and revolt, of public formulae as well as of private judgments, are all subject to some certainty of insight, some poetic pattern to which they are made to conform.

To disentangle and isolate this pattern is a task always difficult and often unrewarding. We need all the evidence we can muster and a great deal which scholars might not accept as evidence. But the problem may be easier if we keep on remembering that every device adopted in a poem must have a poetic justification. The poem itself must give you satisfactory reasons for every element being what and where it is. If it accepts a tradition it is because that tradition is useful, because it helps to say what the poem is trying to assert. If it rejects it, it is because what the poem is saying cannot be said in that manner and it is worth while going against precedent to say it. The decisive evidence for Milton's intention, accordingly, should be available within the limits of the text. Corroborative evidence may sometimes be supplied by his treatment of tradition. But as we do not know enough about Milton's audience to be always certain of the traditions they may have accepted, we should be correspondingly careful in accepting this kind of evidence. Certainly, in the absence of a reasonable poetic explanation, we are not entitled to build our conclusions on it. Bearing in mind these precautions let us now turn to the argument which *Paradise Lost* proposes.

Milton's first few lines tell us about that argument. It is about man's disobedience, his fall and his subsequent redemption. In order to present this action more effectively, certain traditionally sanctioned details are introduced. The fall of the angels is used to motivate the temptation of Adam and Eve, and the creation of man is presented as a divine counter action to remedy the damage done by the fall. The material is familiar enough and I need not harass the reader with examples; but you cannot say the same of Milton's chronology. For as I have already pointed out, the opinion established during the Middle Ages, and all but universally accepted in Milton's time, was that the angels fell *during* and not *before* the creation. You can argue if you like that Milton's version was used by Caedmon and Spenser, that he had the support of several 'ancient Fathers' and that Aquinas and Augustine had labelled the problem as a thing indifferent.[10] Nevertheless here is a possible departure from tradition and one should note that Milton in adopting this chronology has also made possible a certain poetic effect. You have only to look at the scheme attentively to see what it offers to any competent craftsman. In the first place the action now falls into two symmetrical halves. Each half begins with a destructive action which is balanced and atoned for by a creative. The actions resemble each other sufficiently for one to make comparisons, and as it is the business of poetry to encourage such activity, it is worthwhile considering how it can be stimulated. Broadly speaking, we can do any, or all of three things. We can compare the creative phases in each half, or the destructive phases, or we can set up a sustained contrast between the powers of creation and destruction which runs through both halves and thereby pull them together. Milton does all three, and he does them so insistently and with such effect, that it is impossible to maintain that he does them simply by accident.[11]

A comparison between the destructive phases will help to show this. The essential difference between the angelic and human transgressions is indicated clearly at 3.93–134. Satan and his associates fall self-tempted. Man falls because he is deceived by Satan and therefore finds mercy unlike the rebel angels. This is repeated at 3.392 ff. Subject to these reservations, the common sin of Satan and Adam, the *materia prima* so to speak of evil, is disobedience. This may be manifest in many forms. In Satan it is most often displayed as an aspiration to Godhead. He revolts (1.33 ff.) in order to equal the Most High. This is the traditional motivation and it is emphasized again at 4.49–51 and at 5.724–26.[12] Satan's external lineaments reflect his sin. His is a 'god-like imitated state,' his chariot resembles that of the Son, and he sits on a hill with towers of gold and diamond which he calls 'the mountain of the congregation' (2.506 ff.; 5.760–66; 6.99–102).[13] Eve's sin also reflects this aspiration. She is (9.793) 'hightened as with wine.' She fancies herself mature in knowledge 'growing up to Godhead.' Both Adam and Eve, satiated with the fruit, feel 'Divinitie within them breeding wings.' The motif occurs repeatedly in the ninth book. It is mentioned at 3.203 ff., and at 11.84 ff. God the Father talks sarcastically about it.[14] All this is not to deny the importance of other elements such as Eve's unwariness and Adam's uxoriousness. But the accumulating repetitions, the inescapable stress on a disobedience issuing in *hubris* is important because of the comparisons it enforces. You see terribly plainly that history repeats itself. You see that despite the contrasts, the varied nuances and refinements of evil, the sins of Satan, of Adam, and of Eve riot from a common stem of disobedience. There are other correspondences to hammer home this fact. In both phases obedience is claimed to an apparently arbitrary command. For Satan there is the motiveless 'begetting' of the Son, for Adam the unintelligible taboo against eating the fruit. In both phases disobedience is followed by a kind of interior chaos. Satan's face is lined with passion and he feels within him 'the hateful siege of contraries' (4.114 ff.; 9.119 ff.). Adam is represented as tossed in a troubled sea of passions and his mind is shaken by mistrust, suspicion and discord (9.1121–26; 10.718). Both falls result too in lust and sexual indulgence. The intoxication of Adam and Eve with its inevitable aftermath of shame is paralleled by Satan's humiliation after his return in triumph to hell. The divinity our parents imagine they feel within them is burlesqued ruthlessly by Sin and Death (9.1008–11; 10.243 ff.). In citing these similarities I do not wish to argue that the destructive phases in both halves are identical. This is patently untrue. But what can be argued is that the differences rest on an underlying sameness which is part and parcel of what Milton has to say and that the symmetry of his plot is an indirect way of saying it.

The similarities between the creative phases are less numerous. The basis of the comparison is the *felix culpa* which, by Milton's time, had become a poetic commonplace.[15] Strictly speaking this should apply only to the Fall which is good in so far as it occasions the Atonement. But Adam, in speaking of it (12.469 ff.) also makes a specific comparison of the Creation to the Atonement. The supporting paradox of good from evil is a familiar feature of the epic. Satan (1.157 ff.) sees it as characteristic of God's providence,[16] and a little further on it is made a feature of the Archangel's punishment that his malice serves only to assert God's goodness. These passages should be sufficient to compel a comparison of the Creation to the Atonement, but to make matters certain the motif is used twice in the seventh book. It is included in the hymn (182 ff.) which is sung before the Son journeys out into Chaos and it is part of the celebrations (613 ff.) which take place on His triumphant return. The comparison is further strengthened by the fact that the minds of Adam and Eve when fallen (9.1121 ff.) are described in imagery reminiscent of that of Chaos, and by the events of the tenth book which, as I shall subsequently indicate, is a cosmic expansion of this inner, mental catastrophe. The result of this lapse into Chaos is that the Atonement can be more effectively presented as a second Creation, thereby reinforcing the correspondences I have cited.

The similarities between the creative and destructive powers can be considered under two headings. First there is a set based on the traditional comparison of Christ to Adam.[17] Milton alludes to this at 1.4–5 and more explicitly at 11.382–4. At 5.384–7 and at 10.133 he strengthens the association by comparing Mary to Eve.[18] But more important than any of these is 3.285ff. where an elaborate and highly effective comparison is made between Adam's fall and Christ's atonement. The biblical imagery which dominates this comparison would have helped to stamp it on the minds of Milton's audience.[19] But it is also emphasized by being interwoven with a far more complex series of correspondences, namely those worked out between the powers of Heaven and Hell. Here the material is so rich that it is difficult to know where to begin, but perhaps the most striking likenesses and differences are those between the councils of Book 2 and Book 3. In both councils important decisions are taken. The one in Hell initiates the destructive action which is central to the poem, the one in Heaven is told of the Atonement which alone can redeem it. Volunteers are invited. There is silence in Heaven as in Hell. Both Satan and Christ offer themselves for the opposing enterprises, but the one speaks distended by 'monarchal pride,' the other in the fullness of charity and love. The angels bow 'lowly reverent' to the Son and bend towards Satan 'with awful reverence prone.' The 'deafening shout' which marks the dispersal of the infernal council is contrasted with the shout 'Loud as from numbers without number, sweet' with which the heavenly conclave ends. The diverse occupations of the fallen angels can be opposed to the hymn of praise which is sung by all in Heaven. Hardly less striking are the resemblances between the Creation and the building of the causeway from Hell as it is described in the tenth book. Christ comes forth into Chaos from the gates of Heaven. Sin and Death issue from the gates of Hell. They brood over the water in a way reminiscent of the Holy Spirit. But whereas the Son creates through the power of His word, Sin and Death are compelled to make do with substitutes: Gorgonian rigour and asphaltic slime. The finished causeway 'Smooth, easie, inoffensive down to Hell' may be compared to that 'broad and ample rode, whose dust is Gold' which leads through Heaven to the house of God.

Mention of this should remind us of something which is no whit less ingenious. I refer of course to Pandemonium which is constructed with amazing rapidity by Mammon and Mulciber. Surely it is no accident that the *roof* of Pandemonium is made of the same material as the *pavement* of Heaven. The gates of Hell too flying open with 'impetuous recoile and jarring sound' are meant to be contrasted with their heavenly counterparts (2.879–83; 7.205–9). Similarly, while the imperial ensign unfurled by Azazel is emblazoned with 'Seraphic arms and Trophies,' those advanced in Heaven are emblazoned with 'Holy Memorials, acts of Zeale and Love' (1.536–40; 5.588–94). Finally there are a series of resemblances between the Father and the Son and Satan. I have already mentioned the latter's chariot, the mount on which he is 'exalted,' and the fact that both Christ and he are raised to their Stations through merit. In addition the Father's delegation of His powers to the Son is paralleled by Satan's sending Sin and Death to earth as his viceregents (3.317–20; 5.606–11; 10.403–5). Again, the Son sits beside the Father 'in bliss imbosom'd,' while Sin looks forward to sitting at Satan's right hand, 'Thy daughter and thy darling without end' (5.597; 2.866–70). The implications behind these parallels vary. Sometimes we are merely reminded that the fallen angels retain the dignities which were theirs in Heaven. At other times the resemblances are scarred by savage burlesque. Yet this too is the result of Satan's governing obsession – 'Evil be thou my good.' It is this which makes Hell a perverted creation and which ensures that so much that is done in Heaven is jeered at and parodied in Hell. To understand this is to penetrate to the heart of the epic, to seize on that massive and symbolic symmetry to which *Paradise Lost* was intended to conform.

It should be clear from this list of correspondences not only that they bulk large in the epic, but also that they play an important part in establishing and stressing the symmetry of its action. Yet they are used relatively seldom in hexaemeral literature. And when they are used frequently, as in Giles Fletcher's longer poems, they are only used to enforce a rhetorical comparison. It is therefore Milton's peculiar achievement to have employed them en masse and yet to have built them into the architecture of his epic, an architecture all the more satisfying because it is so just to the nature of its material.

The likelihood that such correspondences are more than mere embellishments is also confirmed by some of the other departures from tradition which are made in *Paradise Lost.* Thus, in the battle of Heaven, Milton represents Christ as triumphing over Satan after Michael and Satan had waged an indecisive conflict, when most of his contemporaries would have identified Michael with Christ.[20] He could have argued that this version was not unorthodox and that it was used in the *De victoria verbi Dei* of the Catholic bishop Rupertus Tutiensus.[21] But I think he would also have suggested that in thus dramatizing Christ's intervention, he intended to contrast the power of good with the comparative impotence of evil. It is in this spirit that Christ's miraculous journey into Chaos is set against Satan's difficult and hazardous voyage through it. His act of creation 'more swift than time or motion' is meant to contrast with Satan's laborious stratagems. Finally, Christ's triumph in Heaven is poised against His triumph on the cross. The one is shown in the panoply of military conquest, the other as a battle waged and won in the mind which, while less spectacular, is in no way less effective.

Even more to my purpose, however, is the preliminary temptation in the fourth book. This occurs nowhere else in the range of hexaemeral literature. If it had occurred Professor McColley would have found it. But he has not found it and as a result he is forced to talk of confusions, lack of agreement, and ambiguities in the tradition which Milton is supposed to be exploiting. Briefly, Professor McColley claims that there was a divergence of opinion regarding the date of Adam's fall. Most commentators believed that he fell on the first day of his creation, but a strong minority believed that he fell a week later. Milton tries to have the best of both worlds by assigning a tentative temptation to the first day, and the second, successful temptation to the eighth.[22] It is an ingenious account but I find it unacceptable. The chronology on which it is based is highly dubious[23] and I cannot see what Milton is supposed to be achieving poetically by appealing to the dual tradition which Professor McColley postulates. Moreover only a very erudite and sophisticated reader could have recognized that such an appeal was being made. Finally, the device involves Milton in serious difficulties. He has to find something for Satan to do between the temptations, and the best he can do is to make him wander seven times round the earth, thereby giving Newton his chance to write a learned footnote. However, several poetic reasons can be cited for this procedure, and all of them seem to me more convincing than those put forward by Professor McColley. Eve's dream is effective as an omen, it involves a deft use of supernatural machinery, and besides providing a pretext for a discussion on faculty psychology it makes possible an encounter between Gabriel and Satan which no reader of Milton would like to see omitted. But what is most important for my purpose is that the actual temptation is anticipated in Eve's dream with a detail that is all the more rewarding given the system of correspondences I have outlined.[24] Thus, the appeal to Eve's vanity and Satan's claim that the fruit makes one god-like are common to both episodes. Again, in the ninth book it is the smell of the fruit which finally persuades Eve to taste it. So also in recounting her dream she says:

> ... the pleasant savourie smell
> So quick'nd appetite, that I, methought,
> Could not but taste.

The results of eating the fruit are also similar. Adam and Eve in the ninth book feel 'Divinitie within them breeding wings / Wherewith to scorn the Earth.' This immediately recalls the last phase of Eve's dream.

> Forthwith up to the Clouds
> With him I flew, and underneath beheld
> The Earth outstrecht immense, a prospect wide
> And various.

If the reader feels that these resemblances are trivial, I could refer him to the building of the causeway from Hell to the top of the world in the tenth book of the epic. Here again there is no precedent for the incident in the literature of the Temptation. You can treat it as an eruption of that grim and semi-private sense of humour which runs riot so depressingly in Limbo, or treat it as an innovation deliberately introduced in accordance with the correspondences I have outlined. Again the Sin-Death allegory may be no more than an elaboration of material in Spenser and Fletcher. But with Satan, Sin and Death make a kind of infernal Trinity and the contrast of this with its heavenly counterpart can be defended, even if its results are often not poetically justifiable.

In thus interpreting some of Milton's departures from the hexaemeral tradition, I do not wish to imply that all his innovations should be treated on this basis. Sometimes – Satan's journey through Chaos is an example – his devices need no justification beyond the poetry they make possible. At other times what strikes us as a failure may be traced to the intrusion of a private and irrelevant emotion. Sometimes the cross references I cite may account for only a part of Milton's intention and at other times they may account for nothing at all. I do not deny these alternatives, but I should like to emphasize that, as far as I am aware, nothing that Milton does is incompatible with my hypothesis, and that many of the events in his epic gain in richness if we agree to locate them within this symbolic pattern of repetition and recurrence.

This brings me to what I hope is my firmest argument for the interpretation I am proposing. It seems to me that what matters in a literary 'explanation' is not so much its consistency with the facts – there are other explanations which fit the facts as well and for some readers fit them more readily – as the standard of poetic achievement it implies. It is possible to maintain that the contrast between the Creation and the building of the Causeway from Hell is inconclusive, that there are precedents for Eve's dream in the classic epic, and that Milton's unconventional chronology and unconventional treatment of the battle in Heaven prove only that he is presenting the theology of the *De doctrina* in the poetic trappings of *Paradise Lost.* But an explanation of this kind is really a disguised apology. You cannot justify an event in *Paradise Lost* by pointing out that it is sanctioned by a systematic theology, even if it is Milton's, or a classical epic, even if it is Homer's. The reasons you seek should be poetic reasons and Milton's borrowings, alike from tradition and his own bizarre beliefs, should be inexorably related to some poetic plan. That plan I have tried to discover in the massive contrasts between creation and destruction and in all the more delicate resemblances of detail which the correspondences developed in the epic imply. Much that Milton accepts in the hexaemeral tradition, much that he ignores and much that he obviously violates is justified and ordered by this symmetry. And to certain minds it is important that it is so justified. For there are those to whom symmetry is a token of ultimate order, for whom discipline remains 'the shape and image of virtue' and not merely an unavoidable and harassing restraint. To such men – and there were many such in Milton's England – there would have been an aesthetic satisfaction in contrasting Hell with Heaven and in finding the temptation anticipated in Eve's dream. The sustained massing of comparison and contrast, the moral enrichment of every theme by its analogue, would have helped to typify, for them, that struggle of light with darkness which the Providence of God administers in history.

In writing for such people moreover, Milton had one very formidable asset at his disposal. I refer to that system of comparison and intricate analogy which is so characteristic of the Elizabethan outlook. Hitherto I have avoided discussing the use of this system in *Paradise Lost,* and limited myself to those correspondences which are specific to the epic and do not exist apart from the events which they integrate. But if Milton meant such correspondences to be more than merely decorative, the odds are that he would have reinforced them with analogies which were not peculiar to his argument, and which were part and parcel of the seventeenth century mind. The two sets would then have drawn attention to each other because of their proximity, and together they would have encouraged a certain way of looking at the epic. I think that this method yields valuable results and so in the rest of this chapter I shall try to apply it to our understanding of *Paradise Lost* [...]

III

It will be remembered that after the first and unsuccessful temptation Raphael is sent down to earth to instruct Adam in the ways of righteousness. Why he should need to do so is not clear. For Adam, according to Purchas, was the greatest philosopher that 'ever the Earth bare.'[1] According to Augustine 'his mental powers surpassed that of the most brilliant philosopher as much as the speed of a bird surpasses that of a tortoise.'[2] Moreover he has already given us an indication of his learning by lecturing to Eve on faculty psychology.[3] Nevertheless the angel is sent down to instruct him and is invited to dinner by Adam, who ventures to doubt if the food is satisfactory. Raphael reassures him. Everything that is created needs to be sustained and fed, just as the grosser elements in the universe feed the purer.[4] Having finished these adumbrations of the hierarchic principle the angel falls to his viands 'with keen dispatch / Of real hunger and concoctive heat.'[5] The meal is rounded off with liquor, but this evidently proves harmless in the state of innocence. As the occasion demands an after-dinner speech, Adam asks the appropriate leading question and the angel, with no more ado, delivers his homily on the Scale of Nature:

> O *Adam,* one Almightie is, from whom
> All things proceed, and up to him return,
> If not depraved from good, created all
> Such to perfection, one first matter all,
> Indu'd with various forms, various degrees
> Of substance, and in things that live, of life;
> But more refin'd, more spiritous and pure,
> As neerer to him plac't or neerer tending
> Each in thir several active Sphears assign'd,
> Till body up to spirit work, in bounds
> Proportiond to each kind. So from the root
> Springs lighter the green stalk, from thence the leaves
> More aerie, last the bright consummate floure

Spirits odorous breathes: flours and thir fruit
Mans nourishment, by gradual scale sublim'd
To vital Spirits aspire, to animal,
To intellectual, give both life and sense,
Fansie and understanding, whence the Soule
Reason receives, and reason is her being,
Discursive or Intuitive; discourse
Is oftest yours, the latter most is ours,
Differing but in degree, of kind the same.
Wonder not then, what God for you saw good
If I refuse not, but convert, as you,
To proper substance, time may come when men
With Angels may participate, and find
No inconvenient Diet, nor too light Fare:
And from these corporal nutriments perhaps
Your bodies may at last turn all to Spirit,
Improv'd by tract of time, and wingd ascend
Ethereal, as wee, or may at choice
Here or in Heav'nly Paradises dwell;
If ye be found obedient, and retain
Unalterably firm his love entire
Whose progenie you are.

The best way to understand this passage is to read it as an academic exercise on degree. This is seldom done by critics, who either delve in it for occult information or talk condescendingly about its quaintness. I have tried to answer the charge of unorthodoxy elsewhere. It remains to be added that Milton's assumptions, whether quaint or not, are endemic to the seventeenth century mind and have to be taken as our terms of reference. When we do this we can perhaps appreciate better the skill with which these assumptions are related. Milton first asserts that the whole creation proceeds from one first matter, that each created thing has its place and function, and that created things are more spiritous and pure in proportion as they are nearer to God. Differences between them are of degree and not of kind. Thus, the vegetable creation culminates in fruits and the 'bright consummate floure,' but these in turn form the basis of man's diet and are thereby converted into vital, animal, and intellectual spirits. Milton is here alluding to the everyday theory that the spirits arose from the conversion of food to blood in the liver. As Burton puts it:

> Spirit is a most subtle vapour which is expressed from the blood, and the instrument of the soul, to perform all his actions ... of these spirits there be three kinds according to the three principal parts brain, heart, liver: natural, vital, animal. The natural are begotten in the liver and thence dispersed through the veins, to perform those natural actions. The vital spirits are made in the heart of <i.e. from> the natural, which by the arteries are transported to all the other parts: if the spirits cease, then life ceaseth as in a syncope or swooning. The animal spirits fanned of the vital, brought up to the brain, and diffused by the nerves to the subordinate members, give sense and motion to all.[6]

Milton departs from Burton by leaving out natural spirits, and adding intellectual spirits, which I think are his invention. But he is quite conventional in his insistence that these spirits are the executives of the soul, that sense, fancy, and reason itself, are powerless without them.[7] This insistence on the continuity between the animate and inanimate naturally suggests that body may work up to spirit and that man can be 'improv'd' into an angel. There is nothing that is at all unusual about these conceptions and the suggestion that man may be transformed into an angel makes it all the more tragic that he elects to be a beast. The promise however is linked to a condition – 'if ye be found obedient.'[8] Disobedience hereafter becomes synonymous with the violation of 'degree.' The forthright statement of the basis of order provides a standard by which all defections should be judged. Adam recognizes this easily enough. He congratulates the angel on his exposition of the Scale of Nature, confirms that one can ascend to God 'through contemplation of created things,' and asks what Raphael means by his warning to be obedient.[9] The angel, after touching on free-will, proceeds to instruct Adam in celestial history. Now the fact that the account of Satan's revolt and the Creation is made to follow a text-book exposition of the Scale of Nature implies that a connection is meant to exist between them, and the implication is confirmed by Raphael's repeated allusion the symbols of 'degree.' Thus at 5.574–6 a correspondence is hinted at between earth and heaven. Forty lines later the cosmic dance is made an analogue of the celestial.[10]

> That day, as other solem dayes they spent
> In song and dance about the sacred Hill,
> Mystical dance, which yonder starrie Spheare
> Of Planets and of fixt in all her Wheeles

Resembles nearest, mazes intricate,
Eccentric, intervolv'd, yet regular
Then most, when most irregular they seem,
And in thir motions harmonie Divine
So smooths her charming tones, that Gods own ear
Listens delighted.

There is a suggestion, but no more than a suggestion, that the music of the spheres too may have its heavenly counterpart. But, in the end, it is the poetry itself, the audacious combination of the elaborate and spontaneous which makes us accept the order which it celebrates. Milton has said many things which are more spectacular. But he has never said anything which is more inevitable. That gaiety, innate yet ceremonial, those turning, pirouetting half-rhymes and caesuras, reach to the heart of what discipline can give us. Milton's craft is not always as consummate. But he continues to play on the evocations of degree by references to Satan's 'hierarchal standard' and to triple hierarchies of angels,[11] reaching an ironical climax in Satan's treatment of the Son's exaltation as a violation of the hierarchical principle:

Will ye submit your necks, and chuse to bend
The supple knee? ye will not if I trust
To know ye right, or if ye know your selves
Natives and Sons of Heav'n possest before
By none, and if not equal all, yet free,
Equally free; for Orders and Degrees
Jarr not with liberty, but well consist.
Who can in reason then or right assume
Monarchie over such, as live by right
His equals ... ?

The argument is all the more interesting because it is a perfectly orthodox version of the claim that monarchy is not grounded on the law of Nature. Here, for instance, is a quotation to the same effect from Rutherford's *Lex Rex*:

... princedom, empire, kingdom, or jurisdiction hath its rise from a positive and secondary law of nations, and not from the law of pure nature. The law saith, there is no law of nature agreeing to all living creatures for superiority; for by no reason in nature hath a boar dominion over a boar, a lion over a lion, a dragon over a dragon, a bull over a bull. And if all men be born equally free (as I hope to prove) there is no reason in nature why one man should be king and lord over another.[12]

Rutherford was a Presbyterian but his formulation would have been equally acceptable to the Puritan left wing.[13] Adam appeals to much the same principle in his condemnation of Nimrod in the twelfth book and Abdiel significantly makes no attempt to challenge its logic. He replies tartly that Satan owes his existence to God and has therefore no right to challenge His decrees. Moreover he was created by the Son and has therefore no right to dispute His exaltation. Lastly, obedience to a hierarchic superior is a confirmation not a denial of freedom. The retort strikes us as unconvincing but that is because we start off with the presumption that the devil may be right. To Milton's reader, on the contrary, he was wrong because he was the devil, and doubly damned by quoting Scripture for his purpose. Abdiel's insistence is clear, even brutally clear. You are not reasonable when you disobey God's will. You violate reason by the very fact of your dissent. When you have set yourself thus against the nature of things there remains no alternative except your subordination by force, or your ultimate expulsion from the order you have defied:

... to subdue
By force, who reason for thir Law refuse,
Right reason for thir Law, and for thir King
Messiah, who by right of merit Reigns.

It is a judgment which Satan recollects in Hell. 'Whom reason hath equald, force hath made supream / Above his equals.'[14] But the grounds of Satan's complaint, the affectation of equality with God, the refusal to admit that the Messiah reigns by merit, these things cut him off from the laws he professes to honour. The consequence is not liberty but servitude, for liberty (and it is impossible to emphasize this too strongly) is only secured by obedience to God's command:

Unjustly thou deprav'st it with the name
Of *Servitude* to serve whom God ordains,
Or Nature; God and Nature bid the same
When he who rules is worthiest, and excells
Them whom he governs. This is servitude,
To serve th'unwise, or him who hath rebelld

Against his worthier, as thine now serve thee,
Thy self not free, but to thy self enthrall'd.

Now that the assumptions no longer interest us, it is easy to underrate the skill with which Abdiel makes his indictment. To begin with, he counters Satan's appeal to the Law of Nature, with the impregnable retort that the Law of Nature cannot conflict with the Divine Law. He then goes on to present Satan's sin as a violation of 'degree,' a violation which has to issue in servitude. Given this challenge to the nature of things, this mockery of the very ground of one's being, the only possible consequence is defeat. Satan may commit his rebel hordes to battle. He may delay the onslaught of the inevitable with secret weapons and atrocious puns. But in the end the 'Chariot of Paternal Deity' which as Wilson Knight rapturously remarks 'is at once a super-tank and a super bomber' must move to its terrible victory over God's enemies.[15] It is a brutal climax no doubt, but one which helps to hammer home Raphael's warning:

... let it profit thee to have heard
By terrible Example the reward
Of disobedience; firm they might have stood,
Yet fell; remember, and fear to transgress.

The account of the Creation follows. God is presented as having planned to fill up the 'vacant room' caused by the expulsion of the apostate angels (7.150 ff.). This kind of motivation strikes us as absurd but, as Professor McColley demonstrates, it was accepted without hesitation by Milton's contemporaries.[16] The description of the Creation itself is a compact but inclusive summary of the material embodied in innumerable hexamerons. Milton departs from tradition in assuming a pre-existent chaos but the assumption is obviously essential to his narrative. He also simplifies his account by postponing the dialogue on astronomy till the eighth book instead of associating it, as is usual, with the first, second, or fourth day of the Creation.[17] The dialogue, which has excited as much comment as anything else in the epic, has been referred by McColley to a controversy between Wilkins and Ross.[18] Wilkins was Cromwell's brother-in-law and a founder of the Royal Society. Ross, among other things, was King Charles's chaplain. Perhaps it is worth noticing that Raphael sides with Ross. He is sarcastic about the Ptolemaic System, plays noncommittally with the Copernican, poses the hypothesis of a plurality of worlds and tells Adam to be lowly wise and leave astronomy to heaven. Adam, like a good schoolboy, repeats the lesson after him and proceeds to tell a story of his own. Raphael listens to him 'heavenly meek' – a beautiful touch this of hierarchic courtesy – while Adam talks of his own and Eve's creation. It is a story which we cannot understand without a conscious effort to do so. For since we do not believe with Aquinas that 'order consists in inequality,' since at best we can make only a metaphor of degree, since we look on the hierarchic principle as an ornamental conceit, we are compelled to regard 'Hee for God only, shee for God in him' as one more specimen of Miltonic egoism. On the contrary it typified the deepest and most impersonal feelings of the time. 'Married Folkes,' declares William Perkins with brutal directness, 'are either Husband or Wife. The Husband is he which hath authoritie over the wife.'[19] Simon Goulart goes even further: '... in the dignity and power of man over a woman (as in all other authority and pre-eminence) the glory of God shineth clearly.'[20] Calvin asserts that 'it is a great honour that God has appointed her <the woman> to the man as the partner of his life, and a helper to him, and has made her subject to him as the body is to the head.'[21] Handbook after handbook on matrimony insisted with tireless unanimity that man is to woman as Christ is to the Church. It is against the background of this insistence, the insistence that the woman can only be herself in being subject to man, the insistence of St. Paul that man is 'the image and glory of God' but woman 'the glory of the man,' it is against this reiterated conviction that Adam's narrative needs to be assessed. And when we read it thus we know that he is doomed from the outset. We know that even before he has considered eating the fruit his uxoriousness has sown the seeds of his disaster. When Adam says to God:

> Thou in thyself art perfet, and in thee
> Is no deficience found,

we recognize the admission of God's infinity. But when he says of Eve:

> ... when I approach
> Her loveliness, so absolute she seems
> And in herself compleat, so well to know
> Her own, that what she wills to do or say,
> Seems wisest, vertuousest, discreetest, best.

we must force ourselves to acknowledge the latent blasphemy. Eve is not God, but a creature, and a creature, moreover, whose happiness consists in her being subject to Adam. It is Adam's duty to rule her as his reason rules his passions. As Augustine puts it: 'Just as in the human soul there is one element which takes thought and dominates, another which is subjected to obedience, so woman has been created corporeally for men: for though she has indeed a nature like that of man in her mind and rational intelligence, yet by her bodily sex she is subjected to the sex of her husband much as appetite, which is the source of action, must be subjected to reason if it is to learn the rules of right action.'[22] So when Adam ecstatically confesses:

All higher knowledge in her presence falls
Degraded, Wisdom in discourse with her
Loses, discount'nanc'd, and like Folly shewes;
Authority and Reason on her waite ...

we are required not to applaud but to condemn. We need to remember with Sir Thomas Browne that the temptation of the man by the woman may be 'the seduction of the rational and higher parts by the inferior and feminine faculties.'[23] When we do so we shall realize that, given the values Milton accepts, there can be no more blatant example of abject and grovelling idolatry. It is not surprising that the angel answers 'with contracted brow.' The wonder is that he is as moderate and courteous as he is. He tells Adam that true love 'has its seat in reason.' This may seem paradoxical to us but it is merely Raphael's way of insisting that the order of the universe is ultimately rational and that love has its fulfilment in the ultimate order of things. It leads up to heaven as the order of the creatures leads to their creator. It is the means, the instrument by which body can work up to spirit and man be translated into his heavenly paradise. Love, true love, which guides all things to their destiny is thus not the slave of a corrupt and localized passion, but the symbol and sanctity of an enduring order:

In loving, thou dost well: in passion not,
Wherein true love consists not.

Having said this Raphael can proceed to his final admonition:

Be strong, live happie, and love, but first of all
Him whom to love is to obey, and keep
His great command: take heed lest passion sway
Thy judgment to do aught which else free Will
Would not admit.

The warning, besides reflecting the outlines of Adam's transgression, parallels the warning provided for Eve in her dream. Milton's audience, reading these passages, would have known what would take place and exactly how it would happen. They would know that nothing had been left undone, that all necessary information and counsel had been given. And so, as Milton changed his notes to tragic, they would have read on with an obsessing fascinated interest as Adam and Eve, possessed of everything necessary to preserve their innocence, marched open-eyed and reckless to ultimate disaster.

IV

A week after Raphael's departure the second and successful temptation takes place. John Swan, who likes be precise about such things, insists that it took place on the twenty-second of April.[1] But Milton says nothing about this and since Eden is in a state of eternal spring it is impossible to tell from the state of the vegetation. However, we know that on the previous night Satan disguised as a mist had made an underground entry into Paradise.[2] Light now dawns, the 'Earth's great Altar,' sends up praise to the Creator[3] and Adam and Eve celebrate the occasion by indulging in the pre-lapsarian equivalent to a lover's quarrel. The dispute arises when Eve suggests a division of labour. Adam is to wind the woodbine and direct the clasping ivy while Eve does what she can in a grove of roses 'intermixt with Myrtle.' Adam replies cautiously that such a parting is dangerous, that Satan is awaiting an opportunity for his assault, and that the wife is safest by the side of her husband. Eve, though she replies with 'sweet austere composure,' obviously regards this as a slur on her integrity, so Adam has to assure her that he knows she will not succumb to temptation, but merely wishes to spare her the insult of being tempted. Eve, however, is not interested in a fugitive and cloistered virtue and insists on sallying forth to meet her adversary.[4] Adam then reluctantly lets her go but not before arming her with this advice:

O Woman, best are all things as the will
Of God ordained them, his creating hand
Nothing imperfet or deficient left
Of all that he created, much less Man,
Or ought that might his happie state secure,
Secure from outward force; within himself
The danger lies, yet lies within his power:

> Against his will he can receave no harme.
> But God left free the Will, for what obeyes
> Reason, is free, and Reason he made right,
> But bid her well beware, and still erect,
> Least by some faire appeering good surpris'd
> She dictate false, and missinforme the Will
> To do what God expressly hath forbid.

The warning complements that which Raphael gives to Adam. It makes it clear that Eve sins because her faculty of reason is deceived while Adam sins by surrendering his will to his passions. The two faults taken together – a defective understanding and a disobedient will – make up the mortal sin, the compendium of every possible error.[5] As usual the antithesis is confirmed by other contrasts. The warning on each occasion is given by a hierarchic superior. The temptation on each occasion is the work of a hierarchic inferior. Presented thus these details may seem trivial but they are in fact indispensable to the pattern of transgression. As Goodman glumly remarks:

> Thus at length hee [Satan] perswades the Serpent to be his Agent and factor, desiring to invert and overthrow the whole course of nature, when the basest creature shall give advice and direction to the best, in the highest point of religion; and that the Serpent should deceive the woman, the woman her husband (the feete must guide and direct the head), notwithstanding God's forewarning and threatening to the contrary.[6]

It is this direction of the higher by the lower, this systematic violation of the government of things, which dominates the action of the ninth book. Every phrase drives home the subjection of reason to appetite, the complete enslavement of the mind to the body. Milton does not hesitate to be unconventional in order to secure his effects. He goes out of his way to draw attention to Eve's gluttony.[7] He compares the fruit to an intoxicating wine, minutely describes the carnality it fosters and degrades the romantic love of Adam for Eve into irrational and destructive lust.[8] He does these things although there is no real precedent for doing them so that, when we come to his declaration that 'understanding ruled not,' we may be deeply and inescapably conscious of the terrible significance which lies behind the formula. So as Eve moves on towards her ordeal wrapt in a cloud of perfume and waited on possibly by a pomp of graces, we are required to watch with unrelaxing vigilance the words which record her progress towards catastrophe.

First and foremost we must observe the subtlety of the Serpent's arguments. Milton here is elaborating on a familiar theme of seventeenth century theologians. Andrewes, for example, devotes several pages to discussing the devil's rhetoric.[9] Downame asserts that Satan proceeds by 'equivocations and sophisticall eclenches.'[10] Lawson takes pains to point out that the serpent 'doth not single out any of God's *moral* precepts or prohibitions. For these were too deeply implanted in the soul, and of clearer light, but he makes choyce of that positive precept which was not so obvious to reason, and seemed to have some mystery in it, and to admit some latitude for a *subtle discourse.*'[11] Thus when Milton compares the serpent to an Athenian orator he is doing more than chide his classical leanings. The serpent, after all, has an important job to do. His eloquence helps him to do it better, and he is further helped by being impossibly handsome and greatly superior to anything out of Ovid. Moreover, he knows Eve well enough to play upon her vanity. He fawns on her, bowing his 'sleek enamell'd Neck.' He pays her a preposterous tribute – 'Fairest resemblance of thy Maker faire' – which exalts her subtly above her hierarchic status. A few lines later on he elegantly varies the compliment – 'Sovran of Creatures, universal Dame.' It is little wonder as he gazes at Eve with his carbuncle eyes that his words win 'too easy entrance' into her unwary heart. She makes no attempt to challenge his arguments and in fact uses them to justify her transgression. She errs because she is insufficiently vigilant. Despite Adam's advice her reason does not keep strictest watch and so falls 'into deception unaware.' Yet for all her murderous triviality she is really no more than hapless and much-failing. We sympathize with her as she puts forth her hand to the fruit. We sympathize still as the earth gives signs of woe. We remember the same earth smiling on the nuptials of Eve and Adam and the hills of heaven putting for flowers as the wheels of the Son's chariot moved to victory.[12] We remember these things, and the memory of their beauty blinds us for the moment to the crime that we are witnessing. Then the recollection is shattered by the aftermath of Eve's sin, by her idolization of the tree, her contemplation of murder, and by the confirmation of her soul in the practice of evil. Yet despite all this she is still not alienated from us, and Adam catches some of our own feelings in the forlorn, horror-struck words with which he greets her:

O fairest of Creation, last and best
Of all Gods Works, Creature in whom excell'd
Whatever can to sight or thought be formd,

Holy, divine, good, amiable, or sweet!
How art thou lost, how on a sudden lost,
Defac't, deflourd, and now to Death devote?

The last line is especially poignant with its heavy, heartbroken sequence of d's, its hint of a lost Eden in the overtones of 'deflourd' and its listless acceptance of dedication to death. Yet touching as the words undoubtedly are, they make it evident that Adam is doomed from the outset. Eve may be the last of God's works, but it is Adam, not she, who is the best. When he forgets that this is so, when he calls Eve the 'fairest of Creation,' when the majesty we associate with 'holy' and 'divine' is linked to the romantic pathos of 'amiable or sweet' it is plain to us that he has chosen disaster. Having said this he has to indulge in the heroics of

... I feel
The Bond of Nature draw me to my owne,
My owne in thee, for what thou art is mine;
Our state cannot be severd, we are one,
One Flesh; to loose thee were to loose my self.[13]

and Eve must reply in terms of the same frivolity:

O glorious trial of exceeding love,
Illustrious evidence, example high!

I have used the word 'frivolity' deliberately. It may shock a good many of my readers, but this only proves that the sensibilities of Milton's audience were radically different from our own. For though we are justified in sympathizing with Adam's predicament and though it is to Milton's credit that he finds a human problem where others see only a theological formula, though we may applaud such self-sacrifice as a romantic gesture, we have to condemn it as a responsible act. We cannot approve of what Adam does and we can approve still less the alacrity with which he does it. There is in him no will, no power of resisting temptation. He does not even hesitate as Eve hesitates. His idolatry, all the more offensive because it is clear-eyed,[14] is an insult to the righteousness to which he is meant to conform. Because he sins thus, because he surrenders his judgment to his passions, it follows that 'reason's mintage' within him must become 'the inglorious likeness of a beast.' Everything that follows assumes this degradation. Intoxication follows gluttony and is succeeded by carnal desire. The two, far from regretting what they have done, congratulate themselves on their good sense in doing it. Then, as the spasm of exhilaration expires, their eyes are opened and they find their honour stripped away. Milton drives this home by using a well-known simile:

> So rose the *Danite* strong
> *Herculean Samson* from the Harlot-lap
> Of *Philistean Dalilah,* and wak'd
> Shorn of his strength ...

It is a simile which we treasure chiefly as an anticipation of Milton's future tragedy. So we need to remember that twenty-five years ago, in *The Reason of Church Government,* Milton had talked of Samson as 'disciplin'd from his birth in the precepts and practice of Temperance and Sobriety, without the strong drink of injurious and excessive desires.' Samson's eyes in that elaborate allegory were 'the fair, and farre sighted eyes of his natural discerning' and his hair 'the golden beames of Law and Right.'[15] But these associations are by no means peculiar to Milton. Much the same thing is said for instance by Bishop Reynolds in his discussion of the effects of the Fall.

> We are ... to remember, that there is in Man, by reason of his general *Corruption,* such a distemper wrought, as that there is not onely *crookednesse* in, but *dissension* also, and fighting betweene his parts: And, though the Light of our *Reason* be by Man's Fall much dimmed and decayed; yet the remainders thereof are so adverse to our unruly *Appetite,* as that it laboureth against us, as the *Philistims* against *Samson;* (or rather indeed as *Dalilah,* for Samson's eyes were truly put out before ever the *Philistims* were upon him) it laboureth, I say, to deprive us of those Reliques of Sight which we yet retaine.[16]

The simile therefore has a function to fulfil. It implies that this newly-found knowledge of the flesh is secure and perverted by blindness to the things of the Spirit. Adam and Eve have their eyes opened indeed, but they see no longer with the eyes of natural innocence.

> Bad Fruit of Knowledge, if this be to know,
> Which leaves us naked thus, of Honour void,
> Of innocence, of Faith, of Puritie ...

Purchas grows lyrical as he speculates on this nakedness:

> Their eyes were opened to see their nakednesse: *naked* they were of *divine* protection and favor, naked of *Angelicall* guard and custodie, naked of *Humane* puritie and holinesse, naked of dutifull *subjection* from the rebelling Creatures; naked in *soule*, naked in *Body*, naked of *Happinesse*, naked of *Hopes*, exposed naked to the fierce *Wrath* of that God, from whom to bee hidden was impossible ... and to whom to appeare was intolerable.[17]

If Adam and Eve are really as naked as all this it is little wonder that they cover themselves with banyan leaves (not fig leaves). But in acknowledging their guilt they cannot cleanse it. They cannot revoke the defiance of order which they have set in motion, they cannot rewrite and they can barely recollect the law of nature which their transgression has defaced. Within the microcosm chaos is come again and degree is suffocated in lawless, murderous misrule:

> They sate them down to weep, nor onely Teares
> Raind at thir Eyes, but high Winds worse within
> Began to rise, high Passions, Anger, Hate,
> Mistrust, Suspicion, Discord, and shook sore
> Thir inward State of Mind, calm Region once
> And full of Peace, now tost and turbulent:
> For Understanding rul'd not, and the Will
> Heard not her lore, both in Subjection now
> To sensual Appetite, who from beneathe
> Usurping over sovran Reason claimd
> Superior sway:[18]

Three consequences follow from this usurpation. The first is death: the corruption of the body which proceeds from and reflects the corruption of the mind. As Aquinas puts it:

> God bestowed this favour on man in his primitive state, that as long as his mind was subject to God, the lower powers of the soul would be subject to his rational mind, and his body to his soul. But inasmuch as through sin man's mind withdrew from subjection to God, the result was that neither were his lower powers wholly subject to his reason, whence there followed so great a rebellion of the carnal appetite against the reason; nor was the body wholly subject to the soul; whence arose death and other bodily defects.[19]

The second consequence is the propagation of this depravity in space, the overflowing of sin upon the creatures. Goodman proclaims this with his usual gloomy relish:

> Man, who was principally ordained for God's service, as all other creatures for man; man (I say), being *nexus et naturae vinculum*, it must necessarily follow, that all the rest of the creatures, which were bound and knit together in man, should likewise be inordinate and overflow their owne banks; if the Captaine and guide first break the ranke, no marvell if the soldiers fall to confusion.[20]

Calvin is so excited by the occasion that he breaks all his own rules by indulging in a simile:

> Nor ought it to seem absurd, that, through the sin of man, punishment should overflow the earth, though innocent. For as the *primum mobile* rolls all the celestial spheres along with it, so the ruin of man drives headlong all those creatures which were formed for his sake, and had been made subject to him.[21]

But the relationship is even more clearly defined in these words of a nonentity, Daniel Dyke:

> Man is truely called a little world, and in him wee may see an image of that in the greater world. Now in man, as created of God, the affections called the unreasonable part, as beeing common to us with bruites, were subjected to reason and so shewed how by like proportion in the great world the unreasonable creatures should be subject to the reasonable. But when once order was broken in the little world, then it was broken also in the other, and when reason lost his authority over affection, then man also lost his sovereignty, over the creatures and his slaves became rebels.[22]

The third and best known consequence of this rebellion is the transmission of evil in time, the death of posterity in the loins of Adam. To suggest how the seventeenth century felt about this I cannot do better than quote once more from Purchas:

> As in the Bodie Politike the Act of the Prince is reputed the Act of the whole; the Consent of a Burgesse in Parliament bindeth the Citie which he representeth; and as in the naturall Bodie the whole Bodie is lyable to the guilt of

> that fact which the head or hand hath committed: as a root to his branches, a Fountaine to his streames, doth convey the goodnesse or badnesse which it selfe hath received: so stands it betwixt us and Adam our naturall Prince, the Burgesse of the World, the Head of this humane Bodie and Generation, the Root and Fountaine of our Humanitie.[23]

It is these three consequences considered jointly, this vision of enmity between all created things, this chaos in man's mind and in the cosmos, this intolerable order of events where depravity feeds and propagates depravity, it is against this background of unrelieved pessimism that the action of the last books of *Paradise Lost* is located. Milton has prepared very carefully for this climax. The hostility between reason and the passions is persistently implied before it is asserted. We are told there is hate in the minds of Eve and Adam, before we see it growing up between them. So when the earth during the transgression groans and gives 'signs of woe' we expect the creatures to be drawn headlong into ruin. We may perhaps remember Romans 8.22: 'For we know that the whole creation groaneth and travaileth in pain together until now' – but even if we do not we are still prepared for the omnipresent corruption which St. Paul's words suggest. When the Son descends to deliver judgment these developing discords are further reinforced. There is hostility between Adam and the earth he tills. There is enmity incipient in the 'Despotic Power' which man is given in order to punish woman.[24] It is a conflict which Milton expands and complicates as Sin and Death take up the melancholy story. We find them where we expect to, at the Gates of Hell, sniffing delightedly the scent of carnage on earth. The 'great altar' which that very morning had sent up praise to the Creator now sends up the 'savour of Death from all things there that live.' The omen persuades the two to build a causeway from 'Hell gates' to the top of the world to improve communications in their prospective empire. There is a good deal of jubilant burlesque and then, when the pair meet Satan on his way homeward, some ceremonial manoeuvres by the infernal Trinity. While Satan proceeds to his humiliation in Hell, his accomplices take up the reins of misgovernment. 'Plenipotent on Earth of matchless might.' Sin asks Death what he thinks of his Empire and Death replies indifferently that it would be a better Empire if there were more to eat. Sin then advises him to get to work on the inferior creation while she 'seasons' man as the tastiest dish of the evening. The Angels now begin to make various alterations in the cosmos so as to reflect the depravity of things. Milton is not sure exactly what happened. The sun may have been made to change its course or, on the other hand, the 'Centric Globe' may have been 'push'd oblique.' But anyway the planets are taught to meet in 'Synod unbenigne' in order to produce the Cambridge climate. As a result of these changes we now have snow, hail, gusts, vapours, mists and pestilent exhalations. Milton ornaments the account with a complicated catalogue of winds which, according to Professor Whiting, is really very simple if you look in the right atlas.[25] But even those who cannot afford an atlas can still listen to the proper names as they clash and clang in their superb and symbolic commotion. The climax of this fantastic catalogue of calamity is Adam's long and tortured self-interrogation which leads at last to an unreserved admission of his guilt:

> ... all my evasions vain
> And reasonings, though through Mazes, lead me still
> But to my own conviction: first and last
> On mee, mee onely, as the sourse and spring
> Of all corruption, all the blame lights due;

But even this confession cannot bring Adam peace and it remains, with beautiful aptness, for Eve, who helped to destroy him, to take the first steps towards his restoration. Her approach drives Adam to one more petulant outburst. Then as the poetry quietens down into the secure flowing rhythm of Eve's supplication it becomes evident that the crisis has been passed.[26] In this universe of immense and brooding desolation, against all the horror of the implacable and unknown, the innate chivalry of two ordinary and very frightened people is slowly but invincibly reasserted. There is all the difference in the world between the understanding which Adam here displays and his operatic gestures in the ninth book. There is no comparison possible between the pampered egoism of Eve during the Fall and the self sacrificing majesty which she now exhibits. In this newly found comprehension, this humanity won from the frontiers of defeat, Milton's faith in man's goodness is splendidly affirmed. It is a faith which, if anything, has grown deeper and more tolerant with the years. For in 'Adam Unparadiz'd' Adam does not repent thus. He is as Milton writes 'stubborn in his offence.' Before he can see the error of his ways he has to be reasoned with by Justice, admonished by the Chorus and intimidated by the masque of evils which Milton postponed to the eleventh book of the epic.[27] The draft shows us a criminal driven to confession by fear. *Paradise Lost* shows us two people ennobled by adversity, acknowledging their unworthiness of their own free-will. The twenty-five years which separate the versions, those years which scarred England with the bitterness of civil war, which shattered the glass walls of innumerable Utopias, those years which brought Milton defeat and disillusion have taught him nothing except to believe in Man. It is an unusual lesson and one which ought to qualify the charge of pessimism which is levelled against the last books.

NOTES

[We reproduce here Rajan's enumeration of notes, which starts at the beginning of each section. Rajan refers throughout to the Columbia edition of Milton's *Works*, ed. Frank Patterson et al. (New York, 1931–8) – Eds.]

1 A great deal has been written on the subject. But see especially G. McColley, '*Paradise Lost*,' *Harvard Theological Review* 33 (1939): 181–235.
2 Maury Thibaut de Maisières, *Les Poêmes inspirés du Début de la Genèse á l'Époque de la Renaissance* (Louvain, 1931), 13–17.
3 P.E. Dustoor, 'Legends of Lucifer in Early English and in Milton,' *Anglia* 54 (1930): 213–68.
4 Dustoor, 214–19, 254ff. In the *Lyff of Adam and Eve* the Angels are created on the first day and fall on the sixth. Aquinas considers it probable that the Angels fell in the moment of their creation (*Summa theologica*, Pt. 1, Q. 58, Art. 6). The Caedmonian Genesis is therefore exceptional in dating the fall of the Angels before the Creation.
5 Langland in *The Vision of Piers Plowman*, however, hits on Milton's nine.
6 Thibaut de Maisières, 18–19.
7 For details see Arnold Williams, 'Commentaries on Genesis as a basis for Hexaemeral Literature,' *Studies in Philology* 34 (1937): 191–208.
8 For evidence see Williams, 'Milton and the Renaissance Commentaries on *Genesis*,' *Modern Philology* 37 (1939–40): 263–78, and 'Renaissance Commentaries on *Genesis* and Some Elements of the Theology of *Paradise Lost*,' *PMLA* 56 (1941): 151–64.
9 Thibaut de Maisières, 119.
10 McColley, 184–5. But, in listing the ancient Fathers whom Milton could have quoted, Professor McColley does not make it clear that Milton's contemporaries and near contemporaries were solidly against him. I have consulted eleven of them and only one (Peter Heylyn) believes that the Angels were created before the world. I think this helps to account for the apologetic tone of the argument to the first book of *Paradise Lost.*

11 Some of the material I am using in the following paragraphs can be found in E.M.W. Tillyard, *Milton* (London, 1930), 247–8; Charles Williams, *Reason and Beauty in the Poetic Mind* (Oxford, 1933), 122n; Tillyard, 'The Causeway from Hell to the World in the Tenth Book of *Paradise Lost*,' *Studies in Philology* 38 (1941): 266–70; and Maurice Kelley, *This Great Argument* (Princeton, 1941), 193n.

12 Isaiah 14.14. For further documentation see McColley, 185–6n.

13 The mountain of the congregation is mentioned in Isaiah 14.13.

14 Milton's verses echo Genesis 3.22. Calvin (*Commentary on Genesis*, ch. 3, sect. 22) calls this an ironic comment. Andrew Willet (*Hexaplia in Genesin*, London, 1632, 23) says that God, in saying that man has become like himself, 'derideth man's folly.' So Milton's harshness may, after all, be impersonal.

15 See A.O. Lovejoy, 'Milton and the Paradox of the Fortunate Fall,' *ELH* 4 (1937): 161–79; and McColley, 204–5.

16 For the idea that the permission of evil and its direction to good ends is a feature of God's Providence, see Henry Lawrence, *An History of Angells* (London, 1649), 68; Thomas Sutton, *Lecture upon the Eleventh Chapter to the Romans* (London, 1632), 208 ff.; Elnathan Parr, *The Grounds of Divinitie* (London, 1636), 202; Johan Wolleb, *Abridgment of Christian Divinitie*, translated and revised by Alexander Ross (London, 1660), 58; and John Davies of Hereford, 'Mirum in Modum,' *Works*, 2 vols, ed. Grosart (London, 1878), 1: 30.

17 The Scriptural Sanction is from 1 Cor 15.45 and Rom 5.14. See also Calvin, *Institutes of the Christian Religion*, Bk. 1, ch. 15, sect. 3–4; Donne, 'Hymne to God my God in my Sicknesse,' *Poetical Works*, 2 vols, ed. Sir H.J.C. Grierson (London, 1912), 1:368; Thomas Goodwin, *Christ Set Forth* (London, 1642), 82ff.; Andrew Willet, *Hexapla* (London, 1616), 256–8; Samuel Purchas, loc. cit., infra n.19; and W. Haller, *The Rise of Puritanism* (New York, 1938), ch. 4.

18 There is no scriptural text to support this. See however Crashaw, 'The Himn O Gloriosa Domina,' *Poetical Works*, ed. L.C. Martin (London, 1927), 302–3; and John Swan, *Speculum mundi* (Cambridge, 1643), 497–8. Professor Saurat points out (*Milton: Man and Thinker*, London, 1944, 218) that Milton in *Of Prelatical Episcopacy* upbraids Irenaeus for saying something very similar.

19 The chief scriptural texts incorporated by Milton are Rom 5.17–19; 1 Cor 15.22; Rom 11.16; John 15.25; Gal 2.20; 1 Cor 11.3 and Col 1.18. Milton's elaboration of these texts is supported by Samuel Purchas, *Purchas His Pilgrim. Microcosmus or the Historie of Man* (London, 1627), 150–2, 402–6, 676–8, and 777–82; by Elnathan Parr, op. cit., 321–2 and by the comment on Rom 5.14 in *Annotations upon all the Books of the Old and New*

Testament ... by the labour of Certain Divines thereunto appointed and therein employed (London, 1651), vol. 2. Hereafter cited as *Assembly Annotations.*

20 My interpretation modifies that of Professor McColley, who states (*Paradise Lost,* Chicago, 1940, 22) that, while early theologians interpreted Rev 11.7–9, as naming Michael as the conqueror of Satan, some altered the punctuation so that Christ could be regarded as intervening after Michael and Satan had waged indecisive conflict. This may be true of patristic exegesis but my impression is that commentators in the seventeenth century identified Michael with Christ. See e.g., George Giffard, *Sermons upon the Whole Booke of the Revelation* (London, 1599), 228; William Cowper, 'A Commentary upon the Reveation of St. John,' *Works* (London, 1629), 1023; John Napier, *A Plaine Discoverie of the Whole Revelation of St. John* (Edinburgh, 1645), 150, and Wolleb-Ross, op. cit., 63. Milton in the *De doctrina* admits the authority of this version: 'it is generally supposed that Michael is Christ.' But he goes on to support his version in *Paradise Lost*: 'But Christ vanquished the devil and trampled him under foot singly; Michael, the leader of the angels, is introduced in the capacity of a hostile commander waging war with the prince of the devils, the armies on both sides being drawn out in battle array, and separating after doubtful conflict' (*Works,* 15:105). Accordingly, I have accepted Milton's account of the received tradition from which he is departing and tried to explain the poetic significance of this departure. Admittedly it squares with his beliefs. But I think it is also important that it can be poetically justified.

21 McColley, 'Milton's Battle in Heaven and Rupert of St. Heribert,' *Speculum* 16 (1941), 23–5.

22 McColley, *Paradise Lost* (Chicago, 1940), 158ff. Marianna Woodhull (*The Epic of 'Paradise Lost,'* New York, 1907, 43) notes that no parallel exists for the episode but she does very little to justify the addition.

23 In 'Paradise Lost' (*Harvard Theological Review,* 1939, 210–11n) McColley cites 2.347ff., 4.287ff., 4.623ff., and 4.776 ff. as evidence that the tentative temptation occurred on the first day. None of these references strikes me as at all conclusive and the last of them seems to contradict McColley's theory. In 4.778–9, the Cherubim are described as issuing from their 'Ivorie Port' at the 'accustomd hour.' They could hardly be doing this if this were the first night of Adam and Eve's creation. Moreover if Adam and Eve were created on this day they should be celebrating their nuptials on the night of the tentative temptation. There is every indication that this cannot be so. The arguments against Professor McColley's chronology are further strengthened by Adam and Eve's accounts of their creation and by the evidence cited in Newton's note on 4.449. So in the absence of any further

supporting evidence, Professor McColley's time-scheme must be regarded as unacceptable.

24 This was noted *en passant* by Addison (Todd, ed. cit., 1:321). Bailey, who also sees the resemblance (*Milton*, London, 1915, 186) differs from me about its effect: '... we notice such things as Eve's dream in the fifth book which, anticipating as it does so many of the details of her temptation, renders her fall much less probable, and goes far to destroy its interest when it occurs.'

[Section II of Rajan's chapter does not appear in this selection – Eds.]

Section III

1 *Purchas His Pilgrimage or Relations of the World* (London, 1613), 11. Hereafter cited as *Pilgrimage.*

2 Quoted in C.S. Lewis, op. cit., 113. For the idea see also Simon Goulart trans., Thomas Lodge, *A Learned Summary of Du Bartas* (London, 1637), pt.2, p.18; Henry More, *Conjectura Cabbalistica*, 24 (Printed in *A Collection of Several Philosophical Writings*, London, 1662); Willet, *Hexapla in Genesin* (London, 1632), 30; Alexander Ross, *An Exposition on the Fourteene First Chapters of Genesis* (London, 1626), 51; John Salkeld, *A Treatise of Paradise* (London, 1613), 189; and Lancelot Andrewes, *A Collection of Posthumous and Orphan Lectures* (London, 1652), 212.

3 *Paradise Lost*, 5.100ff. McColley (op.cit., 166–8) concludes that the passage is based on one in Phineas Fletcher's *Purple Island.* But similar poetic descriptions can be found in Davies's *Nosce Teipsum* and Fulke Greville's *Treatise of Human Learning.* Prose counterparts are too numerous to be worth citing but for a selection see K. Svendsen, 'Milton and the Encyclopaedias of Science,' *Studies in Philology* 39 (1942): 303–27.

4 Denis Saurat (op. cit., 264–5) quotes Fludd for the idea. But see also *Timon of Athens*, 4.3.433ff.

5 P.L. Carver ('The Angels in *Paradise Lost*,' *RES* 16 [1940]: 417) here sees a possible allusion to a passage from Duns Scotus. But C.S. Lewis's explanation (*op. cit.*, 106) seems to me adequate. Nevertheless Milton's furious insistence on detail (Tasting, concoct, digest, assimilate / And corporeal to incorporeal turn) seemed to me inexplicable until I ran across the following in Peter Martyr's *Commonplaces*: '*Scotus* thinketh, that to eate, is nothing else but to chawe meate, and to conveie it downe into the belly: but this did the Angels; wherefore he gathereth that they did verilie eate. Others thinke, that to eate, is not onelie to chawe the meate, or to conveie it downe into the bellie; but further to convert it to the substance of his own bodie, by

concoction through the quickening power; which thing seeing the Angels did not, they did not trulie eate' (trans. Anthony Marten, London, 1583, pt. 1, p. 118). Milton is obviously arguing that the angels *did* eat in the second sense, and despite Mr. Lewis's citations and Mr. McColley's (op. cit., 70), it still seems to me to be a drastic thing to say.

6 Robert Burton, *The Anatomy of Melancholy*, pt. 1, sect. 1, memb. 11, subsect. 11.

7 Milton's statement that discursive and intuitive reason differ only in degree may seem extraordinary but I imagine it could be supported from Aquinas (*Summa theologica*, pt. 1, Q. 79, art. 8, trans. of the Fathers of the English Dominican Province): '... in the angels the power of knowledge is not of a different genus from that which is the human reason but is compared to it as the perfect to the imperfect.' Milton uses the distinction with superb effect in 2.557ff. where the fallen angels, *arguing* over fixed fate, free-will, and foreknowledge, do so only because they have lost their powers of intuitive apprehension.

Theodore Spenser (*Shakespeare and the Nature of Man*, London, 1943, 12n) argues that Milton in this passage is identifying understanding with common sense. This is a possible reading but it is incompatible with 9.1121 ff. I think that Milton couples reason with understanding, possibly regarding them as active and passive aspects of the same faculty. Mainly on the evidence of 9.113, I should conclude that Milton is following the Renaissance version of Aristotelian, rather than Platonic, psychology. Everything he says seems compatible with this version. But the matter is not really important. Milton's contemporaries were more muddled about the divisions than scholars like to think and Calvin's presentation (*Institutes*, Bk. 1, ch. 15, sects. 6–7) would hardly have enlightened them. What matters is not the accuracy with which such concepts are employed but the stock responses aroused by their employment.

8 The motif recurs in everything Raphael says. Cp. 5.522, 5.541, 6.911, 8.634. Similarly Augustine argues that obedience is 'the mother and guardian of all the other virtues of the soul' (*De civ. Dei*, trans. M. Dodds, bk. 14, ch. 12). William Perkins asserts that 'the fall is a revolting of the reasonable creature from obedience to Sin' ('A Golden Chaine,' *Works*, London, 1616, 1:18). Calvin concludes that 'the prohibition of the tree of knowledge of good and evil was a test of obedience that Adam might prove his willing submission to the Divine Government' (*Institutes*, trans. J. Allen, Philadelphia, 1936, Bk. 2, ch. 1, sect. 4). Hooker therefore is more than justified in putting the question 'see we not plainly that obedience of creatures unto the law of nature is the stay of the whole world?' (*The Lawes of Ecclesiastical Polity*, 1.3.2).

9 The classical authority for the idea is *Symposium*, 210–12, the scriptural, Rom 1.20. It is discussed by A.O. Lovejoy (*The Great Chain of Being*, Cambridge, Mass., 1936, 89ff.) and by W.C. Curry ('Milton and the Scale of Nature,' *Stanford University Studies in Language and Literature*, 1941, 173–92). See among Milton's near contemporaries Spenser, *An Hymne of Heavenly Beauty*; Stafford, *Niobe* (London, 1611), 3; Goodman, *The Fall of Man* (London, 1616), 152–3; John Smith, *Select Discourses* (London, 1660), 430–1; and Henry Reynolds, 'Mythomestes,' *Critical Essays of the Seventeenth Century*, ed. J.E. Spingarn, 1:174.

10 The relation of the Symbolism of the dance to that of degree is already alluded to in the cosmic dance in describing Satan's journey (3.579 ff.) and in the morning prayers of Adam and Eve (5.175 ff.). Paradise at 4.264 ff. is described in similar language and even the Copernican System is visualized as a dance at 8.122 ff. The correspondence between the cosmic dance and the celestial is suggested at 5.617 ff., and is acknowledged by Satan at 9.99 ff. It reinforces the analogy between earth and heaven which Raphael considers at 5.574 ff. This is further emphasized by the references to a heavenly Paradise at 5.500 and to the removal of amarant from Paradise to Heaven (3.351 ff.). For the former see Henry Ainsworth, *Annotations upon the five Books of Moses* (London, 1627), 10–11; Alexander Ross, *An Exposition on the Fourteene first Chapters of Genesis* (London, 1626), 42; *Annotations upon all the Books of the Old and New Testament* (London, 1651), vol. 1 comment on Genesis 2.9; and Edward Leigh, *A Systeme or Body of Divinitie* (London, 1654), 293. Leigh's comment is particularly striking. 'Paradise was a little model of Heaven, and a sign of the great Heaven, assuring *Adam*, that if he continued in obedience to God, he should be translated into Heaven, to enjoy God supernaturally, as there he did enjoy him naturally.' Milton adds to all this, his notion that man may dwell at option in earthly or celestial paradises. His story of the removal of amarant is probably also his own, though it is intended to allude to 1 Pet 1.4 and 1 Pet 5.4.

11 Dustoor (op. cit., passim) devotes much space to puzzling out the orders of Milton's angels. However I agree with Dr. Tillyard (op. cit., 39) that Milton 'has his various hierarchies but lays down no precise order.' After all Calvin had asserted that 'if we wish to be truly wise, we must forsake the vain imaginations propagated by triflers concerning the nature, order, and multitude of angels ... No man can deny that great subtlety and acuteness is discovered by Dionysius, whoever he was, in many parts of his treatise on the celestial Hierarchy; but if any one enters into a critical examination of it, he will find the greatest part of it to be mere babbling' (*Institutes*, ed. cit., Bk. 1, ch. 14, sect. 4). Or as Bucanus puts it: 'But that there be Hierarchies, and

degrees of Hierarchies among the angels as the Papists imagine, it cannot be proved by any testimony of Scripture' (William Bucanus, *Institutes of the Christian Religion,* trans. R. Hill, London, 1606, 69). See also James Ussher, *A Body of Divinitie,* 4th ed. (London, 1663), 116; Edward Leigh, op. cit., 272; and Samuel Purchas, op. cit., 567. Milton was therefore quite justified in refusing to be exact and in using these angelic titles purely for the sake of their poetic evocations.

12 Quoted in A.S.P. Woodhouse, *Puritanism and Liberty* (London, 1938), 201.

13 Cp. Woodhouse, op. cit., Introduction, 62: 'Once the inferior magistrates have declared against the prince and freed opposition from the stigma of rebellion, so staunch a Calvinist as Rutherford can forge in *Lex Rex* almost every argument of revolution later to be employed by the Levellers.'

14 *PL* 6.40–3 and 1.248–9. There are other phrases which are remembered in Hell. Compare 5.886–8 with 2.327–8, and 6.183–4 with 1.263. The last two are noted by Todd and Newton.

15 G. Wilson Knight, *Chariot of Wrath* (London, 1942), 158.

16 G. McColley, op. cit., 45–7.

17 G. McColley, op. cit., ch. 3.

18 G. McColley, 'Milton's Dialogue on Astronomy: The Principal Immediate Sources,' *PMLA* 52 (1937): 728–62. The 'immediate sources' are John Wilkins's *The Discovery of a World in the Moone* (3rd ed., London, 1640); *A Discourse concerning a New Planet* (London, 1640; bound with the 3rd ed. of the 'Discovery' as a second part) and Alexander Ross's *The New Planet no Planet: or to the Earth no Wandring Star* (London, 1646).

Much misunderstanding exists, especially in annotated editions of *Paradise Lost,* concerning the theories discussed in the dialogue on Astronomy. The received tradition is that the Ptolemaic and Copernican Systems were reigning alternatives for Milton's generation, that the dialogue is devoted to discussing their respective merits, and that Milton, while preferring the latter, bases his cosmography, for poetic reasons, on the former. In fact, four distinct conceptions are discussed: the Copernican system, the Ptolemaic, the theory of a plurality of worlds, and the idea of the diurnal rotation of the Earth. The last of these, usually thought of as part of the Copernican System, was often supported quite independently of it. Thus, among its advocates, William Gilbert ignores the heliocentric hypothesis, and Nathaniel Carpenter, Francis Godwin and Anthony Deusingius reject it. Diurnal rotation is discussed by Milton at five points in the dialogue (8.13 ff., 64 ff., 85 ff., 133 ff., 160 ff.) and also at 4.592 ff. At 8.133 ff. it seems to be proposed as an alternative to the Copernican hypothesis.

Another deficiency in the received explanation is its omission of the theory of the plurality of worlds. The history of the idea has been discussed by

McColley (*Annals of Science*, 1, 1936, 385–430). Milton alludes to it in three forms: (1) that the moon may be like the earth and inhabited; (2) that other parts of the universe may be like the earth and inhabited; (3) that there may be other universes similar to ours. The place of (1) in seventeenth century thought has been discussed by Professor M. Nicholson ('A World in the Moon,' *Smith College Studies in Modern Languages*, 17.2 [1936]: 36–44 et passim). Milton glances at it in 1.286 ff., is critical of it in 5.261–3, and non-committal in the dialogue (8.140 ff.). But in 3.459–62 (strangely ignored by commentators) he is more specific and takes the idea at least as seriously as he takes his limbo. (2) probably lies behind 3.667–70, and is touched on in 3.561 ff., and 7.621–2, while (3) is discussed at some length in the dialogue (8.148 ff.).

The received explanation is correct in stressing Milton's hostility to the Ptolemaic hypothesis. But it does not follow that he supports the Copernican. Since he neither adopts nor rejects the heliocentric theory and since there were alternative systems based on diurnal rotation he may have preferred Purchas's 'learned ignorance' on these matters (*Pilgrimage*, 2nd ed., London, 1614, 10). The received explanation is also misleading when it implies that the Ptolemaic and Copernican hypotheses were the reigning alternatives for Milton's generation. It was the geo-heliocentric Tychonic System which was contending with the Copernican for supremacy; both in learned treatises and in popular almanacs opinion was divided fairly evenly between them. (F.R. Johnson, op. cit., 248–87; G. McColley, 'The Astronomy of *Paradise Lost*,' *Studies in Philology* 34 [1937]: 210–11, 234–8.) The Tychonic System is not mentioned in *Paradise Lost* and the omission greatly affects the value of the dialogue as a record of the options prevailing in Milton's generation.

To conclude it seems probable that Milton's knowledge of astronomy has been overestimated. McColley (op. cit., 232–4) points out that his version of the Copernican System was out of date and Johnson concludes (op. cit., 285) that Milton's 'scientific knowledge in such matters was probably inferior to Donne's, and certainly to Gabriel Harvey's.' But one should also insist that the aim of the dialogue is not so much to decide between rival theories in astronomy as to decide to what extent such theories are worth while. The conclusion is that they are inconclusive, and that we are not to vex our thoughts 'with matters hid' but to concentrate instead on the daily business of living. It is a verdict far from palpable to us, but it is argued too plainly to be otherwise interpreted.

19 William Perkins, 'Of Christian Oeconomie or Household Government,' *Works* (London, 1616), 3:691.

20 Simon Goulart trans. Thomas Lodge, op. cit., pt. 1, p. 297.

21 Calvin, *Commentary on 1 Corinthians*, trans. Rev. John Pringle (Edinburgh, 1848), ch. 11, sect. 7. These quotations should make it clear that Milton's attitude to women is typical of his time. But see also Clinton Powell, *English Domestic Relations* (New York, 1917), 177n et passim; Louis B. Wright, *Middle Class Culture in Elizabethan England* (Chapel Hill, 1935), ch. 7 and especially p. 204; M.M. Knappen, *Tudor Puritanism* (Chicago, 1940), 451–5; and W. and M. Haller, 'The Puritan Art of Love,' *Huntingdon Library Quarterly* 5 (1942): 235–72.
22 *The Confessions of St. Augustine*, trans. F.J. Sheed (London, 1944), 287.
23 Browne, 'Pseudodoxia Epidemica,' *Works*, ed. Charles Sayle (London, 1904), 1:125.

Section IV

1 Swan, op. cit., 498.
2 Lines 157–67 of Satan's Soliloquy at this point are illuminated by this comment of Lancelot Andrewes: 'And the fathers doe think that Almighty God of set purpose, did allot him this creature and restrain him all other, for these two respects: first, thereby to punish the pride and ambitious nature of the Devill, that he might see and all the world perceive, to what his sin of pride had brought him, because he which a little before was so vainglorious as to presume to exalt him in God's throne and be as God, is now cast down in most vile and miserable sort, basely and contemptibly crawling upon he ground and being as the abject and most hated worm on the earth' (op. cit., 253).
3 Perhaps Milton took the idea from Rabbinical sources. See Louis Ginzberg, *Legends of the Jews* (Philadelphia, 1909), 1:25–6.
4 Verity in his edition of *Paradise Lost* (London, 1936, 572) notes the resemblance to *Areopagitica.*
5 For catalogues of sins which are included in the sin of Adam and Eve see Milton, *De doctrina Christiana, Works,* 15:181–3; Augustine, *Enchiridion*, ch. 45; Downame, op. cit., 233–4; Bucanus, op. cit., 160; Leigh, op. cit., 304; Ussher, op. cit., 134–6; Parr, op. cit., 252–3; and Willet, *Hexapla in Genesin*, 47.
6 Godfrey Goodman, op. cit., 429.
7 McColley, who cites Caedmon as a precedent, says (op. cit., 174) that Milton's insistence on Eve's gluttony is unusual. But the following, from Goodman, matches Milton's treatment:

'The first Sinnes of the mind seme to be the disobedience and pride ... And for our bodie, gluttonie seemes to be the wellspring of all our carnall and bodily Sinnes: as a surfeit it is for the most part the beginning of al our diseases, and whereunto man is most subject and prone: it doth undoubtedly argue that the first Sinne was the Sinne of a surfeite and gluttonie, the tasting of forbidden fruit.'

Furthermore Milton's insistence on this aspect of Eve's sin enables him to separate the visions of the eleventh book into a pageant of diseases proceeding from the 'Inabstinence' of Eve and one of licentiousness proceeding from the uxoriousness of Adam.

8 McColley (op. cit., 178) describes as distinctly uncommon the idea that there was lustful cohabitation in Paradise. The matter is not discussed in *De doctrina Christiana.* Plainly Milton intends to contrast this carnality with the purity and reasonableness of wedded love:

> By thee adulterous lust was driven from men
> Among the bestial herds to raunge, by thee
> Founded in Reason, Loyal, Just, and Pure
> Relations dear, and all the Charities
> Of Father, Son, and Brother first were known.

Also unusual is Milton's description of the fruit as an intoxicant (9.793, 837–8, 1008 ff., 1046 ff.). The *De doctrina Christiana* does not imply this. In fact, chapter ten suggests that the fruit had no powers of any kind. Of the fourteen other commentators I have consulted, the majority agree with the *De doctrina,* and none provide any encouragement for the version in *Paradise Lost.* So, if we were to take this version at its face value, it would run counter to tradition and also to what we know of Milton's beliefs. Hence I feel that it is simply a figure of speech, introduced in order to stress still more the gross physical aftermath of Sin that Milton does not believe in the conceit or intend his audience to believe it.

9 Andrewes, op. cit., 255 ff.

10 Downame, op. cit., 235.

11 G. Lawson, *A Body of Divinitie* (London, 1659), 63. On the Devil's rhetoric see also Ussher, op.cit., 130. The serpent's claim to have attained knowledge by eating the fruit is also unusual. I have not come across it except in Beaumont's *Psyche* (Canto 6, stanzas 282–4).

12 *PL* 6.780–4, 8.511–15, 9.782–3, 9.1000–03. The idea is fairly frequent (see McColley, op. cit., 174).

13 Purchas (*Microcosmus,* 226) embroiders on the sentiment. 'Such indeed is the sympathie betwixt Soule and Bodie, that as *Adam* and *Eve,* they will take part with each other, though it be in the forbidden fruit; both tempting and tempted of each other, living and dying together.'

14 Milton claims (9.998–9) that Adam ate 'Against his better knowledge, not deceav'd, / But fondly overcome with femal charm.' It is a version supported by 1 Tim 2.14, and Augustine, *De civ. Dei,* Bk. 12, ch. 11. Calvin (*Commentary on Genesis,* ch. 3, sect. 6) dislikes the opinion, but cites it as

commonly received. Several theologians, following him, concluded that Adam was also deceived. See e.g. Leigh, op. cit., 304; Willet, op. cit., 39 (misnumbered 29); and Gervaise Babington, 'Certaine Plaine Briefe and Comfortable Notes upon every Chapter of Genesis,' *Works* (London, 1637), 16. It is difficult to say what Andrewes (op. cit., 285–6) thinks but he seems, on the whole, to support Milton's version.

15 *Reason of Church Government*, *Works*, 3:276.

16 Edward Reynolds, *A Treatise of the Passions and Faculties of the Soul of Man* (London, 1640), 63.

17 Purchas, *Microcosmus*, 152.

18 Pierre Charron puts the situation as follows: 'These are the Principal Winds that raise all the storms in our souls; and the Cavern (like that of Aeolus) where they are engender'd and from whence they break loose, is nothing else but opinion ... The Will is made by Nature to follow the directions of the Understanding; this is its Guide to instruct, its Candle to give it Light; but when once the strength of Passion hath corrupted, and, as it were laid violent hands upon the Will, then the Will in like manner, corrupts, and commits a violence on the Understanding ... What was at first in the Sensual Appetite only, hath made its way higher and got the Upper Hand of the Understanding; what was merely Passion and Pleasure, hath been advanced into a Principle of Religion and an Article of Faith' (*Of Wisdom*, trans. G. Stanhope, London, 1727, 1:200, 171, and 173). The notion that the conformity of the sensitive appetite to reason was destroyed as a result of the Fall is fairly frequent and can be studied in Leigh, op. cit., 579; Wolleb-Ross, op. cit., 71, 79–80; Edward Reynolds, op. cit., 62–3; Aquinas and Daniel Dyke, infra, n19, n22; Browne, *Pseudodoxia Epidemica*, Bk. 1, ch. 1; and Burton, *The Anatomy of Melancholy*, pt. 1, sect. 1, memb. 2, subsect. 11.

19 *Summa theologica*, ed. cit., pt. 2, Q. 144, art. 1.

20 Goodman, op. cit., 17.

21 Calvin, *Commentary on Genesis*, trans. J. King (Edinburh, 1848), ch. 3, sect. 17.

22 Daniel Dyke, *Two Treatises. The One of Repentance, the Other of Christ's Temptation* (London, 1646), 235 (misnumbered 225). The way in which the depravity of man is mirrored in the Creation is described by Burton at the beginning of the 'Anatomy' in Du Bartas's *The Furies* and by Goodman, op. cit., 218.

23 Purchas, *Pilgrimage*, 23. Calvin's more prosaic version may also be quoted: 'And his <Adam's> guilt, being the origin of that curse which extends to every part of the world, it is reasonable to conclude its propagation to all his offspring. Therefore, when the Divine Image in him was obliterated, and he was punished with the loss of wisdom, strength, sanctity, truth, and

righteousness, with which he had been adorned, but which were succeeded by the dreadful pests of ignorance, impotence, impurity, vanity, and iniquity, he suffered not alone, but involved all his posterity with him, and plunged into the same miseries' (*Institutes*, ed. cit., Bk. 2, ch. 1, sect. 5).

24 According to Goodman: 'It stood with the justice of God, that the woman first enticing and abusing her husband, should now incurre a thraldome, and be made a captive to the will of her great Lord and Master (her husband)' (op. cit., 250). Goodman adds characteristically 'I know not whether I should call this just decree of God either a curse or a blessing.' See also Willet, op. cit., 49, and the Assembly's comment on *Gen.* 3.16. Calvin on the same place is equally severe but Babington (op. cit., 18) and Andrewes (op. cit., 314) are more humane.

25 G.W. Whiting, op. cit., 121. The Atlas is Jansson's *Novus Atlas* published in eleven volumes apparently from 1647 to 1662. But according to Kester-Svendsen ('Cosmological Lore in Late Milton,' *ELH* 9 (1942): 208 ff.) an encyclopaedia will do almost as well as an Atlas.

26 Eve's admission – 'both have sin'd, but thou / Against God onely, I against God and thee' – recalls this comment of Aquinas: '… the woman not only herself sinned, but suggested sin to the man; wherefore she sinned against both God and her neighbour' (*Summa theologica*, ed. cit., pt. 2, Q. 163, art. 4).

27 'Adam Unparadiz'd,' *Works*, ed. cit., 18:231–2.

6 *Areopagitica* and a Forgotten Licensing Controversy*

ERNEST SIRLUCK

I

When the House of Commons in 1695 refused to concur with the House of Lords in renewing the Printing Act of 1662, licensing of the press in England came permanently to an end. But the reasons which the Lower House gave for its action had nothing to do with the desirability of a free press. The Commons' criticism of the act they were allowing to expire was not that its object was bad, but that experience had shown the instrument to be hopelessly inefficient, impossible to administer, and gravely subject to favouritism and abuse.[1] Their intent was clearly not to vacate legislative control of publication but to start afresh with a new law, in preference to protracting yet again the life of the oft-renewed Act of 1662;[2] and in fact they brought a bill to that purpose through a second reading by November,[3] but the session ended without a third reading.

Every historian of the emancipation of the press has been struck by the ironical disparity between the intent of the Commons and the tremendous consequences of their action. Macaulay set the tone of future comment:

> They knew not what they were doing, what a revolution they were making, what a power they were calling into existence. They pointed out ... the absurdities and iniquities of the statute which was about to expire. But all their objections will be found to relate to matters of detail. On the great

* Originally appearing in *Review of English Studies* n.s. 11 (1960): 260–74. Editors' emendations are indicated in square brackets; Sirluck's square brackets have been converted to angled ones.

> question of principle, on the question whether the liberty of unlicensed printing be, on the whole, a blessing or a curse to society, not a word is said.[4]

After listing a number of the Commons' objections, the great admirer of Milton could not resist drawing the contrast: 'Such were the arguments which did what Milton's *Areopagitica* failed to do.' Laurence Hanson, pointing out in the same way that the Commons were motivated by 'no sudden access of enlightenment,' adds: 'That the lapse of the Licensing Act should have been succeeded by no immediate legislation was accidental rather than of set purpose. ... The press indeed remained free, largely because of the quarrel between the two Houses of Parliament ...'[5] So too Fredrick S. Siebert, who also finds that the House was moved by 'the practical reasons arising from the difficulties of administration and the restraint of trade.'[6] Pointing out that the Commons' reply was based on a paper by Locke, Siebert too notices the contrast with *Areopagitica*: 'Unlike Milton, Locke grounded his arguments principally on the unnatural monopolies of the Stationers Company, on the vague and general terms of prohibition, and on the adequacy of prosecutions at common law. Nothing was said about the universal principle of freedom of the press' (261).

What seems not to have been noticed (or rather to have been forgotten, for it was at least partly known as late as 1819) is that when, two years later, a series of efforts was begun to reintroduce licensing, just such a debate was precipitated as was so remarkably absent in 1695. The discussion did not at the outset rise to this level, certainly not in Parliament. The first occasion was the attempt, by a group of financial speculators, to depress the Exchequer Bills by means of a rumour in a venal newspaper named *The Flying Post*. The infuriated Commons instantly arrested the editor, and, without dividing, called for a Bill to prevent the publishing of news without a licence. Pulteney brought the Bill in within two days, and the House's anger carried it through a first reading; but by the second reading the mood had changed and the Bill was rejected. Nicholas Tindal explains that 'though they saw the mischiefs of the liberty of the press, they knew not where to fix the restraint.'[7] Macaulay believes the House's reversal was due largely to the members' reluctance to be deprived of what had become one of their chief out-of-town pleasures, the competitive private newspapers.[8]

But as, during the next few years, bill followed bill – all, for one reason or another, failing to reach enactment[9] – a small pamphlet war developed in which, on the one hand, unlicensed printing was proclaimed the fundamental safeguard of all religious and civil liberty, without which society must sink into ecclesiastical and secular tyranny; and, on the other hand, licensing was defended as the necessary preservative of truth and order in church and state, as much the magistrate's duty as his right. What was responsible for the change in the nature of the discussion from 1695?

Such things are unlikely to be due to a single cause, but, with due allowance made for the complexities of controversy, I think it can be shown that the change is a direct reflection of the influence of Milton's *Areopagitica* (most probably through its republication in the anonymous collection of Milton's English prose of 1697 or in Toland's collection of 1698). Indeed, the form that the controversy over licensing took in 1698, and the difference between what the champion of a free press said in that year and what he had said in an immediately preceding book of the year before, constitute that rare thing in the history of ideas, a case history of the birth of an influence.

II

The central document is a quarto pamphlet of thirty-two pages, published in 1698, entitled *A Letter To a Member of Parliament, Shewing, that a Restraint On the Press Is inconsistent with the Protestant Religion, and dangerous to the Liberties of the Nation,* hereafter cited as *A Letter* (1698). This pamphlet is unknown to Halkett and Laing,[10] and it is not referred to by either Siebert, the best historian of the struggle for freedom of the press in England during the period, or Sensabaugh, whose account of the influence of Milton's prose from the Restoration to the accession of Anne is the most comprehensive so far published.[11]

A Letter (1698) was not always so obscure, however, nor was its connexion with Milton always unrecognized. It provoked at least two full-scale replies in 1698 and 1699,[12] went into a second edition in 1700,[13] was abridged in a pamphlet of 1704,[14] and was reprinted two years later in the very important *State Tracts* of 1705–7.[15] After this initial decade of prominence it seems to have fallen out of sight for a century, until Cobbett reprinted it in 1809 (its last appearance).[16]

The British Museum Catalogue and Wing (L1680) list it without attribution, but it is demonstrably by the celebrated deist Matthew Tindal. T. Holt White seems to have known this, as we may infer from a passage unaccountably neglected by later editors of Milton and by students of his influence:

> Mathew Tindal writing in 1698 against Mr. Pulteney's Bill to provide, with other restrictions on the Press, that no unlicenced Newspaper should be in circulation, transcribed from it <*Areopagitica*> without scruple, with little alteration and without acknowlegement. It is not unlikely he was apprehensive, that the name of MILTON would have been detrimental to the cause for which he ably and anxiously contending![17]

White does not name the work by Tindal to which he is referring, and his documentation here gives no clue;[18] furthermore, *A Letter* (1698) was not written against Pulteney's Bill, which had been killed before the publication of the pamphlet which caused Tindal to write *A Letter* (1698);[19] nevertheless, once it is seen that *A Letter* (1698) is Tindal's it becomes clear that it must be the pamphlet White meant. Hanson, in his bibliography of sources for the relations of government and press during the period, lists *A Letter* (1698) as Tindal's (128), but he neither discusses the pamphlet nor explains his attribution.

What demonstrates Tindal's authorship is that *A Letter* (1698) is the second of a sequence of three works visibly by the same hand, the other two known certainly to be by Tindal. In 1697 he published *An Essay Concerning the Power of the Magistrate, and the Rights of Mankind, in Matters of Religion*, which contains a 'Postscript' promising that his 'next Discourse' will be on freedom of the press.[20] *A Letter* (1698) repeats a good deal of *An Essay* (1697), often transcribing large passages verbatim.[21] Then in 1704 Tindal published *Reasons Against Restraining the Press*,[22] which is an abridgement of *A Letter* (1698).[23] It may be added that *An Essay* (1697) and *A Letter* (1698) were printed and sold by the same men. The former imprint reads 'London, Printed by J.D. for *Andrew Bell* at the Cross-Keys and Bible in Comhil,' and the latter 'Printed by *J. Darby*, and sold by *Andr. Bell* at the Cross-Keys and Bible in Cornhil.'[24]

An Essay (1697) falls into two parts. The main portion (to p. 176) is a well-written, carefully argued plea, in the tradition of Locke, for religious toleration. It does not concern itself with liberty of the press, except that on two occasions the phrase is added to the general argument for liberty of the pulpit.[25] An unlicensed press is certainly implicit in the toleration demanded by *An Essay* (1697), but Tindal was not thinking about it at the moment, and in the main part of the book referred to it only in this very casual way.

After the main *Essay* was written, and apparently after it had been set up in type, Atterbury's famous *Letter to a Convocation-Man* (1697) was published.[26] Atterbury based his demand for a church convocation in the urgent need to suppress what he thought a monstrous new growth of heresy, schism, deism, &c. He foresaw the objection that the means for dealing with these evils already existed, but he denied that such was the case. The powers of the bishops and the universities were far too limited; he was ambiguous and evasive about the powers of the crown; on those of Parliament his position, while put with some caution, was clear enough: Parliament had still not acted in the matter, nor in truth was it proper for Parliament to exercise a function which was ecclesiastical in nature and belonged properly to Convocation.[27]

Tindal read Atterbury's pamphlet in time to delay the appearance of *An Essay* (1697) until he could append to it 'A *Postscript* in Answer to the *Letter to a Convocation-Man*' (176–204), which is obviously hurriedly written, is set in a smaller type than the main body of the book, and generally witnesses that it is indeed a postscript. Its theme is that the clergy cannot have the powers claimed by *A Letter to a Convocation-Man*, and in this context it makes a point, as the main *Essay* had not done, of liberty of the press. Quoting Atterbury's complaint that Parliament had done nothing in defence of religion, it replies:

> But what can Men in a Legislative Capacity do more for Religion, than ... to protect every one in worshipping God as they judg most agreeable to his Will, and give them the best Opportunity of informing themselves of his Mind? And have they not done this, by granting a Toleration, and by refusing a Bill for restraining the Liberty of the Press? (184)

This reference to the Commons' rejection, in April, of Pulteney's Bill to license news helps to explain the nature of the 'Postscript's' argument against licensing. Less than four pages long, this is simply that the power claimed by the clergy belonged elsewhere. Such an argument was obviously a suitable one to oppose to the *Letter to a Convocation-Man*, and the Commons' action in April apparently encouraged Tindal to think that the state would not use the power of licensing; hence the best way to keep it out of the hands of the clergy – who would – was to claim it exclusively for the state. Despite the Reformation, he wrote, the clergy, 'loth to forgo their beloved Empire over the Consciences of Men' (185), remained

> no less zealous to hinder the Liberty of the Press ... but the Powers the Clergy claimed to themselves being inconsistent with the Principles of the Reformation, and in *England* with the Oath of Supremacy, and that Power the Laws have invested the King with, there is nothing so contradictory as

> their pretended Power, and that which they are forced to own does belong to the Magistrate. (186)

Then, after some expansion of this point, Tindal says, 'But of these things more fully in my next Discourse ...' (187).

But Tindal's 'next Discourse,' while certainly a plea for unlicensed printing, is not an argument that the clergy cannot have the power of licensing because it belongs rightfully to the magistrate. Quite the contrary: it argues that the power of licensing in the hands of the magistrate would enable him to impose a secular tyranny as evil as the spiritual tyranny at which a licensing clergy would aim. The position is that while the press must be responsible to the law (i.e., the publisher's name must appear, so that he may be answerable to indictment or suit),[28] licensing is bad, whether used by ecclesiastical or civil authority.

Perhaps the introduction of further licensing Bills in Parliament in late 1697 and early 1698 had lessened Tindal's confidence in the tactic he had adopted against Atterbury,[29] but the main determinant of the new position was Milton's *Areopagitica*. A few parallel readings will establish *A Letter* (1698)'s dependence upn *Areopagitica*.[30]

A Letter (1698)	*Areopagitica*
Were Licensers unbiast, uncorrupt, and infallible, there might be good Reason to trust them with an Arbitrary Power to pass what Sentences they pleas'd on Books; but if we are to judg of the future by the past, they are almost as likely to be one as the other. Men of Sense, (and others ought not to be trusted with it) without being resolved to make the most of it, will not care to be condemned to the drudgery of reading all the Trash that comes to be printed, nothing but necessity will make such persons submit to it, and that necessity will make them less able to withstand Temptation. So that the appointing Licensers	If learned men be the first receivers out of books, & dispredders both of vice and error, how shall the licencers themselves be confided in, unlesse we can conferr upon them, or they assume to themselves above all others in the Land, the grace of infallibility, and uncorruptednesse? (14) He who is made judge to sit upon the birth, or death of books whether they may be wafted into this world, or not, had need to be a man above the common measure, both studious, learned, and judicious ... If he be of such worth as behoovs him, there cannot be a more tedious and unpleasing journey-work, a greater losse of time levied upon his

will be as bad as laying a Tax on Learning ... But this is not the worst, it will be a great hindrance to the promoting of Knowledg and Truth, by discouraging the ablest Men from writing, for such Persons, especially after having once had the liberty of publishing their own Thoughts, will not be content to have their Works lie at the Mercy of an ignorant or at the best of an unleisured Licenser, who upon a cursory view may either condemn the whole to perpetual Darkness, or strike out what he pleaseth, perhaps the most material things. And tho a living Author may subject himself to this, yet none will be content that the Labours of a deceased Friend should be so served; so that the Works of such a Person, tho never so famous in his Life-time, shall be lost to all Posterity. Besides, is it not intolerable, that every time a Man has a mind to make any Alteration or Addition between the licensing of the Copy, and the printing it off, that he must as often hunt after the same Licenser to obtain his leave, for the Printer could not go beyond his licensed Copy, when in the mean time the Press, to his no small damage, must stand still?

In short, tho there might seem to be some reason to condemn a Person that upon a fair Trial had been found guilty of writing immoral things, or against the Government, to the Punishment of never writing again but under the Authority of an Examiner; yet what reason can there be that those that

head, then to be made the perpetuall reader of unchosen books and pamphlets, oftimes huge volumes ... an imposition which I cannot beleeve how he that values time, and his own studies, or is but of a sensible nostrill should be able to endure ... Seeing therefore ... that no man of worth ... is ever likely to succeed them, except he mean to put himself to the salary of a Presse-corrector, we may easily foresee what kind of licencers we are to expect hereafter, either ignorant, imperious, and remisse, or discouragement and affront, that can be offer'd to learning and to learned men. ... Know, that so far to distrust the judgement & the honesty of one hath but a common repute in learning, and never yet offended, as not to count him dignity of Learning. And what if the author shall be one so copious of fancie, as to have many things well worth the adding, come into his mind after licencing, while the book is yet under the Presse, which not seldom happ'ns to the best and diligentest writers; and that perhaps a dozen times in one book. The Printer dares not go beyond his licenc't copy; so often then must the author trudge to his leav-giver, that those his new insertions may be viewd; and many a jaunt will be made, ere that licencer, for it must be the same man, can either be found, or found at leisure; mean while either the Presse must stand still, which is no small damage, or the author loose his accuratest thoughts, & send the never offended, nay that the whole Commonwealth of Learning should be subject to so severe Usage, which too is the way to have none but Fools and Blockheads plague the World with their Impertinence, and make an *Imprimatur* (as it did formerly) signify no more than that such a Book is foolish enough to be printed? (30–2)

book forth wors then he had made it, which to a diligent writer is the greatest melancholy and vexation that can befall. And how can a man teach with authority ... whenas all he teaches, all he delivers, is but under the tuition, under the correction of his patriarchal licencer to blot or alter what precisely accords not with the hidebound humor which he calls his judgement. When every acute reader upon the first sight of pedantick licence, will be ready with these like words to ding the book a coits distance from him, I hate a pupil teacher ... This is some common stuffe ... Nay, which is more lamentable, if the work of any deceased author; though never so famous in his life time, and even to this day, come to their hands for licence to be Printed or Reprinted, if there be found in his book one sentence of a ventrous edge ... they Will not pardon him their dash: the sense of that great man shall to all posterity be lost, for the fearfulnesse, or the presumptuos rashnesse of a perfunctory licenser ... Had any one writt'n and divulg'd erroneous things & scandalous to honest life ... if after conviction this only censure were adjudg'd him, that he should never henceforth write, but what were first examin'd by an appointed officer, whose hand should be annext to passe his credit for him, that now he might be safely read, it could not be apprehended lesse than a disgracefull punishment. Whence to include the whole Nation, and those that never yet thus offended, under such a diffident and suspectfull prohibition, may plainly be understood what a disparagement it is. (19–23)

And if some good men ... had not had the Courage privately to print some Treatises to undeceive the People, and to make them see the fatal Consequences of those Doctrines which by the restraint of the Press pass'd for divine and sacred Truths; the Nation had tamely submitted to the yoke. And as it cannot be denyed but that those Papers in a great measure opened our eyes, so it may justly be hoped that none that saw the miserable Condition that the Act for regulating the Press would have brought us into, will be instrumental in reestablishing that Law. No; those Men sure who so much exclaimed against it in the late Reigns, will take all care imaginable to prevent it now. But if these very men who may justly be said to be written into their places, and owe their Preferments to the freedom of examining those slavish Doctrines of the former Reigns; if these Men, I say, can so far forget themselves as to be for a Law which till themselves were uppermost they thought tended only to inslave us, there cannot be, I think, a greater Argument for all others to oppose it. (26–7)

There have bin not a few since the beginning of this Parliament ... who by their unlicens't books to the contempt of an Imprimatur first broke that triple ice clung about our hearts, and taught the people to see day: I hope that none of these were the perswaders to renew upon us this bondage, which they themselves have wrought so much good by contemning. But if ... neither their own remembrance what evill hath abounded in the Church by this lett of licencing, and what good they themselves have begun by transgressing it, be not anough, but that they will perswade, and execute the most *Dominican* part of the Inquisition over us, and are already with one foot in the stirrup so active at suppresing, it would be no unequall distribution in the first place to suppresse the suppressors themselves; whom the change of their condition hath puft up, more then their late experience of harder times hath made wise. (39)

The Clergy, say they, are so learned, and withal so numerous, that amongst them they could not fail to expose and confound any thing that's writ against

Writing is more publick then preaching; and more easie to refutation, if need be, there being so many whose businesse and profession meerly it is, them, had they but Truth on their side, which they know is, next to the Almighty, strong, and therefore needs no licensing Tricks, or Stratagems, to make it victorious: These are the mean Shifts that Error is forced to use against its Power. (16–17)

to be the champions of Truth; which if they neglect, what can be imputed but their sloth, or unability? (28) For who knows not that Truth is strong next to the Almighty; she needs no policies, nor stratagems, nor licencings, to make her victorious, those are the shifts and the defences that error uses against her power ... (36)

If we must, *early and late*, according to the Wise Man's direction, *seek after Wisdom as after a hidden Treasure*, I cannot see how it will become the *Wisdom* of a Nation to endeavour by a Law to hinder us from knowing more than the scanty Measure of a Party-Licenser will afford us. (7)

What a collusion is this, whenas we are exhorted by the wise man to use diligence, *to seek for wisdom as for hidd'n treasures* early and late, that another order shall enjoyn us to know nothing but by statute. (36)

I can see no reason why they that are for tying Men to that Interpretation of Scripture a Licencer shall approve, and therefore put it into his power to hinder all others from being published, can with any justice condemn the Popish Clergy for not licensing the Bible it self for the Laity to read it. For if the Bible is to be translated into the vulgar Tongue, to what end is it, but that the People by reading it may judg what is their Duty in the most obscure and difficult places? (16)

But then all human learning and controversie in religious points must remove out of the world, yea the Bible it selfe; for that oftimes ... answers dubiously and darkly to the common reader ... For these causes we all know the Bible it selfe put by the Papist into the first rank of prohibited books. (13)

Tho I cannot but presume that our Legislators, were there no other reason, yet out of respect to the Clergy, would not enact such a Law as supposeth the greatest and most learned of them not fit to be trusted with the printing but a Half-sheet in Religion without

This may have much reason to discourage the Ministers when such a low conceit is had of all their exhortations and the benefiting of their hearers, as that they are not thought fit to be turn'd loose to three sheets of paper without a licencer (24) ... But consent of a ... Licenser ... But if they are content with that Disgrace, it must be because either they cannot defend themselves against their Adversaries, or that they have a mind to give themselves up to Laziness and Idleness, and not trouble themselves with the laborious work of controversial Divinity. (23–4)

if his rear and flanks be not impal'd, if his back dore be not secur'd by the rigid licencer, but that a bold book may now and then issue forth, and give the assault to some of his old collections in their trenches, it will concern him then to keep waking, to stand in watch, to set good guards and sentinells about his receiv'd opinions ... And, God send that the fear of this diligence which must then be us'd, doe not make us affect the lazines of a licencing Church. (28)

The argument of *A Letter* (1698) is not precisely that of *Areopagitica*: it is *Areopagitica* adapted to deism. It begins by premising that what distinguishes man from brutes is his reason, 'the only Light God has given him, not only to discover that there is a Religion, but to distinguish the true from the many false ones' (3). Whoever neglects to use his reason to find out for himself the truth of religion is disobedient to God, 'and tho he should light on Truth, the luckiness of the Accident will no way excuse his Disobedience' (4). At the same time, men have a duty to inform others of what they believe to be the truth. Hence the press, the primary means of such communication ought not to be restrained, because such restraint 'tends to make Men blindly submit to the Religion they chance to be educated in,' deprives them of the 'best means to discover Truth, by ... seeing and examining ... different Opinions' (5), 'hinders Truth from having any great influence on Mens Minds, which is owing chiefly to Examination,' and 'tends to make us hold the Truth (should we chance to light on it) guiltily' (6).

Popery quite rightly adopted licensing as the best means of maintaining its empire over men by keeping them stupid and ignorant, and this policy was successful until the invention of printing made it unenforceable (the success of the Reformation was due to printing); but for a Protestant church to ape Rome in this is to betray its fundamental principles and reveal that it is actuated by ambition rather than by love of truth. Licensing is no cure for heresy or schism; to hold a belief on trust is heresy (even if the belief is true), and schism is caused by the attempt to impose on men's minds. The only cure of heresy and schism is freedom for all opinions, for truth is invincible (8–24).

With respect to civil rights liberty of the press is equally fundamental. A licensed press must be subservient to the will of a ruler who aspires to arbitrary power, and thus leave the people without warning or guidance; on the other hand, a free press will alert them to attempted encroachments. 'Secure but the Liberty of the Press, and that will, in all probability, secure all other Liberty; but if that once falls into the hands of ill designing Men, nothing that we hold dear or precious is safe' (27).

Here, then, in a pamphlet which everywhere echoes *Areopagitica*, is a sharp change from the author's last discussion of the subject. It seems impossible that Tindal could have known *Areopagitca* when he wrote 'A Postscript,' and it is therefore most likely that he first encountered it in one of the collections of 1697 and 1698.[31]

III

The first reply to *A Letter* (1698) was *A Modest Plea For the Due Regulation of the Press, In Answer to several Reasons lately Printed against it* (1698), by the well-known divine Francis Gregory, who had been chaplain to Charles II and was now rector of Hambledon. Although Gregory begins *ad hominem*, deducing that the author of *A Letter* (1698) must be 'one of the worst sort of *Hereticks*, I mean a *Socinian*' (3), his tract is for the most part studiedly moderate in tone. His method is to take up in turn each of Tindal's propositions, usually conceding the principle but denying the application. Thus, for example, he concedes that to take up a religion on trust is sinful, and that unhappily many Englishmen calling themselves Protestants have done so; but it is false to blame this condition on licensing of the press: it was a ground of complaint in the days of the apostles, long before the invention of printing, and is due to faults of human nature. Men ought indeed to examine their beliefs, but in England licensing has been no hindrance thereto, since Scripture and orthodox expositors of Scripture are freely published. Only erroneous and heretical commentators, apt to mislead and seduce, are suppressed (11–13). In this manner Gregory runs through *A Letter* (1698) from the viewpoint of the established church, his own position being that 'since this unlimited Liberty of the Press would certainly be ... an inlet to Schisms, Heresies, and a great variety of Opinions and Practices in Matters of Religion; the allowance of it can never consist with that Command of God, contend earnestly for the Faith once delivered to the Saints' (41).

The second reply to *A Letter* (1698) was anonymous. *A Letter to a Member of Parliament, Shewing the Necessity of Regulating the Press ... With A Particular Answer to the Objections that of late have been Advanced against it* (Oxford, 1699), which is not in Halkett and Laing, is attributed by Wing (D837) to Defoe – an attribution which, if correct, would make this the most surprising product of even that prodigal pen (actually, Defoe took the opposite side in this controversy, as will appear below). Sensabaugh, noticing this pamphlet because it refers to Milton by name, is unaware of the controversy to which it belongs and dismisses it in a half-sentence as by some 'loyal old Anglican' (196) – an attribution which, while not very informative, is at least more likely to be correct than Wing's.

A Letter Shewing the Necessity is more uncompromising than Gregory's *Modest Plea.* It argues the case for licensing from basic principles: the duty of the magistrate in matters of religion, considered first in a state of nature and then in a state of Revelation (1–15); the necessity of an established church (15–26); the magistrate's obligation to maintain the true and established church against attacks from misbelievers and unbelievers, and hence his duty to control the press, for which no means short of licensing can be effectual (26–47). Most of the rest of the tract is devoted to answering the chief arguments of *A Letter* (1698), which it does not name but from which it quotes and paraphrases extensively (48–62). The author ends by urging the Member of Parliament to whom his *Letter* is at least ostensibly addressed to use his influence in the House to bring forward a new licensing Bill. The failure of the Bill in the last Parliament 'cannot conclude against the Reasonableness or Necessity of it. I'm confident the Eyes and Heart, the Hopes and Expectations of every *Englishman,* that is acted with a true Concern for the True Religion, are fixed on the ensuing Session' (63).

Since in fact neither the ensuing session nor the one following produced a new licensing Bill, Tindal seems to have troubled himself with no other reply to his two assailants than the republication of his original *A Letter* (1698) in 1700.[32] But in 1702 bills were introduced in both Houses, although neither successfully; in March of 1703 a royal proclamation announced a more rigorous enforcement of existing unrepealed press laws; in December the Commons gave leave for another Bill, and by 18 January 1704 this had passed a second reading.[33] Tindal was sufficiently alarmed to publish *Reasons Against Restraining the Press* (1704). (It was during the same crisis that Defoe composed his plea against licensing, *An Essay on the Regulation of the Press.*)[34]

Reasons (1704) is a systematic abridgement of *A Letter* (1698), but since it is only one-third the length of the original most of the latter's verbal echoes of *Areopagitica* have been squeezed out. A few remain; e.g., 'Nothing can more discourage men of Abilities from writing, than to subject their Discourse to the mercy of an Ignorant, or at least an Unleisured Licenser: such a Hardship on the Commonwealth of Learning, will be apt to make an *Imprimatur* signify no more, than that the Book is foolish enough to be printed' (9–10). But the influence of *Areopagitica* on *Reasons* (1704) is primarily in the structure of ideas, and this is fully visible only through *A Letter* (1698).

The failure of the Bill of 1704 did not end the effort to reimpose licensing and other forms of press censorship, and Tindal continued to fight for freedom of the press; but as his position became increasingly complicated by immediate concerns (e.g., the defence of two men imprisoned for selling one of his books)[35] his argument gave less visible evidence of the influence of *Areopagitica.* That influence was not spent; on the contrary, those of its aspects which Tindal found congenial were so thoroughly absorbed that they became part of his own attitude, and no longer needed to be clothed in Milton's language when they appeared in Tindal's writings. They had done their work, converting one who would have tried to withhold the power of licensing from the clergy by vesting it in the state into the protagonist of an unlicensed press as the basic guarantee of all liberties.

IV

In 1738, when it was thought that the revival of stage licensing might well be followed by an attempt to revive licensing of the press, James Thomson, the poet, edited, with a preface, the first separate republication of *Areopagitica.*[36] It has been thought that *Areopagitica* was thus rescued from a century of virtual oblivion and launched into a second career of almost universal influence. But in fact it seems likely that despite the absence of acknowledgement *Areopagitica* had exerted something like a continuous influence throughout its first century. We have long known that it played a part in the lapse of the Press Act in 1679 and in the attempt, in 1693, to prevent one of the Act's recurrent renewals.[37] We may now add a considerable influence in the decade from 1698 to 1707. There is some reason to think that it had more influence immediately after publication than has recently been thought.[38] Perhaps there were other cases of unacknowledged use, and some to fill the apparent gap between 1707 and 1738?

NOTES

1 *Lord's Journals,* 15:545–6.
2 Renewed 1664, 1665; lapsed 1679; revised 1685; renewed 1692. See F.S. Siebert, *Freedom of the Press in England 1476–1776* (Urbana, Ill., 1952), 237–8, 260–3.
3 *Commons Journals,* 11:340, 354.
4 [Thomas Babington] Macaulay, [*The History of England,* intr. Douglas Jerrold, 4 vols. (London, 1906),] Book 3, ch. 21.
5 [Laurence Hanson,] *Government and the Press 1695–1763* (Oxford, 1936), 7–8.
6 Siebert, 263.
7 [Nicholas Tindal,] *The Continuation of Mr. Rapin de Thoyras's History of England,* 2nd ed. (London, 1751), 1:350.
8 Macaulay, Book 3, ch. 22.
9 Hanson, 8–9.
10 Halkett and Laing, *Dictionary of Anonymous and Pseudonymous English Literature* (London, 1926–56).
11 G.F. Sensabaugh, *That Grand Whig Milton* (Stanford, 1952).
12 See below, [133–4].
13 *Term Catalogues,* 3:181; Wing L1681.
14 See below, [134].
15 *A Collection of State Tracts, Publish'd on Occasion of the Late Revolution in 1688. And During the Reign of William III* [, 3 vols.] (London, 1705–7), 2:614–26.
16 Cobbett, *Cobbett's Parliamentary History of England* (London, 1806–12), 5, col. 1164.
17 T. Holt White, ed., *Areopagitica* (London, 1819), lvii.
18 White's references are to Nicholas Tindal's *Continuation of Rapin* and James Ralph's *History of England* (London, 1744–6). Both give the account of the failure of Pulteney's Bill but neither mentions any publications on the subject.
19 For this, and for the probable basis of White's mistake, see below, [126–7] and [n29].
20 [Matthew Tindal, *An Essay Concerning the Power of the Magistrate* ([London,] 1697),] 187; and see below, [p. 127]. Attribution by Wood, accepted by *DNB* and all bibliographies.

21 Compare *A Letter* (1698), title, 3–4, 14, 12–13, 13, 17, 18, and 22 with *An Essay* (1697), headings of Part 1, ch. 4; and Part 2, ch. 5; 31–2 and 87–8, 119–20, 122–3, 123–4, 32–3, 126, and 155.

22 Attribution by Richard Barron, *Pillars of Priestcraft*, 2nd ed. (London, 1768), 4:281; accepted by *DNB* and all bibliographies.

23 See below, [134–5].

24 Darby also printed John Toland's *Life of John Milton* ([London,] 1699), and since this was reprinted from Toland's edition of Milton's prose works in 1698, Darby may also have been the anonymous London printer of that volume who concealed his work under the false 'Amsterdam' imprint.

25 Tindal, *An Essay* (1697), 104, 122.

26 William Fraser, who edited the pamphlet in 1853, argued that the author was Sir Bartholomew Shower, and this attribution was long accepted; it is now generally agreed that the pamphlet was written by [Francis] Atterbury from materials supplied by Shower. See BM Catalogue.

27 Atterbury, *Letter to a Convocation-Man* (1697), 8–16.

28 Tindal, *A Letter* (1698), 18.

29 That White was wrong in thinking that Tindal was 'writing in 1698 against Mr. *Pulteney's* Bill' is obvious to anyone who recalls the date of that Bill, but the error is explicable enough. It is due to Cobbett, who reprinted *A Letter* (1698) as an appendix throwing light on the Commons' conduct in first calling for, and then rejecting, Pulteney's Bill of 1 April 1697: 'About this time a small tract was published, intitled, "A Letter to a Member of Parliament <&c.>"; for a copy of which see Appendix No. XIII' (5, col. 1164). Appendix XIII gives its source for the tract, which it dates 1697, as *State Tracts*, but in that collection the date appears correctly as 1698. Evidently Cobbett, unaware of the continuing debate on the subject, assumed that *A Letter* (1698) must have been occasioned by Pulteney's Bill, and that the editors of *State Tracts* had mistaken the date; he accordingly 'corrected' this to fit the parliamentary action. The association with Pulteney's Bill remained in White's mind even though he got the date of *A Letter* (1698) right.

30 In this comparison, page references to *Areopagitica* are to the original edition (1644).

31 One phrase, however, suggests that Tindal may also have made use of Charles Blount's adaptation of *Areopagitica*, *A Just Vindication of Learning* ([London,] 1679). Where *Areopagitica* has (22): 'When every acute reader upon the first sight of a pedantick licence, will be ready with these like words to ding the book a coits distance from him, I hate a pupil teacher ... This is some common stuffe,' Blount wrote (7): 'Every Acute

Reader upon first sight of a Pedantick *License*, will be apt to misinterpret the word (*Imprimatur*) and think it signifies no more, but that, this Book is foolish enough to be Printed.' Here *A Letter* (1698) speaks (31–32) of the way to 'make an *Imprimatur* (as it did formerly) signify no more than that such a Book is foolish enough to be printed.' Tindal may well have used Blount's pamphlet for help in abbreviating Milton; he could not have relied wholly on it, for he adopts a good deal from *Areopagitica* which is not in Blount.

The discovery that Blount's *A Just Vindication* was an adaptation of *Areopagitica* was made by Macaulay, who also attributed to Blount the 1693 tract entitled *Reasons Humbly Offered for the Liberty of Unlicens'd Printing*; see Book 3, chap. 19. Holt White had already noticed (cxxi) that the latter tract, whose authorship he did not know, was 'a sort of abridgement of the *Areopagitica*.' Sensabaugh (55–61 and 155–62) discusses at length the relation of Blount's two pamphlets to *Areopagitica* without referring to either White or Macaulay.

32 *Term Catalogues*, 3:188; Wing (L1681) shows a copy in the National Library of Scotland; there is no copy in the BM.

33 In the event Parliament was prorogued without its reaching a third reading; see Hanson, 9–10.

34 Daniel Defoe, *An Essay on the Regulation of the Press*, ed. J.R. Moore, The Luttrell Society (Oxford, 1948).

35 Matthew Tindal, *A Second Defence of the Rights of the Christian Church, Occasion'd by two late Indictments against a Bookseller and his Servant, for selling one of the said Books* (London, 1708).

36 *Areopagitica: A Speech of Mr. John Milton ... First Published in the Year 1644*, with a Preface, by another Hand (London: Printed for A. Millar, 1738).

37 See White, Macaulay, and Sensabaugh, as cited above, [n.31].

38 See *Complete Prose Works of John Milton*, vol. 2, ed. E. Sirluck (New Haven, 1959), 87, 89, 90, 91, 209, 506–7, 545–6, 551.

7 '... And on His Crest Sat Horror': Eighteenth-Century Interpretations of Milton's Sublimity and his Satan*

ARTHUR BARKER

I

Milton's reputation in the eighteenth century has already been so thoroughly examined that another article on the subject must seem superfluous.[1] I am however less concerned with Milton and his influence on literary practice than with the development of certain ideas which played an important part in the evolution of Romanticism and readily found illustration in his work. Few of us still believe that the paradoxical interpretation of *Paradise Lost* set forth by Blake and Shelley, expanded by other early nineteenth-century writers, and given respectability by Sir Walter Raleigh, sprang fully armed from the miraculous marriage of Heaven and Hell effected by Romantic inspiration over the dead body of Neo-classicism. We understand nineteenth-century Romanticism better through seeing it as the fruit of a steady (though complex) growth. I propose to trace and document two minor elements in this complexity which have not, I think, received much attention: the interpretation of Milton's sublimity, and of his Satan.[2] Such a study should throw some indirect light on our own interpretation of *Paradise Lost*; but its purpose is to examine the emergence of the romantic attitude from the neo-classical, not in aesthetic theory or literary practice, but in one specific critical instance.

Milton's influence on eighteenth-century opinion was unique in that he alone among the great English poets was at once sufficiently neo-classical to recommend himself and sufficiently irregular to exert a salutary pressure against inflexible canons. Spenser had to wait till 1754 to be defended in his 'barbarity' by Warton. Shakespeare, though loved, was regarded as a 'natural genius' whose achievements were sometimes remarkable in

* Originally appearing in the *University of Toronto Quarterly* 11 (1942): 421–36.

spite of his ignorance of what was fitting. But Milton had written of poetry in terms which were commonplaces among the Augustans; and Addison could set him among the more correct in Apollo's court, with Virgil, Tully, and others who had 'formed themselves by rules and submitted the greatness of their natural geniuses to the corrections and restraints of art.'[3] *Paradise Lost* was, moreover, the only English epic which could challenge comparison with classical and Italian epics. Throughout the first half of the century attempts were consequently made to refute the criticism of Dryden and Rymer, that it offended against epic rule. Such attempts could be successful only if the rules were liberalized; and even before Shakespeare's influence began to have its full effect, Milton's Italianate Neo-classicism was offsetting the more precise French doctrine. In particular he exemplified that sublimity beyond the reach of regular art for which the treatise of Longinus suggested a critical justification. Boileau, and after him Pope and Addison, endeavoured to fit this elevating and transporting quality into the Neo-classical code.[4] Milton reminded the eighteenth century that the effect could be achieved in English.

This influence is already apparent in Addison's *Spectator* papers on *Paradise Lost* (1712). These admirable essays require no analysis here; but they provide an excellent point of departure: they established the normal eighteenth-century view of the poem,[5] and they indicate the two chief points at which it was to suffer transformation. Addison set out specifically to examine *Paradise Lost* 'by the rules of epic poetry, and see whether it falls short of the *Iliad* or *Aeneid* in the beauties which are essential to that kind of writing.'[6] The result of his critique 'according to Aristotle's method' was a triumphant vindication which showed the *Spectator*'s readers that Milton was sufficiently Augustan to warrant their admiration: the epic possesses 'all the greatness of plan, regularity of design, and masterly beauties, which we discover in Homer and Virgil.'[7]

Yet in some parts of his poem Milton had indulged in flights which could be justified only by appealing beyond the laws and by observing, 'with Longinus, that the productions of a great genius, with many lapses and inadvertencies, are infinitely preferable to works of an inferior kind of author which are scrupulously exact and conformable to all the rules of correct writing.'[8] This observation illustrates both Addison's good sense and the escape from straitness provided by Longinus. Especially in the cosmic parts of the epic, the sublimity justifies the comparative irregularity:

> It is impossible for the imagination of man to distend itself with greater ideas than those which he has laid together in his first, second, and sixth

> books. The seventh, which describes the creation of the world, is likewise wonderfully sublime ... Let the judicious reader compare what Longinus has observed on several passages in Homer, and he will find parallels for most of them in the *Paradise Lost*.[9]

As we shall see, this suggestion was to be remembered, and the idea of Milton's sublimity, especially in the books here mentioned, was to lead to enthusiasms quite beyond the reach of Neo-classicism.

That is also true of a second and closely related method of justification suggested by Addison. As Milton himself had claimed, there is a magnificence in *Paradise Lost* 'much greater than could have been formed upon any pagan system.'[10] This Christian advantage begot not only a sublimity but an originality of invention superior to Homer's, Virgil's, and even Shakespeare's:

> Homer and Virgil introduced persons whose characters are commonly known among men ... Milton's characters, most of them, lie out of nature, and were to be formed purely by his own invention. It shows a greater genius in Shakespeare to have drawn his Caliban than his Hotspur or Julius Caesar: the one was to be supplied out of his own imagination, whereas the other might have been formed upon tradition, history and observation. It was much easier therefore for Homer to find proper sentiments for an assembly of Grecian generals than for Milton to diversify his infernal council with proper characters and inspire them with a variety of sentiments.[11]

Addison has here suggested a contrast between mere imitation of nature and the inventions of sublimely original genius which was to be developed with remarkable consequences, finding support in an interpretation of Milton's devils, and especially their leader, which the author of *Cato* would have repudiated. For the polished Spectator was no Satanist. He suggests directions, but he did not himself pursue them. He felt that 'most readers ... are more charmed with Milton's description of Paradise than of Hell; they are both perhaps equally perfect in their kind; but in the one the brimstone and the sulphur are not so refreshing to the imagination as the beds of flowers and the wilderness of sweets in the other.'[12] It was also his opinion that, because Milton never allowed his sublime originality to overcome his judgment, he kept the balance between 'the probable and the marvellous.'[13] We are to see how this nicely poised judgment was overturned.

II

In general the late seventeenth and early eighteenth centuries accepted Dryden's judgment that *Paradise Lost* was 'one of the most sublime poems which either this age or nation has producéd,' but that it was insufficiently polished and not truly epic in subject.[1] Addison's attempt to disprove the negative part of this opinion was not altogether satisfactory to John Dennis, who somewhat ponderously linked the age of Dryden and the age of Pope. Dennis was torn between admiration for Milton, veneration of Dryden, and hatred of Addison and Pope (who dubbed him 'Sir Tremendous Longinus'). He was annoyed with Addison for subjecting Milton to an examination by rule.[2] He had himself followed Le Bossu's *Traité du poème épique* in evaluating Blackmore's *Prince Arthur*; but whenever he thought of Milton, his enthusiasm for the sublime and his religious ardour came into violent conflict with his neo-classical principles. He believed that 'Virgil has infinitely the advantage of Milton in the wonderful contrivance of his poem ... and in the constant tenor of his majesty and his elevation.'[3] He therefore preferred to admit with Dryden that the epic was full of flats and had two actions instead of one; and then to argue that Milton is to be admired above all 'for one thing, and that is for having carried away the prize of sublimity from both ancients and moderns.'[4]

Enthusiasm for sublimity led Dennis to stress Milton's original and divine inspiration. He had said of *Paradise Lost* that, 'being so very different from what Homer and Virgil had ever thought of, it could not be entirely subjected to their rules'; for Milton's theme 'threw him upon new thoughts, and new images, and an original spirit ...'[5] He surpassed the ancients (according to Dennis's most cherished theory) because of his contemplation of 'those divine ideas that raised his soul and filled it with a noble greatness, which passion expressed makes the greatness of spirit.'[6]

This statement contains significant implications. It was a commonplace of Milton criticism to say with Addison that the epic was the better for being Christian; but there were two quite distinct interpretations of this idea. For an interpreter whose religious opinions were based, like Addison's, on a conception of the reasonableness of the Creator and the regularity of his creation, it meant that Milton had managed to reflect the sublime justness of God's ways.'[7] Henry Felton believed that 'the thoughts which are natural to every sacred theme are so far exalted above the heathen poetry or philosophy that the meanest Christian ... is able to surpass the noblest wits of antiquity in the truth and greatness of his sentiments.'[8] Thus the Scriptures were the source from which Milton 'derived his light, the sacred treasure that enriched his fancy and furnished him with all the truth and wonders of God and his creation, of angels and men, which no mortal brain was able either to discover or conceive.' The element of inspired originality implied by this statement accounts for the 'force and richness of imagination' in which Milton seemed to Felton to surpass Homer; the element of truth, for the 'justness of thought and exactness of work' in which he surpassed Virgil.[9] Sublimity and regularity are thus united.

When, however, the interpreter tended like Dennis towards religious enthusiasm, the emphasis on Milton's Christianity meant that he had managed to suggest a sublimity awful and dynamic. Actually, both views are present and in conflict in Dennis's remarks on Milton. When the neo-classicist is uppermost in him, he remembers that the contemplation of Christianity is a contemplation of revealed truth. The poet thus inspired will be imitating the supernatural, but the result will be like the imitation of nature in quality though not in kind. The ideas of God are just and reasonable; therefore sublime poetry must be just and reasonable; for, said he, in a sentence which clearly echoes Milton, 'If the end of poetry be to instruct and reform the world, that is, to bring mankind from irregularity, extravagance and confusion, to rule and order, then poetry itself may not be irregular and extravagant, and must not swerve from rule, that is, from reason.'[10] Unfortunately, Milton did seem to swerve from Le Bossu's epic rule and order; and the problem was complicated for Dennis by Addison's attempt to show that he did not swerve much, and by his own delight in Milton's extravagance.

Dennis could say of *Paradise Lost*, 'Here is all that is great and sublime in reason.'[11] But 'passion' was also important for him as 'the characteristic mark of poetry'; and he believed 'enthusiasm in poetry is wonderful and sublime' especially when it arises from the contemplation of the supernatural.[12] In spite of himself he tended to emphasize what was awful and vast in Milton's sublimity. He experienced 'infinite' and 'transporting pleasures' at sight of the Alps, and contrasted the 'delights consistent with reason' produced by 'the prospect of hills and valleys, of flowery meads and murmuring streams,' with those 'unusual transports that are mingled with horrors and sometimes with despair.'[13] He experienced unusual transports when he read Milton, especially the description of Satan, his address to the Sun, and the accounts of Chaos and the Creation. Of part of Book VII he said that there was nothing so sublime in Homer and Virgil: 'The reader who sees the inequalities in it will easily perceive that it derives its greatness from the becoming thoughts which it has of the deity.'[14]

As the apologetic reference to inequalities suggests, Dennis would never quite allow himself to say that parts of the epic were eminently sublime *because* they were unequal. With his passion for sublimity and his neo-classical principles, exasperation drove him to term *Paradise Lost* at once 'the most lofty and the most irregular poem that has ever been produced by the mind of man.'[15] But the bolder statement was always on the tip of his tongue; and Pope and Addison drove him to assert that Milton was greater than the ancients because he is 'more terrible, more lofty, more vehement, more astonishing, and has more impetuous and divine raptures.'[16] Annoyance is a prime solvent of dilemmas; and the Milton problem was ultimately to be solved for the eighteenth century precisely as it was solved for Dennis. It is much easier to cry with Satan, 'Hail, horrors, hail!' than to justify the ways of an epic poet.

III

As Mr. Monk has said, 'terror is the first of several qualities that, finding no very happy home in the well-planned ... domain of neo-classicism, sought and found refuge in the sublime, which constantly gathered to itself ideas and emotions that were to be prominent in the poetry and prose of the romantic era.'[1] This process is very clearly adumbrated in Milton criticism. The rules were being undermined when the painter Jonathan Richardson quoted a passage from book 1 to illustrate the contention that 'in writing, the sublime is consistent with great irregularity; nay, that very irregularity may produce that noble effect ...'[2] His son, also Jonathan, linked to this the idea of religious and original inspiration when he maintained that Milton's sublimest passages are 'such as the heathen world were incapable of by infinite degrees, such as none but the noblest genius could attain to, and that assisted by a religion revealed by God himself'; and he added 'Himself was his own rule when in heights where none had gone before, and higher than which none can ever go.'[3] Paul Rolli pressed farther when he said in reply to Voltaire's carpings, 'All great epic poets have been helped by the senses ... but Milton had almost no other help but that of his own fancy. The whole is almost all imaginary, and as he well says, "Invisible to mortal sight."'[4] And these ideas were found to be especially illustrated by those passages dealing with the fallen angels which, according to Patterson, exceeded 'all human imagination, and all the astonishment or consternation that ever was or will be again.'[5]

In spite of Addison, interest in the Satanic books was almost as great in the eighteenth century as in the nineteenth. This is apparent in the two eighteenth-century translations of *On the Sublime*, by Leonard Welsted (1712) and William Smith (1739), who also make clear the important connection between Longinus and Milton. Remembering Addison's suggestion, the translators take from *Paradise Lost* most of their parallels to the illustrative quotations of Longinus.[6] They agree that the loftiness of Milton's theme makes his poem more sublime than the classical epics,[7] but their passages are drawn chiefly from the opening books or the War in Heaven, especially where these are terrible.

Welsted expressed a decided preference for Milton over the correct Waller: 'Waller abounds with a multitude of easy turns and sprightly strokes of fancy; Milton pours upon us a torrent of images, great and terrible; in subjects common to them both, Waller is more fruitful, Milton more natural. I have a fondness for one, but I pay adoration to the other.'[8] It is by Milton's 'unbounded soarings of imagination' that he is excited, especially in such passages as the account of Satan. Homer's description of the goddess Discord is 'undoubtedly very great; but to anyone who has read the prodigious description Milton gives us of Satan, as when he rises from the fiery surge, when he views the host of fallen angels, and particularly when he is apprehended in Paradise, this perhaps will seem but moderately sublime.'[9] Such indeed is Welsted's delight in immoderate sublimity that he 'could almost be content that Virgil himself were less correct, provided he were more sublime.'[10] Milton is more satisfying: 'When I view him thus in his most exalted flights, piercing beyond the boundaries of the universe, he appears to me as a vast comet that for want of room is ready to burst its orb and grow eccentric.'[11]

Smith is rather more conservative. He was not uncomfortable with the rules, and was delighted by the Paradise scenes as Welsted apparently was not.[12] Yet he also enjoyed the terrible sublimity of the War in Heaven, the description of Satan preparing for combat, and, curiously, the account of the Lazar House. Certainly 'the horrible grandeur in which Milton arrays his devils throughout the poem is an honourable proof of the stretch of his invention,' and their answer to Satan's harangue, 'great and dreadfull' as it is, 'at once displays the art of the poet, gives the reader a terrible idea of the fallen angels, and imprints a dread and horror on the mind.'[13] However, though Smith agrees with Welsted that book 1 is a magnificent example of sublimity, he makes a careful and sober distinction: 'The descriptions of Satan and the other fallen angels are very grand, but terrible; they do not so much exalt as terrify the imagination.'[14]

The distinction is typical of the eighteenth century; but the emphasis of Welsted and Smith on Hell indicates how the balance was being shifted to favour the dreadful, and how the conception of Milton's sublimity was being transformed from a theory of religious elevation to a delightful sensationalism. The transition from the uplifting and moral to the exciting and stimulating is complete in Burke's examination of the sublime and the beautiful (1757). Burke was aware of the importance of religious emotion in the sublime; but he found that quality, not in those parts of *Paradise Lost* which (in Dennis's phrase) fill the soul 'with joy and a certain noble pride,'[15] but in those which convey a sense of the terrible and mysterious power of God or Satan. 'Astonishment is the effect of the sublime in the highest degree,' he said; not an awed and worshipping reverence, but a wonder combined with 'delightful horror.'[16]

The description of Satan seemed to Burke 'unsurpassed in its sublimity' because of its confused horror. 'Here is a very noble picture; and in what does this poetical picture consist? In images of a tower, an archangel, the sun rising through mist, or in an eclipse, the ruin of monarchs and the revolution of kingdoms. The mind is hurried out of itself by a crowd of great and confused images, which affect because they are great and confused.'[17] This is to say what Dennis would never say; and so it is also in Burke's examination of the shadowy description of Hell and the 'majesty of darkness' which surrounds the most incomprehensible of all beings. Sublimity is the effect of irregularity and obscurity.

> No person seems better to have understood the secret of heightening or of setting terrible things, if I may use the expression, in their strongest light by the force of a judicious obscurity than Milton. His description of Death in the second book is admirably studied; it is astonishing with what a gloomy pomp, with what a significant and expressive uncertainty of strokes and colouring, he has finished the portrait of the King of Terrors ... In this description all is dark, uncertain, confused, terrible, and sublime in the last degree.[18]

The collocation of words in the final sentence is illuminating; Addison and Voltaire thought Sin and Death absurd.

There is no need to trace this view of Milton farther in the second half of the eighteenth century. At this point it becomes inextricably involved with the revival of interest in mediaeval romance, Spenser and the Italians, romantic scenery, and those other dreadful props of the Gothic novel or tale of terror.[19] One later critic will serve to suggest the consequences of the movement we have been tracing.

Blair's *Lectures on Rhetoric* (1783) are in general academic and conservative; but his view of the sublime, based on Genesis, Milton, and Ossian, is very like Burke's. He distinguishes its effect from the 'gay and brisk emotion raised by beautiful objects,' insists on its 'awfulness and solemnity,' and differentiates it from the kind of writing which Longinus and Smith included under the heading but which he terms 'merely elegant.'[20] It is not produced by regular beauty but by ideas of vastness, of great noise as of earthquakes and torrents, of darkness, solitude and silence, of disorder, confusion and wildness. Much of this is supplied by Ossian; but much also comes from Milton.

It is 'the daring sublimity of his genius' which is most striking in the 'new and very extraordinary road' which he followed with a 'stretch both of imagination and invention which is perfectly wonderful.'[21] Instances of this quality are to be found throughout the poem, but especially in the Satanic books. 'Almost the whole of the first and second books ... are continued instances of the highest sublime. The prospect of Hell and of the fallen host, the appearance and behaviour of Satan, the consultation of the infernal chiefs, and Satan's flight through chaos to the borders of the world, discover the most lofty ideas that ever entered into the conception of any poet.'[22] Blair emphasizes Satan even more heavily than had Welsted. In a passage apparently inspired by Burke, he notes that in the characterization there 'concur a variety of sources of the sublime; the principal object eminently great, a high superior nature, fallen indeed but erecting itself against distress; the grandeur of the principal object heightened by associating with it so noble an idea as that of the sun suffering an eclipse; this picture shaded with all those images of change and trouble, of darkness and terror, which coincide so finely with the sublime emotion ...'[23]

All the elements of the romanticism of terror are here; but it will be observed that Blair's remarks contain a suggestion not found in the critics hitherto considered. Even Dennis and Welsted, impressed as they were by the Satanic books, did not suggest that their sublimity owed something to the character of the superior and courageous figure for which they provide the background. Blair said with Johnson, 'Adam is undoubtedly his hero';[24] but he considered that Satan 'in particular makes a striking figure and is indeed the best drawn character in the poem.'[25] What is more important, he regarded him with a wondering terror not unmixed with sympathetic admiration – an attitude whose emergence in the eighteenth century can also be traced.

IV

The critics and annotators who preceded Blair were certainly not without an interest in Satan; but they did not interpret his character sympathetically. Like Addison, who preferred him to Ulysses because he 'makes a much longer voyage ... puts in practice many more wiles and stratagems, and hides himself under a greater variety of shapes and appearances, all of which are severally detected to the great delight and surprise of the reader,' they remember that Satan is the enemy of God and man.[1] It is true that 'there is no single passage in the whole poem worked up to a greater sublimity' than the description of him; but, as Addison noted (and Johnson after him), Milton has taken pains to make his speeches 'big with absurdity' so that the religious reader will not be misled by his blasphemy.[2] Yet there is discernible in the early eighteenth century a tendency to humanize Satan, partly as a result of the neo-classical demand for probability and partly because of the contrast between Milton's figure and the mediaeval devil, which prepares the way for the nineteenth-century interpretation.

Dryden's insistence that the Devil was the hero of *Paradise Lost* has no real connection with this development.[3] It arose from a somewhat perverse distinction between epic and tragedy, and does not imply admiration. Indeed, Dryden's remarks tend in the opposite direction when he suggests that a Christian epic labours under a disadvantage in its machines because of the difficulty of making them human enough to be probable. This opinion was shared by Dennis,[4] who nevertheless thought that Milton had overcome the difficulty without making his devils, like the gods of Homer, so human as to be without the grandeur proper to spiritual beings: 'The passions and inclinations of the Grecian gods are downright human inclinations and affections. The passions of Milton's devils have enough of humanity in them to make them delightful, but then they have a great deal more to make them admirable, and may be said to be the true passions of devils.'[5]

It is strange that it is precisely this element of humanity in Milton's characterization which is increasingly emphasized by those critics who were also insisting on the horrible sublimity of the Satanic books.

Already in the edition of *Paradise Lost* in 1698, Hume (who had no admiration for the 'blasphemous boastings' and the 'cursed character' of the 'Father of Lies whom the Lord of Hosts had in derision') noted the difference between Satan and the traditional devil in commenting on an illustration:

> From verse 591 to 594 and from thence to this, the designer of Lucifer's picture prefixed to this first book should have taken the noble lineaments of his obscured and yet glorious, haughty looks. He should have expressed his furrowed face and faded check under those lofty brows of steadfast courage and of wary pride, vowing and waiting for revenge. If he had hit these lucky strikes, he might have spared his horns and asses' ears, so unsuitable to the description of the archangel that Milton has afforded him no hint of them.[6]

A similar contrast between Milton and Tasso was developed by Smith in the translation of Longinus:

> Tasso ... has opened a council of devils but his description of them is frivolous and puerile, savouring too much of old women's tales and the fantastic dreams of ignorance. He makes some of them walk upon the feet of beasts and dresses out their resemblance of a human head with twisting serpents instead of hair; horns sprout upon their foreheads ... His devil talks somewhat like Milton's, but looks not with half that terrible pomp, that height of obscured glory.[7]

And much the same opinion was expressed by the painter Richardson when he described how he would depict Satan:

> Devils are usually painted with horns, saucer eyes, ugly faces, tails, cloven-feet, &c. Milton's devils are no such. He must be read without such images. His are seen to be angels still, though scarred and disfigured. 'T is hard, impossible, to conceive a character of beauty proper to a blessed spirit ... More difficult yet is it to imagine a proper idea of a ruined archangel; nor Guido, nor Rafael has succeeded here ... Michael Angelo was more fit for it, and he has done vastly beyond any other and without falling deep into the common follies ... but still they are not what Milton has directed us to imagine. Tasso ... has been avoided by him here; for Tasso has gone into the horns, tails, &c. No man has ever thought in this (as in other respects) like Milton. O that he had painted! and as he conceived! What are we to do in this case? Let us imagine virgin beauty, with masculine strength and vigour, all in the utmost conceivable degree, the strength and vigour little

> impaired, but the beauty withered, ruined, by age, by disease, and scars, and by guile, envy, malice, rage, lust, grief, despair, &c. Then add vastness of proportion, and you have nearly one of Milton's devils, when dressed and armed in a suitable manner, not as an ancient Greek or Roman but in a habit odd and disagreeable, tattered, foul, &c ...[8]

Hume, Smith, and Richardson do not sympathize with Satan; nor are they concerned to develop any radical philosophical or psychological implications from the figure as they see it. Richardson's devil in rags and tatters is anything but a glorious hero; but he is – as in the remarks of Hume and Smith – recognizably the diabolically heroic figure of Milton's text. All three critics are intent on seeing what Milton has described; and because of the misrepresentation of illustrators, all three emphasize the human qualities through which Milton makes his Satan probable. As Newton said, he has followed Aristotle's principle and 'drawn Satan with some remains of beauty' and with 'some of the other perfections of an archangel' because 'a devil all made up of wickedness would be shocking to any reader or writer.'[9]

Yet the emphasis on Satan's probability slipped very easily into a suggestion of his humanity, especially when it was associated with the dreadful and heroic sublimity of the opening books. When in Newton's edition Thyer noted that Milton, 'describing the fierce and unrelenting spirit of Satan, seems very plainly to have copied after the picture that Aeschylus gives of Prometheus,'[10] he did not mean to anticipate Shelley's perversely paradoxical reading of the poem, but he gave a hint of things to come.

The emergence of the new view of Satan may be illustrated from the opinions expressed by James Beattie in writing of the sublimity of terror. Beattie clung to the notion that religion and goodness are the true sources of the sublime; but he left the path of Addison and Johnson to argue that 'a character may be sublime which is not completely good, nay, which is upon the whole bad; for the test of sublimity is not moral approbation but that pleasurable astonishment wherewith certain things strike the beholder.'

> Nay, even Satan, as Milton has represented him in *Paradise Lost,* though there are no qualities that can be called good in a moral view; nay, though every purpose of that wicked spirit is bent to evil and to that only; yet there is a grandeur of a ruined archangel; there is force able to contend with the most boisterous elements; and there is boldness which no power but what

> is Almighty can intimidate. These qualities are astonishing; and though we always detest his malignity, we are often compelled to admire that very greatness by which we are confounded and terrified.[11]

Beattie hastens to add that there is no blasphemy in this 'pleasurable astonishment' since we regard the figure 'not as the great enemy of our souls but as a fictitious being, and a mere poetical hero,' having no reason to think that the Devil 'has really that boldness, irresistible strength, and dignity of form which the poet ascribed to him.'[12] But the excuse is a lame one and suggests whistling in the dark; for Beattie, who thinks that 'in the style of dreadful magnificence, nothing is superior and scarce anything equal to Milton's representation of hell and chaos,' is on the point of echoing Satan's horrible cry.[13]

Blair does echo it; for he adds to the emergent view of Satan the element of sympathetic as well as terrified admiration. Addison had emphasized 'his pride, envy and revenge, obstinacy, despair, and impenitence'; Blair emphasizes his humanity:

> Milton has not described him such as we suppose an infernal spirit to be. He has, more suitably to his own purposes, given him a human, that is a mixed character, not altogether void of some good qualities. He is brave and faithful to his troops. In the midst of his impiety, he is not without remorse. He is even touched with pity for our first parents, and justifies himself in his design against them from the necessity of his situation. He is actuated by ambition and resentment, rather than by pure malice. In short, Milton's Satan is no worse than many a conspirator or factious chief that makes a figure in history.[14]

This is not very far from the contrast noted by Hume, Smith and Richardson, or from Newton's Aristotelian comment; but in Blair's apologetic selection of the extenuating features of Satan's character there is a difference of tone which arises from the element of sentiment in his attitude towards the rebellious angel – a fact made more significant by his academic moderation. With the transference of this ingredient from Paradise to Hell, the way is prepared for Shelley and the other dynamic Satanists of the nineteenth and twentieth centuries. Blair is not a Satanist; he thinks Adam the hero because he still believes with Addison in the validity of Milton's Christian principles. But Satan fascinates him, and seems worthy of pity and admiration; and when the principles which Milton erects against Satan (not only in theological disquisitions but in the description of Paradise and the dramatic account of the Fall) have ceased to be felt as facts, there will be nothing to hinder the triumph of the devil's party. Already Satan may begin to assume a further variety of shapes and appearances, stalking through literature (as Railo and Praz have shown) sometimes as Shedoni, sometimes as Manfred, sometimes as Prometheus, to the terrified delight of readers and with little fear of detection.

NOTES

[We reproduce here Barker's enumeration of notes, which starts at the beginning of each section – Eds.]

1 See E. Dowden, 'Milton and the Eighteenth Century,' and J.G. Robertson, 'Milton's Fame on the Continent' (*Proceedings of the British Academy* [3], 1907–8 [: 275–94; 319–40]); J.W. Good, *Studies in the Milton Tradition*, University of Illinois Studies in Language and Literature 1 ([Urbana, Ill.,] 1913); R.D. Havens, *Influence of Milton* [*on English Poetry*] ([Cambridge,] 1922); Ants Oras, *Milton's Editors and Commentators* [*from Patrick Hume to Henry John Todd, 1695–1801, A Study of Critical Views and Methods*] ([London,] 1931). To all of these I am indebted, and also to Professor A.S.P. Woodhouse, whose course in the Graduate School, The Origins of Romanticism, directed my attention to the subject several years ago.

2 S.H. Monk's *The Sublime: A Study of Critical Theories in the 18th Century* ([New York,] 1935), provides a very full account of the development of the principles in aesthetics. For Satanism in the late eighteenth and the nineteenth centuries, see E. Railo, *The Haunted Castle* ([London,] 1927); M. Praz, *The Romantic Agony* ([London,] 1933).

3 Joseph Addison, *Spectator*, no. 160. I have modernized the spelling in quotations throughout.

4 On the influence of the treatise *On the Sublime* ascribed to Dionysius Longinus, see Monk, *The Sublime*; [Thomas Rice] Henn, *Longinus and English Criticism* ([Cambridge,] 1934); A.F.B. Clark, *Boileau and the French Classical Critics in England* ([Paris,] 1925), 361–79.

5 Johnson said in his *Life* of Addison that the essays made 'readers of every class think it necessary to be pleased' with the epic. Addison's influence is apparent in nearly every eighteenth-century discussion of the poem, in Felton's, Blair's, Johnson's, and Voltaire's English version of his *Essays upon Epic Poetry*.

6 Addison, *Spectator*, no. 267.

7 Addison, *Spectator,* no. 297.
8 Addison, *Spectator,* no. 291.
9 Addison, *Spectator,* no. 279.
10 Addison, *Spectator,* no. 267.
11 Addison, *Spectator,* no. 279. The passage proceeds to the loves of Dido and Aeneas and of Adam and Eve before the Fall.
12 Addison, *Spectator,* no. 418; the eighth paper on the Imagination.
13 Addison, *Spectator,* no. 315.

Section II

1 John Dryden, *Essays,* [2 vols,] ed. Ker, [(Oxford, 1900)] 1:179; 2:29, 165.
2 Introduction to *Remarks upon 'Cato'* [(London, 1713)]; see also *Reflections upon ... an Essay upon Criticism* [(London, 1711)], 3, and [Harry Gilbert] Paul, *John Dennis*[: *His Life and Criticism* (New York, 1911)], 151, 194.
3 John Dennis, *Reflections,* 219.
4 John Dennis, *Proposals for Printing ... the Following Miscellaneous Tracts ...* ([London,] 1721), 2.
5 John Dennis, *Specimen,* prefatory to the *Grounds of Criticism*; quoted in Paul, *John Dennis,* 149.
6 [Dennis,] *Grounds of Criticism* (1704), in [Willard Higley] Durham [ed.], *Critical Essays of the 18th Century*[(London & New Haven, 1915), 143–211], 157.
7 See A.O. Lovejoy, 'The Parallel of Classicism and Deism,' *Modern Philology* [29.3 (1932), 281–99].
8 [Henry Felton,] *Dissertation on Reading the Classics*[, 4th ed.] ([London,] 1730), 192; first published 1713; see R.S. Crane, 'Imitation of Spenser and Milton in the Early 18th Century,' *Studies in Philology* 15[.2 (1918), 195–206]: 195.
9 [Felton, *Dissertation,*] 227.
10 [Dennis,] *Grounds of Criticism,* in Durham, [*Critical Essays,*] 145.
11 Ibid., 160.
12 [John Dennis,] *Advancement ... of Modern Poetry,* quoted in Paul, [*John Dennis,*] 135; and *Grounds of Criticism,* [in Durham, *Critical Essays,*] 162.
13 [John Dennis,] *Miscellanies in Prose and Verse* (1693), quoted in Paul, [*John Dennis,*] 5.
14 [Dennis,] *Grounds of Criticism,* [in Durham, *Critical Essays,*] 158.
15 [Dennis] quoted in Paul, [*John Dennis,*] 193.
16 [Dennis,] *Reflections,* [in Durham, *Critical Essays,*] 234.

Section III

1 Monk, *The Sublime*, 52.
2 [Jonathan Richardson,] 'The Connoisseur: An Essay on the Whole Art of Criticism' (first published 1719); *The Works of Jonathan Richardson* ([London,] 1792), 116.
3 [Jonathan Richardson, father and son,] *Explanatory Remarks and Notes on 'Paradise Lost'* ([London,] 1734), clii, cxlvii.
4 [Paul Rolli,] *Remarks upon M. Voltaire's Essay upon Epic Poetry* ([London,] 1728), 69.
5 Oras, *Milton's Editors*, 196.
6 Welsted also quotes some passages from Spenser and Shakespeare, Smith from Shakespeare.
7 Welsted[, trans.], *The Works of D. Longinus[: On the Sublime]* ([London,] 1712), 151; Smith, *Dionysius Longinus on the Sublime* ([London,] 1770), 38.
8 [Welsted, *Works of D. Longinus*,] 186.
9 Ibid., 148.
10 Ibid., 186.
11 Ibid., 156.
12 I cannot forbear to quote Smith's delightful remarks on our first parents: 'Adam and Eve are the finest picture of conjugal love that ever was drawn. In them it is true warmth of affection, without violence or fury of passion; a sweet and reasonable tenderness, without any cloying or insipid fondness. In its serenity and sunshine, it is noble, amiable, endearing, and innocent. When it jars and goes out of tune, as on some occasions it will, there is anger and resentment. He is gloomy; she complains and weeps; yet love has still its force. Eve knows how to submit, and Adam to forgive. We are pleased that they have quarreled when we see the agreeable manner in which they are reconciled. They have enjoyed prosperity and will share adversity together' (52–3). Nothing could be more fatuous; and nothing could better illustrate the insensibility of the eighteenth century to Milton's conception of the Fall than this reference to it by a Dean of Chester as one of those unfortunate misunderstandings that sometimes occur in the best regulated of families. It is this failure to comprehend the significance of Milton's epic which accounts for the emergence in the eighteenth century, and the continuance in the nineteenth and twentieth, of the Satanic interpretation.
13 [Smith,] *Dionysius Longinus*, 44, 78.
14 Ibid., 26.
15 Quoted in Paul, [*John Dennis*,] 134.

16 [Edmund Burke,] *A Philosophical Inquiry in the Origin of Our Ideas of the Sublime and Beautiful* ([London,] 1757), part 1, section 7.
17 Ibid., part 2, section 4.
18 Ibid., part 2, section 3.
19 See Railo, [*The Haunted Castle*] ([London,] 1927).
20 [Hugh Blair,] *Lectures on Rhetoric*[, 2 vols.]([London,] 1783), 1:58–9.
21 Ibid., 2:471.
22 Ibid., 2:474.
23 Ibid., 1:69.
24 Ibid., 2:422.
25 Ibid., 2:472.

Section IV

1 [Addison,] *Spectator*, no. 273.
2 Ibid., no. 303.
3 [Dryden,] *Essays*, ed. Ker, 2:165.
4 [Dennis,] *Proposals*, 17.
5 [Dennis,] *Grounds of Criticism*, in Durham, [*Critical Essays*,] 205.
6 *Paradise Lost* (1698), note on 1.603.
7 [Smith, *Dionysius Longinus*,] 44–5.
8 [Richardson, father and son, *Explanatory Remarks*,] note on 1.600.
9 [Thomas Newton, ed.,] *Paradise Lost* ([London,] 1778), note on 2.483.
The representations of Satan in the illustrated editions of the epic deserve comment. In spite of the remarks quoted above, the horns and asses' ears of the 1695 edition printed by Tho. Hodgkin for Jacob Tonson reappear in Tonson's edition of 1707 and even in John Marchant's of 1751. In the 1764 edition of L. Hawes and others, Satan is without these marks, but the figure is otherwise unchanged and the face is very ugly, a fault perhaps of the engraver since Adam and Eve are themselves not very attractive. By the 1794 edition of J. and H. Richter, Satan has become Herculean, though with black, serpentine hair. In the editions of 1802 by F.J. Du Roveray, and 1808 by J. Johnson and others, the figure is like Blake's, a Grecian god with fair, curled locks; and in Septimus Prowett's edition of 1827, John Martin presents a marvellously romantic Paradise and a Satan who is a youth of great strength and pure white wings, helmeted as an oriental warrior, and distinguishable from the angels only by his fearful frown and his gloom of countenance.
10 [Newton, ed., *Paradise Lost*,] note on 1.94.
11 [James Beattie,] 'Illustrations on Sublimity,' *Dissertations Moral and Critical* ([London,] 1783), 612.

12 Ibid., 613.

13 Ibid., 622.

14 [Blair, *Lectures on Rhetoric*,] 2: 472–3. This is of course the counterpart of the development in Shakespearean criticism apparent in Morgann's *Dramatic Character of Falstaff*, Mackenzie's comments on *Hamlet*, and to some extent Johnson's notes.

REFLECTION

8 The Study of Milton at the University of Toronto in the Mid-Twentieth Century

HUGH MACCALLUM

The 1950s were interesting years in which to study Milton at the University of Toronto. Close to the heart of the undergraduate program in English was a third-year course on Spenser and Milton that was taught at the four colleges included in the university at that time. (In 1949–50 I studied Milton for the first time in a section of this course taught by Arthur Barker, of whom more later.) The graduate Milton course was given by A.S.P. Woodhouse, who was Head of the English Department at University College and also Head of the Graduate Department of English. Woodhouse began teaching at the University of Toronto in 1928, and continued until his retirement in 1963. He brought to his study of Renaissance and Romantic literature a combination of religious, philosophical, and literary insight coupled with historical knowledge.[1] In teaching as well as writing he was a master of precise and discriminating definition: he could reduce a large and difficult subject to a carefully balanced and integrated description. Yet his style was marked by intellectual energy, judicious evaluation, and wit.

Over the mantel in Woodhouse's office, among the unstable piles of books, were portraits of Samuel Johnson and Matthew Arnold. This was the scene where he met his graduate classes. He had written lectures in a number of notebooks with black covers and sometimes he read from them, but with such dramatic emphasis that there was a sense of performance. Frequently, too, one realized that he had put aside his text without any change of pace. If he liked a student essay that was being read in class, he would interrupt repeatedly, adding a running commentary. Sometimes he read Milton's poetry with high feeling, a process that was well described by a former student and colleague: 'the measured liturgical tones, the emotion controlled and deepened by the sense of form, the huge relish and gusto of it all.'[2]

Another colleague observed that Woodhouse's own literary interests were as firm as were his literary principles and suspicion of the 'wilder vicissitudes of taste,' but any demonstration of vitality, independence, learning, could win his respect and, often, interest.[3] Woodhouse was an apologist for the historical method in literary studies. He believed that literary criticism must deal with the experience, the thought, and the art of the poet, showing each against the age as well as in itself. Arguing against the New Critics in 1950, he explains that historical criticism is concerned with the application of the results of research to the interpretation of a work or an author.[4] He will not be intimidated by 'the autobiographical fallacy' or 'the personal heresy.' One does not get rid of the temporal by ignoring it. Critics who reduce themselves to the level of the ordinary reader neglect their responsibility, which is to uncover the assumptions on which the poet wrote. Otherwise, he observes, false assumptions will always fill the vacuum where true assumptions are lacking. Historical criticism proceeds by hypothesis to explore the world of the poet and his audience; not a mere corrective, it provides new and fruitful ways of looking at the poem under examination, and enables us to understand the terms in which the author did his thinking. Resisting the temptation to bring everything for judgment to the bar of our own age and our own temperament, historical study 'is the necessary preliminary if the judgement of value is itself to be valuable.'[5]

His first publication on Milton introduced the subject of liberty,[6] which was to be a ground-note of Milton studies at the University of Toronto. His position is that Milton has a potent, individualistic conception of liberty, but that the aristocratic principle evident in both his Protestant Christianity and his classical humanism prevents him from adding equality to liberty, and thus bars the road to democracy. Three years later he published *Puritanism and Liberty: Being the Army Debates (1647–9) from the Clarke Manuscripts with Supplementary Documents.*[7] The 100-page introduction remains an indispensable guide to English Puritanism. His unusual powers of summary and condensation are used to provide a map of the varieties of thought and experience within Puritanism. He recognizes that Puritanism is not a unity, but a continuity, and he keeps this idea before the reader as he delineates the features of the Puritan mind. He characterizes with precision the dynamism which controls the growth of the Puritan revolution: the conflict between the passionate zeal for reform and the equally passionate concern for liberty. In the course of this exposition three doctrines or principles are introduced that are crucial to his analysis and to his later criticism.

The first is the dogma of the two orders of nature and grace. Reformation writers assign all experience to one of these two levels. The natural order includes man insofar as he is an inhabitant of the natural world and apprehends that world through the use of reason. While reason can produce natural ethics and even natural religion, it is not adequate to grasp the order of grace, which includes all that pertains to revealed religion and to man's salvation under both the law and the gospel. God rules over both orders, but he does so by different dispensations and to different ends. Only the elect belong to the order of grace. To this a second doctrine can be added. In radical Puritan thought the spiritual is sometimes separated from the secular, the order of grace from the order of nature. This separation Woodhouse names the 'principle of segregation.' Thoroughly applied, it imposes limits on the intrusion of dogma into secular life, and thus requires the separation of state and church. A purely spiritual view of the church is set against a purely secular view of the state. Here Woodhouse sees an opportunity for democracy, for in practice this segregation cannot mean the cessation of all influence. The influence must now work by analogy or parallelism. The liberty and equality of the elect pose a powerful example to the natural man, to the free church, and to the free state.

The third doctrine is closely related in its operation to the first two. Christian liberty is a radical notion based on St Paul and developed by some Reformers, notably Luther. At the heart of the idea is the contrast between the Mosaic law and the gospel. The law, with its impossible demand of obedience, is abrogated by Christ, whose coming replaced it by the liberty declared in the gospel. That liberty is dependent on the inward law of love and the guidance of the spirit.

Woodhouse has the ability, as Roy Daniells once observed, to make ideas more real than facts. In spite of his close attention to religious ideas there is never any doubt of his desire for historical objectivity. His attitude was suggested by a remark he made to Ernest Sirluck in which he compared himself to a flying buttress, outside the Anglican church, but supporting it.[8]

The ideas I have been summarizing serve to interpret Milton's art. In 'The Argument of Milton's *Comus*,'[9] Woodhouse sets out the intellectual frame of reference of the masque in terms of the order of nature and the order of grace. The virtues celebrated in the masque form a scale that leads from one order to the other. The epilogue introduces for the first time the notion of Christian liberty. These historical considerations, supplemented by references to Milton's experience and to the example of Spenser, become the way to a better literary appreciation of the work. Woodhouse pays close attention to detail in his treatment of poetry, but his starting point is usually theme, structure, and patterning. Milton, he emphasizes, was a poet who showed his originality by recreating traditional forms. In his treatments of the major poems, Woodhouse proceeds by drawing comparisons with classical examples, pointing repeatedly to the ways in which Milton transforms the genres that he employs. The idea of heroism, too, is transformed. Nature and grace play a part in these poems about earlier dispensations, as do the law of nature and the idea of liberty. As Woodhouse sees it, when Milton writes about liberty in his true medium, poetry, the defects of his temper are reviewed and conscientiously corrected. The result and perfect symbol of Milton's feeling for liberty is found in poetic creation.[10]

I joined the English Department at University College in 1959. Like others, I realized that Woodhouse intended to draw his interpretations of Milton's poetry and prose – published in essays spread over nearly three decades – into a book. A delay was occasioned by a lecture series he gave for the Frank L. Weil Institute for Studies in Religion and the Humanities in which he treated religion and poetry in England from Spenser to Eliot and Auden. The lectures were published as *The Poet and His Faith.*[11] After his sudden death in 1964, I edited the manuscript of his Milton project, supplementing where necessary with essays previously published. The result was *The Heavenly Muse: A Preface to Milton.* Another project that was unfinished at his death was volume 2 of *A Variorum Commentary on the Poems of John Milton: The Minor English Poems,*[12] which was completed by his friend Douglas Bush. While the two men had been undergraduates at the University of Toronto, they had been at different colleges. Their friendship was established when they were graduate students at Harvard and continued throughout their careers, fed by the respect each had for the scholarship of the other.

Other influences were at play in our thoughts about Milton and history. Two require particular mention. I recall Woodhouse emphasizing the importance of a recent book by Balachandra Rajan called *'Paradise Lost' and the Seventeenth Century Reader.* Rajan was in these years a diplomat in the Indian Foreign Service. He returned to academic life at the University of Delhi in 1961, and in 1966 moved to Canada and to the University of Western Ontario. His study of *Paradise Lost* shows both what would have been accessible to Milton's unlearned contemporaries and the details and nuances that would have invited them into learning. Woodhouse approved of this kind of investigation of assumptions and expectations, and wrote in a review of the book that the author 'has been able to make a notable contribution to our understanding of *Paradise Lost* and, indirectly, to administer a check to those who are more prone to attack than to understand.'[13] Another study that was recommended by Woodhouse was a Toronto doctoral thesis by Ernest Sirluck, 'Milton and the Law of Nature.'[14] At the time Sirluck was at the University of Chicago; he would come back to the University of Toronto in 1962, and leave in 1970 to become president of the University of Manitoba. His study of Milton's treatment of the law of nature explains certain seeming inconsistencies in terms of tactics in the pamphlet wars, and anticipates his rich introduction to the second volume of the Yale edition of the *Complete Prose Works of John Milton*, as well as his essays on the prose.

At the time about which I write the Head of the English Department at Trinity College, University of Toronto, was Arthur E. Barker. After twenty-five years at Toronto, Barker was to leave in 1960 for the University of Illinois where he spent a decade before joining the staff at the University of Western Ontario. Barker's interest in Milton was sealed by his master's thesis entitled 'Milton and the Struggle for Liberty,' which was directed by Woodhouse. After completing a doctoral thesis on Milton at the University of London, Barker wrote *Milton and the Puritan Dilemma*.[15] This detailed study of Milton's thought carefully traces his developing conception of liberty, viewing the process at each stage in the contexts provided by the religious and political discourse of the age. Milton could strike an uneasy alliance with the Presbyterians in his anti-episcopal tracts as he urges the reform of the church and nation, but toward the end of the Protectorate he finds himself among the Puritan extremists. Barker notes that in the later tracts the magistrate wields power in civil but not in religious matters, and that the minister relies on scripture and the illumination of the spirit rather than on a university education. Like Woodhouse, Barker concludes that there are limits to Milton's separation of church and state. While Milton thought of liberty in terms of a humanistic conception of reason, he nonetheless found it impossible to separate the good of the state from Christianity. The extent of the religious liberty which a Christian magistrate might permit and men might claim depends on the regeneration of the natural faculties of the individual. Milton's theory of regeneration thus provides the basis for his interpretation of Christian liberty. Here Barker adds a new element to the analysis of that liberty by the way he emphasizes regeneration, examining Milton's view of the subject in his theological tract, *De doctrina Christiana*.

The poetry is explored by Barker in various essays.[16] Like Woodhouse, he emphasizes theme, structure, and patterning. Thus he provides a definitive analysis of Milton's reworking of *Paradise Lost* from ten books to twelve, and he uses the structural divisions so revealed in his exposition of the importance of regeneration to the epic. The later poems are all representations of experience in pre-Christian dispensations, and yet each provides a mimesis of the doctrine of regeneration. Barker concludes that Milton's theory of regeneration and his theory of poetry are inseparable.

Barker normally taught Milton in the undergraduate course and English Humanism (with emphasis on Sir Thomas More) in graduate seminars. A very fine teacher, one of his skills lay in identifying the special interest of each member of the seminar, and then drawing that out while ensuring that the individual also worked on some quite different project. His seminars became tightly knit groups that pursued selected themes with intensity and pertinacity. While Barker did not to my knowledge teach Milton at the graduate level while he was at Toronto, his supervision included theses on Milton that he undertook jointly with Woodhouse.[17]

Northrop Frye became a member of the faculty at Victoria College in 1939, a position he held for more than fifty years. He taught Milton to undergraduates, and Milton was a strong presence in his famous graduate course on literary symbolism and in his writing. His first book, *Fearful Symmetry: A Study of William Blake*, contains many passages on Milton, and in 1951 he published an introduction to the Rheinhart Edition of *'Paradise Lost' and Selected Poetry and Prose* that has sections on the early poetry, on themes in the prose, and on the major poems. The views that he was developing through the 1950s concerning Milton were given expression in publications of that decade and the next.[18] After 1973 he did not write any further essays on Milton, but his later books have many references to the poet, who continued to play an important role in his thought.

The continuity between teaching and publishing was important to Frye. In the modest disclaimer with which he opened a lecture series at Huron College in 1963 he said that while he did not intend to add to or alter the general shape of Milton scholarship, he had been teaching Milton long enough 'to have incorporated him as a central part of my own literary experience.'[19] His classes were spellbinding. There was a breathtaking sense of discovery, of slicing easily through Gordian knots of criticism, and yet at the same time the reassurance of an unfolding and coherent design. Frye did not usually read longer passages in class, for his remarkable memory enabled him to cite short passages at will, weaving them economically into his argument. When he did perform a longer passage his tone was impersonal, a kind of incantation. His seminars and classes also made a more explicit use of diagrams (levels and circles) than his written studies, although in the latter such organizing structures often have a ghostly presence.

Frye is less concerned with political and social history than Woodhouse and Barker, and yet when such history is relevant to his argument he uses it forcefully. He often draws on Milton's prose and occasionally on the writing of his contemporaries, but his aim is to place Milton's poetry within a larger literary and mythic perspective. For Frye historical criticism is concerned with culture, and culture itself is viewed primarily, though not exclusively, in literary terms. Archetypal criticism, in particular, corrects and gives ethical direction to historical criticism.[20] The treatment of *Lycidas,* for example, explores a literary context that includes examples of the pastoral elegy written after as well as before Milton's monody. The archetypes which the poem uses, he argues, are symbols that recur regularly in many poems of its kind. More important than other historical contexts is that provided by literature as an order of words. *Paradise Lost,* too, is understood in terms of genre and convention. As well as being an epic it is also, like the Bible, encyclopedic. After exploring these two strands in some detail and adding several subgenres, he comes to the conclusion that the Arcadian and pastoral elements in the poem direct attention to the kind of domestic liberty that was Milton's own sphere.

As well as demonstrating the importance of convention through reference and allusion, Frye draws each of the late poems together and demonstrates its unity. Among the tools he uses in this endeavour are some which recall those of Woodhouse, but with a shift from idea and conceptual framework to image and archetype. They include the distinction between the law and the gospel, parody, spatial and temporal elements, the traditional idea of the four levels of existence, and typology. The eight lectures and essays that Frye produced on Milton provide a compact understanding of the major poems in their literary context while at the same time contributing to Frye's enunciation of his literary principles.

Woodhouse and Barker are very close in their practice of historical method. Both scholars trace the evolving position of the poet against the background provided by the climate of opinion and with frequent recourse to biography and political events. Both see Milton as a deliberate artist who finds answers in his poetry to issues that proved insoluble in the prose. This doesn't mean that the poetry lacks the presence of conflict, but that the poet finds organizing structures to contain it. Frye belongs to a different critical camp. He has a place for historical criticism in his system, but it is contained within an order of words that embraces all literature and its archetypes and myths. Frye is less likely to view the poem as a resolution of a problem in the poet's life, and more likely to see it as the resolution of problems arising from the literary context. There is an element of surprise, then, in the recognition that Frye, Woodhouse, and Barker, are in agreement about many central features of Milton's poetry. All three explore his original treatment of genres and find in his poems a rich, imaginative unity. Milton, we might conclude, not only taught his seventeenth-century readers, but his modern ones too.

I have concentrated on the University of Toronto, but of course there were scholars at other Canadian universities who were writing about Milton and to whom a historical perspective was important. Malcolm Ross, Roy Daniells, and Watson Kirkonnell, among others, all made significant contributions to the historical approach to Milton. That approach is now well established, and awaiting further historicisms.

NOTES

1 For a fine overview of A.S.P. Woodhouse's scholarship, see Douglas Bush, 'A.S.P. Woodhouse: Scholar, Critic, Humanist,' in *Essays in English Literature from the Renaissance to the Victorian Age*, ed. Millar Maclure and F.W. Watt (Toronto, 1964), 320–33. The same volume also contains 'Publications of A.S.P. Woodhouse,' by M.H.M. Mackinnon, 334–9.

2 Claude Bissell in an address given at a memorial service for A.S.P. Woodhouse in West Hall, University College, 31 October 1964.

3 Memorial service address, 31 October 1964.

4 Woodhouse, 'The Historical Criticism of Milton,' *PMLA* 66 (1951): 1033. This paper was read before the Milton Group of the Modern Language Association of America on 28 December 1950.

5 Woodhouse, *The Heavenly Muse: A Preface to Milton* (Toronto, 1972), 99.

6 Woodhouse, 'Milton, Puritanism and Liberty,' *UTQ* 4 (1934–5): 483–513.

7 Woodhouse, *Puritanism and Liberty* (London, 1938; 2nd ed., Chicago, 1951, repr., 1965).

8 Ernest Sirluck, *First Generation: An Autobiography* (Toronto, 1996), 74. Sirluck provides a vivid account of Woodhouse as a teacher.
9 Woodhouse, 'The Argument of Milton's *Comus*,' *UTQ* 11 (1941–2): 46–71.
10 *The Heavenly Muse*, 122–3.
11 Woodhouse, *The Poet and His Faith* (Chicago, 1965).
12 Woodhouse and Bush, eds, *A Variorum Commentary on the Poems of John Milton*, vol. 2 part 3 (New York, 1972).
13 Woodhouse, 'Milton and His Readers,' *UTQ* 18 (1948–49): 205.
14 Sirluck, 'Milton and the Law of Nature' (PhD diss., University of Toronto, 1948).
15 Arthur E. Barker, *Milton and the Puritan Dilemma* (Toronto, 1942, repr. 1945, 1964, 1971).
16 Among the most important of Barker's essays on Milton's poetry are 'The Pattern of Milton's *Nativity Ode*,' *UTQ* 10 (1941): 167–81; 'Structural Pattern in *Paradise Lost*,' *Philological Quarterly* 28 (1949): 17–30; 'Structural and Doctrinal Pattern in Milton's Later Poems,' in *Essays in English Literature*, 169–94; '*Paradise Lost*: The Relevance of Regeneration,' in *'Paradise Lost': A Tercentenary Tribute*, ed. B. Rajan (Toronto, 1969), 48–78; and 'Calm Regained through Passion Spent: The Conclusions of the Miltonic Effort,' in *The Prison and the Pinnacle: Papers to Commemorate the Tercentenary of 'Paradise Regained' and 'Samson Agonistes*,' ed. B. Rajan (Toronto, 1973), 3–43. For further studies, see Jane Couchman, 'Selected List of Publications and Lectures of Arthur Edward Barker,' in *Familiar Colloquy: Essays Presented to Arthur Edward Barker*, ed. Patricia Bruckmann (Ottawa, 1978), 227–30.
17 Barker was second reader for Sirluck's MA thesis 'Milton's Political Thought' (1941) and for his PhD thesis 'Milton and the Law of Nature' (1948). He also co-supervised my 'Milton and the Study of Scripture' (PhD diss., University of Toronto, 1959).
18 Northrop Frye, *'Paradise Lost' and Selected Poetry and Prose* (New York, 1951); *The Return of Eden* (Toronto, 1965). Three essays concern Milton: 1) 'Literature as Context: Milton's *Lycidas*,' in *Proceedings of the Second Congress of the International Comparative Literature Association*, University of North Carolina Studies in Comparative Literature 23 (1959): 44–55, reprinted above; 2) 'The Revelation to Eve,' in *'Paradise Lost': A Tercentenary Tribute*, 18–47, repr. in *The Stubborn Structure* (Ithaca, NY, 1970); and 3) 'Agon and Logos,' in *The Prison and the Pinnacle*, 135–63, repr. in *Spiritus Mundi* (Bloomington, 1976). All but one of these publications was given first as a public lecture or a lecture series (the exception is the fifth chapter of *The Return of Eden*, which appeared first in print as 'The Typology of *Paradise*

Regained,' *MP* 53 [1956]: 227–38). See Robert D. Denham, *Northrop Frye: An Annotated Bibliography of Primary and Secondary Sources* (Toronto, 1987); and Angela Esterhammer, ed., *Northrop Frye on Milton and Blake*, vol. 16 of *Collected Works of Northrop Frye* (Toronto, 2005).

19 Frye, *Return of Eden*, 3–4.

20 Frye, *Anatomy of Criticism* (Princeton, NJ, 1957), 346.

NEW ARTICLES

9 Douglas Bush in His Time and Ours

JOHN LEONARD

When Douglas Bush delivered the Alexander Lectures at the University of Toronto in 1939, he began his first lecture, 'Modern Theories of the Renaissance,' with a gracious compliment to his alma mater. 'It is a satisfaction to remember,' he said, 'in an educational world increasingly dominated by gentiles, that the University of Toronto remains a stronghold of the humanities.' 'We whose trade is lecturing,' he continued, 'loathe nothing so much as listening to other men's lectures, and I appreciate the active benevolence and fortitude which my former preceptors and friends have shown in turning out so gallantly today.' At this point he must surely have looked around the room with its many familiar faces and made eye contact with his 'former preceptors and friends' as he drew a witty analogy. 'Like Helen on the wall of Troy,' he quipped, 'a Helen who has at least launched a thousand foot-notes, I can look around and name the leaders of Greece.' The joke is funny but it also warrants attention as a literary allusion. Bush was a master of allusion. One of his finest critical essays (we shall return to it) bears the title 'Ironic and Ambiguous Allusion in *Paradise Lost*.' 'Launched a thousand' clearly echoes Marlowe, but it is a less obvious allusion to Homer that matters most. Bush is recalling that moment in the *Iliad*, just before the single combat of Paris and Menelaus, when Priam, seated 'on the wall of Troy,' asks Helen to sit beside him and name the Greek leaders as she points them out. Bush's next sentence makes the reference clear: 'And, as Helen missed Castor and Pollux, I miss one who towered above others by his white head and broad shoulders, and whose voice when he spoke was like the snowflakes of winter.'[1]

This beautifully compresses three moments from the same long Homeric passage (*Iliad* 3.161–244). Priam asks Helen to identify the tallest Greek hero [Ajax]: 'Who then is this other Achaian of power and stature / towering above the Argives by head and broad shoulders?' (3.226–7). Bush adds the epithet 'white' ('white head and broad shoulders') because he is thinking of a specific white-haired person, but 'white' then leads into a lovely simile: 'whose voice when he spoke was like the snowflakes of winter.' This too is Homeric. Antenor, in the same passage, compares Menelaus to Odysseus and notes that while Menelaus is more physically impressive, none could compare with Odysseus when he 'let the great voice go from his chest, and the words came / drifting down like the winter snows' (3.221–3). But it is the third Homeric element in Bush's allusion that is most moving. Having surveyed the Greek army, Helen remarks the absence of her brothers Castor and Pollux and sadly conjectures that they did not join the expedition against Troy, '"dreading the words of shame and all the reproach that is on me." / So she spoke, but the teeming earth lay already upon them / away in Lakedaimon, the beloved land of their fathers' (3.242–4).[2] Bush omits these lines, but they are the heart of his allusion and he expected his audience ('a stronghold of the humanities') to remember them. What had at first sounded like jocular self-deprecation ('launched a thousand foot-notes') turns with exquisite tact and timing into a poignant tribute to one of Bush's old teachers, probably the classicist A.J. Bell, who had died seven years before Bush delivered his lecture.[3]

The allusion is magnificent, but (as is the way of allusions) it also admits ironies and ambiguities. Specifically, it is hard to tell how Canada fits in. Bush seems out of place as he gazes from 'the wall of Troy' upon 'the leaders of Greece' who have turned out 'so gallantly.' Homer's strong-greaved Achaians came to raze Troy and (re)capture Helen, but *this* Helen sees hospitable hosts, not an invading host. The 'stronghold of the humanities' is under threat, but not from the far-famed Torontonians. They are its gallant defenders. The encroaching 'gentiles' are somewhere else. (In his fourth lecture Bush will locate them in the Faculty of Social Science.) To pursue these tangents may be to inquire too curiously, but the simile of 'snowflakes' encourages a Canadian connection. I suggest that one of the reasons why Bush was drawn to Helen when speaking about Canada was that he, like Helen, was torn between two homes. Helen, gazing upon the Greeks, regrets 'forsaking my chamber, my kinsmen, / my grown child, and the loveliness of girls my own age' (3.174–5). Bush's allusion is repining rather than regretful, but it shares Helen's nostalgia even though it declines to say where home is. Bush speaks of 'Helen on the wall,' not 'Helen of Troy' or 'Helen of

Sparta.' His disorientation is only natural. He spent much of his life in the United States, and most of his career at Harvard. Whatever his sense of personal identity, his institutional loyalty was American. If there is such a thing as a distinctive Canadian tradition or 'voice' in Milton criticism (and it is far from certain that there is), Bush's relationship to it is inevitably complex.

Addressing an American audience, Bush sounds less personal, but also more sure of where he stands. *'Paradise Lost' in Our Time* began as the Messenger Lectures on the Evolution of Civilization, delivered at Cornell University in the fall term of 1944. Like any good lecturer, Bush is aware of his audience, who are mostly American. He repeatedly compares American and British responses to Milton, usually to make the point that most anti-Miltonists are British. This is how he justifies his own intervention in the debate:

> Since this hostility to Milton had developed almost wholly in his own country, and since such Englishmen as Messrs. Tillyard, Charles Williams, C.S. Lewis, and R.W. Chambers – not to mention the work of American scholars – have written sensitive and cogent expositions and defenses of Milton, it may be said, or thought, that there can be no occasion for another and inevitably less sensitive and cogent defense. There is no adequate reply to that. But by way of extenuation, one may say, first, that one has one's own view of Milton and feels moved to express it; secondly, that most 'general readers' here as well as in England seem to rest in the nineteenth-century notion of verbal and musical beauties divorced from obsolete substance; and, thirdly, that a good many bright American undergraduates have been infected by the modernist reaction.[4]

Bush's prime concern is to protect 'American undergraduates' from the British contagion. Naturally, he does not make the point that bluntly. He duly notes some exceptions to the prevailing British 'hostility' ('Messrs. Tillyard, Charles Williams, C.S. Lewis, and R.W. Chambers'), but he also gives the Milton controversy the flavour of a trans-Atlantic dispute.

This binary construction soon runs into difficulty, however, when he is forced to name two of Milton's most hostile critics: Ezra Pound and T.S. Eliot. The latter had become a British subject in 1927, so Bush is able to treat him as one. Pound presents more of a problem. Rather than address it directly, Bush prefers to dismiss Pound as an aberration. 'We might begin,' he writes, 'by naming Mr. Ezra Pound, though we shall pass him by, since his notion of Milton is not of much more value than his notion of, say, his own learning or of Fascism' (6). A little later, when discussing Eliot's notorious claim that '"the only jury of judgement is that of the ablest poetical practitioners" of his own time,' Bush again takes a shot at Pound: 'Who make up this great tribunal Mr. Eliot does not indicate. The only modern poet mentioned in the essay is Mr. Pound, whose infallibility we may be forgiven for doubting' (14). Such sternness is out of character for Bush, but it was understandable in 1945, when Pound's treasonous radio broadcasts were a recent and bitter memory.

The shadow of the Second World War hangs over much of *'Paradise Lost' in Our Time.* Bush frequently has recourse to military metaphors. 'The active campaign against Milton,' he writes at one point, 'has been conducted by younger guerrilla warriors' (6). Bush identifies the chief adversary as Eliot, whom he always treats with respect. 'Whatever the motives of Mr. Eliot's camp followers,' Bush writes, 'his own sniping at Milton has been a kind of oblique – and quite needless – justification of his own poetry' (8). Two pages later Eliot is promoted from sniper to one-man army: 'a commando raid by Mr. Eliot is equivalent to [a] full-scale invasion' (10). These metaphors sound odd at the present time, when critics often speak slightingly of the mid twentieth-century 'Milton controversy.' I have heard more than one critic call it 'a storm in a teacup.' For Bush, however, the debate about Milton was an extension of the global conflict still raging when he addressed his Cornell audience. Early in his first lecture he issues this provocative affirmation of Milton's importance: 'If there be any people who think that the rise or fall of Milton's fame is not of much moment in a war-torn world, we may remember that poetry has outlived many wars and that Milton is one of the great portions of that heritage for which the war has been fought' (2). Writing at a time when the Allied victory was in sight, Bush takes comfort from the thought that Milton too will prevail. 'There is indeed ground for belief,' he writes, 'that the righting of our poetical perspective was under way before the war began, and that the war will be found to have completed the process. Viewed against the scope and stress of a world conflict, Milton's stature, and Donne's, somehow assume their true proportions.' Bush is not primarily concerned to denigrate what he calls 'the cult of Donne.' 'I have as much admiration for Donne,' he writes, 'as is good for anyone' (5). It is nevertheless clear that he sees Donne as a lesser poet than Milton, and he believes that the war will reaffirm their relative merits (as, arguably, it did), and at the end of his final chapter he goes so far as to hope that the war will re-establish the importance of the arts and humanities in general (as it did not). 'We all hope,' he writes, 'and many believe, that the war will be followed by a return to the humanities, a return inspired, not by the notion that we can now afford useless luxuries again, but by the recognition that our modern worship of science and technology has revealed its inadequacy, and that in losing hold of the classical-Christian tradition we have lost our way' (117).

It is easy to find fault with statements like these. At their worst, Bush's references to the war degenerate into self-parody. He is least persuasive when he evokes topical events in an attempt to discredit Milton's Satan. He has no patience with George Rostrevor Hamilton, who had recently defended Satan against the moral strictures of C.S. Lewis. Bush leaps immediately to Lewis's defence. 'Mr. Hamilton,' he writes, 'does not seem to understand that a poet can be, or could be, passionate in his celebration of Law and Order' (62). 'Milton was a great rebel,' Bush admits, but then again, 'he was not.' Milton was 'a rebel like his own Abdiel, the faithful angel' (63). Satan is full 'of nothing but egoistic pride.' Drawing an analogy with his own time, Bush finds in Satan 'the spirit of Hitler': Satan's courage is 'the courage of a wolf at bay, of Hitler again' (70); Satan weeping before his defeated legions is like 'Hitler explaining his later campaigns'; Milton likens 'Satan to a Sultan,' the seventeenth-century 'equivalent of Hitler' (72). There is a strong element of propaganda in all this. Hell does in some ways resemble a fascist rally, and Milton in his prose does deplore 'the Turkish Tyranny,' but Sultans were not 'the equivalent of Hitler.' The Sultan Solimano in Tasso's *Gerusalemme Liberata* is noble as well as cruel. Bush uses Hitler's name to foreclose debate. Empson, writing in 1961, may have had Bush in mind when he deplored 'the pro-Christian polemic' of Milton criticism of the 1940s, which was 'very like the wartime propaganda then current.'[5]

Bush nevertheless eschews the worst excesses of some of his contemporaries. He is justly suspicious of G. Wilson Knight's crude patriotism. Knight had joined the chorus of anti-Miltonists in the 1930s, but turned coat in 1942 when he tried to claim Milton's high moral seriousness for the British war effort. The following is typical of his *Chariot of Wrath: The Message of John Milton to Democracy at War*: 'Satan's sense of injustice under the enthronement of Messiah as God's vice-regent reflects Germany's view of Great Britain's ascendancy ... Satan, like Hitler, is worshipped "as a god" ... Satan's legions attend their leader like hordes of black-uniformed Nazis gathered ... to hear Hitler speak at Nuremberg.'[6]

Bush's objection is not to the sentiments (which he shared), but to the opportunistic way in which Knight makes Milton their vehicle. 'Mr. Wilson Knight,' he coolly observes,

> is a fire worshiper whom *Paradise Lost* leaves cold, or at least with a mixture of chills and fever. In 1939 Mr. Knight produced a long critique, mainly of the epic, entitled 'The Frozen Labyrinth.' In 1942, having felt the impact of the war, Mr. Knight mounted the architect of the frozen labyrinth in a chariot of wrath as the great apostle of national liberty and destiny. One may respect the feeling behind the change while thinking that Milton might have preferred relatively intelligible criticism to a whirlwind apotheosis. (6)

Bush cares too much about Milton to make him an idol.

The stated aim of the Messenger Lectures was to provide annually 'a course or courses of lectures on the evolution of civilization, for the special purpose of raising the moral standard of our political, business, and social life' (vi). The core of Bush's defence of Milton is his earnest belief that 'Milton's vision of life is of abiding value' (88) because it moves us to aspire to a high moral standard. 'Milton's poetry,' Bush avers, 'is inseparable from his vision of life,' and his 'vision of life, in its essentials, remains significant' (29). 'At the present time,' he continues, 'we have a multitude of serious minor poets, who mirror the supposedly overwhelming complexities of the modern world, but we do not hear any voice of heroic magnitude proclaiming that good is good and evil evil, that man is a religious and moral being in a religious and moral universe, and that the destiny of the race depends upon the individual soul' (29–30). Bush's Milton is not for everyone. Like C.S. Lewis, Bush can be preachy, especially when he deplores the evils of the modern world and 'the modern temper,' which he believes 'has been formed largely by writers who have attained a foggy pinnacle beyond good and evil.' Bush reveres Milton because he believes that 'we need the shock of encountering a poet to whom good and evil are distinct realities, a poet who has a much-tried but invincible belief in a divine order and in man's divine heritage and responsibility, who sees in human life an eternal contest between irreligious pride and religious humility' (57). Bush's favourite word 'order' has now fallen out of fashion, and even Milton's admirers find such praise of the poet embarrassing or unpalatable. The term 'Christian humanism,' which Bush elevated to the heart of Milton studies, is now either ignored or dismissed as a euphemism for conservative complacency.

It must be admitted that Bush deprives Milton of much of his political energy. In the second chapter of *'Paradise Lost' in Our Time,* entitled 'Religious and Ethical Principles,' he identifies '"right reason," *recta ratio*' as the 'cardinal principle' and 'basic element of Christian humanism' (36–7). Few would quarrel with this, but Bush is needlessly provocative when he names Richard Hooker and Jeremy Taylor alongside Milton as leading exponents of the doctrine. He is indifferent to the fact that Milton's views on politics and church government were opposed to those of Hooker and Taylor. The latter served as chaplain in ordinary to Charles I and refuted the arguments of Milton's *Of Prelatical Episcopacy* (1641) in his *Of the Sacred Order, and Offices of Episcopacy* (1642).

The point is not that Bush is wrong to identify both Milton and Taylor as advocates of right reason. The point is that he makes 'Christian humanism' a monolithic category by downplaying important differences between the figures he includes in it. Perhaps for this reason, historicist critics now have little interest in 'right reason,' though Milton repeatedly uses the term in both his poetry and prose. My own view is that we do both Bush and Milton an injustice if we dismiss 'right reason' as a bland mystification. Historicist Miltonists have special cause to be open to the term, since it was a rallying cry of many radicals in the civil war, particularly the Levellers. 'No government can be just or durable,' declared John Lilburne, 'but what is founded and established upon the principles of right reason, common and universal justice, equity and conscience.' 'All Formes and Lawes of Governments,' wrote Richard Overton, 'may fall and passe away; but right Reason … shall and will endure for ever; it is that by which in all our Actions we must stand or fall, be justified or condemned; for neither Morality nor Divinity amongst Men can or may transgresse the limits of right reason.' John Cook, prosecutor at the trial of Charles I, insisted that 'the King is servant to all his Subjects; set over them for their good; and this is the voice of right reason.' Right reason is accordingly the sole basis of legal precedent, and 'if it be not reason, the pronunciation of 10000 *judges* cannot make it *Law* no more then the *Venetian Madonnas* can by their huge high heels in reality add one Cubit to their stature.'[7] Bush, with his love of 'Law and Order,' has little time for the radical potential of *recta ratio.* He never mentions Cook, Lilburne, or Overton. He does acknowledge 'the seeds of revolution latent in this Protestant individualism,' but at once hastens to restore due proprieties: 'Properly understood, of course, the doctrine does not make man irresponsible; it vastly heightens his responsibility to God' (218). There is a touch of anxiety in that 'of course,' but in fairness one should recall that it is an anxiety that Milton shared. He was never happy with the word 'rebel,' which he preferred to apply to tyrants such as Nimrod or the Stuart kings and their supporters. Bush makes the concept of 'right reason' appear more conservative than it really was in the seventeenth century, but he is right to stress the importance of the concept in Milton's political and ethical thought.

Bush places more emphasis on the ethical than the political applications of 'right reason.' He is especially keen to rebut the view, unquestioned by earlier twentieth-century critics, that Milton's God is *un*reasonable. Sir Walter Raleigh had called Milton's God 'a whimsical Tyrant, all of whose laws are arbitrary and occasional.'[8] Sir Herbert Grierson had called the prohibition about the apple 'capricious,' 'an arbitrary command, a tabu,' announced with 'no reason.' He found this problematic since Milton's central ethical claim is that sin is a 'revolt against reason.'[9] Eliot and Leavis, the two weightiest anti-Miltonists of the 1930s, agreed. For Eliot, the poem's 'theology' is 'repellent, expressed through a mythology which would have been better left in the Book of Genesis, upon which Milton has not improved.'[10] Leavis complained that Milton 'offers as ultimate for our worship mere brute assertive will.'[11] Even C.S. Lewis, staunch defender of both Milton and God, accepted the prohibition's status as a taboo. As Lewis saw it, readers 'must just accept Milton's doctrine of obedience as they accept the inexplicable prohibitions in *Lohengrin, Cinderella,* or *Cupid and Psyche.* It is, after all, the commonest of themes; even Peter Rabbit came to grief because he *would* go into Mr. McGregror's garden.'[12]

Bush set the debate on a new level by taking head-on Grierson's assertion that the prohibition has 'no reason.' For Bush, God's prohibition is 'not merely a tabu, but the order of nature' (48). It is not reasonless, for 'the supreme manifestation of right reason is God Himself, and what God is in the world, the macrocosm, reason is in the soul of man, the microcosm' (46). It follows that God's sovereignty 'is not the arbitrary and tyrannous sovereignty of absolute will,' but 'the sovereignty of right reason and the law of nature, a sovereignty comprehended by the uncorrupted right reason of man and accepted not as servitude but as the condition of true freedom' (42). It is hard not to bridle at some of this. That passive verb 'accepted' ignores the fact that Adam and Eve (and many readers) do not, in the event, accept obedience as 'true freedom,' and E.M.W. Tillyard has famously doubted whether Milton himself would have done so. Had Milton been 'stranded in his own Paradise,' Tillyard conjectures, he 'would very soon have eaten the apple on his own responsibility and immediately justified the act in a polemical pamphlet.'[13] One suspects that the pamphlet would have invoked 'right reason.' When Bush identifies God with reason ('right reason is God Himself'), he assumes that the identification can lead only to humble obedience, but Gerrard Winstanley had used this very identification to justify *dis*obedience, even of 'God,' when oppressive ministers abuse that name: 'I have been held under darknesse by that word, as I see many people are.'[14]

I admit that Winstanley goes further than Milton in exploring the subversive possibilities of *recta ratio,* but it matters that there are subversive possibilities to explore. Bush obscures this. He also exaggerates Milton's faith in reason. He never quotes the chorus's cry in *Samson Agonistes*: 'Down Reason then, at least vain reasonings down' (322). Notwithstanding these weaknesses, Bush has continuing importance and relevance for the kind of historicist criticism that now dominates Milton studies, but which has had little use for him. He was one of the first critics to give serious attention to Milton's religious and ethical thought, and he did this at a time when Leavis was opining that the term 'Milton's "thought"' was an oxymoron.[15] Bush could be reductive and conservative, but he was also a trailblazer. More than any critic before him, he felt that Milton matters, and his singular achievement was to convince his contemporaries that Milton's ideas, far from being 'dead and repellent' (29), are worthy of serious study.

He is least persuasive when he deploys 'Milton's poetic thought and feeling about man and God' (88) as a defence of Milton's style. He sometimes writes as if 'the modern reaction against Milton' had been spurred not by a distaste for Milton's poetry but by a widespread social and moral 'disease' (3). This is unjust to a critic like Leavis, who had grounded his critique firmly on Milton's words. 'Our objection to Milton,' he had insisted, 'is that we dislike his verse.'[16] Bush likes Milton's verse, but sometimes sounds as if he would rather not talk about it. This is partly because he is distrustful of the kind of aesthetic criticism practised by Victorian critics, who had (for the most part) praised Milton's style but ridiculed his ideas. Sir Walter Raleigh famously called *Paradise Lost* 'a monument to dead ideas.'[17] Bush does not want to 'rest in the nineteenth-century notion of verbal and musical beauties divorced from obsolete substance' (25). He tells us that we must take 'beauties' and 'substance' together or not at all:

> If a reputedly great poet has no other claim upon us than his style and sound, however wonderful these may be, we might better admit that he is

> dead and read poets who still have something to say. But before we assent too readily to the conventional view that *Paradise Lost* is a monument to dead ideas, and the poet's art the decoration on a tomb, we may ask, first, what those ideas were, and, secondly, if they are in essence so remote from us and our world, if they are not, rather, very close to what many modern thinkers have been declaring are necessary to our own necessary regeneration. (27)

Milton indeed has 'something to say,' but Bush is too morally prescriptive in pressing this point. He leaves no room for the reader who is genuinely engaged with Milton's 'ideas,' but does not share them. Some of Milton's best critics have been readers of this kind. William Empson is justly celebrated for his acute and sensitive appreciation of Milton's style (no 'anti-Miltonist,' he), but he was also deeply engaged with Milton's theodicy, albeit not in a way that Bush would have applauded. Maybe Empson was wrong-headed, but he found more in *Paradise Lost* than just 'decoration on a tomb.' Bush sometimes writes as if the only valid Milton criticism were an acquiescent criticism.

At his best, he is a fine close reader, but he fails to press his points home, and so lets opportunities slip through his fingers. He sometimes makes needless concessions. This is most evident when he tries to rebut Eliot's claim that the following lines from *Comus* are '*artificial* and *conventional*':[18]

> their way
> Lies through the perplex't paths of this drear Wood,
> The nodding horror of whose shady brows
> Threats the forlorn and wandring Passinger. (36–9)

To appreciate both the strengths and weaknesses of Bush's reply, we must quote him at length:

> Milton is personifying his symbolic wood by way of heightening its sinister darkness. Mr. Eliot presumably does not like 'nodding horror,' presumably because he sees the phrase as a bit of eighteenth-century poetic diction. But at the time Milton was writing it was a novelty. As Mr. Geoffrey Tillotson has shown, the use of English derivatives in their classical meaning was beginning in the early seventeenth century, and such words – like some of Mr. Eliot's classicisms of diction – had an effect comparable to the metaphysical wit and surprise. Granted that these lines of Milton's have no special distinction, they show already a touch of that suggestive vagueness which can be as essential for its purpose as particularity. (16)

Just as Bush is about to make a significant breakthrough, his last sentence weakly concedes that Milton's verbal wit does lack 'particularity.' The word 'vagueness' is especially disappointing, for the sentences preceding it had promised (and might have delivered) something stronger. The 'classical meaning' that Bush rightly invokes (Latin *horror*, 'shaking, trembling,' and *horridus*, 'bristling') is not vague, but imaginatively precise. The verbal wit anticipates *Paradise Lost*, where angels' spears present a 'horrid Front' (1.563), and Satan, confronting Death, resembles a comet with 'horrid hair' (2.710). Bush senses this, but does not develop his own insight. He never mentions the word 'bristling,' and he fails to make the crucial point that Milton plays on the Latin *and* English senses. By mentioning only the former ('English derivatives in their classical meaning'), he reinforces the idea, central to the anti-Miltonists' case, that Milton exhibits only an antiquarian delight in remote meanings. It will remain for Christopher Ricks to push Bush's insight to its proper conclusion.[19]

Bush is wary of engaging Eliot and Leavis on their own ground as a close reader. He prefers to invoke epic precedent as a ready-made riposte to Milton's detractors. 'Since Milton's art is of the ancient kind,' he writes, 'the charges brought against him must be brought likewise against nearly all the Greek and Roman poets' (91). This misses the anti-Miltonists' point. They had charged Milton with violating English by bending it to classical diction and idiom. The charge might be unjust, but a lofty appeal to classical precedent is not enough to make it disappear. When Vergil wrote Latin, he was not abandoning his own tongue.

Like C.S. Lewis before him, Bush defends the grand style by appealing to epic precedent. Eliot had taken exception to Satan's great speech in heaven exhorting the angels to rebel:

Thrones, Dominations, Princedoms, Vertues, Powers,
If these magnific Titles yet remain
Not meerly titular, since by Decree
Another now hath to himselfingross't
All Power, and us eclipst under the name
Of King anointed, for whom all this haste
Of midnight march, and hurried meeting here,
This onely to consult how we may best
With what may be devis'd of honors new
Receive him coming to receive from us
Knee-tribute yet unpaid, prostration vile,
Too much to one, but double how endur'd,
To one and to his image now proclaim'd? (5.772–84)

Eliot had complained that the lines fail to convey a mind in the act of thinking: 'The dark angel here is not *thinking* or conversing, but making a speech carefully prepared for him; and the arrangement is for the sake of musical value, not for significance.'[20] Bush replies: 'We are told that Satan is not thinking or conversing, as he should be. Of course he is not. He is the leader of a rebellion making a speech of exhortation to his followers. ... In such a situation rhetorical magniloquence is essential to the effect he desires' (19). This duplicates a defence Lewis had offered three years before: 'Satan rises to make a speech before an audience of angels "innumerable as the starrs of night"' and Eliot complains 'that he sounds as if he were "making a speech"' (135). The defence is strong, but it engages with only half of Eliot's point. Yes, an oration is not the same as small talk in a parlour, and this retort is a perfect answer to Eliot's complaint that Satan is not 'conversing.' But it ignores his other complaint: that Satan is 'not *thinking*.' Eliot's italics ('not *thinking* or conversing') had clearly identified 'thinking' as the main deficiency; Bush's reply ('not thinking or conversing ... Of course ... not') shifts the emphasis to 'conversing.' This makes possible his witty (and rhetorically devastating) antithesis between 'conversing' and 'making a speech,' but it comes at a price. Bush, like Lewis before him, tacitly concedes Eliot's main point that Satan 'is not *thinking*.'

This is a pity because one can challenge Eliot on the facts and so give Milton a stronger defence than either Lewis or Bush gives him. *Pace* Eliot, Satan's oration *does* exhibit a mind thinking. The speech is not introspective (in the manner of Satan's soliloquies), but it still shows a keen and lively intelligence. The words are arranged for 'musical value' *and* 'significance.' When Eliot calls the speech 'carefully prepared,' he means that Milton uses Satan as a ventriloquist's dummy to deliver mighty-mouthed harmonies. The speech is 'carefully prepared,' but the organizing intelligence is Satan's as well as Milton's. The key is timing. To appreciate this we must make an imaginative effort to hear the speech as Satan's auditors hear it. The 'thinking' occurs in their minds as well as his. The gathered multitude (they are not yet a host) might not expect an exhortation to rebel. They have followed Satan to the north after his 'next subordinate' (not yet called 'Beelzebub') has stirred them into motion with 'Ambiguous words' (703). Specifically, they have been told 'to prepare / Fit entertainment to receive our King / The great *Messiah*' (689–91). It is possible to hear this innocently. At least one of Milton's critics has done just that.[21] When Satan addresses the multitude, he does not know how they have understood his earlier words, and so does not know what to expect from them – any more than they know what to expect from him. Satan is *sounding out* his audience, some of whom might still be loyal to God. He therefore treads cautiously. He explains the 'hurried meeting' by referring back to the 'Ambiguous words' that have brought the angels here:

> and hurried meeting here,
> This onely to consult how we may best
> With what may be devis'd of honors new
> Receive him coming to receive from us ...

The repeated 'receive' looks back to 'Fit entertainment to receive our king' (689). Abdiel had heard this innocently, and he might still give Satan the benefit of the doubt. Resentment has been audible from the beginning of the speech ('merely titular,' 'ingross't,' 'eclipst'), but the enormity of Satan's plan dawns only slowly through the lines. Rebellion does not come to the fore until the climactic turn into the next line:

> Receive him coming to receive from us
> Knee-tribute yet unpaid, prostration vile,
> Too much to one, but double how endur'd,
> To one and to his image now proclaim'd?

Even this holds something back. At no point in the long sentence quoted by Eliot and Bush does Satan say outright just what he means to do. There are many verbs, but no obvious main verb. Eliot might censure this as another instance of Milton's idiomatic remoteness, but the effect is to make us yearn for some kind of direct statement. Satan's sudden question, two lines later, 'Will ye submit your necks, and chuse to bend / The supple knee?' is timed perfectly to answer this need, flashing like lightning from a sullen cloud.

Satan, in short, is not delivering a prefabricated speech for 'musical value' alone. He uses both sound and sense to incite rebellious thoughts in the minds of angels who have not before had any. Milton conveys the exhilaration of a mind discovering and articulating such thoughts for the first time. Satan thinks and speaks like 'the famous Orators,'

> Those antient, whose resistless eloquence
> Wielded at will that fierce Democratie,
> Shook the Arsenal and fulmin'd over *Greece*,
> To *Macedon*, and *Artaxerxes* Throne. (*Paradise Regained*, 4.268–71)

Satan is a manipulative orator – he takes control of others' thoughts – but he could not do this if he were not himself 'thinking.'

Bush has mixed success, then, as a defender of Milton's style. He shrinks from engaging Eliot and Leavis on their own terms. But he has a complete success when he turns from verbal criticism to Milton's inventiveness with 'the half-concealed or altered allusion' (103). Critics had long been aware of the fact that Milton in *Paradise Lost* alludes frequently to the Bible and previous epics. Editors had accumulated a stock of such allusions since 1695, when Patrick Hume published his *Annotations on 'Paradise Lost.'* But the dominant view, since at least the time of Addison, had been that Milton's allusions serve the simple function of claiming a place in the epic tradition. Bush raises the argument to a new level by noting the role of 'dramatic irony' in Milton's allusions, which are often created out of igniting differences, as well as similarities. By significantly changing another poet's phrase, or its context, Milton can pass implicit moral judgment on his characters, previous epic poets, or both. Bush likens Milton's allusive technique to that of Eliot, and so builds a bridge between the two poets: 'irony is embodied,' he writes, 'as in Mr. Eliot in more or less veiled allusion.' He cites as an example Adam's reply when Raphael warns him of the dangers of excessive passion for Eve. Adam assures Raphael that he is 'still free' and determined to 'Approve the best, and follow what I approve' (8.610–11). Bush is the first critic to catch the allusion to Medea's infamous words in Ovid's *Metamorphoses*: 'video melioraproboque, / deteriorasequor' (7.20), which Sandys had famously rendered: 'I see the better, I approve it too: / The worse I follow.'[22] As Bush notes, 'the altered version of a familiar Ovidian tag has the effect, for the reader, of ironically puncturing Adam's self-confidence and preparing for what is to come' (107). Notice that Bush does not deny that Adam is 'still free.' Adam might yet make the right choice, and (unlike Medea) he means to do so, but the echo of Medea inevitably renders his assurance ominous for the alert and informed reader. This kind of allusion is not merely decorative. Milton makes it an interpretative device.

Bush's work on allusion has had enormous influence. He developed his argument in his landmark 1961 essay, 'Ironic and Ambiguous Allusion in *Paradise Lost*,' which blazed the way for many later studies, including Davis P. Harding's *The Club of Hercules* (1962). He is particularly good on the kind of ironic allusion that makes Satan's doings a grim parody of God's. When Satan arises from the burning lake, and 'on each hand the flames / Drivn backward slope thir pointing spires, and rowld / In billows, leave i'th' midst a horrid Vale' (1.222–4), Bush plausibly detects an allusion to the miraculous parting of the Red Sea. Some might think this far-fetched, and Bush himself admits to being 'doubtful': 'sometimes one is not sure how far the modern appetite for this kind of thing is entitled to go.'[23] In this particular case, I find the allusion convincing. As Bush notes, the parting of Hell's waves is followed, some ninety lines later, by an 'elaborate simile' which explicitly likens Hell's lake to the Red Sea, 'whose waves orethrew / *Busiris* and his *Memphian* Chivalry' (1.306–7). The only thing Bush does not note is that the simile reverses an identification implicit in the earlier allusion. When Satan had passed between the parted 'billows,' Milton's imagery had raised the teasing possibility that the devils, like the Israelites, are fleeing cruel persecution. The subsequent simile casts Satan in the opposite role of the Pharaoh who pursued God's children with 'perfidious hatred' (308). The simile effectively corrects the earlier allusion, taking back what it had merely seemed to concede.

If Bush's argument for 'Ironic and Ambiguous Allusion' has a weakness, it is not (as he fears) that he overstates his case, but that he sometimes *under*estimates Milton's irony and ambiguity. Discussing Adam and Eve's innocence, he brilliantly detects an allusion to Vergil in the following two passages:

> Sleep on
> Blest pair; and O yet happiest if ye seek
> No happier state, and know to know no more. (4.773–5)

> thrice happie if they know
> Thir happiness, and persevere upright. (7.631–2)

'In both utterances,' Bush writes,

> Milton is recalling Virgil's eulogy of the simple Italian farmers who shun ambition and are content with their humble life (*Georgics*, II, 458–60):
> O fortunatos nimium, sua si bona norint,
> agricolas! Quibus ipsa, procul discordibus armis,
> fundit humo facilem victum iustissima tellus.

H. Rushton Fairclough translates: 'O happy husbandmen! too happy should they come to know their blessings! for whom, far from the clash of arms, most righteous Earth, unbidden, pours forth from her soil an easy sustenance.'[24] For Bush, the point of Milton's repeated allusion is to cast an ominous shadow over Paradise. 'The reminder of Virgil's peasants,' he writes, 'adds a note of human actuality to the pathos of idyllic innocence' (637). This is a plausible account of the first of Milton's two allusions, but the second one works quite differently. The lines in book four, spoken by the epic narrator, declare that Adam and Eve will be 'happiest' if they define a limit to what they know; the lines in book seven, sung by a chorus of angels, declare that they will be 'thrice happy if they know.' The implicit question behind all three passages is: 'Can one know one's happiness without losing it?' In Vergil, this question is focused on the one word *nimium* ('too much'). Bush writes as if 'thrice happy' were a faithful recreation of *fortunatosnimium*, but there is a significant difference between the two phrases. Vergil is being ironic, for his farmers will not be 'too happy' (they will not be happy at all) if they 'come to know' (*norint*) their happiness in the moment of losing it. Here I cannot refrain from a modern Canadian parallel:

> Don't it always seem to go,
> That you don't know what you've got
> Till it's gone –
> They paved paradise
> And put up a parking lot.[25]

Vergil would presumably have agreed – but would Milton? He clearly alludes to Vergil, but the point of his book seven allusion might be to turn Vergil's wisdom on its head. Unlike Vergil, Milton's angels mean what they say. So long as Adam and Eve obey God's command ('persevere upright'), they are free to grow in happiness *and* knowledge. As Dennis Danielson has shrewdly observed, Milton's meaning 'is quite the opposite' of Vergil's: 'Adam and Eve, unlike Virgil's peasants, ought to know their happiness; and given the manifold operation of the principle of contrariety in Eden, they *can* know it, and increase it. Moreover, this requires that they be not "far from the clash of arms" but rather in the very midst of spiritual warfare, as indeed they are. To Milton "an easy sustenance" would be anathema' (200). If Danielson is right, as I believe he is, Bush has missed the point of Milton's allusion, but he still deserves our gratitude for alerting us to it, and urging us to ponder the implications.

I shall conclude with one of the most puzzling and complex of Milton's allusions: the reference to Pan in 'On the Morning of Christ's Nativity.'

Strictly, there are two such references, which is why the allusion is troubling. When the shepherds are startled by the angels' singing, Milton comments: 'Full little thought they than, / That the mighty *Pan* / Was kindly come to live with them below' (88–90). The second reference to Pan occurs much later in the poem, and is more oblique. As the oracles cease, and the pagan gods are banished, they raise a mournful cry: 'The lonely mountains o're, / And the resounding shore, / A voice of weeping heard, and loud lament' (181–3). Here the primary allusion is to Matthew 2:18 (to which I shall return in a moment), but Woodhouse and Bush, in their splendid note in the Milton *Variorum*, detect a further allusion to the death of Pan as recounted by Plutarch and adapted by Eusebius. Plutarch, explaining the silence of oracles in his own time, tells how an Egyptian pilot (intriguingly named Thamus)[26] was sailing past the island of Paxi, when a great voice called to him from the island three times by name. The voice told him to announce 'great Pan is dead' when he reached the island of Palodes. He did so, and at once heard the pitiful sound of many voices weeping.[27] Eusebius took up the story, and adapted it for Christian purposes, noting that the event occurred at the very time Christ was banishing devils. He identified Pan as one of the devils Christ banished. Renaissance commentators, including Rabelais and Lavater, followed Eusebius in giving the story a Christian interpretation, but they changed two key details. They placed the event at the time of Christ's crucifixion, and they identified Pan with Christ, not a devil. This is the version that appears in E.K.'s gloss to Spenser's *Shepheardes Calender (May* 54), but E.K. mistakenly cites Eusebius as its source:

> Great Pan, is Christ, the very God of all shepheards, which calleth himselfe the greate and good shepherd. The name is most rightly (me thinkes) applyed to him, for Pan signifieth all or omnipotent, which is onely the Lord Jesus. And by that name (as I remember) he is called of Eusebius in his fiftebooke de Preparat. Evang; who thereof telleth a proper storye to that purpose.[28]

As Woodhouse and Bush succinctly note, E.K.'s 'Gloss is in error: Eusebius regards Pan as a demon and his death as an example of Christ's destruction of such.'[29] E.K.'s revisionist tradition clearly underlies Milton's initial allusion to 'the mighty *Pan*' (89), but it jars with his subsequent allusion to the voices that mourned Pan's death. Milton, unlike E.K., remembers Eusebius correctly when he alludes to the 'voice of weeping' (183).

At issue is the moral status of those mourning voices: do they have a legitimate claim on our sympathy or must we steel ourselves against them? E.K. knows that 'some' take a stern view, but he cannot persuade himself that the voices were evil:

> there was heard suche piteous outcryes and dreadfull shriking, as hath not bene the like. By whych Pan, though of some be understoode the great Satanas, whose kingdome at that time was by Christ conquered ... (for at that time ... all Oracles surceased, and enchanted spirits, that were wont to delude the people, thenceforth held theyr peace) ... yet I think it more properly meant of the death of Christ, the onely and very Pan, then suffering for his flock.

Woodhouse and Bush cite all these sources (and more besides) in their notes to lines 89 and 173 of Milton's poem. They disentangle the separate threads, draw the necessary distinctions, and correct the sources when they misrepresent each other (as E.K. misremembers Eusebius). Such critical rigour is exemplary. Where lesser critics might have presented us with a single, innocuous 'tradition,' Woodhouse and Bush are scrupulous and honest, candidly acknowledging that Milton's Pan is both Christ and devil. 'Here,' they write (referring to line 89), 'Milton is content to relate the classical and the Christian, while in the poem generally ... he repudiates the classical in favour of the Christian and by implication Pan among the rest.' That is finely said, and I hope that I shall not seem ungrateful if I now find fault with Woodhouse and Bush for downplaying the significance of their own discoveries. My objection is not that they sweep things under the carpet, but that they avert their eyes from what they have brought to light. A note of apology is audible when they conclude: 'Milton had, then, abundant precedent for identifying Pan and Christ' (80). This is true, but it sidesteps the real question, which is not whether Milton had 'precedent for identifying Pan and Christ' (he obviously did), but whether he had any precedent (or good reason) for identifying Pan with Christ *and* a devil *in the same poem.*

This, it seems to me, is a serious problem, and one that does not arise in Spenser or any of the other sources noted by Woodhouse and Bush. There would be no difficulty if Milton had identified Christ with 'the mighty *Pan*' and left it at that. The difficulty is that, having made this identification, he goes on to make the opposite one, drawing on the very tradition that E.K. had explicitly rejected. E.K. and all the other sources cited by Woodhouse and Bush are internally consistent. Milton's two allusions clash with each other, and so introduce moral confusion. It only complicates matters that the line 'A voice of weeping heard, and loud lament' (183) also alludes to the slaughter of the innocents. Woodhouse and Bush are once again laudably honest: 'Milton remembers the "piteous outcryes" from the shore of Palodes (above, 173n.), but also (as Warton noted) the phrasing of Matt. 2:18: "In Rama there was a voice heard, lamentation, and weeping, and great mourning."'[30] To my mind, it is deeply disconcerting that the cries of banished devils (cries that should be cause for joy) blend with those of the slaughtered innocents and their bereaved parents. If we are to take Milton's allusions seriously (and Bush, more than anyone else, has taught us that we should), it is hard to resist the inference that the banished devils are innocent. Do not misunderstand me. I am not arguing that these tensions and contradictions are a blemish in the poem. They arguably make it all the more poignant. But they do, I think, lend support to those critics who read 'On the Morning of Christ's Nativity' as a work deeply divided against itself. Woodhouse and Bush would not have welcomed this conclusion, but it is a tribute to their scholarly industry and critical probity that they make it possible.

NOTES

1 Douglas Bush, *The Renaissance and English Humanism* (Toronto, 1939), 13. The preface to this book of 'four lectures' states that 'they are printed exactly as they were read.'
2 *The Iliad of Homer*, trans. Richmond Lattimore (Chicago, 1951).
3 Bush does not name the person he misses, but David Galbraith and Heather Murray of the University of Toronto inform me that A.J. Bell (1856–1932), eminent classicist at Victoria College, is the likeliest candidate. Bell was Professor of Latin (1881–1921) and Professor of Comparative Philology (1882–1922) and continued to teach until 1927. Bush studied under him as an undergraduate and wrote a tribute to him after he retired, in which he speaks of his white hair, massive frame, and deep voice delivering weighty words – details that perfectly fit the unnamed person missing from the Alexander lecture. See Douglas Bush, 'A Classical Scholar,' *Canadian Forum* 9 (September 1929): 423–4.
4 Douglas Bush, *'Paradise Lost' in Our Time: Some Comments* (Ithaca, 1945), 25. See above, 19–20.
5 William Empson, *Milton's God* (London, 1961), 30–1.

6 G. Wilson Knight, *Chariot of Wrath: The Message of John Milton to Democracy at War* (London, 1942), 16, 143.
7 John Lilburne, *Innocency and Truth Justified* (1646), 38. Richard Overton, *An Appeale from the degenerate Representative Body the Commons of England ... to the Body represented, the Free People in General* (1647), 2. John Cook, *Redintegratio Amoris* (1647), 8, 9–10. Pauline Gregg cites these and other relevant sources in *Free-Born John: the Biography of John Lilburne* (London, 1961), 218.
8 Walter Raleigh, *Milton* (London, 1900), 130.
9 Herbert J.C. Grierson, *Milton and Wordsworth* (Cambridge, 1937), 96, 116.
10 T.S. Eliot, 'A Note on the Verse of John Milton,' in *Essays and Studies* 21 (1935 [misdated 1936]): 32–40 (see p. 38).
11 F.R. Leavis, *Revaluation: Tradition and Development in English Poetry* (London, 1936), 58.
12 C.S. Lewis, *A Preface to 'Paradise Lost'* (London, 1942), 72.
13 E.M.W. Tillyard, *Milton* (London 1930), 239.
14 Gerrard Winstanley, *Truth Lifting Up Its Head Above Scandals* (1649), 105. See further, David Loewenstein, *Representing Revolution in Milton and His Contemporaries: Religion, Politics, and Polemics in Radical Puritanism* (Cambridge, 2001), 59.
15 See F.R. Leavis, *The Common Pursuit* (London, 1952), 23: 'it is ... deplorable that literary students should be required to ... devote any large part of their time to the solemn study of Milton's "thought."'
16 Leavis, *Revaluation*, 43.
17 Walter Raleigh, *Milton* (London, 1900; repr. New York. 1967), 85 (page citation is to reprint edition).
18 Eliot, 34. The italics are Eliot's.
19 See Christopher Ricks, *Milton's Grand Style* (Oxford, 1963), 63: 'The extra meaning which Milton finds comes clearly from the fact that he does not discard the English meaning.'
20 Eliot, 36.
21 See John Peter, *A Critique of 'Paradise Lost'* (New York, 1960), 68. Peter himself hears only the innocent sense of 'Fit entertainment' and so is dismayed when the angels are so quickly won over by Satan's oratory. He accuses Milton of cheating. I have argued elsewhere that Satan seduces his legions with deliberate equivocations. See John Leonard, *Naming in Paradise: Milton and the Language of Adam and Eve* (Oxford, 1990), 156–63.
22 George Sandys, *Ovid's Metamorphosis Englished, Mythologized, and Represented in Figures* (1632), ed. Karl K. Hulley and Stanley T. Vandersall (Lincoln, NE, 1970), 306.

23 Douglas Bush, 'Ironic and Ambiguous Allusion in *Paradise Lost*,' *JEGP* 60 (1961): 631–40 (p. 634).

24 H. Rushton Fairclough, trans. and ed., *Eclogues, Georgics, Aeneid I–VI*, vol. 1 of *Virgil in Two Volumes* (London, 1916), 149.

25 Joni Mitchell, 'Big Yellow Taxi,' *Ladies of the Canyon*, Reprise compact disk 7599274502.

26 The name is intriguing because it resembles that of Thammuz, the Phoenician god whose festival of mourning is one of the pagan cults silenced in 'On the Morning of Christ's Nativity.' Bush and Woodhouse do not comment on this resemblance, but Robert Graves has conjectured that Plutarch's pilot 'misheard the ceremonial lament *Thammus Pan-megas Tethnçce* ("the all-great Thammuz is dead") for the message "Thamus, Great Pan is dead!"' See Robert Graves, *Greek Myths* (London, 1958), 103.

27 Plutarch, *De defectu oracularum [The Obsolence of Oracles*] 17, in *Moralia* 419 A–E.

28 Edmund Spenser, *The Shepheardes Calender* (1579), E.K.'s gloss to *May* 54, fol. 21.

29 *A Variorum Commentary on the Poems of John Milton*, ed. Merritt Y. Hughes, vol. 2, *The Minor English Poems*, ed. A.S.P. Woodhouse and Douglas Bush, part 1 (London, 1972), 80.

30 *A Variorum Commentary*, vol. 2, part 1, 98.

10 Radical Company: Milton, the Nostalgia of (Post-)War Criticism, and the Case of A.S.P. Woodhouse's *Puritanism and Liberty*

ELIZABETH SAUER

Long hailed as positive values of modern Western society, liberty, toleration, and democracy have been central themes for political, cultural, and literary historians. One might turn, for example, to such influential works as S.R. Gardiner's *The First Two Stuarts and the Puritan Revolution* (1876) and W.K. Jordan's *The Development of Religious Toleration in England* (1932–40), a four-volume series that exhibits the strains of the turbulent era when it was composed, as 'the very foundations of the liberal philosophy' suddenly fractured.[1] Indeed history has also rewritten such accounts, and like other treatments of liberalisms, toleration as a topic of inquiry 'survived the First World War not in England but in the United States.'[2] Notable American contributions to this field of study consist of William Haller's works, among which are *Tracts on Liberty in the Puritan Revolution* (1933–4), *The Rise of Puritanism ... from Thomas Cartwright to John Lilburne and John Milton* (1938), *The Leveller Tracts, 1647–1653,* edited with G. Davies (1944), and *Liberty and Reformation in the Puritan Revolution* (1955), G.W. Whiting's *Milton's Literary Milieu* (1939), Don M. Wolfe's *Milton in the Puritan Revolution* (1941), and Merritt Y. Hughes's 'Milton as Revolutionary' (1943).[3] To this list should be added the studies of such Canadians as A.S.P. Woodhouse, whose oft-reissued 1938 *Puritanism and Liberty: Being the Army Debates (1647–9) from the Clarke Manuscripts with Supplementary Documents* is the subject of this chapter, and Arthur Barker, whose 1942 *Milton and the Puritan Dilemma* applied the arguments of *Puritanism and Liberty* to a full-length interpretation of Milton's prose.

In boldly challenging the devaluation of Milton's polemical writings by generations of readers and in disregarding even Milton's own hierarchal distinction between left-hand prose and right-hand verse,[4] historicist scholars, including Woodhouse, demonstrated that the prose is 'sufficient of itself to raise' 'higher Argument,' one that treats the redoubtable subject of liberty. Haller, Woodhouse, Whiting, Wolfe, Barker, and Hughes thereby also diverted attention from the earlier twentieth-century portrait of the Renaissance rationalist and humanist, 'an eclectic, an independent thinker ... daring and original in his poetry,'[5] to Milton the Puritan, the controversialist prose writer immersed in the world of political ideas, an engagement deemed 'unpoetic' in the critical tradition of the day. In the 1930s and 1940s, scholarship featuring Milton's prose polemics located Milton in relation to seventeenth-century developments in church politics, private and political liberty, and individual rights.[6] Enduring and influential, investigations by the historicist-minded critics generally relied on evolutionary or teleological models of history which, according to Lord Lindsay of Birker – author of the foreword to the 1938 edition of *Puritanism and Liberty* and of the postscript to the 1951 reprint – established the ideological groundwork for western democracy ('Postscript to the 1950 Edition' [1966 published posthumously]). The historiographical approaches of these scholars exhibited what William Lamont in 2001 classified as a 1930s 'tendency ... to equate Puritanism with liberty,'[7] propelled in part by recourse to Milton's own contributions to the Good Old Cause.

The recent quatercentenary of Milton's birth and the assembly of Canadian-authored essays on Milton in this volume offer an opportune occasion for reviewing the critical reception of Milton in a national and international setting. Prominently represented in Woodhouse's work and in that of his contemporaries, Milton would come to enjoy a reputation in the twentieth century as a champion of liberalism bolstered by the presentism and progressivism that marked the 'great Whig tradition.'[8] Such features of Whig history were perpetuated by the Marxist-informed analyses of Christopher Hill, who re-energized research on the seventeenth-century Good Old Cause of revolution.[9] Even through the 1970s when revisionism dominated British historiography, Hill produced some of his best and most influential scholarship, including *Antichrist in Seventeenth-Century England* (1971), *The World Turned Upside Down: Radical Ideas during the English Revolution* (1972), and *Milton and the English Revolution* (1977).[10] His example would help advance historicist criticism that situated Milton's literary, political, and biographical engagements in relation to movements like Puritan radicalism, liberalism, and republicanism. To this day, Milton's metaphors of 'moderat varieties and brotherly dissimilitudes,'[11] his outcries against persecution, and his role as critic of church government are used in defence of theories on the evolutionary history of toleration.[12] Despite his self-professed post-revisionism, Coffey at the opening of *Persecution and Toleration in Protestant England, 1558–1689* revalidates the 'unfashionably Whiggish claim' that seventeenth-century England gave rise to dramatic transformations from religious persecution and enforced uniformity to toleration and religious pluralism.[13] Furthermore, he concurs with Haller and Woodhouse in arguing that tolerationist ideas originated in radical Puritanism (7), though historians like Jonathan Scott have pointed out that Jacobean uniformity could be more tolerationist than the 'pluralism' of the Left.[14] Woodhouse's seminal contribution to a Whiggish account that bolstered Milton's reputation as a radical liberal is the focus of this chapter. I feature the introduction to *Puritanism and Liberty,* left unchanged from the original essay in the reprints and editions of the volume that followed through to 1992.[15] Woodhouse portrays Milton as an example of the leftist Puritan attitude to custom, toleration, and history (*P&L* 50) in his integrationist study, one that universalizes and contemporizes the seventeenth-century revolution in conjunction with a Whiggish historiography and forges connections among revolutionary movements across the centuries.[16]

Since the original publication of *Puritanism and Liberty,* explains Woodhouse in the 'Preface to the 1950 Edition' that appeared in all reprints beginning with 1951, several works advanced historical research on Puritan ideology: William Haller's *The Rise of Puritanism* (1938); Marxist historian D. Petegorsky's *Left-Wing Democracy in the English Civil War* (1940), which concentrates on Winstanley; and George H. Sabine's edition of the Digger tracts, *The Works of Gerrard Winstanley* (1941).[17] As mentioned, Barker concentrates on the development of Milton's social and political thought as evidenced by the prose, and he probes seventeenth-century efforts to advance a Reformation that would support private and political liberties. Woodhouse's volume also informed countless other literary and historical investigations, though they devote minimal attention to Milton's contributions to the Good Old Cause.[18] Even when *Puritanism and Liberty* is cited by Miltonists, Woodhouse's Milton gets short shrift. References are chiefly not to Woodhouse's introduction but to the excerpted materials in the edition proper, as we find in Hill's *Milton and the English Revolution.* Quoting from the Part I materials on the Putney Debates in Woodhouse's 1938 edition, Hill connects Milton's pronouncement that 'to take away from the people the right of choosing government takes away all liberty' with Rainborough's famous words in the Debates: 'Every man that is to live under a government ought first by his own consent to put himself under that government.'[19]

Likewise, recent studies including Barbara Lewalski's *Life of John Milton* (2000), David Loewenstein's *Milton and the Drama of History* (1990), his co-edition *Politics, Poetics and Hermeneutics in Milton's Prose* (1990), and his *Representing Revolution in Milton and His Contemporaries* (2001), as well as more broadly ranging literary collections like David Womersley's *Companion to Literature from Milton to Blake* (2000)[20] tend to cite not the arguments from Woodhouse's introduction, but rather works in the edition proper, which features excerpts from writings on the Putney Debates, the Whitehall Debates, and on leftist Puritan thinking.

Is it possible in a post-Whig and post-revisionist era to re-establish the historical, historiographical, and literary value of such an overdetermined Whiggish account as Woodhouse's and understand Milton's place therein? This chapter examines the significance of Woodhouse's work in several regards. First I review the comments *Puritanism and Liberty* makes on the historical circumstances of its production. I then consider how Woodhouse made inroads in a literary field dominated by the New Criticism, and established a basis for the rehabilitation of Milton by later twentieth-century historicist critics. By aligning Milton with a liberal Puritanism, Woodhouse revived the revolutionary prose writer, polemicist, controversialist. He recognized the advantages of locating Milton's tracts, notably *Areopagitica,* within a religious, political, and intellectual climate over a decade and a half before the first volume of the Yale edition of the prose was produced. Woodhouse dealt with the Miltonic oeuvre in a thoroughly contextualized manner that was out of line with the tenets of the New Criticism and in resistance to the disavowal or devaluation of Milton's *left*-hand achievements. In doing so, he contributed to what Paul Stevens characterized of late as a 'remarkable renaissance in English literary studies' experienced at the University of Toronto in the 1940s. The renaissance, Stevens continues, was most apparent in Milton studies, which was in turn historicist-oriented and attentive to Milton's religious and political thought. The school of criticism that fostered the Toronto Miltonists' preoccupation with the theme of liberty was indebted to Woodhouse and to a troubling suspicion about violations to liberty abroad.[21]

The original appearance of *Puritanism and Liberty* in the late 1930s is highly suggestive. 'There was a growing awareness of another looming threat to English liberty and democracy,' Lesley Le Claire observes in alluding to the fascism that engulfed Europe.[22] The substantial introductory essay in Woodhouse's edition historicizes the contemporary political climate by studying the nature of Puritanism and Puritan contributions to liberty. Woodhouse's thesis features a radical Puritan-generated revolution intimately bound up with the struggle against despotic church and state power. Had they been 'allowed to prevail,' judges Woodhouse, absolutist systems

> might radically have altered the whole subsequent course of English political development: in so far at least the 'Whig view of history' is correct. Nor is it easy to conceive of this overthrow without the powerful incentive and example of Puritanism, not at one stage merely but at point after point of its course. (*P&L* 61)

Applying both political and social theory, Woodhouse's introduction exposes 'the heart of Puritanism' which Ernest Barker, in a review of *Puritanism and Liberty* contemporaneous with the book's appearance, attributes to Woodhouse's familiarity with 'modern Calvinist theology.'[23] While the introduction is not designed as a complete or final synthesis of the causes of the Revolution, it is 'an exploration of the religious background of Puritan ideology ... without which no final synthesis is possible' (Woodhouse, 'Preface to the Second Edition,' *P&L* 5). Woodhouse's concern is to portray the Puritan mind as it arrives 'at truth and agreement' (*P&L* 11) despite the ideological or political differences among its adherents. His definition of Puritanism is necessarily and suitably all-encompassing: a Calvinist-generated idealized holy community of saints who make up a *discordia concors* comprised of the Parties of the Right, the Centre, and the Left. Together they offer a continuity in Puritan thinking, Woodhouse avers (*P&L* 36–7) with an observation that underwrites much twentieth-century historiography of Puritanism.[24]

Ernest Barker reminds us of the genesis of Woodhouse's *Puritanism and Liberty* 'from an incursion of the [English] philosophers ... into the domain of historians.' A.D. Lindsay's lectures 'The Essentials of Democracy' characterized the Putney Debates of the New Model Army as 'a memorable debate on the principles of democratic government.'[25] Woodhouse produced an edition of the Putney Debates of October 1647 and the Whitehall Debates of the Army in 1648–9, based on the manuscript in the (William) Clarke Papers found in the library of Worcester College, Oxford, and the edition prepared by Sir Charles Firth for the Camden Society (1891–1901). Citing Lindsay's published *Essentials of Democracy* (1929) in support of the idea that the congregation of the radicals was the school for democracy (*P&L* 76), Woodhouse, in the introduction and the book at large, invites a reading of the Putney debates in relation to the Whitehall Debates to reinforce that connection.[26] The result is, as Lamont states, 'We view not Putney, but Putney-in-the-company-it-keeps. And Woodhouse chooses that company for us.'[27] The edition is in fact densely populated with Puritans whose writings are construed as relational: following the tracts on the Putney Debates and Whitehall Debates in *Puritanism and Liberty* are pamphlets from contemporary and earlier writers who contributed to 'Puritan Views on Liberty' and an appendix containing documents on the Army and the record of both sets of Debates.

The pamphlet literature selected for *Puritanism and Liberty* is designed to be highly resonant and transparently current. A 1938 review of *Puritanism and Liberty* in *The New English Weekly* supports Woodhouse's contention that with the 'living voices' of the Putney Debates 'begins the modern world.'[28] Yet Jack Lindsay charges Woodhouse with short-changing the radical tradition. Essentially he accuses Woodhouse of the same oversight as cited by Milton's contemporary, the republican commonwealth-supporter Moses Wall, who concurred with Milton about 'the Nonprogresency of the nation ... and its retrograde Motion of late,' but reproached Milton for not attending to the material, economic causes of the seventeenth-century revolution and its failures.[29] Woodhouse's introduction, though brilliant at points, remains antimaterialist and 'rather academic and rootless,' Lindsay judges (77). Regrettable for Lindsay is Gerrard Winstanley's under-representation in the volume at large and any discussion of the contribution of 'dispossessed farmers and ruined journeymen' who comprised Europe's 'first democratic army,' with parallels in later eras in the French revolutionaries, the Red Army, and the Spanish People's Army (77). Lindsay's reference to Wall's 1659 letter to Milton offers evidence that Milton's contemporaries were not oblivious to the economic reasons for their defeat, nor were they unaware 'of the lines on which the future had to develop before the struggle for liberty could begin afresh on securer ground' (Lindsay 77). The 1938 review thus points to the antimaterialist nature of Woodhouse's approach whose Whiggish historiography is more conceptual and idealist than twentieth-century Marxian historicism, and which advances a teleological model.

Mid-twentieth-century Canada presents a different politico-historical climate to which *Puritanism and Liberty* proleptically speaks. The 'Preface to the Second Edition' justifies the appearance of the 1951 book on the basis of the successful first edition that 'was exhausted (by sales, not by war damage)' (*P&L* 5). A.D. Lindsay observes in his postscript: 'The study of this book is even more important than when it was first published' in the midst of 'the rise and spread of an entirely new idea of democracy in eastern Europe,' from which western democracy and liberty must be distinguished.[30] The theme of liberty in Woodhouse's timely pre-war project acquired a new historical resonance in a Cold War anti-Communist era.[31]

I Milton's Puritanism and Liberty

For literary critics and Miltonists, the original date of the appearance of *Puritanism and Liberty* is noteworthy in light of the concurrent formulation of the New Criticism. Nineteen thirty-eight saw the publication of Cleanth Brooks's *Understanding Poetry*, followed by *The Well Wrought Urn* (1947). In the 1941 collection, *The New Criticism*, John Crowe Ransom coined the term New Criticism while outlining some of the formalist principles behind the movement and its emphasis on close reading. F.R. Leavis published *Revaluation: Tradition and the Development in English Poetry* (1936), and *Education and the University* (1943, 2nd ed. 1948).[32] The Cambridge School had embraced the modern-day Johnsonians, T.S. Eliot and Leavis, who excluded Milton from the canon for his alleged 'unwholesome' influence on the poetic tradition and the alienating effects of his language.[33] In a statement he made just over a decade later (1947), by which Leavis would feel betrayed, Eliot conceded that his 'antipathy towards Milton the man' who aligned himself with the 'party of the Puritans' accounted in part for Eliot's earlier repudiation of Milton's verse.[34] The American New Critics, including Brooks who opened *The Well Wrought Urn* with a chapter on 'L'Allegro' and 'Il Penseroso,' and whose work was furthered by Arnold Stein in *Answerable Style*,[35] had been more generous to Milton from the start.

The editing of Milton's prose, the achievement of the left hand according to Milton's own testimony (*YP* 1:808), was first undertaken by John Toland in 1698, followed by Thomas Birch in 1738, Charles Symmons in 1806, George Burnett in 1809, Robert Fletcher in 1833, Rufus Griswold in 1845, J.A. St John in 1853, and then by the Columbia University Press editors. Not only did the Columbia edition not include annotations, it also offered no historical, intellectual context in which Milton's prose might be set.[36] The Yale edition takes up this challenge. Following on the Columbia edition of Milton's works – only the second American edition (1931–8) – Don M. Wolfe produced what might now be judged a much-needed annotated edition of the prose. The first volume of the major collaboration that became the *Complete Prose Works of John Milton* was published in 1953, following the submission of the first manuscripts for the project in 1949.[37] That Woodhouse initially served on the editorial board for the Yale edition is only fitting.

Puritanism and Liberty prepares the way for that project. Woodhouse recognized the need to position Milton the polemicist within a seventeenth-century religious, political, and intellectual climate, and the results, he reports over a decade later in his preface to the 1951 edition, had yet to be surpassed by any study. By aligning Milton with a liberal Puritanism, Woodhouse revived both the poet and also the *revolutionary* prose writer and polemicist. His University of Toronto colleague and former student, Arthur Barker – whom Woodhouse credits in the preface to his 1951 edition of *Puritanism and Liberty* with carrying out the work of locating Milton in relation to a revolution – would shortly thereafter raise the prose to the status of the poetry, thus giving the former its rightful due.

Woodhouse and Barker dealt with the Miltonic oeuvre in a thoroughly contextualized manner, completely out of line with the tenets of the New Criticism. Woodhouse continued to debate and dispute the merits of the 'dogmatic,' 'narrow' New Critical approach through to the early 1950s, when he reiterated that 'self-possession and deliberation [were the] distinguishing marks of Milton.'[38] Central to the debate in which Woodhouse participated with Cleanth Brooks in 1950 was the question about what qualifies as evidence and the methodology that can best interpret admissible evidence. 'Historicist Critics' – among whom Woodhouse lists Haller, Barker, Hughes, and Arnold Williams (1038n1) – can do most justice to Milton's writings by situating them alongside Milton's extra-aesthetic experiences and research on his life, thought, and intentions, a premise spurned by New Critics as the autobiographical fallacy.

In line with the historicist criticism that he had been practicing long before his head-on encounter with Brooks, Woodhouse in the introduction to *Puritanism and Liberty* puts Milton in the company of Roger Williams who, together with Milton, contributes to the 'progressive movement towards the Left' (*P&L* 18n1). But even before his footnoted reference to Milton, Woodhouse is already speaking Milton's language (from his 1646? poem 'On the New Forces of Conscience under the Long Parliament') in stating that the Independents 'discovered that if new presbyter was but old priest writ large, new Parliament also bore a striking resemblance to old King' (*P&L* 17). Woodhouse generously relates Milton's 'pleas for liberty of conscience' to those of Williams in *The Bloody Tenent,* Henry Robinson in *Liberty of Conscience,* William Walwyn in *The Compassionate Samaritan* (among others), and Samuel Richardson in *The Necessity of Toleration,* when introducing the 1648 Whitehall Debates (*P&L* 35). Certainly later scholarship has developed more nuanced accounts of Milton's relationships to these figures on such questions as civic and religious liberty, disestablishment, and the scale of toleration.[39] Woodhouse, however, marshals evidence from the early prose in support of the contention that Milton's championing of liberty puts him in league with leftist Puritans. Further, while not making Milton the subject of the introduction, Woodhouse entertains (parenthetically) the prospect of Milton being 'our chief concern here' (*P&L* 92).

His source for Milton is the Miltonic texts themselves – from the Bohn edition of the prose (1848–53). Offering brief commentaries on a broad survey of Milton's works, Woodhouse's focus in the introduction and the edition proper is almost exclusively on the prose writings: *Reason of Church Government* (1641), the *Doctrine and Discipline of Divorce* (1643), *Areopagitica* (1644), *Tenure of Kings and Magistrates* (1649), *Of Civil Power* (1659), *The Readie and Easie Way* (1660), and *De doctrina* (c.1658–60; pub. 1825). There is also the occasional brief reference to *Paradise Lost,* as Woodhouse offers a fuller representation of the Miltonic oeuvre. However, the energy and progressive movement of the revolution experienced by Milton are largely reserved for and captured in the polemical writings from which Woodhouse derives the bulk of his evidence for his case on Milton's radicalism:

> No sooner has he attacked the problem of religious liberty and reform than he decides that change cannot be too 'swift and sudden provided still it be from worse to better.' Custom, he discovers, is 'a natural tyrant' in religion and in the state, a tyrant which has an ally in man's fallen nature – 'a double tyranny of custom from without and blind affections within.' Custom, it is assumed as self-evident, always enters into alliance with error, never with truth: '... Error supports custom, custom countenances error, and these two between them would persecute and chase away all truth and solid wisdom out of human life, were it not that God, rather than man, once in many ages calls together the prudent and religious counsels of men, deputed to repress the encroachments and to work off the inveterate blots and obscurities wrought upon our minds by the subtle insinuating of custom and error.'[40]

'In this passage,' Woodhouse judges, 'is implied the Puritan view of history (the view which informs Adam's vision in *Paradise Lost*): deterioration is its note, but deterioration relieved by sudden interventions of God in behalf of truth and righteousness.' For the most part, *Paradise Lost* figures only parenthetically in Woodhouse's remarks on Milton, and usually to support the liberationist statements extracted from the prose. Quotations from the Independent John Cook and from a Levellers' tract are used thereafter to reinforce the identification of Milton's views with those of the radicals (*P&L* 50–1), though Woodhouse stops short of identifying Milton as a democrat, marking him instead as a left-leaning Puritan.

In the introduction, *Areopagitica* is the Miltonic treat most often used to illustrate the experimental and experiential nature of Puritanism. While distinguishing among the various strands of Puritanism, Woodhouse states that for the Independents and especially for the dissenters, there must still be allowances for 'progressive comprehension, progressive interpretation.' In this context 'free discussion can (as Milton maintains in the *Areopagitica*) minister to the discovery of the truth and to agreement in the truth' (*P&L* 45). The theories and discourse of *Areopagitica* also pervade the introduction even when the text is not specifically cited. Thus the Areopagitican pronouncement that, while 'Truth be in the field, we do injuriously by licencing and prohibiting to misdoubt her strength. Let her and Falshood grapple; who ever knew Truth put to the wors, in a free and open encounter' (*YP* 2:561) is modulated into a statement on Puritanism and liberty; Woodhouse writes: 'this eager quest of truth ... with the attendant confidence in truth's power to guard itself and to prevail if given an open field, is the deepest and most abiding element in the Puritan campaign for liberty of conscience' (*P&L* 46). Then specifically referencing both *Areopagitica* and *Of Civil Power*, though produced in different decades, Woodhouse determines that Christian liberty constitutes for Milton 'the very corner-stone of his theory of toleration' (*P&L* 65). Fifteen years of historical and personal change impacts Milton's stance on liberty. While Milton's antiestablishment views can, for example, be traced in the pre-1659 works, they were not paramount until Milton confronted the growing scope and complexity of the crisis over toleration, as Balachandra Rajan reminded us.[41] Beginning with Arthur Barker, Woodhouse's successors offered more nuanced readings of Milton's development.[42] In transferring the task of editing the second volume of the Yale prose to his student Ernest Sirluck, Woodhouse made possible the kind of careful contextualization of *Areopagitica* in the 1959 edition that could not be accommodated in Woodhouse's original thesis on Puritanism and liberty. In the same gesture, Woodhouse diverted that project from Don M. Wolfe's extensively annotated, thickly contextualized Yale edition of Milton's prose in volume 1 (1953).

Woodhouse is at pains to establish Milton's public persona, but constantly confronts the tension between his activism and idealism. Spirituality and religion are the basis for Milton's civic and political theories and commitments, as well as for his program for reform. Milton is located at the vanguard of the Puritan Party's efforts at guarding religious and civil aims. Quoting from the *Readie and Easie Way,* without actually referencing the 1660 work, Woodhouse states that Milton speaks of '"the best part of our liberty, which is our religion"; and the Puritan's whole conception of liberty is (as we shall see) deeply coloured by his religious thought, while the second and partially incompatible object of his concern, positive reformation, is equally so coloured' (*P&L* 43). Woodhouse emphasizes the interconnection between the religious and the public, political spheres to affirm Milton's activist agenda: 'in his hands spiritual concepts like "Christian liberty" are capable of being wrested from the contemplative to the active sphere' (*P&L* 44). Comparisons between Milton and Roger Williams in the introduction allow Woodhouse to keep Milton in radical company while doing justice to the different positions advanced by the two advocates of religious and civil liberties: unlike Milton, Woodhouse explains, Williams assigns 'religion to the contemplative spirit, but to the active reserving all the rest of life' (*P&L* 44). Recourse to Milton's *Pro populo Anglicano defensio* (1651), excerpted in the edition proper of *Puritanism and Liberty,* illustrates the emancipatory nature of the Leftist conception of Christian liberty, the formulation of which involves, furthermore, the seamless translation of the theological and ecclesiastical to the civil sphere (*P&L* 67). Milton, like Williams but unlike Luther, champions disestablishment, which the two seventeenth-century writers identify as the means for securing Christian liberty and freedom of church and conscience. Christian liberty thus conceived complements Puritan thought, which Woodhouse aligns with political change: as Milton 'presses on boldly' from the ecclesiastical sphere to the civil (66), so was the doctrine of Christian liberty 'actually pressed into the service of revolution' (67).

The unifying approach Woodhouse applies to Milton's writings as he moves freely throughout the Miltonic oeuvre complements his treatment of the Puritan revolution and twentieth-century history as continuous. Ernest Barker states that his version of *Puritanism and Liberty* would have included Cromwellian speeches and writings in Part III on the Puritan views of liberty, but the presentation of such material, he recognizes, would have required going 'beyond the limit of 1650 to which Professor Woodhouse ... confined himself' (Barker 241). The fact is that the writings by Milton that Woodhouse edits are indeed outside that time frame: none included in the edition proper is from the civil wars' era: *Of Civil Power in Ecclesiastical Causes* (1659), *Pro populo Anglicano defensio prima (Defensio prima)* (1651) and *Defensio secunda* (1654). Brief selections on Christian liberty from these three treatises are categorized under 'The Law and the Gospel: Christian Liberty' (*P&L* IV, Part III), which is limited to writings by Luther and Milton. Woodhouse justifies the inclusion of the post 1640s sources on the basis that 'in Milton himself [Christian liberty, the theological basis for toleration] occurs from 1642 onwards. I have felt free to illustrate it from Milton's clearest expositions, which happen to occur in the decade subsequent to the Debates' (*P&L* 66n1). Implying a consistency of thought in Milton's views on Christian liberty, Woodhouse defends his approach in locating Interregnum writings alongside the Whitehall and Putney Debates of the previous decade.

It is true, Woodhouse acknowledges, that Milton is 'a little remote from the tumult of practical politics' (*P&L* 71), yet he formulates 'with perfect clarity' the position advanced by the Levellers in the *Agreement of the People*, namely that governmental power be restricted and the individual safe-guarded: 'the function of the state is to preserve peace and order and to guarantee the freedom of the individual' (*P&L* 71). The inner law, 'according to Milton, is the law of nature written in the heart,' Woodhouse explains (*P&L* 71), citing the fundamental and original law of nature mentioned in *De doctrina Christiana* (*Prose.* 4:378). In contrast to the tyrannical outward law, 'The ideal condition is to be able to live without laws because "our reason is our law,"' Woodhouse maintains, borrowing Eve's argument from *Paradise Lost* (9.654). As religious and civic spheres intersect, and poetry is used to further polemics, so do the theoretical positions advanced by Milton's works slide easily into the discussions by his radical-minded contemporaries on institutionalized church and state authority. The Leftist Puritans' proposals for institutional reform would, according to Woodhouse's developmental historiography, take root in the '*laisser-faire* ideal of the state' (*P&L* 70) championed by Jeremy Bentham (*P&L* 71).

Underlying the model of a free state is the model of a more or less democratic church (*P&L* 72). Evidence from the pre-Restoration treatise *Readie and Easie Way* is again marshalled in support of Woodhouse's contention that the Puritans of the Left applied their scripturalism to both church and state politics and by extension to theories of disestablishment. Synonymous with God's law, the law of nature underlies his argument for the establishment of a Christian commonwealth on the eve of the restoration of monarchy and the official reinstatement of a national church. 'Those who would reform the state,' Woodhouse quotes Milton as saying, are '"not bound by any statute of preceding Parliaments but by the law of nature only, which is the only law of laws truly and properly to all mankind fundamental, the beginning and end of all government, to which no Parliament or people that will thoroughly reform but may and must have recourse, *as they had (and must yet have) in church reformation ... to evangelic rules*, not to ecclesiastical canons"' (*Prose*, 2:111; *P&L* 72). The law of God on which 'civil excellence' is founded (*P&L* 72) justifies opposition to or destruction of anything that comes into conflict with the law, with reason, and with the rights of the individual.

These examples demonstrate again that Woodhouse's goal is not to install Milton as a writer with a singular voice, but rather to integrate this major figure fully into the history of liberal Puritanism and the polemical fight for liberty. Here the doctrine of Christian liberty informs Puritan thought through the translation of its spiritual character into the revolutionary cause. This transference, Woodhouse explains is 'clearly' illustrated by Milton who spoke 'the language of the military Saints whom he was defending' (*P&L* 67). The process of assimilation entails the representation of Milton's views as central to radicalism, millenarianism, and the Puritan concept of the unfolding of history: 'we may glance at the Puritan attitude to custom, precedent, and history, taking Milton as our example' (*P&L* 50). Milton's prose works from *Of Reformation* (1641) to *Tenure of Kings and Magistrates* (1649) to *The Readie and Easie Way* (1660) are cited as evidence of the zeal for positive reform. In his concluding remarks on Milton, Woodhouse dissociates Milton's radicalism from a democratic position to account for Milton's privileging of the (regenerate) individual over the collective or the majority: 'Despite his passion for liberty, and his partial application, in the interests of religious liberty, of the principle of segregation, he is, as Wordsworth rightly divined, radical but not democratic' (*P&L* 92–3). From Milton's perspective, Woodhouse explains, the law of nature is a law of liberty designed for the rational, the regenerate, not the majority – a characteristic and 'restrictive emphasis' of Puritan thought that Woodhouse had confronted and attempted to counter earlier in the introduction (*P&L* 67–8), again bringing zeal and toleration somewhat closer. Milton's formulation of the law of nature comes with certain restrictions, Woodhouse concedes, but it is not wholly lacking a liberating influence, which it can exert '*as an ideal.*' In fact, while remaining an ideal, it is 'individualist, and even anarchist, in character' (*P&L* 93). The countervailing forces of Puritanism are not suppressed but rather reconciled in the Whig narrative. In the company of J.S. Mill's *Essay on Liberty, Areopagitica* offers the final gloss on terms of liberty: ideal individualism is not associated only with distrust of the state, as *Areopagitica* reminds us, but must be balanced 'by a sense of the community' (*P&L* 100).

II Afterlife: Puritanism and Liberty Revisited

Of concern in this chapter has been the critical, historical, and historiographical models applied by Woodhouse to a reading of Milton, and the value of revisiting and assessing those models for Canadian and international literary scholars, notably Miltonists. The first edition of *Puritanism and Liberty* enjoyed a long afterlife, having been reprinted as a second edition in 1951, 1965, 1966, and 1968, and appearing with a new preface in 1974, and as a third edition in 1986, 1989, and 1992. The early and mid-twentieth-century response was highly favourable, as reviewers from William Haller in 1939 to Alex Gottfried in 1952 defended Woodhouse's assertion that 'our notions of democracy are rooted in the popular religion of the Puritan age' and that 'many elements in Puritan thinking were conducive to the development of democratic ideas.'[43] M.M. Knappen acknowledged at the outset of *Puritanism and Liberty*'s long reception history the significance of the volume for the champions of liberty in its ancient and contemporary forms. Milton scholars number among those champions. 'While doing their work in such a way as greatly to assist the historian,' Knappen explains, Miltonists 'are also aware of current interests,' notably of 'the antiquity of the liberal ideal, of some of its original implications, and of the sacrifices which were made to bring it into existence' and which will ensure its enduring relevance.[44]

The 1951 edition also evokes a specifically Canadian context, which supplements the aforementioned explanations for the book's appearance in the Cold War era, as supplied by Lindsay in the postscript to that edition. In 1949–51 the Massey Commission on National Development in the Arts, Letters, and Sciences, chaired by the then Chancellor of the University of Toronto, Vincent Massey, recommended federal government policy to bolster the cause of the arts in Canada and help render high culture meaningful for and accessible to Canadian audiences. The

Commission's members (Vincent Massey, Hilda Neatby, Georges-Henri Levesque, Norman Mackenzie, and Arthur Surveyer) attributed the relative isolation of writers in Canada to a cultural and national milieu that failed to nurture Canadian arts. In articulating the need to champion Canadian sovereignty by patronizing the arts in the post-war period, the Commission invoked – by way of E.A. McCourt's study – Milton's desire for artistic fame from an early prose work, *An Apology for Smectymnuus:* 'What explanation, it has been asked, can there be other than their environment for the fact that none of them has produced "a book which, in Miltonic phrase, the world will not willingly let die."' In a climate in which an emerging cultural nationalism and liberal humanism were allegedly under seige by an American-dominated media industry, the reprinting of this Canadian-authored work of historical, literary scholarship which invests cultural capital in Milton as a proponent of liberty takes on new meaning.[45]

The historical and cultural context shifts again with the 1974 edition of *Puritanism and Liberty,* which features a preface in which Ivan Roots explains that studies of Puritanism have certainly diverged from Woodhouse's inclusive concept. Yet it would be 'unthinkable' to exclude in later editions of the volume the 'thought-provoking' introduction that Woodhouse produced in 1938. Roots outlines the challenges posed to seventeenth-century Puritanism and Puritan political thought by scholars like C.H. George who attacked the neo-idealism characterizing earlier twentieth-century conceptions of Puritanism generally.[46] While sharing some of the scepticism about the usefulness of such an elastic concept as Puritanism, Roots reserves judgment about its value, leaving the reader hanging on a negatively formulated but open-ended question of whether 'a concept which does accept differences [in ideas, ideals, programs and class affinities is] quite impossible' (xiii [1974 ed.]). In the 1986 third edition, Roots directly addresses 'the historiographical conflict about radicalism in the English Revolution or the Great Rebellion.' This latest edition of *Puritanism and Liberty* invites us to rethink revisionism – which posits traditionalism and 'even apathy as the enduring characteristics of the political nation' (xx) – and Woodhouse's contribution to the war among historians over the nature of radicalism, revolution, and rebellion. Roots insists that the volume Woodhouse assembled is classical, relevant, 'patient of interpretation,' and worth revisiting.[47] The current and lasting controversy 'over change and continuity among the radicals,' as Roots affirms in 1992, will continue to secure *Puritanism and Liberty*'s future in historical scholarship on the seventeenth-century tradition of dissent.[48]

Recognizing that the theory of a Puritan revolution giving rise to liberal ideals 'has fallen on hard times,' John Coffey over a decade ago offered a balanced response to revisionist attacks both on the thesis advanced by Woodhouse – whom he 'Americanizes' – and the theses of the aforementioned S.R. Gardiner and William Haller, whose approaches revisionists had dismissed as anachronistic.[49] In 'Puritanism and Liberty Revisited,' Coffey demonstrates that the radical Puritan zeal for religious liberty is 'a good deal more genuine than revisionist historians seem to imply' (962), and that the 'hotter sort of Protestants' had indeed reached some 'liberal conclusions' (985). Though cited infrequently in Coffey's article, Milton leaves his mark: he is featured as pro-tolerationist. Still he is not akin in his politics or philosophy to the radicals, and that is certainly one of the significant ways in which Coffey's Milton differs from Woodhouse's. Coffey also acknowledges that the minority of zealous Protestants, who were the subject of his article and Woodhouse's volume, had less influence than did mainstream Protestants like John Locke and Milton (969, 984).[50] Recent literary scholars have likewise offered historical recontextualizations of Milton's politico-religious emphases. David Norbrook, Nigel Smith, Sharon Achinstein, Michael Wilding, and Kristen Poole have interrogated Milton's complex relationship to the culture of dissent along the lines outlined by David Loewenstein, who contends that Milton's radical religious politics resembled that of dissenters from whom he nevertheless maintained a 'polemical and authorial independence.'[51] Each scholar also analyses and applies critical and historiographical approaches specific to our time that raise key questions about the poet-revolutionary's literary, religious, and political commitments. Finally, each resituates Milton in terms of the Puritan movement and the controversial history of liberty – the subject of Woodhouse's major contribution to early modern and modern historiography, political and literary history, Milton studies, and Canadian culture.

NOTES

1 S.R. Gardiner, *The First Two Stuarts and the Puritan Revolution* (London, 1876); W.K. Jordan, Preface, *The Development of Religious Toleration in England,* 4 vols (London, 1932–40; repr. Gloucester, MA, 1967), vol. 3 (1938), 9.

2 Blair Worden, 'Toleration and the Cromwellian Protectorate,' in *Studies in Church History,* vol. 21, *Persecution and Toleration,* ed. W.J. Shields (Oxford, 1984), 199 (199–233).

3 William Haller, *Tracts on Liberty in the Puritan Revolution,* 3 vols (New York, 1934), *The Rise of Puritanism ... from Thomas Cartwright to John Lilburne and John Milton* (New York, 1938), *The Leveller Tracts, 1647–1653,* ed. W. Haller and G. Davies (New York, 1944), and *Liberty and Reformation in the Puritan Revolution* (New York, 1955); G.W. Whiting, *Milton's Literary Milieu* (Chapel Hill, 1939); Don M. Wolfe, *Milton in the Puritan Revolution* (New York, 1941); Merritt Y. Hughes, 'Milton as Revolutionary,' *ELH* 9 (1943): 87–116.

4 Milton characterizes the business of prose writing as an inferior practice in John Milton, *The Reason of Church-Government,* in *Complete Prose Works of John Milton,* gen. ed. Don Wolfe, 8 vols. (New Haven, 1953–82), 1:808. (The Yale prose edition is cited as *YP* hereafter.) Sharon Achinstein reviewed the reception history of the contested relationship between Milton's verse and prose, from Milton's observations on the status of art and statements of independence of the poetry through to the modernists' silencing of the prose writer from the Miltonic poet ('Milton: Poetry vs. Prose,' Northeast Milton Seminar, Princeton University, October 2008). Challenging the approach of Barbara Lewalski and David Loewenstein who in different ways aligned the poetry and prose, Annabel Patterson argues that Milton makes a concerted effort to separate his poetry and prose, and reserves the subject of rights for the latter. See Patterson, 'Why Is There No Rights Talk in Milton's Poetry?' in *Milton, Rights and Liberties,* ed. Christophe Tournu and Neil Forsyth (New York, 2007), 197–209. The dissociation of Milton the poet from the polemicist extends as far back as Restoration and the neoclassical eras. On eighteenth-century efforts to suppress the political identity of the classical poet, see 'Those Grand Whigs, Bentley and Fish,' in William Kolbrener, *Milton's Warring Angels: A Study of Critical Engagements* (Cambridge, 1997), 107–32. Kolbrener reminds us by way of J.G.A. Pocock of the multiple manifestations of eighteenth-century Whiggism represented by Modern Whigs like Low Churchman Richard Bentley to Old Whigs like John Toland, a radical deist (Pocock 'Cambridge Platonists and Scottish Philosophers,' in *Wealth and Virtue: The Shaping of Political Economy in the Scottish Enlightenment,* ed. Istvan Hont and Michael Ignatieff [Cambridge, 1983], 215, 231).

5 In the early century, James Holly Hanford and Dennis Saurat cast Milton as a 'rationalist' and 'humanist,' at the expense of 'all elements of Puritanism' (James Thorpe, *Milton Criticism: Selections from Four Centuries* [London, 1951], 16). Balachandra Rajan offers an overview of the literary critical representations of Milton in the 1930s and 1940s in *'Paradise Lost' and the Seventeenth Century Reader* (London, 1947; reissued 1962), 11.

6 A.S.P. Woodhouse, ed. and intro., *Puritanism and Liberty: Being the Army Debates (1647–9) from the Clarke Manuscripts with Supplementary Documents,* foreword by

A.D. Lindsay (London, 1938, repr. 1951, 1965, 1966); unless otherwise indicated, all quotations from *Puritanism and Liberty* are to the first edition and specifically the 1966 reprint, and cited in the essay as *P&L*. Arthur E. Barker, *Milton and the Puritan Dilemma 1641–1660* (Toronto, 1942). See also A.S.P. Woodhouse, 'Milton and His Age,' *UTQ* 5 (1935): 483–513. The quoted verse is from *Paradise Lost* 9.43, 42.

7 William Lamont, 'Puritanism, Liberty and the Putney Debates,' in *The Putney Debates*, ed. Michael Mendle (Cambridge, 2001), 251. See also W. Lamont, 'Pamphleteering, the Protestant Consensus and the English Revolution,' in *Freedom and the English Revolution*, ed. R.C. Richardson and G.M. Ridden (Manchester, 1986), 72–92.

8 The Whiggish interpretation that converted history 'into our present' was first criticized in Woodhouse's day by Herbert Butterfield who objected to teleological models historians and historiographers projected onto the past (Butterfield, *The Whig Interpretation of History* [1931], 47). Progressive, developmental narratives, Marxist and Whiggish, were later discredited by 'revisionist' historians such as Conrad Russell who exposed continuities underlying English politics, emphasized regional over national interests, resisted theories of a Puritan opposition, and maintained the importance of events in three kingdoms, while tending to underplay the shaping role of culture. Geoffrey Elton, Conrad Russell, John Morrill, and originally Kevin Sharpe were among the best-known revisionists. See Nicholas Tyacke's remarks on the great Whig tradition in 'The "Rise of Puritanism" and the Legalizing of Dissent, 1571–1719,' in Ole Peter Grell, Jonathan I. Israel, and Nicholas Tyacke, *From Persecution to Toleration: The Glorious Revolution and Religion in England* (Oxford, 1991), 17.

9 Christopher Hill and Edmund Dell, eds, *The Good Old Cause: The English Revolution of 1640–1660: Its Causes, Course and Consequences: Extracts from Contemporary Sources* (London, 1949); C. Hill, *Puritanism and Revolution* (1958; repr. in Panther ed. 1969).

10 Hill, *Antichrist in Seventeenth-Century England* (Oxford, 1971), *The World Turned Upside Down: Radical Ideas during the English Revolution* (Harmondsworth, 1972), *Milton and the English Revolution* (New York, 1977).

11 John Milton, *Areopagitica*, ed. Ernest Sirluck, vol. 2 of *Complete Prose Works of John Milton* (New Haven, 1959), 555.

12 Milton of all tolerationists 'was to enjoy easily the greatest posthumous reputation among later liberals' and become the only radical puritan tolerationist to exercise great influence in the eighteenth century, Roger Williams, John Goodwin, and Sir Henry Vane having proven less popular in the mainstream of political thought, reports John Coffey in 'Puritanism and Liberty

Revisited: The Case for Toleration in the English Revolution,' *The Historical Journal* 41 (1998): 969, 984 (961–85).

13 John Coffey, *Persecution and Toleration in Protestant England, 1558–1689* (Harlow, 2000), 5. Recent literary scholars and historians have moved from debates over causation to examining the cultural experience of the period. On post-revisionism, see Peter Lake, 'Retrospective: Wentworth's Political World in Revisionist and Post-Revisionist Perspective,' in *The Political World of Thomas Wentworth, Earl of Strafford, 1621–1641,* ed. J.F. Merritt (Cambridge, 1996), 252–83. Other historians and literary critics who have adopted post-revisionist approaches include David Norbrook, John Marshall, and Kevin Sharpe.

14 James I was in general known for his 'confessional bridge-building' (Jonathan Scott, *England's Troubles: Seventeenth-Century English Political Instability in European Context* [Cambridge, 2000], 98–9).

15 *Puritanism and Liberty* was reprinted by J.M. Dent as a second edition in 1951, 1965, 1966, and 1968, and appeared with a new preface in 1974, published by J.M. Dent and the University of Chicago Press. A third edition with a new preface, again by Ivan Roots, appeared in 1986. A second preface by Ivan Roots and a bibliography were added to the 1989 edition, and a third preface and bibliographical update by Roots appeared in the 1992 edition published by Dent. The pagination of Woodhouse's introduction and edition proper remained consistent throughout the long publication history.

16 Woodhouse mentions Burke on the relationship between the 1649 and 1789 revolutions (*P&L* 70).

17 William Haller, *The Rise of Puritanism* (New York, 1938); David Petegorsky, *Left-Wing Democracy in the English Civil War* (London, 1940); George H. Sabine, ed., *The Works of Gerrard Winstanley* (New York, 1941). Arthur Barker would put Milton at the centre of his 1942 study of the Puritan revolution, *Milton and the Puritan Dilemma.*

18 The reviewers from the 1930s onward tended to be historians who focused on Woodhouse's contributions to studies of Puritanism.

19 Christopher Hill, *Milton and the English Revolution* (New York, 1972), 101; Hill quotes *Puritanism and Liberty* (1938), 53.

20 Barbara Lewalski, *Life of John Milton: A Critical Biography* (Oxford, 2000), 610n89, 612n115; David Loewenstein, *Milton and the Drama of History: Historical Vision, Iconoclasm, and the Literary Imagination* (Cambridge, 1990), 162n18, 166n31; Loewenstein and James Grantham Turner, eds, *Politics, Poetics and Hermeneutics in Milton's Prose* (Cambridge, 1990), 119, 120; Loewenstein, *Representing Revolution in Milton and His Contemporaries: Religion, Politics, and Polemics in Radical Puritanism* (Cambridge, 2001), 304n16, 358n20, 373n74, 376n22, 377n32, and passim; Martin Dzelzainis, 'John

Milton, *Areopagitica*,' in *Companion to Literature from Milton to Blake*, ed. David Womersley (Oxford, 2000), 153, 158 (151–8). See also Anthony Arblaster's citation of Woodhouse's edition in *The Rise and Decline of Western Liberalism* (Oxford, 1984), 363nn41, 44. Arblaster's seventh chapter is heavily indebted to the work of Christopher Hill and includes a section on Milton's liberalism (153–6).

21 Paul Stevens, 'Hugh MacCallum, 1928–2008: In Memoriam,' *Milton Quarterly* 42 (2008): 248 (248–30).

22 Lesley Le Claire, 'The Survival of the Manuscript,' in *The Putney Debates of 1647*, ed. Michael Mendle (Cambridge, 2001), 22.

23 Ernest Barker, review of *Puritanism and Liberty*, *UTQ* 8 (1938–9): 241 (238–41).

24 Mark Goldie, 'Roger Morrice and the History of Puritanism,' in *Religious Identities in Britain, 1660–1832*, ed. William Gibson and Robert G. Ingram (Aldershot, 2005), 11–14.

25 A.D. Lindsay, *The Essentials of Democracy*, 2nd ed. (Santa Barbara, 1980), 11.

26 Putney debates of 1647 refer to meetings of the victors in the first civil war about the form of government that should be established in England. Among the issues on the table were the franchise, the place of the monarchy and the House of Lords in any settlement, and any future role for Charles I. The Army Council convened in late 1648 to participate in debates at Whitehall concerning the new constitution.

27 Lamont reports that much of *Puritanism and Liberty* is devoted to pamphlets illustrating 'Puritan Views of Liberty.' 'Woodhouse never pretends that the connection between the two is unambiguous,' Lamont observes; 'His title and his packaging, however, do his work for him' (Lamont, 'Puritanism, Liberty and the Putney Debates,' 241).

28 Jack Lindsay, 'Views and Reviews: The First Modern Revolutionaries,' *The New English Weekly* (10 Nov. 1938): 76 (76–7). For a contemporary Marxian reading of Milton's antimaterialist position as evidenced in his prose, see David Aers and Gunther Kress, 'Historical Process, Individuals and Communities in Milton's *Areopagitica*,' in *Literature, Language and Society in England 1580–1680*, ed. David Aers, Bob Hodge, and Gunther Kress (Totowa, 1981), 152–83.

29 'Moses Wall to Milton,' in *Complete Prose Works of John Milton*, gen. ed. Don Wolfe, 8 vols (New Haven, 1953–82), 7:511 (510–13).

30 Lindsay's 'Postscript to the 1950 Edition' follows his foreword and constitutes part of the front matter of the edition (p. 3).

31 See Sharon Achinstein's superb analysis of the academic climate and literary critical wars of the mid-twentieth century in 'Cold War Milton,' *UTQ* 77 (2008): 801–26.

32 Cleanth Brooks, *Understanding Poetry* (New York, 1938); Brooks, *The Well Wrought Urn* (New York, 1947); John Crowe Ransom, *The New Criticism* (New York, 1941); F.R. Leavis, *Revaluation: Tradition and the Development in English Poetry* (London, 1936), and *Education and the University* (London, 1943, 2nd ed. 1948).

33 Eliot, 'A Note on the Verse of John Milton,' in *Essays and Studies* (1936), quoted in T.S. Eliot, *Selected Prose,* ed. John Hayward (London, 1953), 123–31. F.R. Leavis, 'Milton's Verse,' *Scrutiny* 2 (1933): 123–36, reprinted in *Revaluation: Tradition and Development in English Poetry* (1936) (London, 1959), 42–61. See Annabel Patterson, *Reading Between the Lines* (Madison, 1993), 245–8.

34 T.S. Eliot, 'Milton' (The Henrietta Hertz Lecture, delivered to the British Academy, 26 March 1947) in T.S. Eliot, *Selected Prose,* ed. Hayward, 134. F.R. Leavis, 'Mr. Eliot and Milton,' *Sewanee Review* 57 (1949): 1–30.

35 Arnold Stein, *Answerable Style* (Minneapolis, 1953); see Woodhouse's discussion of Brooks's essay on Milton's early pastoral poems in Woodhouse, 'The Historical Criticism of Milton,' *PMLA* 66 (1951): 1043 (1033–44).

36 *The Works of John Milton,* ed. Frank Allen Patterson et al. 18 vols (New York, 1931–8).

37 Don Wolfe, gen. ed., *Complete Prose Works of John Milton,* 8 vols (New Haven, 1953–82). The less than favourable reception of volume 1, edited by Wolfe, is surveyed in Achinstein.

38 E. Barker, 238; Woodhouse, 'The Historical Criticism of Milton,' 1041.

39 Thomas N. Corns, 'John Milton, Roger Williams, and the Limits of Toleration,' in *Milton and Toleration,* ed. Sharon Achinstein and Elizabeth Sauer (Oxford, 2007), 72–85. But much earlier, Barker had recognized the differences between Williams's and Milton's locations on the scale of toleration (*Milton and the Puritan Dilemma,* 95). Milton's theory of liberty often takes the form of contempt for custom and resistance to restraints without the raising of liberty to a positive value. See Elizabeth Sauer, 'Milton's *Of True Religion,* Protestant Nationhood, and the Negotiation of Liberty,' *Milton Quarterly* 40.1 (2006): 1–19. Woodhouse's progressivism and tendency to absorb all into a Puritanism-liberty alliance discourages a more nuanced approach to Milton's understanding of liberty.

40 Woodhouse quotes *Of Reformation, The Reason of Church Government, The Tenure of Kings and Magistrates,* and *The Doctrine and Discipline of Divorce* in *P&L* 50. He uses the Columbia University Press edition of Milton's complete works, hereafter cited as *Prose.*

41 Elizabeth Sauer, ed., *Milton and the Climates of Reading: Essays by Balachandra Rajan* (Toronto, 2006), 143. See also Feisal Mohamed, 'Liberty Before and After Liberalism: Milton's Shifting Politics and the Current Crisis in Liberal

Theory,' *UTQ* 77 (2008): 940–60; reprinted as chapter 3 of *Milton and the Post-Secular Present: Ethics, Politics, Terrorism* (Stanford, 2011), 66–86.

42 See Barker, 'Of Christian Liberty,' in *Milton and the Puritan Dilemma*, 236–59, esp. 239, 242, 258; and Corns, 84, 85.

43 William Haller, review, *The American Historical Review* 44.4 (July 1939): 856 (855–7); Alex Gottfried, review, *The Western Political Quarterly* 5.1 (March 1952): 156 (156–7).

44 M.M. Knappen, review of A.S.P. Woodhouse, ed., *Puritanism and Liberty: Being the Army Debates (1647–9), Church Quarterly* (April 1939): 211 (210–11).

45 'Canada. Royal Commission on National Development in the Arts, Letters, and Sciences 1949–51' (Ottawa, 1951), xv, iv, 226. For a balanced assessment of the Commission's impact, see Paul Litt, *The Muses, the Masses, and the Massey Commission* (Toronto, 1992). I am very grateful to Patricia Demers for drawing my attention to the Massey Commission report.

46 C.H. George, 'Puritanism as History and Historiography,' *Past and Present* 41 (1968): 97 (77–104). George identified Woodhouse and Haller as the 'major scholarly architects of the neo-idealist interpretive structure which serves as the museum of English Puritanism' and complained about their 'alchemist tricks' in transmuting the 'stuff of puritan piety into the gold of egalitarianism, individual liberty, and tolerance' (102). George's criticism is directed at modern historiographers who associate Puritanism with a distinctive theology, political theory, and the spirit of capitalism.

47 Ivan Roots, 'New Preface,' in *Puritanism and Liberty*, ed. A.S.P. Woodhouse (London, 1986), xxi.

48 Ivan Roots, 'Preface to the 1992 Edition,' in *Puritanism and Liberty*, ed. A.S.P. Woodhouse (London, 1992), xxi.

49 At the opening of 'Puritanism and Liberty Revisited,' Coffey identifies Woodhouse as a distinguished 'American' scholar (961). Coffey makes judicious use of *Puritanism and Liberty*, both the edited materials and the key claims of the author-editor, including Woodhouse's identification of the 'principle of segregation' as applied by the Levellers (Coffey, 977). On the revisionists, see William Lamont, 'Pamphleteering, the Protestant Consensus and the English Revolution,' in *Freedom and the English Revolution*, ed. G.M. Ridden (Manchester, 1986), 72–92; J.C. Davis, 'Religion and the Struggle for Freedom in the English Revolution,' *Historical Journal* 35 (1992): 507–30; Conal Condren, 'Liberty of Office and its Defence in Seventeenth-Century Political Argument,' *History of Political Thought* 18 (1997): 460–82.

50 Coffey develops his argument about the radical Puritan origins of tolerationism in his *Persecution and Toleration* (2000).

51 David Norbrook, *Writing the English Republic: Poetry, Rhetoric, and Politics,*

1627–1660 (Cambridge, 1999); Nigel Smith, *Perfection Proclaimed: Language and Literature in English Radical Religion 1640–1660* (Oxford, 1989); Sharon Achinstein, *Milton and the Revolutionary Reader* (Princeton, 1994), and *Literature and Dissent in Milton's England* (Cambridge, 2003); Michael Wilding, *Dragons Teeth: Literature in the English Revolution* (Oxford, 1987); Kristen Poole, *Radical Religion from Shakespeare to Milton: Figures of Nonconformity in Early Modern England* (Cambridge, 2000); David Loewenstein, *Representing Revolution in Milton and His Contemporaries*, 11.

11 Milton and the Deist Prelude to Liberalism

NICHOLAS VON MALTZAHN

One of the key questions that has been put to liberalism is whether its universalizing construction of reason has too much lent itself to oppressions of those then deemed less rational, at home or abroad. A dark view of the Enlightenment legacy characterized the historical reflections of the Frankfurt School and a like Marxist critique has informed postcolonial suspicions of instrumental reason, construed as a form of Western thought with hegemonic effect. A critique of modern reason has also exercised natural-law theorists, from Étienne Gilson to Pope Benedict XVI, who decry the separation of 'faith and reason' associated with the Protestant legacy to 'the liberal theology of the nineteenth and twentieth centuries.'[1] Further doubts have been raised about the historical scheme that defines modernity in terms of unreason yielding to reason.[2] We are less and less sure of the view of world-history, given its fullest expression by Hegel, in which statehood completes some grand national rite of maturation into modernity, a progress in national reason often measured on a European yardstick, or more recently an American one. If liberals have long held that the sleep of reason produces monsters, their waking reason has been accused of making monsters too. If liberals have long written Milton into their narrative of emancipation, the questions remain of how far he belongs there and, if that narrative itself be disputed, how far Milton already puts it into doubt.

One famous Miltonist was raising such concerns already two hundred years ago. In the essay on Milton that made his name (1825), the young Thomas Babington Macaulay articulated his own misgivings about subject peoples having thus to pass muster, misgivings renewed by today's postcolonial historians. Brought up in an influential abolitionist household, Macaulay lamented that so 'Many politicians of our time are in the habit of laying down as a self-evident proposition, that no people ought to be free till they are fit to use their freedom.'[3] The position he decried was given memorable expression by John Stuart Mill, who decades later still insisted that 'universal teaching must precede universal enfranchisement.'[4] The contest might develop within a nation or between nations. Hence the great debate, for example, between those heirs of abolitionism, Booker T. Washington and W.E.B. Du Bois, regarding the social, economic, and political progress of African-Americans – Washington aiming for several generations of steady improvement but that deliberate speed seen by Du Bois as too constraining a 'not yet' when what was needed was present emancipation, what Martin Luther King voiced as 'the fierce urgency of Now.' Between nations a like concern may prevail: postcolonial writers have movingly protested against that forbidding 'not yet, not yet.'[5] In later years Macaulay himself retreated toward the more cautious colonial position even as he maintained his high regard for Milton. Famously in his 'Minute on Indian Education' (1835) he demanded the promotion of European and especially English literature at the expense of literature native to India.[6] For this curriculum, he especially valued Milton because British legislation forbade any more evangelical colonial education. *Paradise Lost* might thus serve as a conduit for Anglo-conformity and Christian liberty alike.

Debate remains whether liberalism should be seen as some fulfilment of Christian belief or as a reaction against it. Among the issues is the legacy of early-modern toleration. Was toleration to foster the conversation necessary between believers for the fuller discovery of revealed Truth? Or was it to permit a multiplicity of faiths, or even indifference, in which believers and unbelievers alike might agree to disagree, preferring instead to meet on the more neutral ground of a 'reason' more narrowly understood, however universalized thereafter? Milton plainly held the former position. His expansive claims for liberty of conscience entail the most strenuous religious engagements, to which he gave memorable expression in *Areopagitica*.[7] But in the decades after his death, some of Milton's most ardent admirers held the latter position, reconfiguring religious engagements in a more secular realm, with even *Areopagitica* adapted for deist ends. Macaulay already observed the freethinking Charles Blount's extensive use of the tract in his *Just Vindication of Learning* (1679), where Blount could not 'but herein agree with Mr. Milton': lamenting the plagiarism, Macaulay likened this plundering of 'that noble discourse' (elsewhere he styles it 'that sublime treatise') to the barbarians' misuse of the monuments of ancient Rome.[8] Blount associated the Protestant rationality to be enlarged through liberty of the press with 'white'-ness; the arbitrariness of Roman Catholicism with the 'black Indian,' who was to be denied any governance over his betters.[9] In the early 1690s, as fresh oppressions threatened, appeared *Reasons Humbly offered for the Liberty of Unlicens'd Printing* (1693), likely again by Blount, which Macaulay only somewhat misdescribed as 'made out of the other half of *Areopagitica*.'[10] A few years later, Matthew Tindal also drew on *Areopagitica* for his *Letter to a Member of Parliament, Shewing, That a Restraint on the Press Is inconsistent with the Protestant Religion, and dangerous to the Liberties of the Nation* (1698) – this is the borrowing that Ernest Sirluck brought to our attention in an elegant pendant to his edition of *Areopagitica* for the *Complete Prose Works of John Milton*, volume 2 (New Haven, 1959).[11] Deist too is John Toland's application of *Areopagitica* to his own ends, ardently preferring the promotion of 'all Knowledge and Virtue' in republican Greece and Rome to the decline toward censorship he knew, with Milton, to associate with the Roman Empire and its barbarous legacy to the Inquisition.[12]

As proponents of natural rather than revealed religion, Blount, Tindal, and Toland make strange friends to Milton. His power as a Christian writer plainly challenged their presuppositions, even as he seemed worth adapting for their purpose. By reading *Areopagitica* and other writings of Milton through their eyes, we find how the categories of reason and of nation might be emphasized at the expense of other ontological and moral claims fundamental to his Christian beliefs. The shift anticipates the interpretive thrust of what in later generations would be termed liberalism, a change from liberty of conscience to liberal toleration I have described elsewhere through comparison of Milton to his friend and admirer Andrew Marvell.[13] One of Milton's dearest principles, that separation of church and state which he meant to safeguard the church, became one of the main achievements, perhaps *the* main achievement, of later liberalism. But there it came to be promoted in great part so that a more secular society might benefit from the pacification of confessional conflicts. Blount, Tindal, and Toland participate in a universalizing of reason that came to be attended by a redescription of religion as culture and hence particular.

We are heirs to this redescription, where culture finds acceptance as a necessary political consideration, but also as necessarily particular rather than universal. Liberalism, not least in its Canadian expression, now emphasizes pluralism, though the question remains how far some supervening reason adjudicates contending cultural claims.[14] A related concern is whether liberalism may in its embrace of multiculturalism have invited the revenge of the repressed, in a way that erodes civil liberties even as it proposes to extend them. In rewriting religion as 'culture,' liberalism may have built a Trojan horse that allows absolute faith into the citadel of the multicultural state. As students of literature, and hence priests of Apollo, we can with Laocoon at least hurl a spear against its side.

The heirs of liberalism have much at stake in its prehistory, as I shall argue by way of conclusion with reference to two Canadian Miltonists: Watson Kirkconnell (1895–1977) and Ernest Sirluck (1918–). Publishing on Milton first in the 1950s, they were confronted with the polarization of politics during the Cold War. Their studies reveal the strengths and weaknesses of the liberal Milton on the eve of state-supported multiculturalism. Kirkconnell's contribution lay in his translation of analogues for a number of Milton's works. There his premises prove consistent with his role as one of the fathers of Canadian multiculturalism, however indifferent to the claims of any truer pluralism. Sirluck's chief contribution as a Miltonist is his magisterial introduction to volume 2 of the Yale University Press *Prose Works of John Milton* (1959 [1953–82]), where he also skilfully edited *Areopagitica*, presented in its historical context but also as a key text in liberal tradition. Their examples provoke the question of what we make of Milton's expansive claims for liberty of conscience. Do we accept or recoil from the strenuous religious engagements on which he insists? Or do we seek to remake those engagements in a more secular realm? And do we, in teaching *Paradise Lost*, allow aestheticization or historicization to supersede that epic's truth claims? I have long studied the reception of Milton's works, exploring the process through which especially his religious poetry but also his political prose were pacified and made polite. *Paradise Lost* was adopted by a critical tradition where an eventually Kantian emphasis on the autonomy of the work of art prevailed, a putative disinterestedness not now easily reconciled with the interest politics of multiculturalism. Milton's epic also became central to a literary-historical tradition informed by a strongly progressive view of the development of politics and culture. The resulting redescriptions of Milton's epic were part of a longer redescription of religion as culture, in which the sublime was stripped of the theological riches that Milton had worked so long to impart to it.

I

With Macaulay, the sublime of *Paradise Lost* came to be historicized, though he so fostered our wonder at Milton's achievement that we may overlook this legacy to the great nineteenth-century Miltonist David Masson and to later Milton studies. 'The most wonderful and splendid proof of genius is a great poem produced in a civilized age': so Macaulay extolled Milton's achievement in *Paradise Lost* precisely because the epic had been written in a late, 'philosophical' stage of history, in which 'abstraction' and 'general terms' had prevailed over 'perception' and 'particular images.' Against what Milton might have styled inspiration, Macaulay sets the reason prevailing in 'an enlightened and literary society':

> In an enlightened age there will be much intelligence, much science, much philosophy, abundance of just classification and subtle analysis, abundance of wit and eloquence, abundance of verses, and even of good ones; but little poetry. Men will judge and compare; but they will not create.[15]

Hence 'no poet has ever triumphed over greater difficulties than Milton.' The character of that triumph Macaulay describes in comparisons with Dante and especially with Aeschylus. The latter provides him with a way of evoking what he finds most powerful in *Paradise Lost*. However lamentable his regard for Euripides, Milton has, in Macaulay's view, as much or more of Aeschylus in him: here an 'Oriental' aspect, consistent with the Athenian exposure to the East in the time of Aeschylus and Pindar, forestalls the 'amenity and elegance' associated with Greece. Instead, 'All is rugged, barbaric, and colossal.'[16] Milton's religion, like that of his fellow Puritan revolutionaries, strikes Macaulay as at once retrograde and magnificently enabling, as understood through Scottish Enlightenment theories of the progressive stages of civilization. In thus evoking the 'otherness' of Milton's achievement, Macaulay prepares the political turn in his essay toward the defence of the Puritan as well as the Glorious Revolution, and by extension more present parliamentary Reform.

Macaulay did for the nineteenth-century Milton what Addison had done for the eighteenth-century one: he defined how Milton should be read. Both critical assessments were very much republished and entered into frequent use in schools.[17] Addison had pacified the political and religious Milton by making him into a literary figure, using him thus to invigorate an ostensibly neutral promotion of the pleasures of the imagination, however much those lent themselves to his Whig ideology. Macaulay in turn pacified the Romantic Milton, harnessing the insurrectionary hero proposed variously by Blake, Byron, and Shelley to the moderate ends of representative government, even as he exalted 'this great poet and patriot.' Inimitable as Milton's works were, Macaulay urged his readers to emulate 'the zeal with which he laboured for the public good, the fortitude with which he endured every private calamity, the lofty disdain with which he looked down on temptations and dangers, the deadly hatred which he bore to bigots and tyrants, and the faith which he so sternly kept with his country and with his fame.'[18] The secular categories that prevail in this peroration bespeak the priorities in even the young Macaulay's reforming Whig thinking. He here transposes Milton's 'better fortitude / Of patience and heroic martyrdom' into the key of civil virtue but, unlike older Whig ideals of timeless virtue, that now construed progressively in terms drawn from Scottish stadial thought.[19]

Such progressive thought emphasized the moral gains in sophistications of commerce and manners. With their ever more elaborate dominion over nature, human societies achieved forms of comfort and security for which they deserved congratulation. Macaulay's presuppositions raise concerns at once modern and also anticipated by Milton and others about the failings of an only instrumental rationality, the much-disputed problem of 'Enlightenment reason.' Such ratiocination might be expected to enable our dominion of even a fallen world – 'an autonomous secular realm, completely transparent to secular understanding'[20] – or indeed to help us forge a world of our own subjective making. *Paradise Lost* already construes this as a Satanic forgery, however, and instead promotes an understanding of reason that sees it as expressing the relation between an active Creator and his Creation, a world not made by us but discovered, without and within, through participation.[21]

Milton's view of this human potential darkened over the course of his life, but even in his later writings he promotes a conception of reason not inconsistent with his early assertion in Prolusion 7 that

> God would indeed seem to have endowed us to no purpose, or even to our distress, with this soul which is capable and indeed insatiably desirous of the highest wisdom, if he had not intended us to strive with all our might toward the lofty understanding of those things, for which he had at our creation instilled so great a longing into the human mind.[22]

How far might this drive toward 'lofty understanding' lead? Early and in Latin oration, Milton exalts 'what a thing it is to grasp the nature of the whole firmament and of its stars' and so forth, yielding a knowledge that permits rule even of those stars and 'Mother Nature herself' (*YP* 1:296). Later, in his English epic, Milton has his Raphael instead direct

Adam's attention away from the cosmos to Adam's own experience of it, as if to restore the proportion between his knowledge of the world without and of the world within (*PL* book 8). After the Fall, so Milton's archangel Michael teaches, this relation or *ratio* between creature and Creator is to be revealed by faith and conscience to the postlapsarian mind.

Modern suspicion of such beliefs may extend to the foundational claims for knowledge or representation that often followed from them.[23] But however much that legacy has now come into question, such claims for knowledge made the seventeenth century a heroic age for epistemology. A key issue was the difference in modes of apprehension or comprehension – these we might term more synthetic or more analytic ways of knowing. The distinction finds specific discussion by Milton. His position at first seems to recall that of Pascal, who distinguishes between an *esprit de finesse* and an *esprit de géométrie*, the rapid intuition of the former contrasting with the more methodical deduction of the latter.[24] In thus pitting sudden understanding against more laborious proof, setting revealed against reasoned knowledge, Pascal generates a division important especially for his representation of true religion, which demands each separately.[25]

By contrast, Milton sees the two as operating in a more continuous way. The reach of even unfallen human sense is limited – hence the archangel Raphael's need in instructing Adam to liken 'spiritual to corporal forms' – but that there is some more essential likeness between spiritual and corporal the archangel indicates, with earth perhaps 'the shaddow of Heav'n, and things therein / Each to other like' (*PL* 5.571–6). Milton's Raphael has been held to distinguish the 'simple, undifferentiated, intuitive operation of the contemplating intellect (*mens*)' from the intellect's 'discursive, ratiocinative, piecemeal operation together with reason (*ratio*).'[26] But this claim overlooks Milton's insistence that reason comprises both 'Discursive, or Intuitive ... Differing but in degree, of kind the same' (*PL* 5.487–90) – or so at least he conceives of unfallen reason. That humans 'oftest' reason through 'discourse,' as Raphael teaches, is already known to Adam, who had discursively pleaded with God for the creation of a partner 'fit to participate / All rational delight,' seeking 'Social communication' (8.390–1, 429). That the angels 'most' use intuition, he learns from Raphael. But whether corporeal or spiritual, these reasoning souls, human and angelic, are made of the same matter.[27] Hence the possibility Raphael raises that human 'bodies may at last turn all to Spirit, / Improv'd by tract of time' (*PL* 5.497–8). That reason entails the 'freedom to choose' Milton asserts from *Areopagitica* (*YP* 2:527) to the dialogue between Father and Son in book 3 of *Paradise Lost* ('Reason also is choice,' 3.108). What is to be chosen appears more fully from Raphael's instruction, where human participation in Creation is set against the corrosive effects of disobedience (*PL* 5:501, 507–28). As John Milbank has proposed: 'The mannerist counter-example shows that far from the *factum* (the made) self-evidently staking out an area of secular autonomy, it could, on the contrary, for the heirs of a Christian-humanist sensibility be seen as the gateway to transcendence.'[28] In the grand sweep of Milbank's account, which is focused on political theology, he does not much instance who these 'heirs' were. But in an English setting, Milton usefully exemplifies 'an effortless Baroque integration of the "modern" discovery of human making into a traditional Platonic, participatory framework.'[29]

Should we wonder how 'transcendence' may nonetheless disclose a 'participatory framework'? Milton's vast but finite universe is given its bounds by a creating God who can be described at length and offered a suitably biblicist voice, and who with his also creating Son beholds at once 'past, present, future' (*PL* 3.78). In this 'Baroque integration' the distances are great but not without limit. And the Christianity is everywhere explicit and specific. The later aestheticization of *Paradise Lost* may have followed from its literary accomplishment, not least in recalling classical epic, but may also have resulted from a reaction against the very insistence of both its biblicism and its expansive representation of the *ratio* between Creator and Creation.

Milton's ampler conception of reason, and his confidence about the order in Creation of which it was part, shows especially when he meets the challenge of describing the deranging effects of the Fall, where human passions and environmental destruction are of a piece. Here relation and proportion are put to the test. Rational liberty struggles to survive against 'upstart Passions' (*PL* 12.88), which render more gross those lost to them. Hence Milton's frequent representations of visceral distemper, wind, and fury as more than symbolic representations of unreason. When private interest disconnects us from fuller relationship, our estranging perturbation finds a physical expression that Milton often treats contemptuously. In the literary marketplace of the Restoration, his was a distinctive contribution that might invite 'a deleberate & repeated reading' by way of reassurance when so much else was but 'ridecule.'[30] Comparison may be made, for example, with Milton's younger friend Marvell, who is eager to impugn his antagonists less for having passions than for pretending to be above them; pleasant as it is to mock others' vanities, the greater vanity would be to think oneself without them. Milton seems everywhere hostile to private interest as damaging to rational liberty; Marvell seems much kinder to private interest which, if rightly understood, might supply some rationality within the welter of passions.[31] Milton is capable of harsh sexual satire, as in his rough handling especially of Alexander Morus in *Defensio secunda* and *Defensio pro se.* There liberty is at odds with the degradations that follow from vice. Writing toleration tracts for a very different audience in the 1670s, Marvell's handling of sexuality is more protean. Where liberty and the libertine more nearly converge, the only vice may seem hypocrisy.

Milton's visceral representations of unreason turn up in some surprising places. Of the many bravura passages in *Areopagitica* (1644), one of the most memorable is his personification of the many imprimaturs on Davanzati's *Scisma Inghilterra* (Florence, 1638), which he describes as 'seen together dialogue-wise in the Piatza of one Title page, complementing and ducking each to other with their shav'n reverences' (7–8; *YP* 2:504). Milton reproduces the sequence attesting the permission of first the Vicar of Florence, then the Chancellor of Florence, then the Vicar anew and then the 'Chancellor of the holy office in Florence,' so that Vincent Rabatta gives way to Nicolo Cini, with Rabatta then again yielding to Simon Mompei d'Amelia. He follows this with a Roman example where the vicegerent Belcastro prepares the way for Friar Nicolo Rodophi, Master of the Holy Palace. Not least on the otherwise very fully printed quarto pages of *Areopagitica,* the resulting disruption of the typography is dramatic.

The complex of ideas here is peculiarly revealing of some of Milton's most lasting concerns, which affective and analogical continuities emerge in his poetry from the youthful Gunpowder Plot poems to *Paradise Lost.* In *Areopagitica* he jokes that such Roman restraints might 'barre' Satan down in hell, if he 'had not long since broke prison,' and then wonders whether even farting might not be licensed, as Claudius is supposed to have proposed (in an act allowing for the breaking of wind at table, and whether silent or loud: Suetonius, *Vita Divi Claudii,* 32). But the joke is characteristic enough and revealing. The association of Satan with such a digestive distemper had featured already in Milton's youthful comparison of Satan's domain to the lava-fields of 'Trinacrian Aetna' where, as he later has it, a 'subterranean wind' leaves 'a singed bottom all involv'd / With stench and smoak' ('In Quintum Novembris' 35–7; *PL* 1.231–7). (Dryden would later recall the phrase and its association by way of conclusion in *Mac Flecknoe,* where the wind-swollen 'tympany' issues in a 'subterranean wind,' with 'the prophet's part' proving a 'double portion of his father's art.') In Milton's early Plot epigrams, these are styled the 'foedos ... cucullos' – foul hoodies, or friars – who menace King James and his parliament, threatening 'per flammas triste ... iter' ('In eandem' ['Siccine tentasti'], 7; 'In eandem' ['Purgatorem animae'], 8). They anticipate the wind-swept friars of Milton's Limbo, in book 3 of *Paradise Lost,* which Carmelites, Dominicans and Franciscans are blown 'o're the backside of the World,' with 'Cowles, Hoods, and Habits ... then Reliques, Beads / Indulgences, Dispenses, Pardons, Bulls' (*PL* 3.487–97). Those orders had long been mocked by Milton as 'mendicantum series longissima fratrum,' a servile train enslaved by a whoring Pope ('In Quintum Novembris' 58, 76).

Such distempers, and their association with Roman Catholicism, may have been a staple of Milton's youth, but they point to a psychology, and indeed a cosmology, that finds fullest expression in *Paradise Lost.* It has been noted of this poetry that 'The conflict of winds, reverting to chaos, often symbolized chaotic emotion'; that 'Macrocosmic disorder becomes subjective metaphor.'[32] In keeping with the vitalism of that day, however, there is a fuller relation between the two than these terms 'symbol' or 'metaphor' may indicate. Macrocosm and microcosm are continuous in no incidental way. Milton's archangel Raphael emphasizes this in explaining to Adam the efficiency of angelic digestion, turning 'corporeal to incorporeal,' the vitalist basis for which process he also cares to expound (*PL* 5.404–33, 436–43, 469–500). With the sterner Michael, the fallen Adam witnesses death by disease in his second vision, when his instructor assures him of the diseased that 'Thir Makers Image ... Forsook them, when themselves they villifi'd / To serve ungovern'd appetite,' to which the only answer is 'temperance ... In what thou eatst and drinkst' (*PL* 11.515–32). From Paul's letter to Romans (16:18) derived a lasting suspicion of those who serve not Jesus 'but their own belly.' Already in embarking upon his antiprelatical pamphlets in 1641, Milton had decried the 'carnall' engrossment of the soul in a corrupt church and excoriated the 'belly-cheere' of the bishops guilty of assisting this decline; that this was not only figurative appears from his unloving evocation of 'the many benefice-gaping mouth of a ... canary-sucking, and swan-eating Prelate' (1:519–22, 549, 719; 3:241). He was in 1649 to complain likewise of the Presbyterian divines having 'preach't their own bellies' (*YP* 5:449). To be 'deluded by belly-doctrines into a devout slavery' had been the affliction already of the ancient Jews, 'untill our Saviour for whom that great and God-like work was reserv'd, redeem'd us to a state above prescriptions by dissolving the whole law into charity' (*YP* 2:588).

The obedience required for this redemption contrasts with the slavery of corruption, a slavery that results in the disfiguring of much more than just guilty humankind. Milton insistently describes the disarranging of the cosmos that follows from the Fall as if the human and the geophysical were intimately related. In the moment of Eve's eating the forbidden fruit, 'Earth felt the wound, and Nature from her seat / Sighing through all her Works gave signs of woe, / That all was lost' (*PL* 9.783–4). When Adam thus transgresses, 'Earth trembl'd from her entrails, as again / In pangs, and Nature gave a second groan'; some first thunder also sounds, and rain (*PL* 9.1000–4). Typhoon and earthquake eventuate from the human Fall. Later, loyal angels perform God's 'several charge' by laboriously setting the earth (or sun) on a different axis (*PL* 10.650, 668–87). The result is the buffeting winds from every point of the compass, whether the cold of Siberia and Canadian Norumbega, or the high heat of African Sierra Leone (*PL* 10.693–706). Adam too is 'in a troubl'd Sea of passion tost' (*PL* 10.718).

How did Milton know that the earth had groaned at original sin, that there had been this profound correspondence between human choice and nature? His biblicism guided this determination. The economical narration of Genesis 3 only reports God's judgment after the Fall: 'cursed is the ground for thy sake' (Gen 3:17). Milton seems to have understood this in a double sense. *Paradise Lost* describes this curse operating as if a punishment but also a kindness to humans, who would otherwise be sloughed off entirely by a pure creation in which the impure can have no part. Painful as the harsh climate and other features of the fallen world prove, the law God has given to nature requires these alterations since otherwise 'Those pure immortal Elements that know / No gross, no unharmoneous mixture foule, / Eject him tainted now' (*PL* 11.49–52). For the earth's groaning at this change Milton draws on Romans 8.22. The epic's description of the wider natural effects of Adam's 'distemper' follow from Paul's assertion that as a result of sin 'the whole creation groaneth and travaileth in pain together until now.' The condemnation of Sin in book 10 in *Paradise Lost* draws on Romans 8 for the same purpose. Romans 8 is not one of Paul's easier passages; the chapter met with much close exegesis then, as it has since, and its peculiar interest for Milton is attested by his frequent quotations from it in his *De doctrina Christiana*. The dominion given to humans as the completion of Creation, described with such verve in *Paradise Lost*, book 7, leads at the Fall to the confusion and subsequent incompletion of natural order. Human unreason issues in 'Outrage' in first 'liveless things' and then 'among th' irrational,' as Death expands his ambit (*PL* 10.706–12). From self-giving relationship modelled in the interactions of God the Father and the Son, the decline into self-asserting destruction continues. Where man 'permits / Within himself unworthie Powers to reign / Over free Reason,' the result is that

God in Judgement just
Subjects him from without to violent Lords;
Who oft as undeservedly enthrall
His outward freedom: Tyrannie must be,
Though to the Tyrant thereby no excuse. (*PL* 12.90–6)

Michael's instruction on this point follows from his narration of the confusions of Babel, where the vanity of human making is conspicuous and leads in Milton's representation directly to the violence of Nimrod. Late in book 12, the constraints on true religion that Michael describes show the renewal of religious liberty, not least in the revival at Pentecost of a common language of the Holy Spirit, again subjected to secular power in impositions hostile to reason (*PL* 12.507vv). Against that destruction of relationship God has already prepared in humans his 'Umpire *Conscience*' (*PL* 3.195; italics in original) which will achieve 'peace' not through law alone but in Christ (*PL* 12.296–9). The living reality of 'Faith and Conscience' is set against any pretended infallibility, conciliar or papal (*PL* 12.529–30).

Milton's apocalyptic confidence found little favour with his deist readers, none of whom quicken to that part of the peroration to *Areopagitica* that glories prophetically 'when God shakes a Kingdome with strong and healthfull commotions to a generall reforming,' rejoicing in 'the order of Gods enlightning his Church, to dispense and deal out by degrees his beam, so as our earthly eyes may best sustain it' (*YP* 2:565–6). 'He sees not as man sees, chooses not as man chooses': in such revelation Milton delights, but soon a different kind of Enlightenment governed the application of Milton's works to later controversies.

II

Further to distinguish Milton's conscientious biblicism, we may return to those later patrons of 'rational liberty' and posthumous friends to

Milton, Charles Blount (1654–93), Matthew Tindal (1657–1733), and especially John Toland (1670–1722). The precocious Toland so soon caught up with the older pair that they may be thought of as of one generation, in which works of Blount-Tindal-Toland can seem remarkably of a piece. These figures have been cited as clear instances 'of how Milton's rhetoric, as Royalists in the Restoration feared, made inroads on the minds of men and inspired them to march to the measure of his thought'; thus said George Sensabaugh in the 1950s, in the grips of an emancipatory Whig narrative where Miltonic liberty seemed to reach down through American history to the recent triumph over tyranny in the Second World War. Closer scrutiny proves otherwise.[33]

Even a few examples soon show the profound difference in orientation between the Milton of *Areopagitica* and Blount-Tindal-Toland's later adaptations of that work, with Toland's relation to *Paradise Lost* also revealing less than a 'march to the measure of [Milton's] thought.' Their handling of his religion can verge on contempt. When Milton worries about the destructive influence of licensing even on posthumous publications or republications, he regrets the loss of even 'one sentence of a ventrous edge, utter'd in the height of zeal, and who knows whether it might not be the dictat of a divine Spirit, yet not suiting with every low decrepit humour of [the licenser], though it were Knox himself, the Reformer of a Kingdom that spake it ...' (*YP* 2:534). When Blount expresses a like concern, he regrets the loss instead of 'any one Opinion ... whether it be of a Vacuum, Motion, Air, or never so inconsiderable a Subject' (*Just Vindication*, 8). Or, where Milton protests 'who knows not that Truth is strong next to the Almighty; she needs no policies, nor stratagems ...' (*YP* 2:563), Blount avers only that 'Truth needs no Policics, no Stratagems ...' (*Just Vindication*, 14).[34] Again, where Milton trusts the 'faith and discretion' of 'the common people' (*YP* 2:536), Blount relies only on their discretion (*Just Vindication*, 10).

In 1693, the use of *Areopagitica* in *Reasons Humbly offered for the Liberty of Unlicens'd Printing*, which purports to be 'a Letter from a Gentleman in the Country,' one 'J.M.,' 'to a Member of Parliament,' reveals telling generic differences. Milton impersonates an Athenian citizen into whose address 'humble' does not enter and whose many Attic flourishes his imitators did not soon reproduce. In the 1690s, the author trades on social standing more than civic virtue, with the (Whig) social position imputed to 'J.M.' briefly enlarged upon in the introduction, which mentions 'our Leisure-Minutes (Honoured Sir),' in which 'we have entertained our selves with Discourses about the Printing Act' (*Reasons Humbly offered*, 3). The title 'reasons humbly offered,' very frequently used for such pamphlet petitions to Parliament, also implies a different role for the author. The long borrowing here from *Areopagitica*, soon followed by a briefer one from Marvell's *Mr. Smirke*, bespeaks a lesser vision of what authorship or publication may constitute, with Milton's civic 'speaking' reductively reproduced in such rewritings.[35]

Revealing too is how Milton's arguments against press licensing inform Matthew Tindal's response to the lapse of licensing in the 1690s and to the debate over its renewal that lasted into the first years of the 1700s.[36] Ernest Sirluck observes Tindal's indebtedness to *Areopagitica* – *Areopagitica* converted Tindal from 'one who would have tried to withhold the power of licensing from the clergy by vesting it in the state into the protagonist of an unlicensed press as the basic guarantee of all liberties' (274) – and skilfully situates Tindal's *Letter to a Member of Parliament* (1698) in its historical context at the turn of the century. Where Sirluck was concerned to establish 'something like a continuous influence' of *Areopagitica*, my argument turns on a point he raises only in brief: that the deist Tindal had rather different objectives in view in the 1690s than did the Milton of the 1640s. Sirluck finally wonders whether there are 'other cases of unacknowledged use' of *Areopagitica* to 'fill the apparent gap between 1707 and 1738' – and there are a few, though of modest import[37] – but the real issue remains the character of the cases to which Sirluck draws our attention.

Some competing impulses complicate the work of Tindal and the radical Whigs whose company he kept. Fundamental was their defence of toleration, but toleration to what end? On this matter, John Locke's *Letter Concerning Toleration* (1689) was an influential and oft-cited text. Locke had, in William Popple's translation, averred that 'Every man has commission to admonish, exhort, convince another of error, and by reasoning to draw him into truth,' whereas 'to give laws, receive obedience, and compel with the sword, belongs to none but the magistrate,' whose penalties in religion 'are absolutely impertinent; because they are not proper to convince the mind'; 'It is only light and evidence that can work a change in men's opinions; and that light can in no manner proceed from corporal sufferings, or any other outward penalties.'[38] Tindal and others were prompt to add Lockean improvements:

> as far as the Reasonableness of an Opinion is seen, so far only can it operate on a rational Creature; and the more Examination renders it so, the more force it will have on the Affections, which are not mov'd without some sensible Connexion between the Cause and the Effect. For this reason thinking

> Men, Truth being endear'd to them as the discovery of their own Industry, are for the most part very conscientious; while those that owe their Religion to the chance of Education, have generally no more regard to it, than if they ow'd it to the Chance of a Die.[39]

They were rather less prompt to dwell on Locke's emphasis on our 'commission to admonish, exhort, convince another of error, and by reasoning to draw him into truth.' This was, if recalled, often construed in a more secular way, not least in support of the Protestant succession. When Tindal upholds 'the Protestant Religion' in the same breath as he defends 'the Liberties of the Nation,'[40] he hopes that civil religion might shape a cohesive polity, where patriots rallied to the call of nation, overcoming priestcraft at home and abroad.[41]

Even as they were drawn to more esoteric speculation about God and might seek freedoms not easily reconciled with their exoteric claims, these writers might be guarded in their expression of their views. Some of this was prudence: reactions might be severe especially against anti-Trinitarian writings; moreover, institutions under the control of the Church of England or of Dissent did not soon forgive such transgressions. But some was also a reluctance to enter into fuller debate that might put into question their emphasis on sincerity in religious opinion, the individuality of conscience. On this point, Locke's more scholastic construction of conscience found ready simplification into something much nearer his definition of 'enthusiasm.' Moreover, where the deist Tindal inveighs against the slavery of priestcraft and insists on man as rational and sociable, others, including the influential Miltonist John Dennis, hoped through their statecraft to harness the passions to more rational, and national, ends.[42] But had that rational sociability been impaired only by priestcraft? Their oracle John Locke had not claimed so much.

Toland's influential role as an early Enlightenment figure makes his handling of Milton peculiarly instructive.[43] The response to his 'adaptations' was often hostile in his lifetime, more positive since.[44] As Toland broadened the war against Stuart kingship beyond just James II, he sought to darken even the memory of the sacrosanct Charles, King and Martyr. Here Milton made a useful auxiliary. But that campaign met with only mixed success and I have elsewhere described Toland's subsequent transformation of the regicide 'Calves-head' Milton into Milton 'the apostle of toleration, a more attractive figure to eighteenth-century readers.'[45] Toland's toleration is not Milton's, however, nor is Toland's religion, wedded as it is to his emphases on reason and on nation.

Toland's failings as a poet reveal the instrumental view of the 'force' of eloquence he holds and the flattening conception of reason from which that view follows. In his *Clito: A Poem on the Force of Eloquence* (London, 1700), Toland sought to 'embody "freedom,"' a dramatization of 'an enthusiastic moment of poetic inspiration free from any trace of inspiration,' where 'the poem becomes its own model' in a way that was becoming characteristic of Whig heroic poetry in the reign of William III.[46] Central to Toland's poetics are his hopes for his 'creating pen' (8). His idea of 'invention,' traditionally the first part of rhetoric, shows him shifting away from an older meaning of 'invention' as a finding out or discovery, in the way of the Latin *invenire* (now an obsolete or archaic usage), to the newer (and lasting) use of the word to describe fresh contrivance or origination, or invention, as we now would say.[47] Toland proposes that his 'fertil Brain [will] new Terms produce, / Or old Expressions bring again in use, / Make all Ideas with their Signs agree' in a hugely effective way (6–7); elsewhere he more modestly hopes that 'what in faint Ideas I conceive, / A matchless Hero will by Facts atchieve' (11).

Where Milton is often suspicious of nation, Toland exalts patriotism and vaunts the 'Patriot's tongue' (*Clito*, 11). In the 1670s, Milton might come to see nation as a necessary bulwark against worse evils. In the 1690s and after, Toland shares the perception but seems much readier to make nation an end in itself. Nation seems an inescapable category for even religious belief when Toland, or his publisher 'W.H.,' insists patriotically on 'no national Religion being less interested, or more rational' than that of England. Where Milton had known that the Holy Spirit prefers 'Before all Temples th' upright heart and pure' (*PL* 1.18), the still less Trinitarian Toland agrees that the 'one, true, all-perfect DEITY' has as 'His sacred Temple ... e'ery good Man's Heart' (*Clito* 17). But that deity now gives his 'first Applause' to those 'Who stake their Lives in their dear Contry's Cause' (17), as Toland professes to do. Defending his own role, he notes the role of the press in generating that wider 'imagined community' to which modern nationhood has more recently been attributed, even if with Toland it may seem his own agency that is being promoted rather than any more collective communication. The eloquence that might stir the *polis* he understands now to 'reach more with more success' if brought to 'the Press' (6).

Freedom might seem to require some exaltation of nation as a defence against worse threats to reason. In this world of political economy, where nation vies with nation, a martial note often enters into Toland's 'ranting and *ALMANZOR*-like strain' – Dryden's too individual hero from *The*

Conquest of Granada is thus recalled in the introduction to *Clito*, perhaps by Toland himself, to frame the Tolandian sublime. Excited as he is at the thought of rousing 'sluggish Cowards ... to use their Swords,' Toland might in the wake of the standing-army controversy also fantasize that such 'warlike Troops I shall with ease disband' (*Clito*, 6, 10). To think of Almanzor – rather a one-man army – is in part to wish away the sterner logic and less relenting momentum of the emerging early-modern military-industrial complex, which the Toland of *The Militia Reform'd* (1698) and other such pamphlets confronted in service to 'Public Liberty.'[48] But Toland stops well short of Milton's condemnation as Satanic of this militarism, which Milton conspicuously gave modern expression to in the rebel angels' newly 'invented' artillery in the War in Heaven. Milton had played insistently on the word 'invent' or 'invention' in describing this diabolic innovation, in a way consistent with his suspicious handling of the word elsewhere in the epic.[49] In *Paradise Lost*, such inventing or 'making' was defiantly adversarial rather than participatory, an abrupt expression of unrelation.

The limits of Toland's unmysterious Christianity appear when he ends *Clito* with two famous stanzas from Horace: 'Iustum et tenacem propositi virum ...' (Odes 3.3; *Clito*, 22). This resolution in a just cause is imagined by Horace as unshaken even by the great hand of thundering Jove ('fulminantis magna Jovis manus,' as Toland has it); indeed, the just man is fearless even should the heavens crash down upon him ('Si fractus illabatur orbis, / Impavidum ferient ruinae'). But what Jove, what heavens? Horace had no reason to suppose Jove as pre-existing the heavens or as a Creator shaping a creation where humankind has a completing role and it is God's doing that reason and justice so cohere. In so invoking Horace, Toland shows a readiness again to abandon the 'participatory framework' in keeping with his apparent uncertainty about creation, whether *ex deo* or *ex nihilo*, and with his hope that the cosmos and its contents 'Shall only after me be rightly named,' a somewhat Adamic role that perhaps pointedly overlooks Adam's own history (*Clito*, 8–9; *PL* 8.272–3 and passim).

'With Priestcraft is the war':[50] Toland plainly rejoices in such allies against *l'infâme* as Milton and Marvell, whether he credits them as 'great men' or makes their words his own. But was Milton (or Marvell) quite so outraged by priestcraft? That word, given its present sense by James Harrington, he never uses despite his often inveighing against what might be so styled. Milton's anticlerical writing reveals a preoccupation chiefly with 'hirelings,' with those often discovered along confessional lines, as in his extraordinary flights of rhetoric against episcopacy especially in his tracts of 1641–2, or then also in his famous lament that '*New Presbyter* is but *Old Priest* writ Large' and like fulminations again those 'unhallowed Priestlings' the Presbyterians, whose 'classic Priestship is too gripple' (*YP* 3:322–3 [*Observations*]). But this was for Milton part of an urgent program of reform toward a more effective, freer ministry, a closer communion with Christ. His quarrel was with ministers, not with ministry.

Toland was more reductive in delighting in Milton's anticlerical sallies (and much besides). The prefatory biography of Milton that Toland contributed to the 1698 *Complete Collection* of Milton's prose gave him a chance to air many of his special interests; his contemporaries saw him as casting Milton in his own image. Quoting from Milton's earliest verse, for example, the liberty-promoting Toland seized upon the opening lines of the 114th Psalm, beginning 'When the blest seed ... their Liberty had won'; he also gladly digresses on the career of Milton's brother Christopher, because he can thus make a radical Whig claim for the revolution of 1688–9, when James II 'was depos'd for his Maladministration by the People of England, represented in a Convention at Westminster.'[51] Other asides touched on more recent issues or events, as when he laments the persecution of the wealthy Presbyterian Daniel Williams, who had been accused of Socinianism, as had Toland himself (26); or goes out of his way to applaud among Milton's Genevan acquaintance Ezekiel Spanheim, that 'celebrated Critic and Antiquary,' brother of the Friedrich Spanheim (the younger) who had been Toland's own tutor just a few years before;[52] or grinds some Irish axes mocking the Presbyterians there for their 'Popish Inquisition,' under which Toland had recently suffered.[53] Elsewhere he seems to be recommending the institution of Latin Secretary as if he might himself fulfil the role (26). His omissions too are suggestive, not least his suppression of all reference to Milton's caustic *Character of the Long Parliament*, an awkward text for Toland's republican purposes, and one that he must also have viewed as regrettable owing to its mistaken emphasis on the climatic basis for the English lack of national virtue.[54] With reference to Milton's visit to Rome Toland could intrude his own more present opinion of the sad decline of that city when 'the Ambition of a few Persons corrupted her equal Government.' He was prompt to supply what Milton must have thought about that city:

> no doubt, all the Examples he had hitherto read of the Virtue, Eloquence, Wisdom, or Valor of her antient Citizens, occur'd to his mind, and could

> not but oppress with grief his generous Soul, when with his own eys he saw *Rome* now the chief Seat of the most exquisit Tyranny exercis'd by effeminat Priests ... (9)

Just the same opinion Toland expresses as his own in another tract of this date.[55] His grief at the Roman decline into superstition also animated his lament for the aging Galileo, whom Toland's Milton found 'a Prisoner to the inquisition for thinking otherwise in Astronomy than pleas'd the Franciscan Friers' – Toland here silently quoting *Areopagitica* for a gibe he was glad to make his own.[56]

Toland knew to praise *Paradise Lost* but the terms in which he did so again reveal his uses for the epic and also his likely reservations about Milton's achievement. He adopts the idiom of sublimity that had so soon predominated in discussion of the poem, especially after its republication in 1674: 'the unparallel'd Sublimity and Force of the Expression, with the delicacy of his Thoughts, and the copiousness of his Invention, are unanimously own'd by all ranks of Writers' (40). But the sublime was as yet a rhetorical more than an ontological category. Toland's fascination with Milton's expressive 'Force' is contemporary with his exploration of the force of eloquence in *Clito.* For his biography, however, he does not investigate Milton's method as an epic poet; there is nothing here of Samuel Johnson's later mix of biography with criticism.

Milton had seen rhetoric reaching through language into Being in a way Toland could not master. From *Paradise Lost,* Toland quotes at length only the invocation to book 3: 'Hail, holy Light ...' – the column of these fifty-five lines fills a folio page in his prefatory biography in the 1698 *Complete Collection* of Milton's prose (1:41). In part he does so because Milton thus 'perpetuats the History of his own Blindness.' But here Milton also colours Toland's imagination of what might be done through eloquence. Styling himself the unsuperstitious Adeisidaemon in *Clito,* Toland imagines his own transformative eloquence:

> Thus arm'd, thus strong, thus fitted to persuade,
> I'll Truth protect, and Error straight invade,
> Dispel those Clouds that darken human sight,
> And bless the World with everlasting Light.
> A noble Fancy dos possess my Soul,
> Which all may forward, nothing can controul;
> The fate of Beings, and the hopes of Men,
> Shall be what pleases my creating Pen. (*Clito,* 7–8)

Milton had asked a series of questions in invoking Light as expressing the roles of Father, Son, and Holy Spirit: 'May I express thee unblam'd? ... Or hear'st thou rather pure Ethereal stream, / Whose Fountain who shall tell?' He had tested the limits of language – 'Bright effluence of bright essence increate' – to evoke the relations of Godhead without overdetermining their nature as Trinity. By degrees Milton then turns from his loss of the sun's light to the 'Celestial light' he bids 'Shine inward ... that I may see and tell / Of things invisible to mortal sight' (*PL* 3.21, 51–5). He returns to this language of light in describing the Father's relation to the Son in book 6: 'Effulgence of my Glorie, Son belov'd, / Son in whose face invisible is beheld / Visibly, what by Deitie I am' (6.680–2). By contrast, in his own *furor poeticus,* Toland sees himself as intervening to 'bless the World with everlasting Light.' This is not just a flattering piece of self-assertion, however. For Milton's metaphysics leave Toland cold, as does the poet's representation of Hell.

Toland's campaign against superstition included contempt for Hell and its terrors. And yet the dominant feature of *Paradise Lost* for many of its readers had since its first publication been Milton's description of Satan in Hell. This was a literary triumph that the deist plainly regretted. Milton and Toland were in agreement that 'Hell's always flaming in a Villain's Mind' (*Clito,* 18): compare Satan's boast, 'the mind is its own place' (*PL* 1.254), his lament 'my self am Hell' (*PL* 4.75), and the epic's insistence on 'the hot Hell that alwayes in him burnes' (*PL* 9.467). But Milton had lengthily investigated more material torments of a kind that Toland associated with the impostures of priestcraft. Toland inveighs against 'the vain Terrors of HELL's Court,' which he will expose as the frauds of 'Priests and Poets.' He aims soon to dispel all these and to

> Extinguish all their Flames,
> Dry up their Rivers, break their ratling Chains,
> Poison their Serpents, fright each hideous Form,
> Cerberus choak, and PLUTO's Castle storm,
> Legions of Fiends to Atoms I'll reduce. (*Clito,* 18)

These features of Hell find elaborate representation in *Paradise Lost.* But Toland construes them as empty deceit. The persecutory imagination he laments as a tool of priestcraft; its English literary legacy was considerable and not only in Milton's descriptions of hell.[57] Toland is not averse to imagining himself as a persecutor of these persecutors, as when he proposes to frighten all the pope's 'Vassals into Dens and Caves, /

Then smoak to death the sacrilegious Slaves' (*Clito*, 14). His eagerness to debunk 'all their awful Mysterys' issues from his conviction that 'Sound Reason is the Law that likes him [God] best' (*Clito* 16). Milton, by contrast, had been more confident about the relation between 'awful Mysterys' and 'Sound Reason.'

III

When recruited for the progressive Whig project, Milton was written further into the triumphant history of British imperialism. Though this met with prescient critiques, especially from Samuel Johnson (Tory) and William Blake (radical), such dissenting voices weighed little in the consensus that emerged.[58] In colonial Canada, older Whig views found expression especially by those ardent proponents of 'responsible government' against the patronage system that so dominated colonial administrative appointments. Here the Scottish Enlightenment legacy to Canadian education, not least at the university level, was far-reaching, if as yet incomplete. Just when Macaulay's essay on Milton was meeting with such esteem, a son of the Scottish Enlightenment, the energetic colonial schoolmaster Thomas McCulloch (1776–1843), was eagerly equipping his Pictou Academy with copies of Milton along with Hugh Blair, George Hill, and Adam Smith's lectures respectively on rhetoric, divinity, and political economy, along with many other like publications.[59] These might leaven the critical and rhetorical study of Latin and Greek authors which dominated the first years of the curriculum at his academy, for McCulloch sought a more 'liberal education' beyond what was offered in 'colleges under monkish arrangements.'[60] But this was still an education in eloquence rather than history. Its construction of virtue was timeless, rather than diachronic, consistent with the 'Country' party of yesteryear, where alienated Whigs and Tories might join in their preference for landed virtue over the dangerous speculations of commercial society.[61]

Also like an older Whig, rather than yet an early nineteenth-century promoter of Reform, McCulloch conceded little to Roman Catholicism when he urged non-denominational education against the Anglican establishment in Nova Scotia.[62] Instead, the thrust of McCulloch's work was to carry his strictures against popery also against the Church of England and patronage appointments in the colonies, complaints sharpened by his lament that the Canadas were falling ever further behind the United States.[63] McCulloch became the first president of Dalhousie University, in the founding of which he had played a role. Among his own successful pupils a number went on to become presidents of other Canadian universities being founded on the Scottish rather than the Oxbridge model.[64] Their success followed in part from his Scottish emphasis on natural history: McCulloch's scientific commitments distinguished him, both in the laboratory and in the field (Audubon admired his collections and commissioned specimens from him). But this empirical bent did not yet extend to much historicizing of the study of literature.

That change from a rhetorically to a historically driven reading of literature required much institutional change in the course of the nineteenth century. All the while, Scottish education became at once a means of governing Empire and of fostering postcolonial independence from the metropolitan centre. In the universities formed on the Scottish model, this later development of English Literature came to feature Milton as a central figure. The academic Milton was significantly shaped by later Scots, especially when Carlyle's heroic projection of 'a last glimpse of the godlike' in the English Revolution was brought back to a more Macaulayan and liberal mean in David Masson's monumental *Life of John Milton* (London, 1859–94).[65] When more progressive Whig thought celebrated the politeness fostered in commercial societies in later stages of history, admiration for Milton's sublimity vied with respect for his sophistication of the vernacular, which found study in its own right. Provincial sophistication might seem a prelude to provincial political independence, except that it still deferred so much to metropolitan standards, fundamental to the claims for empire inherent in the progressive Whig view. The elaboration of English Literature as a course of study made it a significant vehicle of Anglo-conformity, especially in the twentieth century. In many parts of the British Empire this entailed the colonial education of native populations. But in Canada where those were in forced retreat (First Nations), or otherwise linguistically separate (French Canada), the emphasis might lie instead on responding to the increasing number and diversity of immigrants with educational policies directed toward their assimilation, soon or late, to a British-Canadian and often Christian norm.

Proponents of rapid assimilation often declared their interest openly. Even as they conceded 'that there are a great many other types than our own, and some just as good, though different,' and suggested they would 'meet these people half way,' they also held that this encouragement 'in every forward movement' must be directed toward 'our Canadian heritage,' with that firmly associated with 'the English race.'[66] But there was a subtler strain in assimilationist thinking in early to mid-twentieth-century

Canada that expressed itself less clearly. Here we encounter in a prominent role Watson Kirkconnell (1895–1977), son of a Scots-Canadian headmaster, diligent Miltonist, and one of the fathers of Canadian multicultural policy. His contribution as a Miltonist lay in three volumes of translation of analogues to Milton's works, a long labour published with the stated purpose of celebrating 'Milton's essential originality and greatness,' since especially 'Milton's epic towers above this nondescript array of forerunners.' By his own account, 'a study of the three volumes of analogues ought only to enhance our awareness of the subtlety, complexity, and powerful originality of Milton's art.'[67] His project was also thus understood by others, with Kirkconnell's 'Some Latin Analogues of Milton' finding praise from Charles S. Osgood at Princeton University: 'it rounds out a massive pedestal which exalts the glory of Milton more than ever.'[68] A prodigious capacity for learning languages allowed Kirkconnell to translate out of forty or more literatures. For many years he reviewed 'New-Canadian Letters' for the *University of Toronto Quarterly*, where he displayed his preoccupation with the immigrants' 'blending loyalty to the new land with racial affection for the traditions of the old.'[69] Kirkconnell exemplifies what may be termed 'soft' assimilation, where the Canadianization of immigrants pays deference to their diversity while underspecifying how the 'civility' they are to achieve differs from a British-Canadian ideal. He has high praise for John Murray Gibbon's *Canadian Mosaic* (1938), which influential work reveals a like contradiction.[70]

After his conversion in his early twenties, Kirkconnell moved through a *cursus honorum* of Canadian Baptist university positions – lecturer at Regent College in Winnipeg, Manitoba; professor at McMaster University in Hamilton, Ontario; president of Acadia University in Wolfville, Nova Scotia. Kirkconnell also threw himself into public affairs, notably as a ferocious anti-Communist early and late and as a significant proponent and institutor of Canadian multiculturalism. Kirkconnell remains concerned with how to impose order on social disorder throughout his career. Early, his Winnipeg writings reflect some of the same strategies for coping with the shock of immigration in that '*storm centre* of this problem in Canada' that had informed Woodsworth's 'notorious' *Strangers Within Our Gates*.[71] Later, his inaugural address at the low-lying Acadia University, 'The Dykes of Civilization' (22 October 1948), drew on long-standing certainties, Baptist and Masonic, also attested in many of his other papers: 'a profound religious awakening' was needed especially to contest 'Communism, a Sarcoma of Civilization.'[72]

Kirkconnell's commitments followed also from his eugenical and economic views, which already found full expression early in the 1920s after his return from a year's study at Lincoln College, Oxford. He was then antitariff and antinationalist, seeing world trade as the only answer to the almost insuperable challenges that population science taught him to see so clearly. In Kirkconnell's writings, the sky is often falling. In his earlier work, the dangerous combination of Malthusian and Mendelian pressures rouses him to lament how overpopulation both fosters and is aggravated by dysgenic tendencies in 'modern Aryan industrialism.' To cope with the resulting great unemployment, Kirkconnell advised the institution of labour camps; he did so without quite explaining their economic logic, not least in such circumstances, but perhaps found them the best means of training or policing those otherwise without work.[73] Measuring his parents' and siblings' skulls, he found their cephalic indices confirming a Mendelian pattern and that extending from 'cranial type' to 'most other characteristics, both somatic and psychic.'[74] Twenty years later he rejected prejudice against French Canadians by observing that their largely Norman descent meant that 'there is a very considerable Nordic element' in them and 'hence they are often more Nordic than the Welsh, Irish or Scottish Canadians who criticize them'; this yielded the reassurance that 'the French-Canadian will often be closer racially to the average English Canadian than is the Welsh, Scotch or Irish Canadian who laments that the French-Canadian is not "British."'[75] He does not much contest the hierarchy of race underlying such an Anglo-centric worldview. Where Milton had protested against his own countrymen as meaning 'Licence ... when they cry libertie,' Kirkconnell joined those Canadians like C.A. McGrath, inclined to fault the new immigrants for failing to 'understand the meaning of liberty, which to them is licence.'[76]

Kirkconnell's translations themselves operate as a form of assimilation, where English iambic pentameter, whether in blank verse, couplet, or quatrain, predominates in response to a wide assortment of original languages and metres. He had long been fascinated by the distinctive laconicism of Germanic languages, where he found English the most laconic of all, a virtue defined by counting the number of syllables in parallel passages of translation (here he much extended previous studies of the syllable-counts of different translations of the Gospel of Matthew).[77] To that quality his own writing does not always attest, but it is characteristic of Kirkconnell that he sees English as supreme, just as he praises Milton's poetry as superior to its antecedents or analogues. He had undertaken the project at A.S.P. Woodhouse's suggestion – how much in Canadian Milton studies has had a like inception – but differences as to how to proceed and how to confine the multiplication of analogues eventually led Kirkconnell to publish alone.[78]

It was during the Second World War that Kirkconnell's preoccupations found expression in his formative role in the development of Canadian multiculturalism. As British Canada struggled to maximize the war effort, Kirkconnell sought to advance the cause using his connections to Eastern European immigrant communities. At issue was the allegiance of immigrant populations whether in the cities or on the land. On their loyalty depended the success of industry, with Kirkconnell suspicious of Communist disruptions, and also effective conscription. His own investment in so many of their languages and literatures extended readily enough to an emollient recognition of their cultures, reflected in the huge print runs of his *Canadians All* (1941) and related productions aimed at 'setting on record the notable contributions to Canadian life of each ethnic group in our population.' Now too he 'had a share, from December 1940 on, in helping to organize a Citizenship Branch of the Federal Government, expressly designed to mediate constructive Canadian ideals to the foreign language communities, especially through their press, and to facilitate their entry into Canadian citizenship with fuller knowledge and greater dignity.'[79] Here, as so often in Kirkconnell's and like writings, the warmth of his commendation of other cultures resolves eventually into the Anglo-conformity, or 'white civility,' that remains an ideal no less prevalent for being less openly expressed, with the concerns of yesteryear over immigration revived by the numerous refugees arriving in Canada after the Second World War.

A son of the Russian migration to rural Manitoba, Ernest Sirluck may seem a poster-child for the assimilation that Kirkconnell was promoting. Of Russian-Jewish stock, Sirluck early and late defied suspicions of his ethnicity, against which anti-Communism and anti-Semitism alike might object. He did so in part by rapidly fulfilling the expectations then proposed by Canadian multiculturalism, such as it was. This centred in the assimilation, fast or slow, of a broad array of European immigrants into the anglophone majority in Canada. The title of his autobiography – *First Generation* – evokes how triumphantly this was achieved in his own case, often against personal and institutional prejudices against immigrant and Jew that at once complicated assimilation and perhaps intensified its appeal. Sirluck's parents were among the thousands emigrating from the Ukraine in reaction to Russian repressions at the turn of the century; they arrived in a Canada transforming itself with aggressively open immigration policies during Wilfrid Laurier's administration, animated by its Minister of the Interior, Clifford Sifton. Those policies were thought to endanger British cultural hegemony in English-speaking Canada and might seem to mock its *mission civilatrice.* In the 1920s, Yiddish was the language of Sirluck's childhood home in Winkler, Manitoba, while that of the playground there was the Plattdeutsch of a predominantly Mennonite population.[80] In the 1930s, Sirluck's coming of age was coloured by the growth of fascism abroad and at home. His success at the University of Manitoba was followed by further success at the University of Toronto, the latter interrupted by Sirluck's distinguished military service (MBE) chiefly in the Low Countries and then the Rheinland late in the Second World War. Even a Watson Kirkconnell could not have wished for more. With the death in action of Sirluck's younger brother, Bert, a bomber-navigator, the immigrant family's commitment to Canada had come at great cost.

Sirluck's career in research centred in successive investigations of Milton's political thought in his MA and PhD theses (Toronto, 1941 and 1948), which a decade later issued in his introduction to volume 2 of the Yale University Press *Complete Prose Works of John Milton,* the jewel in the battered crown of that eight-volume work. Sirluck had begun with the classical antecedents to Milton's political thought, in work plainly meant as complementary to Arthur Barker's study *Milton and the Puritan Dilemma* (Toronto, 1942).[81] Despite an idealizing history-of-ideas approach – 'isolating' the political ideas, and then invoking their classical counterparts, with Plato to the fore, as if all were to be assessed according to some synchronic and transcendent Reason – Sirluck already was alert to Milton's inconsistencies within and across his tracts, even if they go largely unexplained. That Milton sought to answer competing needs as a polemicist found fuller recognition in Sirluck's doctoral dissertation, which offered a more inflected study of the contexts in which Milton made his interventions in the political debates of the 1640s and 1650s.[82] Since Barker saw 'the role of natural law in Milton's thought' as 'largely negated by the theological limits Milton put on it,' Sirluck sought doctoral supervision instead from A.S.P. Woodhouse, whose presentation of the Army debates in *Puritanism and Liberty* (1938) did so much to exhibit those competing and rapidly changing positions on an acceptable constitutional settlement.[83] But like Barker's theological emphasis, Woodhouse's lasting curiosity about 'the Puritan mind' is foreign to Sirluck's eventual concern to show how various and even 'secular' these 'Puritan' opinions might prove, how independent natural-law thought might be of biblical reasoning and how inflected by present circumstance. His determined secularization of this great 'turn' in Milton's thought scants the impassioned use of proof texts from the Hebrew Bible especially in the divorce tracts (1643–5), with Sirluck indifferent to what has been termed 'Milton's felt knowledge of the saving power of the deuteronomic Mosaic law.'[84]

Although the continuities in Sirluck's work appear when materials from his MA thesis in 1941 find publication as late as 1964,[85] there is something of a second act in the rich amplification of his doctoral inquiry evident in his introduction to the Yale *Prose*, volume 2. Here his intensive reading in the Thomason Tracts allows an ambitious account of the 'tactical' aspect of partisan publications in the early 1640s (pages 1–136) and Milton's situation in their midst (137–216). Sirluck's achievement bears comparison with Peter Laslett's ground-breaking analyses in his editions of Robert Filmer (Oxford, 1949) and of Locke's *Two Treatises* (Cambridge, 1960). No longer would scholars be content to analyse the logic of major works of political theory – though Sirluck's contributions retain this strength – without studying more carefully their present occasions amid the welter of controversy. This more critical analysis of formal discourse, now often associated with the 'Cambridge School' in the history of political thought,[86] has a significant antecedent in Sirluck's independent example. In his edition and in related work, Sirluck skilfully situated Milton's pamphlets, and *Areopagitica* especially, in the controversies of Milton's day. Sirluck's more concerted argument has an explanatory force that marks a real departure from the miscellaneous approach of Don Wolfe, general editor of the Yale Milton, for whom Milton's works served to illustrate a broader account of the English Revolution as a time of heroic emancipation (notably in his introductions to volumes 1 and 4 of the Yale *Prose*).

In its emphasis on law and reason, Sirluck's liberal account also marked a corrective to Wolfe's ambition to conceive of Milton as a less trammelled revolutionary, situated among the Levellers.[87] Sirluck published volume 2 in the teeth of Wolfe's disapproval.[88] At Brooklyn College, Wolfe was a holdover from an earlier, pre–Second World War, American Left; at the University of Chicago, the Canadian Sirluck's commitments lay with the progressive liberalism of Adlai Stevenson and Paul Douglas, even as Sirluck might look past his colleague Milton Friedman's reputation as an ultraconservative to find his arguments 'surprisingly pragmatic and persuasive.'[89] Pragmatism and persuasion were the hallmarks of the real second act in Sirluck's academic career when, after fifteen years at the University of Chicago, he became a most influential dean of graduate studies at the University of Toronto in the 1960s. He now played a central part in the much fuller establishment of the graduate school at that hitherto more collegiate university and in the development of graduate studies in Ontario (and Canada) more generally. His further service as president of the University of Manitoba in the 1970s was by Sirluck's own confession much less of a triumph, as he sought against the current of a socialist legislature to establish in his native province a centre of excellence in some way comparable to that which he had helped to develop at Toronto. There he met the revenge of the Old Left, whose crisis-ridden governance as much as its more revolutionary rhetoric were hard to square with his own liberal emphasis on excellence in research as underpinned by a more conservative institutional order.

The drive to build or rebuild institutions of higher learning was especially strong after the horrors of fascism and Stalinism that culminated in the Second World War. But what should govern that renewal? It was not only Sirluck's historicism and the legacy of Victorian liberalism that encouraged his separation of faith and reason in preference for the latter. He seems to have understood the project of the humanities in Canada as requiring professionalization lest it slip back into confessional harness or into Arnoldian generalities about the powers of beauty and conduct. Those alternatives might be susceptible to no liberal construction, and might seem of indifferent worth in view of what Sirluck had experienced as a Jewish immigrant's child in Canada, and as a soldier abroad. They were not what the university was for. Where Watson Kirkconnell proposed the role of the humanities as 'amid paralyzing scepticism to shape a faith by which men may live,' and that mooted in distinctly religious terms,[90] Sirluck was readier to attend to the means – above all critical analysis animating research, peer review, and no parochial standards – and let the end be what it might. This did ask the professor to relinquish the role of 'the guardian of leisure-class wisdom' though it might not require his transformation 'into a harried employee of a culture-processing factory.'[91] When those ideals were then challenged from the Left, the supposedly neutral reason that adjudicated contending claims was itself historicized, in the *marxisant* critique of liberal ideology against which Sirluck later fought such a determined rear-guard action.[92]

Sirluck never much explains why he was attracted to Milton. But whatever his appreciation for Milton's rhetorical range and poetic achievement, he plainly also felt the calling of the institution that is Milton studies, where professional formation might be extended to the full on a writer very eminent in the canon, whose works peculiarly lent themselves to intellectual-historical inquiry. The robust prestige of this scholarly enterprise, centred in no very affective criticism, gave Milton a peculiar status; in an English department, one could thus attain to something of the authority of an historian, while still possessed of significant cultural capital in an Anglocentric curriculum and national culture. It was thus that David Masson, as one of the first British professors of English, had dignified the calling in the heyday of Victorian liberalism. In the mid-twentieth century, at Toronto and indeed in North America, there was still nothing else quite like it and a golden age of Milton studies seemed to open before those embarked on such a project. Where Macaulay had applauded *Paradise Lost* as 'a great poem produced in a civilized age,' Canadians might turn to it as an epic at once pre-eminent but also common property, and that all the more welcome in view of Canada's own 'belatedness in the race for civility.' If 'Canada was born too late,' its compensating expression of Britishness might answer for its being haunted by a lack of ghosts.[93] Something in Sirluck's commitments made it impossible for him to return to Milton after fifteen years of administering the Canadian academy.[94] Specifically that lay in his sense that critical curiosity about Milton now lay elsewhere than his own intellectual-historical contribution, and instead with critical models he found less persuasive, systematic, or prestigious.[95] But more generally, he was faced with a cultural turn in which rationalism and even nationalism grudgingly yielded to a more experiential criticism or phenomenologically driven poetics. It had become ever harder for the literary historian to join in what Northrop Frye posited as 'a future in which Western man has come home from his exile in the land of unlikeness and has become something better than the ghost of an ego haunting himself.'[96]

NOTES

1 For a recent and influential statement, see Pope Benedict XIV's address 'Faith, Reason and the University,' at the University of Regensburg (12 Sept. 2006), notably: 'the faith of the Church has always insisted that between God and us, between his eternal Creator Spirit and our created reason there exists a real analogy, in which – as the Fourth Lateran Council in 1215 stated – unlikeness remains infinitely greater than likeness, yet not to the point of abolishing analogy and its language.' See: http://www.vatican.va/

holy_father/benedict_xvi/speeches/2006/september/documents/hf_ben-xvi_spe_20060912_university-regensburg_en.html.

2 Philip S. Gorski, 'Historicizing the Secularization Debate: Church, State, and Society in Late Medieval and Early Modern Europe, ca. 1300 to 1700,' *American Sociological Review* 65 (2000): 148–50; Jürgen Habermas, 'Religion in the Public Sphere,' trans. Jeremy Gaines, *European Journal of Philosophy* 14 (2006): 1–25, esp.16–20; Charles Taylor, *A Secular Age* (Cambridge, MA, 2007), who touches on Tindal and Toland in his account of the emergence of 'exclusive humanism' through 'providential deism' (221ff.).

3 Thomas Babington Macaulay, *Miscellaneous Works*, ed. Hannah (Macaulay) Trevelyan, 5 vols (New York, 1880), 1:48.

4 J.S. Mill, *Three Essays* [*On Representative Government*, ch. 8] (Oxford, 1975), 278.

5 Dipesh Chakrabarty, *Provincializing Europe: Postcolonial Thought and Historical Difference* (Princeton, 2000), 9.

6 Thomas Babington Macaulay, *Selected Writings*, ed. John Clive and Thomas Pinney (Chicago, 1972), 241–2, 248–9 [237–51].

7 Phillip J. Donnelly, *Milton's Scriptural Reasoning: Narrative and Protestant Toleration* (Oxford, 2009), 15, 31–9, 45.

8 Thomas Babington Macaulay, *The History of England*, intro. Douglas Jerrold, 4 vols (London, 1906), 3:533 (ch. 19); Macaulay, *Miscellaneous Works*, 1:64; Charles Blount, *A Just Vindication of Learning* (London, 1679), 3; George Sensabaugh, *That Grand Whig, Milton* (Stanford, 1952), 58–62; Ernest Sirluck, '*Areopagitica* and a Forgotten Licensing Controversy,' *Review of English Studies* 11 (1960): 271 [260–74], reprinted in the present collection.

9 Charles Blount, *A Just Vindication of Learning* (London, 1679), sig.A2v.

10 Macaulay, *History of England*, 3:533–4. The attribution of this work to Blount has sometimes been questioned, chiefly owing to its absence from his *Oracles of Reason* (1693), from which collection, however, its *Areopagitica*-derived 'Reasons' by 'J.M.' and then ad hoc 'Postscript' against Edmund Bohun might well excuse it.

11 Ernest Sirluck, '*Areopagitica* and a Forgotten Licensing Controversy,' 270 and passim.

12 John Toland, 'The Life of John Milton,' in *A Complete Collection of the ... Works of John Milton*, 3 vols ('Amsterdam' [London], 1698), 1:21.

13 Nicholas von Maltzahn, 'Milton, Marvell and Toleration,' in *Milton and Toleration*, ed. Sharon Achinstein and Elizabeth Sauer (Oxford, 2007), 86–104.

14 The recent Canadian Supreme Court decision in Bruker vs Marcovitz (2007 SCC 54) has been lamented by diverse commentators as a landmark civil imposition on religious law.

15 Macaulay, *Miscellaneous Works,* 1:16–17, 19, 20.
16 Macaulay, *Miscellaneous Works,* 1:25 (its Euripidean aspect diminishes *Samson Agonistes*), 34–5.
17 For the later such use of Macaulay, see for example *The Canada School Journal* 2.11 (April 1878): 86; *Journal of Education, Nova Scotia* 2.5 (April 1898): 59.
18 Macaulay, *Miscellaneous Works,* 1:64.
19 Hugh Trevor-Roper, introduction to Thomas Babington Macaulay, *The History of England* (Harmondsworth, 1979), 7–42.
20 The formulation is John Milbank's, *Theology and Social Theory* (Oxford, 1990), 1.
21 That Milton is instead uniquely poised between these is argued by Gordon Teskey, *Delirious Milton* (Cambridge, MA, 2006).
22 *Complete Prose Works of John Milton* [hereafter *YP*], gen. ed. Don Wolfe, 8 vols (New Haven, 1953–82), 1:291.
23 For example, Richard Rorty, *Philosophy and the Mirror of Nature* (1979; Princeton, 2009), who here and in other of his works cites especially Wittgenstein, Heidegger, and Dewey as exploding 'the notion of knowledge as accurate representation' (6). Some complication of the usual story of the triumph of rationalism emerges also in Susan James, *Passion and Action: The Emotions in Seventeenth-Century Philosophy* (Oxford, 1997).
24 Blaise Pascal, *Pensées,* ed. Philippe Sellier (St-Amand-Montrond, 1976), 344–7 [nos. 669–71].
25 James, 236–40.
26 Alastair Fowler, ed., *Paradise Lost,* 2nd ed. (London, 1998), 312n.
27 Phillip Donnelly, '"Matter" vs "Body": The Character of Milton's Monism,' *Milton Quarterly* 33 (1999): 79 85.
28 Milbank, 12.
29 Milbank, 12.
30 Nicholas von Maltzahn, 'The First Reception of *Paradise Lost* (1667),' *Review of English Studies* 48 (1996): 490–1.
31 Nicholas von Maltzahn, 'Liberalism or Apocalypse? John Milton and Andrew Marvell,' in *English Now,* ed. Marianne Thormählen (Lund, 2008), 44–58.
32 Fowler, ed., *Paradise Lost,* 578, 580.
33 Sensabaugh, *That Grand Whig, Milton,*61; Nicholas von Maltzahn, 'The Whig Milton, 1667–1700,' in *Milton and Republicanism,* ed. David Armitage, Armand Himy, and Quentin Skinner (Cambridge, 1995), 229–53.
34 Another contemporary appropriation of *Areopagitica,* that of the Whig physician William Denton, shows a less decided scepticism but, even so, Denton

just claims that truth 'is as strong as the Almighty': *YP* 2:562; William Denton, *An Apology for the Liberty of the Press* (London, 1681), 6 [appended to his *Ius Caesaris*]; Sensabaugh, *That Grand Whig, Milton*, 61–5.

35 *Reasons Humbly offered ...*, 9: this passage about Laudian censorship from *Mr. Smirke* (*Prose Works of Andrew Marvell*, ed. Annabel Patterson et al. [New Haven, 2003], 2:51–2), may well derive from its intervening use in Toland's (?) *A Letter from Major General Ludlow to Sir E.S.* (Amsterdam [?], 1691), 8.

36 Sirluck, '*Areopagitica* and a Forgotten Licensing Controversy.'

37 Sirluck, '*Areopagitica* and a Forgotten Licensing Controversy,' 274: signal additions include the republication of Tindal's *Letter* (1698) in his *Four Discourses* (London, 1709), pt 2, 293–329, and the *Thoughts of a Tory Author, Concerning the Press* (London, 1712), 8–12, dubiously attributed to Joseph Addison by Thomas Holt White, ed., *Areopagitica* (London, 1819), cxxiii–cxxiv.

38 John Locke, *A Letter Concerning Toleration*, ed. John Horton and Susan Mendus (London, 1991), 19.

39 Tindal, *Reasons against Restraining the Press* (London, 1704), 7; compare Tindal, *Letter to a Member of Parliament* (1698), 6.

40 Tindal, *Letter to a Member of Parliament* (1698), title-page, 3.

41 For Milton's reaction against moves toward state religion under Cromwell and his fortunes amid their revival in the 1690s, see my 'Milton: Nation and Reception,' in *Early Modern Nationalism and Milton's England*, ed. Paul Stevens and David Loewenstein (Toronto, 2008), 401–42.

42 Phillip Donnelly, 'Enthusiastic Poetry and Rationalized Christianity: The Poetic Theory of John Dennis,' *Christianity and Literature* 54 (2005): 236–64.

43 William Kolbrener, *Milton's Warring Angels* (Cambridge, 1997); Abraham Stoll, 'Discontinuous Wound: Milton and Deism,' *Milton Studies* 44 (2005): 179–202.

44 My objective here is to learn from Toland's example rather than to fault it, for which see especially Robert E. Sullivan, *John Toland and the Deist Controversy: A Study in Adaptations* (Cambridge, MA, 1982), e.g., 140–2. For Toland in his milieu, see Justin Champion, *Republican Learning: John Toland and the Crisis of Christian Culture, 1696–1722* (Manchester, 2003) and Edmund Ludlow, *A Voyce from the Watchtower*, ed. Blair Worden (London, 1978), 1–80.

45 von Maltzahn, 'Whig Milton,' 251.

46 The first phrase is Nigel Smith's in 'The English Revolution and the End of Rhetoric: John Toland's *Clito* (1700) and the Republican Daemon,' *Essays and Studies* 49 (1996): 1–18 [6]; the latter characterizations of Whig heroic poetics are David Womersley's, in his edition of *Augustan Critical Writing* (London, 1997), xxvi–xxvii.

47 *OED*: *invention*, 1 and 3.

48 Cf. Smith, 'The English Revolution and the End of Rhetoric,' 9–10.

49 In the War in Heaven: *PL* 6.Argument, 464, 470, 498, 499. Elsewhere in the epic, ranging from Satan in hell to the race of Cain: *PL* 2.70, 4.524, 7.121, 9.767, 11.610.

50 John Toland, *Clito* (London, 1700), 16.

51 Milton, *Complete Collection* (1698), 1:6.

52 Milton, *Complete Collection*, 1:10: this claim can only 'absurdly' apply to the 1630s, as William Riley Parker observes, when Ezekiel was a boy (*Milton: A Biography*, rev. ed. Gordon Campbell [Oxford, 1996], 819, 831), but Toland's Spanheim interest invites this awkward reference to Milton's later letter to him (24 March 1654/5, *YP* 4: 872–4).

53 Milton, *Complete Collection*, 1:30; *An Apology for Mr Toland* (London, 1697).

54 Like some other republicans of his day, Toland rates constitutional arrangements as very much more important than climate – Rome had, after all, the same climate in its most glorious epoch as during the times of its greatest miseries – and these political scientists knew that 'the same Causes will produce like Effects in all Ages,' that 'Men in the same Circumstances will do the same things.' See also John Trenchard, *An Argument, Shewing, that a Standing Army is inconsistent with a Free Government* (London, 1697), 5; *A Short History of Standing Armies in England* (London, 1698), iii.

55 Toland, *The Militia Reform'd* (London, 1698), 71–2.

56 *Complete Collection*, 1:10.

57 John Stachniewski, *The Persecutory Imagination: English Puritanism and the Literature of Religious Despair* (Oxford, 1991).

58 So in 1833 the Baptist Joseph Ivimey could quote with approval the Bishop of Chester, even as Ivimey celebrated especially Milton's 'features as a *patriot*, a *protestant*, and *non-conformist*,' and took up the battle once more against Johnson's 'bigotry': *John Milton: His Life and Times* (London, 1833), iii–iv, viii.

59 Public Archives of Nova Scotia, Halifax: McCulloch papers, MG1, 550/56 (24 March 1826).

60 Public Archives of Nova Scotia, Halifax: McCulloch papers, MG1, 550/69 (1825); MG1, 552/107 (nd).

61 Thomas McCulloch, *The Stepsure Letters* (Toronto, 1960 [originally 1821–3]).

62 Dalhousie University Archives, Halifax: MS2-40-A4, McCulloch to the Senate of the University of Edinburgh. In the event, confessional rivalries led eventually to the foundation of a number of denominational colleges in Nova Scotia rather than one non-denominational university.

63 McCulloch, *Popery Again Condemned by Scripture and the Fathers* (Edinburgh, 1810); Public Archives of Nova Scotia, Halifax: MG1, 553/12, McCulloch to John Mitchell (5 Dec. 1819).

64 Most notably Sir (John) William Dawson (1820–99), principal of McGill University (1855–93) and founding president of the Royal Society of Canada (*ODNB*). This longer legacy is summarized in Marjory Whitelaw, *Thomas McCulloch: His Life and Times* (Halifax, 1985), 38.

65 Thomas Carlyle, *The Letters and Speeches of Oliver Cromwell*, ed. S.C. Lomas, 3 vols (London, 1904); Blair Worden, *Roundhead Reputations* (London, 2001), 264–95. In 1852, Carlyle wrote on behalf of Masson, under consideration for the Chair of English Literature at the University of London, citing especially Masson's recent essay 'The Works of John Milton' (*North British Review* 16 [1852]: 295–335).See *The Collected Letters of Thomas and Jane Welsh Carlyle* (London and Durham, NC: 1970 –), 27:312–13.

66 James S. Woodsworth, *Strangers within Our Gates or Coming Canadians* (Toronto, 1909, 3rd ed. 1911), 288–9.

67 Watson Kirkconnell, *The Celestial Cycle* (New York, 1967), vii, xxii; Kirkconnell, *Awake the Courteous Echo* (Toronto, 1973), xxiv.

68 Acadia University (Wolfville, Nova Scotia), Watson Kirkconnell Collection, WK-9, F-29 (25 June 1947).

69 Kirkconnell, 'New-Canadian Letters,' *UTQ* 7 (1938): 571 [567–71].

70 Kirkconnell, 'New-Canadian Letters,' *UTQ* 8 (1939): 493 [491–3]; Daniel Coleman, *White Civility: The Literary Project of English Canada* (Toronto, 2006), 182–9.

71 J.W. Sparling, introduction in Woodsworth, *Strangers within Our Gates*, 3; the quoted epithet for this influential work is from Daniel Coleman, *White Civility*, 21.

72 Acadia University, Watson Kirkconnell Collection, WK-9, F-33 and 34.

73 Watson Kirkconnell, *International Aspects of Unemployment* (London, 1923), 11.

74 Watson Kirkconnell, 'Mendelism and Cephalic Index,' *American Journal of Physical Anthopology* 8 (1925): 443–4.

75 Ca. April 1947, it seems, in 'Raw Material on the Ethnology of Canada (European),' Acadia University, Watson Kirkconnell Collection: WK-56, F-1. This recalls longstanding racial theories of Canadian character, as in Robert Grant Haliburton's *Men of the North and Their Place in History* (Montreal, 1869), quoted in Coleman, *White Civility*, 148, which might concede still more to Woodsworth's long social-democratic commitment to the needs of Canadian immigrants.

76 Milton, Sonnet XII ('I did but prompt the age ...'); McGrath, *Canada's Growth and Problems Affecting It* (1909), quoted in Coleman, *White Civility*, 11.

77 Kirkconnell, 'Linguistic Laconicism,' *American Journal of Philology* 48 (1927): 34–7.
78 Acadia University, Watson Kirkconnell Collection, WK-8, F-29, letters to and from Woodhouse, 12 May 1937, 24 June 1938, 15 Sept. 1942.
79 Acadia University, Watson Kirkconnell Collection, WK-9, F-34, 'Education for World Brotherhood,' 5.
80 Ernest Sirluck, *First Generation: An Autobiography* (Toronto, 1996), 3–6.
81 Ernest Sirluck, 'Milton's Political Thought: A Survey Preliminary to the Investigation of the Classical Influence' (MA, University of Toronto, 1941).
82 Ernest Sirluck, 'Milton and the Law of Nature' (PhD, University of Toronto, 1948).
83 Sirluck, *First Generation*, 86–7.
84 Jason Rosenblatt, *Torah and Law in* Paradise Lost (Princeton, 1994), 6, 12, 45ff., 79–89, 97–113.
85 Sirluck, 'Milton's Political Thought: The First Cycle,' *Modern Philology* 61 (1964): 209–24.
86 On this point I am grateful for Bernard Bailyn's perspective in his contribution to the conference 'Civil and Religious Liberty: Ideas of Rights and Tolerance in England c. 1640–1800,' Yale University (26 July 2008) and in personal communication.
87 Don M. Wolfe, *Milton in the Puritan Revolution* (New York, 1941).
88 Sirluck, *First Generation*, 200–2.
89 Sirluck, *First Generation*, 203, 205.
90 Watson Kirkconnell and A.S.P. Woodhouse, *The Humanities in Canada* (Ottawa, 1947), 12.
91 Northrop Frye, 'Pelham Edgar,' *Northrop Frye on Canada*, ed. Jean O'Grady and David Staines, vol. 12 of *Collected Works of Northrop Frye* (Toronto, 2003), 232 [230–4].
92 Ernest Sirluck, 'The Neutrality of the University: Institution and Discipline,' in *Nationalism and the University* (Toronto, 1973), 77–101, esp. 87–8.
93 Coleman, *White Civility*, 16–17; Northrop Frye, 'Haunted by a Lack of Ghosts,' in *The Canadian Imagination*, ed. David Staines (Cambridge, MA, 1977), 22–45.
94 The heavy cost of administrative duty shows in Ernest Sirluck, *Paradise Lost: A Deliberate Epic* (Cambridge, 1967), which lecture shows the difficulty of moving from historical to critical work under such circumstances.
95 Personal communication, Canada Milton Seminar, Victoria College, University of Toronto, 5 May 2007.
96 Frye, 'Haunted by a Lack of Ghosts,' 45.

12 Milton as Political Prophet: *The Readie and Easie Way*

ANNABEL PATTERSON

In late 1659 and early 1660, John Milton, having just lost his second wife and the chance for a peaceful retirement, reentered the English public sphere, which was once more in a furor. Oliver Cromwell had died in September 1658, it was clear that his son Richard was not strong enough to inherit the Protectorate, and the press was bursting with suggestions as to what form of government might come next. Although it was not his only response to this crisis, Milton's largest and boldest suggestion was *The Readie and Easie Way to establish a Free Commonwealth*, a title packed with irony, given the circumstances. As he added in the second edition, 'We have all this while say they bin expecting it, and cannot yet attain it' (*YP* 7:429), an acknowledgment of the fact that twenty years of state reconstruction seemed to have resulted in nothing. Every word of Milton's title, as first published in the final week of February, was loaded – 'ready,' 'easy,' 'establish,' and 'Commonwealth,' but above all 'free,' meaning republican. It was an improvement, in terms of efficiency, on the title of a pamphlet by James Harrington, *The Wayes and Meanes whereby an Equal Lasting Commonwealth May be suddenly introduced and Perfectly founded with the Free Consent and Actual Confirmation of the Whole People of England*, a tract which preceded Milton's by about three weeks, and from which he borrowed slightly.

Though there have been several excellent discussions of the *Readie and Easie Way*, whose two editions will hereafter be designated *REW1* and *REW2*, it is still true to say that it is one of the least well-known or understood of Milton's political tracts.[1] Most of us would not dream of introducing it to students, even graduate students, who might be expected to know at least the first of the church reform pamphlets, the divorce pamphlets, and the regicide pamphlets – Milton wrote his polemic in clusters of three or four – and the autobiographical passages in everything else.

The appeal of *REW* is less than all of these by virtue of it being self-evidently, indeed admittedly, an appeal to a cause now lost; and the task of understanding it has been seriously hampered by the fact of Milton's revisions, whereby the tract was increased in the second edition to about twice its original length. Not only was it doubled in size but individual passages were delicately altered, a word or phrase at a time. This was a prodigious task for a man completely blind, and indicated a commitment by Milton so great that we ought to honour it by following his changes attentively. When the new Oxford edition appears, with its side-by-side arrangement, readers will have a somewhat easier task. It seems clear that he must have had help, and Blair Worden's suggestion that the collaborator might have been Marchamont Nedham is extremely plausible.[2]

In addition, Miltonists of liberal persuasion have, over time, been horrified by what they see as the most explicit statement of Milton's political elitism, antidemocratic tendencies, or outright descent into oligarchism. The most important of such reactions, probably, was that by John Adams, second president of the United States, who reread it when writing his *Defence of the Constitutions of America*, written in the late 1780s. Adams did not object to the republican spirit of the pamphlet, naturally, but was shocked by its actual proposal for a new system of government:

> Can one read, without shuddering, this wild reverie of the divine, immortal Milton? ... What! A single assembly to govern England? An assembly of senators for life too? What! Did Milton's ideas of liberty and free government extend no further than exchanging one house of lords for another, and making it supreme and perpetual? ... It would have been an oligarchy ... on the first day of its sitting ... John Milton was as honest a man as his nation ever bred, and as great a friend of liberty; but his greatness most certainly did not consist in the knowledge of the nature of man and of government, if we are to judge from this performance.[3]

And Miltonists old and young have tended to agree with his judgment, with only a few exceptions.

One of the most interesting exceptions is the chapter on *REW* in *Mammon's Music*, by Blair Hoxby.[4] Hoxby approached this much-criticized text through the lens of the history of trade, and attitudes to trade, in the late seventeenth century, and his primary aim was to defend Milton from the charge of being weak on economics. But in looking closely at *REW*, Hoxby noticed the careful way in which Milton defined his potential new republic as a federal system, based less on the Dutch republic than, Hoxby suggests, on news that had seeped into England about the strong forms of local government being developed in the American colonies, the town meetings of New England. Whatever it originally owed to news from the colonies, a suggestion I rather doubt, Milton's perpetual Grand Council was actually conceived more like the American federal government would eventually be, with relatively few powers, those powers being limited to foreign policy, national defence and the raising and management of the public revenue; the rest of government, judicature, or what Milton calls 'all things of civil government between man and man' (7:459), religion and education, would be local, based in the counties and administered in their central towns. Local government, moreover, would become a training ground for those who aspired some day to candidacy for the Grand Council.

In the second edition, Milton carefully revised his description of the limited powers of the Grand Council to make them more limited still. It is worthwhile pausing to compare the two versions, not least because the alterations show how carefully Milton considered what governance consists of and how it should be divided:

REW1:

> This Grand Councel must have the forces by sea and land in thir power, must raise and mannage the Publick revenue, make laws, as need requires, treat of commerce, peace, or war with forein nations; and for the carrying on some particular affairs of State with more secrecie and expedition, must elect, as they have already out of thir own number and others, a Councel of State. (7:368)

REW2:

> In this Grand Councel must the sovrantie, not transferrd, but delegated only, and as it were deposited, reside; with this caution they must have the forces by sea and land committed to them for preservation of the common peace and libertie; must raise and manage the public revenue, at least with som inspectors deputed for satisfaction of the people, how it is imploide; must make or propose, as more expressly shall be said anon, civil laws; treat of commerce, peace or warr with forein nations, and for the carrying on som particular affairs with more secrecie and expedition, must elect, as they have alreadie out of their own number and others, a Councel of State. (7:432–3)

Thus the powers traditionally reserved to the king's prerogative – foreign policy and the making of wars and treaties – were to be combined with the power traditionally reserved to the House of Commons, the raising of public revenue through taxation. But Milton makes it clear that this would be representative government – 'sovrantie, not transferred, but delegated only' – and offers reassurances similar, if much briefer, to those that the *Federalist Papers* of 1788 offered to the states. Indeed, he later added a second passage to alleviate criticism he had heard in the interim:

> And when we have our forces by sea and land, either of a faithful Armie or a setl'd Militia, in our own hands to the firm establishing of a free Commonwealth, publick accounts under our own inspection, general laws and taxes with their causes in our own domestic suffrages, judicial laws, offices and ornaments ... in our own ordering and administration, all distinction of lords and commoners, that may any way divide or sever the public interest, remov'd what can a perpetual senat have then wherin to grow corrupt, wherin to encroach upon us or usurp; or if they do, wherin to be formidable. (7:461)

Particularly in that clause, perhaps easy to overlook, 'all distinction of lords and commoners ... remov'd,' Milton complicated the charge of elitism that has accrued to him from other parts of the tract.

John Adams would have had access to the second edition of Milton's tract, which was the one included in John Toland's edition of Milton's works, published in 1698,[5] and Richard Baron's edition of 1763,[6] both of which were privately exported to the colonies. He was, however, not reading very carefully, being already committed to bicameralism and to congressional elections. Blair Hoxby was reading more carefully than John Adams, but he did not attend to these crucial Miltonic revisions. They are, obviously, very far-sighted in terms of modern political theory, but they are also, I suggest, closely linked to the dark side of Milton's argument, his account of what would happen if his advice were ignored, and the nation insisted on restoring the monarchy.

These dark prophecies are the central part of my argument. Other Miltonists have focused on the prophetic aspect of Milton's rhetoric, especially his summoning up of the spirit of Jeremiah for the pamphlet's peroration, but their focus moves it back into the territory of biblical thinking,[7] whereas what strikes me about it is its extraordinary secularism. His provisions for freedom of religion are themselves secular provisions.

Milton here eschews the continued recourse to biblical history that he still relied on for the *First Defense*, and the result is in striking contrast to Richard Baxter's *Holy Commonwealth*, published in 1659, whose title says it all. And Milton's revisions in the second edition of *REW* here become not part of the problem but part of the solution, since there is no better control for discovering an author's intention than seeing where he changed his mind and his emphasis. One of his revisions, as noted by Stanley Stewart, though he draws the opposite inference from it, was to remove the closing allusion to 'Coniah and his seed,' that is, the worthless king of Judah who surrendered to the Chaldeans under Nebuchadnezzar, and who in the first edition of the tract served as an analogy to Charles II, serving his exile abroad.

I myself have returned to this late tract late in the day. Having cut my teeth on Milton in A.S.P. Woodhouse's famous undergraduate class, and having tried to teach Milton myself at Victoria College in the 1960s, I finally did what long ago Arthur Barker had hoped I would: produce a book of my own on this most intrepid, most elusive, of all early modern writers. In *Milton's Words* I tackled anew the subject of Milton's political vocabulary, and discovered that, if one really looks closely at his revisions in *REW2*, the problem of his oligarchism or antipopulism therein looks a great deal more complicated than Adams thought it did. His use, in particular, of the loaded phrase 'the people,' as in the above revision, indicates that he could not quite decide how representative government could work – but he was working on it! And he actually added two completely opposed statements about democratic values, using the keyword, *democracy*, about whose use he had been unusually careful hitherto, once with a positive and once with a negative valence.

In this essay, however, I offer a different, though compatible, argument. Having recently learned a good deal about the Restoration government, and in particular about how Charles II dealt with his first, improperly long-lived Parliament, I returned to the *Readie and Easie Way* with a start of genuine surprise. How could Milton have predicted so accurately what the political consequences of the Restoration would be? In *The Long Parliament of Charles II*, I had painfully laid out how over eighteen years the central meaning of parliamentary government, as Milton believed in it – government by the most qualified of the people for the people – was gradually eviscerated. For thirteen of those eighteen years Milton was alive, and if not watching, listening. How he avoided writing a new tract, entitled *I Told You So*, I do not know. After his death, Andrew Marvell wrote it for him, in his *Account of the Growth of Popery and Arbitrary Government*.[8]

Let us now return to Milton's positive proposal. He argued that the now doomed Rump Parliament be replaced not by a Senate, though that was what John Adams called it, but by a Grand Council, made up of ordinary persons:

> Wherin they who are greatest, are perpetual servants and drudges to the publick at thir own cost and charges, neglect their own affairs; yet are not elevated above thir brethren, live soberly in thir families, walk the streets as other men, may be spoken to freely, friendly, without adoration. Wheras a king must be ador'd like a Demigod, with a dissolute and hautie court about him, of vast expense and luxurie ... nor at his own cost, but on the publick revenue. (7:360)

This was, obviously, a warning of the financial costs to the nation of bringing back the king, as compared to perpetuating the rule of the respectable gentry, who, Milton implies, would not even take a salary for their senatorial service. This reformed version of a Parliament would elect out of their own number and others a Council of State 'for the carrying on some particular affairs of State with more secrecie and expedition' (7:368). But whereas the Grand Councel would initially be elected, as would the smaller Council of State, Milton's most startling recommendation was that thereafter there would be no more national elections, except for the filling of seats that Death had made vacant. The Grand Council 'should sit perpetual' (7:369).

This proposal was less a return to Plato's *Laws* than it was a natural suspicion of how an ordinary Parliament would be treated by a reinstated monarch, especially a son of Charles I. 'If ther be a king,' Milton continued several pages later, the Grand Councel:

> shall be call'd, by the kings good will and utmost endeavour, as seldom as may be; and then for his own ends: for it will soon return to that, let no man hope otherwise, whatever law or provision be made to the contrarie. For it is only the kings right, he will say, to call a Parlament; and this he will do most commonly about his own affairs rather then the kingdom's, as will appear planely so soon as they are called. (7:375)

This prophecy was easy to make. It was merely a recall of what Milton had charged in the first chapter of *Eikonoklastes* against Charles I, 'who never call'd a Parlament but to supply his necessities; and having supplyd those, as suddenly and ignominiously dissolv'd it, without redressing any one grievance of the people' (3:351).

Like father, like son, but not *quite* like. When Charles II was indeed recalled, and the ground rules of the new-old game had been established by the Convention Parliament of 1660, the newly elected Parliament of 1661 soon discovered that the son had learned from the father to avoid the most rabble-rousing tool, dissolution, and to replace it with prorogation, the temporary suspension of Parliament, recently used to astonishing effect in Canada by Queen Elizabeth II's viceroy, Michaëlle Jean, to avoid the collapse of Prime Minister Stephen Harper's government. The most powerful of the new king's strategies was to manipulate the length of sessions, so as to keep Parliament focused on his financial demands, which were always the first order of business. As soon as the Commons had granted a Supply, they were prorogued, so that they could never proceed on their own business. In the third session, prorogation followed in twelve days; in the sixth session, ten days; in the seventh session, thirteen days; in the ninth session, fifteen days.[9] As early as November 1666, Brome Whorwood complained that 'when we have raised the King's supply we may go home like fools, as we came.'[10]

Most significantly, in March 1664, the king's opening speech asked the Commons to repeal the Triennial Act. The Triennial Act, passed in February 1641, was one of the first achievements of the first Long Parliament. It called for a new Parliament every three years, and set up procedures for writs for elections to be sent out by others if the king did not comply. Milton believed, up to a point, in the Triennial Act. In *Areopagitica*, he had contrasted the 'magnanimity of a triennial Parliament' with the 'jealous hautiness of Prelates and cabin Counsellours that usurpt of late' (*YP* 2:489). But in *Eikonoklastes* he scorned not only Charles I's taking credit for an act which in fact was due to parliamentary pressure, but the act itself:

> The first Bill granted much less then two former Statutes yet in force by Edward the third; that a Parlament should be call'd every yeare, or often if need were; nay from a farr ancienter Law Book call'd the *Mirror*, it is affirm'd in a late Treatise call'd *Rights of the Kingdom*, that Parlaments by our old Laws ought twice a year to be at London. (*YP* 3:399)

And then, in one of the longest additions to the second edition of *Eikonoklastes* in 1650, Milton continued in some heat:

> From twice in one year to once in three year, it may be soon cast up how great a loss we fell into of our ancient liberty by that act, which in the ignorant and Slavish minds we then were, was thought a great purchase. Wisest

> men perhaps were contented, for the present at least by this act to have recoverd Parlaments, which were then upon the brink of danger to be forever lost ... And thus the taking from us all but a Triennial remnant of that English Freedom which our Fathers left us double, in a fair annuity enrowl'd, is set out, and sould to us heer for [that is, as] the gracious, and over liberal giving of a new enfranchisement. (3:399)

In his speech at the opening of Parliament in 1664, Charles II insisted on his personal belief in frequent Parliaments, without explaining what he meant by frequent, and then issued his ultimatum: 'I would never suffer a Parliament to come together by the Means prescribed by that Bill.' The same day it was moved in the Commons that the Triennial Act should be brought up for review, and on 28 March they voted not to repeal it, but to remove its coercive power, leaving it, in effect, merely advisory. Before the vote, however, Sir Richard Temple had argued that the act of Edward III laid down the right to annual Parliaments.[11] One might wonder what he had been reading. In any case, Charles II realized that once he had been able to bend the group to his will, to tame it or work around it, he could accomplish more by keeping the same Parliament theoretically in place, without risking a new election. Thus the Eleven Years of Personal Rule under the father were replaced by the Eighteen Years of Successful Manipulation by the son; and Milton's predictions about the timing and purpose of parliamentary sessions were fulfilled in spades.

It was not only the continuity of the Grand Council, or Parliament, as he alternatively spoke about it in his dark version of the future, that Milton worried about, but also whether a Restoration Parliament would be able to do its job. Even when sitting, he warned, 'what will thir business then be and the chief expence of thir time, but an endless tugging between right of subject and royal prerogative, especially about the negative voice, militia, or subsidies, demanded and ofttimes extorted without reasonable cause appearing to the Commons, who are the only true representatives of the people' (7:375–6). Milton correctly, if loosely, identified what would become the main cause of friction between the new king and the Commons: the endless appeal for funds, which when granted seemed to disappear into thin air, without adequate accounting for them. In December 1666, after three quarters of a million pounds had melted away in an unsuccessful war against the Dutch, William Garroway successfully proposed to attach a proviso to the Poll Bill, the instrument devised to raise a new supply of one million, eight hundred thousand pounds, such proviso to set up a commission of Accounts, in an attempt to verify that all the money granted was actually used for the purposes for which it had been granted. This echoed Milton's revised version of the Grand Councel's accountability, and he was probably informed of the event by Marvell, who had written to his Hull constituents that the bill 'will be of very good service to the publick.'[12] As the Long Parliament lengthened into the mid 1670s, members of the Opposition party in the Commons began to declare publicly that taxpayers' money was being diverted to improper ends, as, for example, financial rewards to the king's mistresses.

As for the 'negative voice,' or royal veto, Charles II only used it once in a policy matter, and that was in relation to the other sensitive issue that Milton had named, the control of the Militia, handed back to the king by Parliament in 1662. But in November 1678, when relations between the king and his Commons had deteriorated to their lowest point over the king's dealings with France, the Commons passed a bill taking control of the Militia back into their own hands. To which the king replied:

> That, as to the Bill for raising the Militia, he did not pass it, because it put the Militia out of his power for a time. For though it were but for half an hour, it was the same thing; for the right of the Militia being in the Crown, he would not consent to any Act that might put it out, though but for half an hour. [13]

What Milton did not anticipate, however, was the far more serious 'tugging' or constitutional struggle between Charles II and the House of Commons that developed in the later 1670s about foreign policy, specifically the king's alliances, public and secret, with Louis XIV of France. In May 1677, driven to exasperation by demands from Parliament that he make alliances with the Dutch *against* France, Charles delivered the clearest and sternest statement of his view of the royal prerogative, in language his father would never have dared to use:

> [In giving this advice] ... you have intrenched upon so undoubted a right of the Crown, that I am confident it will appear in no Age (when the Sword was not drawn) that Prerogative of making Peace and War hath been so dangerously invaded ... Should I suffer this fundamental Power of making Peace and War to be so far invaded (though but once) as to have the manner and circumstances of Leagues prescribed to Me by Parliament, it is plain that no Prince or State would any longer believe that the Soveraigntie of England rests in the Crown.[14]

In other words, and whether or not he had read the *Readie and Easie Way*, Charles II realized that his own Parliament, the one he thought he had hobbled, was trying to assume the very powers that Milton had assigned to his imaginary Grand Council.

Milton had also directed his readers' attention to another fear, that the return of the king would inevitably bring with it the restoration of the House of Lords:

> Besides which, within thir own walls, the sincere part of them who stand faithful to the people, will again have to deal with two troublesome counterworking adversaries from without, meer creatures of the king, temporal and spiritual lords, made up into one house, and nothing concern'd with the peoples libertie.

The House of Lords, of course, had been abolished by the first Long Parliament in March 1649, as 'useless and dangerous.' During the Convention Parliament, the upper House had gradually reconvened itself, absorbing a group of 'young lords' who had been members of the original body,[15] and one of the very first acts of its successor, the Parliament that met in the spring of 1661, was to restore the bishops to the Lords. Note that Milton assumed that a reinstated House of Lords would, given its aristocratic origins and unaccountability, the fatal permanence of its membership, be hostile to legislation designed for the good of 'the people,' a phrase used twice in the sentence I have just quoted. In fact, though the Commons' failure even to discuss 'grievances' was itself a grievance, it was not the fault of the House of Lords, but of the king and his managers in the Lower House. In this respect Milton's prophecy was askew. He simply could not envisage that it would be some of the great lords, Shaftesbury, Buckingham, Wharton, Salisbury, and a few others, who would throw themselves against the impregnable fortress of bishops in the Lords, those who, in league with the earl of Danby, attempted a legislative coup d'etat on the nation's liberties. It would have to be Marvell who, in his *Account of the Growth of Popery and Arbitrary Government*, formally recognized them as heroes.

The mention of the earl of Danby brings me to the next set of Miltonic prophecies in the *Readie and Easie Way*, first edition; that is, the reemergence of a third group of politicians distinct from either the Lords or the Commons, though individually they might be members of one or the other House:

> Next, the Councel of State shall not be chosen by the Parlament, but by the king, still his own creatures, courtiers and favorites; who will be sure in all

> thir counsels to set thir maister's grandure and absolute power, in what they are able, far above the peoples libertie. (7:377)

This sounds like the age-old cynicism about court favourites, and its primary referent was certainly the practice of Charles I in selecting his most intimate counsellors. If we are to believe Kevin Sharpe, the most important advisors of the Caroline regime were not 'favourites' in the old complaining sense, the extreme exception being George Villiers, duke of Buckingham. Weston, Coke, Cottington, Hyde, and Wentworth rose to their positions because of their abilities.

Unsurprisingly, this was not Milton's assessment. In the same opening chapter of *Eikonoklastes* in which he had made Charles I's dislike of Parliaments the first charge against him, Milton wrote: 'Those nearest to this King and most his Favorites, were Courtiers and Prelates, men whose chief study was to find out which way the King inclin'd, and to imitate him exactly' (3:350–1). But Milton's position in *REW1* may also register disillusionment with Oliver Cromwell's shrinkage of the organs of counsel. The original revolutionary Council of State had forty-one members (safety in numbers) who were elected by the Commons. In his *First Defense* Milton had praised this institution, in response to Salmasius's mocking of the English 'Supreme Council' and its President:

> For that Council – figment of your dreams – is not supreme, but appointed by authority of Parliament, for a definite time only, of about forty of its members, anysoever of whom may by vote of the rest be president. It has always been, moreover, a well-established practice for Parliament, which is our Senate, to fix a comparatively small number of its members, choose and appoint them, and delegate to them authority to meet anywhere, and to hold, as it were a kind of smaller Senate. To these often, weightiest matters were turned over and entrusted, to be dispatched the more quickly and quietly; the management or administration of the navy, the army, the treasury – in fine, any and all business of peace and war. This body, call it 'council' or anything else, may be new in name, but is ancient in substance; without it no commonwealth can be managed properly. (*CE* 7:31)[16]

This would reappear in the new edition of the *First Defense* that appeared in early October 1658 – after Cromwell's death – and constituted the first of Milton's published contributions to the suddenly unstable political climate. Reprise of praise of the original revolutionary Council of

State could have been read as a critique of how this ideal had shrunk since 1651. When Cromwell became Protector, the size of the Council of State was roughly halved, though its members were still elected. But subsequently it became known as the Protector's Privy Council, its members appointed by Cromwell, though subject to Parliament's approval. For Milton, the ideal was the large, elected, Council of State, the one whose Secretary he had been; and Cromwell's behaviour merely underlined his fears that the tendency to draw the shutters of policy close around one was human nature, bound to recur in any government led by a single person, when secrecy could be invoked as executive privilege.

On his return, Charles II tactfully appointed a fairly large Privy Council, which included former parliamentarians and Cromwellians; but in fact real decisions were taken in a much smaller group, which became known as the cabinet or cabinet-council. For the first few years of the reign, policy was primarily controlled by Edward Hyde, now made Chancellor (the equivalent of prime minister) and soon to become earl of Clarendon. Clarendon was the most obvious point of continuity between the two Stuart reigns, but his influence with the king was gradually undermined by a small group of lords who came to be known as the Cabal. When rivalries and infighting undermined the Cabal, they would effectively be displaced by Sir Thomas Osborne, the future earl of Danby, a much better politician, an early instance of those who manage, like Dick Cheney, to outsmart and outlast other councillors and assume a great deal of power into their own hands. Danby became Treasurer in June 1673, when Milton was still alive, but Milton did not live to hear how he became the focus of Parliament's suspicion as the source of all the bad advice that Charles must be receiving – advice, that is, which was the polar opposite of their own.

The contest between the Great Council – that is, the House of Commons – the Privy Council, which at least had Tudor precedent behind it, and the cabinet or interior council, whose deliberations were secret and were therefore not subject to any kind of accountability – steadily increased after Milton's death. The Commons won a false victory in 1679 when Charles agreed to reconstruct the Privy Council as a larger group that would include Opposition members; but, as Clayton Roberts has deftly shown, 'within one day Charles revived the hated cabinet council under the name of the Committee of Intelligence, and within a month had placed his confidence in an cabal of three men,' Sunderland, Halifax, and Essex.[17]

Thus a single sentence of the *Readie and Easie Way* opens up, if we pay attention, to an area of genuine constitutional concern, in which the government of Charles II would prove to be far more faulty than that of his father. In this respect Milton, who believed in structural safeguards, guessed right. 'I denie not,' he continued, 'but that there may be such a king, who may regard the common good before his own, may have no vitious favorite, may hearken only to the wisest and incorruptest of his Parlament; but this rarely happens in a monarchie not elective' (7:377). 'A monarchie not elective' was what his nation was about to restore. An elective monarchy was not unthinkable. In July 1674, a few months before his death, Milton translated into English and arranged for the publication of the Latin announcement of the election of Jan Sobieski to the Polish throne, initiating a whole series of allusions to 'the king of Poland' in English political thought for the next decade. But the English monarchy remains hereditary still.

Milton had still other warnings to convey. 'Admitt,' he admitted, 'that monarchy of itself may be convenient to some nations, yet to us who have thrown it out, received back again, it cannot but prove pernicious.' His point was the simple one of the human tendency to turn redistribution into retribution, the series of individual demotions, firings, even indictments that, as we know, still usually follow a complete change of government:

> For the kings to com, never forgetting thir former ejection, will be sure to fortifie and arme themselves sufficiently for the future against all such attempts hereafter from the people [that phrase again], who shall be then so narrowly watch'd and kept so low, as that ... they never shall be able to regain what they now have purchasd and may enjoy, or to free themselves from any yoke impos'd upon them ... Besides this, a new royal revenue must be found, which being wholly dissipated or bought by private persons, cannot be recover'd without a general confusion ... not to speak of revenges and offences that will be rememberd and returnd ... accounts and reperations that will be requir'd, suites and inditements, who knows against whom, or how many, though perhaps neuters, if not to utmost infliction, yet to imprisonment, fines, banishment[.] (7:378)

This was another passage that Milton worked over carefully for the second edition of the pamphlet, showing that he was not only nervous for himself, with good reason, but saw this as one of his strongest arguments. Here is the revised version:

> a new royal-revenue must be found, a new episcopal; for those are individual: both which being wholly dissipated or bought by privat persons or

> assign'd for service don, and especially to the Armie, cannot be recovered without a general detriment and confusion to mens estates, or a heavie imposition on all mens purses ... But not to speak more of losses and extraordinarie levies on our estates, what will then be the revenges and offences rememberd and returnd ... accounts and reparations that will be requir'd, suites, inditements, inquiries, discoveries, complaints, informations, who knows against whom or how many, though perhaps neuters, if not to utmost infliction, yet to imprisonment, fines, banishment, or molestation[.] (7:450–1)

Mentioning how the army leaders had profited was shrewd, and 'molestation' was a nice final touch. The climate of litigiousness that Milton invoked he hoped would scare those who had profited from the revolution. Joan Thirsk has brilliantly described the problem the Restoration government faced when so much of crown or church land, or private estates of 'delinquent' Royalists, had been sold to the victors during the interregnum, and in fact both the king and the Convention Parliament did better than might have been expected in sorting out these problems of landownership fairly, and without recriminations.[18] If anything, it was Royalists who were most disappointed. But it was anticipated 'revenges' that presumably weighed most heavily on Milton's mind. The king's clever Declaration from Breda, drafted by Clarendon, was received in London on 4 April 1660, in the same week, probably, that Milton published *REW2*. It pronounced a free and general pardon for all except such persons as should be excepted by the Parliament that was then in process of being elected, that is, the Convention Parliament. This transferred revenge, and the blame for it, from the king to the Parliament, a stratagem that Milton had not foreseen. On 14 May the Convention Parliament selected twelve men, actual signers of the king's father's death sentence and some others, for execution. On 8 June they named another twenty men, including Milton, for lesser punishments. Under the heading of molestation I think we may include the disinterment and dismemberment of the bodies of John Bradshaw, president of the Council of State, and Henry Ireton, and, of course, Cromwell himself. The first of the regicides to be executed was Thomas Harrison, on 13 October 1660; the last, though not strictly a regicide, since he had had not signed the death warrant, was Sir Henry Vane, beheaded on Tower Hill on 14 June 1662. Almost immediately afterwards, the sonnet that Milton had written in praise of Vane was published, though without of course naming its author, in the defiant biography of Vane compiled by George Sikes.[19] Indeed, Sikes made the sonnet something of a talking point in the biography and the defiance, which must have caused Milton, now released from prison and officially pardoned, to be nervous all over again. In the case of Vane, it was Charles himself, generally less vengeful than the Cavalier Parliament, who insisted on his execution. Needless to say, when Milton recollected his minor works and published them in 1673, the sonnet to Vane, as that to Cromwell and Fairfax, was omitted from the volume.

In his introduction to *REW2* in the Yale *Prose Works,* Robert Ayers remarked that the tone of the second edition was considerably darkened by Milton's revisions, though what he points to is a passage common to both versions, where, at the end of the pamphlet, 'Milton cries out to the earth in the words of Jeremiah' (7:402). As I said earlier, other Miltonists have focused on this moment, which suits their view of Milton as primarily a religious thinker. But it is not the reach backwards to the Old Testament that most darkens the *Readie and Easie Way*; in our hindsight, and if we know our Restoration political history, it is the accuracy of its premonitions of the future. It was not chance, but the logic of political thought and experience that caused Milton to have these premonitions, and he did not exaggerate. However benevolent in some of his impulses, however good-humored (and most historians like him better than his father), Charles II set out to make sure that he, and only he, held sovereign power in England. Even today the American constitution cannot protect us from an imperial presidency, with its historically resonant consequences: ill fought wars, a wasted treasury, civil rights retrenched, decisions made in secret, illegal imprisonments, in short, arbitrary government.

NOTES

1 The first edition appears in February 1660 and is available in *YP* 7:353–88; the second edition appears in April 1660 and is available in *YP* 7:407–63.

2 Blair Worden, *Literature and Politics in Cromwellian England* (Oxford, 2007), especially 347–50.

3 John Adams, *The Works of John Adams,* ed. Charles Francis Adams, 10 vols (Boston, 1851), 4:465–6.

4 Blair Hoxby, *Mammon's Music: Literature and Economics in the Age of Milton* (New Haven, 2002), 77–90.

5 John Toland, ed., *A Complete Collection of the Historical, Political, and Miscellaneous Works of John Milton*, 3 vols ('Amsterdam,' 1698), 1:783–97.
6 Richard Baron, ed., *The Works of John Milton, Historical, Political and Miscellaneous*, 2 vols (London, 1753).
7 See especially Stanley Stewart, 'Milton Revises *The Readie and Easie Way*,' *Milton Studies* 20 (1984): 205–24; and Reuben Sánchez, Jr, *Persona and Decorum in Milton's Prose* (Madison, NJ, 1997), ch. 4.
8 This tract, Marvell's last and most Miltonic, can now be read in the superb edition by Nicholas von Maltzahn, *The Prose Works of Andrew Marvell*, 2 vols (New Haven, 2003), 2:178–377.
9 See Annabel Patterson, *The Long Parliament of Charles II* (London, 2008), 56–8.
10 *Diary of John Milward*, ed. Caroline Robbins (Cambridge, 1938), 41.
11 Paul Seaward, *The Cavalier Parliament and the Reconstruction of the Old Regime, 1661–1667* (Cambridge, 1988), 137–9; Patterson, *Long Parliament*, 48–52; *Journal of the House of Commons*, 534, 535.
12 Marvell, *Poems and Letters*, ed. H.M. Margoliouth, rev. Pierre Legouis, 2 vols (Oxford, 1971), 2:47.
13 Patterson, *Long Parliament*, 220–1.
14 King's speech to the Commons on 28 May 1677; cited by Marvell, *Account of the Growth of Popery*, 367–8.
15 See Andrew Swatland, *The House of Lords in the Reign of Charles II* (Cambridge, 1996), 17–26.
16 References to Milton's defences are to *The Works of John Milton*, gen. ed. Frank Allen Patterson, 18 vols in 21 (New York, 1931–8), cited by volume and page, and indicated by the abbreviation *CE*.
17 Clayton Roberts, 'Privy Council Schemes and Ministerial Responsibility in Later Stuart England,' *American Historical Review* 64 (1959): 564–82; available on JSTOR.
18 Joan Thirsk, 'The Restoration Land Settlement,' *Journal of Modern History* 26 (1954): 315–28.
19 George Sikes, *The Life and Death of Sir Henry Vane, Kt.* ([London,] 1662), 93–4.

13 Northrop Frye, *Lycidas*, and the 'Intense Inane' of History

PETER C. HERMAN

It is easy to forget just how great a shadow Northrop Frye once cast. To say that Frye's peers honoured him would be a vast understatement: the man received almost innumerable honorary degrees, and in 1965, the English Institute organized an assessment of Frye's work, the first such session devoted to a living critic.[1] Both Paul Ricoeur and Geoffrey Hartman seriously compared Frye to Aristotle.[2] While the archetypal approach pioneered by Frye has been largely superseded by, inter alia, post-structuralism and the New Historicism, it would not be an exaggeration to say that Frye's work provided the foundation for the next generation of luminaries, such as Harold Bloom, who called *Fearful Symmetry* 'the best book I'd ever read about anything.'[3] Frye's interest in Canadian painting, along with the parallels he draws between Canadian painting and Canadian literature, distinguish him as interdisciplinary *avant la lettre.* Frye also shunned the insularity that sometimes afflicts academics. He was a public intellectual, appearing regularly on the radio and on television, and pedagogical issues engaged him nearly as much as literary theory.[4] If he no longer dominates bibliographies, we would do well to remember that Northrop Frye anticipated many of the developments in literary criticism from the sixties onward.

Yet certain aspects of Frye's career remain occluded, especially outside Canada.[5] In particular, even though John Milton figured as a constant presence in Frye's thought,[6] his work on this author has not received anywhere near the amount of attention accorded the essays and books he wrote on William Blake, William Shakespeare, and literary theory.[7] Granted, C.A. Patrides thought enough of Frye's 'Literature as Context: Milton's *Lycidas*' to include this essay in the important 1961 anthology-*Milton's 'Lycidas': The Tradition and the Poem*[8] (a book we will return to shortly), yet the essay no longer figures prominently in *Lycidas* scholarship.[9] Also, even though Frye's work on Canadian literature and culture has received significant attention,[10] the relationship of that body of writing to Frye's work on European literature and literary theory has not been extensively explored. In particular, it has not been noted that Frye wrote 'Literature as Context: Milton's *Lycidas*,' while in the middle of writing his omnibus reviews of Canadian poetry for the *University of Toronto Quarterly*. In this essay, I want to bring together these various aspects of Frye's career. After looking at the relationship between 'Literature as Context' and Milton studies up through the 1950s, that is to say, after examining how Frye almost completely fulfills the accepted paradigms of Milton criticism – he departs from this paradigm in one major way – I will then examine the relationship, or rather, non-relationship, between Frye's views on Milton and his views on Canadian culture and literature. As we shall see, there are significant gaps between the two.

I

In his 1951 essay 'The Archetypes of Literature' (published in the *Kenyon Review* under the general title of 'My Credo'), and in his monumental *Anatomy of Criticism* (1957 and frequently reprinted thereafter), Frye proposed that literary criticism should be considered a science, not an art,[11] equivalent in essence to all the other natural sciences. Criticism, Frye writes in his earlier essay, 'as we find it in learned journals and scholarly monographs has every characteristic of a science,'[12] and in the *Anatomy*, Frye asks:[13] 'What if criticism is a science as well as an art? Not a "pure" or "exact" science, of course, but these phrases belong to a nineteenth-century cosmology which is no longer with us' (7), and he proposes that if literary criticism is to exist, it should proceed along Baconian lines: 'it must be an examination of literature in terms of a conceptual framework derivable from an inductive survey of the literary field' (7).

Frye's redefinition of literary criticism as a science has a complex set of filiations. Even though Frye had his differences with the New Criticism,[14] he nonetheless draws on the New Critical project of professionalizing the study of literature by urging literary critics to become, as John Crowe Ransom urges, 'more scientific, or precise and systematic ...'[15] Frye's extensive refiguring of criticism as science also took place over the course of the 1950s, that is to say, over the course of the Cold War. Consequently, it is worth speculating, if only momentarily (the subject deserves much fuller treatment than this essay allows), on the relationship between Frye's 'Polemical Introduction' and the tectonic shifts in university resources taking place at precisely this time.[16] In both Canada and the United States, the Cold War led to a massive influx of research dollars into the university, and these monies found their way mainly, if not exclusively, to the hard and social sciences,[17] leaving literature departments in the dust, a 'poor relation, an indirect beneficiary, at most of scraps of "overhead" redistributed by administrations to the shabbier precincts ...'[18] Insisting on literary criticism's status as a science, however, had the potential to alter that equation. If literary criticism constitutes a 'science,' equivalent to all the other 'natural sciences' as well as the social sciences, then departments of literature should have an equal claim for status and funding. While the primary audience for the 'Polemical Introduction' is literary critics, Frye possibly also has in mind his discipline's competitors for university and governmental largesse.

To return to our main topic, when Frye recasts literary criticism as a science, he has in mind a particular definition of science as the objective progression of knowledge toward a verifiable, objective truth. Thus, he begins 'The Archetypes of Literature' by declaring: 'Every organized body of knowledge can be learned progressively,'[19] which he expands in the *Anatomy* into 'Everyone who has seriously studied literature knows that the mental process involved is as coherent and progressive as the study of science. A precisely similar training of the mind takes place, and a similar sense of the unity of the subject is built up' (10–11). Frye's assumptions about science, however, have been overturned by Thomas Kuhn in *The Structure of Scientific Revolutions.*[20] Frye understands both scientific and critical development as, in Kuhn's terms, 'a process of accretion' (Kuhn 3), each part of the literary puzzle leading inexorably toward truth. The *Hamlet* scholar, for example, will move from 'the pre-Shakespeare play to Saxo, and from Saxo to nature-myths,' and so 'drawing closer to the archetypal form which Shakespeare recreated.'[21] Kuhn, however, demonstrates that science proceeds inside certain 'paradigms,' or 'particular coherent traditions of scientific research' (10), which determine the scope and shape of future inquiry:

> Effective research scarcely begins before a scientific community thinks it has acquired firm answers to questions like the following: What are the fundamental entities of which the universe is compounded? How do these interact with each other and with the senses? What questions may legitimately be asked about such entities and what techniques employed in seeking solutions? (4–5)

I have argued elsewhere about how Kuhn's theory of 'normal' science combined with Stanley Fish's theory of interpretive communities can be profitably used to analyse the dominant paradigms of Milton studies.[22] Right now, however, I want to look more specifically at the 'normal' interpretation of *Lycidas* circa 1959, when Frye first published his essay, 'Literature as Context: Milton's *Lycidas*.' What constituted the 'legitimate problems' for the interpretation of this poem? And what was deemed out of bounds?

II

To answer these questions, we must first turn to Samuel Johnson's caustic, yet extraordinarily influential, comments on *Lycidas*. To say that Johnson did not like this poem would be a gross understatement. First, Johnson believes that in this poem, Milton wrote bad verse: 'the diction is harsh, the rhymes uncertain, and the numbers unpleasing' (Patrides, 56). Second, there is no genuine human feeling in the poem: 'It is not to be considered as the effusion of real passion' (56). Third, Johnson does not like the pastoral form to begin with, and the classical allusions that go along with it distract rather than help the poem's meaning: 'Its form is that of a pastoral, easy, vulgar, and therefore disgusting; whatever images it can supply are long ago exhausted, and its inherent improbability always forces dissatisfaction on the mind' (56). Finally, and for later criticism, most important, Johnson accuses *Lycidas* of disunity, because the poem tries to combine the sacred and the profane: 'With these trifling fictions are mingled the most awful and sacred truths, such as ought never to be polluted with such irreverend combinations. The shepherd likewise is now a feeder of sheep, and afterwards an ecclesiastical pastor, a superintendent of a Christian flock' (57).

Johnson's denunciation of *Lycidas* created for the institution of twentieth-century Milton criticism an 'anomaly' (Kuhn's term), that is, a result that 'violated the paradigm-induced expectations that govern normal science' (52–3). The reigning assumption (which largely still governs) is that a significant poet should not, *cannot*, write a bad poem, especially if that poem is a major one, such as *Lycidas*. As Kuhn noted, when scientists confront an anomaly, rather than changing the theory, they will try to get rid of the troublesome result and preserve the paradigm: 'They will devise numerous articulations and *ad hoc* modifications of theory in order to eliminate any apparent conflict' (78).

Faced with Johnson's criticisms, Milton's critics set themselves the task of demonstrating the falsity of each and every one of Johnson's claims.

This is not to say that all *Lycidas* criticism necessarily takes the same positions over the poem's details. There are areas of controversy, which Kuhn terms 'legitimate problems' (10). Is the poem best understood historically, or without reference to history? Is Milton or Edward King the poem's central focus? Are there archetypal images or not? Critics will come up with very different answers to these questions, just as scientists will disagree as to which approach, which instrument, is best suited to resolve a particular problem. However, for both the scientists and Milton critics, *the result is known ahead of time.* As Kuhn writes, 'Though its outcome can be anticipated, often in detail so great that what remains to be known is itself uninteresting, the way to achieve that outcome remains very much in doubt. Bringing a normal research problem to a conclusion is achieving the anticipated in a new way ...' (36). As we will now see from various representative examples (citing every article on *Lycidas* would be impractical), Kuhn perfectly describes the communal project of *Lycidas* criticism that Frye sought to join. For members of the interpretive community devoted to this project, the 'anticipated' result is that *Lycidas* constitutes a beautiful, unified, emotionally and intellectually satisfying poem. The only question is how to get there.

Let us first take up Johnson's accusation that Milton's verse is harsh, the rhymes 'uncertain, and the numbers unpleasing.' Because beauty is in the eye of the beholder, and there is no disputing taste, many Milton critics leave alone the question of whether the rhymes are pleasing, yet at least two directly confront Johnson's charge of technical incompetence. F.T. Prince, in 'The Italian Element in *Lycidas*,' refers the reader to Milton's absorption and use of 'several different kinds of Italian verse' (Patrides,153–4). Johnson does not understand, writes Prince, that Milton took 'advantage of the technical freedom of the later *Cinquecento*' (156). Ants Oras, basing her study of Milton's rhyme schemes on Prince, similarly argues that *Lycidas* demonstrates 'an increasing mastery in making rhyme express mood and matter with force and precision. It shows a technique growing in range and intricacy but never "irregular" in the negative sense of the poet's letting himself go without knowing exactly what course he is taking.'[23] John Crowe Ransom, of course, disagrees, declaring that there is not in English 'another poem so willful and illegal in form as this one' (Patrides, 71).

Yet while Ransom remains within the fold, as it were, of 'normal' Milton criticism, he does so just barely. Kuhn notes that adherents of a particular paradigm 'are often intolerant of those'[24] who offer differing views, as exemplified by Martin C. Battestin's critique of Ransom.

Battestin does not content himself with disputing Ransom's conclusion; he also puts into question Ransom's professional qualifications: the essay 'contributes nothing of value to an understanding of *Lycidas.* Rather, Mr. Ransom's *undisciplined* impressionism – his fragile hypothesizing on the nature of the creative psychology behind the poem's irregularities – tends toward a depreciation of Milton's justly famous monody by questioning the artistic integrity of its author' (my emphasis).[25] Battestin does not simply disagree with Ransom; he thinks that Ransom has committed the critical equivalent of malpractice, and should be sanctioned accordingly.

Milton critics almost universally disagree with Johnson's sense that *Lycidas* contains no genuine passion, no emotional charge. Nearly every critic who published on this poem in the twentieth century makes some mention of how moving they find the poem, and perhaps the most powerful refutation of Johnson's accusation comes from the pen of Rosemond Tuve, who declares that '*Lycidas* is the most poignant and controlled statement in English poetry of the acceptance of that in the human condition which seems to man unacceptable' (Patrides, 167).

Johnson's charge that the pastoral tradition was 'long ago exhausted, and its inherent improbability always forces dissatisfaction on the mind' (56) spawned a huge amount of criticism devoted to elucidating the range and vitality of pastoral for Milton and beyond. Alluding implicitly, yet unmistakably, to Johnson, James Holly Hanford begins 'The Pastoral Elegy and Milton's *Lycidas*' by acknowledging that 'not infrequently the pastoral imagery continues to be felt as a defect' (Patrides, 27), yet readers believe so only because they have lost contact with this tradition, and we must recover the tradition as it seemed to Milton if we are to read *Lycidas* properly:

> For in Milton's eyes the pastoral element in *Lycidas* was neither alien nor artificial. Familiar as he was with poetry of this kind in English, Latin, Italian, and Greek, Milton recognized the pastoral as one of the natural modes of literary expression, sanctioned by classic practice, and recommended by not inconsiderable advantages of its own. The setting of *Lycidas* was to him not merely an ornament, but an essential element in the artistic composition of the poem. (Patrides, 28)

The rest of Hanford's essay consists of an exhaustive survey of pastoral verse that ranges seamlessly between different languages and ages, from Theocritus to Virgil, from Virgil to Petrarch, Mantuan, and Boccaccio, and then to Spenser, with stops along the way for the Carolingian Renaissance and Marot, among others. The same principle underlies F.T. Prince's 'The Italian Element in *Lycidas*,' which begins with an overt allusion to Johnson – 'Dr. Johnson's severity towards the pastoral convention of the poem has had little effect upon its reputation and its appeal' (Patrides, 153); this principle underlies essays by David Daiches (Patrides), Don Cameron Allen (*Harmonious Vision*), and many others as well.[26]

Lastly, Johnson charges *Lycidas* with disunity, with combining like with unlike, sacred truth with trifling fictions. The immediate object of Johnson's disdain is in all likelihood the denunciation of the contemporary clergy by St Peter, which concludes with the famously ambiguous reference to the 'two-handed engine at the door' (130). Johnson's comment occasioned a small cottage industry on trying to discern what exactly Milton meant by this phrase.[27] But while the specific answer may vary along with the critic, the underlying purpose of each essay is to demonstrate that the line, and the speech it comes from, continues the larger themes of *Lycidas* and is therefore perfectly appropriate. For example, after Harry F. Robins defines 'two-handed engine' as 'an engine with two hands – a man,' he asks: 'How is the problem in *Lycidas* illuminated by this conception of the import of "two-handed"?'[28] The answer lies in the 'duality implied by "two-handed,"' as he defines this phrase as 'having two hands which characteristically perform disparate offices.'[29] The two 'disparate offices' symbolize two discrete classes of shepherds, the good and the bad.[30] St Peter 'is introduced as the archetype of the good shepherd,' and of course he 'bears two keys, one of which promises to reward the virtuous, among whom is Lycidas.'[31] Far from a problem, 'two-handed engine' continues the unity of Milton's poem.

While one may occasionally find a critic who agrees with Johnson's sense that *Lycidas* lacks a fundamental organizing principle, the overwhelming majority seek to prove that if properly understood, *Lycidas* is a completely unified poem, that the so-called digressions are in fact central to the poem's central point. As one might expect, given the New Critical emphasis on resolving antitheses into unities,[32] Cleanth Brooks and John Edward Hardy explicitly take issue with Johnson, although they credit him with raising the right issues: Johnson 'puts his finger firmly on the matter of first importance for a reading of the poem' (Patrides, 136). While Johnson finds 'the pagan-Christian conflict' evidence of the poem's 'clumsy confusion' (Patrides, 136), Brooks and Hardy find unity, devoting their essay to an elucidation of the poem's 'architecture, and an intricate and subtle architecture at that' (Patrides, 137). Yet the project of finding unity in *Lycidas* is far from restricted to New Critical treatments of this poem, and throughout the 1950s, the project of eliminating digression and demonstrating unity seems to intensify.[33] I want to turn to now to how Northrop Frye, in 'Literature as Context: Milton's *Lycidas*,' adds to the scope and precision of 'normal' *Lycidas* criticism, and to isolate the one place where Frye veers outside the parameters of acceptability.

III

In the introduction to *Fables of Identity*, Frye recalls that in the preface to the *Anatomy*, he admitted 'that a work of practical criticism was needed to complement' that 'very theoretical book' (1), and the essays collected in this anthology fulfil that desideratum. Certainly, 'Literature as Context' continues the themes of the *Anatomy*, giving them, as Frye puts it, 'a more specific' embodiment. This essay shares Frye's predilection for taxonomy (e.g., Frye divides the 'framework of images' into 'four levels of existence' [122], and finds in *Lycidas* 'four creative principles of particular importance' [123]).[34] Frye also uses the occasion to argue once again for the primacy of the 'archetype' in literary criticism.[35] Both works concern themselves with constituting 'literature' as a separate, self-enclosed entity (which we will return to shortly). But as much as 'Literature as Context' draws on the *Anatomy*, this essay also draws as much from the accepted paradigm of *Lycidas* studies.

First, like so many other critics who have written on Milton's elegy, Frye sets up Samuel Johnson as the critic whose opinion he must refute. Frye explicitly raises Johnson's accusation that the poem 'is not to be considered as the effusion of real passion' (56). Like the majority of Miltonists, Frye disagrees, declaring that he finds the poem intensely moving. But, as Kuhn would have predicted, and exactly parallel to Battestin's denunciation of Ransom, Frye does not rest with asserting that Johnson was merely wrong. He declares that Johnson was *unprofessional* when he accused *Lycidas* of insincerity, and Miltonists therefore do not have to take Johnson's views of this poem seriously:

> Another form of the same kind of fallacy is the confusion between personal sincerity and literary sincerity. If we start with the facts that *Lycidas* is highly conventional and that Milton knew King only slightly, we may see in *Lycidas*

> an 'artificial' poem without 'real feeling' in it. This red herring, though more common among third-rate romantics, was dragged across the study of *Lycidas* by Samuel Johnson. Johnson knew better, but he happened to feel perverse about this particular poem, and so deliberately raised false issues ... *Lycidas* is a passionately sincere poem, because Milton was deeply interested in the structure and symbolism of funeral elegies, and had been practicing since adolescence on every fresh corpse in sight, from the university beadle to the fair infant dying of a cough. (124–5)

Frye's need explicitly to refute Samuel Johnson is far from an isolated example of his echoing then current thinking on *Lycidas*. When Frye briefly mentions the myth of Arethusa and Alpheus, 'the Arcadian water-spirits who plunged underground and reappeared in Sicily' (121), he notes that 'this myth not only outlines the history of the pastoral convention, but unites the water imagery with the theme of disappearance and revival' (121). Frye's analysis thus draws on the canonical treatment of water imagery in *Lycidas* by Cleanth Brooks and John Hardy. Like Wayne Shumaker, and Ants Oras, who also finds a 'symphonic structure'[36] in *Lycidas*, Frye invokes musical metaphors to describe this poem's structure and effect. 'The body of the poem is arranged in the form ABACA,' Frye writes, 'a main theme repeated twice with two intervening episodes, as in the musical rondo' (121); and the concluding line, 'Tomorrow to fresh woods and pastures new,' brings 'the elegy to a full rich *tierce de Picardie* or major chord' (121). Implicitly alluding to the work of F.T. Prince (Frye did not use any footnotes for this article) and to Johnson's accusation that in *Lycidas* Milton wrote bad verse, Frye notes that 'Even the diction, of which I have no space to speak, shows strong Italian influence' (123). Even Frye's situating *Lycidas* in terms of myths and archetypes, a move that obviously continues the themes of the *Anatomy of Criticism*, expands upon Richard P. Adams's article (originally published in 1949), 'The Archetypal Pattern of Death and Rebirth in *Lycidas*,' which begins, as does Frye's essay, with aligning Milton's elegy with the myths of Adonis and Bion (Patrides, 121; Frye, 129).

The major points of Frye's article also recapitulate the major themes of *Lycidas* criticism. First, like so many before him, Frye insists that Milton did not by any stretch of the imagination write a disunified poem, and the critic's task is to find out *how* the poem coheres. Incoherence, to use Kuhn's terms, constitutes an anomaly, one that must be resolved, and Frye fulfils Kuhn's observation that when an experiment yields an anomalous result, one must look to the investigator, not the object (or text) under investigation:

> The next principle is that the provisional hypothesis which we must adopt for the study of every poem is that that [*sic*] the poem is a unity ... A good deal of bad criticism of *Lycidas* has resulted from not making enough initial effort to understand the unity of the poem. To talk of 'digressions' in *Lycidas* is a typical consequence of a mistaken critical method, of backing into the poem the wrong way around. (123)

Indeed, Frye, like the New Critics,[37] elevates this view into a general principle. '*Every* poem,' Frye writes, without qualification, 'must be examined as a unity' (126; my emphasis).

Frye's belief that every poem should be examined as a unity leads directly to his theory, articulated in this essay as well as the *Anatomy*, that all literature constitutes a unity. When Frye writes that 'Every poem must be examined as a unity ...' (126), he does not exclusively mean, as perhaps the New Critics would have meant, *internal* unity, i.e., the relationships of the individual parts of the poem to the whole. This is not to say that Frye does not believe in the poem's internal unity: he spends a small amount of space toward the beginning of the essay outlining how the different parts of *Lycidas* fit into the whole (e.g., 'The theme of salvation out of water is connected with the image of the dolphin, a conventional type of Christ, and dolphins are called upon to "waft the hapless youth" just before the peroration begins' [121]). Establishing the poem's internal unity, however, is but a way-station to the larger thesis, as Frye expands the principle of unity to include *all* of literature: 'Every poem must be examined as a unity, *but no poem is an isolatable unity*' (126; my emphasis).

At first, it seems as though Frye means that each poem should be considered within the framework of its literary traditions, and so Frye appears to be following in the wake of such scholars as J. Holly Hanford and Don Cameron Allen. Like them, Frye regards *Lycidas* as an intensely intertextual poem. Milton's elegy, Frye writes, 'owes quite as much to Hebrew, Greek, Latin, and Italian traditions as it does to English' (123). Slightly later, Frye returns to this point:

> *Lycidas* is a dense mass of echoes from previous literature, chiefly pastoral literature. Reading through Virgil's Eclogues with *Lycidas* in mind, we can see that Milton had not simply read or studied these poems: he possessed them; they were part of the material he was shaping. The passage

> about the hungry sheep reminds us of at least three other passages: one in Dante's *Paradiso,* one in the Book of Ezekiel, and one near the beginning of Hesiod's *Theogony.* There are also echoes of Mantuan and Spenser, of the Gospel of John, and it is quite possible that there are even more striking parallels with poems that Milton had not read. (124)

Yet Frye will expand this approach in this essay into a theoretical position that will ultimately put him at odds with mainstream Milton criticism.

First, Frye proposes an entirely closed, if coherent, literary universe. A poem may be inspired, Frye admits, by an outside experience or event, yet 'the impulse to write can only come from previous contact with literature, and the formal inspiration, the poetic structure that crystallizes around the new event, *can only be derived from other poems*' (125; my emphasis). Literature may give us 'the illusion of turning from books to life ... But this is never quite what happens' (125). The reason, as Frye states earlier in this essay, is that 'the forms of literature are autonomous: that is, they do not exist outside literature' (123). What is more, these autonomous forms constitute the only legitimate area for investigation: 'There are only archetypes, or recurring themes of literary expression, which *Lycidas* has recreated, and therefore re-echoed, yet once more' (124). This line of thought leads Frye to the central 'critical principle' of 'Literature as Context,' 'the one,' as Frye writes, that he has 'written this paper to enunciate' (126): 'Every poem is inherently connected with other poems of its kind, whether explicitly, as *Lycidas* is with Theocritus and Virgil, or implicitly, as Whitman is with the same tradition, or by anticipation, as *Lycidas* is with later pastoral elegies' (126).

While it may seem that Frye's thesis expands but does not fundamentally differ from Hanford's and Allen's project of elucidating, in Hanford's words, 'those elements of the elegiac tradition which appear in *Lycidas* and to show in detail Milton's indebtedness to each of the greater examples of the type' (Patrides, 28), Frye is in fact proposing something very different from what Hanford et al. had in mind. First, Frye rejects the source-hunting of Hanford et al. because, in his view, it risks turning *Lycidas* 'into a scissors-and-paste collection of allusive tags' (127). Similarly, he rejects the New Critical project of analysing 'the ambiguities and subtleties of [the poem's] diction' because this method 'soon reaches a point of no return to the poem' (127). The latter 'method reduces the poem to a jangle of echoes of itself, the other a jangle of echoes from other poets' (127). The solution to this conundrum lies, Frye argues, in the 'unifying principle' of mythic criticism. But Frye does not mean identifying the stories of gods, goddesses, and spirits. Rather, by 'myth,' Frye means 'the moving formal cause which is what Aristotle called the "soul" of the work and assimilates all details in the realizing of its unity' (127). The mythic element of *Lycidas* constitutes 'the connecting link between what makes *Lycidas* the poem it is and what unites it to other forms of poetic experience' (127).

While the paradigms dominating Milton criticism at the time Frye wrote this essay were, I think, capacious enough to embrace an essay critiquing both New Criticism and source studies as well as Frye's mythopoetic approach to literature, he articulates a position that goes beyond what the paradigm could ultimately allow: his belief that contextualizing, or historicizing, literature produces nothing of value. The mythic approach, Frye argues, will yield greater and greater returns; historical or biographical questions quickly result, so Frye claims, in idiocy:

> We notice that a law of diminishing returns sets in as soon as we move away from the poem itself. If we ask, who is Lycidas? The answer is that he is a member of the same family as Theocritus' Daphnis, Bion's Adonis, the Old Testament's Abel, and so on. The answer goes on building up a wider comprehension of literature and a deeper knowledge of its structural principles and recurring themes. *But if we ask, who was Edward King? What was his relation to Milton? How good a poet was he? we find ourselves moving dimly in the intense inane.* (124; my emphasis)

Frye singles out the mini-industry devoted to the 'two-handed engine' as exemplifying the futility of this approach. If we ask, writes Frye, 'why is the image of the two-handed engine in *Lycidas*? We can give an answer ... that illustrates how carefully the poem has been constructed' (124). But if we ask the historical question that occupied so many Miltonists: 'what is the two-handed engine?' then, Frye concludes, the inability to come up with a definitive answer undermines the credibility of the entire enterprise: 'there are forty-odd answers, none of them completely satisfactory; yet the fact that they are not wholly satisfactory hardly seems to be important' (124) to those who perversely insist upon providing yet more unsatisfactory answers.

Frye refines this point with more subtlety (and less humor) in two essays also collected in *Fables of Identity*. He grants that, initially, a work's political context may be part of its original meaning. In 'Myth, Fiction, and Displacement' (originally published in 1961), Frye allows that Arthur Miller's *The Crucible* 'deals with the Salem witch trials in a way that suggested McCarthyism to most of its original audience' (37), just as both Demosthenes and Byron, at the time they composed their works, 'are talking about the freedom of Greece' ('Nature and Homer [originally published in 1958],' 46). But Frye then argues that a work gains stature, gains meaning, in inverse proportion to its original, political contexts. Immediately after correctly identifying the political overtones of Miller's play, Frye asserts that if *The Crucible* is to matter to subsequent audiences, its meaning must transcend the original impetus: 'But if *The Crucible* is good enough to hold the stage after McCarthyism has become as dead an issue as the Salem trials, it would be clear that the theme of *The Crucible* is one which can always be used in literature, and that any social hysteria can form its subject matter' (37). Frye is even clearer in 'Nature and Homer': 'As time goes on, and historical tradition becomes more tenuous, only the events with conventional poetic associations can carry the thrilling magic of a great name' (46). The farther one gets from the particulars of history, in Frye's view, the more meaningful a work becomes.

Thus we come to the polemic embedded in the *Lycidas* essay's subtitle: 'literature as context.' Frye means that the *only* acceptable context, the only context that will yield an intellectually satisfying result, is what he terms 'literature.' 'Literature as context,' in other words, points to a negative as well as a positive, i.e., *not* history as context, *not* biography as context, *not* anything other than literature as the only proper context for studying literature, because, as Frye writes, '*all other contexts* ... are secondary and derivative' (127; my emphasis). Frye even brings this essay to a conclusion with a witty dismissal of both critical ecumenicism and historically based literary criticism: 'There are critics who can find things in the Public Record Office, and there are critics who, like myself, could not find the Public Records Office. Not all critical statements or procedures can be equally valid' (128).[38]

In later years, Frye complained that the 'Milton establishment' did not appreciate his work. In particular, he believed that *The Return of Eden: Five Essays on Milton's Epics* (Toronto, 1965), would not, as John Ayre, Frye's biographer, puts it, 'come into its own until the current generation of Miltonists died off,'[39] and I suggest one can find the source of this estrangement in Frye's resolute anti-historicism. While such literary historians as Hanford and Allen may have focused their scholarship on investigating the literary traditions informing Milton's work, they never overtly attacked the project of situating Milton's work within its historical framework. In fact, during the period in which Frye wrote 'Literature as Context,' the major project of the Milton establishment was editing the *Complete Prose Works of John Milton*, published by the Yale University Press. As Ernest Sirluck, Frye's eventual colleague,[40] editor of volume 2 of the *Complete Prose Works* (1643–8) and a scholar about as conversant with the location and contents of the Public Record Office as one could imagine,[41] recalls in his memoir, the editorial board, 'which was to have the advice and cooperation of James Holly Hanford and William Haller, constituted a substantial portion of the Milton establishment of the day.'[42] Historically based scholarship, in other words, figured as an essential aspect of 'normal' Milton criticism, and Frye's militant a historicism helps explain why Frye and 'the Milton establishment' mistrusted each other.[43] While in almost every way, Frye adds to the scope and precision of 'normal' *Lycidas* criticism in 'Literature as Context' (i.e., he demonstrates in finer detail the unity of the poem, the quality of the verse, the elegy's relationship to the pastoral tradition, and its emotional impact), the rejection of historical context ultimately rendered it less than entirely acceptable, especially after the emergence of the New Historicism during the 1980s. Consequently, 'Literature as Context' ultimately met the fate awaiting work not in conformity with the paradigms established and maintained by the interpretive community the essay addresses: it has all but disappeared from the list of books and articles considered foundational to the study of *Lycidas*.[44]

IV

A confession: when I started researching this essay, I expected at this point to turn gracefully from Frye's views on Milton to Frye's views of Canadian literature, since he wrote 'Literature as Context' during the period he wrote yearly reviews of Canadian poetry for the *University of Toronto Quarterly*. I assumed that Frye's treatment of Canadian poetry would overlap with his treatment of Milton, that the two areas would constitute two aspects of a single, unified body of thought. I thought I would find the same 'total coherence'[45] that Frye ascribes to both science and literary criticism. To my surprise, however, I found something very different, as Frye's views of Canadian poetry significantly differ from his views of non-Canadian literature and literary theory.[46] More precisely, the questions that Frye banishes as illegitimate in 'Literature as Context' (and the *Anatomy*) are exactly the questions on which he grounds much of his thinking about Canadian literature and culture. When Frye shifted his focus to the literary history of his home country, the critical positions enunciated in his analysis of *Lycidas* no longer predominate.

In 'Literature as Context,' Frye asserts that 'the primary business of the critic is with myth as the shaping principle of a work of literature' (127), and occasionally Frye will return to myth in his analyses of Canadian poetry. In his 1946 essay, for example, 'The Narrative Tradition of English Canadian Poetry,' Frye will praise Isabella Crawford as possessing 'the most remarkable mythopoetic imagination in Canadian poetry' (57).[47] His 1957 omnibus review of Canadian poetry (written in 1956) included a sensitive treatment of Leonard Cohen's first book, *Let Us Compare Mythologies*, which notes Cohen's use of 'mythical patterns' in some of his verse (164–5), and in 'Preface to an Uncollected Anthology' (also first published in 1956), Frye repeated his concern with 'myth as a shaping principle of poetry' (271). But these passages are isolated examples. Even though Frye would later call these reviews 'an essential piece of "field work" to be carried on while I was working out a comprehensive critical theory,'[48] in fact, myth plays a very small role in Frye's analyses of Canadian verse, and it is never the *essential* element. In his 1956 review (written in 1955), he gives respectful notice to Desmond Pacey's *The Selected Poems of Sir Charles G.D. Roberts,* and contra to the argument in both 'Literature as Context' and the *Anatomy* that myth constitutes the sine qua non of *all* poetry, Frye grants that Roberts 'is a subjective and descriptive poet, *not a mythical one,* and the organizing formal principles which give both intellectual and emotional unity to his work come out of his personal life' (138; my emphasis). Not only is myth no longer the central concern, but Frye gives primacy to the poet's 'personal life,' precisely the concern that Frye, in 'Literature as Context,' claims will lead one to move 'dimly in the intense inane' (124).

Frye's comments in his 1958 review (written as always the year before) of Jay Macpherson's Governor-General Award winning book, *The Boatman,* provide the best example of the diminution of myth's importance. Frye writes, 'As for mythology, that is one of poetry's indispensable languages' (172). In 'Literature as Context,' as well as the *Anatomy*, myth is not *one of* poetry's indispensable languages; myth is *the only* language (e.g., 'myth [is] the formal moving cause ... of the work and assimilates all details in the realizing of its unity' [127]). But Frye says that myth is not essential to understanding or enjoying Macpherson's poems. After quoting a lovely quatrain ('Oh wake him not until he please, / Lest he should rise to weep:/ For flocks and birds and streams and trees / Are golden in his silver sleep'),[49] Frye situates these lines in terms of their mythic resonances, echoing exactly the type of analysis one finds on nearly every page of the *Anatomy.* But, Frye then significantly qualifies myth's ultimate importance to Macpherson's verse, and by implication, to Canadian poetry in general:

> For thousands of years poetry has been ringing the changes on a sleeper whom it is dangerous to waken, and the myths of Endymion, of the

> bridegroom in the Song of Songs, of Adam, of Blake's Albion, of Joyce's Finnegan, are a few of the by-products. *Such myths in the background enrich the suggestiveness of the above four lines, but the lines are not dependent on the echoes, either for their meaning or for their poetic value.* (172; my emphasis)

The demotion of myth's importance is not the only shift when Frye changes topics. As if to balance the equation, from the very beginning of his writing about Canadian literature, Frye insists on the primacy of exactly the areas he so vigorously denounced as secondary in 'Literature as Context' as well as the *Anatomy*: i.e., history and extra-literary contexts. In his foundational 1943 essay, 'Canada and Its Poetry,' Frye announces (contra his later assertion that 'literature ... forms the primary context of any given work of literary art' [127]) that 'poetry is not a citizen of the world: it is conditioned by language, and flourishes best within a national unit' (28), and in his 1953 review for the *UTQ* (written in 1952), Frye declares: 'Poets do not live on Mount Parnassus, but in their own environments, and Canada has made itself an environmental reality' (102). By 'environmental reality,' Frye means that Canada's physical geography constitutes the shaping presence of its literature, and he contrasts Canada's topography with that of the United States. Later in the essay, Frye will locate another 'distinctively Canadian' element in the different political histories of the two countries ('a Canadian is an American who rejects the Revolution. Canada fought its civil war to establish its union and its wars of independence which were fought against the United States and not Europe, came later' [106]), a theme he will return to in his 1956 'Preface to an Uncollected Anthology.' In this piece, Frye once more argues that Canadian poetry is shaped by two fundamental forces. The first is geography: 'In older countries the works of man and of nature, the city and the garden of civilization, have usually reached some kind of imaginative harmony. But the land of the Rockies and the Precambrian Shield impresses painter and poet alike by its raw colours and angular rhythms' (256). The second, again, is politics: 'Yet there is, I think, a more distinctive attitude in Canadian poetry than in Canadian life, a more withdrawn and detached view of that life which may go back to the central fact of Canadian history: the rejection of the American Revolution' (258).

Frye's treatment of John McCrae's 'In Flanders Fields' – which he deems 'the best known of all Canadian poems' (58) – demonstrates how history becomes increasingly important to the analysis of Canadian literature. When Frye first mentions this poem in 'The Narrative Tradition in English Canadian Poetry,' he writes that the poem expresses 'the same spirit of an inexorable ferocity which even death cannot relax, like the old Norse warrior whose head continued to gnash and bite the dust long after it had been severed from his body' (58). When Frye returns to this poem in the 'Preface to an Uncollected Anthology' (1956), he repeats the connection to the heroic ethos, but he adds another passage. In complete contradiction to the assertion in both 'Literature as Context' and the *Anatomy* that poems arise from other poems, not life,[50] Frye situates this poem within history: it 'breathes a spirit like that of the Viking warrior whose head continued to gnaw the dust after it had been cut from his body; and it comes from the country of the Long Sault, Crysler's Farm, St. Julien, and Dieppe' (262). Frye connects this poem to battles important to Canadian history, and by doing so, not only goes beyond the 'self-contained literary universe' of the *Anatomy*, but situates the poem within exactly the contexts that he dismisses in 'Literature as Context' as 'secondary and derivative' (127).

What is going on here? How can Frye claim one thing in 'Literature as Context' (and the *Anatomy*) and the opposite in his work on Canadian literature? Frye, evidently, was not unaware of this split, and without explicitly addressing the issue, he offered two overlapping reasons for why his analyses of Canadian and European literature proceeded on opposite tracks, animated by opposite assumptions. First, Frye distinguishes between the cultural legacies available to European writers (a category that includes England and the United States), and those in Canada. The former writers are heir to the literary traditions analysed in 'Literature as Context' and the *Anatomy*, the latter are not, due to the extremely young age of the country. As Frye puts it in 'Canada and Its Poetry':

> To an English poet, the tradition of his own country and language proceeds in a direct chronological line down to himself, and that in its turn is part of a gigantic funnel of a tradition extending back to Homer and the Old Testament. But to a Canadian, broken off from this linear sequence and having none of his own, the traditions of Europe appear as a kaleidoscopic whirl with no definite shape or meaning. (32)

In 'The Narrative Tradition in English Canadian Poetry' (1946), Frye will make the same point: a European's poetry 'cannot be "young," for it is written in a European language with a thousand years of disciplined utterance behind it' (55); a Canadian, on the other hand, is at the very beginning of his tradition, and he (or she) occupies the same position as the anonymous Anglo-Saxon bards: the Canadian poet 'has to deal with a poetic and imaginative environment for which, to find any parallel in England, we should have to go back to a period earlier than Chaucer' (56).

Yet the claim that Canada is too young to have its own tradition makes little sense, since in the *Anatomy* Frye regularly alludes to eighteenth- and nineteenth-century American writers, such as Benjamin Franklin (227), Nathaniel Hawthorne (e.g., 137–9), and Walt Whitman (e.g., 100–3) among his examples of archetypal or mythic literature. Nor will the explanation that no Canadian writer equals Shakespeare, Wordsworth, or Dante suffice, as the *Anatomy* is filled with references to such marginally canonical figures as Vachel Lindsay (279), Gilbert and Sullivan (109), R.D. Blackmore (author of *Lorna Doone* [138]), and P.G. Wodehouse (173). The absence of Canadian writers is even more surprising, given Frye's extreme enthusiasm for E.J. Pratt's verse. When he first read Pratt's poem, 'The Truant,' he told A.J.M. Smith that 'it's the subtlest and maturest piece of symbolism he's done, and he always has been a symbolic poet rather than a chronicler or ballad-spinner.'[51] Frye's enthusiasm for this poem continued through and beyond the period of the *Anatomy*'s composition, when he called it 'the greatest poem in Canadian literature.'[52] One would imagine such a poet would find a place in the *Anatomy*, but while one finds references to, inter alia, Dickens's Podsnap and 'primitive art and literature,' there are none to Pratt.

There is, however, another reason, a more convincing one, that has the added advantage of helping to explain why, despite the claims of universal applicability in the *Anatomy*, repeated at the end of 'Literature as Context,' Frye never refers to Canadian literature when discussing literary theory. To recap, throughout 'Literature as Context,' Frye insists upon the necessity of unity. Bad criticism of *Lycidas* results from not trying hard enough 'to understand the unity of the poem' (123); every poem 'must be examined as a unity' (127); and unless 'we have a unifying principle' (127), source hunting and close reading 'will get out of hand' (127). The same drive for unity will show up in other works. In the *Anatomy*, Frye proposes that archetypal criticism 'prevents each poem from becoming a separate center of isolated scholarship' (342), and in the introduction to his 1971 collection, *The Bush Garden*, Frye declares that 'the imagination is occupationally disposed to synthesis.'[53]

Yet Frye realized from the very start that Canada is far from unified, that his native country comprises an unresolved, perhaps irresolvable, perpetual binary opposition. In 'Canada and Its Poetry,' Frye readily admits that when he speaks of 'Canadian poetry,' he really means '*English* Canadian poetry.' A.J.M. Smith's anthology, *The Book of Canadian Poetry*, addresses only half of the equation, and 'as Mr. Smith says in his Preface, French Canadian Poetry is a separate job' (27).[54] Even more, this division governs Canadian identity. Canada, as Frye says, is a colony, and 'this colonial tendency has been sharpened by the French-English split' (30), and goes beyond linguistic difference: 'the division of language and race is approximately one of religion also' (30). This division not only pits the nation against itself, but perverts Canada's relationship to European traditions: 'It is an obvious paradox in Canadian life that the more colonial the English- or French-speaking Canadian is, and the more he distrusts the other half of his country, the more artificial his relation to the real Britain or France becomes' (31). Frye will return to this theme in his 1956 essay 'Preface to an Uncollected Anthology.' Again, qualifying his assertion in the *Anatomy* and 'Literature as Context' that poems derive only from other poems, Frye allows that 'environment' impacts poets as well, and linguistic duality forms an essential part of the Canadian context: 'A country with almost no Atlantic seaboard, which for most of history has existed in practically one dimension; a country divided by two languages and great stretches of wilderness ...' (256). Even nature is affected: 'The Wordsworth who saw nature as exquisitely fitted to the human mind would be lost in Canada, where what the poets see is a violent collision of two forces [the works of man versus the savagery of nature], both monstrous' (256). In his 1965 essay, 'Conclusion to the First Edition of *Literary History of Canada*,' Frye writes that he sympathizes with efforts to create 'a cultural community' (i.e., a cultural unity) because 'Canada has two languages and two literatures' (343). Furthermore, Frye knows this duality intensely well, because it constituted the most important formative influence of his early life:[55]

> I grew up in two towns, Sherbrooke and Moncton, where the population was half English and half French, divided by language, education, and religion, and living in a state of more or less amiable Apartheid. In the Eastern Townships, the English-speaking group formed a northern spur of New England, and had at a much earlier time almost annexed themselves to New England, feeling much more akin to it than to Quebec. The English-speaking Maritimers, also, had most of their cultural and economic ties with New England, but their political connexion was with New France, so that culturally, from their point of view, Canada stopped at Fredericton and started again at Westmount. There were also a good many Maritime French families whose native language was English, and so had the same cultural dislocation in reverse.

In their critiques of the New Criticism, both Richard Ohmann and Terry Eagleton note that the New Critics tried to create in literature the unity they could not find in reality,[56] and I would suggest that something of the same is going on with Northrop Frye. Confronted with the hostile duality of Canada in both his intellectual and personal life, Frye tried to find in European literature in general, and *Lycidas* in particular, the unity, the synthesis, he so desired. Like the speaker in Milton's *Doctrine and Discipline of Divorce*, Frye was a 'wanting soul' (*YP* 2:251), and the object of his 'wanting,' meaning both desire and lack, is unity. But because Frye was too intellectually honest to transform Canadian literature into something it manifestly was not, he seems to have decided, consciously or not, to create his own division between European and Canadian literature. Hence the absence of Canadian literature in the *Anatomy*, and the contradiction between his approaches to *Lycidas* and to Canadian literature, his banishing history from the former and embrace of it in the latter. But the analysis of *Lycidas* and of Canadian literature do not constitute, to appropriate the title of Hugh MacLennan's novel, 'two solitudes.' Nor do I think that the contradiction between Frye's work on *Lycidas* and his work on Canadian literature is an example of 'poetic' thinking or of Frye's 'penchant for holding diametrically opposed ideas simultaneously ...'[57] Rather, I propose that Northrop Frye's sense of Canada as fundamentally riven constitutes the ground from which the *Anatomy* and 'Literature as Context' arise, and the two areas are in a constant, ongoing dialectic. To paraphrase James Joyce, Canada's history was the nightmare from which Frye tried to wake up, and his efforts resulted in the *Anatomy of Criticism* as well as 'Milton's *Lycidas*: Literature and Context.'[58]

NOTES

1 The essays are collected in *Northrop Frye in Modern Criticism: Selected Papers from the English Institute*, ed. Murray Krieger (New York, 1966).

2 Paul Ricoeur, '*Anatomy of Criticism* or the Order of Paradigms,' in *Centre and Labyrinth: Essays in Honour of Northrop Frye*, ed. Eleanor Cook et al. (Toronto, 1983), 1; Geoffrey Hartman, 'Structuralism: The Anglo-American Adventure,' *Yale French Studies* 36/37 (1966): 155.

3 Quoted in John Ayre, *Northrop Frye: A Biography* (Toronto, 1989), 262.

4 See his collection, *On Education* (Ann Arbor, MI, 1988).

5 Even though Random House published Ayre's biography of Frye, it came out only in Canada, and it is a rare library in the United States that houses all of Frye's collected works.

6 See Angela Esterhammer, introduction to *Northrop Frye on Milton and Blake,* vol. 16 of *Collected Works of Northrop Frye* (Toronto, 2005), xviii–xxvii.

7 For example, neither Ian Balfour (*Northrop Frye* [Boston, 1988]), nor Jonathan Hart (*Northrop Frye: The Theoretical Imagination* [Routledge,1994]) devotes any space to examining this essay. A possible reason might be that Frye's thinking about Milton tended to be directed toward students and non-specialists rather than professional Miltonists. As he writes in the preface to *The Return to Eden* (Toronto, 1965): 'The lectures at Huron College were conceived as an introduction to *Paradise Lost* for relatively inexperienced students, with the hope that they would also have something to interest the general reader' (vii).

8 *Milton's 'Lycidas': The Tradition and the Poem,* ed. C.A. Patrides (New York, 1961). All further references to the essays contained within this edition will be cited parenthetically.

9 For example, while J. Martin Evans cites four essays from Patrides in the 'Suggested Reading' section of his essay on *Lycidas* in *The Cambridge Companion to Milton,* 2nd ed., ed. Dennis Danielson (Cambridge, 1999), 34–53; Frye's is not among them. Nor does Stella Revard cite 'Literature as Context' in her essay on *Lycidas* in *A Companion to Milton,* ed. Thomas N. Corns (2001; Oxford, 2003), 246–60. According to the Arts and Humanities Citation Index, since 1975 (when the online database begins), 'Literature as Context' has been cited only twice, once by a Miltonist (Mary Jane Doherty, 'Ezekiel's Voice, Milton's Prophetic Exile, and the Merkavah in *Lycidas,*' *Milton Quarterly* 23.3 [1989]: 89), and once by an Americanist (R. Tuerk, 'Mythic Patterns of Reconciliation in Emerson's "Threnody,"' *ESQ: A Journal of the American Renaissance* 27.3 [1981]: 181–8).

10 See, for example, the essays collected in section 2, 'Imagined Community: Frye and Canada,' of *The Legacy of Northrop Frye,* ed. Alvin A. Lee, and Robert D. Denham (Toronto, 1994); and Eli Mandel, 'Northrop Frye and the Canadian Literary Tradition,' in *Centre and Labyrinth: Essays in Honour of Northrop Frye,* ed. Eleanor Cook et al. (Toronto, 1983), 288–9.

11 On this aspect of Frye's work, see Frank Lentricchia, *After the New Criticism* (Chicago, 1980), 8–9.

12 'The Archetypes of Literature,' in *Fables of Identity: Studies in Poetic Mythology* (New York, 1963), 7.

13 Frye, *Anatomy of Criticism* (Princeton, 1957; repr. New York, 1969). All further references will be to the reprinted edition, and cited parenthetically.

14 Frye did not like the New Critical nostalgia for a past unity. In a review of Alan Tate's *The Forlorn Demon*, he mocked their sense of cultural decline: 'the great Western Butterslide, the doctrine of a coordinated synthesis in medieval culture, giving place, at the Renaissance to a splitting and specialized schizophrenia which has got steadily worse until it has finally landed all in that Pretty Pass in which we are today' (quoted in Ayre, 240).

15 John Crowe Ransom, 'Criticism, Inc. [1938],' reprinted in *The Norton Anthology of Theory and Criticism*, ed. Vincent B. Leitch et al., (New York, 2001), 1109. See also Jeffrey Williams, 'Theory Change,' *Journal of Cultural and Religious Theory* 4.2 (2003), http://www.jcrt.org/archives/04.2/williams.shtml accessed 4/16/2006, par. 26; and Stephen Schryer, 'Fantasies of the New Class: The New Criticism, Harvard Sociology, and the Idea of the University,' *PMLA* 122.3 (2007): 663–78.

16 For a fascinating example of how the Cold War fundamentally altered the research and disciplinary practices of a particular university, see Rebecca S. Lowen, *Creating the Cold War University: The Transformation of Stanford* (Berkeley and Los Angeles, 1997).

17 While the shifts in university funding were not as marked as they were in the United States, the growth in research dollars flowing to defence work was significant nonetheless. As Martin L. Friedland puts it in *The University of Toronto: A History* (Toronto, 2002), 'The Institute of Aerospace Studies perhaps best illustrates the growing interest in research in engineering in the late 1940s. It also illustrates the continuing involvement of the University in defence work during the cold war' (375). In 1949, McGill University's principal, Dr. Cyril James, defended the university from the charge of incubating communists by becoming 'an impassioned advocate of Cold War preparedness' (Reg Whitaker and Gary Marcuse, *Cold War Canada: The Making of a National Insecurity State, 1945–1957* [Toronto, 1994], 107). For an analysis of the Cold War from a very different perspective, see Richard Cavell's collection, *Love, Hate, and Fear in Canada's Cold War* (Toronto, 2004), which demonstrates how 'Canada's Cold War was not simply an extension of the one waged in the United States; ours had a particularly cultural dimension because it raised issues of national self-representation that went beyond Cold War tensions related to capitalistic versus communistic regimes' (5).

18 Richard Ohmann, 'English and the Cold War,' in *The Cold War and the University: Toward an Intellectual History of the Postwar Years*, ed. André Schiffren (New York, 1997), 74. See also R.C. Lewontin's essay in the same volume, 'The Cold War and the Transformation of the Academy,' 1–34.

19 'Archetypes,' 7.

20 Thomas Kuhn, *The Structure of Scientific Revolutions*, 2nd ed. (Chicago, 1970). All further references will be to this edition, and cited parenthetically.
21 'Archetypes,' 13.
22 See Peter C. Herman, *Destabilizing Milton: 'Paradise Lost' and the Poetics of Incertitude* (New York, 2005), 1–24.
23 Oras, 'Milton's Early Rhyme Schemes and the Structure of *Lycidas*,' *Modern Philology* 52.1 (1954): 21.
24 Kuhn, 24. Frye unintentionally expresses the same point when he notes that 'In literature, as in life, the unconventionally new is a monstrosity' ('Nature and Homer,' in *Fables of Identity*, 43).
25 Battestin, 'John Crowe Ransom and *Lycidas*: A Reappraisal,' *College English* 17.4 (1956): 223.
26 Other examples would include Henry Hitch Adams, 'The Development of the Flower Passage in "Lycidas,"' *Modern Language Notes* 65.7 (1950): 468–72 (Shakespeare as the source for this passage); Edward S. Le Comte, '"Lycidas," Petrarch and the Plague,' *Modern Language Notes* 69.6 (1954): 402–4 (Milton's debt to the ninth of Petrarch's Latin elegies); D.C. Allen, 'Milton's Alpheus,' *Modern Language Notes* 71.3 (1956): 172–3 (Milton's use of Fulgentius for the symbolic meaning of this river); D.C. Allen, 'Milton's Amarant,' *Modern Language Notes* 72.4 (1957): 256–8 (Milton's use of Claudius Claudianus for the symbolic meaning of this flower).
27 See Patrides, 240–1, for a summary of the controversy and a bibliography. This industry continues to this day, although with some recognition that the proliferation of answers has rendered the project somewhat silly. See, for example, David Sansone, 'How Milton Reads: Scripture, the Classics, and that Two-Handed Engine,' *Modern Philology* 103.3 (2006): 332–58.
28 Harry F. Robins, 'Milton's "Two-Handed Engine at the Door" and St. Matthew's Gospel,' *Review of English Studies* n.s. 5 (1954): 29.
29 Ibid, 29. Robins puts his definition of 'two-handed' in quotes, but does not supply a note identifying the source.
30 Ibid.
31 Ibid.
32 As Cleanth Brooks puts it, 'The characteristic unity of a poem (even of those poems which may accidentally possess a logical unity as well as this poetic unity) lies in the unification of attitudes into a hierarchy subordinated to a total and governing attitude ... The conclusion of the poem is the working out of the various tensions – set up by whatever means – by propositions, metaphors, symbols' (*The Well Wrought Urn: Studies in the Structure of Poetry* [New York, 1947], 206–7). See also Richard Ohmann, *English in America: A Radical View of the Profession* (New York, 1976), 75.

33 See, for example, J. Milton French, 'The Digressions in Milton's "Lycidas,"' *Studies in Philology* 50 (1953): 485; Allen, *The Harmonious Vision: Studies in Milton's Poetry* (Baltimore, 1970), 63; Oras, 'Milton's Early Rhyme Schemes,' 17.

34 All references to Frye's essay will be to *Fables of Identity*, and cited parenthetically. Frye's emotional reaction to *Lycidas* was apparently not restricted to scholarship. According to Alvin Lee, 'In class one day in the mid-fifties he recited the last lines of this great elegy and his voice broke, the only time in numerous direct encounters with him that I ever saw such a development' (private correspondence).

35 Frye gives a less expansive definition of 'archetype' in 'Literature as Context' than he does in the *Anatomy*. In the latter work, Frye defines 'archetype' as 'a symbol which connects one poem with another and thereby helps to unify and integrate our literary experience' (99); in the former, an 'archetype' means 'a literary symbol, or cluster of symbols, which are used recurrently throughout literature, and thereby become conventional' (120).

36 Oras, 'Milton's Early Rhyme Schemes,' 21.

37 In, for example, 'The Formalist Critics,' Cleanth Brooks asserts that 'the primary concern of criticism is with the problem of unity,' that the critic's task is to describe 'how the parts of [the poem] are related' (*Norton Anthology of Theory and Criticism*, 1366, 1368).

38 In the *Anatomy*, Frye is even more resolute in his rejection of history: 'Poetry can only be made out of other poems; novels out of other novels. Literature shapes itself, and is not shaped externally' (97). In fact, Frye predicates the study of archetypes on 'the possibility of a self-contained literary universe' (118).

39 Ayre, *Northrop Frye: A Biography*, 290.

40 Sirluck returned to the University of Toronto in 1962; see Sirluck, *First Generation: An Autobiography* (Toronto, 1996), 173.

41 In addition to being the volume's general editor, Sirluck edited *Areopagitica* and wrote the extensively detailed introduction.

42 Sirluck, *First Generation*, 179.

43 According to Ayre, Frye's 'obdurately anti-historical bias' also cost him a position at Harvard in 1949 (229).

44 See above, n. 9.

45 'Archetypes of Literature,' 9.

46 See also Eli Mandel, 'Northrop Frye and the Canadian Literary Tradition,' in *Centre and Labyrinth*, 288–9, and Jean O'Grady, introduction to *Northrop Frye on Canada*, ed. Jean O'Grady and David Staines, vol. 12 of *Collected Works of Northrop Frye* (Toronto, 2003), xxxvi, xl–xliv.

47 Unless otherwise noted, all references to Frye's writings on Canadian literature will be to *Northrop Frye on Canada.* Page numbers will be cited parenthetically.
48 Preface to *The Bush Garden: Essays on the Canadian Imagination* (Toronto, 1971), viii.
49 Frye does not give the title of this poem.
50 For the *Anatomy,* see above, n. 34.
51 Quoted in Ayre, 182. See also Frye's obituary for Pratt, 'Ned Pratt: The Personal Legend' (*Northrop Frye on Canada,* 326–30). Frye even dedicated *Fables of Identity* to Pratt.
52 Ayre, 182.
53 Preface to *The Bush Garden,* x.
54 The division is even more complicated than Frye suggests, as he omits all mention of the First Nations from his discussions of Canadian identity. I want to thank Mary Nyquist and Feisal Mohamed for pointing this out to me.
55 Frye, *The Bush Garden,* v–vi.
56 Richard Ohmann, *English in America: A Radical View of the Profession* (New York, 1976), 75; Terry Eagleton, *Literary Theory: An Introduction* (Minneapolis, 1983), 47.
57 Jean O'Grady, introduction to *Northrop Frye on Canada,* xxxvi.
58 I gratefully acknowledge the aid I received in the course of writing this essay from Alvin Lee, John Denham, and Richard Cavell.

14 Fielding, Jonson, and the Critique of High Mimesis in *Paradise Lost*

FEISAL G. MOHAMED

For a Satyr as it was born out of a *Tragedy*, so ought to resemble his parentage, to strike high, and adventure dangerously at the most eminent vices among the greatest persons ...

– Milton, *An Apology Against a Pamphlet*

In the foreword to his all-Canadian collection marking the tercentenary of *Paradise Lost*, Balachandra Rajan notes the coincidence of that event with the first centenary of Confederation. He leaves it to others to wonder 'what is implied by this Pythagorean harmony,' whilst indicating that suggestive coincidence is the animating force behind the broad range of significant offerings gathered on 'the Canadian shelf in a Milton library.'[1] It must be said that this alignment of centenaries does not seem entirely coincidental: that Milton is born in the same year that Quebec City is founded seems like chance; that *Paradise Lost* is first printed exactly two hundred years before the Dominion of Canada is formed, give or take two months, seems like a forethought of the great clockmaker.[2]

Despite his scepticism regarding a Canadian 'tradition' in Milton studies, Rajan does refer quite comfortably in the same foreword to 'the Woodhouse tradition.'[3] Woodhouse's presence in that collection is certain; Rajan stands alone in its ranks in not being at one time his student or colleague – the other contributors are Arthur E. Barker, Roy Daniells, Northrop Frye, and Hugh MacCallum. But if Woodhouse exerts a ghostly influence over so many Canadian Miltonists, one must wonder if he brings with him those genii of literary criticism whose images hovered among the stacks of books in the office where he held his seminal graduate classes, Samuel Johnson and Matthew Arnold. Though the Canadian

School of mid-twentieth century, if it can be so called, allows for a great deal of variety, it seems at times quietly to suppose that Milton's poetry translates the spirit of the ancients into English and represents the greatest of what is thought and said in Western culture. As such it takes a prominent place in the refining of moral sensibilities described in Watson Kirkconnell and Woodhouse's report *The Humanities in Canada*, which endorses Arnold's sense that 'the "power of beauty" and the "power of conduct" are integral parts of the cultured or liberal personality.'[4]

Frye's deep admiration for Woodhouse is consistently expressed in his diaries, which do not frequently find much to admire in academic company.[5] High regard seems also to have been a desire for approval, as suggested by a dream recorded in his 1949 diary: 'Stumbled at length into an uneasy dozing dream that I was in the Merton Library pointing out the Mob Quad to Woodhouse, very proud of my knowledge, of being able to display it, & of having been connected with it. Curious.'[6] It is commonly observed that Woodhouse approached humanities study with a deep sense of vocation; Frye is a complex figure in this respect. He seems consistently to resist an affective, moralizing response to literature as he equally consistently refers formal patterns to those of the Bible. Under his student editorship in 1932, Victoria College's *Acta Victoriana* stopped printing biographies of Methodist clergymen, but his personal faith, and his desire to spread the word, are indicated by his ordination as a minister of the United Church in 1936.[7] What polemic there is in the 'Polemical Introduction' to the *Anatomy of Criticism* seeks to exorcise the spectre of Arnold from the study of literature. Arnold aims to 'create a new scriptural canon out of poetry to serve as a guide for those social principles which he wants culture to take over from religion'; as such he applies 'a social attitude' where Frye advocates a 'conceptual framework which criticism alone possesses.'[8] Such a framework is not to be found in New Criticism's focus on the texture of individual poems, which Frye identifies as a rhetorical criticism, but instead in the rigorous accounting for the symbolic order of literary expression that he wishes to advance.

In his taxonomy, *Paradise Lost* is firmly in the high mimetic realm of epic and tragedy.[9] Indeed, the language with which Frye describes tragedy seems closely bound to Milton: 'while catastrophe is the normal end of tragedy, this is balanced by an equally significant original greatness, a paradise lost.' Connecting *Paradise Lost* to tragedy, Frye suggestively observes that 'the relation of Milton's God to Adam is the relation of the tragic poet to his hero. The tragic poet knows that his hero will be in a tragic situation, but he exerts all his power to avoid the sense of having manipulated that situation for his own purposes.'[10] High mimetic modes are opposed to irony and satire: where high mimesis presents a stable order of nature governed by reason and idealizing 'human representatives of the divine and spiritual world,' irony and satire 'give form to the shifting ambiguities and complexities of unidealized existence.'[11] Unlike tragedy, irony 'does not need an exceptional figure: as a rule, the dingier the hero the sharper the irony, when irony alone is aimed at.'[12] Though he wishes to expunge value judgments from the science of criticism, he tends to associate Milton with something akin to Arnold's Class One of literary decorum: Frye places Milton in a triumvirate with Homer and Vergil, and opens his *Return of Eden* with a declaration of Milton's 'gigantic' proportions; those who have 'abjectly failed' as readers of Milton 'have tried to cut him down to size – their size.'[13]

Much as we might find such statements to be simply correct, valuing Milton for his literary majesty can also blind us to his literary subversiveness. And the thematic content of *Paradise Lost* should call into question straightforward association of its mimesis with a stable order of nature: it is an epic of the natural world transformed, and of the loss of human ability to be governed by reason. The universe may be governed by divine agency, but unlike classical mythopoeism the full dynamics of divine will remain inscrutable in this Christian poem. We are not shown a race of heroes whence we spring, but the human frailty producing the unidealized realms that Frye associates with irony and satire. Biographical evidence suggests that we should expect Milton to operate in precisely these modes. We often remember Dryden's observation that Milton pronounced the letter 'r' very hard but forget that he took it as a sign of 'satiric wit,' though the two qualities are clearly paired in Milton's poetry – 'thus they relate, / E*rr*ing,' 'G*r*ate on their sc*r*annel Pipes of w*r*etched st*r*aw.'[14] Marvell's famous defence of Milton defers to the force of the older man's satirical grip: 'had he took you in hand, you would have had cause to repent the occasion, and not escap'd so easily as you did under my *Transprosal.*'[15] Such wit is not at odds with the fact that Milton is not the most accomplished of humorists – Cicero recognized the difference between the grace and charm of humour (*facetia*) and the 'shafts of ridicule' hurled by wit (*dicax*)[16] – and indeed Aubrey's note on Milton's conversation suggests that, perhaps despite himself, even the poet's dinner-table satire could tend toward the snarling rather than the smiling: 'Extreme pleasant in his conversation and at dinner, supper, etc; *but* satirical' (emphasis mine).[17]

Satiric wit can often animate Milton's handling of literary genres, which he subjects to a destabilizing scepticism – Balachandra Rajan's observation in this volume that the Ludlow Masque overturns the genre in which it takes part might be applied to several works across Milton's career, from the 'Nativity Ode,' which locates Christ's birth on the traditional calendar only to show how it erases the significance of earthly time (and vaults above the rival efforts of Ben Jonson, Jeremy Taylor, and William Drummond of Hawthornden), to *Samson Agonistes,* Milton's long-intended and much-planned entry into tragedy arriving at the moment when its classical purism and biblical subject is most an indictment of contemporary drama. In engaging genre Milton does not entirely leave his controversialist persona behind. Rather he adopts the satirist's persona of moral rectitude in a corrupt world, which corruption has polluted accepted literary forms. This goes beyond an Eliotean relationship between tradition and individual talent; in making his place in the tradition Milton assails the moral foundation of those modes he engages.

Paradise Lost has not been fully explored in this respect, though its satiric elements seemed somewhat more apparent in the early decades of its reception.[18] That set-piece of ridicule in book 3, the 'Paradise of Fools,' unsurprisingly drew the attention of several Restoration writers, being mentioned in Nahum Tate's poem 'The Match' (1677), Nathaniel Lee's *Ceasar Borgia ... A Tragedy* (1680), and in the preface to Philip Ayres's *Revengeful Mistress* (1696).[19] As Nicholas von Maltzahn notes in this volume, Dryden alludes in *Mac Flecknoe* to the simile in book 1 by which Satan perches himself atop the excrement of Aetna – 'Such *r*esting found the sole / Of unblest feet' (*PL* 1.237–8).[20] But the writer who seems most attuned to this strain in *Paradise Lost* is Henry Fielding. Frye rightly describes Fielding's *Jonathan Wild* (1743) as 'satiric irony,' and in it we undoubtedly see the 'parody of romance' that he associates with irony and satire.[21] A closer look at this work shows that Fielding's approach has a significant provenance. While the novel derives much of its factual material from Daniel Defoe's account of the eponymous 'Thief-Taker General,' its method of presenting an antihero is strongly influenced by Milton's handling of Satan in *Paradise Lost,* and it draws along the way on *Paradise Regained* in its ironizing of received notions of 'greatness.'

The novel opens with the claim that if the misanthrope finds in Newgate 'human nature with its mask off' then one must consider 'the splendid palaces of the great ... no other than Newgate with the mask on,' for the 'great' have as many thieves among them. The especial target of Fielding's equation of the criminal and the nobleman is Robert Walpole, whose long career of double-dealing is subtly in the background of the novel – the arch-Whig is lampooned in the figure of the arch-'prig,' or thief. Drawing on the language and ethics of epic heroism, Fielding proceeds to transform Defoe's account of a public enemy into the story of a 'great man': though Wild 'would not give himself the pains requisite to acquire a competent sufficiency in the learned languages,' he 'was wonderfully pleased with that passage in the eleventh Iliad where Achilles is said to have bound two sons of Priam upon a mountain, and afterwards to have released them for a sum of money. This was, he said, alone sufficient to refute those who affected a contempt for the wisdom of the ancients, and an undeniable testimony of the great antiquity of priggism' (47).

Fielding's irony thus mocks not only his own social and political world but also received traditions of heroism. He finds precedent for the latter in Milton. Conversing with his mentor in 'priggism,' Count la Ruse, Wild remarks that he 'had rather stand on the summit of a dunghill than at the bottom of a hill in Paradise,' to which the more erudite man replies that he had 'often heard the devil used to say, where or to whom I know not, that it was better to reign in Hell than to be a valet de chambre in Heaven' (51–2). Like Satan, Wild often seduces others into advancing his ends with the language of virtue and liberty. In a way recalling Satan's account of the 'Glorious Enterprize' in his dialogue with Beelzebub (1.89), Wild steels the resolve of a would-be henchman reluctant to commit murder by asking, 'Art thou he whom I have selected out of my whole gang for this glorious undertaking[?]' (130).

When Wild finds himself imprisoned, he leads a rebellion against Newgate's chief gang-leader, Robert Johnson, by encouraging an overthrow of tyranny that soon devolves into his own personal rule. Johnson, Wild claims, 'is a fellow ... undermining THE LIBERTIES OF NEWGATE': 'your privileges have been long undermined, and are now openly violated by one man' (172). We must wonder in this repetition of the scene of Satan's rebellion in book 5 how far Fielding's irony extends: does it ironize the supposed freedom of following God, making the liberty of Milton's Heaven as empty as the liberty of Newgate? There is no ontological difference in this scene between rebel and prevailing authority, and no zealous Abdiel present to point out to us the difference between the two; does this have the effect of leaving Milton's Heaven intact or does it dismantle the distinctions fundamental to the sense of right order in *Paradise Lost*?

Fielding sets his ironic portrait of 'greatness' against the 'goodness' of the Heartfrees, a couple whose innocence verges on the prelapsarian, as their name suggests, and who become victims of Wild's stratagems. The qualities of the good man, we learn in the figure of the honest shopkeeper Thomas Heartfree, have no place in a narrative of greatness: 'He was possessed of several great weaknesses of mind, being good-natured, friendly, and generous to a great excess' (84). Mrs Heartfree is equally good natured – and, in the novel's terms, is equally maligned for being a 'low-bred animal' who 'followed no expensive fashions or diversions' (84–5) – and, like Milton's Eve, has a moment of innocent vanity in relishing compliments to her beauty (199–200). Fielding shows his typical concern with the corruption of the law and its officers when Wild succeeds in having Hearftree imprisoned; the 'arch-prig' feels his only pang of guilt when the good man's death warrant is issued. The result is a soliloquy strongly evoking Satan's Niphates speech: wavering from his purpose would cause him to be 'for ever contemptible to the PRIGS, as a wretch who wanted spirit to execute my undertaking' (177), much as Satan dreads 'shame / Among the spirits beneath' (4.82–3). Also like Satan he closes this soliloquy by steeling himself for the destruction of Heartfree, for which the narrative voice duly praises him:

> 'What have I done then? Why, I have ruined a family, and brought an innocent man to the gallows. I ought rather to weep with Alexander that I have ruined no more, than to regret the little I have done.' He at length, therefore, bravely resolved to consign over Heartfree to his fate ... and to banish away every degree of humanity from his mind, these little sparks of which composed one of those weaknesses which we lamented in the opening of our history. (178)

This is Wild's 'Farwel Remorse,' his dismissal of the 'Good' and decision to embrace fully the heroic role he has appointed for himself (*PL* 4.109).

The ironic portrait of greatness in *Jonathan Wild* is not sustained to the end of the novel. Rather, Fielding draws our attention to a shift in literary mode at the moment when the reversal of an unjust legal decision paves the way to comic resolution – as is typical in such works of this jurist-novelist as *Tom Jones.* That rare gem in a Fielding novel, a just and rigorous magistrate, sets things right by freeing Heartfree and condemning Wild, and effects a transformation of the novel's literary voice so that the irony is temporarily dropped and goodness can be an object of praise. It is after this point that we have the first suggestion of Wild's true physical appearance, emerging in an account of his rage over a fellow thief's seduction of his mistress, the 'lovely Laetitia': 'the following accents leapt over the hedge of his teeth, or rather the ditch of his gums, whence those hedgestakes had long since by a batten been displaced in battle with an amazon of Drury' (197). After we learn of the events leading up to Heartfree's release, the novel returns in its final chapters to '*the Contemplation of* GREATNESS' (203) in likening Wild's execution to that of Socrates and invoking other instances of heroic death.

The brief lifting of the narrative's irony serves a purpose much like adding the speech of Clarissa to the version of Pope's *Rape of The Lock* appearing in the 1717 *Works*: '*to open more clearly the* Moral *of the Poem*.'[22] The parallel to Pope, however, also makes clear the difference between each writer's use of Milton. Pope's mock heroic ridicules aspects of *Paradise Lost* – angels changing sex and healing themselves in battle. Fielding's irony, by contrast, is Milton's irony. He mines the vein of *Paradise Lost* that presents us with an antihero and annuls epic heroism, and he explores the conflicted relationship between Milton's bardic voice and the characters of his epic. The just judgment that secures the happy fate of the Heartfrees is equivalent to the judgment of Adam and Eve by the Son in book 10. As in Fielding's novel, the veil in *Paradise Lost* is most fully lifted on Satan's heroism after this point – the moment of his triumph becomes the moment of his greatest humiliation – and books 11 and 12 eschew epic's devices of historical narration in favour of biblical history, drawing attention not to the likes of an Odysseus, or Aeneas, or Roland but to the 'heroes of faith' of Hebrews 11. Michael rises fully to prominence not in the war in Heaven, where he enjoys military triumph over Satan in Renaissance epic, but as minister of Providential history in the spirit of Daniel 10.

These elements of *Paradise Lost* have been recognized as leading us to classify it as an 'epic' in a complex and carefully qualified way – an epic of the defeated, an epic of many potential heroes undermining traditional heroism, an epic whose cosmic truths are at odds with the values of the nation it addresses. They should also lead us to qualify the extent to which we describe it as high mimesis, for they have the effect of consistently limiting the authority to be derived from epic in and of itself. If Michael's narrative has special authority in *Paradise Lost* it is not because of its historiographical virtuosity, but because – to mix Frye's language with Woodhouse's – it provides an account of the irruption of the order of grace into fallen nature in a way possible only for a divine messenger closely following scripture. In this way Michael's history accords primacy to the Word, and those divinely guided to read it aright, as transcending human literary modes. It confirms the limits placed on the conventions of high mimetic modes, epic and tragedy, as embodying a stable centre of authority. These forms of representation are valid as truth insofar as they are governed by biblical master narratives, and *Paradise Lost* arraigns the literary tradition's resistance of this government. We will soon explore the implications of these modal complexities with respect to the bard's claims of divine inspiration in the epic invocations, which Frye describes as indicating 'what tradition his work primarily belongs to and what its closest affinities are with.'[23].

But for a work to be 'mock epic' requires more than some criticism of epic convention. We can take as characteristic of the genre the qualities that Pope suggests in his 1712 Dedicatory Epistle to Arabella Fermor, where he states that 'the ancient Poets are in one respect like many modern Ladies; Let an Action be never so trivial in it self, they always make it appear of the utmost Importance.'[24] This suggests a double movement that parodies unheroic characters by viewing their actions through the standards of epic, and at the same time casts some doubt upon epic's estimation of its heroes – 'They were but men,' in Elizabeth Barrett's sceptical remark.[25] We can add one further element as typical of mock epic: it tends to offer an alternative literary mode as more closely aligned to truth than epic is. Thus Ovid's *Metamorphoses* is a work deeply sceptical of epic in the Vergilian mould, but not necessarily mock epic in that it does not suggest a more stable alternative. In deciding at last to include Clarissa's speech in *The Rape of the Lock*, Pope shows that completion of the work requires a Horatian verse essay on good sense of the sort he prizes; in the comic resolution of the Heartfrees, Fielding offers the domestic rewards of humble decency typical of the novel as superior to the hubris of heroism with its desire for public recognition. In his scepticism of epic's truth claims, Milton similarly presents us with more viable alternatives: the heroism of faith of Abdiel and the biblical history of Michael, each in its own way drawing our attention to the authority of 'those written records Pure' (12.513).

We should recall that mock epic is a mode with a history long antedating Samuel Butler. Aristotle names in the *Poetics* Nicocharus's *Deiliad,* or 'tale of a coward,' as representing characters inferior to ourselves where Homer represents those greater. An otherwise unknown 'Eucleides the elder' is mentioned as one who 'supposing it easy to write poetry if one is allowed to lengthen words at whim, lampooned Homer in his very diction.'[26] Archestratos of Gela's gastronomic poem the *Hedupatheia* appears in the late fourth and third century BCE, seems to have been widely read, and has been recently associated with epic parody, a genre that, according to the second-century BCE literary antiquarian Polemon Periegetes, was invented by Hipponax and sustained by Epicharmos, Kratinos, and especially Hegemon of Thasos.[27] Seventeenth-century Italy, a literary milieu extremely important to Milton, also produced several mock epics: Francesco Bracciolini's 1618 *Lo scherno degli dei*, or 'The Mocking of the Gods'; Carlo de' Dottori's 1652 *L'asino d'oro*, or 'The Golden Ass'; and, most popular of all, Alessandro Tassoni's *La secchia rapita*, or 'The Rape of the Bucket,' first published in Paris in 1622, though with earlier manuscript circulation that seems to have influenced Bracciolini.[28]

These were not unnoticed in England, though much of the notice comes shortly after the first appearance of *Paradise Lost.* Milton's nephew and pupil Edward Phillips lists Bracciolini in his catalogue of poets ancient and modern, the *Theatrum poetarum*, praising especially his *Cruce ricuperata.*[29] Philip Ayres provides a translation of the Endymion and Diana story from the eighth canto of Tassoni's *Secchia rapita* in his 1687 *Lyric Poems.*[30] Dryden refers admiringly to this work in the essay on satire prefacing his translations of Juvenal, describing it as a 'Satire of the *Varronian* kind,' stating that it and Boileau's *Lutrin* (1674) – which he ventures is modelled on Tassoni – are the best examples of 'Burlesque Rhyme,' and admiring the effect of Tassoni's form: 'The first ix lines of the Stanza seem Majestical and Severe: but the two last turn them all into a pleasant Ridicule.'[31] (He refers to the Varro of the *Antiquitates* and *Saturae Menippeae*; also noteworthy are the lost works of Terentius Varro Atacinus, which include both satire and epic.)[32] John Dennis uses Dryden's praise of Tassoni to rescue Butler from the charge of overusing triple rhyme, and concludes that 'if any one would set the Common places of *Tassone* and *Boileau's Lutrin* against those of Butler, it would appear for the Honour of *England*, that neither *French* man nor *Italian* could stand before us.'[33] It is also significant that in defending Butler's 'manly Satyr,' Dennis measures it against the dignity of Tasso and Milton: 'some parts of [the *Gierusalemme*] are so far from being effeminate, that they have incomparably more gravity than any long winded Poem which has been writ by the Moderns, if you only except some passages of the *Paradise lost* of Milton.'[34]

The portion of *Paradise Lost* that seems most explicitly to draw on this long tradition is the war in Heaven of book 6. As has been observed several times, most recently by Paul Stevens and Balachandra Rajan, the deviations from decorum criticized by Dr Johnson and others can be explained by considering it in mock epic terms.[35] The turmoil and confusion of angelic battle paves the way for the triumph of the Son on the third day. But the episode may not necessarily resist ancient models. George deForest Lord reminds us that 'among its many modes Homeric epic includes mock-epic,' and that 'the two principal hand-to-hand engagements in the war in Heaven [Satan's encounters with Abdiel and with Michael] are modeled on Ares' encounters with Diomedes and Athene [in *Iliad* 5].'[36] At the heart of this Homeric mockery is the insight that the gods' immortality precludes them from achieving heroism in the way that their human counterparts do in the glorious death that battle affords; 'hence comes their fascination,' as Lord describes it, 'with the doings and sufferings of the *brotoí*, those who die and who thus can achieve a more than godlike glory in sacrificing their lives in a noble cause ... If games can bring man closer to the divine, war may serve a corresponding function for gods preoccupied with mortals.'[37]

The terms of mortality and immortality in Milton's epic battle are quite different. Raphael is translating invisible exploits to sensual apprehension, which already declares the limits of the high mimetic convention of epic battle. He further calls into question not only the glory of warfare but the entire enterprise of cataloguing its events. The Seraph explicitly tells us after the first day that the fallen angels do not deserve such attention, and that the loyal angels enjoy higher praise in Heaven than earthly records of militarism can bring:

> I might relate of thousands, and thir names
> Eternize here on Earth; but those elect
> Angels contented with thir fame in Heav'n
> Seek not the praise of men: the other sort
> In might though wondrous and in Acts of Warr,
> Nor of Renown less eager, yet by doome
> Canceld from Heav'n and sacred memorie,
> Nameless in dark oblivion let them dwell. (6.373–80)

Unlike Homer's, Milton's mockery comes entirely at the expense of Adam's mortal offspring. It reminds us not only of the true glory enjoyed in abundance by our angelic superiors, but of the pursuit of false glory to which we are prone.

Noted less often is the tendency more fully to interrogate epic in the proem to book 9, in which David Norbrook finds a 'sharp, sceptical wit' overlooked by those 'scholars seeking to turn Milton into a votary of the classical tradition.'[38] Chief among these scholars is Richard Bentley, who in his 1732 edition detects the work of a corrupting hand in the catalogue of classical heroic poems:

Not less but more Heroic than the wrauth
Of stern *Achilles* on his Foe pursu'd
Thrice Fugitive about *Troy* Wall; or rage
Of *Turnus* for *Lavinia* disespous'd,
Or *Neptun's* ire or *Juno's*, that so long
Perplex'd the *Greek* and *Cytherea's* Son[.] (9.14–19; italics original)

Bentley flies contrary to Milton's sense in stating that the poet intends only to state that his 'is *as* Heroic a Subject as the *Iliad* or *Aeneid*,' and is furthermore convinced that in the dilation of this statement into five lines we see the work of his great bogey, 'the Editor.' The passage, Bentley reasons, mischaracterizes the wrath of Achilles as against Hector rather than Agamemnon; describes Turnus's wrath in a way that is 'silly, as if the *Aeneid* was wrote for Turnus's Sake and Fame'; misrepresents the 'principal Subject' of *The Odyssey* in emphasizing '*Neptune's Anger to the Greeks*'; has no more 'distinguishing Title for *Ulysses* than the *Greek*'; and makes a superfluous second reference to the *Aeneid* with '*Juno's Ire to Cytherea's Son*.' 'No Poetaster,' he concludes, 'ever made poorer stuff ... Let me divine, therefore, that Milton clos'd all within one Line, to express both *Iliad* and *Aeneid*,

Not less but more Heroic, than the Wrath
Of stern *Achilles*, or the Arms and Man.'[39]

Bentley's powers of divination might be limited, but his powers of observation are not: Milton's lines do reduce classical epic to a confused 'rubbish' heap in the way he describes. Getting rougher handling still is romance epic, with its cumbrous 'tinsel Trappings ... The skill of Artifice or Office mean' (*PL* 9.36–9). Sensitive to Milton's interrogation of tradition in the passage, Norbrook associates it with 'the adventurous iconoclasm of the republican era.'[40] A possible allusion to Ben Jonson's epigram 'On the Famous Voyage,' however, qualifies this conclusion and suggests Milton's evocation of a literary tradition of mock heroic extending well beyond republican discourse. In this, the longest of his epigrams at 196 lines and the one appearing last in the *Epigrammes* (1616), Jonson narrates a mock heroic barge ride through Fleet Ditch arising from a drunken wager. Preceding 'The Voyage Itself' is a proem placing this adventure above those of classical epic:

No more let Greece her bolder fables tell
Of Hercules, or Theseus going into hell,
Orpheus, Ulysses; or the Latin Muse,
With tales of Troy's just knight, our faith's abuse;
We have a Shelton and a Heyden got,
Had power to act, what they to feign had not. (1–6)

Like book 9 of *Paradise Lost*, the epigram begins with the words 'No more' and proceeds to reduce the classical tradition to confusion, here to emphasize that a journey through hell is less treacherous than a voyage through one of London's most notoriously filthy waterways. Just as Milton presents classical epic as a record of so many temper tantrums – whether 'wrauth' of Achilles, 'rage' of Turnus, 'ire' of Neptune and Juno – Jonson ridicules the pervasiveness of the descent into the underworld, collapsing along the way the very different stories of Hercules, Theseus, Orpheus, Ulysses, and Aeneas. In Jonson's terms, the fictional courage signified by this classical device is subordinated to the 'actual' heroism of Shelton and Heyden.

In noticing this possible allusion one is immediately confronted by the fact that there can hardly be a work further removed from *Paradise Lost* than the 'Famous Voyage,' which is alarmingly dirty even by Jonson's standards and by the standards of epigram. If Martial declares himself pleased when one member of his audience turns red, pales, gapes, and detests, Jonson outdoes him in the revulsion this poem must provoke in all who would read it.[41] As Katherine Duncan-Jones observes, it presents the critic untroubled by bawdy with the further challenge of finding tools with which to analyse its 'relentless jokes about farts and turds.'[42] Such jokes are its polite introduction: among the poem's many reversals, the heroes' journey is a sort of backwards trek through an alimentary canal that begins by navigating excrement before arriving at the much more disgusting food scraps emptied into the ditch by the cooks of Fleet Lane:

All was to them the same, they were to pass,
And so they did, from Styx, to Acheron:
The ever-boiling flood. Whose banks upon
Your Fleet Lane Furies; and hot cooks do dwell,
That, with still-scalding steams, make the place hell.

The sinks ran grease, and hair of measled hogs,
The heads, houghs, entrails, and the hides of dogs:
For, to say truth, what scullion is so nasty,
To put the skins, and offal in a pasty?
Cats there lay divers had been flay'd and roasted,
And, after mouldy grown, again were toasted,
Then, selling not, a dish was ta'en to mince'em,
But still, it seem'd, the rankness did convince'em. (140–52)

Does Milton have Jonson's 'Famous Voyage' in mind, and if so, to what end? The phrase 'no more' opening book 9 and the epigram is common in *Paradise Lost*, where it appears no fewer than twenty-four times. Many of these appearances can be resolved into a divine 'no more' – which *really* means no more – and a more conjectural human 'no more' revealing limited knowledge. In the first class are the Son's and the Father's statements about the apocalypse in book 3 – 'wrauth shall be no more / Thenceforth' (3.264–5) and 'regal Scepter then no more shall need, / God shall be All in All' (3.340–1) – and the Father's statement that the fallen angels are forever cut off from Heaven: 'thir place knows here no more' (7.144). The human 'no more' arises especially after the Fall, as Adam and Eve are learning the terms of death. In her address to the Tree of Knowledge, Eve wonders 'what if God have seen, / And Death ensue? then I shall be no more' (9.826–7). When Adam looks forward to death in his complaint of book 10, he describes it as an escape from God's judging voice: 'There I should rest / And sleep secure; his dreadful voice no more / Would Thunder in my ears' (10.778–80).[43]

The 'no more' with which Milton opens book 9 seems to participate in this imperfect understanding of the nature of the afterlife. Like Adam and Eve, the bard presents the Fall as ending his talk of traffic between Heaven and Earth, and in the process reveals the limits of narrative order:

No more of talk where God or Angel Guest
With Man, as with his Friend, familiar us'd
To sit indulgent, and with him partake
Rural repast, permitting him the while
Venial discourse unblam'd: I now must change
Those Notes to Tragic[.] (9.1–6)

It is worth noticing that even though the bard will no longer be able to tell of such events in the course of this particular narrative, everything listed after the opening 'no more' does in fact occur after the Fall. Angels do sit as guests in friendship and enjoy a repast with Abraham in Genesis 18 and with the family of Tobit (Tobit 12:19). The second of these in particular lends itself to the range of meanings raised by 'familiar' in that the angel Raphael disguises himself as a relation. More significant is the passage's ambiguity: it can be taken to lament that neither god nor angel will sit as a guest or that only an angel will no longer sit as a guest. It troubles Bentley that God was not a familiar guest in Eden, a difficulty not entirely explained away in Zachary Pearce's lawyerly response to his emendations: 'The Sense seems to be this; where God, or rather the Angel sent by him and acting as his Proxy, us'd to sit familiarly with Man.'[44]

Raising the possibility of dining with God reminds us of a benefit not enjoyed in Eden but in the life of Jesus. The ambiguity anticipates the arrival of Christ in a way that qualifies the declared tragedy of the Fall. Like Adam and Eve's 'no more,' the bard's at this juncture does not fully acknowledge the life of the soul that extends beyond the grave and receives its greatest benefit from the Redemption. It evinces the human temptation to impose order on events rather than to wait on God's plan, a limited perception that Milton seems strongly to associate with tragedy: it animates his planned Abraham and Phineas tragedies and the misunderstanding that afflicts the Danites in *Samson Agonistes.*[45] Turning notes to tragic may signal entry into a world of misapprehension in which the bard is implicated. Though the proem has been described as the most stridently confident in *Paradise Lost* in terms of the bard's knowledge of receiving divine guidance, we might see this confidence as somewhat misplaced. In applying the human genre of tragedy to the Fall, one does not sufficiently emphasize that, in Joyce's phrase, the playwright who wrote the folio of the world intends the events of book 9 to be a diverting episode in a long comedy.[46]

In the proem's handling of genre, then, Milton both evokes and outdoes Jonson. Like Jonson he mocks the ancients. He also, however, goes beyond Jonson by calling into question the genres to which he claims adherence. This is done by the allusion to epigram in and of itself, which in its own way breaks with the decorum of high mimetic modes, and also with the implication that the events of the Fall are not fit subject for tragedy after all. Like Jonson's Shelton and Heyden, Adam and Eve are about to embark on a debased voyage of false discovery, and like that drunken pair we will see them indulge intemperate appetites in committing sin and in their lust shortly thereafter. The proem thus not only inveighs against the false heroism of classical epic, but also against the false tragedy of Adam and Eve, leaving us to attribute value neither to divine ire nor to human error, but to 'the better fortitude / Of Patience and Heroic Martyrdom' exemplified especially by Christ (9.31–2). Just as Fielding's mockery of epic in *Jonathan Wild* allows for novelic resolution, so Milton's satiric handling of genres allows biblical history and the promise of Redemption to receive due emphasis. All attempts to impose human literary genre on this divine master narrative fall short.

We can see the proem to book 9 as sustaining the critique of mimesis typical of Milton's invocations. The promise of 'Things unattempted yet in Prose or Rhime' (1.16) is Ariosto's movie-poster line, which advertises his romance as a more spectacular blockbuster than its predecessors; Milton includes the claim to show that he will truly attempt the unattempted where Ariosto does not. But the line also has the effect of depicting the attempt of the unattempted as a convention, and leaves us wondering how much of the bard's aim to do so is driven by the imperatives of literary inventiveness and how much is inspired by piety – our suspicion is deepened when we see that this proem introduces the portion of *Paradise Lost* most dense in its inclusion of material from its forebears. The 'Hail holy Light' invocation of book 3 presents in terms evoking pastoral the representation of the natural world as inferior to poetry inspired by inner light.[47] In the invocation of book 7 the bard raises the possibility of poetic overreaching in the Bellerophon allusion and calls into question the poetic authority over natural order associated with Orpheus – the remarkably succinct 'thou art Heav'nlie, shee an empty dreame' (7.39) far from eliminates the anxieties raised by the images of 'barbarous dissonance' (7.32) and the allusion to the Bacchae's dismembering of the archetypal poet. As Gordon Teskey observes of this invocation, it renders the poem 'an action of the physical body – a jointure of sounds and not a soaring flight – the poet's body has become an issue, a body that is not just strained by the effort of making the poem but actually at risk from attack.'[48] The poet's physical vulnerability, which is also the vulnerability of poetic creation, is likewise at play in the emphasis on blindness in the invocation to book 3 and the susceptibility to climate and age seen in the proem to book 9. Milton's most strident claim to prophecy in *Paradise Lost* is not expressed by the bard, but by Michael's close paraphrase of *A Treatise of Civil Power* in book 12.[49] This moment is doubly removed from human mimesis in that it is articulated by the highest of angels and points to a prose tract on religion as closely embodying truth, and a tract at that in which Milton catalogues his achievements in truth's defence.

The mock epic strain of *Paradise Lost* thus extends significantly beyond its presentation of Satan, who is consistently humiliated in his aspirations to heroism, and beyond the burlesque elements of the war in Heaven. True to the statement on satire in the *Apology* that is an epigraph to this chapter, Milton strikes high by also subjecting Adam and Eve, and his bard, to his sceptical wit, showing the insufficiencies of epic and tragedy in justifying the ways of God to man even as he declares himself to be operating in these genres. To focus on the representation of events is to sustain the famous misreading of Thomas Ellwood, which saw much in it of '*Paradise Lost*' and not enough of '*Paradise Found*,'[50] a reading ignoring the poem's pervasive lessons on the spiritual benefit of Redemption. In a way quite unprecedented in epic, Milton's bard can himself be implicated in the tendency of high mimesis to stray from God's forms. As such *Paradise Lost* might best be viewed simultaneously as epic and mock epic, involving in its capacious inclusion of literary modes both the high seriousness of epic and the mocking scepticism of its twin. The clash of these modes can tend to be lost in an emphasis on patterns connecting Milton's poetry to the classical tradition, which neglects the dust and heat of his confrontation with poetic contemporaries and predecessors.

NOTES

1 Balachandra Rajan, foreword to *'Paradise Lost': A Tercentenary Tribute*, ed. Rajan (Toronto, 1969), ix. Epigraph is from *An Apology Against a Pamphlet*, *YP* 1:916. For their comments on an earlier draft of this essay, I am grateful to John Leonard and Mary Nyquist, as well as participants in the conference 'John Milton: Iconoclast to Icon,' University of Illinois, 6 Nov. 2008.

2 The Stationer's Register entry for the first edition of *Paradise Lost* is dated 20 August 1667. See Barbara Lewalski, *The Life of John Milton*, rev. ed. (Oxford, 2003), 455. Taking into account the transition between Gregorian and Julian calendars, *Paradise Lost* was registered exactly 199 years, 303 days before Confederation.

3 Rajan, foreword, x.

4 Watson Kirkconnell and A.S.P. Woodhouse, *The Humanities in Canada* (Ottawa, 1947), 10.

5 See Northrop Frye, *The Diaries of Northrop Frye: 1942–1955*, ed. Robert D. Denham, vol. 8 of *The Collected Works of Northrop Frye* (Toronto, 2001), esp. 143 ('Woodhouse tries to sound like a pedant, but he's really a great man') and 190 ('nobody here has Woodhouse's intensity').

6 Frye, *Diaries*, 140.
7 See Sandra Djwa, *Professing English: A Life of Roy Daniells* (Toronto, 2002), 10; and Robert D. Denham, *Northrop Frye: Religious Visionary and Architect of the Spiritual World* (Charlottesville, VA, 2004), 1–14.
8 Northrop Frye, *Anatomy of Criticism: Four Essays*, ed. Robert D. Denham, vol. 22 of *Collected Works of Northrop Frye* (Toronto, 2006), 17, 23.
9 See, for example, *Anatomy*, 298: 'In the high mimetic we reach the structure that we think of as typically epic, the form represented by Homer, Virgil, and Milton.'
10 Frye, *Anatomy*, 197.
11 Frye, *Anatomy*, 142, 208.
12 Frye, *Anatomy*, 195–6.
13 Frye, *Anatomy*, 36; *The Return of Eden: Northrop Frye on Milton and Blake*, ed. Angela Esterhammer, vol. 16 of *Collected Works of Northrop Frye* (Toronto, 2005), 36–7.
14 Emphasis mine; *Paradise Lost* 1.746–7, *Lycidas* 124. Further citations are in parentheses, using where necessary the abbreviation *PL* for *Paradise Lost.*
15 Andrew Marvell, *Rehearsal Transpros'd: The Second Part, The Prose Works of Andrew Marvell*, vol. 1, ed. Martin Dzelzainis and Annabel Patterson (New Haven, 2003), 417.
16 Cicero, *Orator*, trans. H.M. Hubbell, in *Brutus and Orator*, Loeb Classical Library (Cambridge, MA, 1942), 87
17 Aubrey's notes available in Andrew Clark, ed., *Aubrey's Brief Lives* (Oxford, 1898), 2:62–72.
18 On the growing association of *Paradise Lost* with the sublime over the course of the eighteenth century, see Arthur Barker's essay in this volume and Nicholas von Maltzahn, 'The War in Heaven and the Miltonic Sublime,' in *A Nation Transformed: England after the Restoration*, ed. Alan Houston and Steve Pinkus (Cambridge, 2001), 154–79.
19 Nahum Tate, *Poems* (London, 1677; Wing T208), p. 70; Nathaniel Lee, *Caesar Borgia ... A Tragedy* (London, 1680; Wing L846), p. 68; Philip Ayres, *The Revengeful Mistress* (London, 1696; Wing A4313), sig. A2[v]. In his recent edition of Marvell, Nigel Smith notes echoes of the 'public resonances' of *Paradise Lost* in the satire *The Last Instructions to a Painter* (*The Poems of Andrew Marvell*, rev. ed. [Harlow, 2007], 367); Gordon Campbell and Thomas N. Corns also suggest that in the poem Marvell 'echoes' *Paradise Lost*, which he likely read in manuscript at some point between March 1665 and the summer of 1667 (*John Milton: Life, Work, and Thought* [Oxford, 2008], 327). For these references I am indebted to John Shawcross's indispensable *Milton: A Bibliography for the Years 1624–1700* (Binghamton, NY, 1984).

20 See Nicholas von Maltzahn, above, 223–4. In *Mac Flecknoe* Dryden also alludes to Satan's 'Throne of Royal State' (*PL* 2.1; cf. *Mac Flecknoe* 107) and uses the stately expression of truth in *Paradise Lost* as a means of accentuating irony, referring to the description of the 'filial Godhead' in Flecknoe's coronation of Shadwell (*PL* 6.722; cf. *Mac Flecknoe* 135–8); Dryden, *Mac Flecknoe*, in *Selected Works*, 2nd ed., ed. William Frost (San Francisco, 1971).

21 Frye, *Anatomy*, 208.

22 Alexander Pope, *The Rape of the Lock*, in *The Poems of Alexander Pope: A One Volume Edition of the Twickenham Pope*, ed. John Butt (London, 1963), n. at 5.7.

23 Frye, *Anatomy*, 229.

24 Pope, *Rape of the Lock*, p. 217.

25 Elizabeth Barrett Browning, *Aurora Leigh*, in *Aurora Leigh and Other Poems*, ed. John Robert Glorney Bolton and Julia Bolton Holloway (London, 1995), 5.147.

26 Aristotle, *Poetics*, ed. and trans. Stephen Halliwell, Loeb Classical Library 23 (1999; Cambridge, MA, 2005), 35 and 111.

27 See S. Douglas Olson and Alexander Sens, introduction to *Archestratos of Gela: Greek Culture and Cuisine in the Fourth Century BCE* (Oxford, 2000), xxxi–xxxii.

28 See Paolo Cherchi, 'The *Seicento*: Poetry, Philosophy and Science,' in *The Cambridge History of Italian Literature*, ed. Peter Brand and Lino Pertile, rev. ed. (1999; Cambridge, 2007), 310–11.

29 Edward Phillips, *Theatrum Poetarum* (London, 1675; Wing P2075), 42.

30 Philip Ayres, *Lyric Poems Made in Imitation of the Italians* (London, 1687; Wing A4312), 30.

31 John Dryden, trans., *The Satires of Decimus Junius Juvenalis Translated into English* (London, 1693; Wing J1288), 30.

32 The most influential references to Marcus Terentius Varro (116–27 BCE) and his *Antiquitates rerum humanarum et divinarum* are found in Augustine of Hippo, *City of God* [*De civitate Dei*], trans. Henry Bettenson (London, 1984), 6.2–10. Terentius Varro Atacinus (b. 82 BCE) has no surviving works, though his satires are referred to unfavourably by Horace, *Satires*, trans. H.R. Fairclough, Loeb Classical Library 194 (1926; Cambridge, MA, 2005), 1.10.46; his epic on Caesar, the *Bellum Sequanicum*, is noted by Priscian in his *Institutiones grammaticae*, in *Opera* (Venice, 1496), fol. 137r–v [book 10]; the copy of Priscian's *Opera* held by the University of Illinois is that of Sir Roger Twysden, member of the Short Parliament.

33 John Dennis, *Miscellanies in Verse and Prose* (London, 1693; Wing D1034), sig. b2^{r}.

34 Dennis, sig. a8v–b1r.

35 Paul Stevens, 'Intolerance and the Virtues of Sacred Vehemence,' in *Milton and Toleration*, ed. Sharon Achinstein and Elizabeth Sauer (Oxford, 2007), 250; Balachandra Rajan, 'Samson Hath Quit Himself / Like Samson,' *Milton Quarterly* 41 (2007): 5. See also Arnold Stein, *Answerable Style: Essays on 'Paradise Lost'* (Seattle, 1953), esp. 20–6; and J.B. Broadbent, *Some Graver Subject: An Essay on 'Paradise Lost'* (New York, 1960), 218–34. On the reception history of Milton's war in Heaven, see Nicholas von Maltzahn, 'The War in Heaven.'

36 George deForest Lord, *Classical Presences in Seventeenth-Century English Poetry* (New Haven, 1987), 173, 178–9. This reprints and expands slightly chapter 2 of Lord's *Heroic Mockery: Variations on Epic Themes from Homer to Joyce* (Newark, 1977).

37 Lord, *Classical Presences*, 173.

38 David Norbrook, *Writing the English Republic: Poetry, Rhetoric and Politics, 1627–1660* (Cambridge, 1999), 440.

39 Richard Bentley, ed., *Milton's 'Paradise Lost,' A New Edition* (London, 1732), p. 267.

40 Norbrook, 440–1.

41 See Martial, *Epigrams*, 6.60:

> Laudat, amat, cantat nostros mea Roma libellos,
> meque sinus omnes, me manus omnis habet.
> ecce rubet quidam, pallet, stupet, oscitat, odit.
> hoc volo: nunc nobis carmina nostra placent.

42 Katherine Duncan-Jones, 'City Limits: Nashe's "Choise of Valentines" and Jonson's "Famous Voyage,"' *The Review of English Studies*, n.s. 56 (2005): 247–62.

43 See also Adam's later comment on death: 'Who knows, or more then this, that we are dust, / And thither must return and be no more' (11.199–200).

44 Zachary Pearce, *A Review of the Text of 'Paradise Lost'* (London, 1733), 289. Jonathan Richardson, father and son, offer a similar view in stating that Genesis 18 provides precedent for referring to God and his messenger, in this case Raphael, interchangeably: 'Read that Chapter and 'twill be seen that This Remarkable Expression is taken from the Ambiguity There. *The Lord* and *the Young Men* (always Understood to be Angels) are used as Words of the same Signification, Denoting that the Divine Presence was so Effectually with his Messengers, that Himself was also There'; see their *Explanatory Notes and Remarks on Milton's 'Paradise Lost'* (London, 1734; ESTC T135898), 386–7 [n. at 9.1].

45 The outline for a Phineas tragedy is available in *YP* 8:558, 560. On the temptation of finality in *Samson Agonistes*, see Ryan Netzley, 'Reading Events: The Value of Reading and the Possibilities of Political Action and Criticism,' *Criticism* 48 (2006): esp. 520.

46 On the confidence of this proem, see Lord, *Classical Presences*: 'the terse assurance of this proem, however, is quite different from the anguish and anxiety in the two preceding ones' (69). I have made similar claims on this proem of which I am now less convinced; see Feisal G. Mohamed, *In the Anteroom of Divinity: The Reformation of the Angels from Colet to Milton* (Toronto, 2008), 162–3.

47 See especially 3.41–4 and 51–5.

48 Gordon Teskey, *Delirious Milton* (Cambridge, MA, 2006), 43.

49 See especially *Paradise Lost* 12.520–30 and cf. *A Treatise of Civil Power*, *YP* 7:241–3.

50 Campbell and Corns, 329.

15 Milton Takes the Veil

ELIZABETH HODGSON

The perspective of history ... is not a master code but still another temptation
– Stanley Fish

I

The Catholic Milton may not exist, but Milton's fantasy of the cloister most interestingly does.[1] In *Areopagitica*, Milton condemns the evils of 'a cloistered ... virtue' but makes himself into a religious acolyte of Truth; in *Il Penseroso*, he makes his muse a melancholic nun. In these opposing representations of sober seclusion, Milton seems to render suspect his citizenship in the radical Protestant nation and also put to question his status as universal man.

The Protestant Milton's citizenship has been awarded by an eminent panel of Milton scholars, several with Canadian passports; it has been reaffirmed by subsequent generations of Miltonists, both here and abroad. Several of the major Canadian Miltonists included in this collection have given their talents to defining Milton's precise march through various Protestant positions and oppositions. A.S.P. Woodhouse, Arthur Barker, and H.R. MacCallum comment on Milton's place in the 'puritan dilemma,' considering among other things his paradigms of liberty, his views on election and regeneration, his attachment to antinomialism, and his use of the doctrine of the inner light, reading Milton 'in the light of the changing climate of opinion among his Puritan associates.'[2] This particular historical tagging of Milton's intellectual allegiances has become a major interpretive tool and trend in Milton criticism.

The same is true in the temptation of ahistoricism in the development of the universal Milton, who has grown up alongside his Protestant doppelgänger as the man for every nation, a writer with diplomatic immunity from his own culture. Arthur Barker, as a historian of Milton's specific Protestantism, resists 'the deceptive ease with which [Milton's] statements can be made to seem applicable to present questions';[3] Douglas Bush and Northrop Frye see this easy applicability not as a problem but as a virtue, de-emphasizing Milton's situatedness to make him larger and more widely relevant. When Bush argues in his Arnoldian way that Milton's popularity reflects 'spiritual health or disease' in modern culture and that 'Milton is one of the great portions of that heritage for which [the world wars have] been fought,' he privileges a 'strenuous and exacting faith' but frames it vaguely: 'Milton is occupied with the far more real and fundamental problem of making one's self better.'[4] Elizabeth Sauer reproduces the universal Milton in 2006: 'Milton scholarship enjoys the advantage of being involved with an author who is at home in any climate and whose ongoing relevance is unquestionable.'[5]

A transient or local Milton might be difficult to envisage given such illustrious interpretive traditions, but that is the goal of this paper: such apparent anomalies as those pro-Catholic images in *Il Penseroso* and *Areopagitica* offer an opportunity to investigate the very notions of a Miltonic career or a Miltonic legacy. *Areopagitica* and *Il Penseroso* depict a 'pensive Nun' who is both cowardly recluse and Orphean messenger of truth, and in so doing they together invite a reconsideration of the role of biography in Miltonic texts. Milton criticism tends either to assume that the local is irrelevant in Milton because his passport is universal, or to develop a very detailed narrative of Milton's intellectual development and then to impose back on his works those learned assumptions about what the Milton of a given text must have believed, or could not have believed. Each tendency – to universalize Milton, or to pin him and his works to specific intellectual cards – frequently turns Miltonic texts into flattened examples of either narrative. The odd anomalous invocations of the cloister in Milton's early works may help us to resist these two interpretive temptations, and make Milton himself (local or global) be less transparent or consistent in his texts.

Many Miltonists have, of course, noted Milton's adoption of Catholic images in these texts and others, a betrayal variously read as politically strategic, youthfully pre-radical, or 'simply' metaphorical. The anti-Catholic Milton of later texts is often the standard against which anomalous moments like those in *Il Penseroso* tend to be read. Milton's 1644 attack on the cloister in *Areopagitica* has, for instance, suggested to many critics that he became increasingly radical through the 1640s, denouncing the Laudian ceremonialism that he once found suggestive and powerful.[6] In this narrative, Milton gradually gave up on the Neoplatonic model of contemplation manifest in *Il Penseroso* and in *The Ludlow Masque* to become a more strenuously aggressive Protestant warrior. Any of these interpretations attaching Milton's works to specific stages in his intellectual development may well be correct, but the problem of these texts is not so much how to fit them into Milton's Protestant trajectory but rather how adequately to acknowledge the challenge they exemplify to the very notion of that trajectory. Milton's texts might sometimes welcome the cloister, regardless of his citizenship in the Protestant nation or his emblematic status as a man for all cultures; the hermeneutic possibilities of this inconsistency are worth understanding.

Pro-Catholic Miltonic gestures do seem almost unimaginable to anyone who has read Milton with any rigour. Milton certainly has many enemies (see almost any paragraph in *Colasterion* for the most attractively vituperative examples), but the arguments in many of Milton's texts suggest that none is more cherished than the 'popish' church.[7] The Roman church is 'the triple Tyrant,' the 'Babylonian' whore ('Massacre,' 12, 14), a nest of 'idolaters' (*YP* 2:664).[8] Milton frequently denigrates Catholicism by linking together charges of error, superstition, criminality, corruption, depravity, and femininity. His unabashed attacks on a wide variety of Catholic practices, beliefs, institutions, and policies do seem to foreclose debate on his views, but the two questions of this paper still remain: first, does Milton's writing lend itself to a biographical narrative about his view of things Catholic, and second, does it matter, what would it mean, if it does not?

A brief case-study of one of Milton's elders will illustrate. John Donne's texts constantly have Protestantism or Catholicism read into them; Barbara Lewalski and Louis Martz, or Jeanne Shami and Dennis Flynn read confessional evidence into his works either via biographical contextualization or through their insistence on the theological affiliations attached to devotion, privacy, intellectualism, or the honouring or dishonouring of marriage. John Donne's 'Canonization' is a helpful example of the difficulties involved in this denominational outing. In this poem Donne both adopts official Catholic terms for the beatification of saints ('canonization,' 'miracles,' 'beg from above') and mocks them, substituting for the Roman pantheon of martyrs a Petrarchan idolization of sexual love which he also belittles.[9] His cross-over hagiography of sexual death and resurrection explicitly invites and repels any theological labelling (other than 'blasphemer,' perhaps). 'For Gods sake hold your tongue, and let me love' enacts a prophane subversion of intimately familiar ideological categories; to be 'canonized for love' is likewise both an affirmation and a challenge to the rules for beatification.

Donne's poem produces a complex metaphorization of the material practices and figures most closely and explicitly associated with Catholicism for most English Protestants, and especially the peculiar myths and associations, slippages and overlaps, in these conceptions of material Catholic practice. Like Tracy Fessenden, I am interested in how and why 'Protestant' texts invoke such Catholic images, and to what ends?[10] What do such usages suggest about the collapse or overlap of these supposedly antithetical theologies? Can we speak of a Protestant or Catholic text at all: how circumstantial, occasional, and local are such traces and tendencies? As Alison Shell argues, 'to identify Catholic elements in a writer's biography is one thing, and to use them to formulate a Catholic aesthetic, quite another ... those arguments ... come from an attic which could do with spring-cleaning.'[11] With Milton the problem is far more complex: identifying either Protestant or Laudian elements, and/or attaching them to Milton's oeuvre, late, middle, early, or entire, requires a set of assumptions about Milton's poetry and prose which I for one am unwilling to make. Miltonic narrators are rarely so self-consciously playful as John Donne's (humour is not Milton's forte at the best of times). But the issue of Milton's shifting invocations and metaphors is no less difficult to map than Donne's wit, and no less important to disentangle from too much or too little religious history.

II

For a vantage point from which to discern the Protestant Milton as he has been constructed, *Areopagitica* is ideal. In this 1644 tract one of the central focal points of the writer's wrath is the prepublication licensing of 'the Inquisition':

> He that can apprehend and consider vice with all her baits and seeming pleasures, and yet abstain, and yet distinguish, and yet prefer that which is truly better, he is the true warfaring Christian. I cannot praise a fugitive and cloister'd vertue, unexercis'd & unbreathed, that never sallies out and sees her adversary, but slinks out of the race, where that immortall garland is to be run for, not without dust and heat. Assuredly we bring not innocence into the world, we bring impurity much rather: that which purifies us is

triall, and triall is by what is contrary. That vertue therefore which is but a youngling in the contemplation of evill, and knows not the utmost that vice promises to her followers, and rejects it, is but a blank vertue, not a pure; her whitenesse is but an excrementall whitenesse. (*YP* 2:515–16)

Milton invokes the metaphor of the cloister to describe the feminized space of cowards and indolents who are and choose to be 'unexercised' while the masculine, athletic, Pauline race remains to be run. The virtue of this 'fugitive' cloister is only an 'excremental whiteness' (like the Pharisaical 'whited sepulchers' of Matthew 23:27). Cloistered virtue is sham interiority, an escape containing only an ironically 'blank' virtue. Milton characterizes this space as 'a youngling in the contemplation of evil,' suggesting innocence, but he then denies such childish virtue: 'we bring not innocence into the world, we bring impurity rather.' He insists upon the doctrine of Original Sin, but Milton's real interest here is not in the origins of sin but in the prevention of its growth; he thinks this resistance impossible in the false refuge of the cloister, a space in which he imagines no intellectual growth or challenge but only timorous vacancy. As Michael Lieb comments drily, 'Monks and the monastical point of view ... do not fare very well in Milton's hands.'[12]

The highly metaphorized scenario of the cloister which Milton imagines may be an academic refuge for scholarly contemplation, which he elsewhere sees as hopelessly infected by Catholic scholasticism: 'it were much better there were not one divine in the university; no school divinity known, the idle sophistry of monks, the canker of religion.'[13] Milton emphasizes in *Areopagitica,* though, a rather more obviously feminine and Catholic space, with its 'contemplation of evil' and virtue, its 'blank virtue' (veiled in white, symbolically innocent, but also vacant, empty), and its feminized virtues and vices (as opposed to the masculine 'warfaring Christian' who sallies out into the world).[14] When the bishop of Carlisle argues against Protestant nunneries by saying that 'to overcome the world is more generous than to fly from it,' he is reflecting Milton's claim that any cloister is a coward's hiding place.[15] The oppositions and negations in Milton's syntax in fact reiterate praise for resistance itself, not just of the cloister but also as a way of being Protestant. He argues 'by what is contrary,' for strife 'not without dust and heat.' Milton's familiar use of reversals and negation pervades the passage: 'unexercised,' 'unbreathed,' 'not without,' 'I cannot praise,' 'not,' 'yet,' and 'but.'[16] Such oppositional terms doubly reinforce Milton's attack on the Inquisition for closing debate and denying opposition.

Milton imagines the proper punishment for such Catholic silencing of dissent by explaining later in the tract that 'popish' texts should themselves be automatically censored: 'popery and open superstition ... as it extirpates all religions and civil supremacies, so itself should be extirpate' (*YP* 2:565). Here the Miltonic project gets increasingly tangled. The conflation of 'popery' with 'superstition,' a standard Miltonic move, makes Catholicism not only guilty of the sin of ignorance which his 'blank virtue' suggests but also a public menace to English nationalism because it challenges 'civil supremacies.' This passage has been of much interest to Milton critics for its justification for only limited toleration,[17] but what is more interesting is that Catholicism, earlier accused of being too private, is now being accused of being too public. Milton charges popery not only by defining it as secretive, hidden, and cloistered, but also for its flagrant, 'open' challenge to certain 'supremacies.' Here, according to Milton, it is popery which sallies forth looking for a fight.

Milton's famous metaphor later in *Areopagitica* of the scattered body of truth is an even more significant inversion of his anti-Catholic metaphors. 'Suffer not these licencing prohibitions to stand at every place of opportunity forbidding and disturbing them that continue seeking, that continue to do our obsequies to the torn body of our martyr'd Saint' (*YP* 2:549–50). Note the shift from '*them* that continue seeking' to '*our* obsequies,' '*our*... Saint,' as the narrator includes himself in the worshippers of Truth. This image of the Miltonic narrator worshipping the relics of a martyred saint is deeply ironic, and a doubling back on his earlier tendentiousness, as the last half of *Areopagitica* defends English Protestantism against the frequently levelled charge that it was itself creating divisions scattering and dismembering the body of Christ.[18] Here he is suturing the body of 'Truth' while also worshipping its remains in a grotesque appropriation of Catholic relics, icons, and liturgical veneration of the host.[19] Milton makes himself here the catacomb worshipper, the censured recusant, in hiding within a secret community of 'true seekers' from 'civil supremacies.'

In *Areopagitica*, then, Milton argues against the closed, cloistered, and cloistering effects of Catholic regulatory practices on books, minds, and virtues, attacking the spurious flight from evil, the hiding behind a rule and a veil, which he associates with the monastic life. He also, however, wishes to accuse Catholicism of being too involved, too brazenly subversive of rules and civil order. This set of somewhat opposite assaults is made more problematic still in his famous passage on the body of

Truth, in which he argues for the clandestine quest and imagines himself a worshipper of Saints. Milton's attacks on popish 'open' challenges and 'prohibitions' becomes an ironic turn in his praise of the unconcealed battle. His image of himself as the mourner on the field of battle in which Truth has been rent makes him far more like the cloistered figure of his earlier anti-Catholic rant, and his adoption of the metaphors of idol-worship indicates how frequently the text can turn on its own images. Milton's potentially contradictory assaults on Catholicism, and his frequent willingness to take condemnatory metaphors and use them to praise himself, makes his language a far less symmetrical or transparent lens than it might at first appear.

III

Areopagitica's oddly contradictory praise of the warfaring intellectual who is also a secret seeker becomes still more complicatedly associated with the cloister in *Il Penseroso*. Though *Il Penseroso* is often treated as a youthful aberration or linked to the young conservative Milton whose politics became more radical in the 1640s, it was published not before but after *Areopagitica*, in the *1645 Poems*. Regardless of the ideological or material conditions behind that publication, *Il Penseroso* demonstrates again this powerful tool of a metaphoric Catholicism. And even if the *1645 Poems* embody an anachronistic and temporary retreat, *Il Penseroso's* subject, and its treatment of its subject, resonates not only with *Areopagitica* but also with the important questions of poetic calling and its temptations which Milton so frequently poses. Its form is perhaps anomalous, but its questions appear in many of Milton's central works.

Il Penseroso, as the second half of Milton's poetic diptych on modes of life, makes the case for a sober, meditative habit of life. I use this last metaphor advisedly, as Milton in this poem describes his muse as a nun and his study a convent. 'Hail divinest Melancholy' (12), the speaker declares:

> Com pensive Nun, devout and pure,
> Sober, steadfast, and demure,
> All in a robe of darkest grain …
> And joyn with thee calm Peace, and Quiet,
> Spare Fast, that oft with gods doth diet …
> The Cherub Contemplation;
> And the mute Silence hist along[.] (31–3, 45–6, 55–6)

But let my due feet never fail
To walk the studious Cloysters pale,
And love the high embowed Roof,
With antic Pillars massy proof,
And storied Windows richly dight (156–60)

What to make of this curious image-set of a fasting nun in her habit, attended by silence and contemplation, is a question few Milton critics have broached. Barbara Lewalski does acknowledge 'surprising affinities with Roman Catholic or Laudian ritual' (50) in the poem, though she sees these primarily as his attempt to reclaim literary 'genres and art forms from debased to valid uses' (50). Annabel Patterson wonders what to make of the 'relation between serious mental work and a religious vocation' which seems tied to 'Laudianism: Melancholy is a "pensive Nun" … the "studious Cloysters" are as much clerical as academic.'[20] But even Patterson sees these moments as Laudian rather than more dramatically Catholic (why is unclear). Several critics have focused on Melancholy herself, as if this renders nugatory the image of the nun,[21] but Milton's conflation of Melancholy with silence, contemplation, and the figure of the nun within the ecclesiastical cloister suggests more interesting fractures.

Protestants of Milton's era certainly had a well-developed habit of comparing Catholic religious with melancholy, not to the advantage of either. In Richard Burton's *Anatomy of Melancholy*, the title-page includes, as types of the melancholic, 'superstition,' figured by a praying monk in his cell.[22] Andreas Laurentius argues that a religious melancholic 'will doe nothing but mumble of his beades, and you shal never finde him out of the Church,'[23] a kind of enactment of the Burton title-page. This correlation between melancholy and Catholic prayer practices goes back to John Calvin: 'Thus it comes to pass, that by praying [the papists] only augment their own sorrows and torments, just as if a man should lay wood upon a fire already kindled.'[24] In Calvin's text papists make themselves martyrs to melancholy, saints to unhappiness, burning themselves at the stake in another fascinating reworking of Catholic hagiographies. Burton lists the ills of religious melancholy: 'Impiety and Superstition, Idolatry and Atheisme … Monkes, Hermites, and c [*sic*] … fight under this superstitious banner:'[25] Melancholy makes them not just sad but dangerously so. More suggestive still is John Donne's gendering of melancholic treachery: 'such a melancholy as makes Witches, makes Papists too.'[26]

If the Catholic's prayers are based on superstition and beget only dangerous melancholy, Milton's invocation of Melancholy seems to be arguing against the grain of the Protestant interpretive tradition. Milton's sober, melancholic nun begets not impiety but higher vision; the cloister generates not an 'excremental whiteness' but a divine vision of the 'rapt soul,' a revalued 'prophetical melancholy.'[27] This attempt to invent an imaginatively generative cloister flies in the face of the argument that 'the easinesse of admitting Revelations, and Visions, and Apparitions of spirits … in the Papist … hath produced … Melancholy.'[28] Melancholy (tagged by the symbols of mourning: cypress, marble, and lead, the nightingale and the moon) in *Il Penseroso* is thus a difficult figure to interpret, especially because her mournful solitude suggests the superstitious fear of papacy so feared by Calvin, Burton, and Donne.

Milton may perhaps wish to suggest another, more positive adaptation of the mournful contemplative woman: her melancholic veiling, her association with retirement and with Orpheus's grief for Eurydice, also shifts her into the iconographic territory of the Protestant widow as well.[29] Widows, like nuns, were to be veiled and clothed in black, 'soberly' and decently attired. Widows, in Vives's influential *Instruction of a Christen Woman,* were ideally to be effectually cloistered, secluded, and private ('a chaste woman desyreth secretnes,' Vives says).[30] Retha Warnicke describes several famous widows who adopted Vives's advice and retired to seclusion and spiritual contemplation.[31] Warnicke cites Lady Falkland's self-chosen 'retirement' after her husband's death, one in which she led 'a more strict course of life,' planning apparently to found a 'place for the retirement of widows' very like a convent.[32] These were women for whom mourning and melancholy were significant features of identity, and whose seclusion in domestic enclosures demonstrated their piety, their loyalty, and their ability to achieve the growth permitted by the melancholic experience.[33]

Il Penseroso investigates and affirms this vision of mourning and contemplation in the figure of the poet:

And may at last my weary age
Find out the peacefull hermitage,
The Hairy Gown and Mossy Cell,
Where I may sit and rightly spell
Of every Star that Heav'n doth shew …
Till old experience do attain
To somthing like Prophetic strain.
These pleasures *Melancholy* give,
And I with thee will choose to live. (167–70, 172–5)

Milton accompanies a nun-like Melancholy into what is evidently an ecclesiastical hermitage, secluded, dark, quiet, and solitary, in order to imagine his own poetic calling as an engagement (vaguely erotic, like so many widows' narratives) with the sublimity of the nun's cloister. In a slightly mocking but also approving adaptation of Ralegh's 'Passionate Pilgrim' and Marlowe's 'Passionate Shepherd,' Milton's narrator claims for himself a sacred solitary space, ruggedly pastoral in nature, in which the company of Melancholy's 'pleasures' will grant 'somthing like Prophetic strain.' Rather than contemplating texts (religious, philosophical, or literary), Milton's hermit will speak because of, not in spite of, his cloistered and natural seclusion, 'spelling' the world as shown to him by Heaven.

Milton's speaker claims for himself by these means the melancholy of genius which causes, as Laurentius says, 'a kinde of divine ravishment, commonly called *Enthousiasma*, which stirreth men up to plaie the Philosophers, Poets, and also to prophesie.'[34] This secluded pastoral narrative generates, through old age and the cloister's sobriety, 'somthing like Prophetic strain,' the same prophetic strain which he claims in *Lycidas*, in *Paradise Lost*, and in many of his prose works, including *Areopagitica*. Milton's invocations of 'old experience' and 'weary age' in *Il Penseroso* suggest that it is a mournful retirement from the fight which will grant him vision.

This use of the sober nun to inspire prophetic poetry seems to rewrite, perhaps through the widow/nun correlative, the Protestant commonplace that Catholic rites produce a perpetual and debilitating state of ineffectual mourning. Here the chief *virtue* of the mourner-role is precisely how it facilitates a prophetic voice.[35] The melancholic narrator in *Il Penseroso* clings to the mourning woman, in a nun's widow-like 'sober' gear and her secluded, cloistered life of contemplation, to enable and imagine the sacred poetic and prophetic voice of the Miltonic author. This nun/widow role in the poem is a choice or even a calling, one which the speaker dedicates himself to, makes a vow to uphold, in order to facilitate his poetic and prophetic voice. Gellert Lyons argues for *Il Penseroso* that 'the fact of the vow, the recognition ... that only one course of life is possible ... is as significant as ... devotion to a religious or contemplative life.'[36] Milton's text I think is invoking precisely this correlation. The melancholy convent of the imagination is here not fugitive at all – or if so, it is a strategic retreat to the cloistered garden in order to enable the warfaring poet's work of becoming 'an imaginative maker of images.'[37] As Georgia Christopher says, the restricted, cloistered spaces the narrator seeks in *Il Penseroso* offer 'an epistemological bonus: access to great invisible reaches of knowledge,' a somewhat secularized but still redolent 'version of the Beatific Vision.'[38] Milton's poet takes the veil, then, as if this is now an appropriate correlative for both purity and poetic inspiration.

Lycidas is an obvious example, but not the only one, of this correlation between devotional mourning and inspiration in Milton's works; in *Paradise Lost* the epic narrator mournfully describes his sight 'veild' with 'dim suffusion' (*PL* 3.26) as the means by which he paradoxically acquires 'Celestial light' (3.51). Adam and Eve too are protected by 'innocence ... as a veile,' which they miss only when it is taken from them (9.1054). The fascinating ambiguities created by Milton's oddly positive use of veiled melancholy and melancholic inspiration, so frequently associated with Catholic superstition, are clearly historically specific rather than general. They also make reading for and through Milton's Protestant biography more problematic than it might already be.

IV

The eminent Canadian Miltonists of this collection are clearly aware of these problematic tensions in Milton's work, and they are certainly aware of the difficulties such neo-Catholic images create for reading Milton either as a Protestant hero or as a man for all seasons, though their explanations of the shifts and changes in Milton's works do tend to pull Milton back into one of these roles. Ernest Sirluck's '*Areopagitica* and a Forgotten Licensing Controversy' is a fascinating example. Sirluck is clearly one of those scholars who 'can find things in the Public Records Office' (Northrop Frye says that he, in contrast, could not even find the Public Records Office),[39] but Sirluck's goal in this particular article is to discover the 'almost universal influence'[40] of Milton's radical policies in historically specific moments. He imagines a very exact taxonomy: 'we can now add a considerable influence [of *Areopagitica*] in the decade from 1698 to 1707 ... Perhaps there were other cases of unacknowledged use, and some to fill the apparent gap between 1707 and 1738?'[41] The integration of Milton's radical politics into broader English culture is clearly his preferred outcome, but he feels compelled to document this lineage decade by decade, laboriously seeking out the influential Protestant Milton where he may be found and continuing to 'do ... obsequies to the torn body of [his] martyred saint.'

Northrop Frye's approach is almost the opposite; his broader interest in the 'critical taxonomy' of myth in a poem like *Lycidas* means that he does not care what 'the poet "had in mind"' or what his 'personal sincerity' might be; 'there are only archetypes, or recurring themes of literary expression.'[42] Frye downplays any poem's place in 'Milton's development; its place in the history of English poetry; its place in seventeenth century thought or history.'[43] His discussions of *Il Penseroso* also fit this idiom. He sees the poet as 'a Platonist' employing the 'analogy of Eros' through magical images of cloisters which 'are appreciated on purely aesthetic grounds':[44] 'the Nonconformist poet sees these tendencies in Christianity as a part of the analogy of Eros, to be enjoyed and appreciated in some contexts and condemned in others. Melancholy herself is a nun, not a Christian nun, of course, but a vestal virgin, being a daughter of Vesta' (144). Frye nods briefly in the direction of the Protestant Milton ('the Nonconformist poet'), apparently thinking it impossible that 'nun' might mean 'nun' on these grounds, but his primary interest is in demonstrating that *Il Penseroso* is about a transcultural 'analogy of Eros.' He argues that the Miltonic narrator seeks in *Il Penseroso* a more aesthetic version of Satan's second temptation in *Paradise Regained*: a pull toward 'what Yeats calls the property of the dead, a wisdom involving a retreat from the world, or what we should now think of as a kind of return to the womb. Such a desire could be readily satisfied ... under the patronage of the virgin goddess ... the shrouding female *hortus conclusus*' (150–1). The language of myth surrounds and defines the particular images which Frye notes are present in the text, drawing *Il Penseroso* itself, like its narrator, out of the realm of historically specific cultures altogether.

Frye and Sirluck in their varying approaches to *Areopagitica* and *Il Penseroso* make evident the difficulty of generalizing about or agreeing on Milton's religious politics. Their arguments demonstrate that the Protestant Milton is neither easily located nor necessarily the Milton whom they equally wish to find. The elders of the Milton tradition are visibly undecided about how radical, how Protestant, how historically specific they wish Milton, even in these two texts, really to be.

If I were in my turn to use *Areopagitica* and *Il Penseroso* as signs of Milton the crypto-Catholic, I would only contribute to what Paul Stevens calls the 'accelerating plurality of different Miltons,'[45] each with its own biography. It is certainly true that my generation has 'been taught to admire [poetry which is] conflicted or tragic or inconclusive or polysemous or paradoxical.'[46] The question of how Milton's works could condemn and then appropriate the cloister, though, is not simply a means to disrupt the Protestantism of Milton (or his universal value); it is rather one small example of the hazards of accepting the assumptions of either an ahistorical approach to Milton or of a totalizing historicist narrative. In *Aereopagitica* and in *Il Penseroso,* Milton uses clearly Catholic images to both praise and blame the solitude of the cloister (religious or intellectual), to both disavow and then embrace the calling of the devotional mourner, to both condemn and appropriate aggressive public challenges to the social realm. His works use all of these devices to create and defend what we might see as his most central positions on politics, on religion, on his own poetic calling. This topical ambiguity, this metaphorical dalliance with the enemy, means then that Milton does not yield himself so easily to being a universal god of liberty, but neither do his works conform to the intellectual history, especially the Protestant bildungsroman, which has so often been constructed for them. In this sense, then, Milton in his own works can once, or yet once more, take the veil.

NOTES

1 Epigraph from Stanley Fish, *How Milton Works* (Cambridge, MA, 2001), 569.
2 Arthur Edward Barker, *Milton and the Puritan Dilemma, 1641–1660* (Toronto, 1942), xi; see also ch. 13. A.S.P. Woodhouse, *Puritanism and Liberty* (Chicago, 1951), introduction; H.R. MacCallum, 'Milton and Figurative Interpretation of the Bible,' *UTQ* 31 (1962): 397–415.
3 Barker, *Puritan Dilemma,* xi.
4 Douglas Bush, 'The Modern Reaction against Milton,' in *'Paradise Lost' in Our Time: Some Comments* (Gloucester, MA, 1957), 3, 2, 4, 27; see above, 6, 7, 21.
5 Sauer, 'The Art of Criticism,' introduction to *Milton and the Climates of Reading: Essays by Balachandra Rajan* (Toronto, 2006), 7.
6 See, for instance, Thomas N. Corns, 'The Nativity, the Circumcision, and the Passion,' in *A Companion to Milton,* ed. Thomas N. Corns (Oxford, 2001), 231; Barbara Lewalski, *The Life of John Milton: A Critical Biography* (Oxford, 2000), 50; and Colin Burrow, '*Poems 1645*: The Future Poet,' in *Cambridge Companion to Milton,* 2nd ed., ed. Dennis Danielson (Cambridge, 1999), 62–6.
7 As Arthur Barker notes, several of Milton's texts from the 1640s are almost entirely composed of 'masses of vituperation and contemptuous wit' (*Puritan Dilemma,* 218).
8 All subsequent Miltonic citations (poetry) are from *Paradise Lost,* ed. Barbara K. Lewalski (Oxford, 2007) and *Complete Shorter Poems,* ed. Stella P. Revard

(Oxford, 2009). Milton's prose will be cited from the Yale edition: *Complete Prose Works of John Milton*, ed. Don M. Wolfe et al. (New Haven, 1953–82), hereafter cited as *YP*, with volume and page numbers given in the text.

9 From *John Donne, The Complete English Poems*, ed. A.J. Smith (Markham, Ontario, 1980), 47–8.

10 Tracey Fessenden, 'The Convent, The Brothel, and the Protestant Woman's Sphere,' *Signs* 25 (2000): 456–7.

11 Alison Shell, *Catholicism, Controversy and the English Literary Imagination, 1558–1660* (Cambridge, 1999), 3.

12 Michael Lieb, 'Milton among the Monks,' in *Milton and the Middle Ages*, ed. John Mulryan (Toronto, 1982), 106.

13 Cited in Barker, *Puritan Dilemma*, 231. Milton adds to this distinction when he associates what he calls the forced sterility of prepublication licensing with the 'new limbo's and new hells' invented by 'inquisiturient Bishops and ... their Chaplains' (*YP* 2:506–7).

14 See also on this battle-metaphor Stanley Fish, *How Milton Works*, 207.

15 Retha Warnicke, 'Private and Public: The Boundaries of Women's Lives,' in *Privileging Gender in Early Modern England*, ed. Jean R. Brink (Kirksville, MO, 1993), 137.

16 'not,''yet,'and 'but' appear thirteen times in these few sentences.

17 See, for instance, Reuben Márquez Sánchez, '"The Worst of Superstitions": Milton's *Of True Religion* and the Issue of Religious Tolerance,' *Prose Studies* 9.3 (1986): 21–38; Ray Tumbleson, '*Of True Religion* and False Politics: Milton and the Uses of Anti-Catholicism,' *Prose Studies* 15.3 (1992): 253–70; Hong Won Suh, 'Belial, Popery, and True Religion: Milton's *Of True Religion* and Antipapist Sentiment,' in *Living Texts: Interpreting Milton*, ed. Kristen A. Pruitt and Charles W. Durham (Selinsgrove, PA, 2000), 283–302; and Don M. Wolfe, 'Limits of Miltonic Toleration,' *JEGP* 60 (1961): 834–46.

18 See for instance *YP* 2:542–3 and 566.

19 Balachandra Rajan discusses the particularly communitarian nature of this Osiris image: 'Warfaring and Wayfaring: Milton and the Globalization of Tolerance,' in *Milton and the Climates of Reading*, 146.

20 Annabel Patterson, '"Forc'd fingers": Milton's Early Poems and Ideological Constraint,' in '*The Muses Common-Weale': Poetry and Politics in the Seventeenth Century*, ed. Claude J. Summers and Ted-Larry Pebworth (Columbia, MO, 1988), 14.

21 See Stella Revard, *Milton and the Tangles of Neaera's Hair: The Making of the 1645 Poems* (Columbia, MO, 1997), 110–14; Casey Finch and Peter Bowen, 'The Solitary Companionship of *L'Allegro* and *Il Penseroso*,' *Milton Studies* 26 (1990): 6.

22 The figure is governed by the cross as well as by the signs of the sun, Jupiter, and Mercury, suggesting (according to Burton) a tendency toward ambition and solitary subtlety; see W.I.D. Scott, *Shakespeare's Melancholics* (Norwood, PA, 1978), 20.

23 Quoted in Margery Lange, 'Humourous Grief: Donne and Burton Read Melancholy,' in *Speaking Grief in English Literary Culture*, ed. Margo Swiss and David A. Kent (Pittsburgh, 2002), 81.

24 Jean Calvin, *Commentaries*, trans. and ed. James Anderson (Edinburgh, 1847–9), vol. 5, *Commentary on Psalms*, 131.

25 Robert Burton, *Anatomy of Melancholy*, 3 vols, ed. Thomas C. Faulkner, Nicolas K. Kiessling, and Rhonda Blair (Oxford, 1989–94), 3:4.1.1.

26 John Donne, *Sermons*, 10 vols, ed. George Potter and Evelyn Simpson (Berkeley and Los Angeles, 1959), 4:108.

27 Donne, *Sermons*, 4:137.

28 Donne, *Sermons*, 8:135.

29 See on Orpheus/Eurydice and loss, Eric C. Brown, 'The Dissolution of Borders in *L'Allegro* and *Il Penseroso*,' *Milton Studies* 40 (2001): 11.

30 Juan Luis Vives, *The Instruction of a Christen Woman*, ed. Virginia Walcott Beauchamp et al. (Chicago, 2002), 174.

31 Vives,137.

32 Warnicke,138.

33 Widowers seem exempt from these cloistering paradigms, though later in the seventeenth century such celebrated widowers as Sir Kenelm Digby are sometimes seen as evidence of spreading masculine appropriation of feminine mourners' conventions. See Ralph Houlbrooke, *Death, Religion, and the Family in England 1480–1750* (Oxford, 1998), 243–4.

34 Quoted in Lange, 79.

35 See my 'Mourning Eve, Mourning Milton in *Paradise Lost*,' *Early Modern Literary Studies* 11.1 (May 2005): 6.1–32; 13 March 2009 http://purl.oclc.org/emls/11-1/hodgmilt.htm. Lange, 76–80 discusses this correlation.

36 Bridget Gellert Lyons, *Voices of Melancholy: Studies in Literary Treatments of Melancholy in Renaissance England* (New York, 1971), 160.

37 Lyons, 160.

38 Georgia B. Christopher, 'Subject and Macrosubject in *L'Allegro* and *Il Penseroso*,' *Milton Studies* 28 (1992): 29. Christopher suggests that this correlation between enclosure and insight also has somewhat Protestant roots 'as the evangelical tradition ... valued hearing over seeing' (28) in the dark spaces the speaker inhabits. I have my doubts, but this is an interesting instance of the difficulties of denominational tagging.

39 Northrop Frye, 'Literature as Context: Milton's *Lycidas,*' in *Fables of Identity: Studies in Poetic Mythology* (New York, 1963), 128; see above, 60.

40 Ernest Sirluck, '*Areopagitica* and a Forgotten Licensing Controversy,' *RES* n.s. 11 (1960): 274; see above, 135.

41 Sirluck, 274; see above, 135–6.

42 Frye, 'Literature as Context,' 127, 124; see above, 60, 56.

43 Ibid., 127.

44 Frye, *Northrop Frye on Milton and Blake* (Toronto, 2005). All subsequent citations in text.

45 Paul Stevens, 'Milton's Janus-faced Nationalism: Soliloquy, Subject, and the Modern Nation-State,' *JEGP* 100 (2001): 249.

46 Fish, *How Milton Works,* 14.

16 Historical Appearance in *Areopagitica*

PHILLIP J. DONNELLY

The writings of Machiavelli are an obvious part of Milton's intellectual context in the 1640s, and 'history' is a central category for Machiavelli; yet Milton's appeal to history in *Areopagitica* (1644) seems unconcerned with what Machiavelli would call the 'effectual truth' of history. At one level neither Machiavelli nor Milton distinguishes sharply between 'history' understood as an explanatory *account* of the past and 'history' understood as the *events* that would constitute the ostensible object of such an account.[1] I suggest that the distinction is absent not because they naively failed to notice the mediated character of historical knowledge, but precisely because they did indeed recognize the intrinsically discursive character of knowledge regarding past events. Where these two writers part company is in what they would mean by saying that all such knowledge is, in effect, 'rhetorical.' Machiavelli, in *The Prince* and *The Discourses*, takes rhetoric to be a persuasive technique whose power must be detachable from any assumptions regarding a human good that would transcend political dominions; by contrast, Milton, in *Areopagitica*, insists that rhetorical practice does not entail a moral commitment to sophistry and can, instead, culminate in the enjoyment of a human good that may be served by but is not limited to the state. Despite extensive critical treatments of Milton's *Areopagitica*, as well as his use of history and his engagement with Machiavelli, these aspects of Milton's writing warrant a united treatment here; their intersection illuminates the way that historical narration in each writer's work differently discloses the capacity of rhetoric, or suasive discourse, to participate in the appearance of reality. The argument here unfolds in three stages. The first part establishes some of the critical contexts that help to explain the challenges posed by historical knowledge generally and by the reception of *Areopagitica* in particular. The second stage considers how

Areopagitica evokes Machiavellian commonplaces regarding political reality and the appearance of history. Finally, I argue that *Areopagitica* deploys key moments in what Milton elsewhere calls 'the story of Scripture' (*YP* 2:387) in order to challenge the Machiavellian assumptions that he imputes to those who would continue to support the Licensing Order of 1643.

I

In his essay 'The "Historical Turn" and the Political Culture of Early Modern England,' Glenn Burgess proposes:

> A critical historiography – for historians and critics – needs to do at least three things. It needs to understand how meta-narratives guide the constitution of facts; it needs to understand how facts constituted under other frameworks can challenge meta-narratives; and it needs to generate some defensible account of the reliability of the ways in which narratives are constructed by historians.[2]

Burgess's aim in that particular essay, as well as his proposals for further study, present what is arguably a model of intellectual clarity and modesty. By developing an argument regarding 'historiography' – that is, a comparative account of the way historical narratives get constructed – Burgess moves beyond the above distinction between 'history' as narrative and 'history' as event. This account may be extended, however, in ways that pertain specifically to the narrative character of both historiography and history, as well as to the role of interpretive assumptions regarding what counts as 'real.' At one level, as Burgess notes, 'it could be argued that all history is reliant, if not exactly on meta-narratives, then on a "great story," or on "meta-historical frameworks."'[3] Despite any individual's purported scepticism of meta-narratives, 'the words themselves,' such as 'bourgeois' or 'absolutist,' can very well 'take us to the metanarratives, even when these are not explicitly endorsed.'[4] This point also applies, however, to the narrative dimensions of critical historiography itself. Insofar as 'defensible' involves naming causes, or giving reasons, and insofar as any 'account' of actions, or 'ways,' implies a story, or emplotment, of some kind, Burgess's third imperative entails recourse to a metanarrative, or, in this case, a metametanarrative. To make such a claim is not to deny the possibility of critical historiography, but to point out that such an approach does not obviate the need for its own dependence upon a further metanarrative of some kind.

Burgess also insists that, notwithstanding the discursively mediated character of all human encounters with the past, the past is not merely fiction: 'To encounter the other, you must first grasp the nature of its otherness. And, for historians and for the past, the only way of doing that is to attempt descriptions and accounts that avoid anachronism.'[5] Each of these historiographical judgments – the constructedness of the past, the imperative to avoid anachronism, and the imperative to give due regard to the historical other – involve characterizations of human action, and are thus implicitly narrative in shape, and require specifically suprahistorical narrative, a metanarrative. Moreover, such narratives necessarily bring with them specific assumptions regarding reality, or the character of the 'other.' Thus, in addition to Burgess's historiographical imperatives, I propose two further claims that will assist our understanding of the differences between Machiavelli and Milton regarding the character of historical appearance. First, notwithstanding the generally principled way that modern historians would disown 'metaphysics,' historical narratives and investigations persistently imply an account of reality, or an ontology, whether atomist or otherwise.[6] Second, to the extent that such ontological assumptions pertain to human action, whether prescriptively (as a hermeneutic imperative) or descriptively (as a narration of past events), the ontology will be manifest to human understanding in narrative form.

Keeping in mind these two claims regarding the role of metanarrative and ontology will help us to distinguish between Machiavelli's modern metanarrative and Milton's understanding of what he calls 'the story of Scripture.' One distinctive aspect of Machiavelli's argument is his insistence that true knowledge finds its purpose in utility, defined as the power to overcome *fortuna*. In this sense, for Machiavelli, the purpose of studying the past is to control the future by reducing the role of chance; all his appeals to history are in service to such immanently defined human ends, whether those of a principality or a republic. This belief is not simply a particle-like interpretive assumption, but involves an imperative dimension whose intelligibility as an imperative for human action depends on a narrative element.[7] As we shall see, Milton's argument in *Areopagitica* appeals to a contrasting narrative regarding the purposes of historical knowledge: not to control the future but to persuade others to the enjoyment of 'knowledge in the making' (*YP* 2:554). My point is not simply that Machiavellian *fortuna* and Miltonic Providence are mutually exclusive. Rather, Machiavelli's conception of reality as an atelic strife between *fortuna* and *virtù* dictates a reduction of all contingent historical events to the universal categories of his taxonomy. His taxonomy subdivides *virtù* into 'laws' and 'force,' the latter of which is further divided into the 'lion' and the 'fox,' or brute force and cunning. Because, however, he also reduces 'good laws' to 'good arms' and has already defined *virtù* as one's own arms, he implies that the lion and the fox are actually two modes of *virtù*.[8] In this respect, 'rhetoric,' the customary sphere of 'law' as an alternative to brute force, is reducible for Machiavelli to the cunning deceptions of the fox. In effect, 'reality' for Machiavelli is always narratable as the strife between random *fortuna* and the imposition of temporary order upon that chaos by means of *virtù*, whether by brute force or cunning. In contrast to Machiavelli's drive to abstraction, *Areopagitica*, as we shall see, appeals to a larger story whose events are contingent and irreducibly unique without being merely random.

Although revisionist readings of *Areopagitica* are now numerous and vary greatly in their approaches and conclusions, they remain, with few exceptions, in general agreement on one point: their rejection of the traditional view that Milton's tract is a manifesto for 'freedom of speech' and liberal toleration.[9] Ernest Sirluck initiated what is arguably the most influential challenge to the liberal account of the *Areopagitica*, by showing the importance of Milton's anticipated audience(s). According to Sirluck, Milton's suasive purpose was to effect a repeal of the 1643 Licensing Order by dividing the Presbyterian majority in Parliament. Milton attempts to do this by convincing a sufficient number of Erastian Presbyterians to side with the Independents and against those Presbyterians who supported the *jure divino* policy of the Westminster Assembly (*YP* 2:176–7).[10] Given such rhetorical aims, we should not be surprised that Milton's appeal to a group of Erastians on their own terms might entail some conflict with his own implicit position. Milton does not, of course, in any of his tracts advocate 'free speech,' as it is commonly understood today.[11] But the apparent stance offered in the tract is complicated not simply by the differences between Milton's Christian humanist view of a 'liberty' based on truth and that of modern liberalism. In Sirluck's account, Milton's attempt to accommodate the anxieties of Erastian Parliamentarians is also potentially at odds with Milton's own view of toleration.[12]

The impulse toward such historical contextualization of Milton's tract arose in part because *Areopagitica* has been 'widely regarded as one of the constitutive texts of modern liberalism' and consequently 'has become a contested site in a larger dispute about liberal values.'[13] Among those united in challenging the liberal interpretation of *Areopagitica*, however, there is little consensus as to what Milton is actually attempting in the tract. As Abbe Blum points out:

> [Milton is alternately viewed as] a brilliant moral instructor who employs irony to move ethically upright, intellectually superior readers (who as kindred liberal Christians will affirm his rhetorical prowess); a conservative party-line Protestant spokesman for intolerance who constructs a conditional restricted freedom tailored for the elect. Most recently *Areopagitica*'s seeming contradictions have been interpreted as Milton's 'manifesto for indeterminacy,' a conversion of various factions' disagreements into a nonoppositional celebration of intellectual energy, and finally and quite differently, as the product of a self-validating monistic ethos which registers the tensions deriving from a bourgeois problematic.[14]

In the twenty years since Blum wrote, critical interpretations have proven this overview to be prophetic rather than dated, as the indeterminacy theme, among others, has been re-enacted over and again.[15] Blum begins her overview by alluding to Sirluck's influential argument: 'Milton is variously seen as a canny tactician who moderates his stance on toleration in order to convey the appearance of solidarity with those who could repeal the 1643 Licensing Act.' Most recently, Markus Klinge has argued directly against Sirluck's account and, in effect, against most other revisionist accounts of *Areopagitica.*[16] Thomas Fulton has also argued along similar lines that *Areopagitica* bears an important genealogical relation to liberal epistemology and ethics, a relation that is obscured by being satisfied with the assertion that the tract's argument is merely 'not liberal.'[17] Both of these arguments challenge the various post-liberal attempts to historicize the tract's rhetorical aims, but Klinge's offers the most detailed engagement with the contextualization first presented by Sirluck.

Klinge points out that the very kind of tactical argument aimed at Erastians that Sirluck describes had indeed been attempted by the anonymous *Apologeticall Narration* (1643), which was extremely irenic and was nearly successful in persuading some Erastians to tolerate moderate Independents.[18] By contrast, Milton's tract was, according to Klinge, as likely to induce distrust, suspicion, and a generally negative reaction among Erastians, as in fact it did among even some who shared Milton's political views.[19] At one level, the tract seems calculated to induce obscurity and doubt, resulting from the shifting rhetorical stance of the speaker and the way that the text signals 'conflicting party allegiances.'[20] In a further way, its use of 'grotesque satire' to portray those who support the Licensing Order, and its use of the grotesque to depict truth, seems guaranteed to offend Erastian Presbyterians.[21] These stylistic features, combined with its central argumentative insistence upon complicating without resolving the disagreements between the four different kinds of printing regulation that it discusses would hardly seem intended to persuade Erastians that they should support such a vaguely defined Independent position.[22] All of this leads Klinge to conclude that, rather than serving an immediate political aim, *Areopagitica* takes the Licensing Order as an occasion for deploying an 'indirect and tentative strategy [that] transcended the tract's apparent logical flaws,' but which aims to persuade readers, in the long run, of the futility of licensing and of religious conformity generally.[23]

Even if we question Sirluck's account of *Areopagitica*'s appeal to Erastians, the tract can still be tactical in some of the more general ways that Sirluck describes. Milton may still be addressing those who do not necessarily share his view of church-state separation, warning them that the Licensing Order is indeed part of the Westminster Assembly's encroaching theocratic tyranny. As Sirluck explains:

> Milton's message to the 'nation' (i.e., to the part supporting Parliament) is this: Parliament, whose power derives from and is dependent upon you, is beginning to legislate at the dictate of a new priestcraft which regard you with contempt and is animated by limitless ambition. The excuses which are offered to justify the present legislation are intended as a screen for developing tyranny, but they are as transparent as the legislation is harmful ... Let Parliament understand that if it threatens your liberty you will have no reason to support it against the king. (*YP* 2:178)

This kind of medium-range, rather than immediate, tactical argument would fit well with Klinge's account of grotesque satire in *Areopagitica*. Such satire is not intended to persuade the tyrants who are the object of satire but to warn others by indirectly exposing the tyranny for what it is.

II

The long-standing recognition that the English political and ecclesiastical crises of the 1640s lent particular relevance to Machiavelli's discussion of de facto political power has given rise to several studies of the relation between Milton and Machiavelli.[24] Despite the important work of Victoria Kahn and, more recently, Paul Rahe regarding *Areopagitica*'s engagement of Machiavelli, there remains a need to consider how the tract addresses Machiavelli's central preoccupation with the ends and reality of historical appearance. We can begin to appreciate the character of the questions surrounding Milton's engagement with Machiavelli if we consider two key passages in *Areopagitica* that directly address Machiavellian commonplaces.

The first passage appears in the initial encomiastic appeal to Parliament, in which Milton allows that England has already made great improvement in civil liberty, despite working 'from such a steepe disadvantage of tyranny and superstition grounded into our principles as was beyond the manhood of a *Roman* recovery' (*YP* 2:487). In the final phrase, Milton alludes to the Machiavellian commonplace regarding the difficulties faced by a people who have been governed under a prince and subsequently recover their liberty.[25] In his *Discourses on Livy*, Machiavelli argues that Rome's ability to 'recover its freedom' in some cases but not in others depended directly on the extent to which the people had either resisted or succumbed to corruption (1.16.5–1.17.1). Machiavelli's summation is worth quoting in full because the passage provides an instance of what he means by the political 'utility' that may be derived from 'true knowledge of histories' (Pref. 2):

> When the Tarquins were expelled, Rome could at once take and maintain its freedom, but after Caesar died, after Gaius Caligula died, after Nero died, when the whole line of Caesar was eliminated, not only could it never maintain but it could not even give a beginning to freedom. So great a difference of results in one and the same city arose from nothing other than that in the times of the Tarquins the Roman people was not yet corrupt, and in these last times it was very corrupt. (1.17.1)

By alluding to this interpretation of Roman history at the outset of *Areopagitica*, Milton's initial point is that the political and religious condition of the English people had been, in effect, so corrupt as to be 'beyond the manhood [*virtù*] of a *Roman* recovery.' Milton's further point is that there has nevertheless been a recovery of liberty in England, which he attributes 'first, as is most due, to the strong assistance of God our deliverer, next to your faithful guidance and undaunted Wisdome, Lords and Commons of *England*' (*YP* 2:487). Milton is pointing out that something more than Machiavellian *virtù* is at work in the political changes in England: he attributes those changes specifically to the combined effect of divine Providence and the moral as well as intellectual virtues of Parliament. The crucial ambiguity here is whether Milton intends to present these causes as a genuine alternative to the Machiavellian vision of reality that he evokes, or whether he expects his readers to follow Machiavelli in reducing Providence to *fortuna* and moral virtue to its mere appearance.[26] I contend that Milton does indeed expect his readers to remember the Machiavellian treatment of Providence and of moral virtue; however, *Areopagitica* does not simply let those reductive possibilities stand. Instead, Milton presents an alternative use of history that inhabits a Providential narrative and presents an account of virtue that subverts the Machiavellian manner of distinguishing between appearance and reality in history.

Before considering Milton's appeal to history, we should note a second key passage in *Areopagitica* where he seems to engage a Machiavellian commonplace. Although Machiavelli disowns the discernment of ends or purposes beyond human intention, he does not conceal the purpose of his own approach to politics: the presumed goal of political action is the self-preservation of political power over time. This sense of purpose then informs Machiavelli's most famous rejection of 'ideals' in political deliberation:

> Since my intent is to write something useful to whoever understands it, it has appeared to me more fitting to go directly to the effectual truth of the thing than to the imagination of it. And many have imagined republics and principalities that have never been seen or known to exist in truth; for it is so far from how one lives to how one should live that he who lets go of what is done for what should be done learns his ruin rather than his preservation ... Hence it is necessary to a prince, if he wants to maintain himself, to learn to be able not to be good, and to use this and not use it according to necessity. (*Prince,* ch. 15)

The explicit purpose of this teaching is to enable a prince to 'maintain himself.' When Machiavelli speaks of republics in *The Discourses on Livy,* his sense of *telos* remains the same as in *The Prince* in this regard. At the same time, Machiavelli is able to make this claim specifically by means of his insistence upon the 'truth' of the historical events that he purports to describe rather than to evaluate morally, a truth that precludes any purposes greater than those of human politics. All of this entails the above disowning of those 'imagined republics' that would impose moral limits upon the means available to rulers whose goal is to preserve political power.

In *Areopagitica*, Milton makes a point that appears similar to Machiavelli's. In contending that licensing cannot accomplish its own alleged purposes, Milton turns, for a second time, to the topic of Plato. After noting the impossibility of attempting to regulate all the sources of temptation that could lead to moral corruption, Milton insists that the 'grave and governing wisdom of a state' is to make such temptations less harmful and less enticing without resorting to coercive measures such as licensing (*YP* 2:526):

> To sequester out of the world into *Atlantick* and *Eutopian* polities, which never can be drawn into use, will not mend our condition; but to ordain wisely as in this world of evill, in the midd'st whereof God hath plac't us unavoidably. Nor is it *Plato's* licensing of books will doe this, which necessarily pulls along with it so many other kinds of licensing, as will make us all both ridiculous and weary, and yet frustrate; but those unwritt'n or at least unconstraining laws of vertuous education, religious and civil nurture, which *Plato* there mentions, as the bonds and ligaments of the commonwealth, the pillars and the sustainers of every writt'n Statute; these they be which will bear chief sway in such matters as these, when all licensing will be easily eluded. (*YP* 2:526–7)

Milton's disowning of '*Atlantick* and *Eutopian* polities' might initially seem like a direct allusion to Machiavelli's rejection of 'imagined republics.' Yet the implications that Milton draws from this claim are ultimately in direct opposition to Machiavelli. At the most explicit level, Milton's argument does not simply dismiss Plato but contends that what '*Plato* meant' was not to extend state censorship beyond his imagined republic (*YP* 2:522).[27] Milton also probably adopts this position in order to forestall allegations that his own opposition to licensing depends on unrealistic idealism. In effect, Milton anticipates and reverses such an argument by contending that the goals of licensing are based on the illusion of mere imagined republics.

In a deeper sense, however, the specific reference to Thomas More's '*Eutopian*' polity also indicates Milton's appreciation for the potential of an 'imagined republic' to serve not as a direct source for political practices but as an indirect source of satire and political criticism.[28] We should not be surprised that the anonymous letter to Samuel Hartlib complained that *Areopagitica* was specifically 'too satyrical.'[29] The direct reference to *Utopia* suggests that More's text exemplifies the kind of satire that Klinge identifies in *Areopagitica*.[30] Such satire, although explicitly directed, in Milton's case, at Catholic licensing practices, also clearly includes the corruptions of episcopacy and the Presbyterian Westminster Assembly.[31] Considered as a rhetorical mode, satire was an indirect means by which Milton could offer a nevertheless clear critique of such ostensibly Protestant tyrannical practices. Moreover, the need for such indirectness arises not simply from the consideration of personal safety but from the very character of the problem posed by political rulers who succeed in appearing to act for the common good while actually performing as tyrants. A direct denunciation of tyranny could indeed incur suspicion. As Giuseppe Mazzotta points out: 'There is nothing more Machiavellian than a thorough profession of anti-Machiavellianism.'[32] In effect, *Areopagitica* demonstrates Milton's appreciation of the need for indirectness in naming tyranny; from this appreciation arises his use of satire and historical narrative.

The Machiavellian commonplaces regarding the need for 'manhood' [*virtù*] to effect a 'Roman recovery' of liberty and the disowning of imaginary republics are part of a deeper set of preoccupations that inform both *The Prince* and the *Discourses*.[33] If we note here two of Machiavelli's other central claims, we can then understand how Milton's appeal to historical argument constitutes an alternative to such a view. The first key point to notice is that Machiavelli advances a proto-Hobbesian narrative regarding the origins of civil society:

> Variations of governments arise by chance among men. For since the inhabitants were sparse in the beginning of the world, they lived dispersed for a time like wild beasts; then as generations multiplied, they gathered together, and to be able to defend themselves better, they began to look to whoever among them was more robust and of greater heart, and they made him head, as it were, and obeyed him. From this arose the knowledge of things honest and good, differing from the pernicious and bad. For, seeing that if one individual hurt his benefactor, hatred and compassion among men came from it, and as they blamed the ungrateful and honored those who were grateful, and thought too that those same injuries could be done to them, [in order] to escape like evil they were reduced to making laws and ordering punishments for whoever acted against them: hence came the knowledge of justice. (*Discourses* 1.2.3)

The most notable feature of this particular version of moral constructivism is the series of causal connections involved in the story. In effect, the threat of violence gives rise to a kind of social contract that, in turn, gives rise to 'knowledge of things honest and good.' Out of such moral judgment arises the need for laws and civil order that make possible the 'knowledge of justice.' In this way, Machiavelli, like Hobbes, posits brute force as the origin of goodness and justice for human beings.[34] Notwithstanding the fact that knowledge of laws will later cause people to choose princes according to prudence, rather than the mere capacity for compulsion, the key point here is that, according to Machiavelli, no good for human beings could predate the violence out of which the social contract arises.[35] In this way, the *Discourses* offers a theoretical account of the *Prince*'s assumption that 'justice' is ultimately reducible to the power of control by means of either coercion ('the lion') or cunning ('the fox').[36] Most important, this causal explanation does not narrate a particular contingent event in the past; it presents a universal explanation for the origin of any and all civil society, as it arises from the ontic strife between *fortuna* and *virtù*. In this respect, the passage quoted above reveals the Machiavellian metanarrative by which all historical contingency is reduced to the abstractions of *fortuna* and *virtù*.

A second key aspect of Machiavelli's position is his insistence upon the political importance of maintaining certain public appearances. Rulers, whether of principalities or republics, will be successful in preserving their political power to the extent that they maintain the appearance of conventional moral virtue and piety.[37] Machiavelli insists that an effective ruler will know the difference between appearance and reality, and specifically how to reduce perceptions of the former to knowledge of the latter by discerning the interplay between fortune, compulsion, and cunning. He thus insists that, although political rulers must use illusory appearances in order to serve the end of preserving power, the knowledge of how best to govern is derived from knowing the truth about history. Such historical knowledge arises not from merely recounting past events but from knowing the real causes of things:

> It *appeared* that in Rome there was a very great union between the plebs and the Senate after the Tarquins were expelled, and that the nobles had put away that pride of theirs, had taken on a popular spirit, and were tolerable to anyone, however mean. This deception remained concealed, nor did anyone see the *cause* of it while the Tarquins lived ... But as soon as the

> Tarquins were dead and fear fled from the nobles, they began to spit out that poison against the plebs that they had held in their breasts. (*Discourses* 1.3.2, emphasis added)

At one level, this passage shows the nobles making effective political use of the difference between appearance and reality. But the most crucial point to notice about this passage is the main inference that Machiavelli draws from this history: 'Such a thing is testimony to what I have said above, that men never work any good unless through necessity, but where choice abounds and one can make use of license, at once everything is full of confusion and disorder' (*Discourses* 1.3.2). This inference is not surprising, given that Machiavelli has already stated that 'every history,' in fact, demonstrates that the makers of law must 'presuppose that all men are bad, and that they always have to use the malignity of their spirit whenever they have a free opportunity for it' (*Discourses* 1.3.1). Underlying this claim is the deeper assumption noted above: that reality – whether social or personal – subsists in a strife between *fortuna* and the *virtù* of compulsion or deception imposing order on such chaos. In this way, Machiavelli consistently reduces the narration of historically contingent events to the universal categories that inform his metanarrative.

The contrast here between Machiavelli and the argument in *Areopagitica* could hardly be more striking. If *Areopagitica* were transposed into the terms deployed by Machiavelli above, Milton would say that 'men will never work any true good unless *freed from* compulsion by civil law' because genuine human virtue, in Milton's account, cannot be compelled by laws. Milton never denies the universality of sin (e.g., *YP* 2:515). Nor does he deny that civil laws play an important role in shaping human behaviour in a fallen world; however, Milton views the best civil law as not compelling human behaviour but as establishing a context where uncoerced human excellence can be pursued and realized. Both Machiavelli and Milton emphasize the universality of sin, but they seem to draw opposing inferences. How does this happen? The difference arises from the contrasting metanarratives that they respectively presume as a context for the meaning of sin. As we shall see, the meaning that each one gives to the universal human tendency toward corruption is shaped directly by whether corruption itself is understood as a result of a contingent event, or whether such corruption is indeed a necessary aspect of reality – that is, the chaos against which the state legitimates itself as a compelled order. Moreover this disagreement is not a merely speculative matter; in each case, the assumption regarding reality issues in a political imperative.

III

The stated structure of the argument in *Areopagitica* involves four stages, the first of which is historical:

> First the inventors of [licensing] bee those whom ye will be loath to own; next what is to be thought in general of reading, whatever sort the Books be; and that this Order avails nothing to the suppressing of scandalous, seditious, and libellous Books, which were mainly intended to be suppress. Last, that it will be primely to the discouragement of all learning, and the stop of Truth, not only by the disexercising and blunting our abilities in what we know already, but by hindering and cropping the discovery that might bee yet further made both in religious and civill Wisdome. (*YP* 2:491–2)

In effect, Milton's argument progresses from consideration of the efficient cause of licensing (who its inventors are) to the material cause of licensing (shifting the subject matter from books to reading). The last two stages both focus on the final cause, or purpose, arguing that the Licensing Order will fail to achieve its own ostensible ends and that the effects of the Order will, in fact, be disastrous for learning in England. As Milton then begins the first argument regarding the 'inventors,' he further explains: 'I refuse not the paines to be so much Historical, as will serve to shew what hath been done by ancient and famous Commonwealths' (*YP* 2:493). As the ensuing stages of argument unfold, however, we discover that the meaning of that first stage becomes transformed, as the later segments situate that history of state-regulated publishing within a still larger narrative.

In the first stage of his argument, Milton presents a brief historical account of the ways in which 'the Magistrate car'd to take notice' of certain published writings. The account considers the evidence for various practices in ancient Athens, Sparta, and Rome, before it describes practices under Christian emperors and later medieval rulers, and then culminates with the Council of Trent. Milton notes various kinds of post-publication censorship, pointing out where some authorities, in Athens for example, banned only blasphemous or libellous texts, but were not concerned with those texts 'tending to voluptuousness' (*YP* 2:494). Among the ecclesiastical authorities, he notes that some permitted the reading of heresies but not 'plain invectives against Christianity,' while for other authorities the permission and prohibition were respectively reversed (*YP* 2:501). Although the ecclesiastical portion of Milton's history of licensing is largely drawn from Sarpi's *History of the Council of Trent*, Milton does not simply adopt Sarpi's forensic arguments about past events uncritically. As Sirluck has shown through detailed comparison, Milton consistently corrects, clarifies, sophisticates, or augments Sarpi's account specifically through recourse to the primary documents concerned.[38] Among the various historical examples of censorship that Milton considers, however, in none of them does he find a systematic attempt at prepublication censorship, or licensing, until the Council of Trent. He then concludes:

> Thus ye have the Inventors and the originall of Book-licencing ript up, and drawn as lineally as any pedigree. We have it not, that can be heard of, from any ancient State, or politie, or Church, nor by any Statute left us by our Ancestors elder or later; nor from the moderne custom of any reformed Citty, or Church abroad; but from the most Antichristian Councel, and the most tyrannous Inquisition that ever inquir'd. (*YP* 2:505)

Only from the 'engendering together' of the Council of Trent and the Spanish Inquisition, according to Milton, did the 'last invention' of licensing arise, before being adopted by the 'apishly Romanizing' Prelates of England (*YP* 2:502–4). At the very outset of this historical account, Milton had gone further in the historical trajectory by referring to licensing as a 'project' that 'crept out of the Inquisition, was catcht up by our Prelats, and hath caught some of our Presbyters' (*YP* 2:493). This larger historical trajectory is repeated in a conditional but explicit way, when Milton later points out that 'if some ... shall come now to silence us from reading, except what they please, it cannot be guest what is intended by som but a second tyranny over learning: and will soon put out of controversy that Bishops and Presbyters are the same to us both name and thing' (*YP* 2:539). Thus, by identifying the Council of Trent as 'the most Antichristian Councel,' Milton is not simply rehearsing Protestant characterizations of the papacy as the Antichrist; he is situating the practice of licensing, and the Westminster Assembly's actions, within a larger biblical narrative – in this case, by referring specifically to the end of that story, or the Eschaton.

Beginning with that reference to the Antichrist at the culmination of his brief history of licensing, Milton then goes on in the remaining stages of his argument to refer to several key moments in the larger biblical story. What Milton, in *Of Education*, calls 'the story of Scripture' (*YP* 2:387) arguably includes the whole of the biblical text, in all of its details; yet *Areopagitica* clearly focuses on pivotal moments in that story in order to show the basic conflict between the practice of licensing and the meanings of the biblical narrative. At one level, this helps to explain one of the most immediate questions arising from *Areopagitica*: why would a political argument against licensing make specific reference to the Creation story, the Fall, Christ's work in Incarnation, Redemption, and Ascension, as well as the Eschaton?[39] Regarding some of these points, multiple examples could be adduced from *Areopagitica*, and we shall not analyse each point in detail here. Milton clearly intends to appeal rhetorically to the entire story, from beginning to end. At the same time, each event is identified here by a proper name specifically because of the unique particularity of each moment. Although Christians are supposed to imitate and participate in the reality revealed by these events, Milton never treats them as constituting a generalized explanatory-predictive narrative. The rhetorical power of Milton's appeal to biblical narrative arises from the fact that his primary political opponents would ostensibly claim to inhabit the same story. In this way, *Areopagitica* argues that the advocates of the Licensing Order, although they claim to be Christians, actually inhabit a Machiavellian metanarrative, because the practice of licensing assumes that political reality is reducible to compulsion or deception and treats religion as merely the most politically useful (or dangerous) deception. In what follows we will focus on how Milton appeals to the moments of Creation, the Fall, and the Eschaton.

In referring directly to an original Creation in *Areopagitica*, Milton revealingly insists that the moral goodness of human beings predates the Fall. As we have already noted, in Machiavelli's account the usefulness of historical knowledge depends on positing a metanarrative regarding the violent origin of human morality and civil society. While Machiavelli might seem to be simply emphasizing the universality of human sin, he is actually doing something quite different. Milton makes that difference apparent when he emphasizes the human capacity for virtue that predates not the possibility of sin but its practice:

> Many there be that complain of divin Providence for suffering *Adam* to transgresse, foolish tongues! when God gave him reason, he gave him freedom to choose, for reason is but choosing; he had bin else a meer artificial *Adam*, such an *Adam* as he is in the motions. We our selves esteem not of

> that obedience, or love, or gift, which is of force ... Wherefore did he creat passions within us, pleasures round about us, but that these rightly temper'd are the very ingredients of vertu? (*YP* 2:527)

Milton's larger point in this passage is that moral virtues, such as 'temperance, justice, continence,' in both the unfallen and the fallen human condition, require the possibility (not the practice) of their contrasting vices in order for the virtues to be embodied as such. By attempting to use the coercive power of civil law to remove the opportunities for vice, licensing depends upon compulsion to control people and thereby limits the opportunity for Christians to practise genuine virtue. Milton's Presbyterian opponents would, of course, readily admit that the original human condition was good. His point here, however, is that regardless of what one might say or appear to believe, the practice of licensing in fact denies that belief: it assumes that if Creation really were good, God should have used force to stop the Fall from happening. In effect, Milton posits that the advocates of the Licensing Order believe in the primacy of compulsion and deny the original goodness of Creation. Moreover, he assumes that Creation is a freely chosen divine action. In this sense Creation is a unique contingent event, in that it could have been otherwise if God had chosen not to act or to act differently, but this is understood as the contingency of an aesthetic act, freely ordered internally toward delight, not mere randomness.

As Milton's opponents would also quickly point out, humans now obviously live in a fallen world whose original goodness has indeed been lost. What about the universality of sin? Milton arguably anticipates such objections by exploring the meaning of the Fall even before referring to the goodness of Creation. The crucial point to notice, which appears in the passage quoted above (*YP* 2:527), is that Milton also insists upon the contingency of the Fall as an event – it is simply not a matter of sheer necessity. In then considering the conditional results of the Fall, Milton emphasizes its meaning for human knowledge. He first observes that 'good and evill we know in the field of this [fallen] World grow up together almost inseparably,' and then proposes that 'perhaps this is the doom which Adam fell into of knowing good and evill, that is to say, of knowing good by evill' (2:514). In this way, Milton modifies his earlier claim that 'to the pure all things are pure' (2: 512).[40] Instead, by observing that no one is actually pure, he argues that virtue is constituted through a process of educative reading: 'Assuredly we bring not innocence into the world, we bring impurity much rather: that which purifies us is triall, and triall is by what is contrary' (2:515). The various ways in which the tract then embodies for readers the opportunity to learn through such a process of trial helps to explain the tract's 'disruptive' quality with respect to its own logic, imagery, and rhetoric.[41] Thomas Fulton suggests that this disruptive 'process of disclosure' by which the tract embodies readerly opportunity for 'knowledge in the making' is itself a 'narrative' that Milton posits as an alternative to the 'nominalistic conception of truth' so characteristic of nascent Enlightenment epistemology.[42] I would extend this point by noting that Milton's engagement with the specifically biblical metanarrative, whose particularities uniquely open onto an infinite aesthetic of concrete particulars in the beatific vision, is the pivotal dimension which keeps the epistemological 'process' from becoming either endless homogenous repetition or mere randomness.

At the same time, *Areopagitica* does not, as we noted, deny the universal presence of sin, but insists that such corruption is simply not necessary among Christians. Milton does not presume that Christians are without moral flaws; rather he assumes that sin is not necessary and that sanctification, or genuinely virtuous action, is possible. As I argue elsewhere, the crux of Milton's oft-repeated argument for religious toleration among Protestants is the correct ordering of the relationship between justification (saving faith) and sanctification (virtue).[43] The mere possibility, and specifically not the necessity, of virtuous action similarly drives Milton's argument for the liberty of unlicensed printing. This is Milton's point in insisting that 'God sure esteems the growth and compleating of one vertuous person, more than the restraint of ten vitious' (*YP* 2:528). In this way, Milton emphasizes how the practice of licensing involves an interpretation of the Fall which takes sin to be inexorable and susceptible to remedy in present human affairs only by means of compulsion or the fear of compulsion.

In effect, *Areopagitica* implies that to support the Licensing Order reveals a primary, rather than secondary, faith in the coercive power of the state to remedy the effects of the Fall. As Arthur Barker has explained:

> [Milton] focused, not on individual liberty, but on the requisite liberty of the good individual who, as a believer accepting the fundamentals of Christianity, would act spontaneously in accordance with the laws of morality, renewed by the Spirit in his heart ... The wicked, on the contrary, would be free only within bounds, and only to increase the hardness of their hearts.[44]

We would be mistaken, however, to infer from Milton's distinction between civil and Christian liberty that he viewed either the gift of Creation's being or the gift of redemption as a function of arbitrary divine edict.[45] When exactly Milton would later become persuaded of the Arminian emphasis upon the conditional character of divine election, based on the human response to the universally sufficient prevenient grace of conscience, remains an open question.[46] By 1644, however, Milton had already parted company with the Presbyterians. Moreover, even before that time, when Milton had still identified himself with such Calvinists, he seemed particularly concerned to avoid letting the doctrine of salvation by grace be construed as divine ukase (*YP* 2:293).[47] In the same way that Milton would later insist that the limited knowledge available to even a corrupted conscience is sufficient to make repentance possible, *Areopagitica* insists that the universal effects of the Fall do not make sin inevitable for the kind of Christian believers that English rulers claimed to be.

The most direct way in which *Areopagitica* transforms the meaning of its own historical narrative, however, is by connecting its culminating event, the invention of licensing, specifically with the Eschaton, or end of the larger biblical story. Eschatology in Milton's England was inseparable from the interpretation of narratives from St John's Apocalypse, which were, in turn, deployed to support a larger Protestant historical narrative.[48] At one level, Milton simply links up the history of licensing with a customary Reformation account of medieval church corruption:

> After which time [800 AD] the Popes of *Rome* engrossing what they pleas'd of Politicall rule into their owne hands, extended their dominion over mens eyes, as they had before over their judgements, burning and prohibiting to be read what they fansied not. (*YP* 2:501–2)

In Milton's account, such practice then became 'stricter policy' at the first signs of the Reformation, in the writings of Wyclif and Husse, and culminated in the work of the Council of Trent and the Spanish Inquisition (*YP* 2:502–3). By describing prepublication licensing as part of the Antichristian practice of religious coercion, he invokes the cosmic battle between the saints and the Antichrist. This larger narrative context then underwrites his argument that unlicensed printing would allow England to continue the process of Reformation and avoid returning to the bondage of pre-Reformed legalism and superstition (*YP* 2:552–3). Just as in his earlier antiprelatical tracts (e.g., *YP* 1:524–5), *Areopagitica* situates its summary of Reformation history within the story of the saints' battle against Antichristian tyranny. Milton's central challenge is to locate the licensing of printing within that history, depicting licensing as a tool used only by the Dragon.[49] This is why Milton describes licensing as a practice issuing 'from the most Antichristian Councel, and the most Tyrannous Inquisition that ever inquired' (*YP* 2:505). The final paragraph of the tract puns on the name of the licensing authority under the episcopacy of William Laud, by describing the 'Star-chamber' as 'now fall'n from the Starres with *Lucifer*' (*YP* 2:569–70). Through this allusion to the biblically unique conjunction of falling 'stars' with the Dragon in Revelation 12, Milton situates the Licensing Order of 1643 within a cosmic battle between the saints and the Dragon, and clearly locates the practice of licensing on the side of the Dragon. Beyond such apocalyptic points in *Areopagitica*, a more general emphasis upon the Eschaton, or end of the biblical story, also recurs throughout the tract. The primary purpose of these references is to emphasize the ongoing nature of the Reformation, and the generally incomplete character of the human apprehension of truth before the Eschaton: 'we have not yet found [all the parts of Truth's beautiful form], Lords and Commons, nor ever shall doe, till her Masters second comming' (*YP* 2:549).[50] Through this passage and similar references to the Eschaton, Milton implies that the practice of licensing, which he extends to enforced religious conformity among Protestants generally, involves both a despair regarding whether the Eschaton will ever come, and a human presumption to judge matters that cannot be known and judged properly except by God. At the same time, beyond the fact that the Eschaton is conditional upon the antecedent contingent divine act of Creation, the particular timing of the Eschaton is also subject to divine will and is, in this further sense, a contingent act, in accord with divine decorum regarding the whole of Creation.

By basing his arguments against licensing upon his interpretation of the Creation, Fall, and Eschaton, Milton ensures that readers situate his initial history of publication censorship within a larger story that informs the meanings of the political events he recounts. Machiavelli disowns 'imagined republics' so that the reader may learn to reduce historical contingencies to knowledge of reality – that is, knowledge of the *virtù* (compulsion or deception) needed to impose an order on *fortuna.* Milton, by contrast, does not claim 'history' as a privileged alternative to imagined republics or abstractions. Instead, his own rhetorical practice suggests that he continues to see an important, if indirect, role for satire and the imagination more generally in guiding political action. Most importantly, to return to Machiavelli's historical explanation of the strife between the plebs and the Senate (*Discourses* 1.3.2), Milton would likely agree that such strife arose for the specific reasons that Machiavelli cites, but Milton would deny the inference that law, or the fear of violence, is necessarily the *only* means by which humans can live peaceably together. In short, Milton posits a metanarrative in which compulsion may occur but is simply not necessary because genuine human virtue is once again possible in the 'Christian liberty' effected by the redemptive work of Christ (*YP* 2:563).

Thus, *Areopagitica* evokes Machiavellian commonplaces regarding the recovery of liberty and the disowning of imagined republics in order to challenge the Machiavellian purposes for studying history. Milton does this by situating his own account of licensing within the unique historical contingencies of a larger biblical narrative, events that he does not reduce to abstractions. In the same stroke, Milton foregrounds the incompatibility between the larger narrative assumed by Machiavelli and the overarching story of Scripture. This kind of narrative indirection that nevertheless engages Machiavelli enables Milton to do two things at the same time: first, it underwrites his satirical indictment of those who would persist in supporting the Licensing Order; second, it enables Milton to reveal the Machiavellian assumptions regarding reality that the Licensing Order embodies. For Milton, reality has an appearance, but one whose intelligibility is not exhausted by the alternatives of random motion and human determinations to control that randomness. Although human participation in reality is presently obscured by the dual effects of finitude and fallenness, Milton insists that 'Truth came once into the world' and that humans are made for participation in the 'beatific vision' (*YP* 2:549). Moreover, he bases his hope for the latter on his claim to partial but genuine knowledge of the former.

The most immediate and striking way in which Machiavelli and Milton differ in their use of historical argument is the extent to which they are willing to be explicit about their own rhetorical aims. Although Machiavelli assumes that the purpose of his political teaching is to preserve political power, his historical claims are never stated in that way. Instead, his persistent rhetorical stance is one of mere historical description regarding 'the effectual truth' (*Prince*, ch. 15), repeatedly implying that he simply describes the way things are, necessarily. By contrast, *Areopagitica* is explicit that its purpose is not simply to describe the truth of past events but to tell that story with a view to further suasive aims. One may well object to Milton's purpose, or one may argue that his goal misleads his selection of evidence, but there is no pretence on Milton's part that he has no rhetorical aim. In this respect, Milton's use of history is more openly rhetorical. Why is this important? At one level, the explicitly rhetorical character of *Areopagitica* reflects Milton's view that created reality is a persuasive act; at another level, the use of rhetoric is central to the way that Milton aims to help educate readers against tyranny.

Milton's appeal to history overtly situates each mode of rhetoric – forensic, epideictic, and deliberative – within the aims of another mode. His initial history of licensing draws upon what would be, considered in themselves, forensic arguments regarding contingent past events.[51] The attempt to verify the character of past events, however, is embedded from the outset in a further epideictic rhetorical purpose, as Milton maintains that his readers will be 'loath to own' 'the inventors' of licensing (*YP* 2:491). The aim of establishing the blameworthy character of licensing's originators is itself, in turn, subsumed by the tract's larger deliberative goal of reversing the 1643 Licensing Order.

What I draw to attention here is that, through rhetorical engagement with the larger biblical story, *Areopagitica* also implicitly unfolds the connections between these rhetorical modes into the world beyond itself. The larger purpose of the main deliberative argument regarding the Licensing Order is to result in historical action whereby Parliament would locate England in a properly co-operative ethical relation to the unfolding biblical metanarrative, specifically between the Ascension and the Eschaton. Any subsequent forensic narration of those contingent ethical actions would find its ultimate fulfilment for Milton in the beatific vision, which is a kind of eternal epideictic. In gesturing toward this larger story, however, Milton's consistent emphasis is upon the possibility of such ethical action, not its inevitability. In this respect, the contrast that Barker identifies, between history as 'progressive degeneracy' in the 1641 prose and 'the future as a progression from truth to truth' in *Areopagitica*, should be qualified, in that, for Milton, the participation of any particular human or group in either the degeneration or the progress is not inexorable.[52] In other words, *Areopagitica* first intimates the seeds of thought that will eventually lead to an Arminian view in which, amid confidence in the realities of the Eschaton and the Beatific vision, the participation of particular humans in those realities remains contingent upon their response to a prevenient grace that is not distributed equally but is universally sufficient for salvation.[53]

Milton is explicitly rhetorical, in a manner different from Machiavelli, because Milton's indirect aim is to teach his readers how to discern tyrannical speech and action in rulers. Beyond simply warning his readers against the danger of tyranny from a Presbyterian Parliament, Milton's other central task in *Areopagitica* is to teach readers how to distinguish between political deception and the authentic manifestations of reality in which moral virtue participates. As Victoria Kahn puts it, Miltonic Truth is 'absolute,' yet not coercive in the sense of being reducible either to the threat of violence or to mere deception.[54] Nevertheless, because of her emphasis upon the coercive potential in Machiavellian rhetoric, the details of Kahn's analysis tend to obscure her own qualifications on this point. Milton's appeal to 'things indifferent' (*adiaphora*) is distinct from both the Independent view that nothing is indifferent and the Episcopal view that the sphere of indifferency is the realm of civil compulsion. In contrast to both, Milton grants the enlargement of the sphere of *adiaphora*, but he does so in order to insist that such a realm precludes rather than permits state-sponsored religious conformity among Protestants.[55] According to Kahn, however, by 'making indifference a matter of individual judgment,' Milton's argument 'illustrates' 'the impossibility of telling the difference between indifference and Machiavellism.'[56] Despite arguing for 'a positive conception of truth as simply different from coercion and falsehood,' Milton, in Kahn's view, conflates 'truth with the realm of things indifferent,' thereby giving a central place to 'individual judgment' but also threatening 'to undermine the notion of truth itself.' She concludes: 'if truth is undermined or uncertain, then the license of individual judgment can only be rhetorical, in the sense of appealing to a contingent configuration of circumstances and interests.'[57] I contend, however, that Milton distinguishes between 'indifference and Machiavellism' on the basis of his belief that both reality and truth (human intellective participation in created reality) are rhetorical, in precisely 'the sense of appealing to a contingent configuration of circumstances and interests.'

Thus, Milton does not conflate 'truth with the realm of things indifferent,' because he assumes that conscience can participate in the gift of the created order. This is why, for Milton, the use of such 'things,' whether food or books, is not merely arbitrary, or an excuse for debauchery; his food-book analogy assumes that the virtue of temperance, discernible by conscience, applies to both eating and reading (*YP* 2:512–13). Milton maintains the distinction between rhetoric and sophistry specifically because he views reality as intrinsically rhetorical, Creation coming into being through divine locution.[58] What distinguishes Milton's rhetorical appeal to the biblical metanarrative from alternative stories like Machiavelli's is the priority of gift over the assumed priority (indeed necessity) of compulsion and cunning in a fallen world.[59] Although events like the Creation, Fall, and Eschaton are emphatically contingent, in Milton's view, in the sense that they could have been otherwise (whether by human or divine will), that contingency is not reducible to the strife between *fortuna* and *virtù*. In this way, Milton's openly rhetorical deployment of historical narration is located within a larger biblical story whose appearance entails a vision of reality that contrasts directly with the assumed meta-narrative and ontology that he attributes to his putatively Machiavellian political opponents.

NOTES

1 George Grant, *Time as History*, ed. William Christian (1969; Toronto, 1995), 8–9.
2 Glenn Burgess, 'The "Historical Turn" and the Political Culture of Early Modern England: Towards a Postmodern History?' in *Neo-Historicism: Studies in Renaissance Literature, History, and Politics*, ed. Robin Headlam Wells, Glenn Burgess, and Rowland Wymer (Cambridge, 2000), 34.
3 Burgess, 'Historical Turn,' 31. In making this claim Burgess cites chapter 2 of Robert Berkhofer, *Beyond the Great Story: History as Text and Discourse* (Cambridge, MA, 1995), as well as Paul Christianson, 'Patterns of Historical Interpretation,' in *Objectivity, Method, and Point of View: Essays in the Philosophy of History*, ed. W.J. van der Dussen and Lionel Rubinoff (Leiden, 1991), 47–71.
4 Burgess, 'Historical Turn,' 33.
5 Burgess, 'Historical Turn,' 36.
6 Regarding, for example, Machiavelli's reliance upon the Epicurean atomist ontology of Lucretius, see Paul A. Rahe, *Against Throne and Altar: Machiavelli and Political Theory under the English Republic* (Cambridge, 2008), 32–45.
7 My thinking on this point is indebted to Paul Ricoeur, *Time and Narrative*, vol. 1, trans. Kathleen McLaughlin and David Pellauer (Chicago, 1984), 31–86.
8 See Niccolò Machiavelli, *The Prince*, 2nd ed., trans. Harvey C. Mansfield (Chicago, 1998), ch. 1 on his initial taxonomy, ch. 12 on the biconditional equivalence of 'good laws' and 'good arms,' and ch. 18 on the apparent division of *virtù* into 'laws' and 'force.' All subsequent quotations from *The Prince* are from this translation and will be cited parenthetically.

9 For example, see Stanley Fish, 'Driving from the Letter: Truth and Indeterminacy in Milton's *Areopagitica*,' in *Re-Membering Milton: Essays on the Texts and Traditions*, ed. Mary Nyquist and Margaret Ferguson (London, 1988), 234–5; John Illo, 'Areopagiticas Mythic and Real,' *Prose Studies* 11.1 (1988): 3–10; William David Kolbrener, 'Plainly Partial: The Liberal *Areopagitica*,' *ELH* 60 (1993): 59–64 (revised as ch. 1 of his *Milton's Warring Angels* [Cambridge, 1997]); David Norbrook, *Writing the English Republic: Poetry, Rhetoric and Politics, 1627–1660* (Cambridge, 1999), 119–20; and Nigel Smith, '*Areopagitica*: Voicing Contexts, 1643–5,' in *Politics, Poetics and Hermeneutics in Milton's Prose*, ed. David Loewenstein and James Grantham Turner (Cambridge, 1990),103–7. A recent exception to this tradition is Markus Klinge, 'The Grotesque in *Areopagitica*,' in *Milton Studies* 45, ed. Albert C. Labriola (Pittsburgh, 2006), 82–128.

10 Sirluck, *YP* 2:176–7. Compare Stephen Burt, '"To the Unknown God": St. Paul and Athens in Milton's *Areopagitica*,' *Milton Quarterly* 32 (1998): 23–8; Paul M. Dowling, '*Areopagitica* and *Areopgiticus*: The Significance of the Isocratic Precedent,' in *Milton Studies* 21, ed. Albert C. Labriola (Pittsburgh, 1985), 49–66; Illo, 'Areopagiticas Mythic and Real,' 4; Norbrook, *Writing the English Republic*, 125–32.

11 Illo, 'Areopagiticas Mythic and Real,' 12–17; Fish, 'Driving from the Letter,' 234–6; Kolbrener, 'Plainly Partial,' 59–64.

12 Compare Sirluck, *YP* 2:170–7; Victoria Kahn, *Machiavellian Rhetoric: From the Counter-Reformation to Milton* (Princeton, NJ, 1994), 173.

13 Martin Dzelzainis, 'John Milton, *Areopagitica*,' in *A Companion to Literature from Milton to Blake*, ed. David Womersley (Oxford, 2000), 151.

14 Abbe Blum, 'The Author's Authority: *Areopagitica* and the Labour of Licensing,' in *Re-membering Milton: Essays on the Texts and Traditions*, ed. Mary Nyquist and Margaret W. Ferguson (London, 1988), 77.

15 See, for example, Peter C. Herman, *Destabilizing Milton: 'Paradise Lost' and the Poetics of Incertitude* (New York, 2005), 23.

16 Markus Klinge, 'Grotesque in *Areopagitica*,' 82–128.

17 Thomas Fulton, '*Areopagitica* and the Roots of Liberal Epistemology,' *English Literary Renaissance* 34 (2004): 42–82. I focus on Klinge in the present essay because of his more detailed engagement of Sirluck's work.

18 Klinge, 'Grotesque in *Areopagitica*,' 85–6.

19 Klinge, 'Grotesque in *Areopagitica*,' 84–9. For a politically sympathetic but rhetorically negative reaction to *Areopagitica*, Klinge cites the well-known anonymous letter to Samuel Hartlib, from Leo Miller, 'A German Critique of *Areopagitica* in 1647,' *N&Q* n.s. 36 (1989): 29–30. Klinge supplies his own corrected translation of the German text (124n22).

20 Klinge, 'Grotesque in *Areopagitica*,' 87–93.
21 Klinge, 'Grotesque in *Areopagitica*,' 93–100, 108–11
22 Klinge, 'Grotesque in *Areopagitica*,' 100–8.
23 Klinge, 'Grotesque in *Areopagitica*,' 122.
24 Regarding Machiavelli's reception in seventeenth-century England, see Zera S. Fink, *The Classical Republicans: An Essay in the Recovery of a Pattern of Thought in Seventeenth-Century England*, 2nd ed. (Evanston, IL, 1962); J.G.A. Pocock, *The Machiavellian Moment: Florentine Political Thought and the Atlantic Republican Tradition* (Princeton, NJ, 1974); Blair Worden, 'Classical Republicanism and the Puritan Revolution,' in *History and Imagination*, ed. Hugh Lloyd-Jones et al. (London, 1981),182–200; Paul A. Rahe, 'Machiavelli in the English Revolution,' in *Machiavelli's Liberal Republican Legacy*, ed. Paul A. Rahe (Cambridge, 2006), 9–35. For an account of Machiavelli's reception in England that gives particular attention to Milton, see Kahn, *Machiavellian Rhetoric*, 85–165, esp. 169–235; and Rahe, *Against Throne and Altar*, 104–78. See also Barbara Riebling, 'Milton on Machiavelli: Representations of the State in *Paradise Lost*,' *Renaissance Quarterly* 49 (1996): 573–97; Paul Stevens, 'Milton's "Renunciation" of Cromwell: The Problem of Raleigh's Cabinet-Council,' *Modern Philology* 99 (2001): 382–9; William Walker, 'Human Nature in Republican Tradition and *Paradise Lost*,' *Early Modern Literary Studies* 10.1 (2004): 6.16–42, available at http://extra.shu.ac.uk/emls/10-1/walkmilt.htm. Compare Blair Worden, 'Milton's Republicanism and the Tyranny of Heaven,' in *Machiavelli and Republicanism*, ed. Gisela Bock, Quentin Skinner, and Maurizio Viroli (Cambridge, 1990), 225–45.
25 Niccolò Machiavelli, *Discourses on Livy*, trans. Harvey C. Mansfield and Nathan Tarcov (Chicago, 1996), 1.16.1–6. In what follows, this translation is cited parenthetically by book, chapter, and paragraph number.
26 For example, in *The Prince*, ch. 18, Machiavelli famously insists upon the political importance of rulers always appearing 'all mercy, all faith, all honesty, all humanity,' and most importantly, 'all religion.'
27 Compare Sirluck, *YP* 2:522n132, 526nn147–8.
28 Thomas More is not, of course, likely to have read Machiavelli's *Prince* before composing *Utopia* in 1515. Although *The Prince* had been composed in 1513, it was not published until 1532. Nevertheless, George M. Logan and Robert M. Adams contend in their introduction to *Utopia*, revised translation (Cambridge, 2002), xxiii, that Thomas More 'certainly knew the tradition of thought that [*The Prince*] crystallised.'
29 Miller, 'German Critique of *Areopagitica*,' 29–30.
30 Klinge, 'Grotesque in *Areopagitica*,' 93–100.

31 Compare *YP* 2:493, 502–7, 539–40.
32 Giuseppe Mazzotta, *Cosmopoiesis: The Renaissance Experiment* (Toronto, 2001), 59.
33 Because Milton's Commonplace Book draws most of its citations of Machiavelli from *The Discourses* (*YP* 1:414–15nn1–2), the discussion here will focus on that text. Any of the points that I make about *The Discourses,* however, may also be adduced from analogous passages in *The Prince.*
34 For an account of how Milton's social contract theory in *The Tenure of Kings and Magistrates* offers a direct contrast to that of Hobbes in *Leviathan,* see Phillip J. Donnelly, *Milton's Scriptural Reasoning: Narrative and Protestant Toleration* (Cambridge, 2009), 11–15.
35 Again, this offers a direct parallel with Hobbes's account of the social contract. See Donnelly, *Milton's Scriptural Reasoning,* 11–12.
36 Compare Machiavelli, *Prince,* ch. 6 and ch. 18 with his *Discourses,* 1.2.3 and 1.12–15.
37 Compare Machiavelli, *Prince,* ch. 18 with his *Discourses,* 1.12–14.
38 Ernest Sirluck, 'Milton's Critical Use of Historical Sources: An Illustration,' *Modern Philology* 50 (1953): 226–31. Sarpi's *Historia del Councilio Tridentio* (1619) had been translated into English twice by the time Milton composed *Areopagitica.* Compare *The Historie of the Councel of Trent,* trans. Nathanael Brent (London, 1620), and *The Historie of the Councel of Trent,* trans. Robert Gentilis (London, 1639). See Sirluck, in *YP* 2:492n23 and 500n54. Milton calls the author, 'Padre Paolo.' As Sirluck explains, 'Paolo Servita is the religious name of Pietro Sarpi (1552–1623),' *YP* 2:501n58.
39 See, respectively, regarding Creation, *YP* 2:527; the Fall, *YP* 2:514–15; the Incarnation *YP* 2:549; the Redemption, *YP* 2:563; the Ascension, *YP* 2:549; and the Eschaton, *YP* 2:549, 564.
40 Milton is quoting Titus 1:15.
41 Dzelzainis, 'John Milton, *Areopagitica,*' 151. Compare David Loewenstein, '*Areopagitica* and the Dynamics of History,' *SEL* 28 (1988): 77; David Loewenstein, *Milton and the Drama of History* (Cambridge, 1990), 35; Fish, 'Driving from the Letter,' 242; Kahn, *Machiavellian Rhetoric,* 175; Dayton Haskin, *Milton's Burden of Interpretation* (Philadelphia, 1994), 185–6, 217–19.
42 Fulton, '*Areopagitica* and the Roots of Liberal Epistemology,' 81–2.
43 In effect, for Milton, Christian virtue (sanctification), as distinct from mere civil conformity, arises from genuine saving faith and, as such, cannot be compelled by others, whereas the very attempt to compel such virtuous action reveals a tacit trust in salvation (justification) by works. See Phillip J. Donnelly, '*Paradise Regained* as Rule of Charity: Religious Toleration and the End of Typology,' in *Milton Studies* 43, ed. Albert C. Labriola (Pittsburgh,

2004), 173–6. Compare Nicholas von Maltzahn, 'Milton, Marvell, and Toleration,' in *Milton and Toleration*, ed. Sharon Achinstein and Elizabeth Sauer (Oxford, 2007), 97, as well as Donnelly, *Milton's Scriptural Reasoning*, 57–66.

44 Arthur Barker, *Milton and the Puritan Dilemma* (Toronto, 1942), 299–300.

45 Milton's view of creation's being (and its redemption) as a 'gift' should not be confused with what John Milbank describes as the 'immanentist parody' of Augustinian participation proffered by Martin Heidegger and subsequently adapted by Jacques Derrida in *Given Time I: Counterfeit Money*, trans. Peggy Kamuf (Chicago, 1991), 34–78, 134–61. See John Milbank, 'Can a Gift be Given?' in *Rethinking Metaphysics*, ed. L. Gregory Jones and Stephen E. Fowl (Oxford, 1995), 119–61.

46 Compare *YP* 6:192–3 and *Paradise Lost* 3.194–7.

47 The unequal distribution of divine election appears in *De doctrina Christiana* but only as election for specific service (*YP* 6:455–6) not for salvation, which is emphatically universal and conditional election (*YP* 6:192–3). Although any formulations in *De doctrina* would be much later than *Areopagitica*, the earlier tract is informed by impulses that could later issue in such doctrinal formulations.

48 As Loewenstein points out in *Milton and the Drama of History*, 49, when compared to Milton's earlier tracts, 'the apocalyptic rhetoric' of *Areopagitica* 'has been mollified to allow for a vision subtler and more generous than that of his earlier radical polemics.'

49 For a discussion of the apocalyptic aspects of *Areopagitica*, see Loewenstein, *Milton and the Drama of History*, 36–41, 48–50. Loewenstein also considers the tract's presentation of trial 'by what is contrary' in order to argue for 'Milton's poetics of history embracing the conflicts and contradictions of a dynamic, revolutionary process' (36). Loewenstein's focus differs from the present argument in that he is most interested in the sense of historical process evoked by Milton's writing, rather than in the uses that Milton makes of particular claims about the past.

50 Compare this with Milton's several allusions to parables and other biblical passages pertaining to the Eschaton, especially at *YP* 2:564–5. These passages are discussed further in Donnelly, *Milton's Scriptural Reasoning*, 35.

51 As Paul Rahe points out, Milton's source for the ecclesiastical part of his history of licensing, Sarpi's *History of the Council of Trent*, had its own rhetorical aims that extended far beyond any strictly forensic argument, most notably to attack the political viability of Christian belief generally, not just Catholicism; see Rahe's *Against Throne and Altar*, 149.

52 Barker, *Milton and the Puritan Dilemma*, 76.

53 See note 47 above.
54 Kahn, *Machiavellian Rhetoric*, 176
55 Kahn, *Machiavellian Rhetoric*, 173–4.
56 Kahn, *Machiavellian Rhetoric*, 174.
57 Kahn, *Machiavellian Rhetoric*, 178–9.
58 For an account of how Milton's view of Creation relates to his view of ontology and Protestant toleration, see Donnelly, *Milton's Scriptural Reasoning*, 49–69.
59 See note 45 above.

17 Ibn Tufayl's Hayy and Milton's Adam

MUHAMMAD SID-AHMAD

With an 'Arabick interest' in early modern England brought to the foreground by several historians and literary critics, chief among whom are G.A. Russell, C.J. Toomer, and Nabil Matar, it may be time to revisit a particular Arabic text: the twelfth-century Arabic mystical-philosophical tale, *Hayy bin Yaqzan.*[1] The tale follows the life of the main character, Hayy bin Yaqzan, which can be translated into Alive son of Awake (or Aware). After two stories of the child's birth – one spontaneous generation from the earth, the other natural – the tale provides Hayy's observations about his natural surroundings and himself: his careful dissection, described in medical terms, of his 'mother,' a roe; his use of reason to reach conclusions on the nature of God, which occupies most of the tale; and finally his mystical visions. Critical discussion of the *Hayy*'s place in seventeenth-century England ranges from its general cultural and intellectual influence to more focused discussion of Daniel Defoe's engagement with the *Hayy* in *Robinson Crusoe.*[2] I would like to begin another discussion, namely that of the *Hayy*'s possible influence on Adam's story of his earliest memories in book 8 of Milton's *Paradise Lost.* The process Adam describes and the conclusions he reaches while in a prelapsarian state so closely parallel the process of natural reasoning Hayy goes through that we might explore the possibility of the *Hayy* having influenced *Paradise Lost.*

I The Seventeenth-Century Interest in Arabic

The seventeenth century corresponds with what Stephen O'Shea describes as the third stage of Islamic-Christian relations. The first, a period of 'mutual ignorance,' begins in the seventh century with the birth of

Islam, and the second, the 'high-water mark of conflict,' extends from around the eleventh to the thirteenth centuries.[3] The third extends from the late medieval to the early modern periods, when commercial interests were on the rise. This, the age of Milton, is also a period of cultural exchange. England joined other European powers to establish trading and diplomatic relations with the Ottoman port as well as other smaller Muslim kingdoms in North Africa. The third period also coincides with increased English biblical and scientific scholarship, which benefited from access to Arabic-speaking lands. The English set up the Levant Company in Ottoman cities, where chaplains were stationed. The resident chaplains in Aleppo and Smyrna wrote travel books and collected manuscripts, especially after Bishop Laud, minister for Charles I, required that all ships returning from the East bring an Arabic or Persian manuscript.[4] There was in fact competition between European collectors and their patrons to acquire as many manuscripts as possible. English and European patrons' and Arabists' collections eventually found their way to Cambridge and Oxford libraries, with Oxford in particular becoming a major centre of eastern learning in Europe.

Why was there such a strong interest in Arabic at this time? First, the Reformation brought about interest in biblical sources, and Arabic was considered ancillary to Hebrew. There were in fact well-established Jewish traditions of biblical exegesis, themselves modelled on Arabic exegesis of the Qur'an, whose science of linguistic analysis produced many lexicons and dictionaries. The Jewish traditions, which developed in Spain, included Hebrew lexicons from which Christian scholars could draw.[5] The polyglot Bibles of the sixteenth and seventeenth centuries are products of these traditions. Trained in oriental languages, including Arabic, theologians and biblical scholars used Old Testament and rabbinical commentaries to interpret biblical passages. In addition to interpretation, members of the Church of England were interested in Eastern Christian churches whose independence from Rome was seen as justification for an English national church. When direct knowledge of Eastern churches replaced the reprinted and often-quoted medieval texts about the east, differences between Protestant and Eastern churches emerged.[6] The second major reason for interest in Arabic was secular. The spirit of experimental science in the early modern period spurred interest in medicine, astronomy, mathematics, and even geography and history. The accuracy of medieval Latin translations of Arabic texts, which contained a synthesis of Roman, Greek, and Arabic knowledge, was questioned; the Arabic originals were sought and new translations appeared. Errors in the medieval translation of Avicenna's seminal medical text the *Canon*, for example, were corrected in the sixteenth-century edition (1595). Arabic texts in mathematics, such as Alhazen, received similar treatment. The new early modern translations showed that errors in the earlier versions resulted from the 'ignorance of the interpreter rather than the inelegance of the Arabe,' according to a contemporaneous mathematician.[7] The need for Arabic manuscripts and translations was practical, as European and English astronomers and doctors, who sought the medicinal uses of plants, compared their observations with more accurately translated texts.

Religious and secular interests combined to spur the early modern interest in Arabic, known as the second Arabic interest, the first occurring in the medieval period. This second period of interest culminated in the institutionalization of Arabic studies at Cambridge and Oxford, but the journey can be traced through some important personages, the first of whom is Robert Wakefield. His *Oratio de laudibus & utilitate trium lingaurum Arabicae Chaldaicae & Hebraicae* was published in 1528, anticipating the introduction of Arabic to the formal training of theologians later in the century.[8] Wakefield's *Oratio* contained Arabic type, probably its first appearance in England.[9] Wakefield learned Hebrew and Syriac, and taught in Tübingen before returning to England in 1519 and becoming chaplain to Henry VIII.

The second major figure, considered the patriarch of Arabic studies in England, is William Bedwell, who produced an Arabic version of the Johannine Epistles. With the encouragement of Lancelot Andrewes, Bedwell produced his 800-page *Arabic-Latin Lexicon*, printed in 1595 through the Dutchman Thomas Erpenius. With French-Ottoman political and commercial links offering access to Eastern Christians, a Maronite College was established in Rome, where the Maronite Gabriel Sionita taught Arabic. He also taught in Paris, where Protestant scholars Erpenius and the German Matthias Pasor studied Arabic in 1609 and 1624–5, respectively. Protestant Orientalism charted its own course, with Erpenius replacing the self-taught Francis Raphelengius as the second professor of oriental languages in Leiden in 1613; when Erpenius died, his pupil James Golius filled his position in 1624. Pasor settled in England where he taught Edward Pococke, whose other teacher of Arabic was Bedwell. After graduating from Cambridge, Pococke became chaplain to the Levant Company in Aleppo in 1630, and in 1637 visited Constantinople with his friend the mathematician John Greaves. In Aleppo, Pococke cemented his knowledge of Arabic; he had two teachers, one Jewish, the other Muslim. He had a local agent in Aleppo, where European collectors and patrons competed for manuscripts in oriental languages. Pococke, Laud, Robert Huntington, Golius, and John Selden's collections became housed at Oxford while Erpenius's large collection found a home in Cambridge. The manuscript of the *Hayy* was brought to England by Pococke on his return to England in 1636.

Edward Pococke and his fellow Cambridge graduate Abraham Wheelocke were the first chairs of Arabic in Oxford and Cambridge, respectively. Though it followed Cambridge in founding the study of Arabic by two years, Oxford, where Arabic was instituted in 1634, became the centre of Arabic learning in all of Europe largely due to Pococke's learning and fame. The main lobbyists for the institutionalization of Arabic at the universities were biblical scholars and physicians. Coinciding with the university reforms in the seventeenth century was another major development: Arabic became a requirement for the Arts Degree, attesting to the status and popularity of the language at the time.[10] In the mid-seventeenth century, London was a centre of sorts for the study of Arabic: it was taught by private tutors and at Westminster, where upper-form students made orations in the language.[11]

The early modern interest in Arabic was so great that, as G.A. Russell notes, it 'permeated English society at all levels, to include the court, the clergy, the colleges of universities, diplomatic service as well as mercantile companies.'[12] Making a similar remark, Nabil Matar emphasizes that Arabic knowledge was common in privileged environments and the 'subculture of the British populace,' especially with Ross's translation of the Qur'an in 1649, when London booksellers' records show people inquiring about copies.[13] Many Arabic manuscripts were translated with the Arabic and Latin appearing side by side. More were translated only in part and were included in larger works, especially histories and scientific encyclopaedias. With such high, widespread interest, it is not surprising that news of new manuscript acquisitions from Aleppo, Smyrna, or elsewhere would circulate, and new translations would be eagerly anticipated. Describing how the Royal Society worked under its first secretary, Henry Oldenberg, M.B. Hall has shown that letters were sent with queries covering a range of topics, the bulk of which enquired about manuscript sources of Islamic and Greek texts (in Arabic), medical or botanical terms, and translations of and commentaries on biblical texts. Others inquired about astronomy, geography, and history. The interest did not start with the establishment of the society, of course, but the society illustrates the reputation England had for oriental learning among Europeans. The German-born Oldenberg exemplifies this, as he travelled to England and mingled with members of Milton's circle before settling in England, where he acted as Boyle's publisher and translator. In fact, Oldenberg met Milton, who commended his fluency in English and asked to be counted as a good friend.[14] Oldenberg also replaced Milton as the tutor of Boyle's nephew.[15]

There is no evidence that Milton knew Arabic. He did, however, have access to Arabic learning, and he definitely saw Arabic in print, not to mention the fact that he was a member of circles that discussed Arabic learning. Milton's use of a variety of encyclopaedias of science is well known, and these encyclopaedias often contained references to Arabic natural philosophers. One example is *De Sphaera* (1608), which included a section in Latin from the Arab astronomer Alfraganus; it is from this section that Milton derives the two names of the planet Venus used in *Paradise Lost.*[16] Also, many of Selden's works contained Arabic in print, such as his *Mare Clausum* (1635), *De successionibius in bona defuncti* (1636), and *De juri naturali* (1642), which Milton studiously read and owned.[17] Milton also owned some of Jacobus Golius's books, including *De veritate religionis Christianae,* which Pococke translated into Arabic.[18] Milton was deeply immersed in Protestant culture, in which knowledge of Hebrew and other oriental languages was commended; he learned Hebrew, Chaldian, and Syriac and taught his nephews the three languages.[19] Milton seems to have relied on the *Polyglot Bible* (1657) – a work containing Arabic and to which Pococke and other Arabists contributed – as a source for the phrase 'Domini ecclesiam' from Syriac for his *De doctrina Christiana.*[20] As for Arabic, Milton seems to have relied on translations, as is the case in book 11 of *Paradise Lost,* where the description of the 'just men' (573–87), as Don Cameron Allen has shown, has as its source Eutychius or Said-ibn-Batrik. Batrik's *String of Jewels* was translated by Pococke and printed in 1658, with the Arabic original and Latin translation appearing side by side. Milton could have had access to Eutychius as early as 1642, when the jurist, Hebraist, and Arabist John Selden printed selections from it in his *Ecclesiae suae Origines.* Many of Selden's works, which discuss oriental, biblical learning, were sources for Milton, as Jason P. Rosenblatt shows.[21] Milton may also have consulted Bochart's work on biblical natural history, *Hierzoicon,* which also contained Arabic commentaries.[22] A more systematic review of Arabic resources available to Milton would uncover many more. It is certain, though, that the fame of Selden and Edward Pococke as Arabic (and Hebrew) scholars could not have escaped him; Pococke held professorships of both Arabic and Hebrew at Oxford, and Selden was his successor in the post. One can imagine that, like his contemporaries, Milton would have heard about newly acquired manuscripts, anticipated forthcoming translations, and discussed the content of the Arabic texts, just as members of his learned circle, Boyle, Hartlib, and many others, did. Milton's close relationship with Hartlib and Boyle is well known. One of the texts discussed by the two prior to its publication is the *Hayy*.

II *Hayy bin Yaqzan*: Circulation

The first translation of the *Hayy* to appear in print in England was in Latin, and this was in 1671 (more below). Over a decade before that, however, members of Milton's circle were enquiring about the *Hayy* in anticipation of Pococke's translation of the Arabic treatise into English. Correspondence in 1659 shows Worthington inquiring about the *Hayy* of Hartlib, who in turn writes to Boyle. Hartlib thanks Boyle for a printed copy of Pococke's translation of an Arabic treatise on coffee, becoming fashionable in England at the time, but also inquires about the *Hayy*.[23] The treatise on coffee shows both the interest in Arabic translations and the degree to which the manuscripts chosen for translation were topical; Hartlib adds that the paper on coffee 'wil be gustful no doubt to our coffee drinkers, and who may add as many more good observations from their own experience.' One can assume similar interest in the *Hayy*. In fact, Hartlib mentions Worthington's 'huge commendations' of the *Hayy* to him in his letter, suggesting, as is expected in these circles, that the *Hayy* was talked about prior to its expected appearance in print. The *Hayy* may have been talked about before 1640, according to Matar, as Pococke returned from Aleppo with the manuscript in the late 1630s, and one can imagine him talking about the *Hayy* to students and other acquaintances. After all, Pococke acquired the manuscript. The correspondence between Worthington, Hartlib, and Boyle continues in 1660, 1661, and 1662. Reference is made to Pococke's translation and publication of an Arabic poem, *Altograi*, with an inquiry again about whether the *Hayy* is 'appended' to the poem. Milton might have heard of the *Hayy* and its themes as early as 1640, or in the late 1650s and early 1660s, the time when he was composing *Paradise Lost*.

Pococke the Elder's English translation of the *Hayy* has never emerged. The first translation to be published was by his son, also called Edward, and, as mentioned above, this translation was published in Latin in 1671, under the title *Philosophus autodidactus sive epistola Abi Jaafar, Ebn Tophail de Hai Ebn Yokdan*. There was a bit of confusion over the translator's identity; at least in Europe, the translation was thought to be the work of the father, who wrote an introduction to it. The Pocockes were royalists for whom the *Hayy* was presented as a good example of rational religion, advocated against enthusiasts; Pococke the Younger dedicated his Latin translation of the *Hayy* to the archbishop of Canterbury.[24] Nonetheless, Latin made the *Hayy* accessible to nonconformists as well. Indeed the first translation into English from the Latin was by the Quaker George Keith in 1674. To him, the *Hayy* confirmed Quaker belief in the inner light inhabiting everyone, including pagans in a natural state, as Hayy was able to gain knowledge of God without the aid of revelation and official church – it is in this spirit that the Quaker apologist Robert Barclay cites it.[25] The *Hayy* also illustrated these teachings in a coherent narrative form, hence its popularity among Quakers. Keith gave a copy of his translation to the Cambridge Platonist Henry More, who gave it to Anne Conway. Thus both proponents of rational religion and enthusiasts used the *Hayy* to bolster their positions. The second translation from the Latin was George Ashwell's, who saw it as instructive, through the light of natural reason, of divine truths. His translation, published in 1686, begins with a preface that censures extremes of religious belief. He seems to have taken the middle ground, for he censures enthusiasts, who believed in direct illumination, scoffers, who ridiculed religion altogether, the 'Covetous Worldlings,' and the 'intemperate,' who were advised to learn from the *Hayy* the 'Virtues of Temperance, and modesty.'[26] Like some of his contemporaries, Ashwell thought Pococke the Elder, '[the] famed professor at Oxford,' the translator of the *Philosophus autodidactus.* The third translation into English was by an Arabist equal in learning to Pococke the Elder. This was Simon Ockley, author of the *History of the Saracens.* Unlike Keith and Ashley, Simon Ockley did not depend on the Latin, but translated directly from the Arabic original into English. It is his translation, published in 1708, that is edited and republished in 1929.[27] Nawal Hassan mentions another abridged translation by an anonymous translator (1696). Hence talk of the *Hayy* prior to its publication as early as the 1640s, two Latin editions of the *Autodidactus* toward the end of the seventeenth century, and several English translations make the *Hayy* a popular text indeed, largely because of its narrative vehicle, which 'at once, appeals to the mind as well as the imagination.'[28]

III *Hayy bin Yaqzan*: Content

Pococke's Latin translation unsurprisingly watered down the *Hayy*'s Islamic content. All translations, however, mention that the author is Muslim and include Qur'anic verses and motifs, especially those with biblical echoes. Ashwell does not translate from the Latin word for word but takes 'more liberty,' as he says in the preface, to keep the sense of the treatise for his English readers. So in a way, Ashwell's translation is closer to an oral discussion of the *Hayy* prior to its publication. One can imagine that commendations of the *Hayy*, such as the ones Worthington makes to Hartlib, spread by word of mouth. The nature of oral transmission involves some fluidity, omission, and especially expansion. Discussants move from one topic to the next, so one can imagine discussion moving from Hayy's spontaneous generation from the earth to the wider topic of the creation of Adam and Eve or comparisons with Christian and Jewish ideas. The different stages of Hayy's life, the circumstances of his birth, which simultaneously recall Adam and the prophet Moses, his observations of nature and his thinking about nature at different stages of his life are other topics that could have been discussed. Comparison of the state of nature with the state of society, which appears toward the end of the *Hayy*, would have certainly invited some comment by seventeenth-century English discussants. Oral discussion of the text would not be as ordered and true to the original as Keith and Ockley's translations are. Because he takes more liberty in his translation, and hence reveals the preoccupations of seventeenth-century readers of the text, I rely on Ashwell's translation in this essay.

It should be noted that Ashwell attempts to make Hayy's spontaneous generation from the earth acceptable by adding that the idea may have originated in Avicenna, well known to seventeenth-century English readers as a philosopher and physician.[29] Ashwell's purpose is to make the unfamiliar notion familiar or acceptable to his readers by associating it with the respected Avicenna. Pococke and Keith had censured spontaneous generation, which Ashwell here tacitly defends, suggesting that the subject had some currency. Ashwell treats another unfamiliar idea in the *Hayy* in a similar way; this is the possibility of stars being 'intelligent bodies,' as he advises his readers that classical philosophers, for example Aristotle and Plato, and church fathers, such as St Jerome and St Augustine, considered this possibility. Ashwell is again trying to make the idea, and by extension the *Hayy*, acceptable. He commends the *Hayy* for dealing with knowledge of God through natural reason in an accessible way. Other writings on the subject, he complains, are 'too subtle, sublime and metaphysical for common understanding,' unlike the *Hayy*, Ashwell adds, which 'uses gentle steps in an easy and familiar way of reasoning' (4, 5). In addition to being a book of natural reason, Ashwell pronounces the *Hayy* a book of nature and of natural theology.

The *Hayy* contains subjects that were very topical in seventeenth- and early eighteenth-century England. The plot is developed to illustrate that one can, without the aid of revelation, know and apprehend God by the observation of nature. The senses, then reason, and finally meditation are the means to knowledge of God. Through meditation one can ascend to the 'supream sphere,' described as 'settled in the highest Degree of delight and Joy, Exultation and Gladness, by reason of the Vision of that true and glorious Being' (144). It is emphasized that none of the senses is used in this meditative state. The apprehension of God, however, is preceded by the knowledge of God through the use of reason. Hayy's detailed speculative reasoning occupies most of the book, and is based on his observation and examination of nature. At this first stage, he uses his senses to observe, contemplate, and analyse his natural surroundings. The movement from the use of the senses in the observation of nature, to the application of natural reason leading to knowledge of God, and finally to meditation, which ends in the apprehension of God, clearly interested seventeenth-century English readers.

Another topical element in the *Hayy* is its treatment of the state of nature and natural man. Medieval writers debated whether pagans could attain salvation. Some entertained the idea that through natural reason, they could become virtuous. The best example of virtuous heathens appears in *Mandeville's Travels*, where they live in a state of nature, without private property and political society. In the early modern period, the main group that followed this tradition were the Quakers, who replaced natural reason with the inner light, which they believed inhabited all human beings. Reformation and mostly mercantile expansion produced another discourse, culminating in John Locke's juxtaposition of the state of nature and the state of society. The two discourses can be explained in terms of the difference between the term 'primitive,' understood as original, simple, and pure, and the term 'savage,' referring to peoples uncivilized and perhaps incapable of becoming civilized.[30] Quakers regarded the Indians of the New World as having inner light,[31] whereas Locke in the *Two Treatises* explains the difference between the state of nature and the state of society in terms of development, characterized by labour, private property, and consent to set boundaries of cities. At the same time, in his second chapter, 'Of the state of Nature,' Locke refers to America as an 'uncultivated wast' and the Indians as 'wretched inhabitants.'[32] He also uses the metaphor of an island that has no commerce with the rest of the world to illustrate his point about the uselessness of private property and civil society in a state of nature.

In the *Hayy*, two islands are juxtaposed. One is uninhabited. This is where Hayy lives. The other island is a city-state ruled by a king who executes laws that protect private property. At the end of the story, Hayy visits the city-state whose inhabitants, he soon discovers, are ruled by their passions and lust for property, incapable of reason and deeper spirituality. He deems them no better than beasts. The *Hayy* inverts Locke's hierarchical relation between nature and civil society. In short, the *Hayy*, on the one hand, appealed to Quakers and other nonconformists by means of what I would call its spiritual discourse, which focuses on Hayy's natural reason and spiritual meditations, while, on the other hand, it challenged theorists occupied with the political and social organization of England, such as Hobbes and Locke.

The *Hayy*'s plot is simple, but the beginning is both interesting and important enough to be censured by Pococke and Keith. It is also memorable. The setting, as we have mentioned, is an uninhabited Indian island 'blest with a most pleasant and temperate Air' beside which is another island filled with 'all the commodities of life ... well inhabited' and 'govern'd by a Prince of a proud and jealous Disposition' (1). The prince rejects all of his sister's suitors, but she marries in secret and becomes pregnant. When she delivers, the princess fears for her son's life, so she places the newborn in a chest and trusts it to the sea. For those familiar with the Qur'an and certainly for seventeenth-century English readers familiar with the Bible, her prayers for the newborn recall both Moses's mother and the Virgin Mary. The chest drifts to the uninhabited island and lodges in a 'shady Grove … thick set with Trees.' It is a 'very pleasant place, sheltered from Wind and Weather, Rain and Sun' (3–4).

Parallels between this setting and Adam's on first gaining consciousness are not clear, but they become apparent when we consider what the *Hayy* narrator calls Hayy's real beginning, spontaneous generation from the earth, which, he says, may be difficult for some readers to accept, and that is why he provides the more acceptable story of the princess who marries in secret. As the narrator anticipates, the *Hayy*'s unexpected seventeenth-century translators Pococke and Keith censured spontaneous generation, which, as we have seen above, Ashwell attempted to make familiar to his readers in the preface to his translation. When he discusses spontaneous generation, the *Hayy* narrator explains how the weather enables this generation, referring to natural philosophy and astronomy. To the unconvinced, the story of the prince's sister is provided, after which the narrator returns to the island whose perfect conditions, he informs us, combine to allow a large piece of the earth to come closest to the 'Temper of Man's Body.' The conditions involve a balance of temperature and dryness; 'the Hot was so equally mix'd with the Cold, and the Moist with the Dry, that none of 'em prevailed.' This piece of the earth receives its 'Light from the highest possible Point in the Heavens.' Heat from the light results in fermentation, and hence 'arose some Bubbles by reason of its [the soil's] viscousness.' The narrator is specific: the heat is attributed to the sun's light or rays. In the midst of the bubbles, a part of the earth is in the right condition to receive a spirit from God. It grows to become Hayy bin Yaqzan, Alive son of Awake or Aware.[33] The main ingredient of Hayy's spontaneous generation, then, is a part of the earth that is viscous, moist, and vaporous, and, heated by the light of the sun, it ferments. This part of the earth is in the perfect condition to receive a spirit from God, and so it grows into a human being.

Once the natural setting and the alternative births are provided, the rest of the *Hayy* is divided into three parts: the discovery of the soul, speculative reasoning, and meditation. In the first section, a roe answers the child's cries for nourishment, and acts as the child's mother. Eventually, though, the roe dies, spurring Hayy to begin his long journey to knowledge of God as he tries to revive her. In his attempts to learn what ails her, Hayy, finding no cause on the outside, decides to dissect her; this process is described with precision, as the twelfth-century author of the *Hayy* is also a physician. Hayy reaches the ribs, which he believes must be protecting the most important part of the body. With some difficulty, he reaches the heart where he finds two cavities, the left empty. Now he begins to think that perhaps there is something in this cavity, and perhaps it has left and gone somewhere else (22–5). Soon Hayy gets the opportunity to catch a wild beast, which he dissects before the animal dies, and, on reaching the left cavity, he finds that it is filled with a 'certain airy or thin vaporous Substance, like unto a white Cloud or mist.' When he touches it, he finds it 'so hot, that it scald[s] him; and the wild Beast instantly die[s].' Perhaps this airy substance is what departed from his mother, and perhaps it is this that showed him love and affection. From this experiment, Hayy makes a generalization: all beasts have an airy substance that leaves when their bodies die (29–35).

The airy substance that beasts have, which Ashwell calls the animal spirit, leads Hayy to begin his speculative thinking. First he compares animals to himself and considers the possibility that he too may have a spirit, which Ashwell announces is the sensitive soul (53–4). Hayy then surveys the whole universe and starts to draw parallels with his own body; the different parts of his body are moved by his spirit, so perhaps the universe is the same with a spirit that moves all of the creatures inhabiting it. He also notices that all things have extension, shape, form, and corporeity (60–2). His observations of water, for example, teach him that it evaporates when heated. Heat is an accident external to the water, yet it changes the water's disposition; heat is also unlike the water's disposition (65–7). Hayy starts to search for the external accident, which he now thinks of as a voluntary agent, but this search, the narrator tells us, is limited to 'things Sensible' as Hayy's attention is mainly focused on the 'sensible world.' Hayy soon realizes that if the whole universe is like a body, then perhaps it too stands 'in need of a voluntary Agent' (67, 75). In other words, a spirit may move the whole universe, and this spirit, or agent, cannot have the same qualities as the things of the universe, that is, extension, shape, form, and corporeity. It should be noted here that Hayy's search for knowledge of the agent is described as a 'vehement desire' (66–7), an interesting comment on Hayy's psychology at this stage of speculative reasoning.

Hayy begins his meditations when he realizes that the voluntary agent cannot be sought among sensible things, i.e., in nature. The way to this realization is reflection upon his thought processes. Although he begins with observations of sensible things, he does not use any of his senses to reach his conclusions. He may have relied on his imagination, which represents the forms or images of things apprehended by the senses, but the apprehension of sensible objects, he reasons, precedes the thought process (78–9). And since the conclusions he reaches are about the agent that moves the universe – just as the animal spirit moves the roe when it is alive – then the agent cannot be a sensible object. In other words, this agent is apprehended 'by somewhat that is not a Body, nor faculty inherent in the Body' because it is an 'Incorporeal Substance' (90–1). If not part of the natural world, then how can the voluntary agent be known? This question troubles Hayy until he is able to draw an analogy with one of his senses: an eye that sees a beautiful and perfect object will desire to see it again, and the desire is proportionate to the beauty and perfection of that object. As for the incorporeal voluntary agent, Hayy's desire for knowledge of it is 'vehement' and since the desire and the thought processes it spurs are not in themselves sensible, Hayy believes that his very essence, his spirit, is of the same nature as the voluntary agent. To satisfy this vehement desire, Hayy decides to purify his thoughts of all sensible things so as to attain fuller knowledge of the voluntary agent.

He therefore decides to follow an ascetic lifestyle, which Ashwell attributes to '*Al-Jonaid,* that eminent Doctor and prince of the *Suphii*' (98–9), suggesting the expectation that seventeenth-century English readers are familiar with the names.

Asceticism brings us to the last stage in Hayy's journey, where he moves from the use of reason to meditation. His first attempts are interrupted by things of the sensible world, such as a 'sound of an animal or pain in his limbs,' so he decides to imitate the heavenly bodies, which he observes are constant in their motion. His experience with fire, which he chances upon, makes him draw comparisons between it and the heavenly bodies, especially the sun, due to the light and heat the fire produces (27–8). He also supposes that these bodies have knowledge of the voluntary agent, so he decides to imitate their action. He circles the whole island and then decides to stand in one place and rotate around himself as heavenly bodies do, but none of these movements enable him to remove sensible objects from his thoughts. He hence changes his routine in a way suggesting a theme common to seventeenth-century English writing: retirement.[34] Hayy sits still in a cave and eventually succeeds in having a vision. The narrator tells us that Hayy 'sit[s] mute and solitary' with his 'head bent down, and his Eyes fixed on the ground' until he succeeds in removing from his thoughts 'all sensible things, and corporeal faculties' (131). The result is a vision: 'the Heavens and the earth, and whatsoever is comprehended between them ... including himself ... were removed out of his Memory and thoughts ... whilst nothing remained with him besides that being, which is the only one, and the True one, and of permanent Existence' (132). Hayy apprehends God, who cannot be apprehended by the senses. Though he gains knowledge of the existence of God through reason, the apprehension of God requires vision in which all the senses, including the imagination, are abandoned.[35] The vision is described in terms of ascension through such cosmological spheres as those of the moon and Saturn to the 'supream sphere' (143–4), but this is only an analogy, as the *Hayy* narrator explains that the experience cannot be articulated in words.

IV Adam's Story: Parallels with the *Hayy*

The *Hayy* ends by confirming the superiority of natural man to civil man, or solitude in a state of nature to the state of society. What is important, though, is that the *History of Hayy bin Yaqzan* follows his journey first from the moment of birth, or spontaneous generation; second to his use of the senses and experimentation; third to his use of speculative reason; and finally to his renunciation of sense and sensible faculty, which completes the spiritual meditation in which he has a beatific vision. As we will see, these stages parallel Adam's in his recounting of his own story from the moment he gains consciousness. In book 8, Adam invites Raphael to hear his story (204–10).[36] Michael Lieb divides Adam's story into three parts. In the first, Adam describes his awakening, in the second his awareness of his natural surroundings and himself, which coincides with his use of reason, and in the third his desire to know and worship the creator whose existence he surmises through the use of reason.[37] There is, in fact, one more stage in which Adam becomes insensible and has a vision of God. In this final stage, Milton emphasizes that Adam does not use any of his senses when he has the vision.

Adam's first recollections are of awakening in a 'flourie herb.' The setting is not similar to the grove in which Hayy's chest lands; it does, however, remind us of the ingredients of Hayy's spontaneous generation. Adam describes the moment of gaining consciousness thus:

As new wak't from soundest sleep
Soft on the flourie herb I found me laid
In *Balmie Sweat,* which *with his Beames the Sun*
Soon dri'd, and on the *reaking moisture* fed (253–6; my emphasis)

There are two interesting elements in these lines. The first has to do with moistness. Adam awakes in 'Balmie Sweat,' which is also described as 'reaking moisture.' While the 'Balmie Sweat' may be a reference to the comfort and ease that Adam's generation from the earth involves, the second description, 'reaking moisture,' suggests fermentation. This is especially true if we think of it as *vaporous* moisture. Adam cannot detail the entire process, as the *Hayy*'s narrator does, because Adam can only describe the final stage(s), from the moment of his waking. In the *Hayy* the beginnings of spontaneous generation are described, from moist, fermenting earth to the point when it is ready to receive a spirit from God. The second element in the lines above is the sun. Milton is very careful to say that it is the sun's beams that dry Adam's moistness. This suggests that the heat from the sun is responsible for fermentation until, in the last stage of Adam's creation, moistness completely dries.[38]

The second parallel is Adam's reading of the book of nature. This parallels Hayy's observation on the natural world and his use of speculative reasoning. After he wakes up, Adam looks at heaven and quickly stands upright. Then he immediately starts to survey nature:

Strait toward Heav'n my wondring eyes I turn'd,
And gaz'd a while the ample Skie, till rais'd
By quick instinctive motion up I sprung,
As thitherward endeavoring, and upright
Stood on my feet; about me round I *saw*
Hill, Dale, and shadie Woods, and sunnie Plaines
And liquid Lapse of murmuring Streams; by these,
Creatures that livd, and movd, and walk'd, or flew,
Birds on the branches warbling; all things smil'd,
With fragrance and with joy my heart oerflow'd. (257–66)

Adam initially peruses natural phenomena, and what he sees makes him happy. However, when Adam peruses himself, 'Limb by Limb' (267), he wonders about his origin: 'But who I was, or where, or from what cause, / Knew not' (270–1). This knowledge should be sought, which suggests that in the preceding lines, Adam is actually thinking about nature and natural phenomena just as he is thinking about himself. He is thinking about origins. He is reasoning.

That Adam uses his senses and also thinks about nature is confirmed in the lines that follow. Adam first addresses nature before he gets the answer to his question, 'who am I?' '*Thou* Sun,' he says,

faire Light,
And *thou* enlight'nd Earth, so fresh and gay,
Ye Hills and Dales, ye Rivers, Woods, and Plaines
And *ye* that live and move, fair Creatures, tell,
Tell, if *ye* saw, how came I thus, how here?
Not of myself; *by some great Maker then,*
In goodness and in power præeminent (273–9; my emphasis)

The poetic address to nature suggests that the answer to the question might be found in reading nature. After describing the setting, Adam uses verbs that denote his use of the senses. He '*gaz'd* a while [at] the ample Skie,' '*saw* / Hill, Dale, and shadie Woods, and sunnie Plaines,' and 'Creatures that livd, and movd, and walk'd, or flew.' Then he '*perus'd*' and '*Survey'd*' himself 'Limb by Limb' (my emphasis). These observations, coming closer to an examination in the last verb, are followed by an interrogation of Adam's natural surroundings so that the conclusion he reaches, 'Not of my self; by some great Maker then,' is the result of his use of reason. This process parallels that of Hayy, who follows his observation of nature with logical conclusions about nature and himself. It is only then that he concludes that there must be a cause, a maker. The difference between the *Hayy*'s and Adam's stories lies in this: in the first we are provided with Hayy's reasoning while in the second only the *sequence* of Adam's reasoning is indicated. Yet like Hayy, whose recognition of a maker makes him both praise God and desire to know him, Adam describes God in terms of goodness and power, and follows this with a desire to 'know' and 'adore' God (8.280).

So far, Adam's story parallels the *Hayy* in generation from the earth, observation of nature, and logical conclusions on the existence of a maker. The next stage is the vision of God. Hayy decides that God has to be incorporeal and hence cannot be perceived sensibly. He retires to a cave, where he meditates in order to go beyond his senses, and this results in his vision of God. This stage occurs after he concludes that there must be a cause, whom he desires to know. It is significant that in this stage, the vision, Hayy has to banish all thought of the sensible world. Hayy's retirement in a cave, where he sits silently, reminds us of Quakers, Familists, and other 'Seekers or Waiters' in Milton's England: they wait in silence for anything that savours of the 'Divine Spring.'[39] In Hayy's case, and unlike Quakers whose visions do not follow the use of reason, the sequence involves the use of reason followed by the insensible stage, when vision is experienced. The same sequence occurs in Adam's story, so that after he avers the existence of a great maker, whom he desires to know and adore, Adam has a vision of God. Before the vision, Adam sits pensively and, significantly, loses consciousness of his senses, passing over to another state, one he 'thought' was 'Insensible,' a state similar to Hayy's (289–91). Adam describes his vision in terms of sleep:

> there gentle sleep
> First found me, and with soft oppression seis'd
> My *droused sense*, untroubl'd, though I thought
> I then was passing to my *former state*
> *Insensible*, and forthwith to *dissolve*:
> When suddenly stood at my Head a dream ... (287–92; my emphasis)

The 'droused sense' and the 'Insensible' condition into which Adam 'dissolve[s]' suggests that the 'former state' is really a new incorporeal state similar to the one Hayy reaches.

There are obvious differences between the visions that Adam and Hayy have. Adam is transported in the vision to the 'Garden of bliss,' and when he 'wak[es]' from the vision, he finds that what he has seen in the vision is 'all real, as the dream / Had lively shadowd' (*PL* 8.309–11). Waking from the dream into what appears to be another sensible world differs from Hayy's visions, which are described in abstract terms. Hayy's visions culminate in a union with God, and when Hayy wakes, he returns to the 'real' world, but in *Paradise Lost,* Adam wakes to find that what is shadowed in the dream is reality. Adam sees the garden, hears God, wanders, and sees the 'Presence Divine.' What Adam sees in the vision is an inspiration from God, but as Paul Stevens explains, Milton does not conceive of a vision in the Platonic sense, where the substance of the vision is intellectual, abstract, or ideal. Because for Milton the God-inspired vision has to have an image that can be seen (or a voice that is heard) to be comprehensible, Adam's vision includes the garden of bliss.[40] At the same time, Milton's use of the word 'shadowd' suggests that the vision itself occurs to Adam's incorporeal self; Adam's spiritual transportation may have accompanied the physical transportation, or it may have occurred before the physical transportation as a kind of foreshadowing. Whatever the case may be, Adam becomes insensible and when the vision begins, it is only his fancy that leads him to believe that he still has being. This points to the annihilation of self, as is explained below.[41]

Though the vision is inhabited with sensible images and God's voice and 'shape,' it could be understood as Milton making Adam's vision comprehensible by adding image and voice to it. So what seems to be a difference between Adam and Hayy's visions may be considered a similarity: both Adam and Hayy have visions of God, in which they lose their individuality, but while Adam's vision is expressed through image and voice, Hayy's vision is articulated in ideal and abstract terms. The *Hayy* narrator actually tells the reader that it is difficult to describe in mortal language the mystical experience that Hayy has; only an attempt to approximate the experience of the vision is provided. So I would suggest that Hayy's vision differs in that it conforms to the abstractness associated with Platonism and may actually be influenced by Neoplatonism. Hayy's vision is abstract; when the narrator describes it in terms of images and mirrors he does so in order to express the inexpressible to a reader who has not had a similar experience. The beatific vision itself is described in figurative, philosophic language; there is no image of God. Another obvious difference is that Adam's vision includes God giving him dominion while Hayy's beatific vision is in itself the purpose and objective of the dream.

Thus the *process* of Adam's vision is similar to Hayy's. First, Adam's sleep seizes him with 'soft oppression'; his sense becomes 'droused'; and he becomes 'Insensible.' Adam thinks he has fallen asleep and that he has had a dream, believing this a return to his former state. It is not a dream, however: the process described is not that of sleeping nor is this a return to his former state. We return to the *Hayy* to clarify. In order properly to apprehend God, Hayy must not mix his meditation with any sensible faculty, and he endeavours to do so by sitting silently and 'alienating himself from all sensible things, and corporeal faculties; his Mind and thoughts being wholly intent on that one necessarily existent Being' (131). When Hayy succeeds in having a vision, he loses consciousness not only of sensible objects but also of his own individual being. This is why Adam says that his 'fancy' led to him to believe he 'yet had being, / And livd' (8.294–5). These lines are significant because they suggest that his vision state necessitates the dissolution of his individual, independent being, but Milton conceives of the vision with the impress of image (and voice), retaining Adam's feeling of an individual identity for the vision to be comprehensible to him. The lines suggest that this vision of individual self is the robe that clothes the actual state in which Adam has no individual and independent being. When we compare the lines with Hayy's vision, we see the parallel. After he rids his thoughts of all sense and sensible faculty, Hayy first realizes that 'his own Being was not excluded [from] his thoughts.' He continues his meditation 'indeavour[ing to] wholly vanish out of his own Sight, and so be wholly taken up with the Vision of that true Being' (132). Thus when Hayy has the vision of God, he does not exist as an individual, independent being, but becomes one with God, a state known in Islamic mysticism as *fana'*, a term Sami Hawi translates as 'melting away' or 'fading away.'[42] This concept may have been alien to Milton's Christianity, but the parallel between Adam's and Hayy's vision processes is nevertheless suggestive of influence.

The parallels between Adam's and Hayy's visions can be made clearer if we consider why the apprehension of God requires the dissolution of the individual self. Hayy needs to remain in essence alone, an essence which he concludes he shares with God, in order to apprehend God, who is an 'Incorporeal Substance' (91). This explains why in his vision, Adam's 'sense' becomes 'droused,' as if in meditation. Only then can he apprehend the 'shape Divine' that raises him 'over Fields and Waters, as in Aire / Smooth sliding without step' (*PL* 8.289, 301–2). Adam's ability to reason and meditate until he becomes senseless stands in contrast to Eve's focus on her reflection on water, which, as Mary Nyquist has shown, suggests that her abilities are limited to the sensual, confirming Neoplatonic readings of the narcissistic act Eve performs.[43] The contrast highlights Adam's superior abilities, both mental and spiritual. Eve's looking down also points to what seems to be a difference between Adam and Hayy, where the latter, just before meditation, sits pensive; Adam, right after his creation, quickly stands up. However, the different directions of these acts of sitting and looking down and of standing and looking up occur in different stages. If we focus on the vision stage, Hayy's is expressed in terms of ascension through several spheres, where the image of God is described in terms of seeing the sun reflected in a series of mirrors, until he reaches direct vision. Adam sees a 'shape Divine' whereas in Hayy's vision, nothing remains to be apprehended but 'the only one, and the True one … of permanent Existence': 'the Heavens and the Earth, and whatsoever is comprehended between them … were removed out of his Memory and thoughts, together with his own Essence also among the rest … whilst nothing remained with him besides that Being' (132–3).

I conclude with a note speculating on how the *History of Hayy bin Yaqzan* may have been received. The early modern period saw the development of spiritual autobiography, of which Adam's story is an early illustration. Hayy's story, on the other hand, is biographical fiction. Yet the translator, George Ashwell, appends to the translation his own *Theologia ruris, siveschola & scala naturæ: Or, The Book of Nature.* The *Hayy* is referred to as a 'natural Theology' that 'expose[s] to our Eyes … the whole Book of Nature to read, with the ways and means, whereby almost all Arts and Sciences came to be invented' (sig.A8^{r}, B2^{r}). The *Theologia* is mostly a didactic echo of the *Hayy*, as Ashwell advises his readers to use their senses to contemplate nature from which they can learn about God. The individual components of nature, he explains, are but letters, which, 'when they are fitly joyned together, (as by Divine Providence, so by humane Meditation) meet as it were in words' (197). What is very curious, though, is that Ashwell addresses nature the same way Milton's Adam does and adopts the autobiographical 'I' in the process – though only in a couple of introductory pages. In other words, the biography of Hayy becomes the personal 'I' of the period. 'O ye pleasant Fields, ye Hospitable Shades, ye green grassy Hills, ye clear running Brooks,' the narrator Ashwell says, addressing nature, when he describes the pleasures he gets from it (195). A few lines after that, he makes an affirmation that echoes what is to be learnt from the *Hayy*: 'But God grant, that I may so fix my Eyes here, and gratifie my Senses, as not to neglect the improvement of my Mind' (196). This is perhaps how the *Hayy* was received: the biographical easily becomes autobiographical.

Ashwell's vocatives to nature can also be considered pastoral, of which two elements are noteworthy. One is song and imitation, where the pastoral shepherd's song is echoed and completed by other shepherds. As Alpers explains it, this exchange can be within a literary work or across literary works.[44] When across literary works, the newer work does not often openly acknowledge the previous one. This element appears in Ashwell's translation, as the narrator's vocatives echo Hayy's survey of nature, even though Hayy never really addresses nature. The knowledge that the Ashwell narrator prays God may grant him points to a desire to draw the same conclusions Hayy does. What is interesting is that in apparently imitating the *Hayy*, Ashwell's narrator condenses the larger part of the biography, where Hayy observes and makes conclusions about nature, into a few lines and does not openly acknowledge the *Hayy*. Of course the *Theologia* is appended to Ashwell's translation of the *Hayy* and hence clearly alludes to it, but my point here is that, first, the larger portion of the *Hayy* is summarized, and the summary does not openly mention the *Hayy*. In this case, it is assumed that the reader has read the *Hayy* and understands the allusion. The second point I would like to make is that the vocatives, in their brevity, are similar to Adam's in book 8 of *Paradise Lost*; it is hence not far-fetched to think that Milton has done the same with Adam, who echoes the *Hayy* in vocative and in summary. Also in the context of the pastoral tradition, the *Hayy* may have been seen as representative of the possibilities of what humankind can and should achieve, and so the allusion in the apparently simple vocatives in Ashwell's *Theologia* on the one hand conceals the complexity of the *Hayy* and, on the other hand, makes the arduous process of reasoning Hayy goes through seem natural. The second element of pastoral to appear in Ashwell's *Theologia* is that of a gathering of speakers, in this case metaphorically, that is, including readers, who are invited to participate in this natural theology, by observing nature, to improve their minds. The invitation to the various sects in Ashwell's preface to learn from the *Hayy* can be read in this context. Once the readers have read the *Hayy*, they can participate in the narrator's 'I' in the appended *Theologia*. In other words, the narrator's vocatives may be a way of calling all readers to participate in this natural knowledge, which leads to knowledge of God. Milton's Adam, of course, is in a prelapsarian condition. In considering Hayy a model for the speakers, Ashwell's narrator in the *Theologia* and Milton's Adam in *Paradise Lost* can be seen as commemorating Tufayl's

Hayy. Yet both Milton and Ashwell are indirectly contributing to an emergent, positive notion of 'natural man.'

NOTES

1 See G.E. Russell, ed., *The 'Arabick' Interest of the Natural Philosophers in Seventeenth-Century England* (Leiden, 1994); G.J. Toomer, *Eastern Wisdom and Learning: The Study of Arabic in Seventeenth-Century England* (Oxford, 1996); Nabil Matar, *Islam in Britain, 1558–1685* (Cambridge, 1998), *Turks, Moors, and Englishmen in the Age of Discovery* (New York, 1999), and *Britain and Barbary, 1589–1689* (Gainesville, FL, 2005).

2 See Matar, *Islam in Britain*, 98–102; Samar Attar, *The Vital Roots of European Enlightenment: Ibn Tufayl's Influence on Modern Western Thought* (Lenham, MD, 2007); Nawal Hassan, *'Hayy Bin Yaqzan' and 'Robinson Crusoe': A Study of an Early Arabic Impact on English Literature* (Baghdad, 1980); Antonio Pastor, *The Idea of Robinson Crusoe* (Watford, UK, 1930); and Thomas A. Lamont, 'Mutual Abuse: The Meeting of *Robinson Crusoe* and Hayy Ibn Yaqzân,' *Edebiyat: Journal of Middle Eastern Literatures* 13 (2003): 169–76.

3 Stephen O'Shea, *Sea of Faith: Islam and Christianity in the Medieval Mediterranean World* (New York, 2006), 8.

4 Colin Wakefield, 'Arabic Manuscripts in the Bodleian Library: The Seventeenth-Century Collections,' in *The 'Arabick' Interest*, 130.

5 Russell, introduction to *The 'Arabick' Interest*, 3 ff.

6 Alistair Hamilton, 'The English Interest in the Arabic-Speaking Christians,' in *The 'Arabick' Interest*, 30–53.

7 Quoted in M.B. Hall, 'Arabick Learning in the Correspondence of the Royal Society 1660–1677,' in *The 'Arabick' Interest*, 153.

8 Robert Wakefield, *Oratio de laudibus & utilitate trium lingaurum Arabicae Chaldaicae & Hebraicae* (London 1528; STC 24944).

9 Geoffrey Roper, 'Arabic Printing and Publishing in England before 1820,' *Bulletin* (British Society for Middle Eastern Studies) 12 (1985): 12–32.

10 Russell, introduction to *The 'Arabick' Interest*, 8–10.

11 Vivian Salmon, 'Arabists and Linguists in Seventeenth-Century England,' in *The 'Arabick' Interest*, 54–69.

12 Russell, introduction to *The 'Arabick' Interest*, 1.

13 Matar, *Islam in Britain*, 84.

14 Hall, 'Arabick Learning,' in *The 'Arabick' Interest*, 148.

15 Angelica Duran, *The Age of Milton and the Scientific Revolution* (Pittsburgh, 2007), 40ff.

16 Allan H. Gilbert, 'Milton's Textbook of Astronomy,' *PMLA* 38. 9 (1923): 300, 304.
17 See Roper; James Holly Hanford, 'The Chronology of Milton's Private Studies,' *PMLA* 36 (1921): 275–6; and Jackson Campbell Boswell, *Milton's Library: A Catalogue of the Remains of John Milton's Library* (New York, 1975), 220–1.
18 See Boswell, 117–18; and Toomer, 145–6.
19 Ivan E. Taylor, 'John Milton's View on the Teaching of Foreign Languages,' *The Modern Language Journal* 33.7 (Nov. 1949): 529, 531 [528–36].
20 Harris Fletcher, 'Milton and Walton's *Biblia Sacra Polyglotta* (1657),' *Modern Language Notes* 42 (1927): 84–7.
21 Jason Philip Rosenblatt, *Renaissance England's Chief Rabbi: John Selden* (Oxford, 2006).
22 Don Cameron Allen, 'Milton's Winged Serpents,' *Modern Language Notes* 59 (1944): 537–8.
23 M. Nahas, 'A Translation of *Hayy Ibn Yaqzan* by Edward Pococke the Elder (1604–1691),' *Journal of Arabic Literature* 16 (1985): 88–90.
24 Matar, *Islam in Britain*, 99.
25 See Robert Barclay, *An Apology for the True Christian Divinity* ([London?], 1678; Wing B721), 126: 'Yea, there is a Book translated out of the *Arabick*, which gives an account of one *Hai Ibn Yokdan*, who, without converse of man, living in an Island alone, attained to such a profound knowledg of God, as to have immediate converse with him.'
26 Ibn Tufayl, Muhammad ibn 'Abd al-Malik, *The History of Hai Eb'n Yockdan, An Indian Prince, or, The Self-Taught Philosopher*, trans. George Ashwell (London, 1686; Wing A151), 12–14. Further references to this edition are in parentheses.
27 Simon Ockley, trans., *The Improvement of Human Reason Exhibited in the Life of Hai Ebn Yokshan*, by Ibn Tufayl, Muhammad ibn 'Abd al-Malik (1708; Hildsheim, 1983).
28 Nawal M. Hassan, *'Hayy ibn Yaqzan' and 'Robinson Crusoe'* (Baghdad, 1980), 1–15.
29 Selden, for example, relies on Avicenna – as well as Averroes and Maimonides – to discuss the divine revelation to prophets through the active intellect; see Rosenblatt, 212–13.
30 See Mary Nyquist, 'Contemporary Ancestors of de Bry, Hobbes, and Milton,' in *Milton in America*, ed. Paul Stevens and Patricia Simmons, spec. issue of *UTQ* 77 (2008): 837–75.
31 See, for example, George Fox, *The Journal*, ed. Nigel Smith (London, 1998), 470.

32 John Locke, *Two Treatises of Government*, ed. Peter Laslett, Cambridge Texts in the History of Political Thought (Cambridge, 1988), 294.

33 Because Ashwell, like Keith, excludes spontaneous generation from his translation of the *Hayy*, I have relied for passages describing Hayy's generation from the earth on Simon Ockley, trans., *The Improvement of Human Reason*, 39, 45–6.

34 Matar attributes the prevalence of the notion of retirement in seventeenth-century England to the *Hayy*; *Islam in Britain*, 99ff.

35 Ibn Tufayl empahsizes in the *Hayy* that while knowledge of God can be attained through nature, with the use of the senses and reason, this kind of knowledge is, as Sami Hawi claims, 'not only insufficient but also remote from the immediate intimacy of the mystical experience' ('Ibn Tufayl's Appraisal of His Predecessors and Their Influence on His Thought,' *International Journal of Middle East Studies* 7 [1967]: 91–2).

36 All parenthetical references to Milton's poetry are to *Paradise Lost*, ed. Barbara K. Lewalski (Oxford, 2007) and *Complete Shorter Poems*, ed. Stella P. Revard (Oxford, 2009).

37 Michael Lieb, 'Adam's Story: Testimony and Transition in *Paradise Lost*,' in *Living Texts: Interpreting Milton*, ed. Kristin A. Pruitt and Charles W. Durham (Selinsgrove, PA, 2000), 24–6.

38 The idea that creation began with fermentation was considered in England in the 1640s and 1650s. The theory, however, was an attempt to explain the first act of the creation of the universe. See John Rogers, *The Matter of Revolution: Science, Poetry, and Politics in the Age of Milton* (Ithaca, NY, 1996), 114ff. The *Hayy* may have suggested the process for the creation of the first man.

39 William Brathwaite, *The Beginnings of Quakerism* (Cambridge, 1955), 22–6.

40 Paul Stevens, *Imagination and the Presence of Shakespeare in 'Paradise Lost'* (Madison, WI, 1985), 32–3.

41 I refer to it as the annihilation of the self because though Hayy's soul remains, a soul that has the beatific vision, Hayy postulates that his essence, his soul, and God's Essence are one and the same. It follows that once the corporeal part of Hayy disappears, one Essence remains, and that is God's. In the Western tradition, Octavio Paz attributes the tradition of the voyage of the soul to Plato and suggests that the tradition was revived in the Renaissance; see Octavio Paz, *Sor Juana: Or, the Traps of Faith*, trans. Margaret Sayers Paden (Cambridge, MA, 1988), 360ff. It may be opportune to mention here that Sor Juana's *First Dream*, whose unknown source Paz speculates about, may draw on the *Hayy*, which became popular throughout Europe once Edward Pococke the Younger translated it in the seventeenth century.

The *Hayy* might be the unknown 'literary echo' that Paz suggests might have been Sor Juana's model (370), but this requires a separate study. I would like to thank Professor Mary Nyquist for pointing out Octavio Paz's *Sor Juana.*

42 Hawi, 233.

43 See Mary Nyquist, 'The Genesis of Gendered Subjectivity in the Divorce Tracts and in *Paradise Lost,*' in *Re-membering Milton,* ed. Nyquist and Margaret W. Ferguson (New York, 1987), 99–127.

44 Paul Alpers, *What is Pastoral?* (Chicago, 1996), 27, 37, 59.

18 Ludlow Revisited: Milton and Eco-Justice

BALACHANDRA RAJAN

Ludlow castle has been revisited in many ways and the many ways testify to the enduring richness of Milton's first essay in the dramatic form. As we ponder the weight of thought in the masque we can ask ourselves if high seriousness is an appropriate burden for so light a vehicle. Asking the question puts us on the brink of a recurrent problem. Is Milton stretching or tearing the envelope? Is the attitude of his individual talent to tradition helpfully revisionary or fulfillingly revolutionary? We can answer that the masque was a form in the making and not a form owned by John Fletcher or Ben Jonson. With 'divine philosophy' given its legitimacy we can turn to Sears Jayne's attempt to place the poem's thinking in a Neoplatonic matrix.[1] We can think of chastity and virginity as different intensities of dedication or think of them like A.S.P. Woodhouse does, as discriminating the realms of nature and grace. We can think of them further as metaphors for Milton's own consecration to his calling. Turning to Demaray's work on the Ludlow performance we can contrast its restrained staging with the addiction of court masques to spectacle.[2] A point is being made about that 'idle show' which the dignified structure of Penshurst sought to avoid. Since a young girl in her teens is the principal performer we can think of the poem both as a celebration and as a warning accompanying her initiation into the way of the world. Monition is emphasized by Barbara Breasted's examination of the Castlehaven scandal and in Leah Marcus's consideration of a rape case in the Ludlow neighbourhood.[3]

The view slowly surfacing in those prefatory remarks is that Milton's masque is the designed antithesis of nearly everything the masque form had come to represent. This is not altogether surprising. A Puritan masque, if it is not to be a contradiction in terms, must rescue the form from misappropriation and reaffirm its potential for thoughtfulness. This is easier said than done and it must be done in order to be said. A masque must be performed and performance needs a patron. A dissident masque calls for a patron resistant to central authority. Centre-circumference relationships are involved here but questions of jurisdiction (which Leah Marcus studies instructively) can pave the way to questioning the ethical basis on which jurisdiction rests. The deft use of regional mythology (as with Sabrina) can strengthen the perception of an inauthentic centre, more concerned with self-fashioning according to court etiquette than with self-making amid the dark wood's entanglements. In addition to local felicity and circumstantial aptness, a dissident masque, like all masques, must celebrate an occasion.[4] That occasion must befit entanglement if a statement of any weight is to be made.

These are tight parameters. Milton was fortunate to find them but he also steps with adroitness into the space that is offered him. In the process he gives us not simply a reformed masque (to quote the current characterization) but an intervention which in taking hold of the masque's potential for thoughtfulness, also asks what the form helps us to think.[5] It is an inquiry as well as an entertainment. In making this inquiry Milton effectively turns the masque world upside down. Scholars once reflected on the oddity of celebrating chastity in a form dedicated to hymen. Today we must reflect not on the oddity but on the sudden and searching relevance of celebrating abstinence in a form that embodies excess. David Norbrook observes that the masque displaying as it does 'the principle of conspicuous waste' is 'the last place where one would expect a serious call for austerity and economy.'[6] Conspicuous waste was once an aesthetic effect. It is now a global preoccupation. The last place may well become a place where the last stand for survival must be made.

The masque as a genre lasted for less than fifty years. It is the transient product of a highly specific moment. New historicists gravitate to that specificity but it also makes the form more than normally vulnerable, once the patronage of the moment has passed. The future of the masque is further weakened by an obsession with spectacle that propels it in the direction of conspicuous consumption and extravagant display. Survival becomes increasingly contingent on a counterstatement highlighting plain living, high thinking, and associated Brahmin virtues. Milton offers this statement with alacrity but also puts in a claim for the masque's life beyond its moment by addressing, with some determination, the identity question implicit in the donning and doffing of disguises. In doing so he reverses his normal version of hybridity which is human to the waist and animal below. Here, it is the face that is otherwise with 'all other parts remaining as they were' (72). Deception deepens into self-deception as we boast ourselves 'more comely than before' (75). The face which, like Eliot's Prufrock, we put on 'to meet the faces we will meet' is the face of institutional and social compliance, of an otherness implanted in ourselves which we must learn to perceive and to disown.[7] We wander through 'this World's vain mask' choosing identities that distract us from our real identities.[8] Radical unmasking must strip away the mask of the world. Revealing the true face is the masque's crucial event and that true face can only be 'reason's mintage.' Milton's achievement is to have seized on the identity question inherent in the masque and to have made it intersect with the right response to nature as the first step in the ladder of self-making. Self-understanding begins with respect for the environment. Pleasure reconciled to virtue is a respectable masque theme. Milton gives it an ecological accent that is unique.

It is time to turn to the central confrontation between Comus and the Lady that is the hinge of so much that Milton subsequently wrote. The preliminaries to this confrontation are notable. Comus, masking himself as a helpful shepherd, unmasks himself as the kind of riotous reveller whom masques are designed to entertain. The Lady, accepting Comus's 'honest offer'd courtesie,' observes that it is more frequent in 'lowly sheds / With smoaky rafters' than it is in 'tapstry halls' and 'Courts of Princes' (321–5). She is, in effect, taking the side of the rural poor against an aristocracy who held those poor to be in a condition not much better than serfdom. Yet it is that very aristocracy that sponsors the masques celebrating the lifestyle Comus represents. The villain of the piece is a stereotypical member of its audience. Milton's interest in turning the form against itself is evident in this paradox. It will be exercised more powerfully in *Lycidas* and most powerfully of all in the ninth book of *Paradise Lost* where Milton changes his notes 'to Tragic' denouncing that 'tedious havoc' in which his own imagination had previously rejoiced (6, 30).

Milton's response to the epic genre is an enormously complicated matter that calls for a book or a very substantial article. In this essay I must restrict myself to differentiating the experimental genre of the masque from an established genre of imperial prestige with Homer and Vergil behind Milton and Camões and Tasso at his side. The epic's imperial claim is reinforced by the tendency to read the *Aeneid* as a civilizational statement, Rome's finest moment in the minds of many. Civilizational statements beget an encyclopaedic urge and that urge blends with the hexaemeral tradition which offers the Christian poet a 'vast design' for containing and locating all knowledge. The result is a powerfully propulsive movement to the maximum of integration and inclusiveness, an imperialism of knowledge affirmed in the Seventh Prolusion, where nature surrenders to the man of learning in a manner strikingly different from the Ludlow masque.[9] When Milton writes his epic he returns to the imperialism of knowledge, seeking it in the assimilative momentum of the poetry but also rebuking what he continues to seek. Hubris is followed by humbling in the invocations, and hubris in the poem's narrative is followed by the most ultimate of humblings, as the quest for forbidden knowledge, the Faustian refusal to acknowledge a just circumference, reaches its disastrous consummation.

The poem is called 'Paradise Lost,' carrying the anguish of what might have been into its title. It can no longer be the poem of an elected nationhood, of God speaking uniquely to his Englishmen. Instead it must contemplate the interregnum's wreckage, that 'bitter tastelessness of shadow fruit' which Satan savours on his return from Paradise.[10] All is not lost and in the text's margins we can dimly discern the elusive coalescence of the second Israel with the second Rome. In the text itself we can see only a sustained and tragic meditation on what the human condition has brought upon itself. The poem implements the epic undertaking with unapproachable grandeur and as it does so sinks a spear into its heart. It is futile to describe so rich and self-subversive an amalgam as revisionary, revolutionary, or anything but itself.

After a digression which was not necessary but may be forgivable, we return to the encounter in the dark wood, with the Lady symbolically imprisoned in her chair and with Comus's 'great hymn to Nature's fecundity' (the phrase is Martin Evans's) delivered to a captive audience.[11] The circumstances scarcely befit a hymn but Evans is right in assigning Comus's speech to that genre. It responds with a matching poetic plenitude to the proposition that the firmament displays the glory of its maker. Those meditating on the display should proceed to revere the divine power that brought it into being. Comus sees it as created for no better purpose than 'to please, and sate the curious taste' (714). Imperialist wars fought in Milton's time over spices (and now fought over oil) lie in the background of this degradation. 'Curious taste' has its cost beginning with Adam and Eve. Milton's audience may also have remembered the massacre of the British in Amboyne which took place in 1621 and established Dutch supremacy in the Indonesian archipelago. The humiliation lasted long enough for Dryden to write a poem on it.

The 'hymn' and the trivializing response to it occupy only one half of Comus's speech. The other half is devoted to the nightmarish fringe which Comus sees as surrounding nature's plenitude, the threat posed by its self-suffocating excess. That threat can only be countered, according to Comus, by unrestrained and even frantic consumption. This is a preposterous remedy though one which big business continues to cultivate. It remains saddening that enthusiasm for Comus as a poet has blinded so many to the falsities of his argument.[12]

The basis for Comus's fantasy is not clear. Europe between the Black Death and Columbus's voyage may not have been in the decrepit state in which Kirkpatrick Sale finds it in *The Conquest of Paradise* but it does not support the vision Comus offers. First encounters with the New World are plausibly suggested by Evans,[13] but by 1634 the sense of wonder in marvellous possessions was beginning to wear off and the difficulties of settlement were becoming apparent. It is the Edenic rather than the current state of nature that Comus is describing, and Milton's ecological thinking can seem mistakenly addressed to primal abundance rather than looming scarcity. Nevertheless the address does have the advantage of underlining temperance as a moral requirement. Its 'holy dictate' (767) should be observed because it is holy and not because the cost of violating it is no longer sustainable.

In the Bridgewater text Comus's speech terminates dramatically as the eruptive energy of an overburdened earth gazes 'upon the Sun with shameless brows' (736; cf. Bridgewater 704).[14] This must have been a high water mark in the actual performance with Comus himself gazing with 'shameless brows' at the Lady.

The Lady's response can be described as measured and probably too measured. Many of us would be happier if some of Comus's passion had leaked into her retort.[15] In its arid exemplariness, contrasted with Comus's burgeoning eloquence, the retort is an early notification that Milton is of the devil's party and knows it. Because he knows it, there is a compulsion to return to the scene of the misdemeanour, to demonstrate that it is an accident not a habit, to show that the flame of 'sacred vehemence' (795) can indeed kindle an incandescent understanding that would put the eloquence of the devil in its place. As the effort discloses the embarrassing strength of an unwanted loyalty, the stakes become higher and the fissures more far-reaching. In the end the poet's signature is in the struggle to dispossess himself.[16]

This said, it must be admitted that the Lady takes the debate to a higher level, replacing the 'lean and sallow Abstinence' which Comus had derided with 'the holy dictate of spare Temperance' (709, 767). Implicitly elevating the secular into the sacred, the Lady treats nature's bounty not as a licence for self-indulgence (Comus had made it a demand), but as an occasion for a moral response that accepts plenitude as a gift and not a temptation.

The response to Comus could have ended at this point but it goes considerably further. The answer to generative excess is not obscene overconsumption by a privileged elite but the more equitable distribution of nature's generosity. The Lady is quite decisive on this point, contrasting just men pining in want with the vast excesses heaped on a few by 'lewdly-pamper'd Luxury' (768–70). Dispensing nature's blessings in 'unsuperfluous even proportion' would result in the giver being thanked and not blasphemed. Pushing intemperance to the point of blasphemy underlines the Lady's view that the generosity of the earth is sacred. Her insistence on social justice not merely in itself, but as an ethical corrective to ecological plundering, marks an unusual moment in Milton and one to which he did not return. Equitable distribution is, of course, no problem in a Paradise with only two inhabitants but the prose could have taken up the matter and did not. Its prevalence in seventeenth-century social thinking remains to be assessed.[17]

The Lady's status as a founding member of the NDP will now be evident. Like the NDP she is unable to garner votes when orators with Comus's proficiency are making right-wing speeches. Her advice should have been adopted in 1634. It is still greeted with delaying tactics at five minutes to twelve on the doomsday clock.

Comus's remarks on virginity are not in Bridgewater which keeps the debate at a socio-economic level, focusing it more pertinently as a text for our times.[18] It can be said at the outset that Comus's view of virginity is straightforward and impervious to that 'high mystery' with which the Lady and the Elder Brother invest it. It is also continuous with Comus's ransacking of the environment. Promiscuity is the internal equivalent of compulsive consumption: 'Beauty is nature's coyn, must not be hoorded' (739). The economic metaphor passes naturally into the sexual one: 'Beauty is natures brag and must be shown' (745). 'Self esteem, grounded on just and right' is a meaningless concept to Comus (*PL* 8.572). It would be an exaggeration to say that he is not on the same spiritual plane as the Lady. He sees no purpose whatsoever in being on any spiritual plane.

This disparity is put to maximum use by the Lady who tells Comus not once but three times that she has no intention of discussing the 'sublime notion' of virginity with him. Her dismissal has to be described as deliciously snooty and redolent of the English memsahib at her finest. Comus, entranced like the Attendant Spirit by the Lady's singing, had previously described her as a 'forren wonder' (265). The Lady's tongue-lashing lays bare the meaning of those words.

Hauteur is dignified but difficult when one is imprisoned in a chair and offered a drink that is undoubtedly laced with ecstasy. These things happened at Castlehaven and continue into today. It is entirely understandable that the Lady should refuse to talk to Comus on matters beyond the right use of nature's bounty. She does warn Comus that nature is on her side not his, and Comus does admit the justice of that warning, implemented in the rescue by Sabrina.[19] None the less one has the uncomfortable feeling that the Lady's threats about what her 'sacred vehemence' can accomplish are really Milton's admission of his own unreadiness to give that vehemence poetic substance. He succeeds in doing so eventually, but in a manner that unravels his success. 'Dye hee or Justice must' goes beyond sacred vehemence to an implacable ferocity that invites his own obsolescence (*PL* 3.210). In the celestial dialectic, the law must be proclaimed with cataclysmic force to generate the necessity and nature of the Gospel. It must consume itself in its excess. 'The rigid satisfaction, death for death' must be made to surrender out of its own inadequacy to a higher satisfaction that takes in and transcends it (3.212). Milton does put poetry at the service of that higher satisfaction but he finds it in the serenity of the Son's sacrifice rather than in sacred vehemence or its Puritan equivalent, zeal.

Since the dramatic situation encourages the Lady's silence, Milton's difficulties in making her a better poet than Comus are not brought to the fore. An expanded Epilogue can be offered as a compensation for that silence. Youth and Joy are confidently promised to those resolute enough to spurn the life of impulse (1005–11). Diagramatically the masque is balanced but the imaginative effect remains askew. *Lycidas* is more troubled in asking whether writing poetry is really preferable to untangling Neaera's hair (67–9). It disposes of this question (as other poems that raise it are obliged to do) but only after a degree of self-torment that is excluded by the masque's reluctance to unsettle itself.

The most important path from Ludlow leads to our current predicament from Paradise. Milton's imagination is deeply committed to the generative power of nature as opposed to an antigenerative, suicidal chaos. In Paradise nature wantons 'as in her prime,' pours forth her 'Virgin Fancies' and offers us an 'enormous bliss,' 'Wilde above Rule or Art'

(*PL* 5.295–7). We are accustomed to associate 'waste' and 'wilde' with chaos and with hell and in fact both epithets are used in a single line on two separate occasions to describe each of these highly avoidable sites (1.60; 7.212). Using them to describe Edenic nature should provide an occasion for thought. The line that separates one elementality from another is fundamental but precarious. In the undertow of the language we are kept advised of this dangerous proximity. It surrounds and sharpens the old Anarch's reassurance that Paradise is within walking distance of chaos (2.988).

As Elizabeth Sauer and Lisa Smith indicate, the enclosed garden is anything but enclosed. The seeds of its otherness are present in its wantonness, its maziness, and its errancy. In their potential slippages these words forecast a possibility which the Fall translates. They are equivocations reflecting a 'just circumference' that is cosmically necessary but socially questionable.[20]

We think of the ecosystem as self-balancing, but as upset by the extent and violence of human intervention. It may be that Milton comes to think of it as self-endangering. The turn in thought can mark a crucial difference in our response to a world which we should participate in rather than seek to direct. A self-balancing nature can both cooperate with and contain the human in a manner appropriate to the genius of the species. A self-endangering nature requires human management to hold it away from the chaos within itself.

Since a primal nature can only be imagined it can be argued that the problems associated with it are also imaginary. This is not quite so. Responses to superabundance persist into our own time long after the premise has disappeared. Extravagant consumption to mop up excess production remains habitual even when growing scarcity has replaced primal excess. Equitable distribution combined with temperance is not difficult in a world of plenitude. In a world of diminishing resources it can only lead to hostile competition for those resources unless temperance is made into a moral imperative and not an imposition laid on us by environmental constraints. Finally, the self-endangering plenitude implicit in the fringe of Comus's speech can lead away from a partnership with nature to a situation in which nature can only be 'tamed' by making it subject to human dominance. Human dominance over the lesser creation is a prominent feature of the Genesis tradition. A self-endangering nature that needs to be protected from its own disposition to suicide is an important reinforcement of this claim. It may also be a Miltonic innovation.

Paradise Lost moves in this direction. Adam's outraged response to Nimrod's behaviour can be read as insisting that all men are equal before God. The other side of this insistence is the 'Dominion absolute' over 'Beast, Fish, Fowl' proclaimed not simply as a 'right,' but as a right sanctified by divine 'donation' (12.67–71). The assertive eco-imperialism of this passage is not challenged by Michael and is confirmed rather than challenged elsewhere. Man, for example, is described as the 'Master work' which the creation needs in order to be governed (7.505–10). Eve is perceived by Adam as inferior to him in the 'prime end' of nature because she is less expressive in proclaiming 'Dominion' absolute (8.540–6). Nevertheless, her creation is necessary, according to Raphael, to prevent man from being 'sunk in carnal pleasure' like the 'Beasts' who for that reason were not fit mates for Adam (8.593–4).[21]

As a veteran Miltonist, I am quite capable of finding a way around these awkwardnesses but I do not propose to look for one. The consequences of installing human dominance over the lesser creation in the structure and fabric of the cosmos need to be investigated and not justified. When C.S. Lewis famously defined the hierarchic principle, he saw it as calling for obedience to what was above and responsibility to what lay below. It is to be admired only in a world of innocence. In the world of history, its inevitable consequence is the abandonment of responsibility for what is below combined with intensified demands for obedience from above that steadily move toward the totalitarian.

The early modern era represents a struggle against the feudal order, which is the political translation of the hierarchic principle. Milton was prominent in that struggle. Hierarchy is now a thing of the past, though it can be argued that it has merely been inverted and not rethought in the populist arrangements that have succeeded it. Human supremacy over the creation on the other hand is very much with us and has become much more dangerous with our growing capacity for interference in an ecosystem of which we should be citizens. Eco-imperialism has also provided the basis for more familiar forms of imperialism since what is good for nature must be good for the natives. It, like hierarchy, should become that island 'salt and bare' to which Paradise was reduced (*PL* 11.834–5). But Milton's own nostalgia for Paradise evident in his prolonged and passionate invocation of a prelapsarian harmony resists the partnership with nature that we ought to seek and which the Ludlow masque can be read as anticipating. It offers us instead the temptation of 'dominion absolute,' of power cut loose from the deep responsibility in which it was once anchored. It also introduces us to a panoply of stresses, strains, and perplexities, a perpetual torsion between the dynamics of change and the character of a permanence which Milton's own continuing interrogation was placing under duress. Because of this torsion Milton's work remains endlessly engrossing but probably not in the manner he intended.

'The Garden is Political' to quote the title of a book of poems published by John Malcolm Brinnin in 1942. Paradise can seem less political than the grounds of Appleton House but it is not impervious to inroads from Milton's world. A river runs beneath it, channelled into a fountain that irrigates the 'mazy error' of the garden's streams. Satan makes his second entrance through this river, contaminating the subsoil before the temptation begins.[22] The contamination spreads worldwide since the river is the source of other rivers. Even if we discount this sinuous subversion, Paradise is still not a place where one stumbles over melons or where ripe fruit drops helpfully into open mouths. Several scholars have commented on the work that seems necessary to prevent Paradise from overgrowing itself. Reflecting on the effort that is needed to control a situation both idyllic and demanding, Evans goes to the extent of describing God as an imperialist with Adam and Eve as indentured labourers.[23] It does seem that the garden reflects some of the travail of pioneering and settlement in a new world closer to Eden than the old one. Milton's point presumably is that the right to residence must be earned even in Paradise, and Western formulations of law insist that entitlement to land is conferred by the proper use of it. There is thus a contemporary background of some richness to the difficulties which Adam and Eve experience as gardeners. Contributing to this background is a trend in recent scholarship in which the universal and mild monarchy of heaven is being increasingly questioned as to its mildness.

In fact, the task of keeping Paradise in order is so onerous that a division of labour is adopted with results quite other than those prophesied by Adam Smith. Milton's double temptation, singular in its treatment of the Fall, hearkens back to Comus's speech. 'Curious taste' is both pleased and sated with not one, but several apples being eaten.[24] Gluttony becomes a metaphor for compulsive consumption. Milton then insists (unlike most of his contemporaries) on lust following gluttony in Paradise so that Comus's stairway of degeneration can be installed at the origin of things. Climate change is then accomplished with catastrophic elegance as the earth's axis is shifted to the position it now occupies. The end of 'Grateful vicissitude' is announced by a clangerous catalogue of winds of which hurricane Katrina seems the natural consequence (6.8).

'Earth felt the wound' is the narrator's first comment as Eve eats the fruit which her 'rash hand' had plucked. The extent of the wound is immediately made apparent with nature 'Sighing through all her Works' (9.780–3).[25] Human intervention had controlled and channelled the exuberance of nature. It now assaults what it had once fulfilled. The fall marks a traumatic turning point at which man, bereft of moral dignity, abdicates from a responsibility which had been that dignity's fountainhead in favour of a delusive self-fulfilment. It is a dereliction of duty to the environment. It is also the death-wish of the human race. As the 'erected wit' of scientific judgment confronts an 'infected will' subservient to the consumer ethos, the realization of that wish draws nearer.[26]

To sum up, eco-justice is an extension of social justice involving justice to other life forms beside the human. It treats the human life form as privileged only because of its extraordinary capacity for intervention in the affairs of this planet. Social justice, in turn, needs to be extended so that natural resources are equitably distributed between as well as within nations and societies. Frugality in the use of natural resources should be regarded as an ethical imperative rather than as a constraint imposed upon us by our own previous plunder of the environment. The Ludlow masque can be regarded as a step in this direction. *Paradise Lost* is a step away from it. Milton's deep imaginative commitment to human dominance over the lesser orders of being can be imagined as creative in a prelapsarian world but can only be exploitative in our own time and predicament. *Paradise Lost* fascinates us with a model that has yet to be washed away with Paradise.

NOTES

The principal explorers of Milton's ecology are Diane McColley and Ken Hiltner. I have benefited from the work of both to an extent far beyond what my text or footnotes indicate. I differ from both in the strong distinction I draw between Milton's ecological thinking in the Ludlow masque and in *Paradise Lost.* I also lay much greater emphasis on the consequences of 'dominion absolute' when it is torn away from its prelapsarian moorings.

I am grateful to Elizabeth Sauer for assisting with the presentation of this paper and for drawing my attention to work on the Ludlow masque which I might otherwise have ignored.

1 Sears Jayne, 'The Subject of Milton's Ludlow *Mask,*' *PMLA* 74 (1959): 533–43.

2 John G. Demaray, *Milton and the Masque Tradition: The Early Poems, 'Arcades,' and 'Comus'* (Cambridge, MA, 1968).

3 Barbara Breasted, '*Comus* and the Castlehaven Scandal,' *Milton Studies* 3 (1971): 201–14; Leah Marcus, 'The Earl of Bridgewater's Legal Life: Notes toward a Political Reading of *Comus*,' *Milton Quarterly* 21.4 (1987): 13–23. Unlike John Creaser ('"The present aid of this occasion": The Setting of *Comus*,' in *The Court Masque*, ed. David Lindley [Manchester, 1984], 134n68), I believe that the Castlehaven Scandal was in the minds of those attending the Ludlow performance. The difference between giving way to coercion and standing firm against it is too striking to be brushed aside. The Elder Brother's remark in 588–9 becomes more pointed in the context of Castlehaven, as does the Lady's warning to Comus in 661–4.

4 The 'occasion' is the earl of Bridgewater's appointment as Lord President of Wales. 'Circumstantial aptness' is felicitously enriched by postponing the main festivities connected with the appointment to Michaelmas (Creaser, 114). Milton makes use of this 'coincidence' on his title page. William B. Hunter's pioneering article ('The Liturgical Context of *Comus*,' *ELN* 10 [1972]: 11–15) demonstrates the intimate links between the Ludlow masque and the Michaelmas liturgies (see also Leah Marcus, *The Politics of Mirth: Jonson, Herrick, Milton, Marvell, and the Defense of Old Holiday Pastimes* [Chicago, 1986], 201–2). Ecclesiastes is among the texts invoked and the insistence in Ecclesiastes that there is a proper time for everything can be contrasted with Comus's insistence that the proper time for everything is now. There is also a proper time for festivity. It is after one has passed through the 'nodding horror' of the wood (37–9) and not amid the wood's entanglements. Given these rites of passage, it is only proper that Michael should instruct Adam on finding his way in the dark wood of the fallen world.

5 David Norbrook in 'The Reformation of the Masque,' in *Court Masque*, 94–110, draws attention to an undercurrent of anxiety about the masque's development that comes to a climax at Ludlow. David Bevington and Peter Holbrook also see the Ludlow masque as 'Seeking to remedy the fundamental values of a court genre perceived as having gone fatally astray' (introduction to *The Politics of the Stuart Court Masque*, ed. David Bevington and Peter Holbrook [Cambridge and NY, 1998], 15). Barbara Lewalski underlines the comprehensiveness of the correction by describing Milton's work as a reformed masque 'in all its stages' ('Milton's *Comus* and the Politics of Masquing,' in *Politics of the Stuart Court Masque*, 307). Marcus in studying the masque as 'anti-Laudian' concentrates on an important item in the agenda of reform (*Politics of Mirth*, 169–212). Maryann Cale McGuire in characterizing the masque as Puritan indicates, even in her book's title, the stresses implicit

in Milton's undertaking (*Milton's Puritan Masque* [Athens, 1983]). The form must be retrieved and placed at the service of a moral dignity which many Puritans believed was contrary to its nature.

The Ludlow masque does much more than restore to normalcy a form that has been hijacked by extremists. In reinventing the genre, it places it within the continuity of Milton's development as a thinker and within his richly complex and evolving response to genres inherited or experimental.

6 Norbrook, 106.

7 T.S. Eliot, 'The Love Song of J. Alfred Prufrock,' in *The Complete Poems and Plays, 1909–1950* (Boston, 1952), p. 4.

8 Milton, Sonnet 22, 'To Mr Cyriack Skinner upon his Blindness,' 13. Milton's remarks on masques are generally adverse and Belial, Comus's cousin, 'Reigns' in those 'Courts and Palaces' where masques are performed (*PL* 1.499–502). It is therefore important to remember that Adam in 'Adam Unparadiz'd' remains 'stubborn in his offence' and cannot be induced to repent until a masque of the world's ills is made to pass before him.

9 The Seventh Prolusion's claim is renounced in the exchange between Michael and Adam (*PL* 12.553–81), which makes evident the implicit connection between knowledge and empire. The temptation of learning in *Paradise Regained* is a farther stage in this renunciation.

10 Eliot, 'Little Gidding,' in *Complete Poems and Plays*, p. 141.

11 J. Martin Evans, *Milton's Imperial Epic: 'Paradise Lost' and the Discourse of Colonialism* (Ithaca, NY, 1996), 47.

12 With Milton's poetry under assault, Leavis's approval of Comus as a poet (*Revaluation: Tradition and Development in English Poetry* [London, 1936], 47–52) was greeted with a relief that has spared Comus's 'hymn' from further scrutiny. His prowess as a poet is not in dispute. The same can be said of Belial (*PL* 2.109–14) who speaks for Milton (2.146–50) with an authenticity unapproached by Comus.

Lewalski, like Cedric Brown, observes that Comus has 'the power and attractiveness of a natural force and a contemporary cultural ideal' (309). Marcus finds 'an unsettling disparity between the grim necromancer described by the Attendant Spirit and the graceful poet appearing before the audience' (*Politics of Mirth*, 185). My view is that the disparity diminishes and possibly disappears as Comus's true colours are revealed.

13 See Evans, 48–9.

14 The Bridgewater *Masque* is available as an appendix to the Revard edition of *The Complete Shorter Poems*.

15 As Marcus notes, 'many have found her [the Lady's] response overly shrill and rigid' (198). Lewalski is not among the many and finds the Lady's

'incisive rejoinder ... couched in trenchant language with a satiric edge' (313). Barker's difficulties with the Lady's retort remain valid for those who feel that the masque suffers from an imaginative imbalance for which diagrammatic rebalancing cannot fully compensate (Arthur E. Barker, *Milton and the Puritan Dilemma* [Toronto, 1942], 10–11).

16 The most memorable of Marlowe's mighty lines are given to members of the devil's party but Marlowe takes this lopsidedness in his stride. Milton struggles incessantly with it, making it the signature of his poetics and a pervasive taint of the fallen imagination.

17 On this matter, see Norbrook (106) and Creaser (128). Lewalski describes the Lady as 'offering (for the time) a remarkable egalitarian argument' (313).

18 The various texts of the Ludlow masque are conveniently presented by Sprott in a side-by-side format. See John Milton, *A Maske: The Earlier Versions*, ed. S.E. Sprott (Toronto, 1973).

19 The last word on Sabrina may belong to Marcus (199–201). Given the masque's deep concern of respect for the environment, it is important that the rescue should come from the world of nature and not from '*Joves* Court' (1), or from the two brothers, even with the Attendant Spirit's assistance. To achieve this result, the Lady has to be allowed to wander away by her brothers and her rescue from a predicament which they have brought about must be bungled. Milton's implicit argument is that the good can hold its own against its enemies but cannot prevail without assistance. In *Paradise Lost* that assistance comes from above. In the Ludlow masque it comes significantly from what in *Paradise Lost* would be deemed below. The view of the human relationship with nature written into the rescue is mutually supportive rather than hierarchic.

20 The enclosure movement is typically held to have reached its maximum in the eighteenth century. In Marx's classic analysis enclosure was necessary to create a landless proletariat as a labour force for the industrial revolution. Blake's *Book of Urizen* can and possibly should be read as the ultimate anti-enclosure poem.

Recent studies (documented by Elizabeth Sauer and Lisa Smith) point to an enclosure movement of considerable magnitude during the seventeenth century ('*Noli me tangere*: Colonialist Imperatives and Enclosure Acts in Early Modern England,' in *Sensible Flesh: On Touch in Early Modern Culture*, ed. Elizabeth D. Harvey [Philadelphia, 2003], 141–58). The basis could include an increased emphasis on property rights so that all land had to be owned by someone, making the concept of common land marginal. The move from a hybrid economy (sustained partly by payments in kind) to a purely monetary one also calls for increasing flexibility in land use. Capital formation rather than a revolution in technology emerges as the driving force in seventeenth-century enclosing. God's gold compasses (*PL* 7.225–31) lend cosmic dignity to enclosure and the enclosed garden of Paradise becomes the apex of that dignity. Enclosure supports the idea of a nature that requires human management to control and direct its otherwise 'wild' productivity.

21 Raphael's crude comment utterly ignores Adam's extraordinary account of his dialogue with God on the need for Eve's creation.

22 The contamination is made more insidious by Satan's vaporizing of himself (9.74–5). The 'rising Mist' in which he enters Paradise is reminiscent of Pandemonium rising 'like an Exhalation' (1.710–11).

23 See Evans, 80, 146.

24 See Balachandra Rajan, *Milton and the Climates of Reading: Essays by Balachandra Rajan*, ed. Elizabeth Sauer (Toronto, 2006), 130, for further comment.

25 For Ken Hiltner's ambivalent response to the wound, see '"Earth felt the wound": Gendered Ecological Consciousness in Illustrations of *Paradise Lost*,' in *Renaissance Ecology: Imagining Eden in Milton's England*, ed. Ken Hiltner (Pittsburgh, 2008), 125–34. I prefer a more straightforward interpretation which connects these lines to 9.999–1000 and to the world 'Under her own waight groaning' (12.539) in contrast to the 'Earth self ballanc't' (7.242) of the pristine creation. Hiltner's emphasis on the wound's redemptive possibilities is too close for comfort to the paradox of the Fortunate Fall and blurs the distinction between the Son's sacrificial wounding of himself and humanity's wounding of nature.

The wound also ends the possibility of stewardship (Anne Lake Prescott, 'Naming and Caring: The Theme of Stewardship in *Paradise Lost*,' in *Approaches to Teaching Milton's* Paradise Lost, ed. Galbraith M. Crump [New York, 1986], 157–64). Stewardship depends on answerability to the divine image within the self. When the connection is wounded, stewardship degenerates into the condition which Lynn White's 1967 article sees as surrounding the concept of overlordship ('The Historical Roots of Our Ecological Crisis,' *Science* 155.3767 [1967]: 1203–7). The macro-microcosmic correspondence, commonplace in Milton's time, strengthens the interaction between humankind and the environment. Thus the winds that result from the dislocation of the earth's axis (10.695–706) are anticipated by the 'high winds worse within' (9.1122) of the fallen self.

26 The phrasing is from Sydney's *Defence of Poetry*.

Milton in the Far North: An Afterword

PAUL STEVENS

By the North – of *Cataio* Eastward, or of *Canada* Westward

Milton, *Areopagitica*

The question this volume most immediately provokes is Balachandra Rajan's: 'You do have to ask whether Canadian Miltonists amount to anything more than Miltonists writing in Canada.'[1] Rajan like many others in the volume is clearly dubious, but the question seems compelling because behind it lies the larger issue of Canadian intellectual life and achievement in general. How exactly is intellectual life in English Canada distinctive or different from that of the two great cultural empires, those of Britain and America, within whose often rival orbits it has struggled to find its own trajectory for so long? Northrop Frye's letters from the 1930s reveal a Canadian intellectual typical in his desire to come up with a formula that would resolve the problem: 'in its determination to apply the old traditions to new surroundings,' he assures his future wife, Helen Kemp, the United Church of Canada epitomizes the nation, a country in the far north at once 'sturdier than England and more coherent than the United States.'[2] But Canada was and is, as Frye at some level always knew, anything but coherent in any traditional sense of what a nation might look like. For Quebec, the bewildering complexity of the issue as it appears in English Canada is further compounded by that province's original and still evolving relationship with France. And even for English Canada, constant pre-war and then massive post-war immigration soon rendered early Frye-like formulations about the nation's mediating role between Britain and America obsolete. Frye's later assertion that Canadians were simply Americans who had rejected the Revolution sounds even less persuasive now than it ever did.[3] On the specific issue of the impact of immigration, Rajan himself is a case in point.

A 'new Canadian' from India in the 1960s, Rajan's forty-year career in Canada illustrates the way the old, often comfortable oscillation between

British and American axes became increasingly, if more than a little fitfully, skewed by various post-colonial and multicultural pressures. For late Rajan, the originator of the 1999 collection *Milton and the Imperial Vision*, for instance, Milton the prophet of both English and American liberties fades before the grim spectre of an imperial poet who authorizes colonial expansion even as he satirizes its abuses:'[m]ore than anyone else,' Rajan came to feel, 'Milton seems to sanction imperial thought.'[4] Even here, in his last essay, as he extols the eco-sensitive Milton of the Ludlow masque for his 'Brahmin virtues,' he remains convinced that Milton's nostalgia for paradise in his greatest poem constitutes a temptation to 'dominion absolute' (468, 478). But there is an earlier Rajan and it is the conflicted young Indian nationalist-cum-Anglophile Cambridge student of the forties who together with Frye somewhat inadvertently opens the way to understanding the historic importance of Milton in Canada. Rajan's early response to the ground-breaking quality of Canadian Milton criticism and Frye's conflicted response to the relation between what he called 'world' literature and an evolving Canadian literature turn out to be critically important. Indeed, Rajan and Frye, so this fascinating volume leads us to suspect, are the errant figures who most clearly allow us to get a fix on the particular cultural significance of the world-class Milton criticism that suddenly flowered in mid twentieth-century Canada. Let me begin with that moment and its achievement.

Woodhouse and the Toronto Renaissance

From the late 1940s into the 1960s, the University of Toronto experienced a remarkable renaissance in English literary studies. According to Robin Harris, these were the 'Woodhouse years.'[5] It was during this period, for instance, that Frye published *Fearful Symmetry* (1947) and *Anatomy of Criticism* (1957) and Marshall McLuhan *The Mechanical Bride* (1951), *The Gutenberg Galaxy* (1962), and *Understanding Media* (1964). Both these highly imaginative and quite literally sensationally successful critics, it became conventional to claim, were isolated visionaries who wrote against the prevailing mood at poor, dull Toronto the Good. But this melodramatic story, as the present volume suggests, is way too easy.[6] It seems increasingly clear that the grain against which Frye and McLuhan wrote, the school's relentless historicism, was in fact an essential and perversely enabling part of the matrix out of which their daring speculations emerged. And nowhere was Toronto's historicist grain more apparent than in Milton studies.

The small and close-knit graduate English faculty of which both Frye and McLuhan were members was dominated by the formidable figure of its chair, Arthur Woodhouse. Despite recurring tensions, Frye remained constant in his admiration of Woodhouse: as Feisal Mohamed so astutely notices, Woodhouse appeared in his dreams as an authority he longed to impress, Frye once noting in his diary, 'Woodhouse tries to sound like a pedant, but he's really a great man' (555). It was Woodhouse who gave Frye his first graduate course, not as one might expect on Blake but on Spenser in 1943, and it was under Woodhouse's aegis that early modern studies at Toronto took off, attracting very early on such brilliant students as Arthur Barker, Malcolm Ross, and Roy Daniells, and through Daniells the Manitobans Ernest Sirluck and, a little later, A.C. Hamilton. As Mary Nyquist and Mohamed explain in their penetrating introduction, Woodhouse became the *fontanus plenitudo* of a national movement (11) and that movement was, of course, overwhelmingly 'historicist,' first in the sense of traditional intellectual history but later in more diverse and complex manifestations. Woodhouse himself, a conservative, albeit independent-minded, Anglican, was preoccupied with the alterity of his own Protestant past. For when he contemplated that past, especially the Puritan revolutionaries who so fascinated him, the people he saw were not so much his forefathers or, in Nyquist's telling phrase, our 'contemporary ancestors,'[7] but much more so the inhabitants of a foreign country: 'even where they differ most markedly [amongst themselves],' he says, '[the English Puritans] talk a common language very foreign to our ears.'[8] The task he and his students, most importantly Barker and Sirluck, set themselves was the onerous one of deciphering that strange language.

Focused as it was on Milton, Woodhouse's critical enterprise was determined to take both his religion and politics seriously. Unlike so many Milton critics then dominant in Britain and the United States, he was convinced that the poetry could not be understood independently of the prose nor the prose independently of the great political upheaval of the English Revolution. As literary criticism, his enterprise was thoroughly revisionist in that it sought to undo the long process of aestheticizing Milton and in this it was remarkably successful. After the 'extra-aesthetic' work of Woodhouse, his students, and their allies in the United States, it became increasingly difficult to dismiss Milton's poetry as W.A. Raleigh's beautiful monument to dead ideas – and indeed, such figures as the radical Milton of Christopher Hill are inconceivable without their ground work. In the shadow of Fascism and under the threat of the Second

World War, Woodhouse's theme was liberty, but the presentism this implies, it needs to be emphasized, was to a large degree coincidental. The concept of 'liberty' did not necessarily mean liberalism and it was unavoidable since it stood at the centre of the particular alterity, the alien Puritan discourse, he and his students wished to understand. With admirable lucidity, Hugh MacCallum, one of Woodhouse's last students, identifies three principal elements in the code the Woodhouse group deciphered (210–11). First, they realized that in their customary way of speaking Puritans, or the people we would now call 'godly,' appeared to assign all experience to the separate orders of nature and grace, the first order being available to unaided reason, but the second only to revelation – that is, only to Luther's *sola scriptura, sola fide, sole gratia.* Next, they perceived that from this distinction comes the principle of segregation, that is, the need that the most radical Puritans felt to separate church from state, the spiritual from the secular. And third, they came to understand that at the heart of Puritan revelation was liberty, freedom from the impossible quid-pro-quo burden of the Mosaic law into the enabling grace of the Gospel, a liberty that *should God so elect* was available to all souls regardless of this-worldly differences. As Woodhouse was well aware, this last point was not as straightforward as it might seem: in its ambiguity or instability it made Puritan liberty simultaneously imply both spiritual democracy and spiritual aristocracy. Unlike Frye's great codes, many of which were explicitly indebted to the work of the Woodhouse group,[9] these discursive patterns were increasingly understood not as universals but as historically specific, contingent, and dynamic particulars. They might constitute the structures of a *langue* but that *langue* was constantly shifting, evolving, under the pressure of quotidian events or what Woodhouse calls the 'demands of actual life' (11).

From the perspective of many contemporary historians, like William Lamont, Woodhouse now appears too willing to reify Puritanism, and it is certainly true, as Elizabeth Sauer suggests in her carefully researched essay, that Woodhouse saw in the common Puritan language he analysed the genesis of modern liberalism. He is, however, not only adamant that this genesis was contingent but that his perception of it was rigorously empirical. There are, for instance, moments in his revealing introduction to the edited collection of the 1647 Putney debates, *Puritanism and Liberty,* when you can hear him counselling himself:

> [Puritanism] is to be understood neither as a resurgence of medieval thought ... nor simply as a harbinger of the modern world, of naturalism

> and democracy . . . It is to be studied in itself – and the penalty for disregarding this counsel is to misunderstand not only the movement, but its relation to the past and future. One's definition must be eclectic and must ignore no fact that is prominent in the period under consideration (35).

What is remarkable is not that Woodhouse sees in the Putney debates a connection between godly notions of liberty and modern liberalism (it would have been astonishing had it been otherwise) or that he deploys an apparently unchanging Milton to amplify that connection, but that he sees so many differences and distinctions, coming to grips with them with unflinching intellectual energy and acuity, always carefully weighing them and surprisingly sensitive to the tactical motives of their articulators, even as he struggles to see a unity in their structural relation. The introduction remains exhilarating to read and the 'intensity' Frye perceived in Woodhouse remains deeply moving (555). As Frye later reflected, it was one thing to be teaching Milton, but quite another 'to be teaching Milton against Woodhouse at U.C. [University College] and Barker at Trinity [College, Toronto], two of the best Milton scholars anywhere.'[10] Just after he had published *Fearful Symmetry*, Frye read the proofs of Woodhouse's article on Milton and creation.[11] As he confided in his diary, no one could doubt the chief's range and imagination: he had done a '[t]errific job of weaving in & out of ex nihilo & ex Deo & the eternity of matter & and so on.' It was a 'formidable article' (*CWNF* 8:114). Even Lamont, Woodhouse's severest contemporary critic, cannot help betraying his admiration: 'Arguably it is Woodhouse, not Clarke or Firth, who has most shaped our ideas about Putney. After Woodhouse, it has proved difficult to think of the Putney debates outside those terms he set for them.'[12] Most importantly, not to say ironically, however, as the historicism of the Woodhouse group develops, perhaps most evidently in the mature work of Sirluck, it comes to anticipate the achievements of Lamont's own practice and the now dominant Cambridge School of Quentin Skinner and his followers.[13] One of the critical moments in the development of the group was Sirluck's doctoral defence in December 1947. Examined by among others Woodhouse, Frye, and Barker, Sirluck argued that many of the contradictions and inconsistencies in Milton's prose could be explained by the tactical need to hold to a party line. While Frye and Barker demurred, Woodhouse perhaps perceiving a continuity with his own emphasis on the Puritans' competing and rapidly changing positions in *Puritanism and Liberty* glowed and immediately suggested that not only should the dissertation be accepted but that it should be published in the same series as Barker's *Milton and the Puritan Dilemma.*[14] In her stimulating essay on Milton's *Readie and Easie Way* in the present volume, Annabel Patterson, one of the most distinguished allies of the present-day Cambridge School, underlines the point, making it clear that it was on the Milton criticism of these people, especially Woodhouse and Barker, that she 'cut her teeth' (318).

More important than defending Woodhouse against contemporary historians, however, it needs to be emphasized for the purpose of our immediate inquiry that in the success of the Woodhouse group, literary-historical criticism produced in Canada, probably for the first time ever, was not perceived as apprentice work, subaltern, or 'colonial' but immediately recognized and accepted as world class.[15] When the 1950 Massey Commission on the Arts, Letters, and Sciences, which Sauer draws attention to, called for 'a book which, in Miltonic phrase, the world will not willingly let die,' their call was more than a little belated.[16] This escape from provincialism leads us back to Rajan and Frye.

Recruiting Rajan

Woodhouse published *Puritanism and Liberty* in 1938, Barker *Milton and the Puritan Dilemma* in 1942, and Sirluck, it was hoped, would complete a major work on Milton and classical republicanism. They thought as a school. To Barker's great annoyance, Sirluck was beaten to the punch on classical republicanism by Zera Fink, but Sirluck went on to incorporate the political implications of his work on natural law into his magisterial introduction to the second volume of the Yale prose in 1958. They were, of course, not alone and their allies in the United States were such figures as Don Wolfe at New York's New School and Brooklyn College, Merritt Hughes at Wisconsin, and Douglas Bush at Harvard. As John Leonard explains in the wonderfully elegant opening of his essay, Bush was himself a Canadian émigré, a Toronto graduate and close friend of Woodhouse, who in his Alexander Lectures of 1939 looks back from Harvard to Toronto as Helen might have from the battlements of Troy to Greece.[17] The moment is especially poignant because as Bush struggles to enlarge his imagined community to embrace Canada and the United States as one in their dedication to the Humanities, the force of his allusion to the *Iliad* effectively pushes the nations apart and compels him to recognize the degree to which he has become an American.[18] The apotheosis of this larger North American movement in a form of re-invigorated historical criticism was the eight-volume Yale edition of

Milton's prose (1953–82).[19] Neither Frye nor Rajan was immediately involved in this project but their relation to the Woodhouse group, as the present volume suggests, is as illuminating as it was frequently agonistic. While Frye's relation to the group was long-standing, Rajan's first contact was with Sirluck at Cambridge in 1944. The meeting was remembered by both of them as singularly fortuitous.[20]

In January 1944, Sirluck, then an officer in the Canadian Army, was on an intelligence course in Cambridge. Completely by accident he met E.M.W. Tillyard at a Jesus College dinner to which he had been invited by an army friend. Conversation turned to Milton and Tillyard mentioned a remarkable young Indian student whose dissertation was being hampered by the inaccessibility of the latest North American Milton scholarship. Sirluck characteristically took the initiative. He had his wife purchase a small parcel of books, including Barker's *Milton and the Puritan Dilemma*, and send it out to England. Just before he set out for Normandy in early July, Sirluck delivered the books to Rajan at Trinity College in Cambridge. They had never met and when Rajan saw Sirluck in uniform, he thought he was about to be arrested for his involvement in the Quit India movement. His fears soon allayed, the impact of these books was considerable and it ultimately led to Rajan's immigration to Canada in the 1960s.[21] Denied a much desired Fellowship at Trinity and deeply wounded by patterns of racism he found difficult to understand,[22] after many years in the Indian diplomatic service, Rajan increasingly came to see Canada as a route back to the centre of English literary studies. Rajan enthusiastically records his debt to Sirluck's books a few years after their meeting in the introduction to *Paradise Lost and the Seventeenth-Century Reader* (1947). As he himself describes it, Rajan is at pains to provide a thorough-going historicist reading of *Paradise Lost*, that is, to see the poem 'through the eyes of Milton's contemporaries.'[23] He feels enabled in his task by a number of crucial scholarly developments, in particular, the new understanding of Puritanism effected by North American scholarship, not least the Woodhouse group, that is, 'a more adequate and charitable understanding than hitherto, of Puritan thought in mid-Seventeenth century England.' Only now, he says, are we beginning to understand 'the meaning of such terms as the "Law of Nature" and "Christian liberty" and the part they played in the planning of *Paradise Lost*' (11–12). The mortality of the religious and political ideas in Milton had turned out to be more than a little exaggerated.

Rajan's response reveals two points crucial to the inquiry implicit in the present volume. First, the work of the Canadian Woodhouse group, especially Barker's book, was felt to be ground-breaking in content, but, second, it seemed utterly indistinguishable in style and orientation from any other North American historical criticism. That it was so suggests the degree to which the problem we have been trying to resolve is itself the point and this in turn suggests that perhaps the real question is not what's distinctively Canadian about Milton criticism in Canada but why did so many brilliant Canadians feel the need to write about Milton, a poet, present-day Canadianists might complain, whose only mention of Canada is as a synecdoche for difficulty and distance, 'an episode in communication,' as Frye might say,[24] or means to get somewhere else through the remote passages of the far north; that is, to undertake an Indian voyage 'by the North of *Cataio* Eastward, or of *Canada* Westward' (*Areopagitica, YP* 2:518–19).

Enabling Frye

Among the many impressive essays in this volume, those by Phillip Donnelly, Elizabeth Hodgson, and Muhammad Sid-Ahmed are especially rewarding in offering fresh insight into Milton's relation to Machiavelli, Catholicism, and Arab literature respectively. Two others, however, are immediately relevant to our inquiry – Peter Herman's absorbing account of Frye and Nicholas von Maltzahn's clever twinning of Sirluck with Woodhouse's collaborator, Watson Kirkconnell. While the tragic Frye Herman offers us is hard to take at face value, the discontinuity he highlights between Frye's work on 'world' literature and that on Canadian literature is striking. Whatever the fate of Frye's brilliant 1959 essay on *Lycidas* (reprinted above), the critic himself never really disappeared from the canon of Milton criticism because that canon was always more flexible, open-minded, or quite simply more disorganized than Herman allows. Even after his heyday, Frye seems to have stood as a powerful point of reference both for those who wished to temper the radical instability of post-structuralism in the 1980s and for those who wished to resist the calcifying effects of the more positivist forms of historicism through the 1990s into the present – as witness his presence in so many recent books on Milton.[25] As for the mistrust of the 'Milton establishment,' it is difficult to imagine a scholar more feted by the airy burgomasters of that over-determined republic than Frye: President of the Milton Society of America in 1963, its Honored Scholar in 1975, and perhaps most tellingly, promoted to the rank of Toronto's first University Professor in 1967 by that grand establishment Miltonist, Ernest Sirluck. As von Maltzahn suggests, Sirluck was almost certainly Toronto's most influential graduate dean and his reasons for promoting Frye were not only intellectual and institutional but nationalist.[26] The promotion meant Frye would not go south to the United States: 'He declined Columbia's offer and his continued presence,' says Sirluck, 'was of enormous benefit to the school [of Graduate Studies], the university, and the country' (260). If Herman's story of Frye's exclusion from the canon of Milton criticism is unpersuasive, his explanation of Canadian literature's exclusion from the canon of Frye's *Anatomy* is genuinely illuminating.[27]

Frye begins his 1971 *Bush Garden* with the cryptic assertion that his principal work on world literature, even at its most universalizing, 'has always been rooted in Canada and drawn its essential characteristics from there.' Frye is a nationalist to the extent that he believes that human beings are like birds: 'the creative instinct has much to do with the assertion of territorial rights,' he says (i). Exactly what territorial rights he is asserting in the *Anatomy* or in his studies of Blake and Milton are not, however, immediately clear. Herman takes up the challenge and thoughtfully suggests that the aesthetically arresting or fearful symmetries so evident in Frye's major work are best understood as a form of displacement; that is, they reveal a deep-rooted desire to overcome his country's quotidian incoherence or debilitating asymmetries in a creative act of imagination: '[he] tried to create in literature,' says Herman, 'the unity [he] could not find in reality' (361). Frye's 1956 'Preface to an Uncollected Anthology' is remarkable in offering insight into the process Herman identifies as it is actually taking place. Confronted with the depressingly chaotic or jarring reality of Canada's history and geography, what Frye, the most musical of critics, hears in his nation's nascent literature – what he half perceives, half creates – is synchronic form or 'myth' rearing itself out of diachronic discord. In E.J. Pratt's poetry, for instance, in 'The Truant,' in *Towards the Last Spike* and *Brebeuf*, he sees the great humanizing archetypes of spring and winter, comedy and irony, already emerging as timeless form out of Canada's 'profoundly unhumanized isolation' (*Bush Garden* 173, 164). In the grand project of the *Anatomy*, Canadian literature was perhaps too much a work-in-progress or too distracting to be assimilated into the harmony of his four quartets. Whatever the case, Herman is acute in directing us toward Frye's sensitivity to what Woodhouse would call the 'extra-aesthetic' categories of history and geography.

Frye was, of course, every bit as much a historicist in his understanding of the world as anyone else in late modern Western culture. To hear him contemplating the alterity of a seventeenth-century writer like the diarist Samuel Pepys, for instance, is not really any different from listening to Greenblatt wanting to speak with the dead, or indeed Woodhouse wanting to decipher the alien language of the godly. 'I can't understand him at all,' Frye says of Pepys in his own diary. In his 'gnomic riddling quality,' the seventeenth-century writer 'makes the dead eerie and transplanetary, not our kind of species at all' (*CWNF* 8:28–9).[28] When he looks at his own country he often sees something equally alien or other and if what we see in his major criticism is the model of music's timeless synchronicity deployed to transcend the messiness of history, it is also there to escape provincialism, what he calls 'the strident shallowness of much Canadian life' (*Bush Garden* 166). Frye's diaries are consumed with rage at the dreary ordinariness of life not only in Toronto the Good but everywhere, even that 'stinking little kraal Moncton' (8:42). Over and again days turn out to be 'desperately dull and gloomy' and when he and a friend try to get a drink in Richmond Hill, the 'natives' expressions, confidently coming out to meet the outside world or else shrinking correctly from it, were exactly what they would have been had we asked for whores' (8:215, 10–11). Despite Frye's deep-seated hostility to the British, galvanized by his two years at Merton College, Oxford, at some level they remain attractive in that they often signify the metropolitan antithesis of provincialism. He can hardly conceal his satisfaction, for instance, when it becomes apparent that the university's guest at what turns out to be a '[w]onderful lunch,' that 'solid-looking aristocrat' Osbert Sitwell 'is deeply impressed by my book [*Fearful Symmetry*]' and 'says he's recommended it to a lot of people including the painter John Piper. Edith is at the St. Regis on East 50th St, New York' (8:62). As the success of Woodhouse and Barker, 'two of the best Milton scholars anywhere,' had already demonstrated, the mastery of canonical English literature was culturally enabling, allowing one, so it seemed, a point of entry into the metropolis and even for a moment reversing circumference and centre. A similar theme, as von Maltzahn's brilliant essay makes clear, is evident in the story of Woodhouse's great Jewish student, Sirluck.

Sirluck's Metamorphosis

The hero of von Maltzahn's story is not Sirluck himself but the particular form of historical criticism he practises, especially as it appears in the 200-page introduction to the 1958 second volume of the Yale prose. It is not difficult to see why von Maltzahn admires it so much. The extraordinary learning and skill with which Sirluck charts the emergence of a new conception of natural law from the heat and dust, the shifting particularity of quotidian debate has much to teach us all: 'No longer would scholars be content to analyze the logic of major works of political theory – though Sirluck's contribution retains this strength – without studying more carefully their present occasions amid the welter of controversy' (307). Unlike von Maltzahn, I do not see this achievement as a radical break with Woodhouse, but, as I have suggested above, much more a development out of elements already implicit in the earlier work of the Woodhouse group – a development surely accelerated by Sirluck's formative wartime experience of 'present occasions,' that is, of sifting vitally important patterns of information from the welter of day-to-day fragments in the midst of a series of fast-moving and rapidly changing battles.[29] Listen to the military metaphors with which he explains the pamphlet debates of 1642: 'This was strong ground for an English party to occupy, and from it Royalist propaganda was for some time able to block every move Parliament made to take the initiative in the controversy.' But already, a lot like the routes the Canadians took on the Verrieres Ridge in July–August 1944, 'the way had been indicated for the Parliamentary propaganda to outflank the royalist position and reach ground from which a new offensive could be launched' (*YP* 2:16, 18). Looked at from another perspective, in the intensity of its intellectual energy, if not in its scope and arresting beauty, Sirluck's work rivals Frye's: there is something curiously similar in the creative way both Sirluck in the Yale introduction and Frye in *The Bush Garden* see form or idea emerging out of shapeless or shoddy particularity – Frye out of the way his country's 'roads and telephone wires and machinery twist and strangle and loop' (164) and Sirluck out of the way obscure pamphlets like the King's *Answer, by Way of Declaration* or Parliament's *A Question Answered* clash and wrangle (*YP* 2:18–19).

The villain of the piece in von Maltzahn's story is unreflective, undiscriminating, secular liberalism, a monstrous Trojan horse against whose flank he directs the speech act of his essay (273). The danger he perceives is that as liberalism transforms religion into culture, its tolerance of religious difference masks its profound indifference to any kind of non-instrumental value, and in that indifference it abandons any intrinsic principle or means by which a national community might refuse entry to various forms of obsessive, illiberal, religious absolutism. It is effectively hung on its own petard. The work of undiscriminating liberalism is evident everywhere, but especially in its general indifference to the alterity of the past and its particular, historic determination to co-opt Milton into the service of many causes he would have found incomprehensible, if not detestable. In the hands of Woodhouse's erstwhile colleague, Watson Kirkconnell, a modernized Milton becomes one of the more potent means by which liberalism can embrace a peculiarly disingenuous form of Euro-centric multiculturalism. And the 'poster-child' (305) for the success of this mode of denying real diversity and assimilating East European immigrants into a provincial-minded British Canada is, so von Maltzahn argues, Sirluck.

As his autobiography *First Generation* suggests, Sirluck's story is indeed remarkable. From the Yiddish-speaking child of relatively poor Russian-Jewish immigrants to distinguished Commonwealth soldier (decorated by Churchill's favourite general), to prized university administrator (in Toronto at least), to great Milton scholar, he personified the kind of assimilation Kirkconnell dreamed of – metamorphosis in one generation. But Sirluck was no dupe nor was he without considerable personal agency. Von Maltzahn sees that agency in his break with the Woodhouse group; I see it elsewhere.

At Toronto's Convocation Hall in 1946 Sirluck was invested as a Member of the Order of the British Empire by the then Governor-General, Lord Alexander, resplendent in his Field-Marshal's uniform. Sirluck chose not to wear his Major's uniform but one of his deceased brother's old civilian suits. Bert Sirluck, an RCAF bomber-navigator, had been killed on take-off for a raid on Germany a few months before Sirluck left for Normandy. Many at the ceremony were unimpressed by Sirluck's wilful gesture; Sirluck himself calls it 'sentimental' (148). It was of course anything but; it was a public demonstration of the degree to which his core identity was rooted in the life of his Jewish immigrant family in rural Manitoba and that he was apparently willing at critical moments to renounce all forms of 'protective colourization' – a term he uses, usually of others, throughout *First Generation*. Von Maltzahn can see little in the way of an affective bond between Sirluck and Milton, the poet he devoted his life to studying (310), and indeed, there is evidence to suggest that Milton functioned for Sirluck like the army as another form of camouflage or protective colouring, that is, another means of passing. This seems to be what he's implying in his account of first studying Milton under Woodhouse:

> Woodhouse, a Conservative and monarchist who thought of himself almost as an English Tory in the Dominions ... had so possessed himself of Milton

> the republican revolutionary, defender of regicide, and radical sectarian that he was able to present his thought and feeling from the inside, a feat I knew how to admire, being a Jew increasingly concentrating on the emphatically Christian literature of the English Renaissance. (74)

In discarding the protective colouring of his army uniform to honour his brother in a very real act of family *pietas,* he was emboldened, so one might argue, by another form of protective colouring in his being an English professor in the making – and not just any kind of English professor but a Miltonist. Von Maltzahn is acute in pointing to the 'robust prestige' of historically oriented Milton studies in a forties English department – it allowed one the authority of a historian together with the cultural capital of a literary figure central to a stubbornly 'anglocentric curriculum and national culture' (310). Sirluck's agency lies in the extraordinary tactical skill with which he deployed and switched these cultural colourings or codes primarily in the service of family, but significantly and increasingly in the service of his family's new country. Yes, he was assimilated but he also played a major role as a scholar and university administrator in transforming Kirkconnell's country into his own.

In 1962 Sirluck gave up the prestige of his professorship at the University of Chicago to return to Canada where he had an enormous impact on the Universities of Toronto and Manitoba – attempting to turn both of them with some success into centres of international and diverse learning. Even though he sometimes had his own doubts and knew that many at Toronto regarded McLuhan as a 'charlatan,' it was Sirluck, for instance, who did the legwork in establishing, among many other centres of excellence, McLuhan's Centre for Culture and Technology.[30] The melodramatic story of Toronto's visionaries struggling to free themselves from the constraints of mindless historicists is further confounded by the correspondence of Sirluck and McLuhan. In April 1964, for instance, McLuhan wrote to Sirluck: 'Dear Ernest: Was fascinated by your article on Milton's prose. One aspect that loomed very large was the use of Hendiadys ... Would like to talk to you about this.'[31] They did talk and frequently.

From Circumference to the Centre

Why did so many brilliant young Canadians in the thirties and forties feel the need or desire to write about Milton? Rajan's story suggests that in the success of the Woodhouse group, Milton studies gave substance to the growing perception of Canada as an intellectual centre – that it was possible to study and teach here at the highest level. Rajan's own desire to get to a place where his intellectual interests, especially those in English literature, might flourish is echoed in the desire of so many home-born Canadians to make that place Canada. That place was not synonymous with Toronto. Throughout the Woodhouse years, both because of him and to some extent in despite of him, Milton studies prospered in numerous universities throughout Canada, most famously perhaps at the University of British Columbia where Roy Daniells became a legend, at Queen's University where A.C. Hamilton emerged as one of the world's pre-eminent Spenserians, and at the University of Western Ontario where Barker and Rajan joined Woodhouse's younger student William Blissett to form an unusually influential group. The stories of Frye and Sirluck as they appear in the present volume suggest the degree to which Milton studies in Canada was driven by a desire similar to Rajan's to get from the margins to the centre – much like Milton's own desire to transform England from Virgil's nation at the edge of the world into another Rome or Athens in the West. Milton for so many gifted young Canadians, like Virgil for Milton, offered an intellectually challenging and culturally prestigious route in from the outside. For Frye being outside or on the edge seems to have meant escaping the tedium of provincialism: Harold Innis's dictum that '[n]ot to be British or American but Canadian is not necessarily to be parochial' speaks directly to him and many others of his generation.[32] For Sirluck being outside meant escaping the routine abuse and humiliation of being a despised minority without betraying that minority's identity. While the study of Milton in Canada was not culturally disinterested, it was equally, so it needs to be underlined, not simply a matter of social prestige or cultural capital. Overemphasizing Milton's value as cultural capital runs the risk of denying him agency. As the present volume makes abundantly clear, Milton studies in Canada could not have worked the way it did without his genius being able to engage emotions and energize minds as complex and sophisticated as those of these Canadian scholars. For all their differences, they appear at one in their distinctive refusal, rightly or wrongly, to doubt Milton's abiding value. Even at their most critical, they offer nothing like the contempt of Eliot and Leavis or the anti-Christian *J'accuse* of Empson. It is clearly this sense of having been enabled by Milton that explains Frye's famous caveat: 'Every student of Milton has been rewarded according to his efforts and his ability: the only ones who have abjectly failed with him are those who have tried to cut him down to size – their size – and that mistake at least I will not make' (*Return of Eden* 4).

All traditions or schools of criticism have their limitations, and the Woodhouse school, like the currently dominant Cambridge School in seventeenth-century studies, is no exception. Woodhouse himself was notoriously Toronto-centric and imperial in his dealings with the English departments of other universities in Canada, and as Frye's possessive pronouns in the quotation above suggest, the Woodhouse generation was peculiarly insensitive to gender issues. Some women were enabled by them, but others clearly felt excluded.[33] If Woodhouse appointed Canada's first Jewish English professor in Sirluck, there is little evidence to suggest he felt especially proactive or even remotely interested in recruiting from ethnic minorities in general. Even Sirluck seems to have grown increasingly suspicious of immigration, especially from those parts of 'Europe and the Middle East' that might sponsor 'the organization of anti-semitic and anti-Israeli activities' (*First Generation,* 387–9). When English literary studies turned first to post-structuralism, and then cultural materialism and new historicism, the Woodhouse generation and so many of their legatees were nonplussed, Sirluck predictably defiant, Frye painfully bewildered, especially by the rise of deconstruction. Their predicament and that of much Milton scholarship at this moment is caught by Mary Nyquist and Margaret Ferguson in the introduction to their 1987 *Re-membering Milton*: 'the conservatism of much Milton scholarship has been apparent in its comparative indifference to the theoretical literature and debates which have been engaging literary critics in both Britain and North America for almost two decades. Much Milton criticism has appeared to wish to preserve its theoretical innocence, or at least to defer as long as possible its inevitable fall into the threatening Babel of theoretical tongues' (xvi). Of the Woodhouse generation itself only Rajan appears to have had the intellectual resilience and flexibility to respond imaginatively to these new forms of scholarly endeavour, *Milton and the Imperial Vision* (edited with Elizabeth Sauer in 1999) and *Under Western Eyes* (also in 1999) standing as valuable models of how the historical interest of the Woodhouse generation might renew itself in the form of engaged political criticism. The same is true of Hugh MacCallum and William Halewood's student, Mary Nyquist, and her work on Milton and gender, her magisterial 1987 essay, 'The Genesis of Gendered Subjectivity in the Divorce Tracts and *Paradise Lost*,' having already achieved the status of a classic.

If the serious limitations of the Woodhouse school need to be recognized, it is equally important to remember, as this volume does so well, its achievements. Let me conclude on a personal note. In August 1976, I left the army to pursue an academic career. I held a regular commission in the Royal Regiment of Wales, but after many years of service, the last two in Ulster and Berlin, I longed to return to university life. Largely innocent of the Woodhouse tradition, but having had a wonderful year at Carleton University in Ottawa and deeply influenced by the very different work of MacCallum and Frye, I set out to pursue doctoral studies at the University of Toronto. Unlike so many earlier generations of British immigrants, however, I had no sense that I was going into exile, leaving for the colonies, or disappearing like Milton's voyagers into the far north. Far from it, I felt as though I was leaping up toward the light. Toronto inhabited my imagination not as an episode in communication or a provincial habitation sprawling along the highway, but as a glistening new metropolis, an exciting centre of intellectual life and new possibilities. That it did so for me and countless others was some measure of the achievement of a great generation of Canadians, not least Woodhouse, his students Barker and Sirluck, and their outliers, Rajan and Frye.

NOTES

In the composition of this essay, I am deeply indebted to the advice and encouragement of David Galbraith, Lynne Magnusson, Feisal Mohamed, Mary Nyquist, Mel Wiebe, and Archie Young.

1 See the introduction above, 10. References to the volume are hereafter cited in the text.
2 Letter to Helen Kemp, 25 August 1932, quoted in John Ayre, *Northrop Frye: A Biography* (Toronto, 1989), 77.
3 See Frye, 'Preface to an Uncollected Anthology' (1956), in *The Bush Garden: Essays on the Canadian Imagination* (Toronto, 1971), 166. As Peter Herman shows, this defiant assertion recurs in Frye's work throughout the 1950s (355–6).
4 Introduction, *Milton and the Imperial Vision*, ed. Balachandra Rajan and Elizabeth Sauer (Pittsburgh, 1999), 6. See also Paul Stevens, '*Paradise Lost* and the Colonial Imperative,' *Milton Studies* 34 (1996): 3–21.
5 See Robin S. Harris, *English Studies at Toronto: A History* (Toronto, 1988), 105–44
6 On the sensational success of Frye and McLuhan, consider Harold Bloom and Woody Allen. While Bloom thought Frye's *Anatomy* the best book he had ever read on any subject, Allen felt McLuhan was such a household name that he needed no introduction when he appeared in his 1977 hit movie

Annie Hall. On Frye as a solitary visionary, see, for instance, John Ayre's racy biography in which Frye and his mentor, George Wilson Knight, stand alone against the obscurantism of Woodhouse, a monstrous figure 'who set a standard of infrequent, soddenly-written works of intellectual history' (112).

7 See Mary Nyquist, 'Contemporary Ancestors of de Bry, Hobbes, and Milton,' in *Milton in America,* special issue of *UTQ* 77.3 (2008): 837–75.

8 A.S.P. Woodhouse, ed., *Puritanism and Liberty* (1938; repr. Chicago, 1951), 11. References hereafter cited in the text.

9 See, for instance, *Fables of Identity: Studies in Poetic Mythology* (New York, 1963), 265, where Frye records his debt to Woodhouse on the relation between the separate orders of nature and grace.

10 Notes for a talk at McGill University, May 1972, in the *Collected Works of Northrop Frye,* gen. ed. Alvin A. Lee, 29 vols (Toronto, 1996–), 25:36. References hereafter cited as *CWNF* in the text.

11 A.S.P. Woodhouse, 'Notes on Milton's Views of the Creation: The Initial Phase,' *Philological Quarterly* 28 (1949): 211–36.

12 See William Lamont, 'Puritanism, Liberty, and the Putney Debates,' in *The Putney Debates of 1647: The Army, the Levellers, and the English State,* ed. Michael Mendle (Cambridge, 2001), 241.

13 See Nyquist and Mohamed, Introduction, 17–23, for a finely nuanced analysis of the development of the Woodhouse group, and Nicholas von Maltzahn on Sirluck, esp. 305–10.

14 See Ernest Sirluck, *First Generation: An Autobiography* (Toronto, 1996), 174.

15 David Galbraith suggests that this honour in early modern studies should go to Malcolm Wallace, *A Life of Sir Philip Sidney* (Cambridge, 1915).

16 See Sauer, 265.

17 See Leonard, 219–20.

18 Bush routinely identifies himself as an American.

19 *The Complete Prose Works of John Milton,* gen. ed. Don M. Wolfe, 8 vols (New Haven, 1953–82). Hereafter cited as *YP* in the text. On the achievement of the Yale edition, see Sharon Achinstein, 'Cold War Milton,' in *Milton in America,* special issue of *UTQ* 77.3 (2008): 801–36.

20 I heard the story directly but separately from both Rajan and Sirluck in May 2006 and April 2007 respectively. Sirluck, who tells the story with characteristic lucidity in *First Generation,* 108–9, was completely unaware of Rajan's fears.

21 See Sirluck, *First Generation,* 109.

22 The loss of the Fellowship, the first in English in Trinity's long history, hurt Rajan enormously and it is hard to believe that racism played no part in Trinity's decision. At the same time, however, it is easy to see why a conserva-

tive college like Trinity would prefer a candidate such as Theodore Redpath over many others regardless of race – a barrister and starred first at St Catherine's College, Cambridge, he was, most importantly, a war hero, having worked on Enigma decrypts at Bletchley Park.

23 B. Rajan, *Paradise Lost and the Seventeenth-Century Reader* (London, 1947), 7. References hereafter cited in the text.

24 See Frye, *Bush Garden*, 164.

25 Consider Frye's recurring appearances in *Re-membering Milton: Essays on the Texts and Traditions*, ed. Mary Nyquist and Margaret W. Ferguson (New York: Methuen, 1987), on the one hand, and his presence in such books as Stanley Fish, *How Milton Works* (Cambridge, MA, 2001), Joseph Wittreich, *Why Milton Matters: A New Preface to His Writings* (New York, 2006), Gordon Teskey, *Delirious Milton: The Fate of the Poet in Modernity* (Cambridge, MA, 2006) and Stephen Fallon, *Milton's Peculiar Grace* (Ithaca, 2007), on the other. Frye taught the *Lycidas* essay to generations of Toronto students and it lives on in ways not accessible to citation indices.

26 See von Maltzahn above and Sirluck, *First Generation*, 260.

27 There are no references to any Canadian literature in Frye's celebrated *Anatomy of Criticism: Four Essays* (Princeton, 1957).

28 Cf. Stephen Greenblatt, *Shakespearean Negotiations: The Circulation of Social Energy in Renaissance England* (Berkeley and Los Angeles, 1988), 1.

29 Sirluck, a member of the Royal Regiment of Canada, distinguished himself first as a junior intelligence officer for the 2nd Canadian Infantry Division in a series of battles fought south of Caen in July–August 1944 and then as the chief of intelligence for the 4th Canadian Armoured Division in Belgium, Holland, and Northern Germany through the fall and winter of 1944 into 1945. He was promoted in the field, cited twice for outstanding service, and finally awarded an MBE at the end of the war.

30 See *First Generation*, 229–30.

31 Quoted from *Letters of Marshall McLuhan*, ed. Matie Molinaro et al. (Toronto, 1987), 298. The article in question is Sirluck's highly regarded and still influential piece 'Milton's Political Thought: The First Cycle,' *Modern Philology* 61.3 (1964): 209–24.

32 Harold A. Innis, *The Strategy of Culture* (Toronto, 1952), 2.

33 See the introduction, 16.

Contributors

Phillip J. Donnelly is Associate Professor of Literature in the Honors College at Baylor University, where he teaches in the Great Texts Program and the English Department. He is author of *Milton's Scriptural Reasoning: Narrative and Protestant Toleration* (Cambridge, 2009). His articles have appeared in *Milton Studies, Milton Quarterly, George Herbert Journal,* and *Christianity and Literature.* He is also a contributor to *Milton in Context,* ed. Stephen B. Dobranski (Cambridge, 2009).

Peter C. Herman's most recent books are *A Short History of Early Modern England: British Literature in Context* (Wiley-Blackwell, 2011); *Royal Poetrie: Monarchic Verse and the Political Imaginary of Early Modern England* (Cornell University Press, 2010), and *Destabilizing Milton: 'Paradise Lost' and the Poetics of Incertitude* (Palgrave, 2005; pbk. 2008). *Royal Poetrie* received a *Choice* Award for Outstanding Academic Title 2010.

Elizabeth Hodgson is an Associate Professor in the English Department at the University of British Columbia. She is the author of *Gender and the Sacred Self in John Donne* (Delaware UP, 1999) and numerous articles and book chapters. Her current book projects include 'The Weapon of Grief for Women Writers of the English Renaissance,' studying a central dynamic of Reformed negotiations with the problem of mourning.

John Leonard has taught at the University of Western Ontario since 1987. He has published widely on Milton and he has won two of the Milton Society's James Holly Hanford Awards as well as the University of Western Ontario's Edward G. Pleva Award for excellence in teaching. He has edited the Penguin editions of Milton's *Complete Poems, Paradise Lost,* and

Selected Poems. His current project (very near completion) is a reception history of *Paradise Lost.*

Feisal G. Mohamed is an Associate Professor in the English Department and the Unit for Criticism and Interpretive Theory at the University of Illinois, as well as a member of the Executive Committee of the Milton Society of America. In addition to scholarly journals, his work has appeared in *The New York Times* and he is a regular contributor to *Dissent Magazine.* His most recent book is *Milton and the Post-Secular Present: Ethics, Politics, Terrorism* (Stanford, 2011).

Mary Nyquist has recently completed *Arbitrary Rule: Slavery, Tyranny and the Power of Life and Death* (forthcoming, University of Chicago Press), and is currently a Faculty Fellow of the Jackman Humanities Institute at the University of Toronto, where she teaches in the Department of English and the Centre for Comparative Literature. With Margaret Ferguson, she co-edited *Re-Membering Milton: New Essays on Texts and Traditions* (Routledge, 1988). She is the Honored Scholar of the Milton Society of America for 2012.

Annabel Patterson is Sterling Professor of English at Yale University. She was born in England and emigrated to Canada in 1957, thus being at least one-third Canadian. She has written extensively and diversely on the literature, history, and culture of early modern Europe, fourteen books in all. The most recent is *Milton's Words* (Oxford, 2009). She is now at work on something completely different, a study of 'the International Novel' since the Second World War.

Elizabeth Sauer, Professor of English at Brock University, has authored *'Paper-Contestations' and Textual Communities in England* (Toronto, 2005) and *Barbarous Dissonance and Images of Voice in Milton's Epics* (McGill-Queen's, 1996). She is also co-editor of ten volumes, including *Reading the Nation,* with Julia M. Wright (Routledge, 2010); *Milton and Toleration,* with Sharon Achinstein (Oxford, 2007); *Milton and the Climates of Reading* (Toronto, 2006); and *Reading Early Modern Women,* with Helen Ostovich (Routledge, 2004). A book on Milton, toleration, and nationhood, funded by a Killam Research Fellowship, is in progress.

Muhammad Sid-Ahmad is a doctoral candidate at the University of Toronto, where he is completing his PhD dissertation, *Negotiating Solitude: Reception and Transformation of Abu Bakr Ibn Tuphayl's 'Hayy bin*

Yaqzan.' He currently teaches in the Department of English at Humber College.

Paul Stevens is Professor and Canada Research Chair in Early Modern Literature and Culture at the University of Toronto and Fellow of Trinity College, Toronto. His area of specialty is seventeenth-century English literature, especially the works of John Milton. Former President of the Milton Society of America and Visiting Fellow at All Souls College, Oxford, his most recent book is *Early Modern Nationalism and Milton's England* (Toronto, 2008), co-edited with David Loewenstein, which won the 2009 Irene Samuel Memorial Prize. He is currently completing a book provisionally called *Sola Gratia: Early Modern English Literature and the Political Ways of Grace.*

Nicholas von Maltzahn (University of Ottawa) has published a number of studies centring in how Milton was received from the seventeenth century to the present day. His work on Milton and Andrew Marvell includes *An Andrew Marvell Chronology* (Palgrave, 2005), an edition of Marvell's *Account of the Growth of Popery and Arbitrary Government* for *The Prose Works of Andrew Marvell* (Yale, 2003), and *Milton's History of Britain: Republican Historiography in the English Revolution* (Oxford, 1991).

Index

www.ingramcontent.com/pod-product-compliance
Lightning Source LLC
LaVergne TN
LVHW090145080826
844660LV00013B/679/J
* 9 7 8 1 4 4 2 6 4 3 9 2 5 *